MW00784251

ליקוטי מוהר"ן

LIKUTEY MOHARAN

ליקוטי מוהר"ן

LIKUTEY MOHARAN

Volume 1 (Lessons 1-6)

by

Rebbe Nachman of Breslov

translated by

Moshe Mykoff and Simcha Bergman

edited by

Moshe Mykoff and Ozer Bergman

annotated by

Chaim Kramer

published by

BRESLOV RESEARCH INSTITUTE

Jerusalem/New York

Table of Contents

Section B:

APPENDIX A

Introductions to Likutey Moharan

Reb Noson's Introduction
Parparaot LeChokhmah's Introduction
Eighteen Rules

Reb Noson's Introduction to *Likutey Moharan*

"O generation, see the word of God" (Jeremiah 2:31). The prophet does not say hear [the word of God], but see it. See that God has given you a precious gift, something which stands at the very summit of the world. As our Sages teach: "*v'limekhaseh atik* (coverings of old)" (Isaiah 23:18)—this is the one who covers over that which *Atik Yomin* (the Ancient One) covered over. And there are those who maintain that this refers to the one who reveals that which *Atik Yomin* covered over (*Pesachim* 119a).

Both are true of this holy work. It both reveals and conceals: revealing and explaining exalted and hidden matters, new insights, rudiments which are precious, awesome and wondrous; providing advice from afar, it is "the work of a master craftsman" (cf. Isaiah 25:1). All these teachings stem from the very exalted and awesome source of living water, [so that] "a wise man scales the city of the strong, and brings down the stronghold in which it trusts" (Proverbs 21:22).

[They teachings are taught to us] through numerous constrictions and diminutions—from the Cause of Causes to the caused, from the upper intellect to the lower one (see Lesson #30)—until they have become clothed in these garments, the cloak of the Sages, in a clear and beautiful manner. They are in the form of pleasant, wondrous and sweet discourses, in the way of wisdom, reason, dialectic and logic, and the way of life—the reproof of ethical instruction, which is like a fire that burns to the very heart of heaven.

All the lessons which Rebbe Nachman revealed to the Chosen People are filled with wonderful and awesome counsel in the true service of the Blessed Holy One. This will be obvious to anyone who studies them, provided he does so in search of the real truth.

For this alone was the Rebbe's holy intention: "to rouse the sleeping and waken the slumbering" (*Shabbat Liturgy*); to make straight the hearts of men, our Jewish brethren, with God; "to tell the imprisoned, 'Go free,' to those residing in darkness, 'Come out'" (Isaiah 49:9); "to give sight to eyes that are blind" (*ibid.* 42:7); 'to redeem those bound in fetters' (cf. Psalms 68:7), to "release the shackled from confinement, those who sit in darkness from [their] prison" (Isaiah 42:7)—those bound to their passions, trapped in their folly, cast out by their sins. [His desire was] to turn their hearts to the Holy One, to

return them to God in truth, along the straight and true path, the path which our forefathers have followed from yore.

And so, even though these points are somewhat obvious and understood from the simple interpretation of the teachings, there is more to them—they are "twofold in insight" (Job 11:6). For the inner meaning of the teachings remain hidden and concealed from all. They are matters that *Atik Yomin* covered over, which we must cover over and reveal in order to bring them into this world.

This is because the covering *is* the revelation, as is explained in the writings of the Ari (cf. *Etz Chaim, Shaar HaKlallim* 2), and as we once heard from the Rebbe's holy lips, when he said that the discourses that he revealed are thousands and thousands of levels lower than the exalted level at which he perceived them (*Tzaddik* #360).

Precisely this is his strength and his awesomeness (cf. *Yoma* 69b): That his holy, lofty intellect succeeded in clothing and bringing down such high and awesome matters as these; holy, subtle and very spiritual matters which he clothed in numerous garments and contractions so that they have become suitable for all. [The Rebbe's intention was] to inform people of God's strength, and to reveal advice, ways and paths for attaining His service in truth, so "that all the peoples of the earth might know that God is the Lord, there is no other" (1 Kings 8:60).

"It is superfluous to go on extolling" (Proverbs 14:23) the great holiness and awesomeness of this book. This is because anyone who is prepared to study it honestly will appreciate and understand the extent of its greatness on his own. But one whose heart is doubtful and who has no interest in perceiving the work's holiness will not be aided at all by these words. Even so, "to all my comrades and friends" (Psalms 122:8) I shall relate a bit of the ways of this holy work, the remainder they will come to on their own—their eyes will see and then their hearts will rejoice.

Each and every lesson of this holy book covers a number of different subjects. [These include] various positive character traits, numerous mitzvot of our holy Torah, as well as learning to keep away from negative traits. And each lesson discusses specific topics not mentioned in a previous teaching.

Thus, the discourse entitled "Speak to the Priests" (Lesson #2) discusses prayer and guarding the Covenant, one being dependent upon the other; and the need to have the quality of judgment in order to know how to do battle with this sword [of prayer]...for which it is necessary to give charity before praying; as well as extraneous thoughts in

prayer, studying the holy Torah, establishing the Tabernacle, and the need for binding prayer to the tzaddik of the generation. In the lesson, all these matters are explained by means of a link that is awesome and amazing, and which has no parallel.

Then, a later discourse, such as "With Trumpets" (Lesson #5), covers entirely different matters: performing the mitzvot with joy, praying enthusiastically, fear and so on. Other lessons deal with different topics, for all the teachings of this holy work are filled with advice which is both good and amazing.

They speak about all the character traits and the mitzvot, and about the keeping away from and breaking of all human desires: primarily lust, avarice and gluttony. [Also discussed is the need for] keeping oneself from honor, anger, impatience and haughtiness, and the great value of truth as opposed to the disgrace of falsehood; keeping away from depression and idleness; keeping from the damage caused by the spoken word through slander and gossip, and from spiritually blemishing one's vision or other senses; sanctifying one's eyes, nose, ears and mouth (Lesson #21), these being "the seven lamps that radiate their light to the center of the holy menorah" (Numbers 8:2).

[Further topics include] the holiness of Shabbat, the Holy Days and the New Moon; the Three Festivals in general and each holiday in particular: Pesach, Shavuot and Sukkot, and the mitzvot which are customarily performed on each one—e.g., eating matzah and the prohibition against chametz, reading the Haggadah and drinking the four cups on Pesach, and similarly the mitzvah of *sukkah* and the Four Species, Hoshana Rabbah, Shemini Atzeret and Simchat Torah, and receiving the Torah on Shavuot—as well as Rosh HaShanah and blowing the shofar, Yom Kippur, Chanukah and Purim.

[Among the daily mitzvot the lessons] deal with are tzitzit, tefillin, reciting the *Shema* and prayer, charity and Torah study, engaging in business honestly, faith in God and faith in the Sages, humility, fear and love, the great value of holy desire and longing. [Rebbe Nachman also discusses the great value] of praying with enthusiasm and concentration, whether it be the three daily prayers or the other, very valuable supplementary prayers, supplications and requests which we must recite each and every day and in abundance. He pays particular attention to the special value of *hitbodedut*—daily expressing one's self before the Holy One, in the language one normally speaks, pouring one's heart out to God that He should make one worthy of coming closer to His service; the importance of reciting the Psalms, through which one succeeds in repenting; the value of crying before the Holy One like a son begging his father for forgiveness.

[The lessons likewise probe] the advantage of a broken heart and avoiding sadness; the benefit of joy, for which the Rebbe offers numerous wondrous suggestions, and for which a person must always strive; the value of the holiness of the Land of Israel, the Tabernacle, the Temple and Jerusalem; the disgrace of contentiousness and the great value of peace, repentance and fasting, of the holiness of thought and shunning of extraneous thoughts; and all the holy ways and means that exist in the world for which we all have need.

[The Rebbe discusses] the great benefit of being close and attached to the tzaddikim (Lesson #123)—the very holiness of a Jew being dependent upon this; [the importance] of melody and musical instruments, and the ten types of song; of clapping and dancing, and of sighing and the "returning voice"*—matters about which the ear has never heard, neither heard nor seen a revelation of the awesome mysteries, [though] the world has great need for matters such as these in which the ways of God are greatly hidden.

Study elsewhere in the Zohar and the writings of the Kabbalists where, from a distance, you will discover and understand the very great concealed mysteries which are present in every human movement, especially when it involves something holy such as clapping one's hands while praying or when it stems from the joy felt from observing a mitzvah and the like (see *Tikkuney Zohar* #69, p.118; *Tzaddik* #504, #507). Open your eyes, see and understand.

Again and again the lessons speak directly to a person's heart, encouraging him in the service of God. He should never despair no matter what, never fall because of anything in the world, but always be very stubborn in God's service and never, under any circumstances, backslide from his achievements. For 'the kindness of God never ends, His mercies never cease' (cf. Lamentations 3:22)—ever.

And in general, [the lessons speak] of the 613 Commandments of the Torah and their offshoots, all the rabbinical edicts; of the Written Law and the Oral Law, revealed and hidden, Halakhah and Kabbalah, secrets and deep secrets. All are mentioned and each is spoken of time and again with amazing approaches and links and new insights. Without exception, they are wonderful suggestions for how to draw closer to the Holy One. [Everything is discussed,] so that there is no mitzvah, holy matter, or good advice

---

* The Zohar acclaims the mystery of the "returning voice," and lauds the esoteric implication of the Jew's *shuckl* [swaying to and fro] when performing some holy deed (*Zohar* III, 168b; 218b).

needed by all the people of the world on all the different levels, which is not mentioned in this holy and awesome work.

For the Rebbe's thoughts are very deep. He speaks of the universality of everything, in general and in particular; including all the universes and levels that exist in the world of each person, great and small alike, from the starting point of creation—the initial point of *Atzilut*—to the ultimate point of *Asiyah*—the physical world in which man resides. Each individual, in accordance with the place and level he is on at that moment, from the greatest of the great to the smallest of the small, and even one who is located on the very lowest rungs of the ten "unholy crowns," having fallen into the farthest reaches and even further because of his sins—Rebbe Nachman arouses, awakens and inspires each one of them so that they never despair, God forbid, from [His] mercy. The Rebbe's words support the one who is falling, he strengthens the one who has weak knees (Job 4:4; as is explained in *Likutey Moharan* II, 7, "The One Who is Compassionate Shall Lead Them.")

In general, each and every topic with which Rebbe Nachman deals, he discusses again and again, each time taking a different approach, suggesting some different advice.

For example: In Lesson #5, "With Trumpets," it is explained that intense prayer corresponds to thunder, and that through such prayer one merits straightening the crookedness of the heart and observing the mitzvot with a great joy stemming from the mitzvah itself. Then, in Lesson #48, "Because You Were Unfaithful," it is explained that through intense prayer one merits sons, and that such prayer corresponds to the *sukkah* and the Land of Israel, whereas elsewhere (Lesson #44) it is explained that intense prayer eliminates haughtiness, self-interests, and foreign thoughts during prayer. And in the teaching "The Deeps Covered Them," Lesson #9, it is explained that by praying intensely one receives the essence of life-force and sustains all the worlds—"lower, second and uppermost"—and merits miracles and wonders, complete faith, the Land of Israel, etc.

The same is true of all the character traits, mitzvot, directives, practices and holy suggestions of which he speaks. The Rebbe discusses all of them over and over again, each time in a novel and amazing way, with a new and amazing link. One time the Rebbe connects and links together guarding the Covenant, through which one merits faith, which is the aspect of Shabbat, through which charity and Torah are made complete...and then one merits a holy desire to be a righteous person so that his eating

corresponds to the showbread of the Temple, as explained in the teaching "We Have a Well in the Desert" (Lesson #31). Another time he connects guarding the Covenant with eliminating haughtiness, which is idolatry, and rectifying the thirty-nine works [prohibited on Shabbat], which are all the business activities in the world, the upper and lower unifications, Halakhah and Kabbalah...and through this, meriting speech that inspires repentance to the point where one merits deep Torah understanding, as explained in "I am God" (Lesson #11). Similar such examples can be found with respect to other mitzvot and character traits.

The Rebbe gave wonderful advice, spreading hope through various new and wonderful ways. Because of our utter weakness, and because of the great force with which man's evil inclination overpowers him, attacking him daily, as our Sages teach (*Sukkah* 52a,b), we therefore need advice and awakening to His service in different ways. This is because sometimes a person will be aroused to a specific path or service through the light of a particular lesson. Other times, he is not aroused by that lesson, but only by a different teaching. Everything depends upon the person: his spiritual level, the place and the time. "Taste and you will see that God is good" (Psalms 34:9). 'Hear the Rebbe's words for they are very pleasing' (cf. Psalms 141:6). They are for anyone who truly desires and is willing to look at himself and take pity on his true life, willing to consider his end and departure from this world: with what sort of face will he ascend before the King...as each person knows in his soul and heart.

Understand and see as well that all the words of each and every lesson in this book contain great depth; there is great profundity in the totality, in the specific, and in the fine details [of the lesson]. As I myself heard from Rebbe Nachman's holy lips, when he said, "There are great depths to my teachings" (*Tzaddik* #347, #348). Why, "the words of this holy work are like a fire and like a hammer splitting a rock" (Jeremiah 23:29; see *Kiddushin* 30b). Each lesson can be divided into numerous new and vital rudiments, and into the various topics and subjects which emerge from each teaching.

For each and every discourse that appears in this holy book is in itself an awesome and mighty structure—"built fortified" (Song of Songs 4:4), a fortress to which all turn (*Berakhot* 30a; *Shir HaShirim Rabbah* 4:11) —comprising many chambers, room within room within room, with windows and openings leading from one to another. And each and every chamber, each explanation, topic and rudiment which appears in a teaching has in it very great depth. The more these explanations and topics expand—as the "waters

cover the sea" (Isaiah 11:9)—the deeper and deeper they get, so that "the clever man studies deeply his way" (Proverbs 14:15).

Each time a person goes from chamber to chamber, from room to room, and from subject to subject within the same topic, he must turn and look back to understand well the sweetness and depth of the words; the end of the matter from its beginning, the beginning from its end. Everything is bound, connected and intertwined; the opening with the conclusion, and the conclusion with the opening, as well as with the body of the text and the marginal points. The reader who traverses the material will increase his understanding, especially with respect to the broader perspective of the lesson, which is bound and sealed, inclusive of many wondrous and deep explanations and topics—'broader than the sea itself' (cf. Job 11:9).

And you, the serious student, should understand in the Rebbe's words that there are times when, in an awesomely intricate and pleasing fashion, he brings two or three proofs for one point. However, due to the cursive style in which the material is presented, it may seem as if there is only one proof. Such is the manner of this book: often using "because" or "for" or some similar word more than once within a single statement, thus making it appear as if it is but a single reason and proof, when in truth there are a number of reasons. But, because each one is linked to the next, it is impossible to separate them. For numerous are the reasons and proofs, set forth in an amazing way, each one fastened and bound to the next (see *Parparaot LeChokhmah's* Introduction).

Indeed, because of the great depth of each and every statement, it would have been fitting to write each time "read carefully," or "understand this," or "study this well," or some similar expression cautioning to the reader to pay close attention to the point being made so as to understand it well. But I realized that if that were the case, it would be necessary to write some such comment following just about every point, considering the abundant sweetness of the intellect and depth contained in every topic and in almost every statement. In general, there is such great depth to the Rebbe's words that none of these expressions could suffice. I have therefore withheld my pen and kept myself from employing any such language, although occasionally and upon rare instances some such expression did escape from the quill.

Anyone who has a brain in his head and studies these teachings with an open mind will, on his own, appreciate their depth. They are 'broader and deeper than the sea' (cf. Job 11:9), 'higher than the sky, deeper than the depths' (cf. Proverbs 25:3). Anyone who wants to taste the sweet nectar of these words should analyze them honestly and in great

depth, understanding each matter in its context as best as he possibly can. "Happy is the one who has found wisdom and who draws insight" (Proverbs 3:13), understanding well the simple meaning of the lessons which appear in this holy book (see *Tzaddik* #353, #361, #362, #365).

Even so, it is something which is suitable for everyone. Even someone whose understanding of intricate matters is limited can find tranquility for his soul in the words of this holy book, in the holy advice and wonderful moral guidance which emerges from each and every lesson—to the degree that God enlightens him in understanding the simple meaning which the Rebbe intended in his holy teachings. Because the truth is, that all the teachings of this awesome book contain extremely exalted and deep insights—infinitely so. Concealed and cloaked within them are very great and fantastic matters which only appear in the Torah by means of an allusion or in an esoteric teaching.

All the writings of the holy Ari and the discourses of the holy *Zohar* and the *Tikkuney Zohar,* as well as all the ways of the Kabbalah, are all included in this holy book. Each and every lesson speaks about the deeper intentions of some mitzvah and of a particular portal in the *Etz Chaim* in some amazing and spectacular fashion. This we have seen with our own eyes and not through another's, for the Rebbe opened our eyes and occasionally revealed a drop of his great intention, as is hinted at every so often in this work. For each lesson contains *PaRDeS: Pshat*—explanation of the simple meaning of the text; *Remez*—explanation of the allusions within the text; *Drush*—explanation of the text using the principles of hermeneutics; and *Sod*—explanation of the text according to its esoteric interpretation. In each approach, there is great depth, though Rebbe Nachman's primary intention is the simple meaning of each lesson.

This is because "study alone is not the main thing—doing is" (Avot 1:17), as has been explained in a number of places (see *Rabbi Nachman's Wisdom* #19, #27, etc.). The essence of his holy intention in each teaching that he revealed and in every statement which issued from his holy lips was only in order to add merit to Israel and bring them to upright actions, to hint to them from far and near, to teach them fantastic counsel and guidance in drawing closer to the Holy One from wherever one is. This the observer will surely notice provided he chooses to view it with an honest and open eye. For the Rebbe's whole intention was only that we diligently work at understanding the service and advice which come out of each lesson, beseeching God, prostrating ourselves before Him and striving, with simplicity, to fulfill all that appears in them.

And we trust in God that anyone who pays close attention to the holy words set forth

in this holy work, his heart will be kindled and his eyes opened, and he will desire and yearn the service of God. He will then return to Him in truth, with his entire heart, soul and strength. A heart as fixed as a rock will be moved from its place. "If it is stone, it will melt; if it is iron, it will splinter" (*Kiddushin* 30b). As we heard from the Rebbe's holy lips: "If a person is prepared to study this work honestly, then without any doubt his heart's obstinacy will be shattered and he will repent totally" (*Tzaddik* #349).

In truth, it is well nigh impossible to speak the praises of this holy and fantastic tome, and certainly of the praises and holiness of its holy author: the exalted, great and precious lamp, our master, teacher and rabbi (the remembrance of the righteous and holy brings blessing). In his case, 'silence is the most fitting praise' (cf. Psalms 65:2), especially because we are well aware of the great conflict—many having stood up against him and us without provocation or cause. Because of this we have had to bridle our mouths and remain silent from the good, from truthfully delineating the praises of his holiness and sanctity, his simplicity, righteousness and humility.

"For in the place of his greatness and exalted wisdom"—his having reached tremendous heights in all aspects of the Torah: in the revealed and the hidden, in the sea of the Talmud, its earlier and later codifiers, and in all the concealed exalted insights, so that "no secret escaped him" (Daniel 4:6), nor did anything remain obscured from him—"there we find his humility!" (*Megillah* 31a). He was forthright, patient, long-suffering, and whole in his deeds; serving God with wondrous self-sacrifice, never ceasing day or night, neither relaxing nor resting from his service of Him with very great and fantastic wisdom and insight, as your eyes will clearly see from this holy work. Because any reader who pays attention to these words will judge favorably, for it is impossible to attain teachings such as these with a full belly. How greatly he toiled, how hard he worked, how many thousands of fasts—time and again from Shabbat to Shabbat—how many mortifications, how many, many years spent in secluded prayer, separating himself in every way from all desires, sanctifying himself with all types of holiness.

And above all, he ascended and sanctified himself with awesome and exquisite holiness through the sanctity of the Land of Israel, for which he endangered his life. He travelled to the Holy Land at a time when [the Napoleonic] War was fiercely raging in those lands through which he passed. How many difficulties he encountered along the way. God is righteous, He judges in the same manner as the flax-dealer: [putting the mighty, not the meek, to the more severe test] (*Bereishit Rabbah* 32:3; *Rashi*, Psalms 11:5). For in

those times the Rebbe was beset by all different kinds of relentless and unceasing adversities and dangers, including the afflictions of plague and the tumult of war which had beset the Holy Land so that no one could be certain that he would live another day, as well as other kinds of severe hardships, physical, spiritual and monetary, which are impossible to explain in writing (see *Rabbi Nachman's Wisdom*, The Pilgrimage). Yet, in His mercy, the Blessed One gave the Rebbe an iron will to endure all this suffering and hardship from every direction, such as no man can bear, so that he merited overcoming all obstacles and entered the Land of Israel. He departed and returned in peace (cf. *Chagigah* 14b), unharmed, having attained that which he did both in the revealed and the hidden.

Because, aside from "those hidden things which are God's" (Deuteronomy 29:28), which he achieved through the Land of Israel and which remain hidden from all living creatures, also in those things manifest, 'we saw that God was with him' (cf. Genesis 26:28). Thus, the teachings which he revealed after having been in the Land of Israel immeasureably eclipsed in insight and level those that he revealed before his journey; despite the fact that even previously his holy lessons had tremendously enlightened the world. The words of his teachings were always amazing, but just as 'the heavens are high above the earth' (Isaiah 55:9), so, too, the ways of the teachings which he revealed after visiting the Land of Israel are high above the ways of the teachings which he had earlier revealed, as we explicitly heard from his holy lips a number of times (see *Tzaddik* #55, #130-135, #357). This work itself is almost entirely made up of lessons which he disclosed after being in the Land of Israel. There are but a few lessons, perhaps two or three pages worth, which are from the lessons given prior to his pilgrimage (these are interspersed among the lessons bearing the mark *leshon chaverim* [written not by Reb Noson but by other followers], which appear between Lessons #73 and #110, and then only a very few of these).

This book was first published thirteen years ago in Ostrog, in 5568 (1808), while Rebbe Nachman was still alive. But, because we were not present when it was printed, the local printers tampered considerably [with the text]. As a result, a good number of mistakes were made during the printing. In a number of places, whole lines went missing or the order was changed, and some pieces were totally exchanged with others. This, aside from other errors in the demarcation between lessons, as well as within the lessons themselves, where a space or a break is occasionally required between different points. In all these areas, the printers introduced considerable distortions. There were places where large gaps were inserted into the text for no reason at all. In other places, where a division

in the text was called for, they combined and put together two separate pieces, sometimes leaving no empty space even at the very beginning of a lesson. Having set my heart and mind on fixing all of this in the best way possible, to the extent that God was with me, I have corrected all the mistakes and distortions that appeared in the first printing.

It should also be mentioned that the first printing took place quite unexpectedly and without my being present, while the Rebbe, of blessed memory, was in Lemberg (Lvov). Thus, although in a number of places in the text it had been necessary to make certain revisions, because of the great rush to print, it was printed the way it had been originally recorded in the initial version. I therefore saw fit and made it my business to make corrections in many places, to expand and explain the material further. I did this in accordance with what I knew and understood to be the intent of the teaching, in line with what I heard from his holy lips. As for the lessons which had been written in the Rebbe's own holy language, I've neither subtracted from nor added to them, not even so much as a single letter. Only in those places where it was absolutely necessary to include some interpretation and explanation, there I presented the material within braces { } so that it would be clear that this was not from the Rebbe himself.

I've also made an effort to research all the references for all the verses quoted from Scripture and the rabbinical teachings from the Talmud, Midrash, the holy Zohar, the Tikkuney Zohar and the writings of the Ari. There are very, very many of these in this work and, with God's help, I've recorded their sources—"where the place of their glory" (Liturgy) is found.

I also marked off each lesson, assigning each teaching a different letter according to the order of the Hebrew alphabet so that it is easier for the student to find what he is looking for. In addition, within each lesson itself, I affixed a letter adjacent to each topic so as 'to indicate a break and a notation between one topic and the next' (cf. *Rashi*, Leviticus 1:1) and to point out that at this juncture the discourse changes topics to teach and explain another rudiment and subject, as will be understood when one analyzes these parts of the text.

Furthermore, in this book there are a number of discourses which are brought twice, one full length and one abridged. The reason for this is as follows: Such was Rebbe Nachman's way. Generally speaking, in those lessons which he recorded himself there were numerous differences between his spoken and written versions. Because of the speed at which his holy mind worked at the time he recorded the teaching, he would either delete

from or add to what he said when he delivered his discourse in public. The same cannot be said of me, because I was careful to write down exactly what I heard from his holy lips, without subtracting or adding. There are also a number of teachings which I transcribed, only to later have the Rebbe's own written version come into my possession. For the reason mentioned earlier, there were differences between these versions and I consequently decided that both were good. The rule is that anything taught twice has only been repeated because of some aspect which is unique to the second (*Chagigah* 3a).

This concludes our limited words which contain a great deal for making known just a modicum of the ways of this holy book—"a little which holds much." It is impossible to go on about and relate any more of the amazing and tremendous holiness which exists in this holy and awesome work. Whole reams of paper would not suffice for telling the praises of even one lesson of this holy book. This is especially so because of the current increase in controversy which has arisen because of our many sins. And, because of our many transgressions, we have witnessed the fulfillment of: "Truth has been thrown down to the ground" (Daniel 8:12); and, "The truth is absent" (Isaiah 59:15)—namely, the truth has been broken into many different groups (*Sanhedrin* 97a), with each group claiming that it alone possesses it. Even so, the truth remains one and testifies for itself.

He that chooses shall choose, while we will put our trust in God. "For there is no one for us to rely upon other than our Father in heaven" (*Sotah* 49b) to Whom we turn. Your mercy and compassion have stood by us up until now, may You never ever forsake or abandon us. "Provide us with Your light and Your truth, they will guide us" (Psalms 43:3). "May God our Lord be with us as He was with our fathers" (1 Kings 8:57), and "may the pleasantness of God our Lord be upon us; establish the works of our hands upon us" (Psalms 90:17). The descendant of David shall come and redeem us, taking us up to our land with rejoicing. May the House of our holiness and splendor be rebuilt speedily in our time. Amen. May it be His will.

These, then, are the words of the transcriber and compiler. "May the Torah be increased and exalted."

The insignificant NOSON: son of my lord, father and teacher, Rabbi NAFTALI HERTZ of Greater Nemerov; son-in-law of the *rav* and sage, the renown pious man, our teacher, Rabbi Dovid Zvi, who was the head of the rabbinical court in Sharograd, Kremenetz and Mohilov.

* * *

Parparaot LeChokhmah's Introduction

"The links and connections within the structure of Rebbe Nachman's lessons literally resemble those in building or weaving. The Rebbe begins by linking two things together. Next, he ties a third thing to the second by means of a number of solid connections. The third thing he then binds to a fourth, and so on. Generally, however, he will return each time so as to bind and connect all four things together. At first they were not all linked with each other; the first was linked to the second, the second to the third and the third to the fourth, but as yet there was nothing tying the fourth to the first. However, the Rebbe next brings a Biblical verse, rabbinical dictum or some other proof through which he binds all four things together until the link is absolutely firm.

"Afterwards, the Rebbe repeats the procedure with a different set of concepts, and then connects the two structures. At first, these two holy structures are only linked insofar as one of the things in the second structure is in some way tied to one of the things in the first. But then, the Rebbe goes back and shows how everything in each structure is bound with everything in the other. He extends girders by which the third item in the first structure is bound to the fourth in the second structure and then to the second item in the third structure. Next, he works on the links between the second and the third structures, and so on, until everything is bound together in a remarkable unity.

"The Rebbe himself discussed this whole subject in my presence the day after Yom Kippur 5571 (1810)—[seven days] before he passed away. It would be valuable to extend this analysis by bringing examples from various lessons in order to enable the reader to properly understand a little of the methods of this holy work" (*Tzaddik* #389).

The compiler [Rabbi Nachman Goldstein, the Tcheriner Rav] writes: I copied the above directly from a manuscript, the holy work of Reb Noson's own hand. It can be understood from his words that he had intended to expand and clarify the point but this never happened. It is likewise clear from this that the Rebbe had also hoped that those who studied his holy work would think into and try to understand well the amazing methods, as well as the wonderful links and connections between each of the topics, found in each and every lesson. I therefore thought to fulfill their holy desire and offer somewhat of an explanation.

Let us begin with the first lesson, "Happy are Those Whose Way is Perfect" which is a short discourse. Rebbe Nachman begins with the general statement that through Torah all prayers and requests are accepted, and the grace and importance of the Jewish people ascends. Afterwards, as he begins to explain the matter in greater detail, he explains that it is necessary to bind oneself to the wisdom and intelligence which exists in every thing. This is the aspect of the sun, the letter *chet*. Yet it is impossible to achieve this except by means of *Malkhut* (Kingdom), which corresponds to the letter *nun*. The Rebbe links this together through the verse, "May his name *yenon* as long as the sun" (Psalm 72:17).

Next, he explains that it is necessary to give strength to the Kingdom of Holiness which corresponds to the good inclination, so that it overcomes the Kingdom of Evil which is the evil inclination. This is achieved by energetically engaging in the study of Torah. We see therefore that Torah study is linked and connected to the rectification of the strength of the Kingdom of Holiness, the aspect of *nun*. Afterwards, the Rebbe explains that through this concept, *nun* is bound to *chet* to form the word *chein* (grace). Thus the Torah is called "*yaalat chein* (a graceful gazelle)." We see with this that the value of Torah study is linked to the two aspects: to Kingdom, which is *nun*, and to the light of intelligence and the wisdom, which is *chet*; in that through these two, *chein* is formed.

Next, the Rebbe explains that through this *chein* an etching and marking is made in the heart of the one being asked to accept the request. This etching is the aspect of the letter *tav*, and through it all the prayers and requests are heard and accepted. This explains and links all of the above, specifically the words of the wise men—those who merit to bind themselves to the wisdom and intelligence. And this is, "The words of the wise men spoken with *NaChaT*"—Nun, Chet, Tav—"are heard." This is because through this [combining of letters] his words are heard, his request is accepted.

Rebbe Nachman then goes back to strengthen the point that through the intelligence one achieves *chein*. In this vein he tells us that Yaakov merited to grace, as did Yosef, and so the Rebbe quotes the verse, "The firstborn of his oxen, grandeur is his." Then, in explaining the story of Rabbah bar bar Chanah, it is explained that the evil inclination, which is the very opposite of intelligence, desires to drown [i.e., subdue] the grace and importance. He also goes back and explains that the primary defeat of the evil inclination is accomplished by means of Torah study, clarifying the reason for this with an amazing explanation. And whereas, in the beginning of the lesson he only brought a proof for

this from the teachings of the Sages, the Rebbe now explains why this is so. Finally, in explaining the verse, "Happy are those whose way is perfect," he links it to the importance of studying the Torah energetically, this being achieved by gazing at the intelligence in each thing; which is how the lesson began.

* * *

Eighteen Rules

for studying *Likutey Moharan* in depth,
by Rabbi Avraham b'Reb Nachman Chazan of Tulchin
(culled from the introduction to his *Biur HaLikutim*)

1) Just as it is possible to expound on and find new insights in the Rebbe's lessons by drawing from one lesson to another—as in the manner our Sages taught with regard to the esoteric and homiletic meaning of the text: The words of the Torah are poor in one place and rich in another—so it is possible to draw from one part of a lesson to another. This is because the beginning, middle and end of the Rebbe's lessons are tightly linked and intertwined, by means of great wisdom and understanding, to the point where one part explains and clarifies the other, and vice versa. Moreover, this is true even for the revealed and simple meaning of the text.

2) Using his wisdom and Divine inspiration, the Rebbe counted and weighed each and every word, both spoken and written, in deciding what to explain briefly and what at length, what to leave out and what to include.

3) In those places which incorporate many concepts and ideas, the Rebbe often chooses one and uses it as a paradigm for all the others—over and over it becomes clear that he had a special intention for selecting the one he did and not another.

4) The Rebbe's insights and holy discourses, as he recited and revealed them, matched the rectifications (*tikkunim*) mentioned in them.

5) Wherever the Rebbe quotes part of a verse from Scripture or of a teaching of the Sages in relation to a particular subject or detail thereof, the entire verse or teaching, in all its details, is applicable to and explained by that subject.

6) As explained in the Kabbalah, the verse "God made one to contrast the other" means that whatever exists on the side of holiness and good has a counterpart on the side of impurity and evil (like a simian aping a man). Thus, it is sometimes possible to learn what is good from its parallel on the side of evil.

7) Whenever the Rebbe mentions the attributes or aspects of a particular thing, we can assume that all the attributes and aspects are encompassed in any one of them; any one quality has in it all the qualities of the others. (The Kabbalah speaks of the *sefirot* in much the same way.)

8) All the levels, from the very lowest to the most infinite, are all considered either a light or a vessel. Of any two levels, the lower level is a vessel, and the higher level is the light that fills it.

9) When the Rebbe speaks about the great perception and knowledge of the tzaddik and his teachings, he is essentially referring to the most unique figures of the generations (such as Rebbe Shimon bar Yochai and the Ari), and almost always he is referring exclusively to Moshe-Mashiach himself, whom we all await.

10) Regarding the explanations the Rebbe gave for a verse from Scripture or a teaching of the Sages, which he based on his holy perceptions: He would first lay out and delineate the perception in all its aspects. Then, he would show how all the points he has mentioned are encompassed in a verse or teaching. And when, as sometimes happens, this pattern has not been adhered to, the reason for the change is to be found in the Rebbe's holy words (other than when he first mentions the verse or teaching in passing, with no explanation).

11) When, in the course of his lesson, the Rebbe concludes expounding the intended insight and then brings a verse from Scripture or a teaching of the Sages in which that insight is explained, it is not his intention to include thereby some new concept not previously mentioned. And, should it at times appear to the reader that this is not the case, he ought to know and believe that what seems to be a new concept in fact already appears in the Rebbe's words. By analyzing and laboring at it, the reader will find, to a lesser or greater degree, that this matter too has already been hinted at within the insight which the Rebbe revealed; he will eventually understand the awesome intention which brought the Rebbe to not openly discuss that concept.

12) At times, the Rebbe will quote only the essence of a familiar Talmudic or Kabbalistic teaching, assuming the reader already knows the material or that he will research the matter on his own.

13) In explaining and expounding a verse from Scripture or a teaching of the Sages, the Rebbe does not reinterpret its simple meaning. On the contrary, the meaning

which the Rebbe gives to the verse or teaching is tied to and is one with the simple meaning, so that the one merely completes and clarifies the other.

14) Simple faith in the absolutely exalted and infinitely deep nature of the Creator's knowledge dictates that there are many things which appear contradictory to the human mind, but which His boundless knowledge and wisdom considers not at all conflicting. The reverse is also true. There are things which His knowledge affirms as contradictory, yet the reason for this affirmation is totally hidden and concealed from human comprehension.

15) The Kabbalistic definition of the *Shekhinah* (Divine Presence) as the drawing of His Godliness into creation at large has led some to conclude that in this sense the Divine Presence is a separate entity. In truth, it is not so. Rather, any mention of the Divine Presence refers only to the immanent aspect of God Himself. Whereas, to assume that the *Shekhinah* is a separate entity borders on idolatry.

16) There is no end or limit to the introductions and definitions needed to explain the Torah that resides in the Infinite One's wisdom in order to bring it into the hearts of limited and physical beings (this being the discourses and lessons the tzaddikim reveal to us). For this is indeed paradoxical: explaining and bringing the Infinite One's knowledge into the heart of something finite. Therefore, in truth, it is impossible to make that entry through convolutions and contractions, except by means of faith and a total nullification of one's own opinion. Likewise, commensurate with a person's faith in the words and counsel of the doctors (tzaddikim) for steadily guarding and healing the mind, so one merits fulfilling their words until that knowledge which was previously unknown shines also for him.

17) There are times when the Rebbe will provide two or three proofs for something, but the reader who fails to sufficiently analyze and study the text will see them as one. This happens because of the very tight connection with which the two proofs are bound to each other.

18) It is not the Rebbe's way to incorporate into the connections he makes in his lessons a totally independent topic. Therefore, when this does in any case happen, it was for reasons known only to him.

* * *

APPENDIX B

Tcheriner Rav's Commentary to Lesson #1

Tcheriner Rav's Commentary to Lesson #1

Reb Nachman Goldstein of Tcherin was the son of Reb Zvi Aryeh of Breslov and grandson of Reb Aharon, who was the *rav* of Breslov during Rebbe Nachman's lifetime. Among the people, Reb Nachman was both affectionately and reverently known as the Tcheriner Rav. He became a close follower of Reb Noson and, like his teacher, was a prolific writer of original Torah ideas and discourses based on the teachings of Rebbe Nachman. His works include the *Parparaot LeChokhmah,* a commentary on *Likutey Moharan;* the collected sources for Rebbe Nachman's *Aleph-Bet Book; Leshon Chassidim* and *Derekh Chassidim,* an anthology of the teachings of Rabbi Yisrael, the Baal Shem Tov (1698-1760), Rabbi Dov Ber, the Magid of Mezritch (1704-1772), and their followers.

Among the Tcheriner Rav's many writings are three works which discuss the concepts of *Likutey Moharan* from three different perspectives. The first, *Zimrat HaAretz,* reviews each lesson from the vantage point of *Eretz Yisrael,* as it were. *Yekara D'Shabbata* shows how each lesson in *Likutey Moharan* speaks about Shabbat. *Yerach HaEitanim* shows how each lesson speaks about the month of Tishrei, with its attendant holidays and rituals/mitzvot. Reb Nachman authored yet another priceless tome, *Nachat HaShulchan,* in which he follows Reb Noson's method of explaining a law found in the *Shulchan Arukh* based on a lesson in *Likutey Moharan.* This work is unique in that the Tcheriner Rav bases it all *solely* on one lesson of *Likutey Moharan.* The name, *Nachat HaShulchan,* is based on the concepts relating to the word *NaChaT* as delineated in the opening lesson of *Likutey Moharan.*

As explained in Reb Noson's introduction to *Likutey Moharan,* the lessons of Rebbe Nachman's *magnum opus* have incredible breadth and depth. The Rebbe himself said that "every one of his lessons can be applied to the entire

Written and Oral Torah (Scripture and the entire corpus of Talmud, Midrash, etc.; *Rabbi Nachman's Wisdom* #201). The Tcheriner Rav's works provide the reader with a glimpse of how this is so. Presented over the following pages are samples from these works. Each is based on the first lesson of *Likutey Moharan*. It would have been preferable to present these treasures after each lesson, but that would have been beyond the scope of this work. (We have inserted the particular section of Rebbe Nachman's lesson [or the notes] to which the Tcheriner Rav's material corresponds.)

* * *

ZIMRAT HAARETZ

...because the air of the Holy Land makes one wise (*Bava Batra* 158b), the Land of Israel was given to Yaakov (Genesis 28:13, see *Rashi*). In our lesson, this corresponds to the wisdom found in each thing.

The mitzvah of proclaiming the new moon, the responsibility of the Sanhedrin, had to be performed specifically in the Land of Israel. This is because the Holy Land is known throughout the holy writings as *Malkhut/nun*—i.e. the moon.

The Holy Land corresponds to the good inclination (cf. *Nedarim* 22a), where one can incite his good inclination to overcome his evil inclination (§2). Therefore, the ideal place for Torah study is the Holy Land, for "there is no Torah like the Torah of the Land of Israel" (*Bereishit Rabbah* 16:7). Moreover, the Holy Land is the place of prayer, for every mouth turns towards the site of the Temple in prayer (*Berakhot* 30a). The Holy Land is the place of true grace and charm, as in the words of the prophet (Isaiah 28:4) who called it "glorious beauty" (§1,2).

We have also seen in the lesson that *chein* creates a *tav* (=400)—the dimensions of the Holy Land: 400 *parsah* by 400 *parsah* (*Rashi*, Numbers 13:25). Therefore, our Sages explained the verse (Ecclesiastes 4:6), "Better a handful of *NaChaT* (calm and quiet) than both hands full of labor and stress"—better a small tract in the Land of Israel than a large tract outside it (*Kohelet Rabbah* 4:6).

This is because the main attainment of *NaChaT* (*chein* and *tav*) is in the Holy Land.

* * *

YEKARA D'SHABBATA

Shabbat, which corresponds to great awareness (*Likutey Moharan* I, 119) and the eyes (*Likutey Moharan* II, 67:2), is an aspect of gazing at the intelligence in each thing (§2). This is why God blessed the Shabbat, so that a person's countenance would glow on it (*Bereishit Rabbah* 11:2)—"A person's wisdom (Shabbat) causes his countenance to shine" (see n.10). In addition, whoever observes the Shabbat is given the heritage of our patriarch Yaakov (*Shabbat* 118b), the personification of intelligence.

By virtue of its connection to *Malkhut*, Shabbat is known as the Shabbat Queen, Shabbat *Malketa*. It is spoken of in the holy writings as a time when the evil inclination is more easily subdued. We have seen in Rebbe Nachman's lesson, that Torah study helps one to subjugate the evil inclination. This is why the main Torah reading of the week is on Shabbat. In fact, the Torah itself was given on Shabbat (*Shabbat* 86b). This is why our Sages taught that on Shabbat the rabbis of each community must gather the people and teach them Torah (*Yalkut Shimoni, Vayakhel* 408).

"And NoaCh found *CheiN* (grace) in God's eyes" (Genesis 6:8). Noach is the tzaddik. His name means "rest," corresponding to Shabbat (*Tikkuney Zohar* #70, p.138b), the Day of Rest. That is, Shabbat refers to *CheiN, chet* and *nun*. The *chein* of Shabbat assists in elevating one's prayers (*Zohar* I, 23b).

Our Sages also explained the verse (Ecclesiastes 4:6), "Better a handful of *NaChaT* than both hands full of labor and stress"—better a little on Shabbat than a lot during the rest of the week (*Kohelet Rabbah* 4:6). This is because Shabbat, *chein,* forms a *tav,* the etching of our prayers upon the Supernal Heart.

Yosef, like Noach, corresponds to the tzaddik (*Yesod*; see Appendix: Seven Supernal Shepherds). Thus we understand the Midrash that tells us Yosef observed the Shabbat even prior to its being given to the Jewish people. Shabbat was "the

day he came to the house to do his work" (Genesis 39:11). What was Yosef's work? To study the Torah teachings he had received from his father Yaakov (*Yalkut* 146). Yosef looked for the intelligence/Yaakov found in each thing. He thereby merited having Yaakov's countenance appear to him, enabling him to withstood the with his master's wife (*see n.60*).

Because Shabbat corresponds to *Malkhut,* the moon, it is customary to bless the New Moon (*Birkat Levanah*) on the Shabbat preceding its appearance (*Mishnah Berurah* 417:1). It is also preferable to sanctify the New Moon (*Kiddush Levanah*) right after Shabbat ends (*ibid.,* 426:2).

When Yaakov returned from Lavan's house to the Holy Land, he camped near Shekhem. Scripture (Genesis 33:18) states that "he *yiChaN* (encamped) near the city." There, he kept the Laws of *Techumin* (the limit one can walk outside a city on Shabbat; *Yalkut* 133). In our context, Yaakov had merited *chein* and was able to establish *techumin.* This is because the limit one can walk is two thousand cubits [approximately 2/3 of a mile]. Each *ELePh* (1,000) cubits corresponds to *PeLEh* (wonder). Both *Chokhmah* and *Malkhut* are called *peleh* (see *Likutey Moharan* I, 28:5). Therefore, the two *elephs* correspond to *Chokhmah* and *Malkhut, chet* and *nun.*

* * *

YERACH HAEITANIM

The New Year is calculated according to the solar calendar, *chet,* whereas the New Moon is calculated according to the lunar calendar, *nun* (see n.52). On Rosh HaShanah, the two come together. Yet, as the *Shulchan Arukh* points out, we make no specific mention of the New Moon sacrifices on Rosh HaShanah (*Orach Chaim* 591:2). This is because *nun*/moon has no light of its own, only that which it receives from the sun (§2). Therefore, any mention of the New Year encompasses the New Moon as well.

On Rosh HaShanah it is also customary to pray for the House of King David and the coming of Mashiach, while at the same time requesting the downfall of the *Malkhut* of Evil. Furthermore, during the first ten days of Tishrei, the

concluding words of the third blessing of the *Amidah* are changed to "the Holy King" (*haMelekh haKadosh*). All this shows the importance of elevating *nun/Malkhut* of Holiness, by attaching it to the wisdom found in everything. We also request that He "remember us for life" (*zakhreinu l'chaim*), because attaching ourselves to the letter *chet* is attaching ourselves to life itself (§2).

It is also customary to travel to tzaddikim for Rosh HaShanah. For the tzaddik is the one who strives constantly to empower the *Malkhut* of Holiness over the *Malkhut* of Evil (see *Crossing the Narrow Bridge*, Chapter 18 and *Uman! Uman! Rosh HaShanah*). We find therefore that the letter *tzaddik* is a combination of two other letters, *yod* and *nun*. For *yod/Chokhmah* illumines *nun/Malkhut*.

Moreover, the battle between Yaakov and Esav is replayed every Rosh HaShanah (cf. *Zohar* I, 137b*ff*), the Day of Judgment. This is why we repeatedly pray for awe and fear of God: to merit the wisdom of Yaakov and to be saved from Esav and his "mitzvot" (see nn.66,67). This is also the reason the *Mussaf* prayer on Rosh HaShanah is based on the three blessings: *Malkhiyot, Zikhronot* and *Shofarot*. *Malkhiyot,* which relates to Kingship, corresponds to *Malkhut*. *Zikhronot,* which relates to remembering, corresponds to attaching one's intellect to God. *Shofarot,* which relates to blowing the ram's horn, begins with a reference to the receiving of the Torah, corresponding to the Torah study which enables *Malkhut* of Holiness to prevail.

After Rosh HaShanah come the Ten Days of Repentance. Empowering *Malkhut* of Holiness and striving to perfect one's ways throughout these ten days enables *Malkhut/nun* to be bound with *Chokhmah,* the wisdom revealed on Rosh HaShanah. As a result, "the light of the moon will be like the light of the sun" (§2). On Yom Kippur, the climax of the Ten Days of Repentance, we recite the *Amidah* prayer five times, which enables us to merit *chein* so that our prayers are accepted. In addition, because the moon is waxing, we sanctify it in Tishrei right after Yom Kippur. The moon's subservience to the sun indicates that the *Malkhut* of Evil is defeated and Esav is subjugated completely. This is why our Sages teach: Satan has no power to prosecute on Yom Kippur (*Nedarim* 32b).

Five days after Yom Kippur we celebrate the Festival of Sukkot. Each of us leaves his permanent dwelling and enters a temporary booth, the *sukkah* (cf. *Sukkah* 2a). This alludes to our having to leave the eternalness of spirituality and enter the fleeting whirlwinds of this temporary world. Our only security is the Torah's advice: Remember! this world is transient. Do not let yourselves be drawn to it (like Esav). Rather, always attach your thoughts and intellect to the World to Come. How? By seeking the Godliness in everything.

The Kaballah teaches that *sukkah* is an aspect of *Binah,* indicative of lofty understanding and intelligence. This being so, the laws of *sukkah* require that its shade be greater than its sunlight (*Sukkah* 2a). This, too, teaches us that to focus on the great inner intelligence of every matter, one must "filter" it through *nun,* a constriction. For the same reason, a *sukkah* whose roof is higher than twenty cubits (37 feet) is invalid, for the eyes cannot readily view it (*ibid.*)—i.e., one is unable to grasp the inner intelligence without the aspect of *nun.* Conversely, a *sukkah* lower than ten *tefachim* (37 inches), a "squalid dwelling" (*ibid.* 4a), is also invalid. This is because at such a low level, one has sunken into Esav's realm of squalor.

The reason we take the Four Species (the palm branch, the myrtle, the willow and the citron) on Sukkot is because they represent a wisdom so great that even King Solomon wondered about its meaning (*Vayikra Rabbah* 30:15). The Talmud teaches that the Festival of Sukkot is the most propitious time to pray for water, and these Four Species all require water to grow (cf. *Taanit* 2b). Water alludes to Torah, as in, "Let all who are thirsty, come for water" (Isaiah 55:1, see *Rashi*). For the main way to attain the lofty wisdom concealed in the Four Species is through Torah study, which subdues Esav and empowers the *Malkhut* of Holiness. Therefore, our Sages teach that when we take the Four Species in our hands on Sukkot, we show that we have been victorious over Esav in the [spiritual] battles of Rosh HaShanah and Yom Kippur (*Vayikra Rabbah* 30:2).

The Midrash teaches further: In reward for taking the Four Species on the first day of Sukkot (see Leviticus 23:40), I will reveal Myself to you first—I will take revenge from the "first" (Esav); build you the "first" (the Holy Temple);

and bring you the "first" (Mashiach) (*ibid.* 30:16). "Taking...on the first" refers to seeking the *reishit*/wisdom. This is taking "revenge from the first," because acquiring wisdom subdues Esav, the spirit of folly. "Build you the first," the Holy Temple, is the revelation of the Godliness in everything, for the Divine Presence was revealed in the Temple. And "bring you the first," refers to Mashiach, who is *nun/Malkhut* of Holiness.

The concluding day(s) of Sukkot, Shemini Atzeret and Simchat Torah, correspond(s) to the proper conclusion of all of our devotions during the Days of Awe. This alludes to Yaakov (see *Likutey Moharan* I, 74), the perfection of wisdom, which a person acquires when he always seeks God. This is why we have the custom to call everybody up to the Torah on Simchat Torah. For perfection can only be attained through studying Torah enthusiastically.

* * *

NACHAT HASHULCHAN

The following is just a sampling from the several hundred passages that appear in *Nachat HaShulchan*. As mentioned, this work shows the relationship between laws appearing in the *Shulchan Arukh* and the first lesson of *Likutey Moharan*. The number of the piece quoted from the *Nachat HaShanah* has been inserted at the end of each passage and corresponds to the chapter quoted from the *Shulchan Arukh*.

*

Orach Chaim

A person should do all he can to rouse himself early in order to serve God, so that he awakens the morning...and studies Torah...and at the very least he must be careful not to oversleep the time for prayer. In other words, a person should not wait for God to arouse him. Rather, he should seek God, even in the darkness—i.e., in those places where the light of understanding is beyond him. By doing so, he will already be awake when morning comes, when the sun/intelligence illumines his path. He will then recite the Morning Prayers. And, by arousing himself and studying Torah, he strengthens *Malkhut* of

Holiness. As a result, as Rebbe Nachman has explained, his prayers are accepted (#1).

*

A person should daily recite the Morning Blessings, which teach us to find the Godliness even in the mundane. Among other things, the last of these blessings requests that we be spared from the evil inclination and that we merit *chein.* Immediately afterward, we also pray that we be saved from brazen-faced people, alluding to Esav and the *Malkhut* of Evil (#46).

*

Before the onset of Shabbat, a person should bathe in warm water. This corresponds to the incineration of the three evil forces, or *kelipot* (see *Likutey Moharan* I, 19:5, n.86). This also corresponds to (Obadiah 1:18), "Then, the House of Yaakov will be fire, the House of Yosef flame, and the House of Esav straw. They will set them alight and consume them." In our context, this refers to Esav, the *Malkhut* of Evil, being subjugated by Yaakov and Yosef, who correspond to those who gaze at the intelligence in everything (#260).

*

Also based on Rebbe Nachman's first lesson, the *Nachat HaShulchan* offers a unique commentary on the text of the Pesach Haggadah (#472, parts of which are quoted in *The Breslov Haggadah.*)

*

Yoreh Deah

It is forbidden to eat the sciatic nerve. Yaakov came away from his battle with Esav's angel limping; the angel had struck and damaged his sciatic nerve. This alludes to Yaakov's constant struggle against the evil inclination, Esav (#64, #65).

*

Before meat may be eaten it must be thoroughly salted and rinsed in order to remove all the blood. This alludes to removing all one's undesirable thoughts. By doing so, a person who truly seeks God can attain Godly wisdom. Yet, he must be patient if he is to utterly remove the "blood" of evil thoughts, the evil inclination, from his heart (the seat of the blood). This is the reason for

the salt: to thoroughly expurgate the blood—symbol of a person's attempt to incite his good inclination against his evil inclination (#69).

*

When one Jew lends money to another, it is forbidden for him to charge interest. Poverty stems from the aspect of the moon, which has nothing of its own (§2). Nevertheless, charity and kindness help to fill this lack. Therefore, our Sages call a loan *halvaat chein* (a loan of grace), where the lender (*chet*) gives from his "light" to the poor (*nun*). Then, as Scripture states (Leviticus 25:35), "Your brother shall *live* with you"—this loan brings him *chet*/life (n.16). However, if the lender charges interest, he is not giving to the poor man—not filling the *nun's* lack—but actually taking from him, for the poor man must now add to his poverty by paying back more than he borrowed (#159).

*

Even HaEzer

Every man is obligated to marry and have children. In our context, man and woman correspond to the sun (*chet*) and moon (*nun*), respectively. The nature of their offspring will depend upon their intentions at the time of union. If their intentions are holy, Godliness will be revealed in the world through their children. This is why our Sages taught: When someone refuses to have children, it is as if he committed murder (*Yevamot* 63b)—i.e., he killed off his chance to reveal Godliness. He is likened to Esav, a murderer. Yet, unlike the other mitzvot, which become obligatory upon a young man at the age of thirteen, the mitzvah to marry can be delayed to eighteen (cf. *Avot* 5:21). The reason is that every young man should first be given the time and opportunity to study Torah. Only then will he be able to empower *Malkhut* of Holiness and create a corresponding union of holiness between himself and his wife, between *chet* and *nun,* and so merit righteous children (#1).

* * *

APPENDIX C

Biographical Sketches

The Life of Rebbe Nachman

Rebbe Nachman's Disciples

The Life of Rebbe Nachman

Rebbe Nachman of Breslov (5532-5571; 1772-1810), great-grandson of the founder of the Chassidic movement, Rebbe Yisrael Baal Shem Tov, was born in Medzeboz, Ukraine, in his great-grandfather's home. As a child Rebbe Nachman was privileged to see many of the great tzaddikim who had been disciples of the Baal Shem Tov. This, together with his noble lineage prepared him for his mission in life: to bring the Jewish people closer to God and prepare the world for the coming of the Mashiach.

After his wedding (5545/1785) Rebbe Nachman lived with his in-laws in Ossatin. When his widowed father-in-law remarried, Rebbe Nachman moved to Medvedevka where he first began to attract a following (circa 5551/1791). While living in Medvedevka, Rebbe Nachman set out for the Holy Land (5558/1798). His visit there brought him to new heights in serving God, such that he later wanted only those lessons he taught after his pilgrimage to be recorded in his *magnum opus, Likutey Moharan.* After his return (summer 5559/1799), Rebbe Nachman remained in Medvedevka for little over a year.

From Medvedevka Rebbe Nachman moved to Zlatipolia where he lived for two years, despite tremendous opposition from the Shpola Zeida and his supporters in the neighboring towns. From there Rebbe Nachman moved to Breslov (fall 5562/1802). It was in Breslov that the Rebbe contracted tuberculosis, to which he ultimately succumbed. And it was in Breslov that the Rebbe's most famous disciple, Reb Noson, first made contact with him.

Immediately after Sukkot of 5568 (1808) Rebbe Nachman traveled to Lemberg (Lvov). Ostensibly this was for the sake of receiving medical treatment for his tuberculosis. In fact, Rebbe Nachman explained to his chassidim, one of his reasons for the journey was to combat atheism. Submitting to medical treatment was merely a tool for doing so. When the Rebbe returned

from Lemberg he spoke more than ever about the importance of strengthening one's faith. He also intimated a number of times that the lessons he gave post-Lemberg were essentially meant as his ethical will.

During the period that the *Likutey Moharan* was being prepared for press (5568/1808), as well as afterwards, Rebbe Nachman often spoke about the importance of this work. He said that one who would study it honestly would have his heartstrings softened so that he would be able to draw himself closer to God. On another occasion the Rebbe said that if necessary one should sell the pillow from under his head in order to purchase *Likutey Moharan.* Most importantly, the Rebbe said that his teachings were *atchalta d'geulah,* the beginning of the Redemption, and that people should study his teachings well enough to be totally conversant in each of the lessons (see *About Rebbe Nachman's Teachings,* pp.41-50).

In the spring of 5570 (1810) Rebbe Nachman left Breslov for Uman, the city he chose as his final resting place. His main efforts for the remainder of his life, less than another half year, were centered on encouraging his followers to remain steadfast to his teachings, getting heretical Jews to return to the faith, and elevating the souls of those already gone from this world. Rebbe Nachman passed away on Tuesday afternoon, the second day of Chol HaMoed Sukkot, 18 Tishrei 5571 (October 16, 1810), and was buried in the old cemetery of Uman amidst the 20,000 Jewish martyrs who had been massacred by the Haidemacks some forty years earlier.

For a more detailed account of Rebbe Nachman's life and teachings see *Until the Mashiach* (Breslov Research Institute, 1985), and *Tzaddik* (Breslov Research Institute, 1987).

* * *

Rebbe Nachman's Disciples

Of all of Rebbe Nachman's disciples, these are the ones whose names appear most often in the lessons' footnotes.

Reb Noson (5540-5605;1780-1844) was born in Nemirov to Reb Naftali Hertz Sternhartz. A young scholar with a real promise for greatness, Reb Noson married the daughter of Reb David Zvi Orbach, a leading rabbinical authority of the Podolia region at that time.

Despite his personal success as a Talmud scholar and his prestige as heir apparent to his father-in-law, Reb Noson felt a spiritual void. He spent many years visiting the great Chassidic masters of the time. Though he gained much from each of them he still felt unfulfilled. Then in 5562 (1802), when Rebbe Nachman moved to Breslov, a friend suggested that Reb Noson meet with Rebbe Nachman. He did and the rest is history.

Under Rebbe Nachman's tutelage Reb Noson's horizons expanded in both the revealed and concealed aspects of Torah. Most importantly, under the Rebbe's guidance Reb Noson learned the art of writing. His ability to distill and clarify Torah novellae, in particular Rebbe Nachman's teachings, became refined to the point of perfection. It was this ability that allowed for the transmission of Breslover Chassidut to this very day.

With Rebbe Nachman's passing in 5571 (1810), Reb Noson slowly but surely grew into his role as the Rebbe's torchbearer. Throughout the remainder of his life Reb Noson devoted himself constantly to ensuring that Rebbe Nachman's legacy would not pass from the world. He did whatever was necessary to that end: building and maintaining the Breslover synagogue in Uman, editing and publishing Rebbe Nachman's works, teaching the Rebbe's lessons and exemplifying them in his own life. This was often done even under the threat of imprisonment and death.

A thorough and comprehensive study of Reb Noson's life can be found in *Through Fire and Water* (Breslov Research Institute, 1992).

*

Reb Shimon, the Rebbe's attendant, was the first of Rebbe Nachman's chassidim. His physical strength and great presence of mind once enabled him to save the Rebbe's life. Apparently, it was Reb Shimon who accompanied Rebbe Nachman on his pilgrimage to the Holy Land. Reb Shimon himself eventually settled in *Eretz Yisrael,* living on the outskirts of Safed, where he spent much time engaged in *hitbodedut.* He is buried in the old cemetery of Safed alongside the path that leads from the grave of the Ari to that of Rabbi Yosef Caro.

*

Reb Yudel of Dashev had been a disciple of Rebbe Pinchas of Koritz. At the time he met Rebbe Nachman, Reb Yudel was the leading figure in his town. He gladly relinquished his stature to become the Rebbe's chassid. An eminent Kabbalist, Reb Yudel was assigned by the Rebbe to take *pidyonot* and intercede on behalf of the sick, the childless, the needy, etc., after the Rebbe's demise. Reb Noson once commented that since Reb Yudel could hear the heavenly summons calling the wicked back to Hell on Saturday night, he, Reb Noson, had nothing to fear from the enemies of the Breslover Chassidim. Reb Yudel passed away in 5598 (1838).

*

Reb Shmuel Isaac was also from Dashev. He was blessed with great physical strength and so among the devotions Rebbe Nachman prescribed for him was to speak to each of his limbs about the true purpose of life. As Reb Noson once remarked, "The Rebbe led Reb Shmuel Isaac [in his Divine service] along the razor's edge." Reb Shmuel Isaac so devoted his great strength to prayer that he himself commented, "If I were to recite the *Shema* today no better than I did yesterday, I would have no reason to live." He passed away in 5587 (1826).

*

Reb Aharon, a young scholar from a long line of distinguished rabbis, was

chosen by Rebbe Nachman to be the official rabbi in Breslov. Some time earlier, while the Rebbe was still living in Medvedevka, Reb Aharon was called upon to adjudicate a business dispute there. Rebbe Nachman sent for Reb Aharon, and the two talked from late afternoon till dawn the next day. Reb Aharon later said that if he had come to this world only to experience that night—a night in which he barely knew that he was in this world—it would have been sufficient. In addition to his natural ability to render halakhic (legal) decisions, Reb Aharon received a blessing from Rebbe Nachman to render his decisions free of any distortions. He passed away on the first of Av, 5605 (August 4, 1845).

*

Reb Naftali was a very close friend of Reb Noson and second only to him in understanding Rebbe Nachman's way. When Reb Naftali first met the Rebbe, he was devoting his entire day to his business ventures. Rebbe Nachman slowly weaned him from this, so that, eventually, Reb Naftali's entire time was spent in Torah and prayer. The Rebbe also advised him that after he, Rebbe Nachman, passed away, Reb Naftali should sit alone for the third meal of Shabbat and recite original Torah discourses. When Reb Naftali expressed his wonder about this, the Rebbe replied, "If I tell you to do this, you need not worry who will hear you." Reb Naftali was later seen faithfully carrying out the Rebbe's instructions. In his later years, Reb Naftali lived in a small room atop the Breslover synagogue in Uman. He passed away on the 19th of Av, 5620 (August 7, 1860).

* * *

APPENDIX D

About Rebbe Nachman's Teachings

About Rebbe Nachman's Teachings

The Rebbe said: "As yet the world has not had the least taste of me. If they were to hear just one of my lessons together with its proper melody and dance, they would pass into a state of total surrender. I mean the whole world—even the animals and plants! Everything which exists would be nullified. Their very souls would expire from the overwhelming delight they would have."

*

The Rebbe said that *Likutey Moharan* was "the beginning of the Redemption. Now that it has come out," he said, "I very much want people to study it. They must study it so much that they know it by heart, because it is filled with guidance and it has the power to stir men to God in a way nothing else can compare with. Those who do so have no need for any other work on ethics and moral guidance." Later on he said explicitly that learning his works was the beginning of the Redemption—may it come speedily in our days. He said the best way to study his works was to follow two separate routines. The first should be to study swiftly so as to become thoroughly conversant with the books. The second should be to study in depth, because his books contain the profoundest depths.

*

Once the Rebbe was encouraging someone to study his book. He said it was a great mitzvah to study it at length, and he told him that one could develop a great mind through doing so, because even in its literal interpretation the work contains profound wisdom and depth. Those who study his works constantly can become pure and holy and will then be worthy of seeing the inner meaning they contain. Beneath the surface there is much that is not evident at all on a literal level. Happy is the one who can study them regularly.

*

He said: "In my teachings there is depth." Some of his lessons were recorded

by others. However, where the text is his own, one should examine it with the same care and precision as a Biblical passage. The Rebbe appears to be constantly repeating himself in a way which seems superfluous. In fact this is intentional and serves a very important purpose. One must examine what he says with great care. Someone who has eyes and devotes himself wholeheartedly to understanding the Rebbe's words will understand a tiny portion of the tremendous depths which his works contain. They are unparalleled by any other work.

*

The Rebbe was once praising *Likutey Moharan* his own book and he said it is possible to become a complete *baal teshuvah* (master of repentance) through learning it. He very much wanted it to be printed over and over again and spread throughout the world.

He said: "There will be people who will learn and pray by means of this book." And he said that if a person is prepared to sit with his works and study them in a spirit of openness and honesty without trying to pick holes and argue for the sake of it, then without any doubt his heart's obstinacy will disappear.

He said that everyone should try to buy the book. Somebody who didn't have the money should sell all his other books in order to buy this work. If the man didn't have books to sell, he should sell the very pillow under his head to buy it. He said the book would prove to have great significance, and it would be in great demand. It would be printed again and again... He said that in the case of the lessons he himself had written down, the language itself was very beneficial, for these lessons were universal.

*

When the manuscript of the first part of *Likutey Moharan* was being bound, the Rebbe said: "To you this may seem like a simple matter, but many worlds depend on this!"

*

He said: "The Evil One has great power to cover peoples eyes. Were it not for this, the book would cause a tremendous arousal in the world."

*

I was told that he said that his lessons come from a place from where no one else has ever received. Once I heard him speaking proudly about the greatness of his teachings and he said: "Don't I know where I take them from!" From what he said and the way he said it, the implication was that he drew his Torah teachings from the highest, most exalted of places.

*

Someone told me that the Rebbe had been praising his Torah teachings and emphasizing their greatness, and he said that people should make great efforts to buy his books. For even if they are just lying in a chest or in a bookcase they are of great benefit. He said that his books have a great protective power in a house and can even protect against loss and damage to one's property and possessions... Elsewhere it is mentioned how much the Rebbe desired that his teachings be spread out amongst all Jews, though not for his own honor, God forbid.

*

He said he did not want any of the teachings he revealed prior to his visit to the Holy Land to be included in his books, only those he gave afterwards. And as for these, they should all be written down, even his casual conversations: everything should be written. He told us many times to record every single conversation we heard from him. "When something is written in a book," he said, "if a person does not remember it today he can always look at it again and learn it another time. But the things you hear from my lips you will never ever hear another time. So you must certainly remember every single word and write everything down—every conversation, every story...everything." (It was because of this that I started writing down some of the things I heard from him personally or second hand, but this was only a tiny fraction.)

*

The Rebbe said explicitly that every single conversation of his had the power to bring us to purity and holiness and even make us tzaddikim of the kind he wanted us to be all our lives. We just had to be prepared to follow what he

said and work with it. Anyone who had the privilege of hearing him in person knows very well that this is the truth. Even today, studying his words has a great power to inspire people to come closer to God and follow His ways. We must just set ourselves to follow the Rebbe's words exactly as they are recorded in this and other works.

Each one of his conversations has a formidable power to inspire people to come closer to God. They contain sound, direct pathways to God—pathways which are accessible to everyone, regardless of their level. Even people on the highest of levels can derive clear guidance and direction from his every word. At the other extreme, even a person on the lowest of levels, God forbid, can also receive direction and guidance on how to save his soul from destruction and return to God in truth. All that is necessary is to pay careful attention to the Rebbe's words and fulfill them honestly and with simplicity, with no attempts at sophistication. Happy are those who hold onto his words.

*

The Rebbe said: "Whatever I tell you of my Torah ideas is only the scraps, and these scraps are thousands and myriads of levels lower than the level at which I perceive them. I am unable to say them any lower."

*

The Rebbe's lessons and discourses are universal. The more you explore them the more you will discover their wonderful freshness and sweetness and radiant light. They possess great depth both in their simple meaning and on the hidden, mystical level. All his lessons contain awesome secrets but this is something which is impossible to explain. Each lesson also deals with the mystical significance of the mitzvot: each lesson relates to some of the mystical devotions as explained in kabbalistic works like the *Etz Chaim* and the *Pri Etz Chaim.*

Regarding the lessons written in his own words, he said they will bear the same minute examination as Biblical verses. They contain many hidden meanings. There are passages where the Rebbe repeats himself apparently for no reason. However, these passages have to be examined thoroughly, because

each of the repetitions has a purpose. The Rebbe also said that the lessons which were written in his own words possess a special power because of their universality. The most important thing is the *mussar*—the guidance and the prescriptions for practical living—which emerges from every one of his lessons. This is besides the hidden secrets they contain, which cannot be explained in writing and must be left for the reader himself to form his own conception.

*

The Rebbe said that students of his works who have a little intelligence believe that the kabbalistic approach of the Ari and others is also alluded to in his books, and they consider it a point in their favor that his works reach such a high level. What such people did not realize is that the opposite is true: the kabbalistic approach of the earlier authorities is also included in his writings. While the Rebbe did not finish the thought explicitly, his meaning was quite clear: His teachings go beyond those of the earlier masters, and the goal of his own teachings is far and away more exalted. Nevertheless, the ideas of the earlier masters are also included in his teachings.

*

The Rebbe said that if the Baal Shem Tov had heard his teachings, he would also have found them original. And if Rebbe Shimon bar Yochai had heard his teachings, he would also have found them original, even for his time.

*

"When I wanted to go to the Land of Israel, I gave my teachings a new direction. When I started my journey, they changed again to a higher level. When I was actually there, I gave my teachings a new direction. And when I returned, I gave them a new direction still."

His awesome perceptions of Torah really began after his visit to the Holy Land and, indeed, he reached a level where he was actually ashamed of his teachings prior to his pilgrimage. Almost all of *Likutey Moharan* consists of teachings dating from after his return from the Holy Land, with the exception of about three or four pages in the middle of the book.

*

"That a single word does not leave my lips without some innovation—that goes without saying. Not even a breath leaves my lips without originality."

*

I once said to him that even his ordinary conversations were quite literally Torah. He said this was correct: Just as it was impossible for a Torah scholar to talk without at least a few words of Torah entering in—expressions from the Talmud and the like—so in his case, no matter what he said, the Torah was bound to come in. Indeed, we saw with our own eyes many times how his ordinary conversations turned into Torah teachings. A quite casual conversation would develop into the most extraordinary Torah teaching. I am only speaking about what was visible to us, quite apart from the many hidden things contained in his conversations, of which people on our level have no conception.

*

The Rebbe said that even those who hear the tzaddik's teachings without understanding them will understand them in the next world. In essence, his teachings are directed at our souls, and when we reach the next world our souls will be well-versed in these exalted teachings. In this world the main thing is to fulfill the tzaddik's teachings to the letter, according to their simple meaning. We should follow them in the way the Rebbe advised us to several times, namely, to go with a particular lesson for a period of time, until all one's devotions from morning till night are in accordance with the lesson in question. After this he should continue with another teaching drawn from a different lesson. He should follow this practice constantly until he has gone through all the Rebbe's lessons. God will help with this. It is very important not to be in too much of a hurry or try to do everything all at once. Proceed calmly, in an orderly way, advancing steadily a little at a time. This is the way to make genuine progress until in the end you will be able to fulfill all the Rebbe's teachings.

*

Countless times we saw with our own eyes how things which were

happening in the world, and especially to the Rebbe's followers, were all included in his lessons. By means of his Torah teachings he drew sweet, positive and salutory influences into all aspects of the world, both in general and in particular, spiritually and physically.

Each of the Rebbe's lessons included any number of events which were taking place at the time... Aside from the hidden aspects of which only God is aware, the teaching also addresses all those present at the time it was given. The concerns, thoughts and affairs, as well as the circumstances and troubles affecting each and every one of the people standing there are to be explicitly found within the words of the lesson. Indeed, the events of the world at large and the wars which were being waged—even whatever was happening throughout all the upper worlds—are all hinted at in his words, their universality being very great from every conceivable point of view. Their remarkableness can neither be expressed in words nor fathomed in the heart. Nothing like it has ever been seen or heard.

*

The Rebbe once told a parable to explain why he revealed so many remarkable teachings and stories and shared so many of his thoughts with us, even though it did not yet seem possible that his words could achieve their purpose.

Once there was a king whose only son became so ill that all the doctors despaired of curing him. Meanwhile, a doctor of outstanding wisdom came. The king begged him to try his best to cure the prince. The doctor told him truthfully that the prince's chances of being healed were very remote. However, there was still a means of last resort. If they tried this, there was a very faint possibility that the prince might be cured. "But I do not know whether I should tell you what this method is," said the doctor, "because it will be very hard indeed to use it." The king pressed him to reveal what the method was. The doctor said: "You should know that your son's illness is so critical that it is now quite impossible to give him even a single drop of medicine to swallow. However, there exist certain remedies which are so priceless that a single small bottle costs thousands and thousands [of gold pieces]. What you have to do is

to fill barrels full of these precious remedies and take bucketfuls of these remedies and pour them over your son. Obviously all these precious remedies will go to waste, but the prince will become very slightly stronger as a result. And it may be that as they pour all this over him, a tiny drop will go into his mouth and then it may thus be possible for him to be healed." The king immediately agreed and gave instructions to do what the doctor had said, and this was how the prince was healed.

The meaning is obvious. It is precisely because we are so crushed by our sickness—the sickness of the soul, God forbid—that the tzaddik, the faithful doctor, is forced to pour such priceless remedies over us, even though it would seem that virtually all of them will go to waste. Nevertheless, the sweet scent is absorbed, and in the fullness of time it may be that we will be able to let a drop penetrate our mouths and our inner being. Then there will be some hope for us to be healed, spiritually and physically.

*

The Rebbe said that if his book *Likutey Moharan* had never come into the world, events would have taken a different course. He had several times felt a desire to produce a halakhic work giving legal decisions on all the laws in the *Shulchan Arukh*. In each detail of the halakhah the work would have given a conclusive decision or stated which previous authority's decision was binding. However, now that *Likutey Moharan* had come into the world the other work would never materialize.

*

"As for me," he said, "I am not part of the present world at all. That is why the world cannot bear me. The role of leader is of no relevance to me at all... Even the little authority I do have goes contrary to nature. I had to force myself to accept it against my nature, because it is only by this means that something I say is able to come into the world. Were it not for the little bit of authority I possess, none of my teachings or conversations or stories would be able to come into the world. If there had been no such generation as the present and my teachings had been given in the time of the Ari, of blessed memory, or even in

the time of Rebbe Shimon bar Yochai, of blessed memory, there would have been a very big commotion."

*

Scripture says: "Depart from evil and do good" (Psalms 34:15). "My way of 'departing from evil' is an extraordinary innovation," the Rebbe said, "and my 'doing good' is also extraordinary, because in truth I do very much good, and my Torah teachings achieve a great deal in the world. All the blessings in the world are brought down to the world through my teachings."

*

I was told that previously he had said that he had certain Torah teachings without garments. This means that he was unable to clothe them in any garment... He said that the reason he had to struggle so much before he taught his lessons was because it was very difficult for him to bring his Torah ideas down and clothe them in garments and words in order to express them and reveal them. Prior to giving his lessons he would sit with us for as much as an hour or two, and from his movements and groaning it was clear that he was struggling. He would sit without speaking, but his movements betrayed the intensity of the struggle. Only afterwards would he open his mouth and begin speaking.

*

At the time *Likutey Moharan* was being printed, he said to me: "Surely you are entitled to feel encouraged seeing that you have such a great share in the book!" He went on to say that the whole book was mine, because without me the book would never have come into the world. He explained to me how it was that the whole book had come about through me. Then he said: "You yourself know something of the true greatness of this book and its holiness. And even more than this, you should have faith in its greatness. They've printed a thousand copies," he said, "and each one will come into the hands of several people." In other words I should take heart from having been privileged to have such a positive influence over the community at large.

*

The above excerpts are from *Tzaddik*, pp.301-327.

APPENDIX E

Printing History

LIKUTEY MOHARAN: Printing History*

1808 — 1st printing, Part I, in Ostrog, by Rebbe Nachman

1811 — 1st printing, Part II, in Mohilov, by Reb Noson

1821 — 2nd printing, Parts I and II, in Breslov, by Reb Noson, including introductions, approbations and additions

1830 — (approximately) 3rd printing, in Lemberg, by Reb Noson

1874 — 4th printing, in Jerusalem, by Reb Pesach Zaslavsky

1876 — 5th printing, in Lemberg, by Tcheriner Rav

1910 — 6th printing, in Jerusalem, by Reb Dovid Zvi Dashevsky

1924 — 7th printing, in Warsaw, by Reb Yehudah Leib Rosenberg and Reb Aharon Leib Ziegelman

1936 — 8th printing, in Warsaw, by Reb Aharon Leib Ziegelman

1938 — 9th printing, in Jerusalem, by Reb Shmuel Horowitz

1938 — 10th printing, in Warsaw, by Yisroel Fried

1947 — 11th printing, in Regensburg, by Reb Zvi Reichman

1958 — 12th printing, in New York, by Reb Bayrach Rubinsohn, Reb Yitzchok Menachem Rottenberg and Reb Zvi Wasilski

1966 — 13th printing, in Bnei Brak, by Yeshivat Breslov

1966 — 14th printing, in New York, by Reb Eliezer Shelomoh Shick, with Rabbi Zvi Aryeh Rosenfeld and his students

Since 1966, *Likutey Moharan* has been printed almost every year, primarily in Israel. Of special note is the 1986 edition, by Agudat Meshech HaNachal, which was the first printing to include vowel signs (*nikud*) for the text; and the 1993 edition, by Torat HaNetzach, which presents the text in an entirely new format.

----

* Other than the last notation, this data on *Likutey Moharan* comes from *Nevey Tzaddikim*, by Rabbi Noson Zvi Keonig, Bnei Brak, 1969.

APPENDIX F

Bibliography

BIBLIOGRAPHY

Advice. *Likutey Etzot* in Hebrew, a collection of concise teachings and advice based on the works of Rebbe Nachman, by Reb Noson of Breslov (see *Fire and Water*), first published in Lemberg, 1840. This English translation by Avraham Greenbaum (b. 1949) was published by Breslov Research Institute, Jerusalem, 1983. A second edition of *Likutey Etzot*, based also on the works of Reb Noson, by Rabbi Nachman of Tcherin, was first published in Lemberg, 1874.

Aleph-Bet Book, The. *Sefer HaMidot* in Hebrew, an alphabetical listing of concise practical epigrams and aphorisms on all aspects of life, by Rebbe Nachman of Breslov, first published in Mohilov, 1811. This English translation by Moshe Mykoff (b. 1951) was published by Breslov Research Institute, 1986.

Alim LeTerufah. Collection of letters by Reb Noson of Breslov (see *Fire and Water*), first published in Berdichev, 1896, and with additions in Jerusalem, 1911. A more complete edition was published by Rabbi Aaron Leib Tziegelman in Jerusalem, 1930. An English translation, by Yaakov Gabel, entitled *Eternally Yours*, is being published by Breslov Research Institute in Jerusalem, 1993-. We have used the annotated and vocalized edition, published by Meshekh HaNachal, in Jerusalem, 1992.

Alshekh. Commentary on the entire Bible, properly known as Torat Moshe, by Rabbi Moshe Alshekh (1498-1560) of Safed. First printed in Venice, 1601.

Anaf Yosef. Commentary on *Eyn Yaakov* (q.v.), by Rabbi Chanokh Zundel ben Yosef (d. 1867), first published with his other commentary, *Etz Yosef*, in the Vilna, 1883, edition of *Eyn Yaakov*.

Ari. Rabbi Yitzchak Luria (1534-1572). Both the Ari, and his disciple Rabbi Chaim Vital (1542-1620), were the leaders of the Safed school of Kabbalah. Many consider the Ari the greatest of all Kabbalists.

Arukh. One of the earliest and most popular Talmudic dictionaries, by Rabbi Natan (ben Yechiel) of Rome (1035-1106), first printed in Rome, 1472.

Avanehah Barzel. Stories and teachings of Rebbe Nachman and his disciples, collected by an important Breslover leader, Rabbi Shmuel Horowitz (1903-1973), first printed in Jerusalem, 1935. We have used the Jerusalem, 1972, edition, printed together with *Kokhavey Or* (q.v.).

Avodah Zarah. Tractate of the Talmud (q.v.).

Avot. Tractate of the Talmud (q.v.).

Avot deRabbi Natan. A running commentary on *Avot*, by the Babylonian sage, Rabbi Natan

(circa. 210 c.e.). It is printed in all editions of the Talmud. We have followed the paragraphing of the Vilna, 1883, Romm edition of the Talmud.

Ayeh?. English translation of *Likutey Moharan* II, 112 and other Breslov literature related to that lesson, published by Breslov Research Institute, Jerusalem, 1984.

Azamra. English translation of *Likutey Moharan* I, 282 and other Breslov literature related to that lesson, published by Breslov Research Institute, Jerusalem, 1984.

Baal HaTurim. Commentary on the Torah by Rabbi Yaakov ben Asher (1270-1343), famed author of the *Tur* (q.v.), of Toledo, Spain. This popular work was first printed in Constantinople, 1514, and has subsequently been included in many editions of the Torah.

Bahir. An important ancient Kabbalistic work, attributed to the school of Rabbi Nechunia ben Hakana (circa 80 c.e.) first printed in Amsterdam, 1651. English translation by Rabbi Aryeh Kaplan (q.v.) was published by Weiser, in York, Maine, 1979.

Bamidbar Rabbah. Section of *Midrash Rabbah* (q.v.) dealing with the Book of Numbers.

Bartenura. Commentary on the entire Mishnah (q.v.), by Rabbi Ovadiah Bartenura (1445-1530), first published in Cracow, 1542.

Batey Midrashot. A collection of ancient Midrashim and similar material from manuscript by Rabbi Shelomoh Aharon Wertheimer (1866-1935), first published in Jerusalem, 1893-97, and with additions in Jerusalem, 1950.

Bava Batra. Tractate of the Talmud (q.v.).

Bava Kama. Tractate of the Talmud (q.v.).

Bava Metzia. Tractate of the Talmud (q.v.).

Belbey HaNachal. Commentary on *Likutey Moharan* (q.v.), by Rabbi Barukh Ephraim (ben Yitzchak), first printed together with *Parparaot LeChokhmah* (q.v.) in Lvov (Lemberg), 1876. It was later printed with *Likutey Moharan*, New York, 1966).

Beitza. Tractate of the Talmud (q.v.).

Bekhorot. Tractate of the Talmud (q.v.).

Bender, Rabbi Levi Yitzchak (1897-1989). Oral teachings, by one of the most prominent elders in Breslov in Jerusalem. Rabbi Bender, a student of Reb Avraham Chazan (see *Biur HaLikutim*), was a major force in building Breslover Chassidut since his arrival in Israel in 1949.

Berakhot. Tractate of the Talmud (q.v.).

Bereishit Rabbah. Section of *Midrash Rabbah* (q.v.) dealing with the Book of Genesis. It is a commentary on Scripture, based on Talmudic material.

Bikkurim. Tractate of the Talmud (q.v.).

Biur HaLikutim. Commentary on *Likutey Moharan* (q.v.), by Rabbi Avraham (Chazan HaLevi) ben Reb Nachman of Tulchin (1849-1917), printed in part in Jerusalem, 1908, and in greater part

in Bnei Brak, 1967. The complete work was published in 1935, by Rabbi Shmuel Horowitz, in Jerusalem. We have used the most recent edition, published in 1989, by Mordechai Frank, in Jerusalem.

Breslov Haggadah, The. Traditional Pesach Haggadah with facing English translation and running commentary based on the teachings of Rebbe Nachman and general sources, by Yehoshua Starret, published by Breslov Research Institute, in Jerusalem, 1989.

Burstyn, Rabbi Nachman (b.1934). Oral teachings, by a leading figure in Breslov in Jerusalem.

Chagigah. Tractate of the Talmud (q.v.).

Challah. Tractate of the Talmud (q.v.).

Charedim. Important work on the commandments and Kabbalistic theology, by Rabbi Elazar Azikri (1533-1600), first published in Venice, 1601. The author was an important Kabbalist and leader of the Safed school.

Chayey Adam. Code of Jewish law based on *Orach Chaim* (q.v.), dealing with prayers, blessings, Shabbat and the festivals, by Rabbi Avraham Danzig (1748-1820). First printed in Vilna, 1810.

Chayey Moharan. See *Tzaddik.*

Chayey Nefesh. Kabbalistic discussion of Breslover principles, by Rabbi Gedalia Aharon Koenig (q.v.), published in Tel Aviv, 1968.

Cheshin, Rabbi Zvi. Oral teachings, by a leading figure in Breslov in Jerusalem.

Choshen Mishpat. Fourth section of *Shulchan Arukh* (q.v.), dealing with judicial law.

Chullin. Tractate of the Talmud (q.v.).

Crossing the Narrow Bridge. A practical guide to Rebbe Nachman's teachings, by Chaim Kramer (b. 1945), published by Breslov Research Institute, Jerusalem, 1989.

D'mai. Tractate of the Talmud (q.v.).

Derekh HaShem. See *The Way of God.*

Devarim Rabbah. Section of *Midrash Rabbah* (q.v.) dealing with the Book of Deuteronomy.

Eduyot. Tractate of the Talmud (q.v.).

Eikhah Rabbah. Section of *Midrash Rabbah* (q.v.) dealing with the Book of Lamentations.

Erkhin. Tractate of the Talmud (q.v.).

Eruvin. Tractate of the Talmud (q.v.).

Esther Rabbah. Section of *Midrash Rabbah* (q.v.) dealing with the Book of Esther.

Etz Chaim. The major classic of Kabbalah, based on the teachings of the Ari (q.v.), by Rabbi Chaim Vital, first published by Rabbi Meir Poppers in Koretz, 1782. We have used the Jerusalem, 1988, edition.

Etz Yosef. See *Anaf Yosef.*

Even HaEzer. Third section of *Shulchan Arukh* (q.v.), dealing with marriage, divorce and related topics.

Eyn Yaakov. Collection of *aggadot* (non-legal portions) of the Talmud, compiled by Rabbi Yaakov (ben Shelomoh) ibn Chabib (1433-1516) and his son Rabbi Levi ibn Chabib, first published in Salonika, 1515-22. We have used the Vilna, 1883, Romm edition.

Fire and Water. A thoroughly researched biography on the life of Reb Noson (ben Reb Naftali Hertz) Sternhartz of Breslov (1780-1844), Rebbe Nachman's scribe and leading disciple (see Biographical Sketches). This is a monumental work on the man who did the most to establish and build Breslover Chassidut, by Chaim Kramer, published by Breslov Research Institute, in Jerusalem, 1992.

Garden of the Souls. Translation and commentary on *Likutey Moharan* I, 65, by Avraham Greenbaum, published by Breslov Research Institute, Jerusalem, 1990.

Gittin. Tractate of the Talmud (q.v.).

Hagah. Gloss on the *Shulchan Arukh* (q.v.), presenting the Ashkenazic customs, by Rabbi Moshe (ben Yisrael) Isserles (1525-1572). Originally known as *HaMappah*, it was first published together with the *Shulchan Arukh* in Cracow, 1578, and in virtually every subsequent edition. The author was a leading rabbinical figure in Cracow, and one of the greatest halakhic authorities of all time.

HaKotev. Commentary on the *Eyn Yaakov* (q.v.) appearing with the first and all subsequent editions, by the compilers of the *Eyn Yaakov*, Rabbi Yaakov (ben Shelomoh) ibn Chabib and his son, Rabbi Levi.

Hekhalot Rabbati. Important meditative work from the Merkava school of Kabbalah, attributed to Rabbi Yishmael (1st century c.e.), and also known as *Pirkey Hekhalot*. First printed as part of *Arzey Levanon*, Venice, 1601. We have used the edition published as part of *Batey Midrashot* (q.v.).

Horayot. Tractate of the Talmud (q.v.).

Idra Rabbah. "The Greater Gathering," Portion of the *Zohar* (q.v.) dealing with the dynamics of the supernal universes, presented as a lecture by Rabbi Shimon bar Yochai to his ten disciples. Found in *Zohar* III, 127b*ff*.

Idra Zutra. "The Lesser Gathering," so called because three of Rabbi Shimon's disciples had passed away. Found in *Zohar* III, 287b*ff*.

Innerspace. An introduction to both the conceptual and meditative aspects of the Kabbalah, by Rabbi Aryeh Kaplan (q.v.), published by Moznaim in Jerusalem, 1990.

Kallah Rabbati. Part of the tractate *Kallah*, one of the Minor Tractates of the Babylonian Talmud.

Kaplan, Rabbi Aryeh (1935-1983). The author of numerous English translations as well as

many original works, he was without a doubt the cardinal force in what is now the burgeoning field of English language Torah material.

Kehillat Yaakov. An explanation of Kabbalistic concepts, alphabetically arranged, by Rabbi Yaakov Zvi Yollish, first printed in Lemberg, 1870.

Keilim. Tractate of the Talmud (q.v.).

Ketuvot. Tractate of the Talmud (q.v.).

Kiddushin. Tractate of the Talmud (q.v.).

Kilayim. Tractate of the Talmud (q.v.).

Kinim. Tractate of the Talmud (q.v.).

Kisey Melekh. Commentary on the *Tikkuney Zohar* (q.v.), by Rabbi Sholom Buzaglo, first printed in Amsterdam, 1768.

Kitzur Likutey Moharan. An abridged version of *Likutey Moharan* (q.v.), focusing on the practical advice that the lessons offer, by Reb Noson of Breslov at the behest of Rebbe Nachman. First published in Mohilov, 1811.

Kitzur Shulchan Arukh. An abridged version of the *Shulchan Arukh* (q.v.), by Rabbi Shelomoh Ganzfried, first printed in Ungvar, 1864.

Kli Yakar. Torah commentary by Rabbi Shelomoh Ephraim (ben Aharon) of Luntschitz (1550-1619), first published in Lublin, 1602, and later in many editions of the Torah. The author was an important rabbinical leader in Poland.

Koenig, Rabbi Gedalia Aharon (ben Elazar Mordechai) (1921-1980). Oral teachings, by a leading figure in Breslov in Jerusalem. Rabbi Koenig transcribed *Tovot Zikhronot* (q.v.) and penned *Chayey Nefesh* (q.v.), as well as many unpublished manuscripts on Breslover thought.

Koenig, Rabbi Noson Zvi. Oral teachings, by a leading figure in Breslov in Bnei Brak.

Kohellet Rabbah. Section of *Midrash Rabbah* (q.v.) dealing with the Book of Ecclesiastes.

Kokhavey Or. Stories and teachings of Rebbe Nachman and his disciples, by Rabbi Avraham ben Reb Nachman of Tulchin (see *Biur HaLikutim*), first printed in Jerusalem, 1896. We have used the Jerusalem, 1972, edition.

Kritut. Tractate of the Talmud (q.v.).

Kramer, Rabbi Shmuel Moshe (b.1937). Oral teachings, by a leading figure in Breslov in Jerusalem.

Kuzari. One of the most important works on Jewish philosophy and theology, by Rabbi Yehudah HaLevi (1074-1141). Translated from the original Arabic to Hebrew by Rabbi Yehudah ibn Tibbon (circa 1120-1190), it was first printed in Constantinople, 1506.

Libermentsch, Rabbi Noson. Oral teachings, by a leading figure in Breslov in Bnei Brak/Immanuel.

Likutey Etzot. See *Advice*.

Likutey Halakhot. Monumental work on Breslover thought and Kabbalah, following the order of the *Shulchan Arukh* (q.v.), by Reb Noson of Breslov (see *Fire and Water*), Rebbe Nachman's foremost disciple. First part was printed in Iasse (Jasse), 1843, with subsequent sections published through 1861. We have used the eight volume, Jerusalem, 1985, edition.

Likutey Tefilot. A classic collection of prayers, based on the teachings found in Rebbe Nachman's *Likutey Moharan*, by Reb Noson of Breslov, first printed in Breslov, 1822. An English translation, entitled *The Fiftieth Gate*, is currently being published by the Breslov Research Institute, in Jerusalem, 1992-.

Likutey Torah. Commentary on the Torah, Prophets and Sacred Writings (*TaNaKh*), by Rabbi Chaim Vital, based on the teachings of the Ari (see Ari), first published in Zolkiev, 1775. We have used the Jerusalem, 1988, edition.

Maaser Sheni. Tractate of the Talmud (q.v.).

Maasrot. Tractate of the Talmud (q.v.).

Maasiot u'Meshalim. Stories about Rebbe Nachman, preserved by his disciple, Reb Naftali (Hertz b'Reb Yehudah Weinberg; 1780-1860). Printed as part of *Sipurim Niflaim* (q.v.) from page 14 on.

Mabuey HaNachal. A monthly journal dedicated to a wide range of topics in Breslov Chassidut. Published in Jerusalem, 1978-1984.

Magen Avraham. Major commentary in *Shulchan Arukh, Orach Chaim* (q.v.), by Rabbi Avraham Gombiner of Ostrog. First published in Direnport, 1692.

Maharchu. Commentary on the *Zohar* (q.v.), by Rabbi Chaim Vital, first printed in Zhitomar, 1862.

Maharsha. Abbreviation of Morenu HaRav Shmuel Eliezer, denoting Rabbi Shmuel Eliezer Aideles's (1555-1632) major commentary on the entire Talmud. The part known as *Chidushey Halakhot* on the legal sections of the Talmud was first printed in Lublin, 1612-1621; the *Chidushey Aggadot* on the homiletical sections in Lublin, 1627, and Cracow, 1631. They were included in the Prague, 1739-46 edition of the Talmud, and in virtually all editions since. The author was one of the most important rabbis and Talmudic scholars in Poland in his time.

Maharzav. Commentary on *Midrash Rabbah* (q.v.), by Rabbi Zeev Volf Einhorn, first printed in Vilna, 1853-1858, and later with the standard editions of *Midrash Rabbah*.

Mai HaNachal. Commentary on *Likutey Moharan* (q.v.), by Rabbi Moshe Yehoshua Bezhilianski (Reb Alter Tepliker). Written in 1897, it was first published by Rabbi Noson Zvi Koenig, Bnei Brak, 1965.

Makkot. Tractate of the Talmud (q.v.).

Makhshirin. Tractate of the Talmud (q.v.).

Matnat Kehunah. Commentary on *Midrash Rabbah* (q.v.), by Rabbi Yissachar Ber Katz (Ashkenazi), first printed in Cracow, 1587-8, and later with the standard editions of *Midrash Rabbah*.

Matok Midvash. Commentary and explanations on the *Zohar* and Tikkuney Zohar (q.v.), by Rabbi Daniel Frisch, printed in Jerusalem, in 1986 and 1991, respectively.

Mayim. English translation of *Likutey Moharan* I, 51 and other Breslov literature related to that lesson, published by Breslov Research Institute, Jerusalem, 1987.

MeAm Lo'ez. Monumental running commentary on the Torah, written in Ladino (Judeo-Spanish) by Rabbi Yaakov (ben Makhir) Culi (1689-1732), first published in Constantinople, 1730-33. A Hebrew translation by Rabbi Shmuel Yerushalmi (Kreuser) was published under the title *Yalkut MeAm Lo'ez* in Jerusalem 1967-71, and an English translation, begun by Rabbi Aryeh Kaplan (q.v.), under the title *The Torah Anthology*, in 1977, is still being published. Rabbi Culi was born in Jerusalem, and later moved to Constantinople, where he was a leading figure in the Sephardic community.

Megillah. Tractate of the Talmud (q.v.).

Megillat Taanit. Compendium of important dates in Jewish history when fasting was forbidden, by Rabbi Chanania ben Chezkiah (circa 70 c.e.; cf. *Shabbat* 13b). First printed in Amsterdam, 1659.

Me'ilah. Tractate of the Talmud (q.v.).

Mekhilta. The earliest commentary on the Book of Exodus, by the school of Rabbi Yishmael (circa 120 c.e.), often quoted in the Talmud. First printed in Constantinople, 1515.

Menachot. Tractate of the Talmud (q.v.).

Metzudot. A pair of commentaries on the Books of Prophets and the Sacred Writings (NaKh) known as *Metzudat Zion* and *Metzudat David*, by Rabbi David Altschuler, completed and edited by his son Rabbi Yechiel Hillel, first published in Levorno, 1753 (or Berlin, 1770), and later with the standard editions of *Mikraot Gedolot*.

Mevo Shearim. A detailed exposition of the foundational principles of the Kabbalah of the Ari, first published by Rabbi Yaakov Zemach, in Koretz, 1783.

Midot. Tractate of the Talmud (q.v.).

Midrash Aggadah. A Midrashic collection based on the works of Moshe HaDarshan (circa 1050), compiled around 1150 and published by Shelomoh Buber in Vienna, 1893-94. Moshe HaDarshan is often quoted by Rashi (q.v.).

Midrash Rabbah. The most important collection of Midrashic literature, assembled during the Gaonic period. The component Midrashim vary widely, from the almost pure commentary to pure homily, all, however, based on the teachings of the Talmudic Sages. The *Midrash Rabbah*

on the Torah was first printed in Constantinople, 1512, while that on the five *megillot* was printed in Pesaro, 1519.

Midrash Shmuel. Commentary on *Avot*, by Rabbi Shmuel (ben Yitzchak) Uceda (1538-1602), first printed in Venice, 1579. The author studied under the Ari and Rabbi Chaim Vital (see *Ari*), and established a major yeshivah in Safed.

Midrash Tadshe. Ancient Midrash attributed to Rabbi Pinchas ben Yair (circa 130 c.e.). First published in Johannesburg, 1858, and later printed in *Beth HaMidrash* 3:164 and *Otzar Midrashim* p.475*ff.*

Midrash Tehillim. See *Shochar Tov*.

Mikdash Melekh. Commentary on the *Zohar* (q.v.), by Rabbi Sholom Buzaglo, first printed in Amsterdam, 1564.

Mikvaot. Tractate of the Talmud (q.v.).

Mishnah. The earliest code of Jewish law, edited by Rabbi Yehudah the Prince (circa 188 c.e.). The Mishnah serves as the basis for the Talmud (q.v.).

Mishnah Berurah. Important Halakhic work by the *Chofetz Chaim*, Rabbi Yisrael Meir (HaKohen) Kagan (1838-1933), on *Shulchan Arukh, Orach Chaim*, begun in 1883.

Mishnat Chassidim. An important Kabbalistic work by Rabbi Immanuel Chai Riki (1688-1743), first published in Levorno, 1722.

Mo'ed Katan. Tractate of the Talmud (q.v.).

Nachat HaShulchan. Insights into a wide variety of halakhic topics based on the first lesson of *Likutey Moharan*, by Rabbi Nachman of Tcherin, first published in Jerusalem, 1910. We have used the Jerusalem, 1968, edition.

Nazir. Tractate of the Talmud (q.v.).

Nedarim. Tractate of the Talmud (q.v.).

Negaim. Tractate of the Talmud (q.v.).

Nevey Tzaddikim. Historical bibliography of all Breslover works, by Rabbi Noson Zvi Koenig (q.v.), published in Bnei Brak, 1969.

Niddah. Tractate of the Talmud (q.v.).

Nitzutzei Orot. Commentary and explanations on the *Zohar* (q.v.), by Rabbi Chaim Yosef David Azulai (Chida), first printed in Levorno, 1815.

Oholot. Tractate of the Talmud (q.v.).

Olat Tamid. An explanation of the Kabbalistic meditations for the year-round prayers by Rabbi Chaim Vital (see Ari), first published by Rabbi Yaakov Zemach in Salonika, 1854. We have used the Jerusalem, 1988, edition.

Oneg Shabbat. Collection of letters and lessons explaining Breslover teachings, by Rabbi

Ephraim Zvi (ben Alter Benzion) Krakavski of Pshedbarz (1880-1946), published in New York, 1966.

Onkelos. See Targum.

Orach Chaim. First section of *Shulchan Arukh* (q.v.), dealing with prayers, blessings, Shabbat and festivals.

Orlah. Tractate of the Talmud (q.v.).

Otiot deRabbi Akiva. Commentary on the letters of the Hebrew alphabet, attributed to Rabbi Akiva (circa 100 c.e.), first published in Constantinople, 1516. We have used the edition published as part of *Batey Midrashot* (q.v.).

Outpouring of the Soul. *Hishtapkhut HaNefesh* in Hebrew, a handbook on Rebbe Nachman's teachings on prayer, collected by Reb Alter Tepliker (see *Mai HaNachal*), first published in Jerusalem, 1905. This English translation includes a scholarly introduction on the topic of *hitbodedut*, by Rabbi Aryeh Kaplan, published by Breslov Research Institute, in Jerusalem, 1980.

Parah. Tractate of the Talmud (q.v.).

Pardes Rimonim. Major Kabbalistic work, by Rabbi Moshe Cordovero (1522-1570), first published in Salonica, 1583. The author was the head of the Safed school of Kabbalah before the Ari (q.v.).

Parparaot LeChokhmah. Major commentary on *Likutey Moharan* (q.v.) by Reb Nachman of Tcherin, first published in Lemberg, 1876.

Peah. Tractate of the Talmud (q.v.).

Pesachim. Tractate of the Talmud (q.v.).

Pesikta d'Rav Kahane. Ancient Midrashic text on various Torah and *haftarot* portions read on holidays and special Shabbats, attributed to Rav Kahane, compiled circa 500 c.e. Many, including compilers of other Midrashic collections and the authors of the *Tosafot* (q.v.) drew from this seminal work which was first published by Shelomoh Buber in Lemberg, 1868.

Pesikta Rabbati. Not to be confused with *Pesikta d'Rav Kahane* (q.v.), this medieval Midrashic collection, circa 845 c.e., consists of homilies on portions of the Torah and *haftarot* read on holidays. First published by Meir Ish-Shalom (Friedmann) in Vienna, 1880.

Pinto, Rabbi Yoshiah (1565-1648), author of *Meor Eynayim* on the *Eyn Yaakov* (q.v.), published in Amsterdam, 1643, and as the "Rif" in the 1883 Vilna edition of *Eyn Yaakov*. An important Talmudist and Kabbalist, the author lived in Damascus, and then migrated to Jerusalem and Safed.

Pirkey deRabbi Eliezer. Important Midrashic work by the school of Rabbi Eliezer (ben Hyrcanos) HaGadol (circa 100 c.e.), first published in Constantinople, 1514.

Pri Etz Chaim. Important Kabbalistic work on meditations for various prayers and rituals, based

on the teachings of the Ari (q.v.), by Rabbi Chaim Vital, first published in Koretz, 1782. We have used the Jerusalem, 1988, edition.

Rabbi Nachman's Stories. Annotated English translation of Rabbi Nachman's famous *Sippurey Maasiot* (stories and parables; q.v.), by Rabbi Aryeh Kaplan (q.v.), published by the Breslov Research Institute in Jerusalem, 1983.

Rabbi Nachman's Tikkun. *Tikkun HaKlali* (q.v.) with an English translation and transliteration. First edition published by the Breslov Research Institute in 1980. Second revised edition, 1982.

Rabbi Nachman's Wisdom. Translation of *Shevachey HaRan* and *Sichot HaRan* (q.v.), by Rabbi Aryeh Kaplan (q.v.), published in New York, 1973.

Radak. Acronym for Rabbi David Kimchi (1157-1236), denoting his major commentary on the Bible, first printed with the *Mikraot Gedolot*, Venice, 1517. The author, who lived in Narbonne, Provence, sought to ascertain the precise meaning of the scripture.

Radal. Acronym for Rabbi David (ben Yehudah) Luria (1798-1855), author of an important commentary of *Pirkey deRabbi Eliezer* (q.v.), first published in Warsaw, 1852.

Rambam. See *Yad HaChazakah*.

Ramban. Acronym for Rabbi Moshe ben Nachman (1194-1270), denoting his commentary on the Torah, first printed in Rome, 1472. The author was a major spiritual leader of his time, writing over fifty major works on Bible, Talmud, Jewish law, philosophy, Kabbalah and medicine. He lived in Gerona, Spain, where he maintained a yeshivah.

Rashba. Acronym for Rabbi Shimon ben Avraham Aderet (1235-1310), denoting his commentaries on the Talmud, many of which were published together with *Eyn Yaakov* (q.v.) in Salonika, 1515. A student of the Ramban (q.v.), the author was rabbi of Barcelona and one of the major Jewish leaders of his time.

Rashbam. Acronym for Rabbi Shmuel ben Meir (circa 1080-1174), author of an important commentary on the Torah and commentaries on portions of the Talmud. He was a grandson of Rashi (q.v.) and elder brother of Rabbi Yaakov Tam, leader of the school that produced the Tosafot (q.v.).

Rashi. Acronym for Rabbi Shelomoh (ben Yitzchak) Yarchi (see *Shem HaGedolim*) or Yitzchaki (1040-1105), author of the most important commentaries on the Bible and Talmud, printed in almost all major editions. His commentary on the Torah was the first known Hebrew book to be published (Rome, circa 1470). He headed yeshivot in Troyes and Worms, France. His commentaries are renowned for being extremely terse, immediately bringing forth the main idea of the text.

Reishit Chokhmah. An encyclopedic work on morality (*mussar*), drawing heavily on the *Zohar* (q.v.), by Rabbi Eliyahu (ben Moshe) de Vidas (1518-1592), first published in Venice, 1579. A

student of Rabbi Moshe Cordovero (see *Pardes Rimonim*), the author had a reputation as a sage and a saint.

Restore My Soul. *Meshivat Nefesh* in Hebrew, a handbook on the teachings of Rebbe Nachman and Reb Noson of Breslov on how to combat hopelessness and draw from the wellsprings of joy, collected by Reb Alter Tepliker (see *Mai HaNAchal*), first published in Lemberg, 1902. This annotated English translation was done by Avraham Greenbaum, published by Breslov Research Institute, in Jerusalem, 1980.

Rif. See Pinto, Rabbi Yoshiah.

Rif. Acronym for Rabbi Yitzchak (ben Yaakov) Al-fasi (1013-1103), author of an abridgement of the Talmud meant to serve as a practical legal code, first printed as *Hilkhot Rav Alfasi*, Hijer, Spain, circa 1845. Born in Algeria, he settled in Fez and is thus known as Al-fasi (the person of Fez). His code, which was the most important before Maimonides' *Yad*, brought the Gaonic period to a close.

Rimzey Maasiot. Commentaries on *Sippurey Maasiot* (q.v.), by Rabbi Nachman of Tcherin. First printed in Lemberg, 1902, and with all subsequent editions of Rebbe Nachman's stories.

Rimzey Maasiot, Hashmatot. Additional commentaries on the stories of Rebbe Nachman, by Rabbi Avraham ben Nachman of Tulchin, printed in the Lemberg, 1902, edition of *Sippurey Maasiot*.

Rokeach. An important code of Jewish law and pietistic practice, by Rabbi Elazar (ben Yehudah) Rokeach of Worms (1164-1232), first printed in Fano, 1505. Besides being a leading authority in Jewish law, the author was one of the foremost masters of Kabbalah in his time.

Rosen, Rabbi Eliyahu Chaim (1899-1983). Oral teachings, by one of the most prominent elders in Breslov in Jerusalem. Rabbi Rosen, a student of Reb Avraham Chazan (see *Biur HaLikutim*), was dean of the Breslov Yeshivah in Jerusalem, which he founded in the old city of Jerusalem in 1937.

Rosenfeld, Rabbi Zvi Aryeh Benzion (1922-1978). Denoting the marginal notes and numerous tapes of lessons given by Rabbi Rosenfeld, who was one of the leaders of the Breslover Chassidim in America. He was a descendant of Rabbi Aharon, the *rav* of Breslov in Rebbe Nachman's time, and a disciple of Rabbi Avraham Sternhartz (q.v.).

Rosh (1250-1327). Acronym for Rabbi Asher (ben Yechiel), denoting the *Piskey HaRosh*, an important legal work, first published with the Talmud, Venice, 1523, and in most subsequent editions. The Rosh was the leading talmudist in Germany, but after a period of persecution, he became rabbi of Toledo, Spain.

Rosh HaShanah. Tractate of the Talmud (q.v.).

Ruth Rabbah. Section of *Midrash Rabbah* (q.v.) dealing with the Book of Ruth.

Saadia Gaon, Rav (882-942). The greatest scholar of the Gaonic period, he authored an Arabic

translation/commentary to the Torah, which was published in Paris, 1893, and as *Keter Torah*, Jerusalem, 1894-1901. A Hebrew translation of key parts was published by Rabbi Yosef Kapach, in Jerusalem, 1963. The author was the greatest scholar of the Gaonic period, and as head of the yeshivah in Pumbedita, Babylonia, was the leader of world Jewry.

Sanhedrin. Tractate of the Talmud (q.v.).

Sefer Baal Shem Tov. Anthology of the teachings of Rabbi Yisrael, the Baal Shem Tov (1698-1760), founder of the Chassidic movement and great-grandfather of Rebbe Nachman, compiled by Rabbi Shimon Mendel Vednik, and first published in Lodz, 1938.

Sefer Chassidim. Laws and customs of Chassidei Ashkenaz (German pietists), by Rabbi Yehudah (ben Shmuel) HaChassid (1148-1217), first printed in Bologna, 1538. The author, who lived in Speyer and Regensburg, was a master Kabbalist and a leading rabbinical authority.

Sefer HaLikutim. Commentary on the Torah, Prophets and Sacred Writings (*TaNaKh*) based on the teachings of the Ari, by Meir Poppers, Jerusalem, 1913. We have used the Jerusalem, 1988, edition.

Sefer HaMidot. See *Aleph-Bet Book*.

Sefer HaTekhunah. Astronomical work by Rabbi Chaim Vital (see Ari, q.v.), first published in Jerusalem, 1866. We have used the Jerusalem, 1967, edition.

Sefer Yetzirah. One of the earliest and most important mystical works, thought to have been written in Talmudic times or earlier. (There are some who attribute its authorship to the Patriarch Abraham.) First printed in Mantua, 1562, it has been the subject of over a hundred commentaries.

Shaar HaGilgulim. A detailed work on reincarnation, the last of the *Shemoneh Shearim* (q.v.), by Rabbi Chaim Vital, first published in Jerusalem, 1863. We have used the Jerusalem, 1988, edition.

Shaar HaKavanot. Kabbalistic meditations on the prayer services and rituals, the sixth of the *Shemoneh Shearim* (q.v.), by Rabbi Chaim Vital, first published in Salonika, 1852. We have used the Jerusalem, 1988, edition.

Shaar HaHakdamot. A detailed exposition of the foundational principles of the Kabbalah of the Ari, the first of the *Shemoneh Shearim* (q.v.), by Rabbi Chaim Vital, first published in Jerusalem, 1850. We have used the Jerusalem, 1988, edition.

Shaar HaMitzvot. Kabbalistic interpretations of the commandments, the fifth of the *Shemoneh Shearim* (q.v.), by Rabbi Chaim Vital, first published in Salonika, 1852. We have used the Jerusalem, 1988, edition.

Shaar HaPesukim. Biblical interpretations of the Ari, fourth of the *Shemoneh Shearim* (q.v.), by Rabbi Chaim Vital, first published in Salonika, 1852. We have used the Jerusalem, 1988, edition.

Shaar Maamarei Rashby. Commentary on teachings from *Sefer Yetzirah, Zohar, Tikkuney*

Zohar and discourses of Rabbi Shimon bar Yochai (Rashby), the second of the *Shemoneh Shearim* (q.v.), by Rabbi Chaim Vital, first published in Salonika, 1862. We have used the Jerusalem, 1988, edition.

Shaar Maamarei Razal. Commentary on teachings of the Sages, the third of the *Shemoneh Shearim* (q.v.), by Rabbi Chaim Vital, first published in Salonika, 1862. We have used the Jerusalem, 1988, edition.

Shaar Ruach HaKodesh. Meditative methods, the seventh of the *Shemoneh Shearim* (q.v.), by Rabbi Chaim Vital, first published in Jerusalem, 1863. We have used the Jerusalem, 1988, edition.

Shaarey Orah. Major Kabbalistic classic, by Rabbi Yosef (ben Avraham) Gikatilla (1248-1345), first printed in Riva de Trento, 1561. The author, who lived in Italy, was a student of Rabbi Avraham Abulafia.

Shaarey Tzion. Important collection of Kabbalistic prayers, by Rabbi Natan Nata (ben Moshe) Hanover (died 1683), first published in Prague, 1662. The author was a leading Kabbalist.

Shaarey Zohar. Index and commentary to the Talmud, cross-referenced to the *Zohar*, by Rabbi Reuven Margolios (1889-1971), published in Jerusalem, 1956.

Shabbat. Tractate of the Talmud (q.v.).

Shakh. Abbreviation for *Siftey Kohen*, an important commentary on *Yoreh Deah* and *Choshen Mishpat* (q.v.), by Rabbi Shabbetai (ben Rabbi Meir) HaKohen (Rappaport), a leading disciple of Rabbi Heschel of Cracow. A major leader of European Jewry, he was instrumental in reorganizing the Jewish communities immediately after the Chmelnitzky massacres of 1648-49. First published in Cracow 1646-47 and later with most standard editions of the *Shulchan Arukh* (q.v.).

Shapiro, Rabbi Shmuel (1913-1989). Oral teachings, by one of the most prominent elders in Breslov in Jerusalem.

Shechter, Rabbi Yaakov Meir (b. 1932). Oral teachings, by a leading figure in Breslov in Jerusalem.

Shekalim. Tractate of the Talmud (q.v.).

Shemoneh Shearim. The "Eight Gates": *Shaar HaHakdamot, Shaar Maamarei Rashby, Shaar Maamarei Razal, Shaar HaPesukim, Shaar HaMitzvot, Shaar HaKavanot, Shaar Ruach HaKodesh, Shaar HaGilgulim*; an eight volume collection of the teachings of the Ari (q.v.), by Rabbi Chaim Vital, edited by Rabbi Shmuel Vital. (Published between the years 1850-1863, in either Salonika or Jerusalem, each is listed here separately.)

Shemot HaTzaddikim. A list of the names of tzaddikim from Adam to the present day, compiled by Reb Noson of Breslov in compliance with Rebbe Nachman's advice in *The Aleph-Bet Book, Tzaddik*, A:19, "Whoever cherishes God, will record all the names of the tzaddikim and the

God-fearing in a book, in order to remember them." First printed in 1821 as an appendix to the *Sefer HaMidot* (q.v.). Subsequent editions include additional names.

Shemot Rabbah. Section of *Midrash Rabbah* (q.v.) dealing with the Book of Numbers.

Shevachey HaAri. Stories about the birth and life of the Ari and his disciples, taken from the introduction to the Kabbalistic work *Emek HaMelekh* by Rabbi Shelomoh Shimmel (b'Reb Chayim Meinstril). First published in Spalov, 1795.

Shevachey HaRan. See *Rabbi Nachman's Wisdom*.

Shevachey HaBaal Shem Tov. A collection of stories of the Baal Shem Tov and some of his closest followers, whose accuracy Rebbe Nachman confirmed. Compiled by Reb Dov Ber (b'Reb Shmuel) Shubb of Linetz, the son-in-law of the Baal Shem Tov's scribe. During Rebbe Nachman's life the book was distributed in manuscript form. It was first printed in Berdichev in 1815.

Shevachey Moharan. Anecdotes and teachings of Rebbe Nachman, compiled by Reb Noson of Breslov, printed together with *Tzaddik* (q.v.). Parts also appear in *Gems of Rabbi Nachman*, by Rabbi Aryeh Kaplan (q.v.), New York, 1980.

Shevi'it. Tractate of the Talmud (q.v.).

Shevuot. Tractate of the Talmud (q.v.).

Shir HaShirim Rabbah. Section of *Midrash Rabbah* (q.v.) dealing with the Song of Songs.

Shiur HaKomah. Book of Kabbalistic concepts by Rabbi Moshe Cordovero (see *Pardes Rimonim*), published in Warsaw, 1883.

Shlah. An abbreviation for *Shney Lichot HaBrit*, an encyclopedic Torah work, by Rabbi Yeshaya Horowitz, first printed in Amsterdam, 1698.

Shochar Tov. Also known as *Midrash Tehillim*. An ancient Midrash on Psalms, first printed in Constantinople, 1515. A critical edition, based on manuscript was published by Shelomoh Buber, Vilna, 1891.

Shulchan Arukh. The standard code of Jewish Law, by Rabbi Yosef (b'Reb Efraim) Caro (1488-1575), first published in Venice, 1564. Divided into four parts, *Orach Chaim, Yoreh Deah, Even HaEzer*, and *Choshen Mishpat*. Born in Spain, the author migrated to Turkey after the expulsion in 1492, and then to Safed, where he served as chief rabbi. With the addition of the *Hagah* (q.v.), the *Shulchan Arukh* became the standard work on Jewish law for all Jewry.

Siach Sarfei Kodesh. Anecdotes and teachings involving Rebbe Nachman, Reb Noson and the Breslover Chassidim, as well as previously unpublished stories, from the Breslover oral tradition. These were transcribed by Avraham Weitzhandler from conversations with Rabbi Levi Yitzchak Bender (q.v.). Five volumes were published to date in Jerusalem, 1988 and 1994, by Meshekh HaNachal. Other volumes currently being prepared.

Sichot HaRan. Short teachings and sayings of Rebbe Nachman, collected by Reb Noson of

Breslov, first published together with Sippurey Maasiot, in Ostrog, 1816. An expanded edition, including much new material, was published in Zolkiev, 1850. Translated into English as part of *Rabbi Nachman's Wisdom* (q.v.), pieces also appear in *Gems of Rabbi Nachman*, by Rabbi Aryeh Kaplan (q.v.), New York, 1980.

Sichot v'Sippurim. Exposition of Rebbe Nachman's teachings, by Reb Avraham Chazan, published in Jerusalem, 1913. Reprinted as part of *Kokhavey Or* (q.v.).

Siddur Ari. There are a number of prayer books that go by this title: a) prayer book printed together with the *Mishnat Chassidim* (q.v.), Zolkiev, 1744; b) prayer book with the meditations of the Ari, Zolkiev, 1781; c) the *Siddur of Rabbi Asher*, by Rabbi Shelomoh Margolios, Lvov (Lemberg), 1788; d) the *Kol Yaakov*, Koretz, 1794; e) the *Siddur of Rabbi Shabbetai* (Rashkover), Koretz, 1797 (which included the unifications of Rabbi Yisrael, the Baal Shem Tov).

Sifra. Also known as *Torat Kohanim*, one of the *Midrashey Halakhah*. It is one of the earliest commentaries on Leviticus, written by Rav (circa 220 c.e.), and often quoted in the Talmud. First published in Constantinople, 1530.

Sifri. One of the *Midrashey Halakhah*, it is the oldest commentary on Numbers and Deuteronomy, written by Rav (circa 220 c.e.), and often quoted in the Talmud. First published in Venice, 1546.

Siftey Chakhamim. Supercommentary on Rashi's commentary (q.v.), by Rabbi Shabbetai Bass (1641-1718), first published in Frankfort am Main, 1712, and reprinted in many editions of the Torah.

Siftey Kohen. See *Shakh*.

Sippurey Maasiot. The stories of Rebbe Nachman. First published in Ostrog, 1816, and with a new introduction in Lemberg, 1850. Translated as *Rabbi Nachman's Stories* (q.v.).

Sippurim Niflaim. Anecdotes and teachings involving Rebbe Nachman, as well as previously unpublished stories, collected by Rabbi Shmuel Horowitz (see *Avanehah Barzel*). First published in Jerusalem in 1935.

Sotah. Tractate of the Talmud (q.v.).

Spector, Rabbi Elchonon (circa 1898-1984). Oral teachings, by a leading figure in Breslov in Jerusalem.

Sternhartz, Rabbi Avraham (Kokhav Lev) (1862-1955). Oral teachings, by one of the most prominent elders of Breslov in Uman and Jerusalem. A great-grandson of Reb Noson of Breslov, author of *Tovot Zikhronot* (q.v.), and founder of the *kibutz* in Meron for Rosh HaShanah, he was mentor to many of the previous generation's and today's leading Breslovers.

Sukkah. Tractate of the Talmud (q.v.).

Sulam. A translation into Hebrew, with explanation and annotation, of the *Zohar* (q.v.), by Rabbi Yehudah HaLevi Ashlag, first published in Jerusalem, 1945.

Taamei HaMinhagim. An encyclopedic collection and explanation of Jewish customs, by Rabbi Avraham Yitzchak Sperling (1851-1901), first published in Lvov (Lemberg), 1891.

Taamei Mitzvot. Kabbalistic interpretations of the commandments, first published in Zolkiev, 1775. We have used the Jerusalem, 1988, edition.

Taanit. Tractate of the Talmud (q.v.).

Talmud. The redaction of the Oral Torah, as taught by the great masters from approximately 50 b.c.e. until around 500 c.e. The first part to be codified was the Mishnah, set in its present form by Rabbi Yehudah the Prince, around 188 c.e. Subsequent discussions were redacted as the *Gemara* by Rav Ashi and Ravina in Babylon around 505 c.e., and it is therefore often referred to as the Babylonian Talmud. Next to the Bible itself, it is the most important work on Jewish law and theology. Individual volumes of the Talmud were printed in Soncino, Italy, as early as 1482, but the entire Talmud was first printed by David Bomberg in Venice, 1523, along with the commentaries of Rashi and Tosafot (q.v.). A second compilation of the Talmud, thought to have been redacted around 240 c.e. by Rabbi Yochanan (182-279 c.e.) and his disciples in Tiberias with the concurrence of the Sages of Jerusalem, is the Talmud *Yerushalmi* (Jerusalem Talmud). It is a work of major importance, although considered secondary to the Babylonian Talmud. It was first printed in Venice, 1523.

Tamid. Tractate of the Talmud (q.v.).

Tana deBei Eliyahu in two parts, Rabba and Zuta. An early Midrash attributed to the teachings of the prophet Elijah, first printed in Venice, 1598.

Tanchuma. An early homiletic Midrash on the Torah, attributed to Rabbi Tanchuma bar Abba (circa 370 c.e.), but added to until around 850. First printed in Constantinople, 1522.

Targum. Authorized Aramaic translation of the Torah, by the proselyte Onkelos (circa 90 c.e.). In Talmudic times, it was read along with the Torah, so that the congregation could understand the reading.

Targum Yerushalmi. Ancient Aramaic translation of the Torah, usually included alongside *Targum Yonatan* (q.v.) and probably written around the same time or somewhat earlier.

Targum Yonatan. Aramaic translation of the Torah, attributed by some to Yonatan ben Uzziel (circa 50 c.e.). Portions appear to have been amended in the Gaonic times.

Taz. An abbreviation of the halakhic work *Turey Zahav*, one of the principal commentaries on the *Shulchan Arukh*. Written by Rabbi David b'Reb Shmuel HaLevi, a leading disciple of Rabbi Heschel of Cracow. First published in Lublin, 1646.

Tefilin. Translation of Reb Noson of Breslov's classic discourse, *Likutey Halakhot, Tefilin 5*, by Avraham Greenbaum, discussing the deeper meaning of practically every aspect of the mitzvah of tefilin. Published by the Breslov Research Institute in Jerusalem, 1989.

Temurah. Tractate of the Talmud (q.v.).

Terumot. Tractate of the Talmud (q.v.).

Tevul Yom. Tractate of the Talmud (q.v.).

The Fiftieth Gate. See *Likutey Tefilot.*

Tiferet Yisrael. Important commentary on the Mishnah by Rabbi Yisrael Lipschutz (1782-1860), first published in Hanover, 1830.

Tikkun HaKlali. The Ten Psalms prescribed by Rebbe Nachman as a "General Remedy" for sexual and other sins, first published by Reb Noson in Breslov, 1821. Translated into English as *Rabbi Nachman's Tikkun* (q.v.).

Tikkuney Zohar. Part of the Zoharic literature, consisting of seventy chapters of commentary on the first word of the Torah, by the school of Rabbi Shimon bar Yochai (circa 120 c.e.), first printed in Mantua, 1558. However, a second edition, Orto Koy, 1719, provided the basis for al subsequent editions. The work contains some of the most important discussion in Kabbalah, and is essential for understanding the system of the *Zohar* (q.v.).

Tikkuney Zohar Chadash. Additions to the *Zohar Chadash* (q.v.) in the manner of the *Tikkuney Zohar.*

Tohorot. Tractate of the Talmud (q.v.).

Torah Temimah. Encyclopedic Torah commentary, by Rabbi Barukh Epstein (1860-1942), first published in Vilna, 1904. The work is noteworthy for quoting all the main Talmudic references to a verse, and offering extensive commentary on them. The author lived in Russia, and was the son of Rabbi Yechiel Michel Epstein, author of *Arukh HaShulchan.*

Torat Natan. Commentary on *Likutey Moharan* based on *Likutey Halakhot* (q.v.), by Rabbi Noson Zvi Koenig, Bnei Brak.

Tosafot. Collection of commentaries using Talmudic methodology on the Talmud itself. The work was a product of the yeshivah academies of France and Germany between around 1100 and 1300, begun by the students of Rashi (q.v.) and his grandsons, most notably, Rabbi Yaakov Tam (circa 1100-1171). It is printed in virtually all editions of the Talmud.

Tosefta. Additions to the Mishnah (see Talmud) by Rabbis Chiya and Oshia (circa 230 c.e.), published together with most editions of the Talmud and often quoted therein.

Tovot Zikhronot. Breslover traditions, by Reb Avraham Sternhartz (q.v.), transcribed by Reb Gedalia Aharon Koenig (q.v.), and published in Jerusalem, 1951. We have used the Bnei Brak, 1978, edition, published together with *Yerach HaEitanim.*

Tsohar. English translation of *Likutey Moharan* I, 112 and other Breslov literature related to that lesson, published by Breslov Research Institute, Jerusalem, 1986.

Tur. Or *Arbaah Turim* ("Four Rows"), by Rabbi Yaakov (ben Rav Asher, the *Rosh*; q.v.) of Toledo, Spain. The first systematic code of Jewish law based on the Talmud and the works of the Gaonim and Rishonim. The *Tur* is the forerunner of the *Shulchan Arukh.* First printed in Mantua, 1476.

Turey Zahav. See *Taz*.

Tzaddik. *Chayey Moharan* in Hebrew, an important biographical work on Rebbe Nachman, including his pilgrimage to the Holy Land, by his chief disciple, Reb Noson of Breslov, first printed in Ostrog, 1816, and again, with notes by Rabbi Nachman of Tcherin, in Lemberg, 1874. Translated, annotated and published as *Tzaddik*, by Breslov Research Institute, Jerusalem, 1987.

Uktzin. Tractate of the Talmud (q.v.).

Uman! Uman! Rosh HaShanah!. A collection of information about Rebbe Nachman's Rosh HaShanah in Uman, published by the Breslov Research Institute in Jerusalem, 1992.

Under the Table. Jewish pathways of spiritual growth, by Avraham Greenbaum, based on Rebbe Nachman's humorous but profound parable of the prince who thought he was a turkey. Published by the Breslov Research Institute in Jerusalem, 1991.

Until The Mashiach. A definitive, chronological account of Rebbe Nachman's life, by Rabbi Aryeh Kaplan (q.v.), published in Jerusalem, 1985, by the Breslov Research Institute.

Vayikra Rabbah. Section of *Midrash Rabbah* (q.v.) dealing with the Book of Leviticus.

Way of God, The. *Derekh HaShem* in Hebrew, a key work on Jewish thought by Rabbi Moshe Chaim Luzzatto (1707-1746), first printed in Amsterdam, 1896. The author was considered one of the most important of all Kabbalistic thinkers, and is best known for his *Mesillat Yesharim, The Path of the Just*. Translated into English by Rabbi Aryeh Kaplan (q.v.), published by Feldheim, New York, 1977.

Yadayim. Tractate of the Talmud (q.v.).

Yad HaChazakah. Also known as *Mishnah Torah*, the monumental Code of Jewish Law by Rabbi Moshe ben Maimon (Maimonides; 1135-1204), better known as the Rambam. The work was so named because of its fourteen divisions, the numerical value of *YaD*. It was the first systematic codification of Jewish law, and the only one that encompasses every branch of the laws of the Torah. Considered one of the great classics of Torah literature, it was first printed in Rome, 1475. It has been printed in many editions, and is the subject of dozens of commentaries.

Yalkut Shimoni. Also known as *Yalkut*, one of the most popular early Midrashic collections on the Bible, compiled by Rabbi Shimon Ashkenazi HaDarshan of Frankfurt (circa 1260), first printed in Salonika, 1521-1527. Many Midrashim are known only because they are cited in this work. The author was a preacher in Frankfurt.

Yemey HaTlaot. A history of the difficulties faced by Reb Noson of Breslov and his followers during the years 1835-39, including some sections of *Chayey Moharan* and *Yemey Moharnat* (q.v.) that were deleted from the printed editions. Written by Reb Avraham Chazan (see Biur HaLikutim), first published as the fifth section of *Kokhavey Or*, 1933, and subsequently in limited editions as a separate pamphlet.

Yemey Moharnat. Autobiography of Reb Noson of Breslov. The first section was printed in

Lemberg, 1876, and the second part, dealing with Reb Noson's pilgrimage to the Land of Israel, in Jerusalem, 1904. We have used the Meshekh HaNachal vocalized edition, Jerusalem, 1982.

Yerach HaEitanim. Breslover teachings about the month of Tishrei and it attendant holidays and rituals based on *Likutey Moharan*, by Rabbi Nachman of Tcherin, published in Jerusalem, 1951. We have used the Bnei Brak, 1978, edition, published together with *Tovot Zikhronot*.

Yekara D'Shabbata. Breslover teachings about Shabbat based on Likutey Moharan, by Rabbi Nachman of Tcherin, published in Lemberg, 1876. We have used the Jerusalem, 1968, edition.

Yerushalmi. Or *Talmud Yerushalmi*. See Talmud.

Yevamot. Tractate of the Talmud (q.v.).

Yoma. Tractate of the Talmud (q.v.).

Yoreh Deah. Second section of the *Shulchan Arukh* (q.v.), dealing with dietary laws and other areas requiring rabbinical decision.

Zavim. Tractate of the Talmud (q.v.).

Zevachim. Tractate of the Talmud (q.v.).

Zimrat HaAretz. Breslover teachings about the importance of the Land of Israel based on *Likutey Moharan*, by Rabbi Nachman of Tcherin, published in Lemberg, 1876. We have used the Jerusalem, 1968, edition.

Zohar. The primary classic of Kabbalah, from the school of Rabbi Shimon bar Yochai (circa 120 c.e.), compiled by his disciple, Rabbi Abba. After being restricted to a small, closed circle of Kabbalists and hidden for centuries, it was finally published around 1290 by Rabbi Moshe (ben Shem Tov) de Leon (1239-1305). After considerable controversy, Rabbi Yitzchak Yehoshua (ben Yaakov Bonet) de Lattes (1498-1571) issued an opinion that it was permitted to print the *Zohar*, and it was published in Mantua, 1558-1560. It has been reprinted in over sixty subsequent editions, and is the subject of dozens of commentaries.

Zohar Chadash. The "New *Zohar*," by the school of Rabbi Shimon bar Yochai, consisting of manuscripts found in the possession of the Safed kabbalists, assembled by Rabbi Avraham (ben Eliezer HaLevi) Barukhim (1516-1593), and printed in Salonika, 1597. It was called the "New *Zohar*" because it was printed after the original *Zohar* (q.v.).

Zohar HaRakia. Commentary on the *Zohar*, by the Ari (q.v.), and edited by Rabbi Yaakov Zemach, first published in Koretz, 1785.

ליקוטי מוהר"ן

LIKUTEY MOHARAN

ליקוטי מוהר"ן

LIKUTEY MOHARAN

Volume 1 (Lessons 1-6)

by

Rebbe Nachman of Breslov

translated by

Moshe Mykoff and Simcha Bergman

edited by

Moshe Mykoff and Ozer Bergman

annotated by

Chaim Kramer

published by

BRESLOV RESEARCH INSTITUTE

Jerusalem/New York

for further information:
Breslov Research Institute
POB 5370
Jerusalem
Israel
or:
Breslov Research Institute
POB 587
Monsey, NY 10952-0587
USA

cover design: Ben Gasner

ספר
ליקוטי מוהר"ן

ממאמרות טהורות של הרב החסיד המפורסים צדיקא קדישא מהו' נחמן נ"י

כאור הבהיר נכדו של הרב הקדוש הבעש"ט זצוק"ל לקוטי מאמר מאמר
אמרות ה' טהורות נפנת פעגה מגלה נסתרות לעורר ישנים ולהוציא אסורים
בכושרות בתוכחת מגולה ואהבה מסותרת לסקל הדרכי' ולפקוח עינים עורות
הלובש מאבני מהצב הבנים יקרות כל הרוצה לסמוך עליה' בנינים גדולים ע"פ
הקדמות ישרות דברי הכמים נצועים כמשמוחן' בהם ימלא מרגוע לנפשו ועצות
ישרות ויזכו לראות ביאות מורה צדק לקבץ מפוזרו' ויכון על תשפטס ק"ק
והיכל והולם ועזרות

גם אלה להחכמים יבינו מדעה' : כי לא נגוים שהיו בימי חכמי הש"ס ז"ל הגוי' האלו
אשר אנו מתגוררים בארצותם כי המה היו עובדי כובבים ומזלו' דבקים בכל
התועבות לא ידעו את ה' ואת דבר קדשו לא הכירו אבל העמים שבזמנינו את ה'
הם יריאים ונותני' כבוד לתורתו עושים חסד ומשפט בארצותם וחסד עם היהודי'
נחוסי' תחת כנפיהם וחלילה לנו לדבר או לחשוב שום גנאי עליהם וכ"מ שנזכר
בספרים גוי או נכרי או הומות העולם וכדומה הכוונה על עכו"ס מותם שהיו
בימי המשנה :

גדרוקט אין אוסטרהאג און וואלינישען גיבערטמאט מיט בעויליגונג אייגר העכסט
פעררר דענטן קייזערליכן לעמ"ר און ווילנא :

ברפום מהור"ר שמואל במהור"ר ישכר בער סג"ל

באוסטרהא

תחת ממשלת אדוניט סקיסר האדיר החסיד מוושע
פריסוטפליוושי דערזמזוונישע וילקי האסידר אהר הימפירלמעהר
אלעקסנדר **פאולאוויטש** סאמיע דער, עם אווסע
רלהסיסקי האסידר מוושע מילעסטיוושע י"ה :

לסדר ולפרט הנני נותן לו את **ברייתי שלום** לפ"ק

LIKUTEY MOHARAN

From the pure discourses of the prominent sage and man of piety, the
holy lamp and clear light, our master

REBBE NACHMAN

great-grandson of the holy sage,
the **BAAL SHEM TOV**
of blessed memory.

Teaching upon teaching we have recorded, they are the pure words of God. Revealing
secrets, uncovering mysteries, to awaken the sleeping and free those bound in
fetters, with open rebuke and hidden love. To clear the way and open the
eyes of the blind. Hewn from a quarry of precious gems. For anyone
who wishes to support himself upon them, they are great edifices
built upon firm foundations: the immutable words of the Sages.
In them he will find tranquility for his soul and sound advice.
May we merit to see the coming of the advisor of
righteousness to gather in the exiled. Then the
holy of holies, the chamber, the meeting hall
and the courtyards will all be established
upon their rightful places.

The wise will understand on their own that the
gentiles in whose lands we currently reside are not
like those who were in the time of the Sages of the Talmud.
The latter were idolaters who worshipped the stars and the constellations,
and were attached to all forms of abomination. They knew not God nor recognized
His holy words.But the nations of our day fear God and honor His Torah; doing kindness
and justice in their lands, and charity with the Jews who take refuge under their wings. Heaven
forbid that we should either say or write anything disrespectful about them. Thus, any reference to nations,
gentiles and peoples of the world and the like, refers only to those idolaters that lived in the time of the Mishnah.

Printed in Ostrog the Province of Volhyn
With the approval of the government censor in Vilna
In the printing house of R' Shmuel son of Yissachar Ber Segal
OSTROG

Under the rule of our master, the exalted and pious **Czar Alexander Pavlovitch**

In the year of: *"Behold, I give him My covenant of peace"* (5568/1808)

Publisher's Preface

"It is good to praise God and sing to His Exalted Name" (Psalms 92:2).

Reb Noson writes in his Introduction to *Likutey Moharan*: "It is superfluous to go on extolling the great holiness and awesomeness of this book. This is because anyone who is prepared to study it honestly will appreciate and understand the extent of its greatness on his own." He explains that each and every lesson of this holy book covers a number of man's characteristics—how to develop the good traits and distant oneself from the negative tendencies. The discourses focus on Torah, prayer and the other mitzvot, and how each and every individual can attain these devotions. The *Parparaot LeChokhmah,* in his Introduction, directs the reader to another realm within this one—namely, how one can attain, from one's seemingly insignificant position in this world, levels that even the angels cannot reach. Many other tzaddikim have praised the *Likutey Moharan* in a similar vein.

Accordingly, we are very thankful to God for having granted us the opportunity to work on the translation of this treasure, Rebbe Nachman's *magnum opus.* Ever since the first edition of this volume of *Likutey Moharan,* which was published back in 1984, we have received numerous letters of thanks from a varied readership for opening up this most important tome of Torah and Chassidut to the English speaking world. We hope that this revised, second edition of the first volume will prove even far more effective in achieving that aim.

The Breslov Research Institute gratefully acknowledges the unparalleled support and encouragement of Stan and Sara Kopel, whose interest, dedication and encouragement have made possible the ongoing project to translate and publish the entire *Likutey Moharan..*

We extend once again our heartfelt thanks to Mr. Manny Plotsker, whose foresight and benevolence initiated this project fourteen years ago.

Acknowledgement is due once again to Moshe Mykoff for a supreme translation of the *Likutey Moharan* text and an even greater editing job of the notes. And to Ozer Bergman, for his tenacious review and helpful suggestions.

Rebbe Nachman's lessons, in the main, center on several main concepts: Torah, prayer and the tzaddik. These are all concepts and ideals that *can* be achieved by man—if he but tries! All the mitzvot we do, all the good deeds we perform, help bring us to the great levels that the Rebbe inspires us to achieve. Would it be the will of the Almighty that we put life and spirit into our Torah, prayers and mitzvot, with attachment to the tzaddik, so that we may merit to see the Coming of Mashiach, the Ingathering of the Exiles and the Rebuilding of the Holy Temple, speedily, in our days, Amen.

Chaim Kramer
Adar I, 5755

Translator's Introduction

In lieu of the more traditional style of translator's preface, the reader to is asked to consider the following:

> After *Likutey Moharan* was printed for the very first time, Rebbe Nachman spoke of the great benefits which studying his teachings afford. He said this was especially so for those worthy of originating some insight based on his lessons. When a follower of the Rebbe then related one such novel interpretation to him, Rebbe Nachman chuckled and said, "You can twist my book in any way you choose, just as long as you don't depart from so much as a small passage of the *Shulchan Arukh*" (*Oral tradition*; cf. *Rabbi Nachman's Wisdom* #267).

> "One should never pride oneself in his intellectual capabilities or good deeds, which all come through the tzaddik of the generation. He is to the tzaddik what a pen is in the hands of a scribe" (*Aleph-Bet Book, Gaavah* A15).

A translation of any of Rebbe Nachman's teachings, particularly his *Likutey Moharan*, cannot help but be a "twisting" of his words. Rendering these complex discourses into English necessitates a certain amount of interpretation and inevitably a certain degree of distortion. It is therefore my hope that nothing which appears here will lead anyone to depart from even the most minor principle of Jewish law. And, whereas the deficiencies which are certainly present in this translation are my own, all credit belongs solely to the tzaddik.

*

My thanks are to all those who assisted in this project. In particular, I want to express my gratefulness to Simcha Bergman for teaching me how to do this work when we labored together on the first edition of this volume, and to Ozer Bergman who proved an indispensable aid, ally and ear. May they and theirs be blessed. And to Chaim Kramer, Director of the Breslov Research Institute, go my sincerest gratitude and appreciation. Without his "broad shoulders" it is hard to see how this work would have been nursed into existence. As in the past, may HaShem continue to grant him the ability to "do for the Rebbe," heart and soul. Above all, I thank the Holy One for bringing me closer to Him by guiding me, through no merit of my own, to Rebbe Nachman's path.

Moshe Mykoff
Adar I, 5749/1995

Table of Contents

GUIDELINES

Reb Noson writes:

"Rebbe Nachman's lessons and discourses are universal. The more one explores them, the more one discovers their radiant light and great depth, both in simple meaning and on the hidden, mystical level" *(Tzaddik #362).*

As author of *Likutey Halakhot* and *Likutey Tefilot,* works based on *Likutey Moharan,* there was no one in a better position than Reb Noson to appreciate the depth and beauty to be found in Rebbe Nachman's teachings. Elsewhere, he writes that each of the Rebbe's lesson can be likened to a palace containing halls and chambers, anterooms and entranceways—all of the most awesome beauty, with storey upon storey, each with its own unique style. No sooner do you enter one room and start examining it, marveling at the extraordinary novelty of its design, than you notice an amazing opening leading to another room. And so it goes from one room to the next, then on to another storey—everything linked and bound to everything else with the most profound wisdom and supreme beauty *(Ibid. #389).*

Yet, for all their radiance and brilliance of design—indeed, precisely because of these qualities—the halls and chambers of *Likutey Moharan* seem genuinely impenetrable and inaccessible to most people. The text of the lesson, with its complex structure and many abstruse concepts challenges, even confounds, the advanced Torah scholar; how much more so those of us who are unfamiliar with the style and language in which Rebbe Nachman taught. And yet, even with entry into the palace proper still beyond our reach, the light which emanates from its windows draws us. Its beauty, once discovered, is impossible to resist.

Because of this, a good number of people interested in studying the *Likutey Moharan* but in need of assistance, have written to Breslov Research asking that we open the way for them to explore these treasures. To the extent that such a thing is possible, this translated version with accompanying notes attempts to do just that. In order to fully benefit from this work, the reader is advised to carefully review and then put into practice the following guidelines for study. It is our belief and hope that these suggestions will enhance your understanding of the text and notes.

1. **First, read just the text itself from beginning to end.** As a rule, Rebbe Nachman begins the lesson (and often each section of a lesson) by setting forth the objective of that particular teaching. The remainder of the lesson (or section) is a series of statements and proofs substantiating that point and showing how it can be attained. It is thus common in *Likutey Moharan* for the Rebbe to connect one concept to a second and third concept, and then to return to connect the second concept to the third one and so on. Because Rebbe Nachman weaves together many different and difficult concepts, the reader can easily lose the lesson's flow. The theme which binds paragraph *a* with paragraph *b* may become unrecognizable. Therefore, it is advisable to begin by reading through the text of the lesson from beginning to end. This will help you absorb the concepts on a simple level. Don't try to understand them all at once. Read the entire lesson through once, twice, perhaps even three times, to familiarize yourself with the ideas. Once this has been done, you are ready to study the lesson with its notes.

2. **Try to flow with the lesson's structure.** In general, explanations of the Torah are said to exist on four planes or levels. They are known collectively as *PaR DeS*: *Pshat*—explanation of the simple meaning of the text; *Remez*—explanation of the allusions within the text; *Drush*—explanation of the text using the principles of hermeneutics; and *Sod*—explanation of the text according to its esoteric interpretation. Rebbe Nachman employs all of these methods, crossing from one area of the *Pardes* to the other, sometimes within a single paragraph or even sentence. It is important to be sensitive to this and to realize that what seems to the reader a sudden turn towards the unexpected was, for the Rebbe, the obvious and most natural next step. Particularly the beginner, if you haven't studied Rebbe Nachman's discourses and become familiar with his style, don't concern yourself with analyzing their structure; there's plenty of time for that later on. For now, staying attuned to the flow of the text is challenge enough.

3. **Pay close attention to connections/relationships between concepts, terminology and spelling.** One of the things which the reader notices almost at the outset is the predominance of "connections and relationships." In Hebrew, the word for this is *bechinah* (pl. *bechinot*). Rebbe Nachman once said, "My Torah teachings are made up entirely of *bechinot*." Indeed, the most often used phrase in his lessons has to be, "this is a *bechinah* of that." It also happens to be one of the hardest to translate. After considerable consideration, it was decided to use interchangeably any of the following: "corresponds to"; "synonymous with"; "relates to"; and perhaps the most

literal choice, "this is an aspect of that." No matter which option has been selected in English, Rebbe Nachman's intention in using the word *bechinah* is to highlight some quality which *aleph* has in common with *bet*. In focusing on this quality or aspect, he builds a bridge between the two concepts, crosses it, and carries on from the other side. The reader is strongly advised to pay particular attention to these connections—following the flow of the lesson ultimately depends upon this.

The reader would also do well to direct his attention to the connections which Rebbe Nachman makes between similarities in terminology. Whether it is two Hebrew words with a common root or one word with two divergent meanings, the Rebbe will emphasize their interrelationship to prove the point he is trying to make. Thus, for example, *TZITZit* (ritual fringes) corresponds to *mei'TZITZ* (looking) in that their root letters are the same. The word *kanaf* means corner or wing, and the Rebbe uses both, associating the corners of the earth with the flying of a bird. Yet, it is obvious that in translation, these similarities disappear. How could the reader be expected to notice that slander corresponds to foot? It was therefore necessary to incorporate the Hebrew transliteration into the text. This, together with the capitalization of the letters the two words have in common, makes it quite clear that *RoGaL* (slander) and *ReGeL* (foot) share the same root letters. This also explains why occasional use has been made of the ligature (the combination Æ and Œ) to highlight the connection between *ÆMuNaH* and Amanah, or *ŒMeiN* and *EMuNah*.

Along these same lines, it is worth mentioning that the translation has, at times, been "bent over backwards" so as to retain the relationship which Rebbe Nachman has focused on. Thus, when the Rebbe mentions kingdom and connects it to a previously quoted verse which speaks of the houses of royalty, the earlier reference has been translated "houses of kingship"—somewhat awkward, but clearly more in keeping with the relationship which the lesson seeks to highlight. This, in fact, has been the general rule followed for translation: Felicity to the style and tone of Rebbe Nachman's Hebrew text is paramount, even where this necessitated a somewhat stilted English rendition. Often times the reader will realize the reason for a particular phraseology only after completing the lesson, when all the pieces have fallen into place.

4. **General points to keep in mind concerning the lesson and its translation.** Most lessons in *Likutey Moharan* have a title. Generally speaking these titles have been taken from the first words of the opening verse. Where the lesson's title does not come from the opening verse, it has invariably been taken from the major theme of the

first section. In either case, the lesson's name appears in the English version in transliteration. Remembering these titles may not seem important at first, but as you advance in your understanding, the ability to refer to a lesson by name becomes a valuable tool for recalling its major themes and is also helpful when researching the commentaries on the Rebbe's teachings.

Wherever Rebbe Nachman uses the phrase "as is known," he is clueing the reader that the thought or concept just discussed has its source in the Kabbalah, Judaism's esoteric teachings, including the *Zohar*, the writings of the Ari and others.

Four separate pairs of markers appear in the translation, each indicative of a different insertion to the text. The first, simple parenthesis ( ), are reserved for sources quoted from the Bible, Talmud, Midrash, Kabbalah, etc. Square brackets [ ] indicate either insertions by the translator to enhance clarity, or the completion of a reference which Rebbe Nachman quotes only in part. Angle brackets < > enclose material quoted from the hand-written manuscript of *Likutey Moharan* as opposed to the more widespread printed version (see end of first note to Lesson #2). Lastly, braces { } are applied either when the text is Reb Noson's parenthetical addition to the lesson, or when a verse or passage has been inserted by way of introduction so that the reader can see it in its entirety before encountering Rebbe Nachman's explanation (which often comes piecemeal).

Another point worth noting concerns Rebbe Nachman's distinctive way of interpreting Scripture and rabbinic literature. In this regard, it must be made clear that the *pshat*, the simple interpretation of the text, is not always the same as its literal meaning. Rebbe Nachman will often explain a verse according to *pshat* which differs from the literal translation. It would therefore benefit the reader to carefully consider the way Rebbe Nachman approaches a verse or Talmudic passage rather than presume knowledge of the material based on previous study. This is particularly so with regard to the way the Rebbe incorporates into his teaching points from rabbinic literature for which there are more than a single opinion. Rebbe Nachman will weave together what seems to be two or more mutually exclusive positions, showing how, in fact, both are simultaneously applicable—both are "the words of the Living God."

Two further points concerning the text, and more specifically its translation. In order to make the text read as simply as possible, many words and concepts which should have been either capitalized or italicized were not. Doing so would have occasionally necessitated presenting the reader with an entire sentence of capitalized

words, or every other word in italics. Thus, when Rebbe Nachman talks about the fountain which waters the garden, or the conceptual wisdom, understanding, knowledge etc., no capitalization has been used. Similarly, the use of quotation marks to indicate a non-literal meaning has been held to a bare minimum. Instead, quotation marks are reserved almost exclusively for when Rebbe Nachman quotes from Scripture or rabbinic literature; italics are employed only for Hebrew transliteration and for a few select English words when particular emphasis was needed; and capitalization is limited to its common usages and for the highlighting of certain letters to show interrelationships, as explained above.

Finally, a note about the sections and paragraphs which appear in this translation. Early editions of *Likutey Moharan* already had the text sectioned and paragraphed, the work of Reb Noson (see Reb Noson's Introduction). However, in the process of translating the Rebbe's lessons, it became obvious that further paragraph breaks were necessary in the English. These were duly added—even liberally, to enable the reader to digest the text in smaller and more manageable chunks. As for the sections, we have not tampered with Reb Noson's original divisions, other than at the end of some lessons (which most often is a review of earlier material, or an interpretation of the opening verse or some major theme), where Reb Noson allowed the text to run on without partition. Then, too, there are some lessons for which Reb Noson provided no section breaks, and those that appear have been added for this translation.

5. **Make certain you understand the purpose of the footnotes.** Once the reader has reviewed the text satisfactorily, he will be able to take full advantage of the footnotes. However, before beginning, it would be worthwhile understanding what these notes are intended to accomplish and what not.

The footnotes have been designed to guide the reader through Rebbe Nachman's lesson, explaining the text, proofs and bases that the Rebbe uses in designing the lesson. We have assumed that the reader is acquainted with the Biblical narratives referred to and have not elaborated upon them. However, references made to Talmudic, Midrashic, Kabbalistic and Rabbinic literature have been explained. Second, the footnotes will prove helpful in connecting concepts from the different sections and paragraphs, while serving as a "road map" showing the reader from where he has come and where he is headed. Third, the footnotes will occasionally show how the lesson's themes connect with material from Scripture and Jewish history. Seen from Rebbe Nachman's perspective, passages from the different branches of Torah take on whole new meaning

and open the reader to aspects of Torah of which he was previously unaware. In addition, some notes make reference to aspects of contemporary society and current events. The hope is that, through these few examples, the reader will come to understand how, in fact, all the Rebbe's discourses remain ever relevant and ever alive. Finally, the footnotes attempt to add that which the Rebbe himself considered most valuable: suggestions for putting the Rebbe's ideas into practice—in our Torah study, prayer, fulfillment of the mitzvot and, indeed, every aspect of our lives.

In contrast, the footnotes were not designed to explain what is not immediately or directly relevant to the text. Concepts have been clarified in so far as their elucidation is required to help the reader understand that with which he is unfamiliar. The aim is to help you have a better appreciation for what Rebbe Nachman is teaching and not to provide exhaustive source material about the branches of the Torah with which you are less familiar.

6. **Read the notes one at a time and apply them to the text.** The reader should be aware that each lesson is self-contained and, as such, its footnotes are meant to explain its ideas as they are put forward *there* and not as they may be presented in a different lesson. Although checking cross references will prove beneficial and enhance your overall understanding, all attempts have been made to provide sufficient information for understanding a lesson without requiring the study of any other lesson or its notes. Read the text, read the note, and then see if you understand what it seeks to add to your comprehension of that particular portion of the Rebbe's teaching. Once you've determined this, you're ready to go on. If the point isn't clear, try again. Because the sections of the lesson are so intertwined and interdependent, reading further without having understood a particular point may prove even more frustrating later on. Omission of a building block of the structure will inevitably limit your comprehension of the various points made in the lesson.

Wherever a note refers to elsewhere within the same lesson, it is worthwhile checking there unless you are clear about the point being made. Even then, it may prove rewarding to reread a note when suggested. There are layers upon layers of interconnected thoughts and ideas in each teaching which you may unearth upon review of that which you already know. Note, also, the difference between the reference "*Likutey Moharan*" #5 and *Likutey Moharan* I, 5. Whereas the first format is used when the lesson referred to is found in the same volume the reader is presently

studying, the latter format is used when the reference appears in one of the other volumes of the translated *Likutey Moharan*.

In the course of study the reader will certainly come across ideas about which he would like to know more. To this end we have annotated all sources in the text and notes, and provided appendices relating to some of the references made to the more esoteric aspects of the Kabbalah. In addition, a chart of the numerical values of the letters of the Hebrew alphabet has been included for those unfamiliar with *gematria* (numerology).

7. Remember: Rebbe Nachman's lessons are universal, our footnotes are not. Reb Noson described Rebbe Nachman's lessons as universal. Actually, the Hebrew word he used was *k'laliyut* which on the one hand indicates generality and on the other an all encompassing nature. Indeed, the Rebbe's teachings are applicable to everyone and at the same time comprehensive in the scope of what they are designed to achieve. Thus, if the lesson speaks of Torah study, then Rebbe Nachman's advice on this topic is universal: relevant to every place, time and person, no matter where it is, when it is, or who he is. The same is true of those lessons which focus on prayer, giving charity, faith in God, and so on.

The advice and Torah insights in Rebbe Nachman's lessons are very precise prescriptions for spiritual growth. Aware of the implication which each and every one of his words carried, the Rebbe was very exacting when selecting the version of his teaching he wished to have recorded. Even so, because of their *k'laliyut*, the correct ways to explain a lesson are many. Accordingly, the interpretations given in the footnotes are, in a sense, a personal choice. Another annotator could have taken an entirely different route in following the Rebbe's lesson-design, chosen an entirely different set of explanatory notes and, even so, arrived at exactly the same destination. Thus, these notes are neither meant to preclude the insights of others nor are they in any way intended to diminish the universality of Rebbe Nachman's words.

Please feel free to send us questions you may have on any of the lessons. We would gladly welcome any suggestions you care to make pertaining to the presentation of Rebbe Nachman's teachings.

* * *

ליקוטי מוהר״ן

LIKUTEY MOHARAN

לְכוּ חֲזוּ מִפְעֲלוֹת ה׳ הִתְגַּלּוּת נִפְלָא מְסוֹד גְּדֻלַּת הַתַּנָּא הָאֱלֹקִי רַבִּי שִׁמְעוֹן בֶּן יוֹחַאי זַ״ל:

רַבִּי שִׁמְעוֹן בֶּן יוֹחַאי. הִבְטִיחַ שֶׁלֹּא תִשְׁתַּכַּח תּוֹרָה מִיִּשְׂרָאֵל עַל יָדוֹ. כַּמּוּבָא בְּדִבְרֵי רַבּוֹתֵינוּ, זִכְרוֹנָם לִבְרָכָה (שבת קלח:) ׳כְּשֶׁנִּכְנְסוּ רַבּוֹתֵינוּ לַכֶּרֶם בְּיַבְנֶה אָמְרוּ: עֲתִידָה תּוֹרָה שֶׁתִּשְׁתַּכַּח מִיִּשְׂרָאֵל וְאָמַר רַבִּי שִׁמְעוֹן בֶּן יוֹחַאי שֶׁלֹּא תִשְׁתַּכַּח. שֶׁנֶּאֱמַר: "כִּי

unity between Rabbi Akiva's 24,000 students was made up for by Rabbi Shimon ben Yochai and his disciples. The *Zohar* often praises this closely knit group and makes clear it was the love between them that enabled Rabbi Shimon to reveal the most esoteric teachings of the Hidden Torah. In this sense, Reb Noson adds, Rashby and his disciples were a rectification for those that died (*Likutey Halakhot, Rosh Chodesh* 6; see *The Breslov Haggadah*, Appendix C: *Lag B'Omer: In Praise of Rabbi Shimon*).

3. **yeshivah in Yavneh.** When the Temple stood, the Sanhedrin, the supreme rabbinic court, had its own hall adjacent to it. Even before the Temple's destruction (in 68 c.e.), Roman oppression forced the Sanhedrin to begin a series of ten exiles, under the aegis of the President of the Sanhedrin (see *Rosh HaShanah* 31a). Yavneh was twice the home of the Sanhedrin, the first time during the lifetime of Rabbi Yochanan ben Zakkai. With his passing, the Sanhedrin moved to Usha, where Rabban Gamliel presided. Ten years later, the Sanhedrin, still under the aegis of Rabban Gamliel, returned to Yavneh. Rabban Gamliel's Sanhedrin consisted of Rabbi Eliezer, Rabbi Yehoshua, Rabbi Akiva and his colleagues, the Ten Martyrs (Rabbi Akiva's five disciples were still students at the time). Forcing the Sanhedrin to constantly relocate was part of the Roman Empire's attempt to destroy the Jewish religion by uprooting the established yeshivot. The presidents of the Sanhedrin, descendants of the House of King David, were particularly viewed with enmity by the Romans, who saw them as a symbol of independent Jewish sovereignty; their continued leadership was thus considered a threat to the empire (*Galiyut Sanhedrin*).

4. **be forgotten....** After the Temple's destruction, the Romans issued very harsh decrees against the Jews, including prohibitions against Torah study, and the observance of Shabbat, family purity and circumcision—all mitzvot which kept the Jews socially apart from their Roman masters. Even keeping mitzvot that were not as obvious—e.g., tefillin, matzah and lulav—made one liable for the death penalty (see *Shabbat* 130a; *Mekhilta, Yitro* 6). Rabbi Shimon's generation was thus known as the Generation of *Shmad* (destruction and apostasy), during which the Jews suffered incessantly at the hands of their Roman conquerors. After witnessing the upheaval wreaked upon the Jewish way of life by their oppressors, the leading rabbis predicted that the suffering and oppression would inevitably lead to a spiritual holocaust of assimilation, as well—i.e., a total forgetting of the Torah and the mitzvot (see *Ri Pinto, Shabbat, loc. cit.*). The Sages based their argument on the prophecy (Amos 8:11-12): " 'Days are coming,' says God, 'when I will send a famine to the world; not a hunger for bread, nor a thirst for water, but to hear the word of God. They will search...to find the word of God, but will not find it.' "

PROLOGUE [1]

Come and see the works of God: an amazing revelation
concerning the mystery of the greatness of the godly sage, Rabbi
Shimon ben Yochai.[2]

Rabbi Shimon ben Yochai gave assurances that through him the
Torah would not be forgotten from the Jewish people. As our
Sages teach (*Shabbat* 138b): When our rabbis entered the yeshivah in
Yavneh,[3] they said, "The Torah will one day be forgotten by the
Jews."[4] But Rabbi Shimon ben Yochai said that it would not be

---

1. **Prologue.** This teaching was given on 4 Iyar, 5570 (May 8, 1810). Four days earlier, on
Shabbat night, Rebbe Nachman's house in Breslov burned down in a major fire which
devastated most of the city. On Sunday, the Rebbe received word that the arrangements for
his move to Uman had been finalized. Having previously expressed his desire to be interred in
the Uman cemetery, burial site of thousands of martyrs from the Uman massacre of 1768,
Rebbe Nachman understood that the news was Heaven's way of telling him his time was
close at hand. It was Tuesday when they set out for Uman, and on the journey Rebbe
Nachman gave this lesson (*Tzaddik* #82, #86). The significance of its timing will become clear
below (see n.11:end).

    This Prologue did not appear in the initial printing of *Likutey Moharan*, in 1808, as the
lesson wasn't even taught until two years later. It was first included in the first printing of
Part II by Reb Noson in 1811, a year after the Rebbe's passing.

2. **Rabbi Shimon ben Yochai.** Rabbi Shimon the son of Yochai (RaShBY, or bar Yochai; circa
120 c.e.) was a leading disciple of Rabbi Akiva and himself one of the most distinguished
Tannaim (sage of the Mishnaic period). He authored both the holy *Zohar* (compiled by his
followers) and the *Sifri*, a Midrash on the books of Numbers and Deuteronomy. The Ari
comments that of all of Rabbi Akiva's disciples, Rashby is most closely identified with him.
This is what enabled Rabbi Shimon to realize and reveal the deep mysteries of the Torah and
the Kabbalah more than anyone else (see *Shaar HaGilgulim* #26, p.71).

    The Talmud relates that Rabbi Akiva had 24,000 students, all of whom were great rabbis
in their own right. Yet, over the course of just thirty-three days during the Omer Counting
period (between Pesach and Shavuot) all 24,000 died because they did not act respectfully
toward one another. When they died, the world was left bereft of Torah, until Rabbi Akiva
came and taught five new students: Rabbi Meir, Rabbi Yehudah, Rabbi Yosi, Rabbi Shimon
ben Yochai and Rabbi Nechemiah. Through these great tzaddikim, who were later the Sages
of the Mishnah, the entire Torah was restored to the Jewish people (*Yevamot* 62b; *Sanhedrin*
86a). Reb Noson explains that that which was lacking because there was no fellowship and

לֹא תִשָּׁכַח מִפִּי זַרְעוֹ". וְכַמְבֹאָר בַּזֹּהַר (ח"ג קכד:) : 'בְּהַאי חִבּוּרָא
דְּאִיהוּ הַזֹּהַר יִפְקוּן בֵּהּ מִן גָּלוּתָא'.
וְעַתָּה בּוֹא וּרְאֵה וְהָבֵן. נִפְלָאוֹת נִסְתָּרוֹת שֶׁל תּוֹרָתֵנוּ הַקְּדוֹשָׁה. כִּי
עַל כֵּן סָמַךְ רַבִּי שִׁמְעוֹן בֶּן יוֹחַאי עַצְמוֹ עַל זֶה הַפָּסוּק כִּי לֹא

purified and cleansed of any admixture). Thus, when the time comes that all Israel will taste from the Tree of Life—which is this Book of the *Zohar*—they will be redeemed from exile through kindness and mercy [and not through the bitterness of "question and answer," as happens to those who study only the Revealed Torah] (*Zohar* III, 124b; see *Matok Midvash, loc. cit.*).

Whereas the Hidden Torah corresponds to the Tree of Life, the Revealed Torah corresponds to the Tree of Knowledge. This is particularly true for the Oral Law (Mishnah and Talmud). Although the Torah is pure in all its aspects, because the Oral Law deals with the permitted and the forbidden (good and evil), it is referred to as the Tree of Knowledge of Good and Evil. This is not to say that a Jew should avoid studying the Revealed Torah. Quite the reverse. Only through its study is it possible to ascend to great levels of good and subdue one's own evil traits, and evil in general. This cleansing process is necessary. It opens the way to a higher level of Torah, the Hidden Torah, which contains the mysteries of the Kabbalah. These mysteries focus on the inner meaning of the Torah's laws and concepts, and have the power to forge a much stronger bond between a Jew and God—Who is Himself hidden. With the arrival of the Mashiach, evil will be completely subdued. This is because the mysteries of Torah, the Tree of Life, will then be revealed to all. Attaining and understanding the Hidden Torah corresponds to attaining and understanding the hidden God, as will happen when Mashiach comes. This revelation of God will, by definition, expose all falsehood and evil. The Hidden Torah is thus the means for subduing evil completely. It is this hidden power of Torah, drawn from the highest of levels, that Rabbi Shimon was able to attain and—even more importantly—transmit for future generations. His teachings and revelations are what enable the Jews to seek God and find Him even in the most concealed places. Therefore, it was only Rabbi Shimon—the one granted permission from Above to reveal the Torah's mysteries—who was able to state with certainty that the Torah would not be forgotten by the Jewish people.

Reb Noson connects this to the Talmudic teaching that the world was created with Ten Sayings, the first of which was "*Bereishit*" (see *Megillah* 21b). That is, the opening chapter of Genesis contains ten utterances, each a verbal expression of some aspect of Creation. However, careful reading of the text shows that the word "*vayomer* (and He said)," which introduces each Saying, appears only nine times. Our Sages therefore teach: The first word, "*Bereishit* (In the beginning)," is also an utterance—the Concealed Saying. Whereas the nine Revealed Sayings all manifest Godliness, corresponding to remembering Torah, the one Concealed Saying denotes forgetting Torah, as if the Torah were concealed from the person. Yet, the Concealed Saying is also the first of the ten, the loftiest of all. As such, it is the Concealed Saying that sustains all the others, even those aspects of Creation which are very removed from God. For only the light of that which is most exalted can shine all the way down to that which is most distant. By searching for this Hidden Light, the Concealed Saying, one can ultimately return to God (*Torat Natan* #1). In our context, this Concealed

forgotten, as is written (Deuteronomy 31:21), "It will not be forgotten from the mouth of his offspring."[5] And, as is explained in the *Zohar* (III, 124b): Because of this work, the Book of the *Zohar,* [the Jews] will be redeemed from exile.[6]

So now come, see and understand the hidden wonders of our holy Torah. This is why Rabbi Shimon ben Yochai based himself on this verse: "It will not be forgotten from the mouth of his offspring." For,

5. **Rabbi Shimon....** Rabbi Shimon stood alone against the leading rabbis of his time in his conviction that the Torah would never be forgotten. He based his opinion on one verse: "It will not be forgotten from the mouth of his offspring." The commentaries explain that the Sages understood this verse to be limited to the Song of Moshe (*Haazinu*; Deuteronomy 32). Only it would remain eternally with the Jews; not so the rest of the Torah. Rabbi Shimon, on the other hand, saw this verse as pertaining to the entire Torah. True, he conceded, the time would come when clarity in the Torah would be extremely rare due to all the disagreements between the rabbis—this being the hunger and thirst for the word of God—but the Torah itself would never be forgotten in its entirety. Rebbe Nachman next explains what gave Rashby the confidence to take this position, in opposition to all the leading rabbis.

The question is raised as to whether this dispute about the Torah's future took place when the Sanhedrin was in Yavneh, or at a later date, after the Sanhedrin moved to Usha a second time and then on to Shfaram. Logically, it seems more likely that this happened when the Sanhedrin was in Shfaram, as then Rabbi Shimon was already universally recognized as one of the outstanding Jewish leaders, even by the Romans, who sought to have him killed (see *Shabbat* 33b). However, in Yavneh, Rabbi Shimon was just one of Rabbi Akiva's young disciples, albeit a formidable and foremost one (see *Berakhot* 28a). It is therefore a bit difficult to imagine that Rabbi Shimon would at that time stand up against all the leading rabbis. However, if that were the case, this makes Rashby's statement all the more powerful. So positive was he of his interpretation of the verse that, even at that stage, he was willing to challenge the predominant view of the time.

6. **Book of the Zohar....** This appears in the *Raaya Mehemna,* the name given to those sections of the *Zohar* revealed and studied in the heavenly yeshivah of Moshe Rabbeinu. It was said by the prophet Eliyahu during a discussion about the laws of *sotah*, a woman suspected of immorality, whose claim of innocence can be verified by the test of the bitter waters (Numbers 5:11-31). The prophet likens the Jews in exile to the *sotah*—they are tested by the bitterness of exile to determine if they have remained true to God or not. He also attributes the Jewish people's trials and tribulations to the influence of the Tree of Knowledge of Good and Evil, as a result of which the Jews assimilated with the Mixed Multitude and so are themselves a mixture of good and evil, sweet and bitter. Those who survive exile with their faith in God intact—i.e., they accept it as a means of purification—become bound to Him. Conversely, those who fail are those who have tasted the bitter waters of exile and fallen even further from faith—their souls go lost, and will not return to the Holy Land at the Ingathering of the Exiles.

Eliyahu continues: But there are those who "eat" from the Tree of Life, and so attain deep understanding. These are the mysteries of Torah [the Kabbalah], from the *zohara* (splendor) of *Binah*, which is the source of all repentance. Those who attain these mysteries do not have to be tested by the bitterness of exile (for through the Hidden Torah the soul is

תִּשָּׁכַח מִפִּי זַרְעוֹ. כִּי בֶּאֱמֶת בְּזֶה הַפָּסוּק בְּעַצְמוֹ. מְרָמָז וְנִסְתָּר סוֹד
הַזֶּה. שֶׁעַל־יְדֵי זַרְעוֹ שֶׁל יוֹחַאי. שֶׁהוּא רַבִּי שִׁמְעוֹן בֶּן יוֹחַאי. עַל
יָדוֹ לֹא תִשְׁתַּכַּח הַתּוֹרָה מִיִּשְׂרָאֵל. כִּי סוֹפֵי תֵבוֹת שֶׁל זֶה הַפָּסוּק כִּי
לֹא תִשָּׁכַח מִפִּי זַרְעוֹ הֵם אוֹתִיּוֹת יוֹחַאי.

וְזֶה שֶׁמְרָמֵּז וּמְגַלֶּה הַפָּסוּק. כִּי לֹא תִשָּׁכַח מִפִּי זַרְעוֹ, מִפִּי זַרְעוֹ
דַּיְקָא הַיְנוּ מִפִּי זַרְעוֹ שֶׁל זֶה בְּעַצְמוֹ שֶׁהוּא מְרָמָז וְנִסְתָּר בְּזֶה
הַפָּסוּק. שֶׁהוּא הַתַּנָּא יוֹחַאי. כִּי עַל־יְדֵי זַרְעוֹ שֶׁל יוֹחַאי שֶׁמְרָמָז
בְּזֶה הַפָּסוּק בְּסוֹפֵי תֵבוֹת כַּנַּ"ל. שֶׁהוּא רַבִּי שִׁמְעוֹן בֶּן יוֹחַאי. עַל
יָדוֹ לֹא תִשָּׁכַח הַתּוֹרָה. כִּי בְּזֹהַר דָּא יִפְּקוּן מִן גָּלוּתָא כַּנַּ"ל:
וְדַע שֶׁסּוֹד רַבִּי שִׁמְעוֹן בְּעַצְמוֹ. הוּא מְרָמָז בְּפָסוּק אַחֵר. כִּי דַע כִּי
הַתַּנָּא הַקָּדוֹשׁ רַבִּי שִׁמְעוֹן הוּא בְּחִינַת (דָּנִיֵּאל ד) : עִ׳יר וְ׳קַדִּישׁ מִ׳ן
שְׁ׳מַיָּא נָ׳חִית – רָאשֵׁי־תֵבוֹת שִׁמְעוֹן וְכוּ׳:

This is why it is said of Rabbi Shimon and his disciples that they were the rectification for Rabbi Akiva's 24,000 students who died (n.2). Although those students had studied the deep mysteries of the Torah, including the Breaking of the Vessels, they were lacking in their comprehension of the subsequent *tikkunim*. This explains why their generation foresaw the Torah's being forgotten by the Jews—symbolic of the Broken Vessels of Creation. Rabbi Shimon, on the other hand, was versed in the rectifications and was therefore able to proclaim that the Torah would not be forgotten (*Torat Natan #2*).

10. **another verse.** In the first verse, Rashby is alluded to only as the offspring of his father, Rabbi Yochai. Here Rebbe Nachman presents his second insight: the verse which alludes to Rabbi Shimon proper.

11. **Ir V'kaddish...ShIMON....** The first letters of the verse from Daniel, "*Ir V'kaddish Min Shemaya Nachit*" (עיר וקדיש מן שמיא נחית), spell ShIMON (שמעון; the letter *vav* can be voweled as an "O" or a "V"). This, Rebbe Nachman says, alludes to none other than Rabbi Shimon ben Yochai. Moreover, the connection is not limited to this acrostic. The words of the verse are those of the wicked Babylonian king, Nevukhadnezzar. He had a dream in which he saw a beautiful tree stretching towards the heavens. The tree, laden with fruits, was huge enough to provide sustenance and shelter for all the different forms of life in Creation. Nevukhadnezzar then described how "an angel, a holy one, descended from heaven" calling for the destruction of the tree.... Daniel was called upon to interpret the dream. The tree, he said, was Nevukhadnezzar himself. As ruler of the entire world, all forms of life were dependent upon him for their food and shelter. However, because of his wickedness, Nevukhadnezzar was to be "cut down" and punished. He was to be transformed into an animal for a period of seven seasons (Daniel 4:6-23). Who was the angel that called for the

in truth, this mystery is hinted at and concealed in this very verse.[7]
Through the offspring of Yochai, this being Rashby, the Torah will
not be forgotten by the Jews. This is because the final letters of the
words in this verse *"kI loA tishakhaCh mipiY zar'O"* are the same
letters as *YOChAI.*[8]

This is what the verse hints to and reveals: "It will not be forgotten
from the mouth of his offspring"—specifically "from the mouth of *his*
offspring." That is, "from the mouth of the offspring" of the one who
is himself alluded to and hidden in this verse, this being the sage
Yochai. Because of the offspring of Yochai, who is hinted at in the
final letters of the words in this verse—this being Rashby—the Torah
will not be forgotten; for with this *Zohar* they will be redeemed from
exile, as above.[9]

And know! the mystery of Rabbi Shimon himself is alluded to in
another verse.[10] Know that the holy sage Rabbi Shimon corresponds
to (Daniel 4:10): *"Ir V'kaddish Min Shemaya Nachit* (An angel, a holy
one, descended from heaven)"—the first letters of which are
ShIMON[11] . . . .

Saying corresponds to the Hidden Torah/the Book of the *Zohar*. Both *"Bereishit"* and the
teachings of Rashby sustain that which is furthest removed from holiness.

7. **this mystery. . . .** Here, Rebbe Nachman presents the lesson's first insight: The choice of
verse was not arbitrary. Rather, hidden within the verse itself is proof that specifically
because of Rabbi Shimon and the *Zohar*, the Jews will not forget the Torah and so merit to
be redeemed from exile.

8. **the offspring of. . .YOChAI.** The verse which Rabbi Shimon quotes as proof for his
position: "It will not be forgotten from the mouth of his offspring," in Hebrew reads: *"kI loA
tishakhaCh mipiY zar'O"* (כי לא תשכח מפי זרעו). Whose offspring? As Rebbe Nachman says next,
the offspring of that one whose name is alluded to in the final letters of each of these words—
namely, YOChAI (יוחי). And, of course, that offspring was none other than Rashby himself.

9. **. . .as above.** Because Rabbi Shimon is alluded to in the verse, "It will not be
forgotten. . . ," he was able to stand up, regardless of the eminence of the rabbis gathered,
and proclaim that the Torah will not be forgotten. What would guarantee this? "From the
mouth of his offspring"—i.e., it would be guaranteed by the teachings and revelations that
were to come from the mouth of R. Yochai's offspring. By means of the *Zohar*, the Jewish
people will merit to be redeemed from exile.

Reb Noson writes: Rabbi Shimon put great effort into revealing the deepest mysteries of
the Torah, especially those found in the sections of the *Zohar* known as *Idra Rabba, Idra
Zuta* and *Sifra DeTzneuta*. These sections explain the mysteries of the beginning of Creation,
including the Breaking of the Vessels and the subsequent construction of the Divine personas.
Above all, Rashby's teachings show that despite the fall and flaws implied by the Breaking of
the Vessels, *tikkun* (rectification), through the revealed mysteries of Torah, is still possible.

has a numerical value of 501, the same as NaChMaN ben SiMChaH" (*Sichot V'Sipurim*, p.166).

The rabbi's explanation is a powerful statement in its own right. Yet, equally telling are the different parallels that can be drawn between the lives of these two great tzaddikim.

When Rebbe Nachman passed away some five months after revealing this teaching, he was only thirty-eight and a half. Despite his relatively few years, he had been teacher and rebbe to accomplished Torah scholars, men of piety, some of whom were many years his senior. Opposition notwithstanding, the Rebbe was recognized as one of the leading "elders" of his time. The parallel to Rabbi Shimon is obvious. He was only a young disciple when he gave his assurance that the Torah would not be forgotten. His prominence as one of Rabbi Akiva's exceptional students was well acknowledged, so much so, that in his case it was not considered unbefitting for one so young to take issue with the accepted position of sages many years his senior.

Rebbe Nachman lived at the beginning of 19th century, a time when a tidal wave of atheism flooded the world. For the Jews living in Eastern Europe, this was manifested by the inroads made by the *Haskalah* (Enlightenment) movement against traditional Torah Judaism. The heretical ideas preached by those who saw the need for Jews to "expand their horizons" and adjust to the changing world around them threatened the very core of Jewish belief. Rebbe Nachman recognized this and foresaw the massive assimilation and flight from Torah that would result from the *Haskalah's* so-called enlightenment. In many ways, it was a time very similar to Rabbi Shimon's Generation of *Shmad* (above, n.4). Then, too, the planned Romanization of the Jewish people was to promote massive assimilation and an uprooting of the Torah. When Rashby proclaimed that the Torah would not be forgotten because of the "offspring of Yochai," he was in fact saying that *he* and his teaching, the holy *Zohar*, would guarantee the Jewish people's survival in exile. If anything, guaranteeing the Jewish people's survival in exile was the Rebbe's mission as well. His concluding words here indicate that *he* and his teaching, *Likutey Moharan*, are a response—a *tikkun* (rectification)—to the tidal wave of secularization that has engulfed the Jewish people ever since his time. Just as there was an *"ir v'kaddish min shemaya nachit,"* there is now a *"nachal novea mekor chokhmah"*—a brook, a wellspring, from which to draw the wisdom and guidance that will ultimately lead to the Jewish people's redemption. Incidentally, this mission of leadership which Rebbe Nachman and Rashby had in common is alluded to by the shared numerical value of their names, 501, which is also the numerical value of the Hebrew word *ROSh* ("head" or "leader").

Although Rabbi Shimon's greatness is unfathomable, we do know that of all the leading Sages of the Talmud, he alone was given permission to reveal the mysteries of Torah. As indicated by the passage from the *Zohar* quoted above (see n.6), the Hidden Torah has the power to elevate the Jews who have assimilated—cleanse them of the influences of the Mixed Multitude—and bring them back to Torah and purity. This power of repentance is drawn from the *sefirah* of *Binah* and can penetrate the heart and mind of every Jew, to arouse his inherent faith. Thus, Rabbi Shimon, the master of Hidden Torah, is most closely identified with *Binah* and repentance.

In describing himself as the *"nachal novea mekor chokhmah,"* Rebbe Nachman, too, was identifying with the qualities of Hidden Torah/*Binah*/repentance. The Kabbalah teaches that the *sefirah* of *Chokhmah* (Wisdom) refers to the water source, whereas "the brook" corresponds to the *sefirah* of *Binah*. By stating, "But now, there is 'a flowing brook, a wellspring of wisdom,' so that even 'a holy one descended from heaven' must also receive

tree's—Nevukhadnezzar's—destruction? This "holy one," Rebbe Nachman reveals, alludes to Rabbi Shimon. In the passage quoted earlier from the *Zohar* (n.6), we saw that the powers of evil are "cut down" and destroyed by the mysteries of Torah/the Tree of Life. From both the Talmud (*Shabbat* 33b; *Me'ilah* 17b; etc.) and the holy *Zohar* (III, 15b; *ibid.,* 106b; *Tikkuney Zohar* #21, 61b, etc.) we see how Rabbi Shimon struggled time and again against the forces of evil. Thus, the Rebbe's choice of this verse is based on more than the acrostic. The verse's allusion to Rabbi Shimon also encompasses Rabbi Shimon's mission in this world—i.e., the revelation of God through the revelation of the Torah's mysteries, as a result of which evil is subdued.

The commentaries (*Rashi, Metzudat David,* etc.) point out that the word *ir,* here translated as "angel," literally means "awake." This is because an angel is always awake—always conscious of God (see *Torat Natan* #3). The word *v'kaddish* ("a holy one") also applies to an angel, whose holiness can never be defiled. Rebbe Nachman taught that being spiritually "awake" is a condition for heightened awareness and holiness, for the one who is "asleep" cannot hope for expanded consciousness. These concepts, which appear in *Likutey Moharan* I, 60 (§§3-6), are based on Rabbi Shimon's teachings concerning the Hidden Torah, the mystery of *Atik Yomin.* Thus, the reference to Rabbi Shimon specifically as "an angel (sleepless), a holy one," is not incidental. On the contrary, Rabbi Shimon's heightened awareness made him especially sensitive to the suffering of those exiled, just as it gave him the ability to remedy their plight through the revelation of the Hidden Torah.

* * *

After revealing this amazing teaching about Rashby and his father Yochai, Rebbe Nachman concluded: "But now, there is '*nachal novea mekor chokhmah* (a flowing brook, a wellspring of wisdom)' (Proverbs 18:4), so that even 'a holy one descended from heaven' must also receive from this brook."

The Rebbe's reference to "*Nachal Novea Mekor Chokhmah*" (נחל נובע מקור חכמה) is an allusion to himself. After showing how the names of Rabbi Yochai and Rabbi Shimon are alluded to in Scripture, Rebbe Nachman quotes a verse whose first letters spell NaChMaN (נחמן; see *Tzaddik* #86).

To better understand Rebbe Nachman's last statement, and its significance as part of the Prologue to *Likutey Moharan,* consider the following anecdote:

A Breslover Chassid once found himself alone in a distant city, not knowing anyone or having where to lodge for the night. He went to the house of the local rabbi, a man known not only for his good name but also for his Torah erudition and mastery of Kabbalah. Upon arriving, the chassid noticed a copy of *Likutey Moharan* on the rabbi's table and asked his host where he got the book.

"Do you know this book and its author?" the rabbi wondered.

"I knew the author. I am a Breslover Chassid."

"Do you understand what's written in it?" the rabbi asked.

"To the best of my ability," the chassid answered.

"In my opinion," the rabbi said, "nobody can truly grasp this work. Just look at the Prologue. What place has this teaching as the opening piece to *Likutey Moharan?*"

"You tell me," the chassid replied.

"It would appear," the rabbi suggested, "that Rebbe Nachman is alluding to his having the same soul as Rabbi Shimon. For the name ShIMON ben YOChAI

In fact, rectification of souls—not only for the dead but also for the living—had been foremost in Rebbe Nachman's thoughts ever since his return from Lemberg, nearly two years earlier. In his own words, he had journeyed there, among other reasons, to combat the spread of heresy. Lemberg (Lvov), the largest city in eastern Galicia, had for centuries been a major center of Torah erudition. During the late 1700s and early 1800s, the *Haskalah* had found a foothold amongst the roughly 30,000 Jewish residents. The Rebbe saw it his mission to combat this—then, and for the future. It is therefore not coincidental that while in Lemberg Rebbe Nachman instructed two of his followers to reveal some of his teachings, which had hitherto been kept from the public eye, as well as initiated the first printing of *Likutey Moharan*. His intention in this regard became even clearer after his return, from which time he repeatedly stressed how his teachings would endure for future generations (*Until the Mashiach* p.153*ff*). As explained above, Rebbe Nachman saw his *Likutey Moharan* as a response—a *tikkun*—for the tidal wave of heresy and secularization that has engulfed the Jewish people ever since his time.

So, now, as Rebbe Nachman and those accompanying him were on their way to Uman, the Rebbe's thoughts must have been on the rectification of souls when he said, "Still, God helps the Jewish people at all times. 'There is no orphaned generation' (*Chagigah* 3b). This is what Rabbi Shimon ben Yochai answered . . . ." He then taught this lesson.

On that same journey Rebbe Nachman spoke to Reb Noson about how God is constantly bringing things to their completion and rectification. Reb Noson writes: To explain all this would take pages and pages. Briefly, he [the Rebbe] had thought originally, when we first became close to him, that he would accomplish the *tikkun* immediately, and many of the things he said indicated this. But later on, because of our many sins, the sins of the generation and the tremendous determination of the Satan which led to all the opposition against the Rebbe, everything was upset and he was unable to accomplish what he wanted in his lifetime. Yet, he still said that he *had* accomplished and *would* accomplish. For after his return from Lemberg, he found a path and spoke in such a way as to ensure that his light would never ever be extinguished. The Rebbe himself said, "*Mein fierel vet shoin tluen biz Moshiach vet koomen!*—My fire will burn until the Mashiach comes!" (*Tzaddik* #126).

from this brook," the Rebbe indicates that, presently, the aim of Rabbi Shimon's teachings can only be achieved when they receive from "the brook"—i.e., the Rebbe's teachings. The lessons in Rebbe Nachman's *Likutey Moharan* are taken from the very source of the "water," *Chokhmah,* and it is specifically these teachings which are needed in order to penetrate to the lowest of levels, instilling faith and a desire for repentance in even those most distant from God. As explained, this was precisely the Rashby's stated goal: to ensure that the Torah would not be forgotten and to ensure Jewish survival in exile. But, now, as a result of Romanization and secularization—and all of history's "-izations" in between—there are many Jews for whom Rabbi Shimon's teachings are beyond their grasp, for whom the light of the Hidden Torah which he revealed is too bright. Hence the need for what is essentially an extension of the rectification begun by the "*ir v'kaddish min shemaya nachit,*" the teachings of "*nachal novea mekor chokhmah.*"

Thus, Breslover Chassidim were wont to quote the passage, "Because of this work, the Book of the *Zohar...,*" and say, "Because of *this* work—*Likutey Moharan,* which is the *Zohar*—we will be redeemed from exile. For, NaChMaN ben SiMChaH (נחמן בן שמחה) has the same numerical value as ShIMON ben YOChAI (שמעון בן יוחאי)" (see Appendix: Gematria Chart).

*

It should now be clear why Rebbe Nachman gave this lesson at the time he travelled from Breslov to Uman. As mentioned (n.1), the Rebbe saw his being called to Uman as a sign that he was soon to die. He was by no means shocked or unprepared for this. On the contrary, as Reb Noson writes: His whole purpose in choosing Uman as his place to die and be buried was to accomplish the rectification of innumerable souls which had been in need of this for several hundred years. For Uman had been the scene of the slaughter of countless souls.... And on the day before he died, he said to me, "For a long time now they've had their eye on me, to get me here. There are not just thousands of souls here, but myriads upon myriads...souls which did not know me at all are awaiting the *tikkun* I can give them" (*Tzaddik* #48, #88).

בְּעֶזְרַת אֵל עֶלְיוֹן

אֲשֶׁר שָׁמַיִם וָאָרֶץ קָנָה.

וְנָתַן לָנוּ אֶת תּוֹרָתוֹ

מִמִּדְבָּר מַתָּנָה.

נַתְחִיל לְהַדְפִּיס

חִדּוּשִׁים נִפְלָאִים וְנוֹרָאִים

עַל מַאַמְרֵי בַּר בַּר חַנָה.

בִּזְכוּת זֶה נִזְכֶּה לַעֲלוֹת

לְצִיּוֹן בְּרִנָּנָה.

אֶל קִרְיַת מֶלֶךְ דָּוִד חַנָה:

When Rebbe Nachman first revealed these teachings, he disclosed that Rabbah bar bar Chanah had come to him saying, "Why don't you pay attention to my stories? If you do, I will reveal to you the most awesome and wonderful new insights" (*Tzaddik* #131).

The first eighteen lessons of *Likutey Moharan* are based on the stories found there in *Bava Batra* (15 based on Rabbah bar bar Chanah's stories and the final 3 on stories told by other Sages). Additional stories appear in *Likutey Moharan* II, Lessons 4, 5 and 7.

4. Paraphrase of Isaiah 29:1.

With the help of the Exalted God,
  Possessor of heaven and earth;[1]
Who gave us His Torah
  From the wilderness to Matanah;[2]
We shall begin to print
  Revelations, wonderful and awesome
  On the stories of Rabbah bar bar Chanah.[3]
In this merit may we ascend
  To Zion with song;
  To the city where King David encamped.[4]

---

1. Paraphrase of Genesis 14:19.

2. See Numbers 21:18, where Matanah is the name of a place. Our Sages (*Eruvin* 54a) interpret it literally, "a gift." Reb Noson, author of these introductory lines, implies that this appellation also applies to Rebbe Nachman's teachings.

3. The incredulous stories of Rabbah bar bar Chanah are recounted in *Bava Batra* (73a*ff*). "Though one cannot deny the veracity of these anecdotes," says the Maharsha in his commentary, "much deeper meanings are to be found within each story" (*Maharsha, s.v. ishta'iy*). He then proceeds to expound on the stories at great length.

ליקוטי מוהר״ן סימן א׳

אַשְׁרֵי תְמִימֵי דָרֶךְ הַהוֹלְכִים בְּתוֹרַת ה׳ (תהלים קי״ט):

דַּע, כִּי עַל יְדֵי הַתּוֹרָה נִתְקַבְּלִים כָּל הַתְּפִלוֹת וְכָל הַבַּקָּשׁוֹת, שֶׁאָנוּ
מְבַקְשִׁים וּמִתְפַּלְלִים. וְהַחֵן וְהַחֲשִׁיבוּת שֶׁל יִשְׂרָאֵל נִתְעַלֶּה
וְנִתְרוֹמֵם בִּפְנֵי כָּל מִי שֶׁצְּרִיכִין, הֵן בְּרוּחָנִי הֵן בְּגַשְׁמִי.

Jewish populace of Eastern Europe created by the dispute between the mitnagdim and the chassidim was still very much in evidence. A major point of contention was the study versus prayer controversy. The mitnagdim argued for the primary importance of Torah study, whereas the chassidim placed greater emphasis on prayer. Commenting on this dispute, the Rebbe said, "The mitnagdim argue that Torah study is a Jew's main devotion. The chassidim argue that prayer is the main devotion. But I say, 'Pray and study and pray!' " (*Aveneha Barzel,* p.52, #10; *Siach Sarfei Kodesh* 1-87). Accordingly, the relationship between prayer and Torah study is a major focus of the lesson.

No less significant is what the lesson has to say about what was, and remains even today, a much more divisive issue for the Jewish people. During Rebbe Nachman's lifetime, the *Haskalah* (Enlightenment) movement had begun making serious inroads into Eastern European Jewry. The leaders of the *Haskalah* argued that for Jews to be accepted by their gentile neighbors—the goal of which was to better their financial and social status—they would have to adapt to modern, non-Jewish society. Couched within the lesson is Rebbe Nachman's rejection of this outlook. He teaches that the *only* way for a Jew to be accepted and respected by the non-Jew is by his adherence to Torah values and study. Only the Torah can enhance the grace and reveal the importance of Israel. This is typical of Rebbe Nachman's lessons: to reflect on the issues of the time—indeed, of all times—and teach how a Jew is to properly relate to them and succeed.

2. **...are accepted.** Rebbe Nachman's opening statement is not merely a response to the follower who came seeking to improve the quality of his prayers. As will become clear in section 2, it is also the Rebbe's advice for anyone who feels his prayers go unanswered. For at one time or another, all those who would serve God experience the frustration expressed by the Rebbe's follower. What happens is that occasionally a person can pray and pray for something, yet fail to see any results. Unless his trust in God is exceptional, he inevitably begins to lose faith. As a result, he slackens in his efforts in prayer, which in turn makes them even less acceptable. Rebbe Nachman's advice for all those to whom this happens is, "Know! by means of the Torah, all the prayers and all the requests that we request and pray are accepted."

3. **matters spiritual or physical.** In general, a person's "physical matters" includes his financial needs, as well as all that relates to his physical and emotional health. A Jew's "spiritual matters" includes his need for eliminating bad character traits, ascending the spiritual ladder of holiness, and an ever increasing recognition of God.

LIKUTEY MOHARAN #1[1]

"Ashrei T'mimei Darekh (**Happy are those whose way is perfect**), **who walk with the Torah of God."**

(Psalms 120:1)

K now! by means of the Torah, all the prayers and all the requests that we request and pray are accepted.[2] The grace and importance of the Jewish people are thus enhanced and elevated in the estimation of all of whom they may have need, whether in matters spiritual or physical.[3]

---

1. **Likutey Moharan #1.** This lesson was given in Medvedevka, the town in which Rebbe Nachman lived for approximately a decade until the end of 5560 (fall of 1800). Although the exact date of the teaching is unknown, it can be surmised that it was given sometime during the final year the Rebbe spent there. In 1798, Rebbe Nachman left on his pilgrimage to the Holy Land. He returned in the summer of 1799 (not long before Rosh HaShanah 5560) and at the end of the following summer moved to Zlatipolia (see *Until The Mashiach*, pp.53-59). Rebbe Nachman was insistent that any lesson he had given prior to his pilgrimage was not be printed in *Likutey Moharan*. Although Reb Noson did later include a few of those teachings when he reprinted *Likutey Moharan* after the Rebbe's passing (these are found among Lessons #73-108, see Lesson #108:end), as the opening lesson to the Rebbe's *magnum opus*, it is highly unlikely that this teaching was one of them. Rather, it must have been given after the Rebbe's return from the Holy Land. And, since it is certain that the lesson was given in Medvedevka, prior to Rebbe Nachman's move to Zlatipolia, it must have been given sometime during 5560.

The current version of this lesson differs slightly from that which appeared in the first printing of *Likutey Moharan*. Found later on by Reb Noson, it was incorporated into the Lemberg (Lvov) reprint of *Likutey Moharan*, in 1830, and has appeared in all subsequent editions (*Aveneha Barzel*, p.74, #62).

One of Rebbe Nachman's followers came to him seeking advice. It seemed to this follower that his prayers were not acceptable before God. The Rebbe advised him to study Torah, preferably Mishnah or Talmud, immediately after praying (see *Orach Chaim* 155:1). The man did as he was told but soon became discouraged. Again he came to the Rebbe, this time complaining that he could not achieve a clear understanding of his studies. "Force yourself to study," the Rebbe said to him, "even without a clear understanding. In time you'll see that it will become very clear, like the sun's light." Rebbe Nachman then remarked, "What else is there to do in this world except to pray and study and pray?!" (*Tovot Zikhronot,* #1, p.103; see *Rabbi Nachman's Wisdom* #287). The main themes of the lesson are: grace and importance; finding Godliness in all things; Torah study and prayer. Also touched upon are Yaakov and Esav, and their battle over the birthright and the blessings.

At the same time that Rebbe Nachman's lesson is a response to that particular follower's personal quest for closeness to God, it also addresses a wider issue of the time. The rift in the

כִּי עַכְשָׁו בַּעֲוֹונוֹתֵינוּ הָרַבִּים הֶן וַחֲשִׁיבוּת הָאֲמִיתִּי שֶׁל יִשְׂרָאֵל
נָפַל, כִּי עַכְשָׁו עִקַּר הַחֲשִׁיבוּת וְהַחֶן הוּא אֶצְלָם. אֲבָל עַל־יְדֵי
הַתּוֹרָה נִתְעַלֶּה הַחֵן וְהַחֲשִׁיבוּת שֶׁל יִשְׂרָאֵל, כִּי הַתּוֹרָה נִקְרֵאת:
"אַיֶּלֶת אֲהָבִים וְיַעֲלַת חֵן"; שֶׁמַּעֲלָה חֵן עַל לוֹמְדֶיהָ (עירובין נ״ד:).
וְעַל־יְדֵי־זֶה נִתְקַבְּלִין כָּל הַתְּפִלוֹת וְהַבַּקָּשׁוֹת:

כִּי אִישׁ הַיִּשְׂרְאֵלִי צָרִיךְ תָּמִיד לְהִסְתַּכֵּל בְּהַשֵּׂכֶל, שֶׁל כָּל דָּבָר,
וּלְקַשֵּׁר עַצְמוֹ אֶל הַחָכְמָה וְהַשֵּׂכֶל שֶׁיֵּשׁ בְּכָל דָּבָר, כְּדֵי שֶׁיָּאִיר לוֹ
הַשֵּׂכֶל, שֶׁיֵּשׁ בְּכָל דָּבָר, לְהִתְקָרֵב לְהַשֵּׁם יִתְבָּרַךְ עַל־יְדֵי אוֹתוֹ

each section of the lesson) by setting forth in the opening paragraph the objective of that particular teaching. The remainder of the lesson (or section) is a series of statements and proofs substantiating that point and showing how it is attained (*Rabbi Eliyahu Chaim Rosen*). In our lesson, Rebbe Nachman sets about to show how "by means of the Torah all prayers...are accepted." This is the lesson's primary objective. The Rebbe begins this second section stating the type of Torah study needed for this: the study which "focuses on the inner intelligence of every matter."

It is common knowledge that throughout his works Rebbe Nachman places great emphasis on the need for a Jew to live by simple faith. Many question—even criticize—this approach as xenophobic, arguing that such emphasis on faith denies a person the use of his intellect to understand the world around him. This very first lesson in *Likutey Moharan* (as well as many others) obviously belies such a conclusion. The Rebbe teaches here that there is nothing in life which doesn't demand deeper study; one must look into the inner intelligence of each matter, understanding it to the fullest of his abilities (see also *Biur HaLikutim*). However, whereas others maintain that understanding supersedes faith in God, Rebbe Nachman teaches that each and every aspect of Creation exists only to bring a person closer to God—i.e., to enhance his faith. Consequently, whenever a person is capable of comprehending the inner intelligence, the Godliness, found in some matter, he can—he must—seek it out. Yet, whenever the Godliness is obscured, when understanding is lacking, he should rely on faith. The difference between Rebbe Nachman's approach and that of his critics is perhaps best seen when it comes to performing the mitzvot. The latter insist, as did the proponents of the *Haskalah*, that one should first understand the Torah's commandments before performing them. Of course, the upshot of this is that when one doesn't understand a mitzvah or doesn't approve of it, one doesn't comply with it. The Rebbe strongly disagreed and, as will be shown shortly in the lesson, explained why this approach cannot be right. True, one *must* seek to comprehend, but there are obstacles that must first be overcome before one can attain a full understanding. Until then, a Jew must rely on simple faith, performing the mitzvot even if he fails to comprehend them.

For presently, as a result of our many sins, the true grace and importance of the Jewish people have fallen. Now, most of the importance and grace are found with others.[4] By means of the Torah, however, the Jewish people's grace and importance are enhanced. For the Torah is called "a beloved doe and a *yaALat chein* (graceful gazelle)" (Proverbs 5:19) — she *maALah chein* (bestows grace) upon those who study her (*Eruvin* 54b).[5] And through this, all prayers and requests are accepted.[6]

2. For the Jew must always focus on the inner intelligence of every matter,[7] and bind himself to the wisdom and inner intelligence that is to be found in each thing. This, so that the intelligence which is in each thing may enlighten him, that he may draw closer to God

---

4. **found with others.** True grace and importance by right belong to God's chosen people. When they sin, however, these qualities are to some degree taken from the Jews collectively and from each Jew personally. This is the definition of exile. The grace and importance is transferred to others. Instead of there being admiration and respect for "things" Jewish, people, including Jews themselves, are drawn to the values and ideals that are part of other cultures and societies.

5. **yaALat...maALah grace....** To show the connection between Torah and *chein* (grace, חן), Rebbe Nachman brings a proof-text from the Talmud. Our Sages explain that Scripture likens the Torah to a *grace*ful gazelle (יעלת חן) because the word of God has the power to bestow grace (מעלה חן) on those who study it.

The Maharsha teaches that "too much of a good thing" does not apply to the Torah. Although anything done with great regularity tends to get boring, sometimes even repugnant, this is not so with regard to the study of God's word. There is always something to be discovered in the Torah—some new *chein*—no matter how many times one goes over its teachings (*Eruvin 54b, Maharsha, s.v. af divrei Torah*). Proof of this comes from all those who are constantly learning and reviewing their lessons in Scripture and Rashi, Talmud, Halakhah, etc. At the same time, one cannot deny that there are those who become weary of Torah study, saying, "I've heard this already," or, "Let me hear something new...," and so on. Rebbe Nachman indirectly answers this in section 3, where he explains that studying Torah enthusiastically provides one with a measure of grace and charm that enhance his words.

6. **And through this**... The "this" to which Rebbe Nachman refers is the Torah study capable of bestowing grace and importance, as a result of which prayers are deemed acceptable.

In review: One's prayers and requests go unanswered because they lack grace and importance. The way to instill these qualities into one's words is by means of the Torah.

7. **inner intelligence of every matter.** As a rule, Rebbe Nachman begins each lesson (and often

הַדָּבָר. כִּי הַשֵּׂכֶל הוּא אוֹר גָּדוֹל וּמֵאִיר לוֹ בְּכָל דְּרָכָיו, כְּמוֹ שֶׁכָּתוּב

(קהלת ח): "חָכְמַת אָדָם תָּאִיר פָּנָיו":

וְזֶה בְּחִינַת יַעֲקֹב. כִּי יַעֲקֹב זָכָה לַבְּכוֹרָה שֶׁהוּא רֵאשִׁית, שֶׁהוּא

growing pains associated with the process of expanding *mochin* (mentalities) or intellect. Moreover, each person, commensurate with the "pain" he is prepared to undergo in order for his intellect to grow, will cry out to God to help him attain his goals (*Likutey Halakhot, Giluach* 5:5).

11. **Yaakov.** Having introduced the concept of "the inner intelligence of every matter," Rebbe Nachman now provides a series of proof-texts which tie this concept to other like concepts. This method of expanding the initial theme through association enables the reader to expand his own understanding of the particular subject under discussion. Although common to Midrash, the writings of the Ari and many Chassidic works, Rebbe Nachman's *Likutey Moharan* is arguably the finest example of this methodology. The Rebbe will introduce a subject, bring a proof-text to tie it to a second subject, tie the second subject to a third, and then tie them all together with yet additional proofs and illustrations. This happens throughout the lesson, so that at its close, the entire teaching is bound together from beginning to end. Reb Noson further explains this method in his introduction to *Likutey Moharan,* and it is also illustrated in the Tcheriner Rav's introduction. In our lesson, Rebbe Nachman opened with the concept of wisdom/inner intelligence. He next connects this to Yaakov, the birthright, the *sefirah* of *Chokhmah* (Wisdom) and life itself. Afterwards, the Rebbe will focus on the antithesis of Yaakov—namely, Esav—and bring support through proof-texts to show how he is in fact the antithesis of all the other concepts introduced in the lesson.

Throughout Rebbe Nachman's writings and those of his followers one finds references to all the major personalities appearing in the Bible. Fundamental to all Breslov teaching is the personal practical application of the Torah to each and every individual. There is no episode (or law) recorded by Scripture which does not embody some relevant teaching for each and every one of us. In this very first lesson of *Likutey Moharan,* Rebbe Nachman shows how the argument between Yaakov and Esav over the birthright (as related in the Bible and based on Talmudic accounts), as well as Yaakov's subsequent fleeing to the house of Lavan, can be explained in this manner.

12. **YaAKoV...firstborn...wisdom.** The concept of firstborn is symbolic of *reishit,* which means "first" or "beginning." Based on teachings from the *Tikkuney Zohar* (#14) and the *Zohar* (II, 121b), Rebbe Nachman relates these two concepts to *Chokhmah* (Wisdom), the first of the manifest *sefirot.* (Although *Keter* is actually the first *sefirah,* it is on such a lofty level that it is often not included in the general hierarchy of the *sefirot.* Rather, the quasi-*sefirah* of *Daat* is included, so that the Ten *Sefirot* in descending order are: *Chokhmah, Binah, Daat, Chesed...Malkhut.* Thus, the first or beginning of the *sefirot* is *Chokhmah.* See Appendix: Order of the *Sefirot.*) Therefore, the person who merits focusing on the inner intelligence of some matter, to the point where he binds himself to its inner wisdom, that person perceives that matter or thing at its highest level—i.e., its *Chokhmah/reishit.* This was Yaakov. He merited the rights of the firstborn, or, as the Rebbe explains, he attained the concept of wisdom.

through that thing.[8] For the inner intelligence is a great light that shines for a person in all his ways.[9] As it is written (Ecclesiastes 8:1), "A person's wisdom causes his countenance to shine."[10]

This is the concept of Yaakov.[11] For YaAKoV merited the rights of the firstborn, which is *reishit* (beginning), the concept of wisdom,[12]

---

8. **draw closer to God....** The purpose of the entire Creation is "in order to know Him" (*Zohar* II, 42a; see *Torat Natan* #8). Attaining this awareness of Godliness is a three step process: one must focus on the wisdom in the thing; then, he must bind himself to that wisdom; finally, as a result of his uniting with that wisdom, it enlightens him and enables him to draw closer to God.

9. **inner intelligence is a great light....** Having attained this inner intelligence, a person finds that it clarifies all his decisions and illuminates all his actions and deeds.

10. **wisdom...countenance to shine.** From this verse we see that wisdom is a light. Rashi (*loc. cit.*) associates the verse with Moshe. After receiving the Torah from God, Scripture relates that his face glowed with a brilliant inner light (see Exodus 34:30). His attainment of true wisdom was such that God's existence was manifest to him from every aspect of creation. As a result, Moshe's attachment to God was on such a lofty level that wisdom's great light actually illuminated his countenance.

Scripture states: "You created everything with wisdom" (Psalms 104:24). Every physical object and all concepts in creation consist of both material substance and spiritual form. With our physical eyes we see its outer makeup, its shape, color, etc. With our spiritual eyes we see its inner makeup, its "wisdom," wherein lies its grace and charm. There's nothing appealing or particularly captivating about a clod of earth. But for those who have the eyes to see the earth's inner value—whether that be the precious stones or the life supporting nutrients it contains—its charm and grace are radiantly clear (cf. *Be'Ibey HaNachal*). The same is true of everything God created. Each thing is unique in its outer and inner makeup, unique in the way it reveals Godliness and God's greatness to the world (*Mai HaNachal*; see also *Likutey Moharan* I, 17:1).

Reb Noson writes: The concept of looking deeply into the inner intelligence found in every aspect of creation is very profound. Each creation has a *chitzoniyut* (an external wisdom or logic) and a *pnimiyut* (an internal wisdom or logic). Man's goal should be to understand all of creation by means of the inner intelligence, the Godliness, found in it. This, Reb Noson emphasizes, is only possible through the Torah. Only by means of the Torah is it possible to free oneself of the physical desires and attachments that dim one's ability to perceive the spiritual. As Rebbe Nachman explains further on in the lesson, only through Torah can a person control his materialistic desires and subdue his evil characteristics (*Torat Natan* #1).

Reb Noson himself demonstrates this "focusing on the inner intelligence of every matter" in several of his discourses in *Likutey Halakhot*. For example, in *Hilkhot Yom Tov* (5:1) he explains how the mechanical gears of a watch embody a deeper wisdom, a spiritual process. In *Hilkhot Pikadon* (5:16) he shows how the same is true of the printing press and technology generally. In fact, over the course of his many discourses he discusses virtually every aspect of creation—mineral, vegetable and animal—showing how one can learn from them how to come closer to God. Take, for example, the crying of a baby. Reb Noson explains this as the

בְּחִינַת חָכְמָה. כְּמוֹ שֶׁכָּתוּב (תהלים קי"א): "רֵאשִׁית חָכְמָה". וְזֶה

בְּחִינַת: "וַיַּעְקְבֵנִי זֶה פַעֲמַיִם". וְתַרְגּוּם אוּנְקְלוֹס: וְחַכְּמַנִי,

וְזֶה בְּחִינַת שֶׁמֶשׁ. כִּי הַשֵּׂכֶל הוּא מֵאִיר לוֹ בְּכָל דְּרָכָיו כְּמוֹ הַשֶּׁמֶשׁ.

וְזֶה בְּחִינַת: "וְאֹרַח צַדִּיקִים כְּאוֹר נֹגַהּ הוֹלֵךְ וָאוֹר עַד נְכוֹן הַיּוֹם":

וְזֶה בְּחִינַת חֵית – לְשׁוֹן חִיּוּת. כִּי הַחָכְמָה וְהַשֵּׂכֶל הוּא הַחִיּוּת שֶׁל

כָּל דָּבָר, כְּמוֹ שֶׁכָּתוּב (קהלת ז): "הַחָכְמָה תְּחַיֶּה" וְכוּ'.

אַךְ מֵחֲמַת שְׁאוֹר הַשֵּׂכֶל גָּדוֹל מְאֹד, אִי אֶפְשָׁר לִזְכּוֹת אֵלָיו כִּי אִם

עַל-יְדֵי בְּחִינַת נוּן שֶׁהוּא בְּחִינַת מַלְכוּת, כְּמוֹ שֶׁכָּתוּב (תהלים ע"ב):

surpassed all the other prophets: "They are all to Moshe as the moon is to the sun" (*Zohar* III, 155b). Cf. Lesson #2 and note 62, where Moshe and Yaakov are shown to have in common a quality of *Tiferet*, though there, too, they each signify a different aspect of that quality.

16. **CheT...ChiuT, life.** The letter *chet* (ח), when written out in full (חית), can also be read *chiut* (חיות), which means life. As Rebbe Nachman explains next, this is: "Wisdom gives life...."

The *Zohar* (III, 245b) teaches that the letter *chet*, the eighth letter of the *aleph-bet*, represents *Binah*, eighth in the general hierarchy of the *sefirot* (ascending from *Malkhut*; see Appendix: Order of the *Sefirot*). As opposed to the seven lower *sefirot*, which correspond to this world (with its seven-day week), a world where death has dominion, the *sefirot* from *Binah* upward all signify life. In fact, *Binah* is known as the Tree of Life. All of life is sustained through *Binah*, the *chet*. This, however, seems to negate the Rebbe's earlier connection between the letter *chet* and the *sefirah* of *Chokhmah*. The resolution comes from a teaching in the *Tikkuney Zohar* (#65, p.96a): All the life found in *Binah* has its source in *Chokhmah*, which fills *Binah*. Thus, the letter *chet*, which indicates life, actually alludes to *Chokhmah* hidden within *Binah*. (An important axiom of Kabbalistic teaching is that the upper level always resides within the lower level in order to sustain it. Rebbe Nachman applies this, in different forms, throughout *Likutey Moharan*.)

17. **Wisdom gives life....** Rebbe Nachman has thus far introduced the concepts of Yaakov, birthright, wisdom, sun, *chet* and *chiut* (life). All these apply to the person who uses his intellect to focus on the great light—the spirituality—found in each aspect of creation. In the next paragraph, the Rebbe addresses an obvious question: If the inner intelligence is so very great, with its radiance likened to that of the sun, how can one focus on it? The light must be much too strong to look at!

18. **NuN...Malkhut, Kingship.** *Malkhut*, the lowest of the *sefirot*, is indicative of limitation and constriction. Because the light of the inner intelligence is so great, it is only possible to absorb and incorporate it by degree, through the aspect of *Malkhut*, which corresponds to the letter *nun* (*Torat Natan* #9; *Parparaot LeChokhmah*). (The nature of *Malkhut* and how it filters the great light of inner intelligence/*Chokhmah* will be explained below, in n.20.)

as in (Psalms 111:10), "The *reishit* is wisdom."[13] This corresponds to "and *YaAKVeiny* (he obstructed me) these two times" (Genesis 27:36), which Onkelos renders: "he outwitted me."[14]

And this is the concept of sun. For the inner intelligence shines for him in all his ways, like the sun. This corresponds to (Proverbs 4:19), "The path of the righteous is like radiant sunlight, shining ever brighter as it approaches noon."[15]

And this is the concept of the *CheT*. It suggests *ChiuT* (life).[16] For the wisdom and the inner intelligence are the vitality of all things, as in (Ecclesiastes 7:12), "Wisdom gives life to those who possess it."[17]

However, because the light of the inner intelligence is so very great, it is impossible to attain except through the concept of *NuN*, which is an aspect of *Malkhut* (Kingship).[18] As it is written (Psalms

---

13. **reishit is wisdom.** Having introduced the concepts of wisdom, Yaakov, firstborn and *reishit*, Rebbe Nachman proceeds to bind each concept with the other. He begins with the verse "The *reishit* (beginning) is *Chokhmah* (Wisdom, the *sefirah*)/*chokhmah* (wisdom, the quality)."

14. **YaAKVeiny...outwitted me.** Bemoaning the loss of the blessings to his brother YaAKoV (יעקב), who had outwitted him, Esav cried out, "*YaAKVeiny* (יעקבני) these two times." Thus we see that Yaakov was the personification of wisdom. As Rebbe Nachman shows here, not only does his name signify wisdom but he also merited the birthright, which is *reishit*/wisdom. What's more, anyone who seeks the intelligence hidden within each thing corresponds to Yaakov, by virtue of the wisdom he attains.

15. **sun...noon.** Just as the sun lights a person's way so that he can see where to go and where not, the inner intelligence enlightens a person's way so that he can see which path to follow and which not. The *Metzudat David* (*loc. cit.*) explains that the verse refers to the light of Torah. It is this light which illuminates the way. In our context, this relates to perceiving the spiritual component within the matter, as it is this which enables a person to find the proper path.

With this Rebbe Nachman has added another element, the sun, to the parallel concepts of Yaakov, wisdom and firstborn. The verse quoted in the text from Proverbs shows the connection between sun and the inner intelligence. Scripture also states (Genesis 32:32): "And the sun shone for [Yaakov]." That is, the sun shone *because* of Yaakov, for he personifies that which the light of the sun signifies: the inner intelligence or wisdom (see *Torat Natan #4*). The *Mai HaNachal* quotes the Midrashic teaching that Yaakov is himself the sun: In relating his dreams to his brothers, Yosef said, "I just had another dream. Behold the sun, the moon, and eleven stars..." (Genesis 37:9). When Yaakov heard this, he wondered, "Who told Yosef that my name is 'sun'?" (*Bereishit Rabbah* 84:11). This was the reason Yaakov took his son's dream seriously. By means of his dream Yosef had come to know that Yaakov is the sun—i.e., the true inner intelligence that guides a person upon the right path. Yaakov was thus certain that the dream would come true (*Matnat Kehunah, ad. loc.*).

Earlier (n.10), we saw that Moshe attained such a lofty level of wisdom's great light that it actually illuminated his countenance. This aligns with the *Zohar's* teaching that Moshe far

"לִפְנֵי שֶׁמֶשׁ יִנּוֹן שְׁמוֹ", וּפֵרֵשׁ רַשִׁ"י: 'לְשׁוֹן מַלְכוּת'.
וְזֶה בְּחִינַת לְבָנָה, כִּי הַלְּבָנָה אֵין לָהּ אוֹר מֵעַצְמָהּ כִּי אִם מַה
שֶּׁמְּקַבֶּלֶת מֵהַשֶּׁמֶשׁ (זהר ח"ג רל"ח.). וְזֶהוּ בְּחִינַת מַלְכוּת, דְּלֵית לָהּ
מִגַּרְמָהּ כְּלוּם, אֶלָּא מַה שֶּׁמְּקַבֶּלֶת מִן הַחֵית, שֶׁהִיא בְּחִינַת חָכְמָה,
בְּחִינַת שֶׁמֶשׁ כַּנַּ"ל, וְנַעֲשָׂה: "אוֹר הַלְּבָנָה כְּאוֹר הַחַמָּה":

moment, it is still possible for him to pursue the right course. That is, if even after focusing on the matter and failing to perceive its spiritual quality he still firmly believes that it embodies Godliness/true inner intelligence, he will nevertheless learn from that matter how to draw closer to God. This, too, is indicative of *Malkhut* being an aspect of limitation or constriction. As faith, *Malkhut* signifies that the person lacks understanding—i.e., that his degree of comprehension is limited. At the same time, his faith/*Malkhut* fosters in him the belief that a greater level does exist, and with additional effort on his part he might eventually attain it. The great light of inner intelligence is thus filtered down judiciously so that a person can perceive it in a limited measure. Reb Noson explains that this additional effort required of him entails his working to subdue his lusts and physical desires. To the extent that a person does this, he attains greater levels of both faith and inner intelligence (*Torat Natan #1*; *Parparaot LeChokhmah*). This last point will be further clarified below (see nn.25,26), where the Rebbe introduces the aspect of Esav, who represents the very antithesis of inner intelligence and the Kingdom of Holiness. The *Mai HaNachal* adds that *Malkhut*/faith has the power to guide a person even when things appear dark and confusing, because it reflects the great light of *Chokhmah*/inner intelligence.

21. **moon has no light of her own....** *Malkhut* is likened to the moon, which does not shine on its own but only reflects the sun's light. Faith, too, only reflects the greater light of the inner intelligence. This is Reb Noson's premise for stating that one's faith must reflect the true inner intelligence, Torah. At the same time, faith only reflects the inner intelligence to which it pertains, just as the moon reflects inner intelligence/light of the sun. Therefore, a person whose faith is in falsehood, foolishness and the like, will actually reject true inner intelligence. Just as the inner intelligence he seeks is distorted, his faith is distorted. It will lead him astray, as the Rebbe explains shortly. But a person who believes in the truth seeks and searches for absolute truth and won't allow himself to be misled. This person has true faith, which will lead him to find God in every situation and in every thing.

It is worth noting that the *Zohar* (*loc. cit.*) relates this teaching about the moon to the kingdom of the Mashiach. Earlier we saw that the *NuN/yeNoN* refers to the Mashiach (n.19). This identifies the Mashiach's kingdom as one built on faith—i.e., that people will come to believe in and accept him. His power to draw mankind under his rule will come from his ability to reveal great inner intelligence, *Chokhmah*, which points to the Godliness suffusing all of creation.

22. **...receives from the chet...wisdom/sun.** For *Malkhut* receives its vitality from *Chokhmah*, the *chet*. *Malkhut* of Holiness, true faith, thus reflects the true wisdom found in everything.

23. **light of the moon will be....** At Creation, the sun and the moon were created equal in size; their lights were of equal intensity. The moon objected to this and complained that it was impossible "for two kings to wear one crown." How would people be able to differentiate

72:17), "may his name *yeNoN* (be perpetuated) as long as the sun,"[19] and Rashi explains that ["*yenon*"] means kingship.[20]

This is also the concept of the moon. For the moon has no light of her own, only that which she receives from the sun (*Zohar* I, 238a). And this corresponds to *Malkhut*.[21] It has nothing of its own other than what it receives from the *chet,* the aspect of wisdom/sun.[22] As a result, "the light of the moon will be like the light of the sun" (Isaiah 30:26).[23]

19. **yeNoN...the sun.** Literally, the verse reads: "*Lifnei shemesh* (before the sun), *yenon....*" In our context, this indicates that before the level of sun/inner intelligence, one must first attain the level of *yenon/Malkhut.* Any attainment of *Chokhmah* must be preceded by an attainment of *Malkhut* (*Torat Natan* #11). Rebbe Nachman is also alluding here to the fact that finding the inner spirituality of each thing is not actually possible for everyone at the present time. The words "his name *yenon*" refer to the Mashiach, whose arrival will usher in a time when "the world will be filled with the knowledge of God..." (Isaiah 11:9). Then, everyone will be able to clearly see the Godliness in every thing, in every aspect of creation. But until then, only those who perfect their aspect of *Malkhut* will be able to attain this *Chokhmah,* each according to his spiritual level (*Torat Natan* #1).

20. **yenon means kingship.** At this point, a broader exposition of *Malkhut* is in order. The word *malkhut* means kingdom, kingship or government. The *sefirah* by the same name thus connotes Kingship or, more specifically, the Kingdom of Holiness, *Malkhut d'Kedushah.* It is only through *Malkhut* that mankind can perceive God's Kingdom. God Himself is unfathomable; this quality being reflected by the most exalted of the *sefirot, Keter* (Crown). In order that He in some way be known and comprehended in this world, God's great and awesome light is constricted, as it were, through a series of filters or delineations. These ten filters, which are anthropomorphized as attributes, are known to us as the Ten *Sefirot* (for a fuller explanation see *Innerspace,* by Rabbi Aryeh Kaplan, Moznaim Pub. 1990, Chapter 4). God's great light is initially filtered through the *sefirah* of *Chokhmah,* then *Binah,* and in descending order through *Chesed...* until *Malkhut.* Each additional descent produces a further revelation. Yet only in *Malkhut* does His light become sufficiently contracted so that His attribute of sovereignty, His Kingship, becomes fully knowable to man. This is what is meant by *Malkhut* being an aspect of limitation and constriction. The *Mai HaNachal* adds: To the degree that a person accepts the yoke of Heaven, God's *Malkhut d'Kedushah,* he is accordingly able to climb the ladder of wisdom until he can perceive the inner intelligence— i.e., the Godliness—of everything.

Reb Noson explains: *Malkhut* corresponds to the concept of faith (cf. *Likutey Moharan* I, 7:1). Only with faith can a person enter the realm of true inner intelligence. This is so because the Torah is really an extension of God's intellect. It is a "Torah of truth" (Malachi 2:6), wherein one finds all true inner intelligence. This relationship between Torah (mitzvot) and faith is indicated in the words of the Psalmist, "All Your commandments are faith" (Psalms 119:86). When a person understands what he should do and how he can go about doing it in a permitted way, according to the Torah, he is attached to the inner intelligence of that particular situation. But if he has yet to attain true knowledge and so fails to understand how he should proceed in the situation in which he finds himself, his only recourse is to turn to faith. When a person has faith, even if he doesn't understand what is required of him at that

אֲבָל מִי שֶׁאֵינוֹ מְקַשֵּׁר עַצְמוֹ אֶל הַשֵּׂכֶל וְהַחָכְמָה וְהַחִיּוּת, שֶׁיֵּשׁ
בְּכָל דָּבָר, זֶה בְּחִינַת עֵשָׂו שֶׁבִּזָּה אֶת הַבְּכוֹרָה, כְּמוֹ שֶׁכָּתוּב: "וַיִּבֶז
עֵשָׂו אֶת הַבְּכוֹרָה"; דְּהַיְנוּ הַשֵּׂכֶל כַּנַּ"ל, בְּחִינַת: "לֹא יַחְפֹּץ כְּסִיל
בִּתְבוּנָה כִּי אִם בְּהִתְגַּלּוֹת לִבּוֹ". וְזֶה בְּחִינַת מַלְכוּת הָרְשָׁעָה,

25. He despised the birthright...inner intelligence. As explained, the rights of the firstborn is *reishit*, which is *Chokhmah* (see nn.12,13). Esav, in despising the birthright, indicated his contempt for true wisdom.

Reb Noson makes the point that "despising wisdom" does not necessarily signify a rejection of inner intelligence and intellectual pursuit. On the contrary, it can apply as well to a person who engages most assiduously in the search for greater knowledge. If he does this without faith, without focusing on the spiritual, without searching for God, then he, too, "despises wisdom." For in that case, his pursuit of wisdom is influenced—at times even governed—by his lusts and material desires. Instead of true wisdom, his intellectual pursuits lead him to what is in fact foolishness. This is because the only complete and eternal wisdom is Torah—which teaches faith and brings one closer to God. Other wisdoms, whether in the arts, the sciences, or the like, are filled with inaccuracies and are temporary at best. They serve a purpose for several years, maybe even several generations or centuries, but are eventually cast aside for more "up-to-date" and "accurate" approaches. Therefore, any pursuit of knowledge which fails to include a focus on the spiritual is, at best, foolhardy, and even grievously wrong. And the same can be said of the pursuit of Torah wisdom, when that pursuit is influenced by an attitude of concession and alteration. When people study the Torah's truths only to then say, "Why don't we try it this way," or, "Let's develop more acceptable Torah ideas to meet the needs of the time," then they, too, are "despising wisdom." The Torah is the eternal word of God. Tailoring it for one's own benefit, inventing one's own mitzvot—as well-intentioned as they may be—can only produce negative results, including ultimately turning people away from God (see *Torat Natan* #14). See next note.

26. fool...only to bare his heart.... As explained earlier (n.20), a person has to be willing to subjugate his lusts and physical desires for spiritual advancement. Only by doing so can he merit seeing the inner intelligence/spirituality within each matter. However, one who chases after the desires of his heart, rather than subjugating his heart to his intellect, comes to despise true wisdom (see *Biur HaLikutim* 11). He relates only to the *chitzoniyut* (see n.10), choosing instead to delight in the ephemeral physical enjoyment or emotional gratification that the object of his heart's desire provides. This was Esav. Instead of studying Torah and focusing on the Godliness in creation, as Yaakov did, Esav chose to while away his time in the fields, hunting animals.

Scripture further relates how, once, when he returned home hungry, Esav failed to control his physical desires and willingly traded his birthright for the instant gratification of a bowl of porridge. Nor could this behavior be justified as the desperate request of a starving man, for the Torah itself bears witness: "Esav despised the rights of the firstborn." He had no interest in the *reishit*/wisdom, but openly displayed his gluttony by saying to Yaakov, "Please, *haliteini* (give me a swallow) of that red stuff" (Genesis 25:30).

It was in no way coincidental that Esav's selling his birthright centered around the issue of food. The act of eating is a medium which, when engaged in properly, binds the spiritual

However, the person who does not bind himself to the inner intelligence, wisdom and vitality that is in each thing corresponds to Esav.[24] He despised the birthright, as is written (Genesis 25:34), "And Esav despised the rights of the firstborn"—i.e., the inner intelligence.[25] This is (Proverbs 18:2), "The fool does not desire understanding, but only to bare his heart."[26] And this corresponds to the Kingdom of

---

between day and night? God's response to the moon's complaint: He made the moon smaller (see *Rashi,* Genesis 1:16; *Chullin* 60b). The verse from Isaiah which Rebbe Nachman quotes refers to the Future, to the era of the Mashiach, for then all the worlds will be rectified and the moon will return to its original size and intensity.

Similarly, man was originally created with the ability to perceive the Godliness that is within everything. But Adam sinned, and this led to a diminishing of this ability. Man must therefore struggle in order to attain the level where he can perceive this inner intelligence. At present, just as the moon waxes and wanes, so, too, man must struggle with his intellect and faith. Nevertheless, just as the Future guarantees that the moon's light will shine as intensely as the sun's, so, too, the Future guarantees that man will return to the level at which he will fully perceive the spirituality in everything (cf. *Torat Natan* #1).

The *Parparaot LeChokhmah* shows how this teaching applies in our lesson. He says: Every person must accept limitations on his mind and intellectual pursuits. His physical desires must also be curbed and broken and he must accept the yoke of God's rule with the utmost simplicity and faith. When he succeeds in accepting his limitations and curbing his appetites, he can at every moment look forward to achieving, by means of these limitations, the aspect of *Malkhut*/moon—and automatically a truer understanding of the inner intelligence/*Chokhmah*/sun. This in itself forms a unity between the sun and the moon, so that the light of the moon becomes as intense as the light of the sun. The *Mai HaNachal* adds that all this can be attained by accepting upon oneself the yoke of Heaven. Accepting God's *Malkhut* enables one to gain a glimpse of the great inner intelligence that will only be fully revealed in the Future, when the Mashiach comes.

The *Biur HaLikutim* asks: We know that the *nun,* which has a numerical value of fifty, generally signifies the Fifty Gates of Wisdom (cf. *Rosh HaShanah* 21b). This is the level of *Chokhmah,* as mentioned above (n.16). That being so, why does Rebbe Nachman connect the *nun* to *Malkhut*? The answer comes from the verse quoted in the lesson. The prophet says, "And then the light of the moon will be as the light of the sun; and the light of the sun will increase seven-fold...." When the light of the moon (*nun*) becomes as intense as that of the sun (*chet*), it will have increased seven times seven or forty-nine-fold. In other words, in the process of completing and rectifying his aspect of the *nun,* a person ascends forty-nine gates and stands at the *nun,* the fiftieth of the Fifty Gates of Wisdom.

In review: One's prayers and requests go unanswered because they lack grace and importance. The way to instill these qualities into one's words is by means of the Torah (§1). For this he must focus on the *pnimiyut,* the spirituality, found in everything in creation. This inner intelligence corresponds to the concepts of Yaakov, firstborn, *Chokhmah,* sun, the *chet* and *chiut* (life), and can only be attained by means of the *nun, Malkhut* (§2).

24. **Esav.** As explained earlier, Yaakov symbolizes all that is good. He is the one who seeks the inner intelligence/*Chokhmah* to illuminate his ways—this being life itself. Here, Rebbe Nachman introduces the concept of Esav, the very antithesis of all that Yaakov represents.

בְּחִינַת לְבָנָה דְּסִטְרָא אָחֳרָא, שֶׁעָלֶיהָ נֶאֱמַר (ישעיהו כ"ד): "וְחָפְרָה הַלְבָנָה" וְכוּ'.

וְזֶה בְּחִינַת יֵצֶר טוֹב וְיֵצֶר הָרָע. כִּי הַיֵּצֶר טוֹב נִקְרָא "מִסְכֵּן וְחָכָם" (קהלת ד), בְּחִינַת מַלְכוּת, שֶׁהִיא בְּחִינַת עֲנִיָּה וְדַלָּה דְּלֵית לַהּ מִגַּרְמַהּ כְּלוּם כִּי אִם מַה שֶּׁמְּקַבֶּלֶת מֵחָכְמָה. וְיֵצֶר הָרָע נִקְרָא "מֶלֶךְ זָקֵן וּכְסִיל" (שם), בְּחִינַת מַלְכוּת דְּסִטְרָא אָחֳרָא, שֶׁאֵינָהּ חֲפֵצָה בְּחָכְמָה וָשֵׂכֶל, בְּחִינַת "לֹא יַחְפֹּץ כְּסִיל בִּתְבוּנָה" וְכוּ', כַּנַּ"ל.

its only light is that which it receives from the sun. In other words, the good inclination attempts to steer a person on the proper path, to illuminate him with the inner intelligence of each thing as with the light of the sun. But the power of the good inclination is weak; enfeebled by the body's desires, which it must first overcome. In this weakened state, the great inner intelligence, *Chokhmah*, cannot illuminate *Malkhut* of Holiness, the good inclination. It therefore is said to be "poor." Nevertheless, the good inclination is "wise" because it knows that the great inner intelligence exists, and desires and strives to attain it (cf. *Parparaot LeChokhmah*).

31. **old and foolish melekh.** Rashi explains that the evil inclination is called a *melekh* (king) because it rules over the entire body. It is called foolish because it leads a person astray, away from God. And it is called old because it accompanies a person from birth.

32. **Malkhut of the Other Side....** Being an "old and foolish *MeLeKh*," the evil inclination corresponds to *MaLKhut* of the Other Side, which prefers folly to understanding. Thus, to one who follows the evil inclination the *Zohar* applies the phrase "the fool walks in darkness" (Ecclesiastes 2:14). Like an old fool, he stumbles and falls along the way. After having followed the evil inclination, he finds it difficult to guard himself against further folly (see above, n.30). In contrast, a person who follows the good inclination, which is "a youth," constantly feels young. In this he resembles the moon, which is constantly renewing itself as it waxes and wanes. He is also called poor, like the moon, but wise, because he has inner intelligence (*Zohar* I, 179b). In our context, this relates to a person who focuses on the inner intelligence of everything and seeks its spiritual quality. He ultimately finds "light." And even if at the moment he cannot locate that inner illumination, he has the faith and determination of youth. But a person who fails to seek out the spiritual quality focuses only on his heart's desires. He "walks in darkness."

The *Mai HaNachal* explains that this is the main battle between the good and evil inclination. The good inclination constantly seeks to guide a person away from alien ideologies and wisdoms, those that will lead him astray, and to help him overcome his evil desires. It seeks to get him to accept upon himself the yoke of Heaven, by means of which he will come to bind himself to the wisdom and inner intelligence—the spiritual quality—found in everything. He will then come to recognize God's greatness. As for the evil inclination, it obviously seeks to achieve the reverse.

This was in fact the battle between Pharaoh, the "old and foolish king," and the Jewish

Evil, to the moon of the Other Side,[27] of which it is said (Isaiah 24:23),
"The moon shall be disgraced."[28]

{**"Better a youth, poor and wise, than an old and foolish** *melekh* **(king) who no longer knows how
to care for himself"** (Ecclesiastes 4:13).}

This is the concept of the good inclination and the evil
inclination.[29] The good inclination is called "poor and wise,"
corresponding to *Malkhut,* which is an aspect of poor and needy,
with nothing of her own other than what she receives from *Chokhmah*
(Wisdom).[30] But the evil inclination is called "an old and foolish
melekh."[31] This is *Malkhut* of the Other Side, who has no desire for
wisdom and inner intelligence, as in, "The fool does not desire
understanding...."[32]

(soul) with the physical (body). (That is, one can focus on the spiritual component through its
physical embodiment.) Had Esav desired wisdom, he would have related to eating as a
spiritual experience. Instead, he asked Yaakov to stuff him (*Be'Ibey HaNachal*).

27. **Other Side.** This is the literal translation of the term *Sitra Achra* and refers to the realm of
the forces of evil. Scripture states: "God made one to contrast the other" (Ecclesiastes 7:14).
Every creation has a parallel or opposing side to it. It is this which presents man with free
will—i.e., the need for choosing between good and evil.

28. **...moon shall be disgraced.** Just as the concepts of sun and moon have corresponding
holy aspects, they have corresponding evil aspects. As opposed to focusing on the true
wisdom and inner intelligence, the sun of the *Sitra Achra* signifies turning to purely secular
wisdom and alien ideologies. As opposed to faith and the proper limiting of the intellect, the
moon of the *Sitra Achra* signifies the rejection of wisdom and the casting aside of inner
intelligence; this is the person who follows his impulses in doing whatever his heart desires.
As opposed to the moon that corresponds to the *Malkhut* of Holiness, this moon corresponds
to the *Malkhut* of Evil. What's more, just as the sun and moon of holiness support one
another—faith and the contraction of the intellect increases intellect—the sun and moon of
evil also support one another—the casting aside of wisdom and following one's heart's
desires increases heresy and the pursuit of alien wisdoms (*Parparaot LeChokhmah*).

29. **This is the concept....** That is, Yaakov, wisdom, the Kingdom of Holiness, etc., all
correspond to the good inclination. Esav, foolishness, the Kingdom of Evil, etc., correspond
to the evil inclination. Rebbe Nachman's proof-text is the verse he quotes from Ecclesiastes.
The *Biur HaLikutim* adds that the Rebbe equates *Malkhut* with the two inclinations in order
to teach that one must use his self-control—his dominion and rule—to empower his good
inclination over his evil inclination.

30. **good...poor and wise...Wisdom.** King Solomon taught: "Better a youth, poor and wise,
than an old and foolish king who no longer knows how to care for himself." Rashi (*loc. cit.*)
explains that the good inclination is called "a youth" because it comes to a person only after
he's reached the age of thirteen (as opposed to the evil inclination which is older, for it is with
him from birth). It is "poor" because the body parts refuse to follow it, and "wise" because it
directs the person on the proper path. In our context, this ties in with the moon being poor as

וְצָרִיךְ כָּל אֶחָד לִתֵּן כֹּחַ לִבְחִינַת מַלְכוּת דִּקְדֻשָּׁה לְהִתְגַּבֵּר עַל
מַלְכוּת דְּסִטְרָא אָחֳרָא. וּכְמוֹ שֶׁאָמְרוּ רַבּוֹתֵינוּ, זִכְרוֹנָם לִבְרָכָה
(ברכות ה.) : 'לְעוֹלָם יַרְגִּיז אָדָם יֵצֶר טוֹב עַל יֵצֶר הָרָע'. וְעַל־יְדֵי מַה
נוֹתֵן כֹּחַ לַמַּלְכוּת דִּקְדֻשָּׁה? עַל־יְדֵי הַתּוֹרָה, שֶׁהוּא עוֹסֵק בְּכֹחַ (כְּמוֹ
שֶׁאָמְרוּ רַבּוֹתֵינוּ, זִכְרוֹנָם לִבְרָכָה, שָׁם: 'לְעוֹלָם יַרְגִּיז וְכוּ' – אִי אָזִיל־מוּטָב,
וְאִם לָאו – יַעֲסֹק בַּתּוֹרָה'). וּכְמוֹ שֶׁאָמְרוּ רַבּוֹתֵינוּ, זִכְרוֹנָם לִבְרָכָה:
'אִם פָּגַע בְּךָ מְנֻוָּל זֶה, מָשְׁכֵהוּ לְבֵית־הַמִּדְרָשׁ'.
כִּי עַל־יְדֵי הַתּוֹרָה נוֹתֵן כֹּחַ לַמַּלְכוּת דִּקְדֻשָּׁה. וַאֲזַי מְקַבֶּלֶת
הַמַּלְכוּת, שֶׁהִיא בְּחִינַת נ, חִיּוּת מִן הַחָכְמָה, שֶׁהִיא בְּחִינַת ח,

35. **with enthusiasm.** Literally, *b'koach* means "with strength" or "forcefully," and can be understood in a number of ways: 1) It can refer to the Torah a person studies under difficult circumstances, as when he is poor, ill, or under stress. 2) It can refer to the need for pronouncing the words audibly when studying Torah. 3) It can also imply complete mental concentration when studying. All of these and similar concepts indicate his enthusiasm for Torah study and may thus be considered "forcefully."

The *Parparaot LeChokhmah* adds: "If you follow My [Torah] laws... I will provide [for] you" (Leviticus 26:3,4). Rashi comments: "provided you labor in Torah"—i.e., study it with *enthusiasm*. This is what will bring all the blessings.

36. **If it leaves, good....** The passage in Talmud reads: A person should always incite the good inclination against the evil inclination. If it leaves, good; if not, he should engage in Torah study. If it then leaves, good; if not, he should recite the *Shema*. If it then leaves, good; if not, remind it of the day of death (*Berakhot, loc. cit.*). From this passage we learn that when the evil inclination attempts to overwhelm a person, there are times when a single rebuff is enough to chase it away. Yet there are also times when the evil inclination comes back again and again. Then, to chase it away, it is necessary to study Torah. It is Torah study that gives strength to the good inclination, which then assists a person in overcoming his evil desires (see Reb Noson's comment on this passage in next note).

37. **rogue...house of study.** Our Sages taught often and in many ways that the only thing which truly has the power to help a person overcome his evil inclination is Torah study. Rebbe Nachman quoted two such teachings. The first urges us to incite against the evil inclination; our actively working to empower the good by following the Torah's counsel. The second calls the evil inclination a rogue and advises that we *drag* it to the house of study—this, too, being one of the ways to "study Torah forcefully" (see n.35). The full passage reads: "If this rogue accosts you, drag him to the house of study. If he is like stone, he will dissolve; if he is like iron, he will shatter." Such is the Torah's power to counter the evil inclination. In our context, this aligns with focusing on the inner intelligence of each matter. The evil inclination appears in one material form or another to entice a person and arouse his physical desires. If he is drawn after his lusts, entrapped by physical pleasures, the evil inclination has succeeded in empowering the Kingdom of the Other Side. But if he resists by focusing on the

Each person is required to give strength to the Kingdom of Holiness so that it may overpower the Kingdom of the Other Side.[33] As our Sages taught: A person should always incite the good inclination against the evil inclination (*Berakhot* 5a).[34] And how is strength given to the Kingdom of Holiness? By means of the Torah study that a person engages in with enthusiasm.[35] {As our Sages taught: A person should always incite.... If it leaves, good; if not, he should engage in Torah study (*ibid.*).[36]} And, as our Sages taught: If this rogue accosts you, drag him to the house of study (*Kiddushin* 30b).[37]

For it is by means of the Torah that strength is given to the Kingdom of Holiness. Then, *Malkhut/nun* receives vitality from *Chokhmah/chet*. The *chet* and the *nun* are joined and bound together,

---

people. God called the Jews "My firstborn, Israel" (Exodus 4:22)—they had always looked for the *reishit*/inner intelligence/Godliness of everything. But after more than two centuries of bondage, many had lost their faith and subsequently assimilated. As a result, a full eighty percent of the Jewish people died together with the Egyptians during the plague of darkness (*Rashi,* Exodus 13:18). In our context, this plague corresponds to the concepts of Esav/darkness/despising wisdom and Godliness; concepts which were best personified in Pharaoh. Pharaoh was also a firstborn (*Rashi,* Exodus 12:32), but as opposed to those Jews who kept their faith, he was a foolish firstborn for he denied the existence of God (Exodus 5:2). As a firstborn of evil, Pharaoh attempted to subjugate the firstborn of holiness, the Jews, just as the evil inclination attempts to subjugate the good inclination (cf. *Shaar HaKavanot, Pesach* 1, p.147).

33. **give strength to the Kingdom....** Having explained that the battle between true inner intelligence and alien ideologies and lusts is the battle between the good and evil inclination—the battle between the Kingdom of Holiness and the Kingdom of the Other Side—Rebbe Nachman proceeds to show how one can empower the Kingdom of Holiness.

34. **always incite....** The Talmud (*loc. cit.*) teaches that it is not enough for a person to sit back and passively allow each of life's situations to develop into a battle between his inclination for good and evil. Rather, he must actively rouse himself to good, always inciting his good inclination against his evil inclination. By doing so, he strengthens the Kingdom of Holiness, which even after having been strengthened once needs to be supported and strengthened again and again. It is like exercising to stay fit. As long as a person keeps to his regimen, his body remains firm and in shape. But if he grows lax and eases off his schedule, his body will weaken and grow flabby. This is why a person must always actively support and strengthen the Kingdom of Holiness. It is not enough to sit back and hope that the Kingdom of the Other Side will desist and abandon the battle of its own accord. Only by actively engaging the Other Side, the evil inclination, can it be defeated. Reb Noson writes: Giving strength to the Kingdom of Holiness is imperative. The forces of the Kingdom of Evil do their work during the night—i.e., in a time of darkness and uncertainty. In the daytime—i.e., in a time of light and clarity—they are restrained. It is thus vital that one focuses on the inner intelligence/sun which illuminates one's ways. For this is the "daylight" that has the power to repel the forces of evil (*Torat Natan* #13).

וְנִתְחַבֵּר וְנִתְקַשֵּׁר הַח וְהַנ, וְנַעֲשֶׂה אוֹר הַלְּבָנָה כְּאוֹר הַחַמָּה:
וּכְשֶׁזֶּה קָם, זֶה נוֹפֵל. וַאֲזַי נוֹפֵל וְנִתְבַּטֵּל מַלְכוּת הָרָשְׁעָה, כְּמוֹ
שֶׁכָּתוּב (הושע י"ד): "כִּי יְשָׁרִים דַּרְכֵי ה', צַדִּיקִים יֵלְכוּ בָם,
וּפֹשְׁעִים יִכָּשְׁלוּ בָם". הַיְנוּ עַל-יְדֵי דַּרְכֵי ה', הַיְנוּ הַתּוֹרָה, עַל-יְדֵי-

days after leaving Egypt before they could receive the Torah. The Torah is *Chokhmah*, God's Divine Wisdom. Due to its exalted nature, it can only be received through the *nun* (= 50)— i.e., the fifty days from the Exodus until the Revelation (*Likutey Halakhot, Pikadon* 4:2).

When Rebbe Nachman gave this lesson, he advised his follower to be sure to study Torah (see above, n.1). When the follower later complained that he couldn't fully understand his studies, Rebbe Nachman said to him, "Force yourself to study even with unclear understanding. You'll see that things will eventually become very clear, like the sun's light." We can now understand the Rebbe's intention. A person's initial grasp of his studies does not always reflect its inner meaning. Such was the case with this follower. Yet he faithfully followed the Rebbe's advice and kept up his studies. This enabled him to increase his comprehension of the deeper, inner meaning, so that, subsequently, his studies became very clear, "like the light of the sun."

Reb Noson writes: Rebbe Nachman very much wanted everyone to take upon themselves a daily program of Torah study, and to keep to that program consistently, without fail. Even those who are very far from holiness will benefit from this. For even if they are caught in evil's trap and sin habitually, the strength of Torah is so great that it can extricate them from their sins. In fact, through the Torah it is possible to accomplish everything, literally (*Rabbi Nachman's Wisdom* #19; see also *Likutey Halakhot, Betziat HaPat* 5:22).

39. one rises, the other falls. When after many years of barrenness our matriarch Rivkah became pregnant (with Yaakov and Esav), she found her great joy offset by a most disturbing occurrence. Whenever she passed a house of Torah study, the fetus inside her would begin to stir as if it wanted to exit. Yet, whenever she passed a house of idol worship, the fetus would do exactly the same thing. Rivkah was perplexed. Would her child follow in the footsteps of its parents, or, God forbid, would it be an idolator, or both? She went to the sage, Shem, for an explanation. Shem informed Rivkah that she would give birth to twins, two sons who were destined to engage in an eternal battle over domination of this world. And, Shem added, because they cannot rule simultaneously, two kings cannot wear one crown, it will always be that "when the one rises, the other falls." In the context of our lesson, the conflict between Yaakov and Esav is the conflict between the good inclination and the evil inclination. When the good inclination is empowered and strength is given to the Kingdom of Holiness, the Kingdom of Evil falls and the evil inclination is defeated. Conversely, if the evil inclination rises, the good inclination declines. For their battle, too, is eternal, and for the two to rule simultaneously is impossible (cf. *Biur HaLikutim*).

40. ways of God...in them. "The ways of God" to which the verse refers are actually one: the way of Torah. Scripture indicates that this single path has a twofold power. It strengthens the righteous—the good inclination—while at the same time causes the sinners—the evil inclination—to stumble.

and as a result, "the light of the moon will be like the light of the sun."[38]

And "when the one rises, the other falls" (*Rashi,* Genesis 25:23)[39]; thus the Kingdom of Evil falls and is nullified. As is written (Hosea 14:10), "The ways of God are upright, the righteous walk in them whereas the sinners stumble in them."[40] That is, by means of "the ways of

---

spiritual component within the material form, he repels the evil inclination's enticements and instead empowers the Kingdom of Holiness. This focusing on the spiritual, on the inner intelligence, is in essence the aim of all Torah study and the source of the Torah's power to "dissolve" and "shatter" the evil inclination (cf. *Maharsha, s.v. im even*).

Reb Noson asks: What if a person is on the road or in some other similar situation where he cannot study. What should he do then to vanquish the evil inclination? The answer is that he should turn his mind into a house of study (*Likutey Halakhot, Minchah* 7:65). In other words, he should focus his mind on holy matters. It is then as if he were studying from the works of Torah, and with this, too, he can defeat the evil inclination.

Elsewhere, Reb Noson asks: Our Sages taught that to vanquish the evil inclination a person must study Torah. Should this fail, he should recite the *Shema* or recall the day of death (see n.36). The question is, if, as implied by the Talmudic passage, the latter two methods are the more effective, why not go straight to them? Why resort to them only after Torah study has failed to repel the evil inclination? Then again, is recalling the day of death really more effective? Many people talk of their death and yet are not aroused by this to the fear of sin? Reb Noson answers that, in truth, Torah study is the lone remedy for repelling the evil inclination. But the evil inclination knows this and therefore does all it can to prevent a person from studying the word of God. And even when a person succeeds in fending off this opposition and studies Torah, he sometimes finds the evil inclination still with him. Sooner or later, the ensuing frustration becomes too much and he gives up the battle. This is where recalling the day of death comes in. When a person remembers that his sojourn in this world is transient and that he will one day be called upon to give a reckoning for his every deed, he is loath to pay heed to his evil inclination. Even though there are times when he falls, times when even reciting the *Shema* is beyond him, still, because his attitude toward the day of death is based on Torah ideals and a desire to study Torah, he will ultimately overcome the evil inclination (*Likutey Halakhot, Betziat HaPat* 5:22).

We can now further explain this passage in the terms of our lesson. As we have seen, Torah study gives strength to the Kingdom of Holiness. By strengthening the Kingdom of Holiness one attains the level of *Malkhut* in which the inner intelligence from *Chokhmah* is revealed. However, there are times when a person cannot comprehend this great *Chokhmah*. For this, he must recite the *Shema,* the quintessential declaration of faith. By affirming his faith, he maintains his attachment to the Kingdom of Holiness.

38. **Malkhut...receives vitality....** Rebbe Nachman explains that studying Torah with enthusiasm gives strength to *Malkhut* of Holiness, which in turn enables the person to focus on the wisdom in each aspect of creation. When he does this, a person unites *Malkhut* with *Chokhmah,* the spiritual element of that matter, so that "the *chet* and *nun* join and are bound together...." Reb Noson adds that this alludes to why the Jewish people had to wait fifty

זֶה הַצַּדִּיקִים, שֶׁדְּבֵקִים בַּמַּלְכוּת דִּקְדֻשָּׁה, הֵם נִתְחַזְּקִים וּמְקַבְּלִים
כֹּחַ עַל־יְדֵי־זֶה. "וּפשְׁעִים יִכָּשְׁלוּ בָם" בְּחִינַת מַלְכוּת הָרְשָׁעָה,
בְּחִינַת הַיֵּצֶר הָרָע, שֶׁנּוֹפֵל וְנִכְנָע עַל־יְדֵי הַתּוֹרָה, כַּנַּ"ל.

וְעַל־יְדֵי־זֶה נִתְקַבְּלִים כָּל הַתְּפִלּוֹת וְהַבַּקָּשׁוֹת, כִּי עִקַּר מַה שֶׁאֵין
נִתְקַבְּלִין הַבַּקָּשׁוֹת הוּא מֵחֲמַת שֶׁאֵין לְהַדְּבָרִים חֵן, וְאֵין נִכְנָסִין
בַּלֵּב שֶׁל זֶה שֶׁמְּבַקְשִׁין מִמֶּנּוּ, כְּאִלּוּ אֵין בְּלִבּוֹ מָקוֹם שֶׁיִּכָּנְסוּ
הַדְּבָרִים בְּלִבּוֹ, מֵחֲמַת שֶׁאֵין לְהַמְבַקֵּשׁ חֵן, שֶׁיִּכָּנְסוּ הַדְּבָרִים בְּלִבּוֹ
שֶׁל זֶה, שֶׁמְּבַקְשִׁין מִמֶּנּוּ.
אֲבָל עַל־יְדֵי הַתּוֹרָה, שֶׁעַל־יְדֵי־זֶה נִתְחַבְּרִין וְנִתְקַשְׁרִין הַנ וְהַח
כַּנַּ"ל, וְנַעֲשֶׂה חֵן, וְעַל כֵּן נִקְרֵאת הַתּוֹרָה: "יַעֲלַת חֵן", וַאֲזַי זוֹכֶה
שֶׁדְּבָרָיו הֵם דִּבְרֵי חֵן, וַאֲזַי נִתְקַבְּלִין דְּבָרָיו וּבַקָּשׁוֹתָיו, כְּמוֹ מִי

explains that when one's heart is open to receiving *Chokhmah*, his heart is also open and ready to receive the requests and petitions of others. But one who chooses to follow the desires of his heart fills his heart with folly. His heart no longer has any room to reflect the *Chokhmah*. On the contrary, his heart is laden with foolish thoughts and nonsense. The heart is thus a passageway that either reflects or obstructs the greater wisdom. This is because the heart is the seat of both the good and evil inclination. When one is worthy, the good inclination causes *Chokhmah* to be revealed. But when evil prospers, then foolishness... (*Biur HaLikutim* 11). From this we learn that for a person's request to be accepted, the heart of the one being implored must have room for the request. As for how one's own grace and charm makes an impression and room in another's heart, the Rebbe will explain this next.

44. **yaalat CheiN.** "The Torah bestows grace upon those who study her" (above, §1, n.5). This is because the Torah gives strength to the Kingdom of Holiness, the *nun*, enabling it to draw *Chokhmah*, the *chet*. It is therefore taught that the Torah bestows *CheiN* (חן), grace and charm. The *Yekara D'Shabbata* adds that the mitzvah of Torah study applies both in the day and at night (cf. Joshua 1:8). As mentioned, day is symbolic of inner intelligence, whereas night is symbolic of faith. Studying Torah day and night thus joins the *chet* and *nun*, creating *chein*.

As explained (n.32), although Pharaoh hoped to destroy the Jewish people, all thoughts of despair were dispelled when Moshe revealed that God was intending to give them the Torah (the *chet*) following their redemption. With their faith (the *nun*) they were able to overcome Pharaoh. As Scripture relates, "God caused the Jewish people to find *chein* in the eyes of the Egyptians" (Exodus 12:36). As a result, they took with them all the blessings—i.e., the booty of Egypt—when departing.

God"—i.e., the Torah—"the righteous," who adhere to the Kingdom of Holiness, are fortified and receive strength. "...whereas the sinners stumble in them" corresponds to the Kingdom of Evil—i.e., the evil inclination—which falls and is humbled by means of the Torah, as above.[41]

3. It is through this that all the prayers and petitions are accepted.[42] For the main reason the requests are not accepted is that the words lack grace and do not penetrate the heart of the one being asked.[43] It is as if there were no place in his heart for the words to enter, because the petitioner is lacking the grace needed for the words to enter the heart of the one he petitions.

But, by means of the Torah—through which the *Nun* and the *Chet* are joined and bound together—*CheiN* (grace) is produced. This is why the Torah is called *"yaalat CheiN."*[44] The person then merits that his words are words of charm, and so his words and requests are received. As is the case when someone speaks with *chein*, the matter

---

41. **by means of the Torah, as above.** In review: By means of the Torah, a person's words acquire grace and importance so that his prayers and requests are accepted (§1). For this he must focus on the *pnimiyut*, the spirituality, found in everything in creation. This inner intelligence corresponds to the concepts of Yaakov, firstborn, *Chokhmah*, sun, the *chet* and *chiut* (life), and can only be attained by means of the *nun*, *Malkhut*. However, there is also a *Malkhut* of the Other Side, which leads people to follow their lusts rather than focus on the inner intelligence found in creation. Only by studying Torah with enthusiasm is it possible to overcome this *Malkhut* and give strength to the *Malkhut* of Holiness, thereby uniting the *nun* with its source, the *chet* (§2).

42. **through this...accepted.** Rebbe Nachman opened this lesson by speaking about the *chein* (grace) and importance of the Jewish people being elevated and enhanced. In the previous section he explained the two components of the word *chein* (חן): the *chet* (ח) and the *nun* (נ). When these two letters are joined—by means of enthusiastic Torah study—the Kingdom of Holiness becomes strengthened. Here the Rebbe explains how this causes the grace of the Jews to be enhanced and how their prayers and requests are therefore accepted.

43. **not penetrate the heart....** Rebbe Nachman began with *Chokhmah*, inner intelligence, and then discussed *Malkhut*, faith, the vessel necessary for receiving inner intelligence. Here, he introduces the concept of heart. As previously mentioned in the notes (n.16), the *chiut*/ *Chokhmah* is hidden within *Binah*, and *Binah* corresponds to the heart (see *Tikkuney Zohar*, Second Introduction). Rebbe Nachman also referred to the heart when explaining that Esav typifies those people whose sole interest is to follow their hearts' desires (see nn.25,26).

The Talmud teaches: When a person has fear of Heaven, his words are heard (*Berakhot* 6b). This fear, accepting the yoke of Heaven, is perfecting the *nun*. The *Biur HaLikutim*

שֶׁמְדַבֵּר דִּבְרֵי חֵן, שֶׁנִּכְנָסִין הַדְּבָרִים בְּלֵב הַמִּתְבַּקֵּשׁ, דְּהַיְנוּ זֶה שֶׁמְבַקְשִׁין מִמֶּנּוּ.

וְזֶה בְּחִינַת ת. הַיְנוּ עַל-יְדֵי שֶׁנִּתְחַבְּרוּ וְנִתְקַשְּׁרוּ הַחֵי"ת וְהַנּוּ"ן וְנַעֲשָׂה בְּחִינַת חֵ"ן – עַל-יְדֵי-זֶה נַעֲשָׂה בְּחִינַת תָּ"ו, שֶׁהוּא לְשׁוֹן חֲקִיקָה וּרְשִׁימָה, כְּמוֹ שֶׁכָּתוּב: "וְהִתְוִיתָ תָּ"ו", כִּי עַל-יְדֵי הַחֵן נֶחְקַק וְנִרְשָׁם מָקוֹם בְּלֵב הַמִּתְבַּקֵּשׁ לְקַבֵּל הַבַּקָּשָׁה, כִּי עַל-יְדֵי הַחֵן נִתְקַבְּלוּ דְּבָרָיו.

נִמְצָא, שֶׁבְּחִינַת הַחֵ"ן חָקַק מָקוֹם בְּלֵב זֶה שֶׁמְבַקְשִׁין מִמֶּנּוּ, כְּדֵי שֶׁיִּכָּנְסוּ דְּבָרָיו בְּלִבּוֹ, וִיקַבֵּל בַּקָּשָׁתוֹ. וְהַחֲקִיקָה וּרְשִׁימָה זֶה בְּחִינַת תָּ"ו כַּנַּ"ל וְזֶהוּ: "דִּבְרֵי חֲכָמִים בְּנַחַת נִשְׁמָעִים". נַחַת דַּיְקָא, הַיְנוּ בְּחִינַת חֵן הַנַּ"ל וְהַת הַנַּ"ל, וְעַל-יְדֵי-זֶה נַעֲשָׂה אוֹתִיּוֹת נַחַת, וְאָז נִשְׁמָעִים דְּבָרָיו, וְנִתְקַבֵּל בַּקָּשָׁתוֹ כַּנַּ"ל:

strengthened by those who seek the wisdom and inner intelligence of everything; **are heard** — and as a result, their prayers and requests are accepted, **for they are spoken b'nachat** — for the Torah they study brings *chein* and makes a *tav*. The *Parparaot LeChokhmah* adds that therefore Targum renders "the words...*b'nachat* (calmly)" as: "the words/prayers of the wise are accepted before the Master of the Universe." The *Biur HaLikutim* points out that the greater the lack in spiritual development that a person has to overcome, the greater is his advancement when he overcomes it and has filled his lack. We can learn this from the *nun*, which, although initially symbolic of a lack, *Malkhut*, when completed, is united with the *chet*—expanding to two letters. What's more, together these two letters form a *tav*, the letter with the greatest numerical value. Thus, the product of *nun* (= 50) and *chet* (= 8) is *tav* (= 400; see Appendix: Gematria Chart).

In this as well the *Be'Ibey HaNachal* sees the inter-relationship between Torah and prayer. Torah is true wisdom, the *chet*. Prayer is *Malkhut*, the *nun* (see *Likutey Moharan* I, 7:1). Binding Torah and prayer produces the grace so vital for Jewish survival. He recalls that this was Rebbe Nachman's directive: to turn Torah into prayer. That is, a person should always formulate prayers out of whatever Torah he studies; entreating God that he merit to fulfill the teaching to the fullest (see *Likutey Moharan* II, 25).

This, in fact, was Moshe's great feat. Moshe spent forty days on Mount Sinai receiving the Torah (the *chet*). When he returned to the people, he found that they had sinned against God by making the Golden Calf. Apparently, he had received the Torah for himself; the Jews were unable to attain the necessary level of holiness (see *Likutey Moharan* I, 190). Moshe therefore ascended a second time, to pray for the people and their spiritual lack (the *nun*). He thereby attained *chein*, the combination of *chet* and *nun*. This explains what he later said, on his third ascent to Heaven. Moshe prayed to God, beginning with the words, "You said

penetrates the heart of the one petitioned—i.e., the one being asked.

This is the concept of the *tav*. That is, by the *Chet* and *Nun* being joined and bound, producing *CheiN*, the *TaV* is made.[45] This suggests etching and marking, as in (Ezekiel 9:4), "and *hiTVita TaV* (inscribe a mark)."[46] By means of the *chein*, a space is carved out and marked in the heart of the one who is petitioned to accept the request. For as a result of the grace, his words are accepted.[47]

Thus it is that the *chein* etches a place in the heart of the one who is being petitioned, so that the other's words may enter his heart and cause the request to be accepted. This etching and marking is the concept of the *tav*. This is the meaning of (Ecclesiastes 9:17), "The words of the wise are heard [for they are spoken] *b'nachat* (gently)." Specifically *nachat*—i.e., the aspect of *CheiN* and the *Tav*, which together spell *NaChaT*. Then, his words are heard and his request is accepted.[48]

---

45. **the TaV is made.** By affixing the letter *nun* (נ) to the left leg of the *chet* (ח), the letter *tav* (ת) is formed (*Be'Ibey HaNachal*). The Rebbe next explains its significance.

46. **inscribe a mark.** God instructed the angel Gabriel to inscribe a mark on the foreheads of the righteous in Jerusalem. This *tav* would be a protective sign, to see them through the time of destruction that was at hand. The letter *tav* thus denotes inscribing or engraving. Elaborating on God's command to Gabriel, the Talmud concludes that in fact the letter *tav* was inscribed upon all the residents of Jerusalem. Why? Because the letter *Tav* stands for *Tichyeh* (you will live), and *Tav* stands for *Tamut* (you will die) (*Shabbat* 55a). In our context, the letter *Tav* alludes to the Torah, of which Scripture says, "The ways of God...the righteous walk in them whereas the sinners stumble in them." As explained, by combining *Chet* and *Nun*, one attains *CheiN*. And this combination makes the *Tav*. More specifically, when one observes the Torah, when he walks in God's ways, his *tav* is a source of life. But when one uses his knowledge to go against God and His Torah, when he despises true knowledge, then his *tav* only leads to death, as happened to Esav (*Biur HaLikutim*).

47. **By means of the chein....** "By means of the Torah"—i.e., studying Torah with enthusiasm—one attains a measure of grace and charm, which enhance his words. The *Parparaot LeChokhmah* points out that the reverse is also true. When one despises wisdom— i.e., distancing himself from Torah—his grace and charm fall away and his petitions go unaccepted and unanswered.

48. **CheiN and the Tav...NaChaT....** Rebbe Nachman concludes this section by explaining how "by means of the Torah..." one's prayers and requests are accepted. The *CheiN* (חן) and *Tav* (ת) combine to form the word *NaChaT* (נחת). As Scripture states, "The words of wise men are heard [for they are spoken] *b'NaChaT* (calmly)." They have charm (*chein*) and make an impression (*tav*) upon the heart of the one being petitioned. His words are therefore heard and accepted. In our context, the verse thus reads: **The words** — *Malkhut* of Holiness (which corresponds to the mouth, see *Tikkuney Zohar*, Second Introduction) **of wise men** — is

וְעַל כֵּן יַעֲקֹב שֶׁהוּא בְּחִינַת הַשֵּׂכֶל כַּנַּ"ל, עַל כֵּן זָכָה לְחֵן, כְּמוֹ
שֶׁכָּתוּב: "כִּי חַנַּנִי אֱלֹקִים" וְכוּ'; וְעַל כֵּן בֵּרַךְ אֶת הַשְּׁבָטִים בְּחֵן,
כְּמוֹ שֶׁכָּתוּב: "הַיְלָדִים אֲשֶׁר חָנַן" וְכוּ'; וּבְנְיָמִין לֹא הָיָה אָז. וְעַל
כֵּן בֵּרְכוֹ יוֹסֵף בְּחֵן, כְּמוֹ שֶׁכָּתוּב: "אֱלֹקִים יָחְנְךָ בְּנִי".

וְדַוְקָא יוֹסֵף הָיָה יָכוֹל לְבָרְכוֹ בְּחֵן, כִּי יוֹסֵף הָיָה כָּלוּל בְּיוֹתֵר

where you were born'...Rescue me, I pray, from the hand of my brother, from Esav...lest he smite mother and child alike" (see Genesis 32). Yaakov feared that Esav would use his own *tav* (= 400)—the mark of the sword, death and destruction—as opposed to the life-giving mark which he himself typified. His prayer for help in returning to the land of his fathers was thus a request to fulfill his Torah study (God's directive). In this way, Yaakov achieved both Torah study and prayer prior to meeting Esav. As a result, he merited *chein*. And so instead of harming Yaakov, Esav fell upon his brother with hugs and kisses (*Be'Ibey HaNachal*).

51. **children...graced your servant.** Having prayed that Esav not harm his children, Yaakov blessed them with *chein* in order to thwart Esav's plot to destroy them (*Be'Ibey HaNachal*). In our context, this verse can alternatively be read as a subtle warning by Yaakov to Esav that God had already provided Yaakov's children with the necessary protection by granting them *chein*.

52. **Binyamin...grace, my son.** The Midrash teaches: The attribute of *chein* was bestowed upon the progenitors of each of the eleven tribes (who were with their father when Yaakov encountered Esav). What about Yaakov's twelfth son, Binyamin, who had not yet been born? It was left for Yosef to later bless his younger brother with *chein* (*Bereshit Rabbah* 78:10).

The importance Scripture ascribes to *chein*, relating that both Yaakov and Yosef made a point of bestowing this blessing upon Israel, calls for deeper study. The *Biur HaLikutim* offers the following very unusual insight: Yaakov, as we have seen, personifies wisdom, inner intelligence. He thus corresponds to the *chet*, the sun. As the sun, he illuminates the moon, enlightening it with his wisdom. The moon, the *nun*, is personified in Yaakov's twelve sons, who correspond to the twelve lunar months. (Hence the Jewish people follow the lunar calendar.) In the Jewish calendar, a leap year is signified by a thirteenth month, indicating the division of the tribe of Yosef into two: his sons Menashe and Efraim (who were allotted full representation among the tribes). Now, the reason for the extra lunar month is to align the lunar cycle with the solar cycle, so that the holidays of Pesach and Sukkot fall in their proper seasons. In the context of our lesson, this is the joining of the *nun* (lunar) with the *chet* (solar). This also explains why the letter *nun* appears twice in the name BiNyamiN (the last of Yaakov's children): to complete the *nun/Malkhut* (the last *sefirah*) to its fullest. It can also be inferred that Binyamin, not yet born when Yaakov conferred the blessing of *chein*, symbolizes all of Yaakov's future descendants. Thus, the Jewish people as a whole correspond to the *nun*, faith, reflecting the wisdom of their Patriarchs, who attained the true inner intelligence. This is why it was obligatory for each tribe to have *chein*, for each tribe (in its own unique way) reflected the great wisdom/inner intelligence of Yaakov (cf. n.20-23).

53. **specifically Yosef....** Here Rebbe Nachman addresses why specifically Yosef, more than any of the other brothers, had to be the one to confer *chein* upon Binyamin.

4. Therefore, Yaakov, who is the aspect of inner intelligence, merited grace.[49] As is written (Genesis 33:11), "God has *ChaNani* (granted me grace)."[50] He, therefore, blessed the tribes with *CheiN,* as in (*ibid.,* 33:5), "The children with whom the Lord has *ChaNan* (graced) your servant."[51] And Binyamin, who was not there at the time, was therefore blessed by Yosef with grace, as is written (Genesis 43:29), "May the Lord *yaChNkha* (grant you grace), my son."[52]

And it was specifically Yosef who was able to bless him with *chein.*[53] This is because Yosef, more than anyone else, embodied the

---

that...I have found *chein* in Your eyes. Now, if I have indeed found *chein*..." (Exodus 33:12,13). With this, he formed the *tav*—the *Tav* indicating *Teshuvah* (repentance; cf. *Bereishit Rabbah* 22:12, *Shabbat* 55a). Consequently, the Second Tablets were given on Yom Kippur, the Day of Repentance. Then, all the Jews merited *chein* through their acceptance of the Torah and the numerous Yom Kippur prayers (see below, *Yerach HaEitanim*). This also explains why Moshe could only attain a glowing countenance (n.10) after his third ascent to God, only after he had received the Torah for *all* the Jewish people.

In review: By means of the Torah, a person's words acquire grace and importance so that his prayers and requests are accepted (§1). For this he must focus on the *pnimiyut,* the spirituality, found in everything in creation. This inner intelligence can only be attained by means of *nun, Malkhut.* However, there is also a *Malkhut* of the Other Side, which leads people to follow their lusts rather than focus on the intelligence found in creation. Only by studying Torah with enthusiasm is it possible to overcome this *Malkhut* and give strength to the *Malkhut* of Holiness, thereby uniting the *nun* with its source, the *chet* (§2). The *chet* and *nun* then unite to form the *tav,* through which a person's words become etched and engraved upon the heart of the one petitioned. This is because *chet* and *nun* form *chein,* and with the *tav, nachat,* by means of which the words of the wise are heard and accepted. Thus, by means of the Torah (studied with enthusiasm), the *chet,* a person's prayers and requests are accepted and the grace and importance of the Jews are enhanced (§3).

49. **Yaakov...inner intelligence, merited grace.** As explained (§2), Yaakov is the personification of inner intelligence. Scripture relates that when Yaakov set out for Lavan's house, the sun set early (Genesis 28:11). Reb Noson comments: This was a sign that he should not expect to intellectually grasp what was about to take place. He would have to lay aside his wisdom and rely on faith (*Torat Natan #6*). Yaakov thus had both the *chet* and the *nun,* and so merited grace.

In this section, Rebbe Nachman will show how the lesson also ties in with the historical context of Yaakov's perpetual battle for survival against Esav. As mentioned (n.11), Breslov teachings place particular emphasis on the contemporary application of Torah. In this lesson, the Rebbe teaches how to enhance the grace of the Jew, who is Yaakov, in the eyes of modern-day Esavs.

50. **granted me grace.** While Yaakov was still in Lavan's employ, God appeared to him and instructed him to return home (Genesis 31:3). In essence, this vision was an attainment of new wisdom, new Torah. On the return trip Yaakov was told of Esav's nefarious plan to avenge his loss of the birthright and the blessings by descending upon Yaakov with 400 hundred men. Yaakov prayed: "O God of my father...You Yourself told me, 'Return to the land

מִבְּחִינַת יַעֲקֹב, כְּמוֹ שֶׁכָּתוּב: "אֵלֶּה תֹּלְדוֹת יַעֲקֹב־יוֹסֵף"; כִּי הוּא הָיָה עִקַּר תּוֹלְדוֹתָיו. כִּי יַעֲקֹב וְיוֹסֵף כְּחַדָּא חֲשִׁיבֵי.

וְעַל כֵּן נֶאֱמַר בְּיוֹסֵף (דברים ל"ג): "בְּכוֹר שׁוֹרוֹ הָדָר לוֹ". 'בְּכוֹר' הוּא בְּחִינַת הַשֵּׂכֶל כַּנַּ"ל. וְזֶהוּ 'שׁוֹרוֹ' – לְשׁוֹן הִסְתַּכְּלוּת, כִּי צְרִיכִין לְהִסְתַּכֵּל בְּהַשֵּׂכֶל שֶׁיֵּשׁ בְּכָל דָּבָר כַּנַּ"ל. וְזֶהוּ הָדָר לוֹ – תִּרְגֵּם אוּנְקְלוֹס: זִיו לֵיהּ – לְשׁוֹן אוֹר. כִּי הַשֵּׂכֶל מֵאִיר לוֹ בְּכָל דָּבָר; אֲפִלּוּ בְּמָקוֹם שֶׁהָיָה אֹפֶל וַחֹשֶׁךְ, מֵאִיר לוֹ הַשֵּׂכֶל, כְּשֶׁזּוֹכֶה

on the wisdom, Yosef attained the birthright.

58. **radiance...luminance.** Rashi explains that the word *bekhor* (the firstborn) implies both greatness and kingship (*malkhut*). In our context, this indicates that greatness, the luminance of *Chokhmah*, can only be attained when joined with *Malkhut*. This was why Yosef, the *bekhor*, later merited to untold grandeur as viceroy of Egypt. Rashi also adds that the *bekhor* is a reference to Yehoshua. He was the moon, as Rebbe Nachman mentions elsewhere, and Moshe was the sun (*Likutey Moharan* I, 6:5). Yehoshua, too, merited grandeur, as leader (king) of the Jewish people. This was because of his ability to reflect the great light and wisdom of his teacher Moshe (above, n.10), through the aspect of the moon, the *nun*.

59. **inner intelligence shines...in each thing.** The verse thus translates in our text as follows: Yosef attained **the firstborn** — the birthright/*Chokhmah*/*reishit* because **of his shor** — because he always focused on finding the inner intelligence (Godliness) of each thing; and as a result, **grandeur is his** — this wisdom illuminates his way and guides him on the proper path.

60. **place that had been dark and obscure.** Our Sages taught: Yosef sanctified the name of Heaven and had one of the letter's of God's name added to his own (*Sotah* 36b). This was when Yosef found himself in a "dark and obscure" place, alone with Potifar's wife, who sought to seduce him. The Talmud (*ibid.*) relates that at the last minute, Yaakov's countenance appeared to Yosef and this enabled him to overcome his evil inclination. By focusing on the inner intelligence—i.e., Yaakov's countenance—which was to be found even in this situation, Yosef withstood the test and sanctified God's name (*Parparaot LeChokhmah*).

In the next section, where Rabbah bar bar Chanah's story is explained, Rebbe Nachman discusses one of the more ruthless ways in which the evil inclination seeks to entrap people: by disguising itself as a mitzvah. This adds much to our understanding of Yosef's test. Potifar's wife had been told by her astrologers that she was destined to have descendants from Yosef. What was unclear was whether this would be through her or her daughter (as later happened; Genesis 41:45). In that case, her intention to have relations with Yosef was for the "sake of Heaven" (*Rashi,* Genesis 39:1). She saw her seductive behavior as a mitzvah! In the end, however, Yosef's fear of Heaven saved him. "How could I commit this evil act and transgress against God?!" he said to her (Genesis 39:9). Yosef always focused on the wisdom found in every matter and used it to come closer to God. He was therefore able to see through the "mitzvah" Potifar's wife had proposed. Instead of succumbing to sin, he sanctified God's name (cf. *Likutey Moharan* I, 7, n.47).

aspect of Yaakov, as in (Genesis 37:2), "These are the chronicles of Yaakov: Yosef."[54] He was the essence of [Yaakov's] chronicles, for Yaakov and Yosef are considered as one (*Zohar* I, 176b).[55]

It is therefore said of Yosef: "The firstborn of his *shor* (oxen), grandeur is his" (Deuteronomy 33:17). "Firstborn" corresponds to the inner intelligence, as above.[56] And this is "his *shor*," it suggests gazing. For it is necessary to focus on the inner intelligence of every matter.[57] Onkelos renders "grandeur is his," as "radiance is his," an expression of luminance.[58] For the inner intelligence shines for him in each thing.[59] Even in a place that had been dark and obscure,[60] the inner intelligence shines for him—when he merits focusing on the

---

54. **chronicles of Yaakov: Yosef.** There are several reasons that the chronicles of Yaakov's life and those of the generations that he begat were hinged on Yosef. First, the essential factor which brought Yaakov to work for Lavan was his wish to marry Rachel, Yosef's mother. And Yosef's facial features closely resembled those of his father. What's more, the events of Yosef's life paralleled those of Yaakov. Just as the one was hated, so, too, the other; Yaakov's brother attempted to kill him and Yosef's brothers attempted to kill him, etc. (*Rashi, loc. cit.*).

55. **are considered as one.** The *Zohar* teaches that on the hierarchy of the *sefirot* Yaakov parallels *Tiferet* and Yosef parallels *Yesod* (see Appendix: Seven Supernal Shepherds). *Tiferet* is alternatively referred to as the *vav* (= 6), for it encompasses the six *sefirot* of *Z'er Anpin*. *Yesod* itself is also known as a *vav*, it being the sixth of the seven lower *sefirot* (see Appendix: The Divine Persona). In the Kabbalah, these are known as the "large" *vav* and the "small" *vav*. They parallel each other and are inseparable. That which *Tiferet* can do, *Yesod* can also do (on a lesser scale). This is suggested in the letter *vav* itself. It cannot be enunciated without pronouncing a second *vaV* (*Zohar* I, 182b; *Nitzutzei Orot*, 1). In these ways Yaakov and Yosef are considered as one. Thus, just as Yaakov had the power to confer *chein*, Yosef could confer *chein*. The *Parparaot LeChokhmah* adds that this is why we find that in blessing Yosef, Yaakov referred to him as "a son with *chein*" (*Rashi*, Genesis 49:22).

   Throughout the different branches of Torah teachings, Yosef is seen as the personification of the true tzaddik. This is because Yosef parallels *Yesod*, the *sefirah* that denotes the qualities embodied by the tzaddik. Rebbe Nachman teaches elsewhere that the tzaddik is always attempting to reveal and enhance the true beauty of every Jewish soul (*Likutey Moharan* I, 17:1). By stating here that it was specifically Yosef who conferred *chein* upon Binyamin, the Rebbe indicates that only the true tzaddikim of each generation have the power to enhance the grace of the Jewish people.

56. **firstborn...as above.** See section 2, note 12. Yosef is called the firstborn because he of all the brothers acquired the birthright when it was denied Reuven, Yaakov's eldest. Yosef thus took the twofold portion that accompanies the birthright; his sons Menashe and Efraim took two places among the tribes.

57. **shor...suggests gazing....** The word *ShoR* (ox) also connotes gazing and focusing, as in (Numbers 24:17), "...*aShuRenu* (I behold it), but it is not near." This suggests focusing on the *Chokhmah* in every matter. "I behold it"—at the level of *Malkhut/nun*—"but it is not near"—for the level of *Chokhmah* is very lofty and exalted. By virtue of this quality, *focusing*

לְהִסְתַּכֵּל עַל הַשֵּׂכֶל שֶׁיֵּשׁ שָׁם בְּכָל דָּבָר וּמְקָרֵב אוֹתוֹ לְהַשֵּׁם יִתְבָּרַךְ.

וְזֶה פֵּרוּשׁ מַה שֶׁאָמַר רַבָּה בַּר בַּר חָנָה (בבא בתרא עג.):

its source in the supernal worlds Above. Thus, the material can be bound to the spiritual, provided, that is, that one recognizes the wisdom and intelligence therein. God then promised Yaakov that He would safeguard him, for guarding the intellect is the only way to properly attain the spiritual wisdom in every matter; the work of connecting the material to the spiritual is where this protection is needed most. This is why when Yaakov arrived at Lavan's house, he became a shepherd, "guardian" of the sheep, focusing on the inner intelligence of each thing and connecting it to its source. But Lavan was a knave. He looked for every opportunity to trick Yaakov and used his cunning against his nephew. However, as Rebbe Nachman taught earlier, the name *Yaakov* suggests wisdom. This includes the ability to outwit another person when necessary. Because he connected everything to its source, Yaakov was able to anticipate Lavan's ploys and overcome them.

Returning home after twenty years in Lavan's house, Yaakov was informed that Esav was heading his way together with a band of 400 men. Yaakov sent Esav the following message: "I lived with Lavan, yet guarded the entire Torah. I have cattle and donkeys, sheep...." That is, he wanted Esav to know that throughout all the years they had not seen each other, he, Yaakov, had successfully guarded his intellect by focusing on the inner intelligence and spirituality found in everything. What's more, he had abundant blessings to show for it. He had thereby elevated the *chein* and so Esav would not be able to harm him. His "*tav*," formed by the *chein*, would overcome Esav and his *tav* (= 400) men. And so, on the contrary, because of his grace Yaakov found favor in Esav's eyes (*Torat Natan* #12).

The *Be'Ibey HaNachal* points out that Esav had spoiled the *chet*, wisdom. Doing so also blemished the *nun*, the vessel one needs to receive inner intelligence. He had thus denied himself the possibility of receiving the blessings.

In review: By means of the Torah, a person's words acquire grace and importance so that his prayers and requests are accepted (§1). For this he must focus on the *pnimiyut*, the spirituality, found in everything in creation. This inner intelligence can only be attained by means of the *nun*, *Malkhut*. However, there is also a *Malkhut* of the Other Side, which leads people to follow their lusts rather than focus on the inner intelligence found in creation. Only by studying Torah with enthusiasm is it possible to overcome this *Malkhut* and give strength to the *Malkhut* of Holiness, thereby uniting the *nun* with its source, the *chet* (§2). The *chet* and *nun* then unite to form the *tav*, through which a person's words become etched and engraved upon the heart of the one petitioned. This is because *chet* and *nun* form *chein*, and with the *tav*, *nachat*, by means of which the words of the wise are heard and accepted. Thus, by means of the Torah (studied with enthusiasm), the *chet*, a person's prayers and requests are accepted and the grace and importance of the Jews are enhanced (§3). Because when a Jew (Yaakov) seeks this inner intelligence, he attains grace for himself and for all his future descendants (Binyamin); provided that he also turns to the true tzaddikim and true leaders (Yosef), as they are the only ones who can confer the blessing of *chein* (§4).

62. **This is the....** Rebbe Nachman now shows how the concepts of this lesson are alluded to within the framework of Rabbah bar bar Chanah's story.

inner intelligence that is found in each thing—and brings him closer to God.[61]

5. This is the explanation of what Rabbah bar bar Chanah said[62]:

61. **closer to God.** Also in light of this lesson we can better understand the struggle between Yaakov and Esav, as well as the ensuing stories which Scripture relates. Their battle was not just over the birthright, but a struggle over which of them possessed true wisdom and would therefore inherit all the blessings and bounty that wisdom affords. Previously (§2), Rebbe Nachman quoted the verse (Ecclesiastes 7:12), "In the shelter of wisdom, in the shelter of wealth; yet the advantage of knowledge is that wisdom gives life to those who possess it." Wisdom is life-giving. It was over this blessing that Yaakov and Esav fought. The *Biur HaLikutim* points out that the letters of *BeKhoR* (בכר, firstborn) and *BeRaKhah* (ברכה, blessing) are the same. Whoever attains wisdom, blessing is his.

Reb Noson writes: Esav totally rejected belief in the World to Come. "I'm about to die," he said, "what good is the birthright?" (Genesis 25:32). Instead of life, he chose death—a spurning of the birthright, a rejection of wisdom. He could not conceive of there being anything more to creation than the material reality which his eyes perceived. Rashi (*loc. cit.*) explains that the priestly service of God, including atoning for sin by sacrificing animals upon the altar, was originally the right of the firstborn. (Only after the sin of the Golden Calf were they replaced by the Kohanim.) Esav, however, never believed that it was possible to elevate something material to the realm of the spiritual, as by offering a sacrifice. In this he was gravely mistaken. The Hebrew term for sacrifice, *KoRBan,* is similar to *KaReV* (without a vowel point the letter *beit* is read *veit*), which means "to bring close." For the sacrifice symbolizes elevating an animalistic quality, a base desire or lust, to a higher level; the one who brings the offering rises above his attachments to materialism and comes closer to God. What was it that caused Esav to reject all of this? His lust for the material world, as in the verse from Proverbs (18:2) which our lesson applies to Esav: "The fool does not desire understanding, but only to bare his heart." Esav assumed that by renouncing the rewards of the World to Come he would better enjoy all the benefits and bounty of this world (food, wealth, etc.). But, as Scripture relates, it was in fact Yaakov, by acquiring the birthright— choosing the World to Come over this world—who received also the blessings for material prosperity. Rather than seeking to satisfy his heart's desires, he chose the path of understanding, the path in which the material is secondary and subsidiary to the spiritual. Yaakov chose wisdom, which encompasses all. This was why when Esav realized that also the blessings for material prosperity had been taken from him, he became enraged and sought to kill his brother Yaakov.

Scripture then relates that Yaakov fled from Esav, intending to seek refuge in the home of his uncle, Lavan. On the way he stopped off at the Torah academy of Shem and spent fourteen years immersed in study. When he resumed his journey to Lavan's house, he came upon the site where the Holy Temple would one day be built, the site where the sacrifices would be offered. While there, the sun set, a sign that Yaakov should not expect to intellectually grasp what was about to take place. He would have to lay aside his wisdom and rely on faith (see n.49). And there he dreamt about a ladder standing on the ground with its top reaching up into heaven—to convey to Yaakov that even the worldly and corporeal has

הַאי גַּלָּא דְּמַטְבַּע לִסְפִינְתָּא מִתְחֲזֵי כִּי פֵּרֵשׁ רַשְׁבַּ"ם:
צוּצִיתָא דְּנוּרָא חִוַּרְתָּא בְּרֵישָׁא: וּמֵחֲנָן אֵשׁ לְבָנָה וּמַלְאָךְ מַזִּיק הוּא.
לֵיהּ בְּאַלְוָתָא דְּחָקִיק עָלֵיהּ "אֶהְיֶה אֲשֶׁר אֶהְיֶה"

גַּלָּא – הוּא הַיֵּצֶר הָרָע:

דְּמַטְבַּע לִסְפִינְתָּא – הוּא הַחֵן וְהַחֲשִׁיבוּת, לְשׁוֹן סָפוּן וְחָשׁוּב,
(מוֹעֵד קָטָן כ"ח. מַאן חֲשִׁיב מַאן סְפוּן). כִּי הַיֵּצֶר הָרָע רוֹצֶה
לְהַטְבִּיעַ וּלְהַשְׁפִּיל, חַס וְשָׁלוֹם, בְּחִינַת הַחֵן וְהַחֲשִׁיבוּת שֶׁל
יִשְׂרָאֵל, בְּחִינַת מַלְכוּת דִּקְדֻשָּׁה:

וּמִתְחֲזֵי כִּי צוּצִיתָא דְּנוּרָא חִוַּרְתָּא בְּרֵישָׁא – כִּי מִתְּחִלָּה הַיֵּצֶר הָרָע
מִתְלַבֵּשׁ עַצְמוֹ בְּמִצְווֹת וּמַטְעֶה אֶת הָאָדָם כְּאִלּוּ מְסִיתוֹ לַעֲשׂוֹת

importance and grace of the Jewish people, which the evil inclination hopes to sink by causing them to neglect the inner intelligence of every matter.

66. **disguises itself in good deeds...mitzvah.** The evil inclination will not take a direct approach and openly propose to a person that he sin (see n.60). Instead, it makes use of certain mitzvot and good deeds for its own ends. This is comparable to Esav, who deceived his father Yitzchak. He would ask, "How does one tithe salt and straw?" (which are in fact not subject to tithing), leading his father to believe he was meticulous in the performance of mitzvot (*Rashi*, Genesis 25:27).

As explained, because the inner intelligence is so very great, one can only attain it through the aspect of the *nun*. This *nun* indicates the constriction a person places on his intellect; his knowledge is predicated on an appropriate restraint of the intellect in its striving for greater perceptions. Quite simply, he does not attempt to reach for that which is beyond his ability to comprehend. This constriction is actually in and of itself a mitzvah. But the evil inclination turns it around and uses it to convince a person that focusing on the inner intelligence is beyond him and therefore forbidden for him to attempt. By doing so, it misleads people through what appears to be righteousness and good deeds (*Parparaot LeChokhmah*).

We learn from this how inner intelligence, though essential, can be distorted so that it causes a person to digress from the truth. Yaakov represents true inner intelligence. Yet Scripture refers to him as "a simple man" (Genesis 25:27)—a man who acted without sophistication. Whatever directive the Torah issues, we, like the simple man, should accept it without question. This is true faith. (Consider, on the other hand, the example of King Shaul. God ordered him to totally annihilate the Amalekite nation. But Shaul intellectualized the decree, theorized on its true meaning, and left Agag, the Amalekite king, alive. Generations later this nearly led to the destruction of the Jewish people at the hands of Agag's descendant, the wicked Haman.) For the only real way to attain true knowledge is through absolute simplicity (*Parparaot LeChokhmah*).

Reb Noson writes: In fact, it is actually quite difficult for the evil inclination to openly

That wave which would sink a *sephinta* **(ship) appears to have a spark of white flame at its crest. We beat it with a staff on which was etched** *Ehyeh asher Ehyeh* **(Bava Batra 73a).**[63]

Rashbam:

spark of white flame - white fire; it is a destroying angel:

wave — This is the evil inclination.[64]

which would sink a SePhINta — This is the grace and the importance, as suggested by *"SePhIN* and important" (*Moed Katan* 28a). The evil inclination desires to sink and subdue, God forbid, the grace and importance of the Jewish people, the aspect of the Kingdom of Holiness.[65]

appears to have a spark of white flame at its crest — Initially, the evil inclination disguises itself in good deeds. It misleads a person, as if it were urging him to perform a mitzvah.[66] This is the meaning of a

---

63. **Ehyeh asher Ehyeh.** Ehyeh is the holy name with which God revealed Himself to Moshe at the burning bush (cf. *Shavuot* 35a). As Scripture relates (Exodus 3:13,14):

> Moshe said to God, "So I will go to the Israelites and say: 'Your ancestors' God has sent me to you.' They will immediately ask me what His name is. What shall I tell them?"
>
> God replied to Moshe, "*Ehyeh asher Ehyeh* (I Will Be Who I Will Be)."
>
> [God then] explained, "This is what you should say to the Israelites: '*I Will Be* sent me to you.' "

The Kabbalah explains that this name parallels the *sefirah* of *Keter*, the Crown of Creation—i.e., God's very first thought or impulse, so to speak, that initiated the creative process. Hence the future tense, "I *Will Be*," for at the time of the impulse everything was still in the future. From the Midrash, Talmud and *Zohar* we learn that this first thought is identified with the concept of Israel (*Bereishit Rabbah* 1:4; *Berakhot* 6a; *Tikkuney Zohar* 17a). This ties in with what Rebbe Nachman teaches above (§1, see also nn.11-13), that Yaakov corresponds to *reishit* (first) and the birthright of the firstborn. From the Kabbalah we know that with regard to the more exalted level, Yaakov is known by his alternate name, Israel. In addition, as mentioned above, God called the Jewish people "My firstborn, Israel" (see n.32). (Identifying both Yaakov and Israel with *reishit* is similar to defining both *Chokhmah* and *Keter* as the first *sefirah*.)

64. **wave....** The evil inclination is called a *gal* (wave) because it forms a screen and a separation in front of holiness (*Kehillat Yaakov, Gal*). The evil inclination seduces a person into ignoring the inner intelligence. This causes a fall in grace and importance, in the aspect of *Malkhut* (*Parparaot LeChokhmah*).

65. **SePhiNta...SePhiN....** The Hebrew term for ship, *sephina* (Aramaic, *sephinta*), resembles the Aramaic term for importance, *sephin*. The ship in the story alludes to the

מִצְוָה. וְזֶהוּ בְּחִינַת צוּצִיתָא דְּנוּרָא חִוַּרְתָּא – אֵשׁ לְבָנָה, אַף־עַל־
פִּי־כֵן מַלְאָךְ מַזִּיק הוּא.

וּמְחִינָן לֵיהּ בְּאַלְוָתָא דְּחָקִיק עֲלֵהּ אֶהְיֶה וְכוּ', הַיְנוּ שֶׁעִקַּר הַכְנָעָתוֹ
שֶׁל הַיֵּצֶר־הָרָע הוּא עַל־יְדֵי הַתּוֹרָה, שֶׁהִיא כְּלַל שְׁמוֹתָיו שֶׁל
הַקָּדוֹשׁ־בָּרוּךְ־הוּא. וְהַתּוֹרָה הִיא בְּחִינַת וָא"ו. כִּי הַלּוּחוֹת, אָרְכָּן
וָי"ו וְרָחְבָּן וָי"ו. וְזֶהוּ בְּחִינַת אַלְוָתָא,
דְּהַיְנוּ מַקְלוֹת דְּחָקִיק עֲלֵהּ אֶהְיֶה וְכוּ', הַיְנוּ שֵׁמוֹת, בְּחִינַת הַתּוֹרָה,
שֶׁהִיא בְּחִינַת וָי"ו, וְהַוָּי"ו הוּא צוּרַת מַקֵּל, וְהִיא כְּלַל שְׁמוֹתָיו שֶׁל
הַשֵּׁם יִתְבָּרַךְ,

commandments, one must *perform* them (*Berakhot* 17a). This is because the Torah was given to be studied, so that we know what God's will is and how to implement it. The person who does this will seek the Godliness in everything, for his sole intention is to serve His Creator through the Godly wisdom he attains. He will practice true mitzvot and not be misled by the "whiteness" of pseudo-mitzvot. Conversely, the knowledge of the person who studies for personal benefit, even if it is for the expansion of his intellect, becomes the source for misguided performance of mitzvot. This is why it is essential that one first acquire the *nun*, the fear of God.

68. **principal defeat....** See above, section 2 and notes 35-37.

69. **names of God.** The Kabbalah is replete with examples of how certain combinations of Hebrew letters or words allude to one of the numerous variations of God's holy names. For example, as Rebbe Nachman explains in *Likutey Moharan* I, 15:5, the words *MI EiLeH* (מי אלה) can be transposed into the holy name ELoHIM (אלהים). With sufficient expertise, it is possible to see how the entire Torah is made up of God's holy names. This principle also has an application in Halakhah. When taking an oath, a person takes hold of a Torah scroll. Doing so indicates an awareness that his oath is in the name of God, and so he would not dare swear falsely. The *Shulchan Arukh* (*Choshen Mishpat* 87:15-17) states that any of the sacred scrolls—e.g., tefillin or one of the Books of the Prophets—are acceptable, for they, too, are made up of God's holy names. See also the commentary of the Rosh on *Nedarim* 3:2.

70. **Torah...vav...six cubits wide.** The Tablets of Law (which embodied the entire Torah) that Moshe received at Sinai were six cubits by six cubits. The Torah is therefore likened to the letter *vav*, which has a numerical value of six.

　　These last two concepts, that the Torah comprises the holy names of God and that it is likened to a *vav*, are new to the lesson. Rebbe Nachman now explains them within the context of Rabbah bar bar Chanah's story.

71. **Ehyeh...stick...names of God.** The holy name Ehyeh here represents all the different holy names found in the Torah. The letter *vav* is shaped like a staff. Thus, the staff with holy names that was used to beat the wave (the evil inclination) was in fact the Torah.

spark of white flame. The flame is white; even so, it is a destroying angel.[67]

We beat it with a staff on which was etched Ehyeh asher Ehyeh — That is, the principal defeat of the evil inclination is accomplished by means of the Torah,[68] which is comprised entirely of the names of God.[69]

The Torah corresponds to the *vav*. For the Tablets were six cubits long by six cubits wide (*Bava Batra* 14a).[70] This is the aspect of **the staff**— i.e., sticks.

on which was etched Ehyeh — That is, holy names—the aspect of Torah, which corresponds to the *vav*. The *vav* has the shape of a stick, and [the Torah] is comprised entirely of the names of God.[71]

suggest to a person that he commit a sin. The Jew, at his source, is very distant from sin. The evil inclination therefore takes a underhanded approach—trying to convince the person that what he is about to do is a mitzvah. The evil inclination is thus the very antithesis of Yaakov. It is Esav, who typified evil at its core, and at the same time it is Lavan, who exemplified the trickery and chicanery by which a person is fooled into performing pseudo-mitzvot. The methods employed by the evil inclination are many. It will relentlessly insist that what it professes is "the absolute truth." It will also promote strife and then convince a person that he must not listen to others but be willing to fight for his principles... Moreover, no one is immune. Consider what happened to Korach. Greatness had been prophesied for his family, and so, thinking he was above the evil inclination's machinations, Korach rose up in rebellion against Moshe, the true tzaddik... Or else, the evil inclination will use false piety to get its way. It will convince a person that he is distant from God, that his efforts to come closer are of no avail. "I can never truly repent," he will piously say of himself, "so what's the use trying?" Then again, the evil inclination has also learned the art of substitution, of how to replace good with bad. This is why conversion (out of the Jewish religion) is known as *l'HaMeR dat*, from the Hebrew for substitute, *HaMaRah*. The evil inclination will not even stop at this to achieve its aims (*Torat Natan* #15).

67. **flame is white...a destroying angel.** The color white, which in Hebrew is *lavan*, denotes purity. Accordingly, it alludes to the true tzaddik and to the very beginning, the *reishit*, of creation. But "God made one to contrast the other" (see n.27). The shylock Lavan thus presents himself as white and pure, as if he were one of the true tzaddikim. However, Lavan is the other manifestation of white: the pure whiteness which indicates leprosy (Leviticus 13). This teaches that a person must be very wary of his personal perceptions of the truth. It is necessary to seek and search for the inner intelligence of everything, until the truth becomes self-apparent (*Torat Natan* #22).

With this we can better understand the words of the Psalmist: "The beginning of wisdom is the fear of God; all who practice it gain sound intelligence" (Psalms 111:10). Rebbe Nachman earlier quoted only the opening of the verse, showing, through the literal reading, that *reishit* is wisdom. Now we understand that the means for acquiring that *reishit*/wisdom is the fear of God/the *nun*—i.e., by accepting God's Kingdom. As for the mitzvot, the Talmud points out that they provide intelligence to "all who practice them"—it is not enough to study the

הַיְנוּ שֶׁהַתּוֹרָה הַקְּדוֹשָׁה הִיא מַכְנִיעַ אֶת הַיֵּצֶר הָרָע שֶׁרוֹצֶה לַעֲשׂוֹת
אֶת הָאָדָם מְשֻׁגָּע מַמָּשׁ, חַס וְשָׁלוֹם. כִּי בַּעַל־עֲבֵרָה הוּא מְשֻׁגָּע,
כְּמוֹ שֶׁאָמְרוּ רַבּוֹתֵינוּ, זִכְרוֹנָם לִבְרָכָה: 'אֵין אָדָם עוֹבֵר עֲבֵרָה אֶלָּא
אִם כֵּן נִכְנַס בּוֹ רוּחַ־שְׁטוּת'. וּכְמוֹ שֶׁהַמְּשֻׁגָּעִים צְרִיכִים לְהַכּוֹתָם
וְלָשׂוּם עֲלֵיהֶם שֵׁמוֹת, כְּמוֹ כֵן מַמָּשׁ הַתּוֹרָה שֶׁעוֹסְקִין הוּא בְּחִינַת
מַקְלוֹת וְשֵׁמוֹת, שֶׁבָּזֶה מַכִּין וּמַכְנִיעִין אֶת הַיֵּצֶר הָרָע וּמְגָרְשִׁין מִן
הָאָדָם אֶת הַשִּׁגָּעוֹן וְהָרוּחַ שְׁטוּת שֶׁנִּכְנַס בּוֹ, בְּחִינַת 'וּמָחִינָן לֵיהּ
בְּאַלְוָתָא, דְּחָקִיק עָלֵיהּ שֵׁמוֹת' וְכוּ', כַּנַּ"ל:

aside his foolish desire. Even though he wants something illegal or sinful, he realizes that it is not worth the beating he will have to suffer. But where one confuses evil with good and vice-versa, as do those in the first category, this treatment will not help. Such a person will always think that there is what to be gained by the "good deed" and will always try to do it. In that case, one must use amulets and holy names to banish his foolishness. (Kabbalistic teachings, including those of the Ari, are filled with stories of how spirits possessed people and drove them insane. In many cases these spirits were ultimately banished by means of amulets and oaths using God's holy names; see *Shaar HaGilgulim*, p.186; *Sefer HaChezyonot*, Rabbi Chaim Vital). The same is true of the evil inclination, which at first convinces a person to engage in pseudo-mitzvot, the substitution of evil for good. Afterwards, once such substitution has become ingrained, the person desires evil of his own accord. In this way the evil inclination seeks to make him totally and literally insane. As Rebbe Nachman teaches, the only way to subdue the evil inclination is with Torah study. For the Torah is a staff, sticks, and is composed entirely of holy names—the two treatments for relieving a person of his insanity (*Parparaot LeChokhmah*).

The *Be'Ibey HaNachal* explains this as follows: There are aspects of the sun and the moon both from the *Sitra d'Kedushah* (Side of Holiness) and from the *Sitra Achra* (Other Side; see §2). The sun and moon of holiness represent Torah study; the sun is Torah/inner intelligence, the moon symbolizes the constriction needed to receive the Torah. When a person's understanding of Torah is predicated on proper restraint of the intellect in its striving for greater heights, he is not fooled or tricked into believing that a sin is a mitzvah. On the other hand, the sun of unholiness represents one's intellectual ability to substitute evil for good, while the moon of the Other Side symbolizes one's electing to constrict his intellect with folly. The holy names and amulets of Torah, which correspond to true inner intelligence, are then used to subdue a person's inclination for substitution. And the staff of Torah, that which one studies Torah with enthusiasm, subdues a person's fondness for folly. There are thus two ways in which the evil inclination attempts to suppress the grace and importance of the Jewish people: through its pseudo-mitzvot and through actual sin. Nevertheless, these two ways can be overcome by Torah study, which joins the *chet* and the *nun* so that the *chein* and importance of the Jewish people ascend.

Thus, Rabbah bar bar Chanah's story translates in our lesson as follows: **That wave** — the evil inclination, **which would sink a ship** — which would devour the grace and importance of the Jewish people, **appears to have a spark of white flame at its crest** — begins by convincing a

   In other words, the holy Torah subdues the evil inclination, which wants to drive a person literally insane, God forbid.[72] For a sinner is insane, as our Sages taught: A person does not commit a sin unless a spirit-of-folly has entered into him (*Sotah* 3a).[73] And, just as the insane must be struck and have [amulets bearing] holy names placed upon them, the Torah study one engages in is likewise an aspect of sticks and holy names. With it we beat and subdue the evil inclination, and dispel from the person the insanity and foolishness that have entered into him. This is, **We beat it with a staff on which was etched** holy names... (cf. *Vayikra Rabbah* 25:1).[74]

---

72. **literally insane, God forbid.** As the manifestation of God's will, the Torah is true inner intelligence. The opposite of this is the transgression of God's will, sin, which is folly, as the Rebbe will next explain. When the evil inclination wants to lead a person to follow the passions of his heart, it attempts to drive him insane with his own foolishness.

73. **spirit-of-folly....** Once possessed by a spirit-of-folly—i.e., a person yearns to follow his heart's desires rather than his intellect—sin is all but inevitable. Then, after getting him to sin once, this spirit-of-folly returns and with even greater ease causes him to commit additional sins, driving him further insane. Reb Noson asks: There are many people who have for years followed their hearts and sinned a great deal. Seeing as each additional sin produces additional mental imbalance, should not the number of bizarre and absolutely crazy people in the world be far greater? The answer Reb Noson gives is that in the true scheme of things, yes. The numbers don't match up. The reason is that the Holy One's mercy is infinite. God takes pity on the sinner and allows him to maintain a semblance of normalcy in order that he be able to return to Him. For even with a minimum amount of intelligence a person has the ability to refrain from the foolishness that leads him to sin (*Torat Natan* #24).

   The *Parparaot LeChokhmah* explains this in the following manner: Sin is generated by a spirit-of-folly. How then can the evil inclination even suggest to a person with intelligence that he commit a sin? It's impossible. Therefore, the evil inclination uses the guise of mitzvah-performance, and with this leads him to sin. This ruse prevents even the person with intelligence from focusing on the inner intelligence and spirituality of each matter; thereby distancing him from God and leading him to further sin. Nevertheless, all Jews, as descendants of Yaakov (the inner intelligence), are born with an inherent ability to focus on the intelligence of everything. This modicum of inner intelligence remains with a person no matter what, directing him to the proper path if he would but heed its call. The *Mai HaNachal* adds that this is why there are many different types of mental illnesses and imbalances. Each person suffers insanity in accordance with the sins he has committed. But when one studies Torah, when he focuses on the spirituality in everything and tries to come closer to God, he acquires wisdom and can rid himself of all foolishness.

74. **Torah study...beat and subdue....** Insanity can be divided into two categories. The first is the insanity which results when a person is overwhelmed by a spirit-of-folly, so that he unintentionally confuses evil with good and good with evil. The second category is the insanity which results when a person knowingly pursues foolishness and desires sin. For each form of insanity a different treatment is prescribed. It is possible to strike fear into an insane person by beating him or by threatening him with physical harm. This forces the person to set

וְזֶהוּ: "אַשְׁרֵי תְמִימֵי דָרֶךְ".

אַשְׁרֵי – לְשׁוֹן הִסְתַּכְּלוּת.

תְּמִימֵי דָרֶךְ – בְּחִינַת: "יַעֲקֹב אִישׁ תָּם"; שֶׁהוּא בְּחִינַת הַשֵּׂכֶל כַּנַּ"ל. הַיְנוּ לִזְכּוֹת לְהִסְתַּכֵּל עַל הַשֵּׂכֶל שֶׁיֵּשׁ בְּכָל דָּבָר, שֶׁהוּא בְּחִינַת "יַעֲקֹב אִישׁ תָּם" – זֶה זוֹכִין עַל-יְדֵי הַתּוֹרָה: וְזֶהוּ:

הַהוֹלְכִים בְּתוֹרַת ה'. כִּי עַל-יְדֵי שֶׁלּוֹמֵד תּוֹרָה בְּכֹחַ, עַל-יְדֵי-זֶה נוֹתֵן כֹּחַ לַמַּלְכוּת דִּקְדֻשָּׁה בְּחִינַת נוּ"ן, לְקַבֵּל מִן הַשֵּׂכֶל, שֶׁהוּא בְּחִינַת חַיִּ"ת, וַאֲזַי נַעֲשֶׂה חֵן וְנִתְקַבְּלִים דְּבָרָיו כַּנַּ"ל, וַאֲזַי נִתְעַלֶּה הַחֵן וְהַחֲשִׁיבוּת שֶׁל יִשְׂרָאֵל, וְכָל הַתְּפִלּוֹת וְהַבַּקָּשׁוֹת נִתְקַבְּלִים:

understand some new approach in his service of God, well and good. If not, he must constrict his intellect and rely on faith. Eventually, once he has sufficiently purified his physical nature, he will understand. But until then he must continue to believe with complete faith that everything in the world does indeed embody wisdom and great inner intelligence. In the words of the Psalmist, "You created everything with wisdom" (Psalms 104:24)—that is, the purpose of everything is to help man draw closer to God and believe in Him (*Likutey Halakhot, Pikadon* 4).

The opening verse thus reads: **Ashrei are those whose way is perfect** — those who focus on the inner intelligence of every matter, to find the spirituality of each thing and so draw closer to God; **who walk with the Torah of God** — can attain this intelligence by studying Torah with enthusiasm, which enlightens the mind and guides it on the proper path. Fortunate are they.

* * *

Reb Noson, in his commentary on this lesson, ties these ideas to the concepts related to *Sefirat HaOmer* (Counting of the Omer). As we've seen in the lesson, a person must focus on the inner intelligence of everything that exists in this world. Similarly, the Counting of the Omer emphasizes the importance of counting each new day—i.e., making certain that every single day of life counts. In addition, the forty-nine days of Omer Counting have to be *tmimot* (complete)—i.e., perfected days. A person can achieve this by focusing on the inner intelligence found in everything he encounters during the course of that day. And even if moments or hours passed during which he failed to remain focused, when awareness slipped from his consciousness, it is still not too late. He can begin to look for the spirituality found in every matter from that moment on. Therefore, even if a part of the day was lost, he can still make it count. It takes no more than suddenly becoming aware that each day is important, even the rest of that day. Doing this leads one to Torah, for the counting (awareness) is the path that precedes the receiving of Torah, as on Shavuot (*Likutey Halakhot, Pikadon* 4:5-7).

6. And this is [the explanation of the opening verse][75]:
"Ashrei **(Happy) are those whose way is perfect, [who walk with the Torah of God]."**

aShRei — This suggests gazing.[76]

whose way is perfect — This corresponds to "Yaakov, a man of perfection" (Genesis 25:27). [Yaakov] is the aspect of inner intelligence, as above.[77] That is, to merit focusing on the inner intelligence of each thing—the aspect of "Yaakov, a man of perfection"—is achieved by means of the Torah. And this is:

who walk with the Torah of God — By studying Torah with enthusiasm, strength is given to the Kingdom of Holiness/*Nun,* [enabling it] to receive from the inner intelligence, the *Chet. CheiN* is then produced and his words are accepted, as explained.[78] As a result, the *chein* and importance of the Jewish people are enhanced,[79] and all the prayers and petitions are accepted.[80]

Jew to perform pseudo-mitzvot. **We beat it with a staff on which was etched Ehyeh asher Ehyeh** — The way to subdue the evil inclination is by studying Torah with enthusiasm.

75. **And this is....** Rebbe Nachman now explains how the entire lesson is embodied within the opening verse.

76. **aShRei...gazing.** As explained, the combination of *Shin* (ש) and *Reish* (ר) as root letters indicates gazing or focusing.

77. **way is perfect...Yaakov...perfection....** See above, section 2, that Yaakov personifies the person who focuses on the inner intelligence of every matter. In describing Yaakov as a man of perfection, Scripture refers to him as an *ish tam* (literally, "a man of simplicity"). Rebbe Nachman sees this as an indication that to attain true inner intelligence—i.e., perfection—a person must initially act with total simplicity. That is, he must first put into effect the concept of *nun*, constriction, by setting aside his own intellect. He must begin by truly accepting the *Malkhut* of Heaven. Only then can he receive the true *chet*, inner intelligence. Moreover, the greater his subservience to *Malkhut* of Holiness, the greater will be his attainment of *Chokhmah* (*Parparaot LeChokhmah; Mai HaNachal*).

78. **as explained.** See above, section 2.

79. **chein and importance...are enhanced.** For the *chet, nun* and *tav* which they form, produce the *NaChaT* that enables a person's words to be heard and accepted (as above, §3).

80. **...are accepted.** The main objective of wisdom and true inner intelligence is the perfection of belief in God, which encapsulates the whole of the Torah, as in, "All Your commandments are faith" (Psalms 119:86). In other words, a person must conduct all his affairs according to the dictates of the Torah. When considering or studying any matter, he must know and believe with total faith that great intelligence is encompassed within that thing, and that it is possible to draw closer to God through it. If he is then able to deduce and

ליקוטי מוהר"ן סימן ב'

לְשׁוֹן רַבֵּנוּ, זִכְרוֹנוֹ לִבְרָכָה:

וַיֹּאמֶר ה' אֶל מֹשֶׁה: אֱמֹר אֶל הַכֹּהֲנִים בְּנֵי אַהֲרֹן וְאָמַרְתָּ אֲלֵיהֶם: לְנֶפֶשׁ לֹא יִטַּמָּא בְּעַמָּיו:

אִיתָא בְּסִפְרָא דִּצְנִיעוּתָא, פֶּרֶק ב': 'מְנוּקְבָא דְּפַרְדַּשְׁקָא מָשַׁךְ רוּחָא דְּחַיֵּי לִמְשִׁיחָא'.

Nachman.) It was then that Reb Shmuel Isaac remembered what he'd been told in the dream: "Who knows if they'll open the door for you?"

When, at last, Reb Shmuel Isaac found Rebbe Nachman's house and knocked, there was no answer. Not about to give up, he continued knocking, until after a while he heard the Rebbe answer softly through the closed door. "Shmuel Isaac, it is impossible to open the door for you right now." Reb Shmuel Isaac was brokenhearted. For the next hour he remained outside the door, crying bitterly. Finally, Rebbe Nachman opened the door and said to Reb Shmuel Isaac, "Weren't you informed, even before setting out on your journey, that you might not be let in?! True, all Heaven's gates are sealed except for the gates of tears (*Bava Metzia* 59a). But, there are numerous clouds surrounding you...." From this Reb Shmuel Isaac understood that the Rebbe knew exactly why he had come. Yet, he was so awed by Rebbe Nachman's *ruach hakodesh* (divine inspiration), that he couldn't work up the courage to say anything about the dream.

That Shabbat, other chassidim came to visit Rebbe Nachman from nearby Medvedevka. The Rebbe taught this lesson, *Emor el haKohanim*. A careful reading shows that he included in his words a full explanation of Reb Shmuel Isaac's dream. From that time on, Reb Shmuel Isaac's devotions especially focused on perfecting his prayers—a fundamental element of this lesson (*Tovot Zikhronot* #2, pp.103-104).

The text of the lesson is *leshon Rabbeinu z'l*. Any lesson designated as such was copied verbatim from Rebbe Nachman's manuscripts, which Reb Noson had in his possession. The remaining lessons (excluding the few which were written down by some of the other followers) were either transcribed by Reb Noson at Rebbe Nachman's dictation, or reconstructed by Reb Noson after he had heard the teaching from the Rebbe in public. He would prepare a written version and present it to Rebbe Nachman for approval.

2. **Siphra DeTzneuta.** This is "The Book of the Hidden," a Kabbalistic treatise comprising five chapters, corresponding to the Five Books of Moses, which is included in the text of the *Zohar* (II, 176b*ff*). Every word of *Siphra DeTzneuta* is carefully weighed, as they reveal the deepest mysteries of the Kabbalah. A phrase from each of the five chapters is expounded upon in *Likutey Moharan*, Lessons #2 and #19-22. This passage is from the Second Chapter of *Sifra DeTzneuta*.

3. **Nukva DePardaska...Mashiach.** *Nukva DePardaska* is the Aramaic term for the apertures of the nose. The Kabbalah speaks of a Divine persona known as *Arikh Anpin*, which

LIKUTEY MOHARAN #2[1]

"God said to Moshe, '*Emor El HaKohanim* (Speak to the priests), the sons of Aharon, and say to them: Let no [priest] defile himself by [contact with] the dead among his people.' "

(Leviticus 21:1)

In *Siphra DeTzneuta*[2] we find: From *Nukva DePardaska* the breath of life is drawn to Mashiach *(Zohar* II, 177a).[3]

---

1. **Likutey Moharan #2.** This lesson was given on a Shabbat in the winter of 5561 (1801), in the town of Zlatipolia. Rebbe Nachman lived there from just prior to Rosh HaShanah 5561 until he moved to Breslov almost two years to the day, in 5563 (see *Until The Mashiach,* p.60). When the Terhovitza Magid (Reb Yekusiel, d.1811), a prominent Chassidic leader in his own right, later saw the lesson in writing, he remarked, "What can I say about this teaching? That it is *Zohar?* It's loftier than the *Zohar!* That it is *Tikkuney Zohar?* It's loftier than the *Tikkuney Zohar!*" (*Aveneha Barzel* p.74, #62). The main themes of the lesson are: prayer; guarding the Covenant; binding oneself to the tzaddik; charity; *mishpat* (justice); and Torah study. The Rebbe revealed this teaching following a visit from one of his closest followers, Reb Shmuel Isaac of Dashev (1765-1827), who had dreamt a most disturbing dream.

In his dream, Reb Shmuel Isaac saw himself inside an endless forest. There he encountered a man carrying a double-edged sword. Although initially frightened, Reb Shmuel Isaac agreed to follow the man. They soon came to a large house and the man told him that inside there were many swords similar to his own, only smaller. Reb Shmuel Isaac could take one, but he would have to know how to wield the sword in a judicious manner. Reb Shmuel Isaac entered the house. Inside, he was confronted by an old man who warned him against taking any of the swords unless a) he was absolutely free from sexual blemish, and b) he knew how to handle the sword. Suddenly, Reb Shmuel Isaac found himself being enveloped by layer upon layer of dark clouds. The old man then pushed Reb Shmuel Isaac out of the house, saying, "Look how you are still surrounded by these clouds! You are not yet ready for the sword! Nevertheless, further on in the forest you'll come upon a beautiful building. There you'll find a master craftsman who sharpens these swords. If you manage to get there...But who knows if they'll open the door for you?"

Reb Shmuel Isaac was shaken by this dream. His first thought was to discuss it with Rebbe Nachman. Although he had no money for the journey from Dashev to Zlatipolia (about 200 kilometers), and despite the impossible travel conditions of the Ukrainian winter, Reb Shmuel Isaac immediately set out. Traveling part of the way by coach and part on foot, he reached his destination only to realize that he had no idea of where the Rebbe lived. Rebbe Nachman had moved to Zlatipolia a few months earlier, and this was Reb Shmuel Isaac's first visit. "Why do you want to see him?" he was asked by the townspeople from whom he sought directions. "Don't you know there's great controversy surrounding Rebbe Nachman?" (This was just after the Shpola Zeide began his relentless opposition to Rebbe

א כִּי עִקַּר כְּלֵי־זֵינוֹ שֶׁל מָשִׁיחַ הוּא הַתְּפִלָּה, שֶׁהוּא בְּחִינַת חֹטֶם,
כְּמוֹ שֶׁכָּתוּב: "וּתְהִלָּתִי אֶחֱטָם לָךְ", וּמִשָּׁם עִקַּר חִיּוּתוֹ. וְכָל
מִלְחַמְתּוֹ שֶׁיַּעֲשֶׂה וְכָל הַכְּבִישׁוֹת שֶׁיִּכְבֹּשׁ – הַכֹּל מִשָּׁם, כְּמוֹ
שֶׁכָּתוּב: "וַהֲרִיחוֹ בְּיִרְאַת ה'" וְכוּ'. זֶה בְּחִינַת חֹטֶם,
וְזֶה עִקַּר כְּלֵי־זֵינוֹ, כְּמוֹ שֶׁכָּתוּב: "בְּחַרְבִּי וּבְקַשְׁתִּי". וּפֵרֵשׁ רַשִׁ"י:

anointed one) is so called because of the *shemen haMiShChah* (anointing oil), which yielded a sweet fragrance, as in (Songs 1:3), "Your ointments give off a pleasant fragrance." Mashiach will bring a fresh "breath of life" and vitality to the world by enhancing people's recognition of God's Kingdom (*Torat Natan*#5).

6. **For My praise, eChToM....** Literally, "I will plug My *ChoTeM* (nose)" so as to prevent the smoke of anger from escaping (see *Rashi, loc. cit.*; cf. *Likutey Moharan* I, 20:10, note 98). "My praise" refers to the words of prayer we recite in praise of God. Seeing that "My praise"—i.e., prayer—is used in conjunction with the nose, we understand that prayer is connected to the *chotem*. Furthermore, we can infer that since "My praise" restrains God's anger, it is prayer that mitigates the judgments. The more one engages in prayer, the greater his ability to mitigate the judgments in *Malkhut*. This will become clearer in section 8, below.

7. **wars...conquests...from there.** From the nose. This refers to the breath of Mashiach, which comes from the left nostril, the side of judgment. Yet, precisely from this side of judgment, God will withhold His anger. Instead of anger and judgment, vitality will emanate from the nose, and with it Mashiach will conquer the world.

Rebbe Nachman once said, "Mashiach will conquer the entire world without even one shot of gunpowder" (*Siach Sarfei Kodesh* 1-67).

8. **breathe...fear of God...chotem.** From this verse we learn that Mashiach's *yir'at HaShem* (fear of God) will afford him a perfected sense of smell. It also connects prayer to *yir'at HaShem*, as the fear of God is the foundation for sanctifying the way one speaks and for using the Holy Tongue perfectly (see *Advice*, p. 120). In our context, this also corresponds to the concept of nose, which is Mashiach's source of vitality in that all his power descends through the nose of *Arikh Anpin*. By means of his perfected sense of smell, Mashiach will distinguish the righteous from the wicked (see *Rashi, Metzudat David, loc. cit.*). Rebbe Nachman thus concludes that a perfected sense of smell is actually perfected prayer—the source of all Mashiach's conquests (see next note).

9. **essential weapon.** The very next verse in Isaiah (11:4) clarifies: "...and [Mashiach] will smite the [guilty] of the earth with the staff of his mouth, and with the breath of his lips he will slay the wicked." Thus, Mashiach's essential weapon, his sword, is prayer; symbolized in the earlier verse as his breath, the nose. Through his sense of smell, his power of prayer, all battles will be won and all obstacles overcome.

10. **sword...bow.** When Yaakov blessed Yosef and his two sons, he said, "I have given you one portion more...which I took out of the hand of the Emorites, with my sword and my bow." The additional portion which Yosef inherited was the birthright, a double portion (see below, §2). Yaakov had taken the birthright from Esav, who is called "the Emorite" (*Maharsha, Bava Batra* 123a, *s.v. Shekhem*). Specifically, Yaakov was referring to the city of

For the basic weapon of Mashiach is prayer.[4] This is the aspect of *ChoTeM* (the nose),[5] as is written (Isaiah 48:9), "For My praise, *eChToM* (I will restrain My anger) from you."[6] [Mashiach's] main vitality is from [the nose]. All the wars he will wage, and all his conquests, will be from there,[7] as is written (Isaiah 11:3), "He shall breathe of the fear of God." This is the aspect of *chotem*.[8]

And [prayer] is his essential weapon,[9] as is written (Genesis 48:22), "with my sword and my bow."[10] < Onkelos renders this: "with my

---

corresponds to the *sefirah* of *Keter* (Crown, or the head of Primordial Man; see Appendix: The Divine Persona). Each particular segment of the upper worlds is also given its own name. Thus *Nukva DePardaska* is the name of the world found in *Arikh Anpin* corresponding to the nostrils of the head of Primordial Man. The *Zohar* describes it as "the hollow"—a passage through which the exalted intellect found in *Arikh Anpin* descends to the lower levels. This "nose" is so exalted, it is totally independent of the lower worlds. In other words, it serves only as a benefactor, giving the breath of life to the lower worlds and requiring nothing in return. From *Nukva DePardaska* life descends to the seven lower *sefirot*. The right nostril transports life to the six *sefirot* of *Z'er Anpin;* the left to the last *sefirah, Malkhut*. At present, however, the judgments found in *Malkhut* are of such severity that the life-force passed on from there to this world is lacking. These judgments will be totally mitigated only when Mashiach comes. Then, through *Nukva DePardaska*, Mashiach will receive the wisdom and vitality necessary to bring the entire world under the *Malkhut* (Kingdom) of God—i.e., perfection. The wisdom and mysteries of Torah will then be revealed to all (*Zohar* III, 130b, 289a; see *Matok Midvash, ad. loc.*). The meaning and application of this passage will be explained over the course of the lesson.

4. **basic weapon...is prayer.** When Mashiach comes, the Holy Temple will be rebuilt. It will then be "a house of prayer for all nations" (Isaiah 56:7). The personification of perfected prayer is King David. Thus Mashiach, as a scion from the House of David, is symbolic of a very exalted level of prayer (*Torat Natan #7*). For when Mashiach comes, he will rule over the entire world. To do so, he will require a very powerful weapon. We know, however, that it will not be a weapon of mass-destruction, which Rebbe Nachman derided as "the foolishness of the nations" because they use their wisdom to invent better and better ways to kill each other (*Tzaddik #546*). Rather, as the Rebbe teaches here, Mashiach's basic weapon is prayer.

Reb Noson writes: Our Sages teach that the strength of a Jew is his mouth (cf. *Yalkut*, Isaiah 450). With this weapon, the mouth, the Kingdom of God can be revealed. As the *Tikkuney Zohar* (Introduction, p.17a) teaches: "*Malkhut* is mouth," which in our context is prayer. Moreover, just as Mashiach's power is prayer, so, too, the tzaddikim in each generation, who draw their power from Mashiach, wage their battles with prayer (*Torat Natan #1*).

5. **the nose.** Rebbe Nachman likens prayer to the nose. This is because a person's life depends on the breath he constantly draws in through his nostrils, as in (Genesis 2:7), "[God] breathed into his nostrils the breath of life" (*Mai HaNachal*). A continuous connection with the Creator through prayer is just as necessary. Prayer is thus the breath of life and symbolized by the nose (*Rabbi Yaakov Meir Shechter*). Reb Noson explains that MaShiaCh (literally,

'תְּפִלָּה וּבַקָּשָׁה'. וּכְמוֹ שֶׁכָּתוּב: "כִּי לֹא בְקַשְׁתִּי אֶבְטַח וְכוּ'
בֵּאלֹהִים הִלַּלְנוּ" בְּחִינַת: "תְּהִלָּתִי אֶחֱטָם לָךְ".

ב וְזֶה הַכְּלִי־זַיִן צָרִיךְ לְקַבֵּל עַל־יְדֵי בְּחִינַת יוֹסֵף, הַיְנוּ שְׁמִירַת
הַבְּרִית, כְּמוֹ שֶׁכָּתוּב: "חֲגוֹר חַרְבְּךָ עַל יָרֵךְ". וּכְמוֹ שֶׁכָּתוּב:
"מִפְּרִי בִטְנְךָ אָשִׁית לְכִסֵּא לָךְ" – זֶה בְּחִינַת מָשִׁיחַ, בְּחִינַת תְּפִלָּה.

ever attain it. The average Jew, even if he is pious, is really very distant from perfected prayer. How then can he ever hope to make use of this most powerful weapon? The answer is that he too can pray, and his prayers will be answered provided a) he attaches himself to the tzaddikim who know how to use their prayers effectively (see below, §6), and b) he engages in prayer constantly, and refuses to give up (*Torat Natan* #4-5).

In review: The main weapon of Mashiach, and indeed of every single Jew, is prayer.

14. Yosef. Tradition speaks of two Mashiachs: the first, a descendant of Yosef; the second, a descendant from the royal House of David. Mashiach ben Yosef is the personification of the battles the Jewish people must wage to bring an end to their exile. He himself will be killed in the final battle with Gog and Magog. Mashiach ben David will then bring the Final Redemption and usher in the era of peace for the entire world (*Sukkah* 52a; see also *Likutey Moharan* I, 16). The Talmud calls these two Mashiachs "master craftsmen" whose task it will be to rebuild the Holy Temple (*ibid.* 52b). The significance of this will become clearer in section 6. Rebbe Nachman next explains that Mashiach ben David, who will conquer the entire world through prayer, receives his power through Mashiach ben Yosef, the aspect of the Covenant.

15. brit, Covenant. The *brit* (covenant) that God made with Avraham and his descendants after him is sealed through the circumcision of the foreskin. This is the sign of the Covenant (Genesis 17). As such, the Jewish people's covenant with God is centered on sexual purity. Guarding the *brit*—the Covenant or, alternatively, the organ of procreation—thus implies a high standard of moral behavior in thought, word and deed. Yosef is the personification of this "guarding" because, while he was a slave in Egypt, he withstood the advances of his master's wife and remained steadfast in his refusal to sin sexually (Genesis 39). In the terminology of the Kabbalah, *brit* parallels the *sefirah* of *Yesod* (Foundation).

16. Gird your sword.... The verse concludes, "this is your splendor and majesty." The entire Psalm (45) was written in praise of the Torah scholar (*Rashi* on v.1). The *Zohar* asks: Is it splendor and majesty for a Torah scholar to have a sword upon his thigh? The answer is yes, because "thigh" alludes to the *brit*. A person must call upon all his self-constraint to control his lusts and keep from sinning with the *brit*. The Torah scholar who attains the level of guarding the Covenant is one who is worthy of "splendor and majesty." In our context, Rebbe Nachman teaches that to attain the weapon of prayer, "the sword," one must first attain the level of guarding the Covenant. This is the connection between sword/prayer and *brit*.

prayer and my supplication,"[11] and likewise > Rashi explains: prayer
and entreaty. The same idea is expressed in the verse (Psalms 44:7,9),
"For I trust not in my bow, nor shall my sword save me... [but
rather,] in those who praise the Lord all day long."[12] This
corresponds to "For My praise, *echtom* from you."[13]

2. Now, this weapon must be received by means of the aspect of
Yosef[14]—i.e., guarding the *brit* (Covenant),[15] as in (Psalms 45:4), "Gird
your sword upon your thigh."[16] It is also written (Psalms 132:11,12), "Of
your offspring I will set upon your throne"—this refers to Mashiach,

---

Shekhem, which he had conquered "with my sword and my bow." It was this that he
bequeathed to Yosef.

11. **prayer...supplication.** In Hebrew, "with my bow" is *BeKaShty*. These are the same letters
as *BaKaShaty* (my supplication). This indicates that the weapon Yaakov used to conquer
Shekhem was, in fact, prayer and supplication. Should one nevertheless insist that Yaakov
meant the sword and bow literally, Rebbe Nachman quotes from Psalms.

12. **For I trust not in my bow....** The bow, the Psalmist says, is not to be trusted, and so
Yaakov's weapons must have been prayer and supplication (*Bava Batra* 123a; *Mai
HaNachal*). Maharsha (*ibid., s.v. u'vkashti*) explains that both "sword" and "bow" are
necessary for countering the enemies of the Jews. Prototypically, the enemies of the Jewish
people (Yaakov) are two: Esav (Rome, Christendom) and Yishmael (the Arab nation). Esav
was blessed (Genesis 27:40), "You shall live by your sword." Yishmael was blessed with
mastery of the bow (cf. Genesis 21:20). To counter them, Yaakov must employ his own
sword—namely, prayer—and his own bow—namely, the *brit* (see next section).

13. **...My praise, echtom....** With this, Rebbe Nachman ties together the concepts of
praise, the sword and bow, and the nose.
   Rebbe Nachman has shown that Mashiach's main weapon will be prayer. In the abridged
version of this lesson, which appears in *Kitzur Likutey Moharan* (see also *Advice,* p.275), Reb
Noson writes: "The basic weapon of *every* Jew is prayer." The Rebbe himself alludes to this
by introducing Yaakov—the prototype of all Jews—into the lesson. For, in fact, each and
every Jew has within himself the power to conquer evil. Whatever negative trait overwhelms a
person, whatever obstacle keeps him from serving God, can be overcome through prayer.
Anyone who takes this to heart and sincerely believes that prayer is his main weapon, will
certainly be diligent in praying to God for his salvation. He knows that with prayer he can
overcome everything that stands in his way. And even those whose belief is lacking and so do
not feel the power of prayer, they, too, have a way to battle "the enemy." They should see
themselves as simple foot soldiers, as members of a troop under the charge of commanding
officers—i.e., the tzaddikim. This is why Rebbe Nachman chose the metaphor of weaponry,
so that each person should know that, no matter what his spiritual level, he can arm himself
with the weapon of prayer (*Mai HaNachal*).
   Reb Noson adds that because perfected prayer is so exalted, only the very great tzaddikim

"אִם יִשְׁמְרוּ בָנֶיךָ בְּרִיתִי", הַיְנוּ עַל־יְדֵי בְּחִינַת יוֹסֵף.

וְיוֹסֵף שֶׁשָּׁמַר אֶת הַבְּרִית, נָטַל אֶת הַבְּכוֹרָה, שֶׁהוּא בְּחִינַת עֲבוֹדַת הַתְּפִלָּה* בְּחִינוֹת פִּי שְׁנַיִם, כִּי הַתְּפִלָּה הוּא פִּי שְׁנַיִם. שְׁנַיִם שֶׁיֵּשׁ בָּהֶם שִׁבְחוֹ שֶׁל מָקוֹם וּשְׁאֵלַת צְרָכָיו. וְהוּא בְּחִינַת: "וְחֶרֶב פִּיפִיּוֹת בְּיָדָם". בְּחִינַת שְׁתֵּי פִיּוֹת, בְּחִינַת פִּי שְׁנַיִם. וְנָטַל מֵרְאוּבֵן עַל־יְדֵי שֶׁחִלֵּל יְצוּעֵי אָבִיו, כִּי הִיא תָּלוּי בִּשְׁמִירַת הַבְּרִית:

[Marginal note]

וְעַל כֵּן יוֹסֵף בִּשְׁבִיל שֶׁזָּכָה לִבְחִינַת תְּפִלָּה, שֶׁהִיא בְּחִינַת "תְּהִלָּתִי אֶחֱטָם" בְּחִינַת חִיּוּת הַנִּמְשָׁךְ מִנּוּקְבָּא דְּפַרְדַשְׁקָא כַּנַּ"ל, עַל כֵּן נִקְרָא בֶּן פּוֹרָת יוֹסֵף, שֶׁהֵם בְּחִינַת תרפ"ו אוֹרוֹת שֶׁהֵם שִׁבְעָה שֵׁמוֹת: ע"ב, ס"ג, מ"ה, ב"ן, קס"א, קנ"א, קמ"ג, שֶׁעוֹלִין תרפ"ו, שֶׁמְּקַבֵּל מִנּוּקְבָּא דְּפַרְדַשְׁקָא, כִּי פַּרְדַשְׁקָא בְּגִימַטְרִיָּא תרפ"ו.

(AB, SaG, MaH, BaN), which together have a numerical value of 232. Ehyeh has three expansions (KSA, KNA, KMG), which together equal 455 (see Appendix: Expansions of the Holy Names; Gematria Chart). Their sum total is 687. (Although these numbers are not exactly equal, the rules of gematria allow the value of 1 to be added for the word itself.) These 686 lights emanate from the apertures of the nose of Arikh Anpin, the pardaska (see above, n.3). Thus PaRDaSKA, which equals 686 (when adding 1 for the word), is the root of the TaRPO lights. (End marginal note.)

Thus, because Yosef guarded the Covenant, he merited prayer—i.e., the TaRPO lights which emanate from Nukva Pardaska/the breath/the source of life/God's holy names.

The significance of the names YHVH and Ehyeh can be understood as follows: The ineffable Tetragrammaton YHVH is often read as HaVaYaH, the Hebrew term for "existence" and "being." Ehyeh means "I will be" (Likutey Moharan I, 6:2). In our context, we can associate YHVH with our praising God for all the good He's already given us, the good already in existence. Ehyeh can be associated with requesting our needs—i.e., our prayers and entreaties for what we hope will be. We see, then, that these two holy names encompass the entire concept of prayer, the breath of life which emanates from Nukva Pardaska.

25. **Reuven...bed.** When Rachel passed away, Yaakov moved his bed to Bilhah's tent. Reuven, Yaakov's firstborn, defended his mother's honor by bringing Yaakov's bed into Leah's tent. Scripture denounces his act as a defiling of Yaakov's bed—i.e., a blemish of the Covenant. As explained, the birthright belongs only to one who guards the Covenant. Therefore, because of what he did, Reuven lost his claim to the birthright. It was subsequently given to Yosef, who did guard the Covenant.

26. **birthright...guarding the brit.** In the lesson, Rebbe Nachman explains the connection between the birthright's double portion and prayer. He does not, however, address why the firstborn deserves a double portion, or what specific significance we derive from the nature of prayer being twofold. Reb Noson takes up these two issues.

who is the aspect of prayer—"if your children will guard My *brit*"[17]—by the means of the aspect of Yosef.[18]

Yosef, who guarded the *brit,* gained the rights of the firstborn.[19] This corresponds to the divine service of prayer,[20] which is an aspect of the double portion [inherited by the firstborn].[21] For prayer is itself twofold, as it is comprised of both praise of God and requesting one's needs.[22] This corresponds to "a double-edged sword in their hand" (Psalms 149:6)[23]—i.e., two edges, a double portion.[24] It was taken from Reuven, because he defiled his father's bed (Genesis 49:4)[25]; for [the birthright] is dependent upon guarding the *brit.*[26]

17. **offspring...Mashiach...brit.** This connection between prayer and *brit* also appears in God's oath to King David regarding his dynasty: "Of your offspring I will set upon your throne, if your children will guard my *brit.*" Prayer—symbolized by Mashiach, an offspring of the House of David—can only be attained through guarding the *brit.*

18. **aspect of Yosef.** As explained, a person who guards the *brit* merits the sword of prayer. This was the level of Yosef. Conversely, one who sins in matters concerning the *brit* has the ability to pray taken away from him.

19. **rights of the firstborn.** The firstborn rights entitle the first child, provided it is a male, to a double portion of the inheritance. Instead of receiving a share of the Land of Israel equal to that of his brothers, Yosef inherited a double portion. His tribe was separated into two: Menashe and Efraim, his two sons. Each received a portion together with all the brothers. Yosef merited this special birthright because he guarded the Covenant.

20. **of prayer.** Divine service included sacrificial offerings, prayer and the duties of the priesthood in general. Traditionally, this was the right of the firstborn. However, because they worshiped the Golden Calf, the firstborns lost this privilege. The divine service was then transferred to the tribe of Levi, who had not participated in the sin (*Rashi,* Numbers 25:13).

21. **inherited by the firstborn.** "He must acknowledge...the firstborn, by giving him a double portion of all that he has...." (Deuteronomy 21:17).

22. **...praise of God...one's needs.** The Talmud states: A person should always begin by praising God, and only then entreat God for his needs (*Avodah Zarah* 7b). The nature of prayer is thus twofold.

23. **double-edged sword....** The Psalmist also speaks of prayer as "doubled" (praise of God and requesting one's needs), likening it to a double-edged sword: "The lofty praises of the Almighty are in their throats, and a doubled-edged sword...."

24. **double portion.** Thus prayer, like the birthright, is a double portion. As was the case with Yosef, one attains it by guarding the Covenant.

The following appears as a marginal note in all the original texts of *Likutey Moharan*: Yosef [because he guarded the Covenant] merited the aspect of prayer, which is "For My praise...*echtom.*" This is the concept of the vitality drawn from *Nukva dePaRDaSKA* (the apertures of the nose). He is therefore called "*ben porat* (a fruitful bough)" (Genesis 49:22). *PORaT* (פורת) corresponds to the *TaRPO* (תרפו = 686) lights which emanate from the seven different expansions of God's holy names *YHVH* and *EHYeH*. *YHVH* has four expansions

ג. וּמִי שֶׁזָּכָה לַחֶרֶב הַזֶּה, צָרִיךְ לֵידַע אֵיךְ לִלְחֹם עִם הַחֶרֶב, שֶׁלֹּא יַטֶּה אוֹתָהּ לְיָמִין אוֹ לִשְׂמֹאל, וְשֶׁיְּהֵא קוֹלֵעַ אֶל הַשַּׂעֲרָה וְלֹא יַחֲטִא:

world. As explained, the birth of new bounty can only be accomplished when there is a means for containing it. This means, or vessel, is created through prayer. Thus, when a person works at creating a vessel, when he puts effort into praying properly, he receives bounty—i.e., the answer to his prayers. Having witnessed the efficacy of his prayers, his faith is strengthened and he prays again and unceasingly, until he sees even more births. Indeed, all subsequent births are easier to come by because of his "firstborn" prayer. Consequently, the birthright is a double portion: the firstborn claims a portion in all subsequent births (*Torat Natan* #10).

Reb Noson also connects this to the Rebbe's statement that a person must achieve the level of guarding the *brit* in order to merit perfected prayer. He writes: Avraham named his son Yishmael, as the angel said, because "God heard your anguish" (Genesis 16:11). In this sense "Yishmael" alludes to the notion that everything we need comes to us because of God's kindness. Although true, it leads to the mistaken conclusion that we need not work to achieve it. If everything is gratis, why bother praying? Esav—who asked, "Why do I need the birthright (prayer)?" (Genesis 25:32)—conversely represents a denial of God, and hence a negation of prayer. "Esav" leaves one asking: Why pray when my prayers are useless? These two perspectives, which must be rejected, are symbolized in the *brit milah* ceremony (cf. *Likutey Moharan* I, 19, n.155). The mitzvah of circumcision has two stages: *milah*, removing the foreskin; and *periyah*, peeling back a thin membrane to reveal the corona. Removing the foreskin without revealing the corona is tantamount to not having performed the circumcision (*Yoreh Deah* 264:4). Symbolically, the foreskin is Esav, that part which is entirely evil and so must be totally rejected and removed. Yishmael is symbolized by the thin membrane that needs to be peeled back so that the corona can be revealed. A person might conclude that it is enough just to remove the foreskin, the evil. This is not so. For even if he is free of outright evil, there is no guarantee that he possesses good. This is why even if *milah* has been performed on the penis (*brit*), *periyah* is still required. Otherwise, the *brit* is considered unguarded (*Torat Natan* #20).

Interestingly, God calls the Jewish people "My firstborn, Israel" (Exodus 4:22), because they were the first to reveal the power of prayer in the world (*Torat Natan* #11). Prior to that, both Yishmael and Esav claimed the birthright for themselves. Just as Yishmael was Avraham's first child, Esav was the first child born to Yitzchak. But, as we have seen, both actually rejected the birthright (prayer). Symbolically, they've come to represent the very antithesis of prayer and are responsible for people abstaining from praying.

In review: The main weapon of Mashiach, and indeed of every single Jew, is prayer (§1). A person cannot come to true prayer unless he first attains the level of guarding the Covenant (§2).

27. ...at a hair and not miss. Scripture describes the exceptional skills of the warriors from the tribe of Binyamin. This same accolade, Rebbe Nachman teaches, can be applied to a person who merits perfected prayer. He guards the Covenant and knows how to direct the sword/prayer in an exacting fashion, without deviating, even in the slightest, to either side. (The concept of sides will be explained shortly).

3. One who is worthy of this sword must understand how to do battle with it. He should not deflect it to the right or to the left, but be able to "strike at a hair and not miss" (Judges 20:16).[27]

He writes: God is constantly providing *shefa* (material and spiritual bounty) for this world. But in order for mankind to receive and contain this *shefa,* they must possess a vessel. This is where prayer comes in. By praying we create vessels for receiving and containing God's bounty. Elsewhere, Rebbe Nachman teaches that prayer and faith are synonymous (see *Likutey Moharan* I, 7:1). Perfected prayer implies perfected faith, and vice versa. Specifically, perfected faith postulates unequivocal belief that God created the world, and that He continuously controls and oversees every aspect of His creation. Everything is under God's dominion, for Him to do as He pleases. Perfected faith also posits unequivocal belief that God hearkens to every plea and prayer a person utters, and that every person has the ability—commensurate with the extent that his prayers are honest and sincere—to have his entreaties answered by God. However, to the degree that this faith is incomplete, the vessel with which to receive the blessings of *shefa* is incomplete and therefore cannot contain the bounty. Accordingly, there are two elements to prayer: praise of God and requesting one's needs. By praising God, a person strengthens his faith in Him. The greater his appreciation of God, the more he praises Him and the more he believes that God answers his requests. This belief, or faith, is the key, because with it the vessel is perfected.

In fact, Reb Noson points out, we go through this process each time we recite the *Amidah* (the Eighteen Benedictions). We begin by recalling the virtues of the three Patriarchs and mentioning God's benevolence. In the merit of the Patriarchs and God's Lovingkindness, we trust that our prayers will be accepted, and that we will also merit seeing the ultimate salvation. This first set of the Eighteen Benedictions is thus essentially praise of God. The next set consists of a series of requests, both personal and national, in which we ask God to provide us with such things as forgiveness, health and healing, prosperity, redemption, etc. In conclusion, we close this middle set with the words, "Blessed are You, God, Who hears prayers." That is, after setting forth God's praise and praying for our needs, we express our faith that God will hear our prayers. In so doing, we create the vessel necessary for receiving the *shefa.*

Of course, achieving this requires much faith and perseverance. Many people become too easily frustrated when they don't see their prayers being answered as swiftly or in the way they would have wanted. This is especially so in the beginning stages of prayer, before a person can pray with full concentration. As a result, many despair of ever seeing the salvation they hoped for and so stop praying for it. But the person who remains steadfast in his efforts *does* get to see the effectiveness of his prayers. And once he does, his faith in God, and in himself—in the efficacy of his prayers—is strengthened. His initial success supplies him with added encouragement and additional faith. God answered him once, why not again? And so he keeps praying, thereby creating the vessel needed to receive Heaven's *shefa.*

From this, Reb Noson says, we can understand why prayer is likened to a firstborn. As the Ari explains, the first sexual union between husband and wife transforms her into a vessel for receiving bounty from him. The births of all their children, and of their firstborn child in particular, are predicated on that first union, with the firstborn taking the spiritual energy of that union and apportioning it to all subsequent offspring (*Shaar HaKavanot, Tzitzit* 1). In our context, having one's prayers answered is like a birth—something new has come into the

וְזֶה אִי אֶפְשָׁר אֶלָּא עַל-יְדֵי בְּחִינַת מִשְׁפָּט, כִּי מִשְׁפָּט הוּא עַמּוּדָא דְּאֶמְצָעִיתָא, הַיְנוּ שֶׁקּוֹלֵעַ עִם כְּלֵי-זֵינוֹ אֶל הַמָּקוֹם הַצָּרִיךְ, וְאֵינוֹ מַטֶּה לְיָמִין וְלֹא לִשְׂמֹאל, אֶלָּא לָאֶמְצַע. וְזֶה בְּחִינַת: "יְכַלְכֵּל דְּבָרָיו בְּמִשְׁפָּט".

וּבִשְׁבִיל זֶה קִבֵּל יוֹסֵף אֶת הַבְּכוֹרָה דַּוְקָא מִיַּעֲקֹב, כְּמוֹ שֶׁכָּתוּב (בראשית מ״ח): "וַאֲנִי נָתַתִּי לְךָ" וְכוּ' – 'אֲנִי' דַּיְקָא, שֶׁהוּא בְּחִינַת מִשְׁפָּט. וְזֶה (תהלים פ״א): "כִּי חֹק לְיִשְׂרָאֵל הוּא", בְּחִינַת בְּרִית, כְּמוֹ שֶׁכָּתוּב: "חֹק בִּשְׁאֵרוֹ שָׂם"; "מִשְׁפָּט לֵאלֹהֵי יַעֲקֹב", הַיְנוּ

---

that since everything is from God, he really doesn't have to do anything. Being that God created all and sustains all, man is therefore totally dependent upon His kindness. If so, why go through the motions of prayer? Concerning this, the Rebbe teaches that we should not turn to the right (the side of *Chesed*, Lovingkindness). Conversely, a person ought not conclude that his prayers are valueless and for naught, God forbid. Every single prayer makes an impression Above; every single word uttered in supplication and pleading to God is very important. Lest a person think that his efforts are in vain, the Rebbe teaches that we should not turn to the left (the side of *Gevurah*, Judgment). Rather, one must judiciously follow the middle path. That is, while realizing that we are totally dependent upon God's kindness, at the same time, we pray to God for all our needs. This is *mishpat*. We have to do ours, by praying as best we can; God, in His kindness, sends us the salvation as He sees fit (*Torat Natan #12*; *Parparaot LeChokhmah*).

32. **d'varav with mishpat.** *D'varav* ("his affairs") can also mean "his speech," from the word *dibur* ("word"). A person must judiciously weigh his speech, his prayers, so as not to turn left or right, but remain centered through *mishpat* (see n.43, below).

33. **Yaakov...aspect of mishpat.** Each of the three Patriarchs personifies a particular trait. Avraham is lovingkindness (*Chesed*); Yitzchak is judgment (*Gevurah*); and Yaakov is balance and beauty (*Tiferet*). As mentioned (n.30), the perfect balance between *Chesed* and *Gevurah* is achieved by means of *Tiferet*. This is Yaakov, *mishpat*, the center pillar. As Rebbe Nachman has explained, the sword/prayer is only attained through guarding the *brit* (*Yesod*), personified by Yosef (see nn.15,18,24). But knowing how to properly use the sword requires *mishpat*. Therefore, Yosef received the birthright specifically from Yaakov; the *brit/Yesod* receiving from *mishpat/Tiferet* (for the positions of these *sefirot* see Appendix: Structure of the Sefirot).

34. **a chok was placed....** This proof-text is from the blessing recited over circumcision (*Shabbat* 137b). The term *chok* thus refers to guarding the *brit*.

35. **Yaakov.** It is a general rule that each lower spiritual level is included in the spiritual level above it. Therefore, Yaakov/*mishpat* also possessed the virtue of Yosef/*brit* (*Rashi*, Genesis 49:3; see also *Likutey Moharan* I, 1, n.55).

And this is impossible[28] without the attribute of *mishpat* (justice).[29] For *mishpat* is the center pillar (Tikkuney Zohar, Introduction 17a).[30] That is, to strike with one's weapon at the precise point, inclining to neither the right nor the left, but at the center.[31] This corresponds to "He orders his *d'varav* (affairs) with *mishpat*" (Psalms 112:5).[32]

{"It is a *chok* (statute) for Israel, a *mishpat* of the Lord of Yaakov" (Psalms 81:5).}

This is the reason Yosef received the rights of the firstborn specifically from Yaakov, as in (Genesis 48:22), "I have given you...." "*I*," < because Yaakov is > the aspect of *mishpat*.[33] And this is: "It is a *chok* for Israel." < "*Chok*" > suggests *brit*, as in (Shabbat 137b): A *chok* was placed on his flesh.[34] [Therefore,] "...a *mishpat* of the Lord of Yaakov."[35] Yosef must receive this sword from the aspect of *mishpat*,

---

28. **this is impossible.** To direct one's prayers accurately.

29. **mishpat, justice.** A person who guards the Covenant and has perfected his faith in prayer merits the sword of prayer (see n.26). This weapon is so potent, that the Talmud sees fit to issue a warning: "It is not good for a tzaddik to punish others" (rephrasing of Proverbs 17:26; see *Berakhot* 7a). By means of his prayers, the tzaddik has the power to mete out judgment against whomever he desires, and so must be careful. Alternatively, he might use his power of prayer to bring about salvation for those unworthy or unready for it (as was Avraham's prayer for Yishmael, which God bemoans daily; see *Maharsha, Sukkah* 52b, *s.v. Yishmaelim*; cf. *Zohar* II, 32a). In that case, his prayers are the cause of ruination, not rectification (*Be'Ibey HaNachal*). What is needed, therefore, is *mishpat*—justice in the sense of true and properly balanced judgment (see next note).

30. **mishpat...center pillar.** In the terminology of the Kabbalah, the name of each *sefirah* indicates its function: *Chesed* (Lovingkindness) manifests benevolence, *Gevurah* (Strength) manifests strict judgments, and so on. But these attributes are not always absolute. Frequently there are extenuating circumstances which moderate the judgment of the guilty, just as there are often ulterior motives which minimize the credit due for acts of kindness. Thus, for proper justice to be done, one needs a balance between *Chesed* and *Gevurah*, between lenience and severity. The *sefirah* in which this is manifested is *Tiferet*, the nucleus of the center column of the *sefirot* (see Appendix: The Structure of the Sefirot). More precisely, the balancing element within *Tiferet* is the quality of *mishpat* (*Tikkuney Zohar*, Introduction p.17b). Perhaps a less abstract way to clarify this is by considering these concepts as they relate to the Patriarchs (see below, n.33). Avraham, the embodiment of *Chesed*, fathered Yishmael—who inclined too far to the side of kindness. Yitzchak, the embodiment of *Gevurah*, fathered Esav—who inclined too far to the side of judgment. It took Yaakov, the balancing center pillar, to father the twelve righteous sons from whom the Jewish people descended (*Biur HaLikutim*).

31. **right...left...center.** Rebbe Nachman has already spoken about praise of God and requesting one's needs, the two elements of prayer. Reb Noson explained this as God's having created the world and His ability to rule it as He pleases, while at the same time encouraging man to pray for his needs as if he thereby controls the bounty he receives (n.26). Here, we have another dimension to this "double-edged sword." A person might conclude

שֶׁצָּרִיךְ יוֹסֵף לְקַבֵּל זֹאת הַחֶרֶב מִבְּחִינַת מִשְׁפָּט, כְּדֵי שֶׁיְכַלְכֵּל
דְּבָרָיו בַּמִּשְׁפָּט. וְזֶה: "מִשְׁפָּטֶיךָ לְמֶלֶךְ תֵּן". שֶׁמָּשִׁיחַ יְקַבֵּל
מִבְּחִינַת מִשְׁפָּט:

ד וְעַל יְדֵי מַה זוֹכֶה לִבְחִינַת מִשְׁפָּט? עַל יְדֵי צְדָקָה. שֶׁעַל יְדֵי
צְדָקָה אוֹחֲזִין בְּמִדַּת הַמִּשְׁפָּט, כְּמוֹ שֶׁכָּתוּב: "צְדָקַת ה' עָשָׂה
וּמִשְׁפָּטָיו". וּכְמוֹ שֶׁכָּתוּב: "מִשְׁפָּט וּצְדָקָה בְּיַעֲקֹב" וְכוּ'.
כִּי צְדָקָה הוּא עַל יְדֵי מִשְׁפָּט, כְּמוֹ שֶׁכָּתוּב: "אֱלֹהִים שׁוֹפֵט, זֶה
יַשְׁפִּיל וְזֶה יָרִים". שֶׁמּוֹרִישׁ לָזֶה, וּמַעֲשִׁיר לָזֶה. וּכְשֶׁנּוֹתֵן צְדָקָה
הוּא בִּבְחִינַת 'זֶה יַשְׁפִּיל', שֶׁמְּחַסֵּר מָמוֹנוֹ, וּבִבְחִינַת וְזֶה יָרִים,
שֶׁמַּעֲשִׁיר לֶעָנִי. נִמְצָא, שֶׁאוֹחֵז עַל יְדֵי זֶה בְּמִדַּת מִשְׁפָּט:

worshipped the Golden Calf, or sent the spies, or any of the other instances in which they angered God and so deserved severe punishment, Moshe found merit in the Jews and judiciously presented their case before God. As a result, his pleas were accepted and the Jewish people were spared. Scripture indicates that Moshe's compassion for the Jewish people was a supreme act of charity, God's charity, and an application of the quality of *mishpat*.

39. **You execute mishpat and charity....** This Psalm refers to the days of Mashiach, when God's Kingdom will be revealed (*Metzudat David*, Psalms 99:1). The subject of the verse quoted here is the Torah's commandments, the mitzvot. They are a balance; their essence is justice and charity (*ibid.* v.4). In our context, this indicates that Mashiach's prayers, through which he will conquer the entire world and bring it under God's Kingdom, will adhere to the principal of "orders his words with *mishpat*."

40. **charity...product of mishpat.** That is, by exercising justice and judiciousness, charity is performed. Rebbe Nachman now shows why the act of charity is equated with executing *mishpat*.

41. **...impoverishes...enriches....** This is based on the Midrashic reading of the verse. When two people of different stations and classes are destined to marry, God judges how best to bring them together. He might impoverish one, or enrich the other. Sometimes, He even takes from one person's wealth and gives it to another so as to facilitate a match between them (see *Bereishit Rabbah* 68:4). Reb Noson adds that by sympathizing with the pain of the poor man and giving him charity, a person can rid himself of arrogance and come to humility. Humbling oneself and elevating another is in essence executing *mishpat* (*Torat Natan* #18).

42. **...mishpat.** As the Rebbe has shown, giving charity is literally executing *mishpat*. And through *mishpat*, one knows how to do battle with his sword (see §3).

so that he might "order his words with *mishpat*."[36] This is the meaning of (Psalms 72:1), "O Lord, give Your *mishpatim* to the king" — i.e., that Mashiach will receive from the aspect of *mishpat*.[37]

4. And how does one merit the aspect of *mishpat?* through charity. In giving charity one embraces the attribute of *mishpat*. As it is written (Deuteronomy 33:21), "He executed the charity of God and His *mishpatim*"[38]; and as in (Psalms 99:4), "You execute *mishpat* and charity in Yaakov."[39]

For charity < is itself > a product of *mishpat*,[40] as in (Psalms 75:8), "The Lord is judge, He brings down one and lifts up another" — He impoverishes one and enriches another.[41] And when a person gives charity, he corresponds to "brings down one < and lifts up another >." < He "brings down one," > because he subtracts from his own money; and he "lifts up another," because he enriches the poor man. Consequently, through this he embraces the attribute of *mishpat*.[42]

In the previous section (§2), Rebbe Nachman showed the connection between *brit* and prayer. In this section, he has introduced *mishpat* and shown how Yosef receives from Yaakov, for "I [Yaakov] have given you [Yosef]...." By quoting this verse from Psalms (81:5), which includes the words *chok...mishpat...*Yaakov, the Rebbe has directly connected *mishpat* to the *brit* (in addition to the connection through Yaakov and Yosef).

36. **Yosef...sword...mishpat.** With this, Rebbe Nachman sums up the lesson to this point, showing how all the concepts interconnect. Yosef/the *brit* must receive his power of prayer/ the sword from Yaakov/*mishpat* so that he might order and set out his words of prayer judiciously. By doing so, his prayers are beneficial for all (see n.29).

37. **king...Mashiach...mishpat.** "The king" in this verse is an allusion to Mashiach (*Targum Yonatan, loc. cit.*). This proof-text establishes the link between Mashiach and *mishpat*, showing that even Mashiach must draw his weapon of prayer from *mishpat*. In the next section, Rebbe Nachman will show how it is possible to acquire the attribute of *mishpat*.

Below (§6), Rebbe Nachman will explain that Moshe and Mashiach are one and the same aspect. The Ari teaches that Moshe is also called king, as in (Deuteronomy 33:5), "He was a king in Yeshurun" (*Sefer HaGilgulim*, 13).

In review: The main weapon of Mashiach, and indeed of every single Jew, is prayer (§1). However, a person cannot come to true prayer unless he first attains the level of guarding the Covenant (§2). And even when one guards the *brit* and attains the power of prayer, he still needs the attribute of *mishpat*. That is, his weapon (prayer) must be wielded judiciously (§3).

38. **He executed the charity...mishpatim.** Rashi explains the verse as speaking about Moshe (*loc. cit.*). Whenever the Jewish people sinned, Moshe prayed on their behalf. When they

וּבִשְׁבִיל זֶה צָרִיךְ לְהַפְרִישׁ צְדָקָה קֹדֶם הַתְּפִלָּה, כְּדֵי שֶׁיּוּכַל לְכַלְכֵּל
דְּבָרָיו בְּמִשְׁפָּט. שֶׁיְּהֵא קוֹלֵעַ אֶל הַשַּׂעֲרָה וְלֹא יַחֲטָא:

וְזֶה שֶׁאָמְרוּ חֲכָמֵינוּ, זִכְרוֹנָם לִבְרָכָה: 'לָמָה נָתַן יַעֲקֹב אֶת הַבְּכוֹרָה
לְיוֹסֵף? בִּשְׁבִיל שֶׁכִּלְכֵּל אוֹתוֹ. מָשָׁל לְבַעַל הַבַּיִת שֶׁגִּדֵּל יָתוֹם
בְּתוֹךְ בֵּיתוֹ' וְכוּ'...

כְּמוֹ שֶׁכָּתוּב: "וַיְכַלְכֵּל יוֹסֵף אֶת אָבִיו וְאֶת אֶחָיו לֶחֶם לְפִי הַטָּף".
כְּמוֹ: "הַטֵּף אֶל דָּרוֹם" (לְשׁוֹן דִּבּוּר) "לְפִי הַטָּף", הַיְנוּ שֶׁהָיָה
שָׁגוּרָה תְּפִלָּתוֹ בְּפִיו עַל־יְדֵי הַצְּדָקָה, וְעַל יְדֵי הַצְּדָקָה שֶׁעָשָׂה, נָתַן
לוֹ יַעֲקֹב, שֶׁהוּא בְּחִינַת מִשְׁפָּט, אֶת הַבְּכוֹרָה שֶׁהוּא בְּחִינַת תְּפִלָּה,
כְּמוֹ שֶׁכָּתוּב: "וַאֲנִי נָתַתִּי לְךָ שְׁכֶם", 'אֲנִי' דַּיְקָא, שֶׁהוּא בְּחִינַת
מִשְׁפָּט:

ה וְעִקָּר שֶׁל הַמַּחֲשָׁבוֹת זָרוֹת הֵם עַל־יְדֵי קִלְקוּל הַמִּשְׁפָּט, כִּי

46. **lephiy...lips.** The root of the word *lephiy* is *PeH* (mouth). In the context of our lesson, the verse thus reads: **Yosef provided his father...with bread** — because Yosef performed charity, he merited **lephiy hataf** — a mouth that speaks and orders the words of prayer with ease.

47. **charitable deed...the aspect of mishpat.** Reb Noson writes that charity is itself considered guarding the Covenant. This is because, on the physical level, when one guards the Covenant, he gives his bounty exclusively to the one worthy recipient, his spouse. This is similar to giving charity: one gives from his own bounty to a worthy recipient (see also *Likutey Moharan* I, 264). In our context, therefore, performing charity is guarding the Covenant. By executing *mishpat* in this way, he can direct his prayers properly (*Torat Natan #13*). Furthermore, the essence of *mishpat* is truth (see n.29). Thus it is particularly Yaakov who personifies truth, as in (Micah 7:20), "Give truth to Yaakov." A person must make certain to perform his deeds of charity with truth (*Torat Natan #15*; see *Likutey Moharan* I, 251:2).

In review: The main weapon of Mashiach, and indeed of every single Jew, is prayer (§1). However, a person cannot come to true prayer unless he first attains the level of guarding the Covenant (§2). And even when one guards the *brit* and attains the power of prayer, he still needs the attribute of *mishpat*. That is, his weapon (prayer) must be wielded judiciously (§3). To attain *mishpat*, he must give charity (§4).

48. **corruption of mishpat.** As explained, by giving charity a person merits *mishpat*. This is especially so when the charity is given before praying. His prayers then flow easily and hit their mark. The question Rebbe Nachman addresses next is, How is it that a person who has

This is the reason it is necessary to donate charity before praying; so that he will "*y'KhaLKeiL d'varav* (order his words) with *mishpat*" — he can "strike at a hair and not miss."[43]

Our Sages taught: **Why did Yaakov give the rights of the firstborn to Yosef? because he provided for him. This is like the parable of the householder who supported an orphan in his home...** (*Bava Batra* 123a).[44]

It is written (Genesis 47:12), "And Yosef *y'KhaLKeiL* (provided)[45] his father and brethren and all his father's household with bread, *lephiy hataf* (according to their little ones)." {The word "*HaTaF*" also denotes speech,} as in (Ezekiel 21:2), "*HaTeiF* (preach) to the south." *Lephiy hataf* indicates that [Yosef's] prayers flowed from his lips.[46] And, because of [Yosef's] charitable deed, Yaakov, the aspect of *mishpat,* granted him the rights of the firstborn — the aspect of prayer. As is written, "I [Yaakov,] have given you one portion...." Specifically "*I,*" for he is the aspect of *mishpat.*[47]

5. Now, the main cause of foreign thoughts < during prayer > is the corruption of *mishpat.*[48] For *mishpat is an aspect of AYNin (eyes),* as

---

43. **donate charity before praying....** See *Bava Batra* 10a; *Orach Chaim* 92:10. One can give this charity before praying by placing a few coins in a charity box in his home. Or, he can do so in the synagogue before beginning his prayers.

By giving charity prior to praying, one executes *mishpat.* He can then wield his sword — direct his prayers — so that he strikes at precisely the center and core of his target. This is why when a person gives charity before praying, his prayers flow easily from his lips. Giving charity prevents extraneous thoughts from disturbing his prayer. This allows him to pray properly; not turning his prayer to the right or the left. Rather, he is able to order his words judiciously, with *mishpat* (*Mai HaNachal*; see note 32).

44. **Our Sages....** The passage reads: Why did Yaakov give the rights of the firstborn to Yosef? because Yosef provided for him in Egypt. This is like the parable of the householder (Yosef) who supported an orphan (Yaakov) in his home. (For Yaakov was without food, which Yosef provided.) Eventually the orphan (Yaakov) became wealthy (he reacquired the birthright, for Reuven lost it and Yaakov could give it to whomever he wished) and said, "Let me benefit the householder with my possessions" (*Bava Batra* 123a, with *Rashbam's* commentary). The *Be'Ibey HaNachal* explains that this is the charity and *mishpat* that Rebbe Nachman just referred to. The "possessions" were the rights of the firstborn. Reuven lost them because he defiled his father's bed. He was lowered in stature, or impoverished, by Yaakov/*mishpat.* On the other hand, Yosef, by guarding the Covenant, became worthy of the birthright. Therefore, he was elevated in stature, or enriched, by Yaakov/*mishpat.* For once the birthright was taken from Reuven, Yaakov/*mishpat* was able to grant it to whomever he wished.

45. **y'KhaLKeiL, provided.** This is similar to "*y'KhaLKeiL* (order) his words." Because Yosef performed charity he merited ordering his words, the quality of *mishpat.*

מִשְׁפָּט הוּא בְּחִינַת עֵינַיִן. כְּמוֹ שֶׁכָּתוּב: "וַיָּבֹאוּ אֶל עֵין מִשְׁפָּט".
זֶה בְּחִינַת: "עֵין יַעֲקֹב".

וְעַל־יְדֵי קִלְקוּל מִשְׁפָּט בָּא קִלְקוּל לָעֵינַיִן, כְּמוֹ שֶׁכָּתוּב: "כִּי הַשֹּׁחַד
יְעַוֵּר עֵינֵי חֲכָמִים", זֶה בְּחִינַת מַחֲשָׁבוֹת זָרוֹת שֶׁבַּתְּפִלָּה, שֶׁהֵם עֲנָנִין
דִּמְכַסְּיָן עַל עֵינַיִן, כְּמוֹ שֶׁכָּתוּב (איכה ג): "סַכֹּתָה בֶעָנָן לָךְ" וְכוּ'.

וּלְעָתִיד שֶׁיִּתָּקֵּן בְּחִינַת מִשְׁפָּט, כְּמוֹ שֶׁכָּתוּב: "צִיּוֹן בְּמִשְׁפָּט
תִּפָּדֶה". אֲזַי יִתְעַבֵּר עֲנָנִין דִּמְכַסְּיָן עַל עֵינָא. כְּמוֹ שֶׁכָּתוּב: "כִּי עַיִן
בְּעַיִן יִרְאוּ בְּשׁוּב ה' צִיּוֹן", וּבִשְׁבִיל זֶה נִקְרָא יוֹסֵף: "בֵּן פֹּרָת עֲלֵי
עָיִן":

Amos prayed that bounty descend for the Jewish people gratis, even when they sinned (*Makkot* 24a). Ayn Yaakov thus corresponds to corrupting *mishpat* by inclining it to the right side. From these proof-texts concerning the *ayin* (eye) we can also understand why Rebbe Nachman equates prayer specifically to the nose. Like the nose, which is in the center of the face and between the two eyes, prayer must be centered, balanced perfectly between right and left.

50. **bribery blinds....** It is forbidden for a judge to allow himself to be influenced in any way whatsoever. Even in a clear case where he can exonerate the innocent and charge the guilty, taking a bribe prejudices his decision—i.e., corrupts his sense of *mishpat*. Thus the verse Rebbe Nachman quotes refers to the blinding, or blemishing, of the eyes.

51. **clouds covering the eyes.** That is, when *mishpat* is blemished—when the eyes are beclouded—a person is distracted by foreign thoughts which obstruct his prayers. This is because the words of prayer can only be ordered properly if one has the quality of *mishpat* (as in §3).

52. **cloud...not pass through.** The *Zohar* teaches: The clouds that cover a person's eyes, spiritually obscuring his sight, correspond to the *kelipot* (forces of evil) that stop the prayers from ascending (*Tikkuney Zohar #21, p.50b*). Reb Noson explains further, that in our context these *kelipot*/clouds are Esav and Yishmael, the detractors who corrupt *mishpat* (*Torat Natan #19*).

53. **Zion...mishpat....** That is, by means of charity, they will be able to execute proper *mishpat*. Then, "Zion shall be redeemed." In the Kabbalah, Zion is identified with the *sefirah* of *Yesod,* the *brit*. Thus, giving charity rectifies *mishpat,* and so redeems prayer for those who have attained the level of guarding the *brit* (cf. *Biur HaLikutim; Mai HaNachal*). Moreover, attaining *mishpat* by giving charity enables a person to attain the level of guarding the *brit* (n.47), and so rectify his prayers.

54. **for eye to eye....** At that time, there will no longer be any clouded or unclear vision of Godliness. Rather, we will be able to concentrate totally on the words of prayer as we recite them, and do so without any doubt as to Whom we are praying. This is as the Rebbe once

in (Genesis 14:7), "They came to AYN Mishpat." This corresponds to "[Israel will dwell securely, apart,] AYN Yaakov..." (Deuteronomy 33:28).[49]

And through the corruption of < the > *mishpat,* the eyes are impaired, as in (Deuteronomy 16:19), "For bribery blinds the eyes of the wise."[50] This is the concept of foreign thoughts during prayer. They are like clouds covering the eyes,[51] as is written (Lamentations 3:44), "[God,] You have covered Yourself with a cloud, so that prayer should not pass through."[52]

But in the Future, the concept of *mishpat* shall be restored, as in (Isaiah 1:27), "Zion shall be redeemed through *mishpat* < and her captives through charity > ."[53] Then, the clouds that cover the eyes will pass, as in (*ibid.* 52:8), "for eye to eye they will see God returning to Zion."[54] And this is why Yosef is called *"bein porat aley AYiN* (a

given charity still encounters distracting thoughts and has difficulty praying? He explains here that these foreign thoughts stem from *mishpat* which is lacking or corrupted (*Mai HaNachal*). One way this happens, as indicated in the previous note, is by giving charity to unworthy causes. This corrupts *mishpat,* causing foreign thoughts to disturb one's prayers.

This was why in his dream, Reb Shmuel Isaac found himself surrounded by clouds. He had yet to perfect his personal level of *mishpat.* It is known, however, that years later Reb Shmuel Isaac achieved a truly incredible level of concentration and devotion in his prayers. Reb Noson said about him, "The Rebbe led Reb Shmuel Isaac on the edge of the sword." Reb Shmuel Isaac himself was heard saying, "If today I pray the *Shema* as I did yesterday, I no longer have any reason to live" (*Oral Tradition*).

49. **AYN Mishpat...AYN Yaakov.** Generally, *AYiN* is "an eye," but it also means "a well" — the Well of Mishpat, the Well of Yaakov. In our lesson, Rebbe Nachman brings two verses, one connecting *ayin* to *mishpat,* the other connecting *ayin* to Yaakov. The Rebbe goes on to explain that spiritually perfecting one's eyes is akin to perfecting *mishpat.* Conversely, a spiritual obfuscating of the power of sight corresponds to a corruption of *mishpat.*

Though *mishpat* and Yaakov are one and the same (§3), Rebbe Nachman brings two proof-texts: "Ayn Mishpat" and "Ayn Yaakov." This is because the detractors of *mishpat* are two: the right and the left. The first verse refers to a place known as Ayn Mishpat, the site where the four kings battled the five kings (Genesis, *loc. cit.*). Rashi explains there that its name was derived from an event that would only take place in the future, as that was where Moshe and Aharon would turn the rock into a well by striking it instead of speaking to it — a display of imbalanced *mishpat.* Ayn Mishpat thus corresponds to corrupting *mishpat* by inclining it to the left side. The second proof the Rebbe brings refers to Ayn Yaakov: "Israel will dwell securely, apart, Ayn Yaakov in a land of grain and wine. Your heavens shall also drip with dew" (*loc. cit.*). However, Scripture qualified its promise of abundant blessing for the Jewish people; they would only receive it when all of them were united and righteous. Unfortunately, such a perfected state has proven to be as rare as it is lofty. With the passage of time and the realization that the nation was falling away from this ideal rather than drawing closer to it, the prophet

ו. וְצָרִיךְ כָּל אֶחָד לְכַוֵּן בִּתְפִלָּתוֹ, שֶׁיְּקַשֵּׁר עַצְמוֹ לַצַּדִּיקִים שֶׁבַּדּוֹר,
כִּי כָּל צַדִּיק שֶׁבַּדּוֹר הוּא בְּחִינַת מֹשֶׁה מָשִׁיחַ, כְּמוֹ שֶׁמָּצִינוּ,
שֶׁהַצַּדִּיקִים קוֹרִין זֶה לָזֶה מֹשֶׁה, כְּמוֹ 'מֹשֶׁה שַׁפִּיר קָאֲמַרְתְּ': וּמֹשֶׁה
זֶה בְּחִינַת מָשִׁיחַ, כְּמוֹ שֶׁכָּתוּב: "עַד כִּי יָבֹא שִׁילֹה" – 'דָּא מֹשֶׁה
מָשִׁיחַ'.

וְכָל תְּפִלָּה וּתְפִלָּה שֶׁכָּל אֶחָד מִתְפַּלֵּל הוּא בְּחִינַת אֵיבָר מֵהַשְּׁכִינָה,
שֶׁהֵם אֵבְרֵי הַמִּשְׁכָּן, שֶׁאֵין אֶחָד שׁוּם אֶחָד מִיִּשְׂרָאֵל יָכוֹל לְאַעֲלָא שִׁיפָא

entails giving charity to tzaddikim and in general having them benefit from one's possessions (*Ketuvot* 111b). Another explanation, found throughout Reb Noson's writings, is that a person should simply *attach* himself to the tzaddik's teachings by studying them and following their directives. Doing so binds one to the tzaddik. See *Crossing the Narrow Bridge*, Chapter 17, pp.326-334, where this concept of binding oneself to the tzaddik and its application are explained in greater depth.

57. **Moshe, you said it well.** This is how the leading Sages of the Talmud would compliment one another. They would refer to each other as Moshe, the implication being: "You are to your generation what Moshe was to his" (*Rashi, loc. cit.*). In our lesson, we have seen that the tzaddikim of every generation are an aspect of Mashiach, for they draw their power from Mashiach (see n.4). The Rebbe teaches here that Mashiach and Moshe are one concept. See next note.

58. **Shilo...Moshe....** Quoting Onkelos, Rashi comments that Shiloh is another name for Mashiach. ShILoH (שילה) and MoShE (משה) both have a numerical value of 345 (see Appendix: Gematria Chart).

The words "until Shiloh will come" are part of Yaakov's blessing to Yehudah that, starting with King David and until the Mashiach, the royal dynasty would be solely from Yehudah's descendants (*Rashi, loc. cit.*). Being that Shiloh corresponds to Moshe (in *gematria*), and that Shiloh is Mashiach, we can draw a connection between Moshe and Mashiach—the concept of Moshe-Mashiach (see below, §8; *Likutey Moharan* I, 9:4), from which all the tzaddikim draw their power.

After beginning the lesson by discussing the significance of an individual's prayer, Rebbe Nachman now turns to another of prayer's dimensions: one's words and requests being bound to the tzaddik so that they can ascend to their proper place together with all the prayers of the Jewish people. As will be explained, this is symbolized in the Torah's account of the erection of the holy Tabernacle. Everyone took part. But it was only Moshe, the tzaddik of the generation, who was capable of assembling the Tabernacle properly.

59. **Tabernacle.** God issued numerous and precise instructions for how the Tabernacle was to be built. Each Jew contributed. Some provided materials, others donated their skills. In some cases, a single person contributed an entire part on his own. In other cases, a number of people jointly contributed a single part. Together, *they* provided all the components for the construction of the Tabernacle. Once built, it was to serve as an abode for the Holy

fruitful bough by the well)" (Genesis 49:22).[55]

6. < Therefore, before praying > it is necessary for each individual to < attach himself to the true > tzaddikim of the generation.[56] For each < true > tzaddik is an aspect < of Mashiach, an aspect of Moshe >. Thus we find the tzaddikim addressing each other as Moshe (*Shabbat* 101b): "Moshe, you said it well."[57] Also, Moshe is identified with Mashiach, as in (Genesis 49:10), "until Shiloh will come" — this is Moshe, < as they have the same numerical value > (*Zohar* I, 25b).[58]

And every single prayer that each person prays is a < separate > component of the *Shekhinah* (Divine Presence). They correspond to the components of the Tabernacle.[59] There was no one in Israel who

said, "Mashiach will have to work perseveringly just to bring a single pure *Amidah* prayer into the world" (*Siach Sarfei Kodesh* 1-20).

Targum Yonatan reads this verse as: "They sing praise together, for those who *served* the Lord will see with their eyes God's return to Zion." Earlier in the lesson (§2 and n.20), Rebbe Nachman associated Divine service with prayer. Moreover, as *Mai HaNachal* explains, this reading ties in with what the Rebbe will shortly explain, that all rectified prayers come together and unite to become the weapon with which Mashiach conquers the world.

55. **Yosef...aley AYiN.** When one merits guarding the *brit* through the quality of *mishpat*, he has the ability to overcome the clouds that impair his vision. Like Yosef, he is "*aley AYiN*" (literally, above the eye), above a clouded vision. He can therefore direct his prayers to the target. This is why Yosef, who also attained *mishpat*, merited the *tarpo* (686) lights mentioned in note 24. There is also another connection that Yosef has with the two proof-texts which the Rebbe just quoted. As explained above, Yosef personified guarding the *brit* and so corresponds to the *sefirah* of Yesod. Both verses from Isaiah speak of Zion, which, as mentioned (n.53), also corresponds to Yesod. Zion (ציון) also has the same numerical value as Yosef (יוסף).

56. **attach himself to the true tzaddikim....** We've seen that the main weapon of every Jew is prayer (see §§1 and 2, and n.13). Yet, it is impossible to achieve perfection in prayer without perfectly guarding the *brit,* something which takes a great deal of effort and self-mastery. If so, how can people ever attain their salvation if their prayers are lacking? Rebbe Nachman's answer is that each individual must bind his prayers to the tzaddikim of the generation, for they are the true guardians of the *brit.* They alone know how to raise up each prayer to its proper place.

Attaching oneself to the tzaddikim is a concept that many people find foreign and difficult to understand. Actually, this idea appears in the earliest teachings of our Sages. They taught: Scripture states, "Attach yourselves to Him" (Deuteronomy 11:22). Is it possible to attach oneself to the *Shekhinah* (Divine Presence)? It is not. Rather, attach yourself to Torah scholars and tzaddikim, and it will be as if you attached yourself to Him (*Sifri, ad. loc.; Rashi, ad. loc.*). What does "Attach yourselves" mean? One opinion brought in the Talmud is that it

בְּשַׁיְפָא כָּל חַד לְדוּכְתֵּיהּ, אֶלָּא מֹשֶׁה בִּלְחוֹד, בִּשְׁבִיל זֶה צָרִיךְ
לְהָבִיא וּלְקַשֵּׁר כָּל הַתְּפִלּוֹת לְצַדִּיק הַדּוֹר, כְּמוֹ שֶׁכָּתוּב: "וַיָּבִיאוּ
אֶת הַמִּשְׁכָּן אֶל מֹשֶׁה". וְהוּא יוֹדֵעַ לְאַעֲלָא שַׁיְפָא בְּשַׁיְפָא וְלַעֲשׂוֹת
אוֹתָהּ קוֹמָה שְׁלֵמָה, כְּמוֹ שֶׁכָּתוּב: "וַיָּקֶם מֹשֶׁה אֶת הַמִּשְׁכָּן".

וְכָל הַתּוֹרָה שֶׁאָדָם לוֹמֵד לִשְׁמֹר וְלַעֲשׂוֹת, כָּל הָאוֹתִיּוֹת הֵם נִיצוֹצֵי

indicate that it is Moshe who corresponds to *Tiferet*. Further study reveals that Moshe parallels the inner essence (*neshamah*) of *Tiferet*, whereas Yaakov parallels its outer aspect (body). In other words, Moshe signifies the attribute of *Tiferet/mishpat* on an even more perfected level than Yaakov. In addition, as just explained, Moshe is Mashiach, the true tzaddik, who also corresponds to *Yesod*, the *brit*. The Tabernacle, meanwhile, corresponds to *Malkhut* (*Zohar* II, 238b). Thus, in the context of our lesson, Moshe is the tzaddik/*brit* who merited prayer/*Malkhut*/Tabernacle. How did he merit this? through *mishpat*. It was therefore Moshe who judged the Jewish people daily (Exodus 18:16).

The *Zohar* speaks of another aspect (other than *gematria*) that Moshe and Mashiach have in common: a unique power to judge. As explained, Mashiach will have the power to judge by means of his sense of smell (above, n.8). Moshe's capacity to judge was also singular. Blessed with having the *Shekhinah* accompany him at all times, Moshe was able to judge by sight. Just by looking at someone, he was immediately able to discern whether that person was telling the truth and thereby pass true judgment (*Zohar* II, 78a). In our context, Moshe's perfected sight alludes to a perfected quality of justice, when there is no beclouding of the eyes (§5). We can therefore understand why only Moshe, the tzaddik—by virtue of his having attained the level of perfected *mishpat*—was able to erect the Tabernacle. He alone knew where each part—each prayer—belonged.

In review: The main weapon of Mashiach, and indeed of every single Jew, is prayer (§1). However, a person cannot come to true prayer unless he first attains the level of guarding the Covenant (§2). And even when one guards the *brit* and attains the power of prayer, he still needs the attribute of *mishpat*. That is, his weapon (prayer) must be wielded judiciously (§3). To attain *mishpat*, he must give charity (§4). Conversely, the major disturbances to one's prayers, one's foreign thoughts and lack of concentration, stem from a corrupted sense of *mishpat* (§5). And to ensure that one's prayers are accepted, one must bind himself to the tzaddikim. They alone know how to elevate each prayer to its proper place (§6).

63. **observing and fulfilling.** For this is the main purpose of Torah study—observing the mitzvot, fulfilling them to the best of one's abilities. In adding this clarification, Rebbe Nachman excludes those whose study of Torah is not for the purpose of observing, but merely an intellectual pursuit.

64. **sparks of souls.** The intellect is often identified as the seat of the soul within the human body (cf. *Likutey Moharan* I, 61:3). This is especially true of the intellect one acquires from any wisdom or insight that brings a person closer to God. Primarily, therefore, it is the study of Torah that gives a person this kind of intellect. When a person studies Torah with the

was able to place all the various parts in their proper positions, just Moshe alone.[60] For this reason it is necessary to bring and bind all prayers to the < tzaddikim > of the generation, as is written (Exodus 39:33), "They brought the Tabernacle to Moshe."[61] He is the one who understands how to connect one part to the next and so erect the complete structure, as in (ibid. 40:18), "Moshe erected the Tabernacle."[62]

7. Now, all the Torah a person studies for the purpose of observing and fulfilling[63]—all these letters are sparks of souls,[64] and they are

Shekhinah (see Exodus 39:32-43). A similar process occurs in the upper worlds. All the different prayers of the Jewish people are components for the building of exquisite spiritual chambers Above. God's Divine Presence, which is *Malkhut* (see Appendix: The Divine Persona), dwells in them. When the moment arrives that all these structures are completed, they will descend to this world as the Third Temple (*Torat Natan #22*; *Rabbi Yaakov Meir Shechter*).

60. **just Moshe alone.** As Scripture relates, the task of assembling all the parts of the Tabernacle belonged exclusively to Moshe (see Exodus 40:2,18). See next note.

61. **Tabernacle to Moshe.** Although all work on the parts of the Tabernacle had been completed, when the Jews tried to piece it together, they couldn't. They came to Moshe and he assembled it (*Rashi, loc. cit.*). Had the Jews insisted on assembling the Tabernacle themselves, they could not have succeeded. All the physical strength and expertise in the world would have made no difference. Rather, simply by attaching their work to Moshe, their efforts were rewarded. The structure was completed and God's glory filled the Tabernacle (cf. Exodus 40:33,34). So, too, when people attempt to direct their prayers to God on their own, without attachment to the tzaddikim, they run the risk of having their efforts prove in vain. If, on the other hand, they bind their prayers to the tzaddikim, the tzaddikim will direct each prayer to its proper place Above. In so doing, they build the structure of the *Shekhinah* and hasten the coming of Mashiach.

Someone once asked Reb Noson, "Who is greater? The simple person who attaches himself to a tzaddik, or the person who is great in his own right?" Reb Noson answered, "When a person contributed even something great to the Tabernacle, if he did not bring it to Moshe, it was not acceptable. But even the smallest, most insignificant contribution, once brought to Moshe, took on great value" (*Aveneha Barzel* p.74, #62).

Accordingly, before praying Breslover Chassidim are accustomed to recite the following passage: I hereby bind myself, for the purpose of this prayer, to all the true tzaddikim in our generation, and to all the true tzaddikim who "dwell in the earth"—i.e., the holy ones who have passed on. In particular, I bind myself to the tzaddik who is the foundation of the world, *Nachal Novea Mekor Chokhmah*, Rebbe Nachman the son of Feiga, may his merit protect us and all Israel, Amen. (Cf. *Rabbi Nachman's Wisdom #296.*)

62. **Moshe erected the Tabernacle.** We have seen above that Yaakov corresponds to *Tiferet* (n.33). At the same time, there are numerous statements throughout the holy writings which

נְשָׁמוֹת, וְהֵם נִתְלַבְּשִׁים בְּתוֹךְ הַתְּפִלָּה, וְנִתְחַדְּשִׁים שָׁם בִּבְחִינַת

עִבּוּר. (כַּמּוּבָא בַּגִּלְגּוּלִים, שֶׁכָּל הַנְּשָׁמוֹת בָּאִים בְּתוֹךְ הַמַּלְכוּת בִּבְחִינַת עִבּוּר

וְנִתְחַדְּשִׁים שָׁם).

וְזֶהוּ: "הַשָּׁמַיִם מְסַפְּרִים כְּבוֹד אֵל", הַיְנוּ הַתּוֹרָה שֶׁהוּא אֵשׁ וּמַיִם,

הַיְנוּ בְּחִינַת הַנְּשָׁמוֹת. וּבָאִים בְּתוֹךְ הַתְּפִלָּה, שֶׁהוּא בְּחִינַת כְּבוֹד

אֵל, כְּמוֹ שֶׁכָּתוּב: "שִׂימוּ כָבוֹד תְּהִלָּתוֹ", בְּחִינַת: "תְּהִלָּתִי אֶחְטָם

לָךְ".

וְהַנְּשָׁמוֹת עִם הַתְּפִלָּה, הַנִּקְרָא כָּבוֹד, (נ"א נִקְרָא כָּבוֹד, מָצָאתִי). עַל

שֵׁם שֶׁהִיא מַלְבֶּשֶׁת אוֹתָנוּ (בכת"י אוֹתָם), כִּי 'ר' יוֹחָנָן קָרָא

לְמָאנֵיהּ מְכַבְּדוּתָא', וְעַל־יְדֵי־זֶה נִקְרָאת כְּבוֹד אֵל. וְהֵן מְאִירִין זֶה

לָזֶה; הַנְּשָׁמוֹת מְאִירִין לְהַתְּפִלָּה בִּבְחִינַת הַעֲלָאַת מַיִן נוּקְבִין,

68. **Make glorious His praise...My praise, echtom....** At the beginning of the lesson (and nn.5,6) we saw that praise is associated with the nose, *echtom*. Rebbe Nachman now shows that praise also suggests glory. Thus, within the context of our lesson, the verse the Rebbe quoted from Psalms (19:2) reads as follows: **The heavens** — the Torah/souls **declare the glory** — are elevated through praise, i.e., prayer.

69. **prayer's clothing them.** When the souls are clothed in prayer, within *Malkhut,* the combination of the two is termed "glory" by virtue of prayer's own element of glory.

70. **...my glorifiers.** Having stated that prayer, which is glory, is an aspect of clothing, the Rebbe brings support from the Talmudic Sage, Rabbi Yochanan, who called his clothing "my glorifiers." Like Rabbi Yochanan's receiving glory from his clothing, the letters of Torah/souls acquire the element of glory from *their* clothing, the prayers.

This reference to Rabbi Yochanan and glory/prayer has a further connection with our lesson. Rabbi Yochanan was the leading tzaddik of his day and, as explained above (§6), one must bring one's prayers to the tzaddikim of the generation.

71. **it is...glory of the Almighty.** "It" is apparently the unit created by the combining of Torah/souls with prayer rather than either of them alone. This unit is also an aspect of "the glory of the Almighty," because God's glory is greatest when fallen souls are rectified. See *Likutey Moharan* I, 14:2.

72. **illuminate each other.** Torah and prayer serve to strengthen and illuminate each other. A person is therefore required to engage in both. All the letters of Torah one studies for the purpose of putting into practice are sparks of souls. They are clothed within our prayers and are renewed there in an aspect of pregnancy. In return, encompassing the souls/Torah within our prayers produces a further perfection of the prayers. Having said this, the ultimate perfection can only be reached when we bring our prayers to the tzaddik of the generation. Then, the Torah illuminates our prayers and strengthens them, so that they become the

clothed within the prayer. There, they are renewed in an aspect of prayer.[65] {As is brought in the *Sefer HaGilgulim:* All the souls enter *Malkhut* (Kingship) in the aspect of pregnancy and are renewed there.}

This is the meaning of (Psalms 19:2), "The *ShaMaYiM* (heavens) declare the glory of the Almighty." This refers to the Torah, which is *aiSh* (fire) and *MaYiM* (water)—the aspect of souls.[66] These [souls] enter into the prayer,[67] which is an aspect of "the glory of the Almighty," as is written (Psalms 66:2), "Make glorious His praise"— corresponding to "For My praise, *echtom* from you."[68]

Thus, these souls together with prayer < are termed > "glory" on account of [prayer's] clothing < them >.[69] Just as Rabbi Yochanan, who called his clothing "my glorifiers" (*Shabbat* 113a).[70] As a result, it is called "the glory of the Almighty."[71] And they illuminate each other[72]: the souls shine to prayer in an aspect of raising feminine

intent of observing its commandments and drawing closer to God, he gains new insights and wisdom which may then be called souls. (A further explanation of sparks of souls is found in *Likutey Moharan* I, 14:13).

65. **aspect of pregnancy.** During pregnancy, what begins as an embryo grows and develops to maturity. In the Kabbalah, the concept of pregnancy, *eybur*, is defined as the development of anything small and lacking completion. This especially applies to intellectual matters, because all ideas start off as just a spark in the mind and need to be enlarged upon. The new insights a person gains from Torah study (see previous note) are at first unformed and fragmentary. But by praying after studying, the wisdom he gains is nurtured and grows to completion.

The Ari teaches that when Adam sinned, nearly all the souls of future mankind were adversely affected. And whereas some souls were only slightly affected, others fell to the lowest levels of the *kelipot*. Thus, when the time comes for a soul to be renewed and rectified, it must go through a stage akin to pregnancy within *Malkhut* before it can enter into this world paired with a physical body. The Ari teaches further that the only way these souls can be elevated to the aspect of pregnancy is through the prayers and mitzvot of a Jew (*Shaar HaGilgulim*, 12-13). In our lesson, Rebbe Nachman teaches that "the Torah a person studies for the purpose of observing..." elevates these fallen sparks of souls. This refers to a Jew's prayers and mitzvot, which have the power to elevate the lost souls into *Malkhut* so that they can receive rectification. *Malkhut*, as we've seen earlier (n.4), is prayer. This is why prayer has the power to renew and rejuvenate the soul—provided, that is, that the prayer is enhanced with Torah study.

66. **Torah...fire and water...souls.** Both the Talmud (*Chagigah* 12b) and Rashi (Genesis 1:8) point out that the elements which make up the firmament are alluded to in the Hebrew term for "the heavens," *ShaMaYiM* (שמים)—the elements being *aiSh* (אש, fire) and *MaYiM* (מים, water). The Torah, too, is likened to fire and water, as in (Jeremiah 23:29), "Behold, My word is like fire," and (Isaiah 55:1), "Let all who are thirsty, come for water" (see *Kiddushin* 30b). And, as just explained, the Torah contains the souls. *Shamayim* ("the heavens") thus connotes Torah and souls.

67. **enter into the prayer.** In the aspect of pregnancy, as explained (n.65).

וְהַתְּפִלָּה מְאִירָה לְהַנְּשָׁמוֹת בִּבְחִינַת חִדּוּשִׁין, שֶׁהִיא מְחַדֶּשֶׁת אוֹתָם בִּבְחִינַת עִבּוּר,

וְהַנְּשָׁמוֹת הַמְלֻבָּשִׁין בַּתְּפִלָּה, הַמּוּבָאוֹת לַצַּדִּיק שֶׁבַּדּוֹר הֵם בִּבְחִינַת: "בְּתוּלוֹת אַחֲרֶיהָ רֵעוֹתֶיהָ מוּבָאוֹת לָךְ".

אָמַר רַבָּה בַּר בַּר חָנָה: זִמְנָא חֲדָא הֲוָה קָאָזְלִינָן בִּסְפִינְתָּא, וְחָזִינָן הַהוּא כַּוְרָא דְּיָתְבָא לֵיה חָלְתָא אַגַּבֵּיה, וְקָדְחָה אֲגַמָּא עֲלוּיהּ. סְבַרִינָן יַבֶּשְׁתָּא הוּא, וְסָלְקִינָן וְאָפִינָן וּבַשְׁלִינָן אַגַּבֵּיהּ. וְכַד חַם גַּבֵּיהּ אִתְהַפִּיךְ, וְאִי לָאו דַּהֲוָה מִקָּרְבָא סְפִינְתָּא, הֲוָה טַבְעִינָן.

פֵּרוּשׁ רַשְׁבַּ"ם: דְּיָתְבָא חָלְתָא אַגַּבֵּיה, שֶׁהָיָה נִקְבָּץ עַל גַּבּוֹ: וְקָדַח עֲשָׂבִים עַל הַחוֹל: וְסַבְרִינָן יַבֶּשְׁתָּא הִיא אִיֵּי הַיָּם הִיא:

prayers so that prayer elevates them in the aspect of *mayin nukvin* (see *Shaar HaGilgulim*, 13).

74. **renews them....** The Hebrew term for "new insights," *chidushin*, has the same root as *m'chadesh*, "renew." The souls are renewed—i.e., the Torah yields new insights—when they are elevated through prayer into the aspect of pregnancy. See above, note 65.

75. **...brought to you.** The Psalmist says (*loc. cit.*): "In embroidered garments [the princess] shall be brought to the king; maidens, her companions who follow her, shall be brought to you." The major commentators explain this as referring to the time of Mashiach, when all Jews, even those who have fallen and become very distant from God, will be brought back to serve Him. The verse thus translates in our text as follows: **In embroidered garments** — clothed within the prayers, **the princess** — the soul **shall be brought to the king** — to the aspect of Moshe-Mashiach (see n.37); and, again, **maidens** — through *Malkhut*/prayer **her companions who follow her** — the fallen souls **shall be brought to you** — are elevated. As explained, elevating fallen souls requires binding one's prayers to the tzaddikim—i.e., Mashiach, to whom all the prayers will be brought. Then, with his prayer-weapon whole and primed, Mashiach will triumph over the entire world and bring it under God's dominion (*Mai HaNachal*).

In review: The main weapon of Mashiach, and indeed of every single Jew, is prayer (§1). However, a person cannot come to true prayer unless he first attains the level of guarding the Covenant (§2). And even when one guards the *brit* and attains the power of prayer, he still needs the attribute of *mishpat*. That is, his weapon (prayer) must be wielded judiciously (§3). To attain *mishpat*, he must give charity (§4). Conversely, the major disturbances to one's prayers, one's foreign thoughts and lack of concentration, stem from a corrupted sense of *mishpat* (§5). And to ensure that one's prayers are accepted, one must bind himself to the tzaddikim. They alone know how to elevate each prayer to its proper place (§6). One must also study Torah, specifically with the intent of observing the mitzvot he studies. This enables him to elevate fallen souls (including his own) and renew them through his prayers (§7).

76. **Rabbah bar bar Chanah....** Rebbe Nachman now shows how the concepts of this lesson are alluded to within the framework of Rabbah bar bar Chanah's story.

waters,[73] and prayer shines to the souls in the aspect of new insights. For she renews them in an aspect of pregnancy.[74]

And the souls, when clothed in prayer and brought to the tzaddik of the generation, are an aspect of "maidens, her companions who follow her, shall be brought to you" (Psalms 45:15).[75]

8. Rabbah bar bar Chanah recounted: Once, while traveling on a ship, we saw this fish. *ChoL* **(sand)** *yatva* **(had settled) on its back and a meadow sprouted up. Thinking it to be dry land we ascended,**

Rashbam:

Sand yatva on its back - sand had gathered on its back: sprouted up - grass on the sand: Thinking it to be dry land - an island:

and we baked and cooked on its back. When its back became hot, it turned over. Were it not that we were near the ship, we would have drowned (*Bava Batra* 73b).[76]

---

weapon through which each individual Jew wins his personal battles, and, ultimately, Mashiach wins his (see *Mai HaNachal*).

Reb Noson writes that this is the great value of what Rebbe Nachman refers to elsewhere as "turning one's studies into prayers" (*Likutey Moharan* II, 25). Whatever Torah a person studies becomes sparks of souls that are renewed when they are then incorporated into his prayers. This is so even if he studies one subject and prays to properly observe another. All the more so if he prays to be able to observe what he has just studied. Then, his studies and prayers are truly united, illuminating one another in a most awesome fashion. Thus, for example, the more a person desires to attain true, everlasting life, the more he will strive for a life bound up with Torah and prayer (*Torat Natan* #23).

73. **feminine waters.** The Kabbalah speaks of the two complementary concepts known as *mayin dukhrin* and *mayin nukvin* (literally, "masculine waters" and "feminine waters"). Essentially, *mayin dukhrin* denotes spiritual energy which descends from Above. It symbolizes the flow of *shefa* (bounty) which God benevolently provides for mankind and the world. *Mayin nukvin*, on the other hand, denotes spiritual energy ascending from below and is symbolic of man's fulfillment of God's will. This energy from below arouses a reciprocal energy from Above (see *Likutey Moharan* I, 185, n.12 for the meaning of "waters" in connection to this term). Consider the following metaphor:

A mother will display her well cared for children to her husband. She proudly demonstrates how she has utilized the resources he has given her. This naturally gains her husband's favor, and he is encouraged to give her more of his bounty. The raising of *mayin nukvin* suggests such a concept. One spiritual level or world will display that it has guarded and developed the bounty it has been given. Then the higher world, seeing that what has been given to the lower world bears fruit, is inclined to bestow more (*Rabbi Yaakov Meir Shechter*).

In our context, raising feminine waters relates to the souls that are rectified by means of a Jew fulfilling God's will through Torah study and the performance of mitzvot. That is, the Torah has brought the souls to a more rectified state, to a state where they can illuminate the

וְזֶה שֶׁאָמַר רַבָּה בַּר בַּר חָנָה: חֲזֵינָן לְהַאי כּוּרָא וְכוּ', כִּי בְּגָלוּתֵנוּ, כִּבְיָכוֹל, הַקָּדוֹשׁ־בָּרוּךְ־הוּא בְּהַסְתָּרַת פָּנִים, כְּמוֹ שֶׁכָּתוּב: "הִסְתַּרְתָּ פָנֶיךָ", שֶׁהוּא בְּחִינוֹת רַחֲמִים, וּפָנָה עֹרֶף שֶׁהוּא בְּחִינוֹת דִּין. וְכָל תְּפִלּוֹתֵינוּ וּבַקָּשָׁתֵנוּ, עַל זֶה שֶׁפָּנָה עֹרֶף אֵלֵינוּ, שֶׁיַּחֲזֹר אֶת פָּנָיו, כְּמוֹ שֶׁכָּתוּב: "פְּנֵה אֵלַי". וּכְמוֹ שֶׁכָּתוּב: "יָאֵר ה' פָּנָיו".

וּכְשֶׁאָנוּ רוֹאִים אֹרֶךְ הַגָּלוּת, וּבְכָל יוֹם אֲנַחְנוּ צוֹעֲקִים אֵלָיו וְאֵינָם נוֹשָׁעִים, – וְיֵשׁ מֵעַמֵּנוּ בְּנֵי־יִשְׂרָאֵל שֶׁטּוֹעִים, חַס וְשָׁלוֹם, בְּלִבָּם, שֶׁכָּל הַתְּפִלּוֹת הֵם לָרִיק, אֲבָל בֶּאֱמֶת כָּל הַתְּפִלּוֹת – הַצַּדִּיקִים שֶׁבְּכָל דּוֹר וָדוֹר, הֵם מַעֲלִים אוֹתָם, וּמְקִימִים אוֹתָם, כְּמוֹ שֶׁכָּתוּב: "וַיָּקֶם מֹשֶׁה אֶת הַמִּשְׁכָּן". וּמַעֲלִין כָּל שַׁיְפָא וְשַׁיְפָא לְדוּכְתֵּיהּ, וּבוֹנִין קוֹמָתָהּ שֶׁל הַשְּׁכִינָה מְעַט מְעַט, עַד שֶׁיִּשְׁתַּלֵּם שִׁעוּר קוֹמָתָהּ, אָז יָבוֹא מָשִׁיחַ, דָּא מֹשֶׁה, וְיַשְׁלִים אוֹתָהּ, וְיָקִים אוֹתָהּ בִּשְׁלֵמוּת.

echtom (I will restrain My anger)" (§1). Just as God withholds His anger and does not mete out deserved suffering, so, too, the Jewish people must exhibit patience while waiting for their prayers to be answered. In fact, the more patience we exhibit, the greater our ability to mitigate God's anger (*Biur HaLikutim*). As Reb Noson explained, Esav personifies the view that there is no reason for prayer (see n.26). For nearly the past 2,000 years we have been exiled under the domination and influence of Edom/Rome, whose progenitor was Esav. Accordingly, there have been many occasions for the Jewish people to despair of prayer. This is why the Rebbe emphasizes patience as a vital element when praying to God. As he goes on to say, "But in truth...The tzaddikim of each and every generation...."

80. **erecting it perfectly.** Reb Noson writes: It is important to realize that the same evil inclination which entices a person to sin, later taunts him for having succumbed, and then sets about convincing him that he has no hope of salvation. The person who has sinned is left wondering why he should pray. "Of what use is prayer to me now that I've sinned?" he asks himself. "There's no hope for me anymore." In this way, the evil inclination succeeds in its ultimate goal: bringing man to despair. This, in fact, is the reason the present exile has extended on and on. The Jews have despaired of prayer!

Nevertheless, Reb Noson concludes, each generation has its share of true tzaddikim; righteous individuals who encourage people's faith in the efficacy of their prayers. Because of these tzaddikim, salvation will ultimately come to the Jewish people. And this is true of the individual as well. Each Jew's personal salvation only comes when he does not despair of praying; when he is patient and believes that each of his prayers bears fruit (*Torat Natan* #24).

Rabbah bar bar Chanah recounted...we saw this fish — For in our exile the Holy One has, as it were, hidden His countenance. < As is written (Deuteronomy 31:18), "and I will utterly hide My face," and > as in (Psalms 30:8), "You hid Your face." < It is known that the face > is an aspect of compassion, < and conversely the back > is an aspect of stern judgment.[77] Thus, all our prayers and petitions are < only > concerned with His having turned His back to us; that He should return His countenance. As < King David requested > (Psalms 86:16), "O turn to me < and show me mercy >," and as in (Numbers 6:25,26), "May God make His countenance shine < upon you and grant you mercy. May God turn His countenance to you. > "[78]

When we see the length of < this bitter > exile and how each day we cry out to Him and yet are not saved, there are those of our people, the Children of Israel, who err in their heart, God forbid. < They say > that all the prayers are for naught.[79] But in truth, < it is not so >. The tzaddikim of each and every generation raise < all the prayers > and erect them, as in, "Moshe erected the Tabernacle." They raise each and every part to its place and build the structure of the *Shekhinah* bit by bit, until the full measure of it structure is realized. Then Mashiach, who is Moshe, will come and consummate it, by erecting it perfectly.[80]

---

77. **hidden His countenance...stern judgment.** The Kabbalah often uses "face" and "countenance" to denote kindness. It is like when one person feels compassion and concern for another, and so turns to him and eagerly listens to what he has to say. Conversely, "back" denotes stern judgment. It is like when one person wants nothing to do with another, and so turns his back to him and refuses to be of any assistance. Therefore, Rebbe Nachman teaches, when exile was decreed upon the Jews, God's attribute of kindness—His face— became hidden, leaving stern judgment—His back—in its place.

There is also a deeper intention here. The Rebbe quotes the verse "You hid Your face," indicating that even if God's countenance is turned to us, we might not benefit from it because it is hidden. "Hidden" and "turned away" thus represent two separate levels. As opposed to a revealed countenance, which denotes a flow of *shefa* (bounty), a hidden countenance indicates an absence of bounty, but not necessarily the presence of suffering. Suffering, which stern judgment implies, is indicated rather by God's having turned His countenance away from us.

78. **O turn to me...His countenance shine....** In the first verse, the Psalmist (*loc. cit.*) pleads with God to turn His face to us—i.e., the negation of stern judgment. The second verse, part of the Priestly Benediction, is a blessing that "God make His countenance shine" on the Jewish people—i.e., supply them with abundant *shefa*. This is the mission of a Jew: to mitigate decrees and *turn* them into blessings for abundant bounty.

79. **...prayers are for naught.** With this, Rebbe Nachman introduces into the lesson the virtue of patience. Both prayer and patience correspond to the nose, as in, "For My praise,

וְזֶה פֵּרוּשׁ:

חֲזִינָא לְהַאי כַּוְרָא – הוּא בְּחִינַת צַדִּיק הַדּוֹר, הַנִּקְרָא דָּג: זֶה בְּחִינַת מֹשֶׁה מָשִׁיחַ.

דְּיַתְבָא לֵיהּ חַלְתָּא אַגַּבֵּיהּ – הַיְנוּ הַתְּפִלּוֹת שֶׁאָנוּ מִתְפַּלְלִים עַל זֶה, שֶׁכְּבִיכוֹל פָּנָה עֹרֶף אֵלֵינוּ.

יַתְבָא לֵיהּ – הַיְנוּ: "וַיָּבִיאוּ אֶת הַמִּשְׁכָּן אֶל מֹשֶׁה", כִּי צָרִיךְ לְהָבִיא וּלְקַשֵּׁר אֶת הַתְּפִלָּה לְהַצַּדִּיק שֶׁבַּדּוֹר.

וְקַדְחִי עֲלֵהּ אַגְמָא – הַיְנוּ הַנְּשָׁמוֹת הַבָּאִים עִם הַתְּפִלָּה, בְּחִינַת "בְּתוּלוֹת אַחֲרֶיהָ רֵעוֹתֶיהָ" וְכוּ', כִּי הַנְּשָׁמוֹת הֵן נִקְרָאִין עֲשָׂבִין כְּמוֹ שֶׁכָּתוּב: "רְבָבָה כְּצֶמַח הַשָּׂדֶה נְתַתִּיךְ".

וְסָבְרִינָן יַבֶּשְׁתָּא הוּא – הַיְנוּ שֶׁהַתְּפִלּוֹת אֵינָם עוֹשִׂים פֵּרוֹת, אֲבָל בֶּאֱמֶת אֵינוֹ כֵן, אֶלָּא

סַלְקִינָן וַאֲפִינָן וּבַשְׁלִינָן – הַיְנוּ כָּל הַתְּפִלּוֹת סַלְקִינָן וְעוֹלִין. וְכָל מַה שֶּׁמַּרְבִּין בִּתְפִלָּה, נִבְנֶה הַשְּׁכִינָה בְּיוֹתֵר, וּמְכִינָה אֶת עַצְמָהּ לְזִוּוּג, וְזֶה 'אֲפִינָן וּבַשְׁלִינָן', כִּי אֲפִיָּה וּבִשּׁוּל הֵם הֲכָנָה לַאֲכִילָה,

"had brought." Rashbam translates it as "had gathered." Thus, in our context, *yatva* relates to the concept of bringing and binding one's prayers to the tzaddikim, as has been explained in section 6.

84. **her companions....** The souls that are elevated through the aspect of pregnancy, as explained in section 7.

85. **foliage of the field.** The prophet Ezekiel describes the children of Israel during their sojourn in Egypt, when, because they multiplied very rapidly, they went from a single family to an entire nation. The "foliage of the field" thus refers to the Jewish souls. This has a further connection to our text, to the fallen souls mentioned earlier. The Ari teaches that the Jews born during the Egyptian exile had fallen souls, and so were in particular need of rectification (*Shaar HaPesukim, Shemot*).

86. **union.** The *Shekhinah* is *Malkhut*, the last of the *sefirot* and the one symbolic of this world (see Appendix: The Divine Persona; Levels of Existence). The term union indicates that *Malkhut* is ready to unite with the Divine persona *Z'er Anpin* in order to bring *shefa* down to this world. This is God shining His countenance upon us.

The concept of building the *Shekhinah* is fundamental in the Kabbalah. The Ari teaches that the Breaking of the Vessels at Creation especially caused blemish in *Malkhut*. The

This is the meaning [of Rabbah bar bar Chanah's statement]:

we saw this fish — This alludes to the tzaddik of the generation, who is called a fish, < as is known >.[81] This is the aspect of Moshe-Mashiach.

ChoL, sand, had settled on its back — < "*ChoL*" suggests prayer, as in, "Then Moshe *ChaL* (began to plead)" (Exodus 32:11). **Sand...on its back:** > These are the prayers we pray because He has, as it were, turned His back to us.[82]

yatva, had settled — This is, "They brought the Tabernacle to Moshe." For it is necessary to bring and bind the prayers to the < tzaddikim > of the generation.[83]

a meadow sprouted up — These are the souls which accompany the prayers, "her companions who follow her...."[84] For the souls are called grass, as is written (Ezekiel 16:7), "I caused you to increase like the foliage of the field."[85]

Thinking it to be dry — That is, that the prayers [are dried out and] do not bear fruit. But in truth, it is not so. Rather:

We ascended, and we baked and cooked — All the prayers ascend and rise upward. And the more we pray, the more the *Shekhinah* is built up. She then prepares herself for union.[86] This is **we baked and cooked.**

---

81. **fish, as is known.** In the writings of the Kabbalah, the tzaddik is likened to a fish (see *Zohar* III 42a; *M'orey Ohr, dag*). Water is symbolic of Torah and wisdom, as in, "Let all who are thirsty, come for water" (see n.66), and, "The earth shall be filled with the knowledge of God as the waters cover the sea" (*Isaiah* 11:9). Thus, just as fish live in water and cannot survive outside it, the tzaddik is totally submersed in Torah and cannot survive without it. Moreover, to the degree that any Jew guards the Covenant, he is likened to a fish, the aspect of Moshe-Mashiach.

The *Biur HaLikutim* points out that the Hebrew letters for "fish" (דג), *dalet* (=4) and *gimel* (=3), have a numerical value of seven. These correspond to the seven expansions of God's holy names: four expansions of the holy name *YHVH* and the three expansions of God's holy name *Ehyeh*. The tzaddik is called *dag* because he is an aspect of Yosef, who merited the *tarpo* lights (see n.24).

82. **ChoL...on its back....** *ChoL* (חל, sand) is phonetically similar to *ChiLah* (חלה, to entreat). Scripture (*loc. cit.*) relates how Moshe pleaded with God to restrain His anger at the Jewish people. Literally, the verse reads: "Then *ChaL* Moshe the countenance of God." Thus, "sand had settled on its back" alludes to our prayers and entreaties because God has hidden His countenance by turning His back to us.

83. **yatva...bind the prayers....** The Aramaic term *yatva* ("had settled") can also mean

לִבְחִינַת זִוּוּג, כְּמוֹ שֶׁכָּתוּב: "כִּי אִם הַלֶּחֶם אֲשֶׁר הוּא אוֹכֵל".

כְּשֶׁיִּשְׁתַּלֵּם קוֹמָה שֶׁל כָּל הַשְּׁכִינָה, הַיְנוּ עַל־יְדֵי רֹב הַתְּפִלּוֹת,

יִכְמְרוּ רַחֲמָיו, וְיִתְהַפֵּךְ מִדַּת הַדִּין לְמִדַּת הָרַחֲמִים.

וְזֶה כַּד חַם – הַיְנוּ כַּאֲשֶׁר יִכְמְרוּ רַחֲמָיו.

גַּבֵּיהּ אִתְהַפֵּךְ – הַיְנוּ שֶׁיִּתְהַפֵּךְ מִדַּת הַדִּין לְמִדַּת הָרַחֲמִים.

וְאִי לֹא הֲוֵי מְקָרְבִינָן לִסְפִינְתָּא – הַיְנוּ: "לְמַעֲנִי לְמַעֲנִי אֶעֱשֶׂה

זֹאת," כִּדְאִיתָא בַּמִּדְרָשׁ: "מִי הִקְדִּימַנִי וַאֲשַׁלֵּם לוֹ". 'מִי עָשָׂה לִי

מְזוּזָה קֹדֶם שֶׁנָּתַתִּי לוֹ בַּיִת' וְכוּ'. נִמְצָא, שֶׁכָּל מַעֲשִׂים טוֹבִים

שֶׁלָּנוּ וְכָל הַתְּפִלּוֹת – הַכֹּל מֵאִתּוֹ, וְאֵין רָאוּי לַחֲשֹׁב לְקַבֵּל שָׂכָר

עַל שׁוּם דָּבָר.

וְאַף־עַל־פִּי שֶׁנִּרְאֶה, שֶׁעַל־יְדֵי תְּפִלָּתֵנוּ וְתוֹרָתֵנוּ יִהְיֶה הַגְּאֻלָּה, אַף־

עַל־פִּי־כֵן צְרִיכִין אֲנַחְנוּ לְחַסְדּוֹ, שֶׁבְּחַסְדּוֹ יִגְאַל אוֹתָנוּ. וְזֶה:

אִי לֹא מְקָרְבִינָן לִסְפִינְתָּא. זֶה בְּחִינַת חֶסֶד, כְּמוֹ שֶׁאָמְרוּ חֲכָמֵינוּ,

---

89. **For My own sake...I will do it.** Scripture states that God will redeem the Jewish people not because they proved meritorious but for His own sake—for the glory of His holy name. Rebbe Nachman will explain the apparent contradiction between this verse and our notion of salvation: If God will redeem us for His own sake, what is the point of our prayers? Why must we pray for salvation? Whereas if our prayers and Torah study do earn us salvation, as has been explained in the lesson, why does God say He will redeem us for His own sake, and not because of anything we might do?

90. **Who preceded Me....** One the one hand, man is commanded to perform the mitzvot; on the other hand, it is literally impossible for him to perform the mitzvot unless God first grants him the opportunity to do so. The Midrash (*loc. cit.*) lists some ten examples showing how a person cannot fulfill the commandments unless he first receives God's bounty, for "whatever is under the entire heaven is Mine." This is as the Rebbe now explains, "From this we can conclude that all our good deeds...."

91. **not proper to consider receiving reward....** For, in truth, we did not merit reward by virtue of anything we did first.

92. **through our prayers and study....** Having said this, it is still true that when we pray, study Torah and perform mitzvot—all of these earn us reward and bring closer our salvation.

93. **in His kindness He will redeem us.** As in, "For My own sake...I will do it." This is one of the paradoxes of life: We must pray, yet realize that all depends solely on God! We must do our part, yet accept that God does it "for My own sake..." alone!

Baking and cooking are preparations for eating, which is [a metaphor for] union, as is written (Genesis 39:6), "except for the food he himself ate."[87]

< **When its back became hot** — That is, > when the structure of the entire *Shekhinah* is completed through the multitude of prayers, < then God's > compassion will warm. The attribute of stern judgment is transformed into the attribute of compassion.[88] This is:

became hot — When His compassion warmed.

its back...turned over — That is, the attribute of stern judgment is transformed into the attribute of compassion.

Were it not that we were near the ship < **we would have drowned** > — This is (Isaiah 48:11), "For My own sake, for My own sake I will do it."[89] As is found in the Midrash < concerning the verse, > "Who preceded Me that I should reward him?" (Job 41:3)—who has made a mezuzah for My sake before I gave him a house (*Vayikra Rabbah* 27:2)?[90] From this we can conclude that all our good deeds and all the prayers are entirely from Him. Thus, it is not proper to consider receiving reward for any < mitzvah or prayer >.[91]

And although it appears that through our prayers and study of Torah the redemption will come, even so, we are in need of His kindness[92]; that in His kindness He will redeem us.[93] This is:

Were it not that we were near the ship — This corresponds to kindness. As our Sages taught: The majority of sailors are benevolent (*Kiddushin*

mission of the tzaddikim, indeed of all humanity, is to restore and rebuild *Malkhut*, the *Shekhinah*. Once this is accomplished, Mashiach will come.

87. **baked and cooked...the food he himself ate.** Scripture states that Yosef's master, Potifar, "left all his affairs in Yosef's hands, except for the food he himself ate." This "food" is a euphemism for Potifar's wife, for the Torah speaks in a refined language (*Rashi, loc. cit.*). Just as baking and cooking are necessary when preparing food for consumption, so, there must be a "baking and cooking" of the seed for a successful union. In our context, this refers to the souls that are elevated through the aspect of pregnancy. Their rectification depends upon the prayers of the Jewish people. Thus, even when it seems to a person that his prayers go unanswered, he should know that no entreaty is ever lost. His prayers are being used for another purpose: to rectify and elevate other souls, which are the building blocks of the Tabernacle, *Malkhut*.

88. **stern judgment...compassion.** A union for producing *shefa* only takes place "face to face." Therefore, when, as a result of our many prayers, God's compassion is aroused and His countenance turns to us, a union occurs. An abundance of bounty then descends to the world.

זִכְרוֹנָם לִבְרָכָה 'הַסַּפָּנִין רְבָּן חֲסִידִים', אִי לֹא חַסְדּוֹ, טָבְעִינָן, חַס
וְשָׁלוֹם, בַּגָּלוּת.

וְזֶה פֵּרוּש:

אֱמֹר אֶל הַכֹּהֲנִים – בְּחִינַת תְּפִלָּה. כְּמוֹ שֶׁכָּתוּב: "אֶת ה' הֶאֱמַרְתָּ
הַיּוֹם".

כֹּהֲנִים – הֵם בְּחִינַת תּוֹרָה, בְּחִינַת נְשָׁמוֹת כַּנַּ"ל, כְּמוֹ שֶׁכָּתוּב: "כִּי
שִׂפְתֵי כֹהֵן יִשְׁמְרוּ דַעַת וְתוֹרָה" וְכוּ'.

אַהֲרֹן – בְּחִינַת מִשְׁפָּט, כְּמוֹ שֶׁכָּתוּב: "וְנָשָׂא אַהֲרֹן אֶת מִשְׁפַּט בְּנֵי
יִשְׂרָאֵל". כִּי צָרִיךְ לְהָבִיא כָּל הַתְּפִלּוֹת לִבְחִינַת מֹשֶׁה מָשִׁיחַ. וְהוּא
יָקִים אֶת הַמִּשְׁכָּן.

Reb Noson explains that we have no way to understand this paradox. Yet, what we can understand from the Rebbe's teaching is that a person must be very diligent in his prayers, believing that his efforts will be rewarded handsomely. At the same time, each person must realize how dependent upon God's compassion he really is (see above, n.31). The more a person practices *mishpat,* the more he is guided by charity, the closer he will be to realizing his goals—through the weapon of prayer. This is why we need to attach ourselves in prayer to the tzaddikim. On their own, our prayers lack potency. However, the tzaddikim take each prayer and elevate it to where it is needed most, so that, with the proper balance of justice, our prayers do have great efficacy and worth.

96. ...he'EMaRta this day. Rebbe Nachman now shows how the concepts of this lesson are alluded to in the opening verse.

EMoR ("speak to") indicates prayer. In *Likutey Moharan* I, 259, Rebbe Nachman explains that the root *e-m-r,* as in the words *he'emarta* and *he'emircha,* denotes prayer in the form of expressive conversation. That is, when a person speaks to God and confesses his sins, the *Shekhinah* responds and consoles him.

97. priests...Torah...souls.... The connection between Torah and souls was explained in section 7. This verse from Malachi (*loc. cit.*) shows that "the priest" corresponds to Torah. Thus, "priests" alludes to the souls. These souls are elevated through *e-m-r,* prayer (see §7).

98. mishpat...on his heart. In his capacity as high priest, Aharon wore the *choshen mishpat* (breastplate of judgment) while performing the Temple service. It contained twelve precious stones, each engraved with the name of one of Israel's tribes (which correspond to prayer; see *Likutey Moharan* I, 9:2). Aharon thus corresponds to the aspect of *mishpat,* which is necessary in order to attain perfected prayer (as explained in §§3 and 4).

99. **Moshe erected the Tabernacle.** As explained in section 6.

82a).[94] Were it not for His kindness, we would, God forbid, have drowned in exile. < But, by means of His kindness, He will soon redeem us. Amen. >[95]

9. This is the explanation [of the opening verse]:

{"**God said to Moshe, 'Speak to the priests, the sons of Aharon, and say to them: Let no [priest] defile himself by [contact with] the dead among his people.'** "}

{**The purpose of this verse is to** *hazhir* **(warn) the grown-ups concerning the little ones** (*Rashi*).}

Speak to the priests — *EMoR* suggests prayer, as is written (Deuteronomy 26:17), "For God *he'EMaRta* (you have spoken out) this day."[96]

priests — They represent the Torah, the souls, as is written (Malachi 2:7), "For the priest's lips guard knowledge, and they seek Torah from his mouth."[97]

Aharon — He is the aspect of *mishpat,* as is written (Exodus 28:30), "Aharon shall bear the *mishpat* of the Israelites [on his heart]."[98] For it is necessary to bring all the prayers to the aspect of Moshe-Mashiach. He will then raise < them, as in, "They brought the Tabernacle to Moshe," and, "Moshe erected > the Tabernacle."[99]

---

94. **sailors are benevolent.** The Sages said: A ship on the high seas is often in danger. This causes the sailors to be contrite and inclined to kindness. "Near the ship" thus symbolizes kindness.

95. **He will soon redeem us. Amen.** Our prayers are extremely beneficial and absolutely necessary. Still, were it not for God's kindness, it would be impossible to survive this long exile.

Thus, within the context of our lesson, the story reads:

Rabbah bar bar Chanah recounted: Once, while traveling on a ship, we saw this fish — We saw the tzaddik of the generation.

Sand had settled on its back — The tzaddik encouraged us to pray so that God would turn to us and bless us with bounty. We complied, and attached our prayers to the tzaddik.

and a meadow sprouted up — We were thus able to elevate the fallen souls. This led us to believe that our efforts and prayers would provide us with all that we asked for and bring about our redemption.

Thinking it to be dry land — But when this did not happen, when salvation did not come, we concluded that our prayers were of no value.

we ascended, and we baked and cooked on its back. When its back became hot, it turned over — Nevertheless, the tzaddik encouraged us not to give up, because all our efforts did count. Eventually, as a result of our prayers, God's compassion was aroused and He turned to us.

Were it not that we were near the ship, we would have drowned — Yet it was not our merit, but God's kindness, that caused us to be redeemed.

וְזֶה פֵּרֵשׁ רַשִׁ"י: 'לְהַזְהִיר הַגְּדוֹלִים עַל הַקְּטַנִּים', הַיְנוּ צַדִּיק הַדּוֹר,
שֶׁהוּא בְּחִינַת מֹשֶׁה מָאוֹר הַגָּדוֹל יַזְהִיר וְיָאִיר אֶת הַתְּפִלָּה, שֶׁהִיא
בְּחִינַת מָאוֹר הַקָּטָן.

וּלְנֶפֶשׁ לֹא יִטַּמָּא בְּעַמָּיו – הַיְנוּ עַל־יְדֵי שְׁמִירַת הַבְּרִית כַּנַּ"ל,
כַּמּוּבָא בַּזֹּהַר: 'עִקָּרָא דִּיְצָרָא בִישָׁא – עַל עֲרָיִן וְהִיא עִקָּרָא
דִּמְסַאֲבוּתָא'.

וּכְשֶׁיִּשְׁמֹר אֶת הַבְּרִית, זוֹכֶה לִבְחִינַת תְּפִלָּה כַּנַּ"ל, וְזוֹכֶה לִבְחִינַת
"תְּהִלָּתִי אֶחֱטָם לָךְ", כִּי עִקַּר הָרֵיחַ תָּלוּי בַּטָּהֳרָה, כְּמוֹ שֶׁאָמְרוּ
חֲכָמֵינוּ, זִכְרוֹנָם לִבְרָכָה (סוטה מח.): 'מִשֶּׁבָּטְלָה הַטָּהֳרָה – בָּטְלָה
הָרֵיחַ'. כַּמְבֹאָר מַעֲשֶׂה בַּגְּמָרָא (שם מט.)

'שֶׁאָמַר: רֵיחָא דְּחַנּוּנִיתָא אֲנִי מֵרִיחַ. אָמַר לֵיהּ: בְּנִי, טָהֳרָה יֵשׁ בְּךָ':

---

103. **echtom from you.** See above, sections 1 and 2.

104. **sense of smell...purity.** For only with sexual purity, guarding the *brit*, is one able to attain prayer, corresponding to the nose.

105. **When purity was lost, fragrance was taken away.** Rashi (*loc. cit., s.v. botlah*) explains that because earlier generations conducted themselves with purity, God blessed them with pure and especially sweet smelling fruits. However, the subsequent decline in moral purity has brought about a loss of this pure, sweet smell. *Etz Yosef* (*loc. cit., s.v. taharah yesh*) explains that, in fact, what God did was not remove this special fragrance entirely, but rather He concealed it within the inner aspect of the fruit—within its spiritual quality. Thus, only someone who has purified his corporeality and cleansed himself of physical desires—who has himself acquired an inner purity—is able to derive pleasure from this pure, sweet smell.

Maharsha (*loc. cit., s.v. taharah*) points out that olfaction is more a spiritual sense than a physical one. The Talmud asks: How do we know that we recite a blessing over fragrances? We learn this from the verse (Psalms 150:6), "Every soul shall bless God." What is it that gives pleasure to soul and not the body? the smell of fragrance! (*Berakhot* 43b). This has a further connection with our text in that it is a person's soul which derives pleasure through the concept of nose—i.e., prayer. However, as explained, for the soul to enjoy a perfected sense of smell—the benefit of perfected prayer—one must attain the level of guarding the *brit*.

106. **Hynunus dates.** An especially juicy and fragrant variety.

107. **...you possess purity.** Because Rava had attained purity, his sense of smell was not spoiled (*Rashi, loc. cit., s.v. taharah*). He was immediately able to sense the sweet smell of the Hynunus dates. The same applies to anyone who has purity. His sense of smell—i.e., his prayer—is potent and bears fruit.

Thus, Rashi explains: **to haZHiR, warn, the grown-ups concerning the little ones.** This refers to the tzaddik of the generation, the aspect of Moshe, the great light.[100] He *yaZHiR* (shines) into and illuminates the prayer, which is the aspect of a small light (see *Zohar* II, 238b).[101]

Let no priest defile himself...the dead among his people — This is accomplished by guarding the *brit*. As is brought in the *Zohar* (III, 15b): The basic drive of the evil inclination is for sexual promiscuity, this being the fundamental source of defilement.[102]

And when a person guards the *brit,* he merits prayer—the aspect of "For my praise, *echtom* from you."[103] This is because the sense of smell is mainly dependent upon purity.[104] As our Sages taught: When purity was lost, fragrance was < taken away > (*Sotah* 49a).[105] As in the incident which the Talmud relates:

[Rav Huna found some Hynunus dates[106] and wrapped them in his shawl. Rava, his son, came by] and said to him, "I smell the scent of Hynunus about you." "My son," he replied, "you possess purity!"[107]

---

100. **Moshe, the great light.** "Moshe's face [shone] like the face of the sun" (*Bava Batra* 75a)— i.e., the great light. As an aspect of the great light, the tzaddik of the generation, who is Moshe-Mashiach, has the power to shine into and illuminate the lesser lights. In the terminology of the Kabbalah, Moshe/the great light/the tzaddik corresponds to *Z'er Anpin,* while the lesser light is *Malkhut.*

101. **the prayer...small light.** The root *z-h-r* indicates both "warning" and "shining." The tzaddik gathers the prayers and shines into them—elevating each prayer to its proper position in the Tabernacle, the *Shekhinah/Malkhut.*

102. **guarding the brit....** A person can only merit perfected prayer after attaining a level of true purity in guarding the *brit.* Because the main urge of the evil inclination is for sexual sin, a person who can guard himself from this source of defilement will certainly be able to guard against lesser sins. Therefore, one who guards the *brit* is protected from defilement and merits prayer.

The verse thus translates in our text as follows:
And God said to Moshe, Speak to the priests — That is, there are souls within the Torah a person studies which are elevated through prayer. But, this prayer needs...
the sons of Aharon — the aspect of *mishpat* (corresponding to the breastplate worn by Aharon).
and say to them: Let no [priest] defile himself by [contact with] the dead among his people — When a person maintains his purity by not defiling himself sexually, this guarding of the Covenant helps him attain prayer that is balanced by the attribute of *mishpat.* Even so, he must bind his prayers to the tzaddik of the generation, the great light, who will illuminate the prayers and elevate them to their proper place.

to the right. In truth, a person must take the balanced path, doing both. He must constantly increase his efforts at prayer, believing that not one of his entreaties is ever in vain. And at the same time, he must bear in mind that without God's kindness he is incapable of achieving anything despite all his efforts and devotions. When we Jews do our part and constantly pray for salvation, then God surely does His part and for His own sake bestows kindness upon us and redeems us. The way to attain this balance, or *mishpat,* is through charity. This is why we give charity before praying (see §4). Just as we distribute bounty through our acts of charity, and this enables us to pray, so, too, our prayers give God cause and reason to answer our entreaties and send us the bounty we seek (*Likutey Halakhot, Nachalot* 4).

In discussing a number of the concepts mentioned in this lesson, Reb Noson concludes: A person worthy of the sword of prayer must understand how to do battle with it; deflecting it neither right nor left. We learn from this that when a person considers the seemingly endless nature of the present exile, he must not mistakenly conclude that all the Jewish people's prayers for salvation are for naught, God forbid. This would be inclining to the left; turning God's attribute of compassion into cruelty, as though the Holy One turns a deaf ear to our prayers. Conversely, a person should not mistakenly conclude that since without God's kindness it is impossible to accomplish anything through prayer, there is no point in expending any effort on prayer. Relying totally upon God's kindness is inclining, mistakenly,

ליקוטי מוהר"ן סימן ג'

רַשְׁבַּ"ם

אַקְרוּקְתָּא צְפַרְדֵּעַ: כְּאַקְרָא
דְּהַגְרוֹנְיָא גָּדוֹל הָיָה כְּאוֹתָה
כְּרָךְ: וְאַקְרָא דְּהַגְרוֹנְיָא כַּמָּה
הֲוֵי? שִׁתִּין בָּתֵּי תַּלְמוּדָא
קָאָמַר לָהּ: אָתָא תַּנִּינָא רַבָּה
קָאָמַר לָהּ: פּוּשְׁקַנְצָא עוֹרֵב
נְקֵבָה:

אָמַר רַבָּה בַּר בַּר חַנָּה: לְדִידִי חֲזִי לִי
הַהִיא אַקְרוּקְתָּא דְּהַוֵי כְּאַקְרָא
דְּהַגְרוֹנְיָא, וְאַקְרָא דְּהַגְרוֹנְיָא כַּמָּה הֲוֵי
שִׁתִּין בָּתֵּי, אָתָא תַּנִּינָא בַּלְעָהּ אָתָא
פּוּשְׁקַנְצָא וּבַלְעָהּ לְתַנִּינָא, וְסָלִיק יָתִיב
בְּאִילָנָא. תָּא חֲזִי כַּמָּה נָפִישׁ חֵילֵיהּ
דְּאִילָנָא:

הִנֵּה מִי שֶׁשּׁוֹמֵעַ נְגִינָה מִמְּנַגֵּן רָשָׁע, קָשֶׁה לוֹ לַעֲבוֹדַת הַבּוֹרֵא.
וּכְשֶׁשּׁוֹמֵעַ מִמְּנַגֵּן כָּשֵׁר וְהָגוּן, אֲזַי טוֹב לוֹ, כְּמוֹ שֶׁיִּתְבָּאֵר.

This time, the *chazan* didn't even show up. This callousness incensed several members of the community and they sent a delegation to bring the cantor, so that the poor man would not be embarrassed. But when they arrived at the cantor's home, they were surprised to find only his wife there. The cantor had gone out, telling her that he was on his way to the *sholom zokhor*. On their way back, the delegation decided to look for the *chazan* at the home of his best friend. When they got there, however, they were again disappointed. The house was dark and no one responded to their knocking. They were about to leave, when they spotted the cantor running out of the back door. For some time, there had been talk about the cantor and his friend's wife. But the rumor had never been substantiated. The cantor's friend had birds nesting near his house, and the cantor attributed his frequent visits there to his desire to hear their melodious chirping. Now, however, the truth was out. The news spread fast and the cantor fled from Ladizin in shame.

After this incident it was clear to the people of Ladizin what the Rebbe meant when he said, "Then I'll just have to give him a voice," and why the Rebbe quoted the verse about associating with prostitutes. The town's inhabitants were awed by Rebbe Nachman's prophetic vision. Many became his followers and, inspired by this lesson, formed groups to study Mishnah and Talmud nightly (*Tovot Zikhronot* #3, p.104*f*).

2. **But when he listens...it helps him....** The following is Reb Noson's explanation of the concepts of voice and speech. His insights are fundamental to understanding the thrust of this section in particular, and the entire lesson generally. He writes: The voice is an extraordinarily potent means for arousing a person from spiritual slumber. This is the import of the teaching: The voice arouses concentration (*Orach Chaim* 61:4; see *Rosh, Berakhot* 3:40; see Lesson #5, n.57 and *Likutey Moharan* I, 21:7, n.64). Yet, the main arousal of one's mind, one's intellect, comes when a person's heart is aflame with a burning desire for holiness. For when the mind is bound to an inspired heart, the result is holy speech. This is as in (Psalms 39:4), "My heart was hot within me, with my contemplation a fire blazed—I spoke out." Thus, as important as the voice is to spiritual

LIKUTEY MOHARAN #3[1]

Rabbah bar bar Chanah recounted: I myself saw this *akrukta* that was as *akra deHagrunia* (the city of Hagrunia). And how large was the city of Hagrunia? Sixty houses. A serpent came by and swallowed it. A *pushkantza* came by and swallowed the serpent. It ascended and perched on a tree. Come, see how great the strength of that tree is! (*Bava Batra* 73b).

Rashbam:

akrukta - [Aramaic for frog; in Hebrew] *tzephardeah*: as the city of Hagrunia - it was as large as that city: **And how large was the city of Hagrunia? Sixty houses -** the Talmud says this: **A serpent came by -** Rabbah says this: **pushkantza -** a female *orev* (raven):

B ehold! when someone listens to the singing of a singer who is wicked, it is detrimental to his serving the Creator. But when he listens to a singer who is virtuous and worthy, it helps him, as will be explained.[2]

---

1. **Likutey Moharan #3.** This lesson was given on Shabbat, 7 Elul 5562 (September 4, 1802), in Ladizin, a town some 19 miles from Breslov. Rebbe Nachman had been accepted as the spiritual leader of Breslov and this lesson was given en route from Zlatipolia, where the Rebbe had lived the previous two years (*Until The Mashiach*, p.77). The lesson's main themes are: song, holy and profane; the study of Torah, especially Talmud, at night; and judging people favorably. This teaching is a prime example of the Rebbe's ability to explain profound Kabbalistic concepts simply and within the context of our daily lives.

While living in Zlatipolia, Rebbe Nachman had encountered unrelenting opposition, particularly from the Shpola Zeida and his followers. Ladizin, some several hundred kilometers to the west, was very different. There, he was received with considerable honor by the local inhabitants. As it happened, that Friday night one of the locals, a follower of the Rebbe, was making a *sholom zokhor* (the customary celebration in honor of a newborn son). Many of the townsfolk were present, including Ladizin's cantor, who was expected to lead the singing at the celebration. However, being a follower of Rebbe Nachman's opponents, the *chazan* had taken a seat at the far end of the table and showed no intention of initiating the singing. The Rebbe sent his host to find out why. "I just don't have a voice right now," the *chazan* insisted. Even the threat of losing the customary financial remuneration made no difference. He kept insisting he had lost his voice. "Then I'll just have to give him a voice," the Rebbe countered when told the cantor's excuse. Others began to sing instead. Later, as the celebration was about to conclude, Rebbe Nachman made a comment that left everyone perplexed. Quoting from Proverbs (29:3), he remarked, "Doesn't Scripture teach that anyone 'who keeps company with prostitutes loses his wealth'—his voice?" The next day, Shabbat, Rebbe Nachman taught this lesson, and left for Breslov early the following week.

The following Shabbat, one of the poorer residents of Ladizin also made a *sholom zokhor*.

כִּי הִנֵּה קוֹל הַנְּגִינָה נִמְשֶׁכֶת מִן הַצִּפֳּרִים, כִּדְאִיתָא בַּמִּדְרָשׁ: מִפְּנֵי מָה מְצֹרָע – טָהֳרָתוֹ תְּלוּיָה בִּשְׁתֵּי צִפֳּרִים חַיּוֹת טְהוֹרוֹת? יָבוֹא קַלָּנְיָא וִיכַפֵּר עַל קַלָּנְיָא. כִּי נִלְקָה מֵחֲמַת קוֹלוֹ שֶׁדִּבֶּר לָשׁוֹן הָרָע.

נִמְצָא, מִי שֶׁהוּא כָּשֵׁר, נִמְשֶׁכֶת הַנְּגִינָה שֶׁלּוֹ מִן הַשְׁתֵּי צִפֳּרִים חַיּוֹת טְהוֹרוֹת. וְכָתוּב בַּזֹּהַר, שֶׁהַשְׁתֵּי צִפֳּרִים הַנַּ"ל, יוֹנְקִים מֵאֲתַר דִּנְבִיאִים יַנְקִין. לְכָךְ נִקְרָא הַמְנַגֵּן חַזָּן מִלְּשׁוֹן חָזוֹן, הַיְנוּ לְשׁוֹן נְבוּאָה, כִּי לוֹקֵחַ הַנְּגִינָה מֵאֲתַר דִּנְבִיאִים יַנְקִין.

Holy Ark with the cherubs stood in the Holy of Holies, *Netzach* and *Hod*, and the relationship between *Z'er Anpin* and *Malkhut,* was complete; prophecy was prevalent in the world.

Moreover, just as prophecy and the *chayot* are identified with *Netzach* and *Hod*, so, by extension, we can conclude that the two birds mentioned in our lesson correspond to *Netzach* and *Hod*. This is true although it appears to contradict the Ari's teaching that the two birds correspond to the two *sefirot* known as the *mochin* (mentalities or brains), namely, *Chokhmah* and *Binah* (see *Etz Chaim* 48:2; see Appendix: The Sefirot and Man). However, this will be clarified later in the lesson (§2), where the Rebbe introduces the concept of building up the *mochin* of *Malkhut* of Holiness.

So far we have seen that the two birds, the cherubs, *Netzach* and *Hod*, and *Z'er Anpin* and *Malkhut* are all corresponding concepts. Rebbe Nachman next adds song to this group and, over the course of the lesson, shows how all these concepts are inter-connected. Having said this, it must be made clear that regarding the structure of the *sefirot*, *Netzach* and *Hod* are in no way parallels of the Divine personas *Z'er Anpin* and *Malkhut*. Allusions to both as corresponding aspects of the two birds must be understood within their particular contexts, as will be clarified below.

A reminder: These notes are provided to assist the reader in navigating the deep waters of Rebbe Nachman's lessons. They are not intended as a source for the study of Kabbalah. Rather, emphasis has been placed on developing the esoteric concepts specifically as they relate to the lesson. Neither in this lesson, nor in any of the others in which Kabbalistic terminology appears, has there been an attempt to thoroughly explain the Kabbalah and its significance. (See *Likutey Moharan* I, 11, note 42:end, for the *Zohar's* warning against revealing the hidden teachings of the Torah.) For further insights into the concept of the two birds, and also into some of the other Kabbalistic teachings mentioned in our text, see *Etz Chaim, Shaar HaKelipot* (*Shaar* 48), especially Chapters 2 and 4.

7. ChaZaN...ChaZoN.... The Hebrew term for cantor, *chazan* (חזן), and that for vision, *chazon* (חזון), share the same root letters. Scripture uses the term *chazon* to denote prophetic vision several times, as in (Isaiah 1:1): "The *chazon* of Yeshayahu...."

8. takes his song...prophets nurse. The connection between prophecy and song is further highlighted by the practice of the prophets to listen to music in order to enter a prophetic state. As it is written, "a group of prophets...preceded by a lyre, a timbrel, a flute, and a harp; and they will be prophesying" (1 Samuel 10:5). And, again, Elisha says, "Now, bring me a musician," after which Scripture states: "As the musician played, God's Hand came upon him..." (2 Kings 3:15). We see, then, that holy song and prophecy have a common root. Therefore, listening to holy song,

The reason for this is that the voice of song is drawn from the birds.[3] As we find in the Midrash: Why is the purification of a leper dependent upon two live pure birds? Let the chatterer come and atone for the chatterer (cf. *Vayikra Rabbah* 16:7). For he was stricken on account of his voice, which spoke *lashon hara* (slander).[4]

We see, then, that the virtuous person draws his song from the two live pure birds.[5] Thus it is written in the *Zohar* (III, 53b) that these two birds nurse from the same place that the prophets nurse.[6] This is why a singer is called a *ChaZaN,* from the word *ChaZoN,* which connotes prophecy.[7] [The *chazan*] takes his song from the same place that the prophets nurse.[8]

growth, it must ultimately be harnessed with the power of speech (*Torat Natan* #1). We see, then, that voice can kindle a burning desire within the one who listens to it. That burning desire, for holiness or otherwise, manifests in speech.

Reb Noson adds: Holiness is an attribute associated with the World of Unity. Profanity is associated with the World of Separation. When a person listens to holy song, his arousal and desires bring him to *unite* voice with speech. This enables him to come closer to God. But if a person listens to profane music and song, to song that draws him to the vanities and desires of this world, he *separates* voice from speech. This leads to his becoming distant from God (*ibid.*).

3. **drawn from the birds.** In Kabbalistic terminology, the two birds represent *Z'er Anpin* and *Malkhut,* which correspond to voice and speech, respectively. The birds also symbolize the two cherubs that were on the Holy Ark. These cherubs were the source of prophecy in the Temple: "When Moshe entered [the outer section of] the Communion Tent to speak with [God], he would hear the Voice speaking to him from between the two cherubs on the ark's cover over the Ark of Testimony" (*Rashi,* Numbers 7:89; *Mai HaNachal*). Thus, the voice of holiness has its origin in the two cherubs, the two birds. Conversely, the voice of profanity also has its origin in two birds. But these are different birds, as the Rebbe will explain.

4. **lashon hara.** Rabbi Yochanan said in the name of Rabbi Yosi: "Slanderers will be smitten with leprosy" (*Erkhin* 15b). The leper, who blemished his voice by speaking slander, must afterwards bring two birds in addition to the sacrifices necessary for his purification (see Leviticus 14:4). Rebbe Nachman explains that since speech has its source in voice/the two birds, and these birds were blemished by tainted speech, rectification, too, must come by means of two birds. The nature of these two birds of rectification will be explained below. Here, the Rebbe has shown the connection between blemished voice, speech and the two birds.

5. **two live pure birds.** As mentioned in Leviticus 14:4. When a person is virtuous and pure, he can draw his voice from an unblemished source, from purity, from the cherubs.

6. **place that the prophets nurse.** The *Zohar* (*loc. cit.*) asks: Why does Scripture emphasize that the leper brings "*live* pure birds." From the continuation of the verse itself I understand that these birds are *chayot* (alive)? However, the term *chayot* in the verse alludes to other *chayot*: the angels that accompany God's Chariot. From Ezekiel (1:5) we know that these *chayot* are identified with the source of prophecy.

Commentaries to this passage in the *Zohar* add that these *chayot* correspond to the two *sefirot* that are the source of prophecy, namely, *Netzach* and *Hod* (*HaGaot MaHarchu,* 1). As long as the

וּכְשֶׁהַמְנַגֵּן הוּא רָשָׁע, אֲזַי הוּא לוֹקֵחַ הַנְּגִינָה שֶׁלּוֹ מִצִּפֳּרִים אֲחֵרוֹת
שֶׁבַּקְּלִפָּה. וְכָתוּב בַּזֹּהַר: כִּי הַצִּפֳּרִים שֶׁבַּקְּלִפָּה יוֹנְקִין מִדַּדֵּי
הַמַּלְכוּת. וְכַד אִתְפָּלֵג לֵילְיָא כְּדֵין כְּרוֹזָא כָּרִיז: "כַּצִּפֳּרִים הָאֲחוּזוֹת

Light, commensurate with its own level, and draw from it the degree of vitality or bounty it needs for its existence. In terms of the *sefirah* hierarchy (see Appendix: Structure of the Sefirot), the Light descends through *Keter* to *Chokhmah*, through *Chokhmah* to *Binah*...through the six *sefirot* that make up *Z'er Anpin* to *Malkhut*. It has then traversed one entire world and is ready to descend on to the *Keter* of the next world. More generally, the ten *sefirot* of each world are divided into three (or four) groupings. The highest grouping of any particular world is its *mochin* (mentalities). The mnemonic by which this grouping is known is *ChaBaD* (*Chokhmah, Binah, Daat*). Its function with regard to the Infinite Light is to receive from the world above it. After doing so, *ChaBaD* filters that which it received and passes it on to the second grouping. The mnemonic by which this next grouping is known is *ChaGaT* (*Chesed, Gevurah, Tiferet*), the heart and center of that particular world. *ChaGaT* receives the Light from *ChaBaD* and filters it on to the third grouping. The mnemonic for this group, the lower regions of that world, is *NeHiY* (*Netzach, Hod, Yesod*). After receiving this twice-filtered Light from *ChaGaT*, *NeHiY* passes it on to what is the lowest *sefirah* of any given world, *Malkhut*. The *Zohar* teaches that, unlike the other *sefirot*, *Malkhut* has no substance (light) of its own, only that which it receives from the *sefirot* above it (*Zohar* I, 249b; see Lesson #1, §2). Therefore, the culmination of this process — *Malkhut's* receiving from *Netzach* and *Hod*—is known as the nourishing or building up of *Malkhut*, with the Light itself becoming *Malkhut's mochin*.

The need for drawing vitality from the Infinite Light also applies to the forces of evil. The *kelipot*, too, are God's creation and so depend upon His Infinite Light for existence. Were they unable to sustain themselves by drawing from the Light after it has passed through the filters of holiness and descended into *Malkhut*, the *kelipot* could not survive. Thus, in the context of our lesson, the two birds of the *kelipah* also draw their nourishment from *Malkhut* (more specifically, *NeHiY* of *Malkhut*).

Expanding on the metaphor of nursing or suckling an infant (human or animal), the Kabbalah teaches that the breasts which nourish the *kelipot* are found in the lower extremities of *Malkhut* (as an udder; *Etz Chaim* 48:2). In the structure of the *sefirot*, the breasts correspond to the area of *Netzach* and *Hod*, paralleling the source of nourishment of the two birds of holiness (as above, n.6). The reason for this is that these two birds of the *kelipah* represent the *mochin* of *Malkhut* of the Other Side, and, as explained, the *mochin* of *Malkhut* are built through *Netzach* and *Hod* (see below, §2, n.32).

The Ari explains further (*ibid.*) that while it is true that the *mochin* of the *kelipot* draw nourishment both day and night, the evil forces are most dominant at night. During the day, the attribute of lovingkindness from the *sefirah* of *Chesed* prevails, and so the *kelipah's* nourishment, and therefore its strength, is minimal. At night, however, the attribute of judgment from the *sefirah* of *Gevurah* prevails. Then, the two birds of the *kelipot* are able to draw a greater amount of nourishment. See next note.

12. **...a cry goes out.** The night, which signifies judgment and *gevurot* (severities), has two parts: before and after midnight. The initial period of the night is the harsher half, a time when the *kelipot* have access to higher levels and draw greater nourishment. Were this to continue unchecked, the forces of the Other Side would become extremely powerful and adversely affect the creation even more than they already have. However, the process by which the *kelipot* nurse and

But when a singer is wicked,[9] he takes his song from other birds, [from] those of the *kelipah* (evil forces).[10] Thus it is written in the *Zohar* (I, 217b) that the birds of the *kelipah* nurse from the breasts of *Malkhut* (Kingship)[11]: When midnight comes, a cry goes out,[12] "As

especially from a singer who is virtuous and worthy, assists a person in serving God.

The *Mai HaNachal* takes this a step further. He says that through holy song a person can even attain an element of prophecy. Elsewhere (*Likutey Moharan* I, 54:10), Rebbe Nachman explains that prophecy is an aspect of attaching one's thoughts to the World to Come. That is, the prophet would shed his corporeality, his attachment to this world, and attach himself to God. By doing so, he attained prophecy. And, although prophecy has ceased to exist in the world, the source of prophecy still exists. Only now, the way to reach it, the way to shed one's attachment to the vanities of this world, is through holy song. When someone listens to the singing of a virtuous person, he can attach himself to God. If the song is joyous, he attaches himself to God in joy. If the song is meditative, he attaches himself to God through yearning. Holy song is thus extremely beneficial to his attaining an element of prophetic vision. The *Yekara D'Shabbata* adds that this is why Shabbat is so closely associated with song. Shabbat is the time of the week when one can best contemplate his relationship with God, and so song is an intrinsic element of the day.

9. **singer is wicked.** Rebbe Nachman now addresses the converse to holy song: listening to profane song, or even holy song but from an unworthy person. The source of a virtuous person's song is of a spiritual nature and not readily observable. The same can be said of the wicked person; his song is also rooted in hidden sources. King Solomon referred to this as "The Lord made one to contrast the other" (Ecclesiastes 7:14). However, in the wicked person's case, his inspiration comes from the unholy and the impure.

The *Mai HaNachal* defines a wicked singer as one whose singing is motivated by personal gain: for great wealth, honor, fame, etc.

10. **song...birds...of the kelipah.** Just as there are two holy birds/*Netzach* and *Hod*, from which prophecy emanates, so, too, there is an opposing pair of birds whose source is the evil forces of the Other Side, the *kelipot* (*Etz Chaim, Shaar HaKelipot* 48:2). These two birds are the source of prophecy for the Other Side, as well as the source of song for the wicked.

In essence, these two birds of the *kelipah* are the source of all forms of false prophecy. In a modern-day context, they are the source from which false leaders derive their ill-conceived, ill-intentioned teachings that lead people astray. For only those with a pure *daat*, the faculty by which man filters and incorporates the light (awareness, knowledge) provided by the *mochin*, can teach and guide others in the proper way. As Reb Noson explained (above, n.2), the voice has the power to arouse one's mind to great levels. But making proper use of this expanded mentality requires *daat*. Lacking this, the song of a wicked person is profane, and thus easily misleads those who listen to it. Reb Noson therefore states that it is the lack of interaction between voice and speech that allows evil to develop to the point where wicked singers are able to draw people away from God (*Torat Natan* #1).

11. **nurse from the breasts of Malkhut.** Fundamental to the Kabbalah's understanding of the Act of Creation is a system of so-called filters that God established in order to enable His awesome light to descend to the farthest reaches of existence. This Infinite Light is the source of life and vitality that sustains everything, from the holiest of holies to the most ungodly of all His creations. But for this Light to be beneficial, it must undergo a series of contractions, passing through so-called filters of *sefirot* and spiritual worlds. Only then can each creation receive the

בַּפֶּה כָּהֶם יוֹקְשִׁים בְּנֵי־אָדָם״.

וְהַתִּקּוּן הוּא שֶׁיּוּכַל לִשְׁמֹעַ נְגִינָה מִכָּל אָדָם, הוּא עַל־יְדֵי שֶׁיִּלְמַד בַּלַּיְלָה תּוֹרָה שֶׁבְּעַל־פֶּה, הַיְנוּ גְּמָרָא שֶׁהִיא בְּחִינַת לַיְלָה. כְּדְאִיתָא בַּמִּדְרָשׁ, 'כְּשֶׁהָיָה מֹשֶׁה בָּהָר אַרְבָּעִים יוֹם וְאַרְבָּעִים לַיְלָה, לֹא הָיָה יוֹדֵעַ מָתַי יוֹם וּמָתַי לַיְלָה, רַק עַל־יְדֵי־זֶה כְּשֶׁהָיָה לוֹמֵד תּוֹרָה שֶׁבִּכְתָב, הָיָה יוֹדֵעַ שֶׁהוּא יוֹם, וּכְשֶׁלָּמַד תּוֹרָה שֶׁבְּעַל־פֶּה, הָיָה יוֹדֵעַ שֶׁהוּא לַיְלָה'.

נִמְצָא, שֶׁהַתּוֹרָה שֶׁבְּעַל־פֶּה הִיא בְּחִינַת לַיְלָה. וּכְמוֹ שֶׁאָמְרוּ רַבּוֹתֵינוּ, זִכְרוֹנָם לִבְרָכָה: "בַּמַּחְשַׁכִּים הוֹשִׁיבַנִי" – 'זֶה תַּלְמוּד בַּבְלִי'. וּכְתִיב: "וְלַחשֶׁךְ קָרָא לַיְלָה".

Elsewhere, the *Zohar* (I, 242b) teaches that the entrapment and defeat of the *kelipot* at midnight is mainly on account of those who rise and study Torah at that time (*Parparaot LeChokhmah*). This will become clearer from the next paragraphs.

15. **ensnared.** In review: Listening to the singing of a virtuous person is beneficial to serving God; listening to the singing of a wicked person is detrimental. The reason is that song, which corresponds to prophecy, stems from *Netzach* and *Hod*, the two *sefirot* that nurse *Malkhut*. A person is sustained by the vitality he receives from one of the two manifestations of *Malkhut*. Commensurate with his deeds, he draws either from *Malkhut* of Holiness or *Malkhut* of the Other Side.

16. **The remedy....** That is, not that a person should intentionally listen to profane songs or singers, but rather, should he hear and be attracted by them, he will not be adversely affected. The *Mai HaNachal* adds that if one does listen to such songs, he might even benefit from them by elevating the profane into holiness (provided he uses the remedy).

17. **Written Torah...day...Oral Torah...night.** Written and Oral Torah correspond to *Z'er Anpin* and *Malkhut*, and to day and night, respectively (see *Zohar* II, 205b). Thus, the study of Torah brings rectification to *Z'er Anpin* and *Malkhut*. In our context, we have seen that *Malkhut* is the arena for either the rectification or blemish of song. Rebbe Nachman reads the passage he quotes from the Midrash as a proof-text that Moshe's studying Oral Torah at night was a rectification for night/*Malkhut*.

18. **and the darkness He called night.** The Sages themselves equated the Oral Law, the Talmud, with darkness. Rashi (*loc. cit.*) explains that this is because the Babylonian Talmud contains many disputed points of law. These difficulties in clarifying the *halakhah* are the "dark places" mentioned in the verse. Therefore, darkness/night alludes to the Talmud. Rectification of night/*Malkhut* is by means of night/Talmud, the Oral Law.

birds are caught in a trap,[13] so are the children of man ensnared" (Ecclesiastes 9:12).[14]

< And if the singer is wicked, then when a person hears him and is attracted by his singing, he, too, becomes trapped in that evil snare. As is written in the *Zohar* (*ibid.*): "...so are the children of man ensnared."[15] >

The remedy, which makes it possible to listen to the < voice > of any individual < without being harmed >,[16] is studying the Oral Torah at night. This refers to the Talmud, which is an aspect of night. As is brought in the Midrash (*Shochar Tov*, 19): When Moshe was on Mount [Sinai] for forty days and forty nights, he had no way of knowing whether it was day or night. Except, that when he was taught the Written Torah, he knew it was day, and when he was taught the Oral Torah, he knew it was night.[17]

We see, then, that the Oral Torah is an aspect of night. As our Sages taught: "He seated me in dark places" (Lamentations 3:6) — this is the Babylonian Talmud (*Sanhedrin* 24a). And it is written (Genesis 1:5), "and the darkness He called night."[18]

---

gain strength — that same process also lures them into being ensnared in the lower realm. This happens at *chatzot* (midnight), when the first traces of *Chesed's* light begin to manifest in the world. As a result, the *kelipot* cry out at midnight, at the time they become trapped.

13. **As birds are caught in a trap.** "Birds" alludes to the two birds of the *kelipah*, which become caught in the trap at midnight.

14. **the children of man ensnared.** Those people who are associated with these two birds draw their nourishment from the *kelipot*. Their choice of this source of nourishment causes them to become trapped in their evil desires and lusts. Listening to a wicked singer, who draws from these two birds, and listening to profane song is therefore detrimental to serving God. Moreover, this strengthening of *Malkhut* of the Other Side invariably adds strength to the *kelipot*. On the physical level, this results in corrupt kingdoms and governments (*malkhut*) growing stronger and the exile being extended (*Mai HaNachal*).

Conversely, through song that is holy *Malkhut* of Holiness is uplifted and elevated, so that God's Kingdom is revealed in the world (*Mai HaNachal*). Thus King David, the personification of *Malkhut* of Holiness, rose from sleep to the sound of song: at midnight, the harp that hung above his bed began playing on its own and he would awake. In his words as the Psalmist: "Awake, my glory; awake, O harp and lyre! I will awaken the dawn" (Psalms 57:9). After praying, he would spend the rest of the night in study, for nighttime study corresponds to rectified song (*Parparaot LeChokhmah*). As the personification of *Malkhut* of Holiness, it was most fitting that King David also said, "At midnight, I will rise..." (Psalms 119:62). Why specifically midnight? We know that *Malkhut* corresponds to night. Why not another hour of the night? However, the rectification of *Malkhut* starts specifically then, when the judgments are stayed and lovingkindness begins to be revealed (see *Zohar* I, 92b).

הַיְנוּ עַל־יְדֵי שֶׁיִּלְמַד שַׁ"ס יְתַקֵּן הַשֵּׁשִׁית עִיזְקָאִין שֶׁבַּקָּנֶה, שֶׁמֵּהֶם

יוֹצֵא הַקּוֹל. וְזֶהוּ: "קוּמִי רֹנִי בַלַּיְלָה", הַיְנוּ שֶׁתִּהְיֶה תְּקוּמָה

לְהָרֹנָּה, הַיְנוּ עַל־יְדֵי הַלַּיְלָה שֶׁהִיא גְמָרָא שַׁ"ס.

אַךְ כְּשֶׁלּוֹמֵד שֶׁלֹּא לִשְׁמָהּ, הַיְנוּ בִּשְׁבִיל שֶׁיִּתְקָרֵא רַבִּי, הַלִּמּוּד אֵינוֹ

at the time of the Holy Temple's destruction, Jewry's darkest hour. This shows that even when *Malkhut* of the Other Side (wicked singers) prevails, a person can elevate evil (profane song) by studying Talmud. This is because studying the Oral Law gives strength to *Malkhut* of Holiness (holy song).

22. **Song...night...Talmud.** See *Targum* (*loc. cit.*), who renders the verse as referring to waking up to study Mishnah. In our context, therefore, the verse reads: **Rise, sing out** — raise and elevate song, **in the night** — by studying Talmud, which is an aspect of night.

See also *Megillah* 32a, where the Sages criticize "those who study without song...." *Tosafot* comments that it was customary when studying Oral Torah to recite the words with a melody. This ties in with our lesson, in that Rebbe Nachman teaches that Talmud study rectifies song. The *Zohar* also points to the connection between the two, quoting Song of Songs (2:12): "The time for singing has arrived and the voice of the *tor* (turtledove)"—this is the Oral Torah—"is heard in the land" (cf. *Zohar* III, 4b).

23. **studies not for learning's own sake.** In Hebrew, "its own sake" is *lishmah*; "not for its own sake" is *shelo lishmah*. The *Parparaot LeChokhmah* writes: There are three general categories for the things we do in the service of God: there are those things that are obligatory and a mitzvah; there are those things that are permissible, concerning which we are free to choose; and, finally, there are those things that are prohibited.

These three categories are also applicable to the study of Torah. Studying solely for the sake of fulfilling the precepts of the Torah is obligatory and a mitzvah—the ultimate perfection of holiness. Studying Torah so as to be able to argue with and irritate other scholars, with no intent of following the Torah's guidance or performing its commandments, falls into the category of prohibited acts—the totally impure *kelipah*. Concerning such study the Talmud states: It would have been better had he never been born (*Berakhot* 17a).

When one studies Torah with the intent of performing and fulfilling the commandments but also has in mind some personal benefit—e.g., wealth, or to be called rabbi—he falls into the middle category. His study is *shelo lishmah*, which has two sides to it. Sometimes, this type of study degenerates into the totally impure sort of learning. Hence the Talmudic dictum: When someone studies *shelo lishmah*, he would be better off had he never been born (*Berakhot* 17a; see also *Tosafot, Pesachim* 50b, *s.v. v'kan*). Other times, it rises to the level of selflessness and perfection, *lishmah*. Hence the Talmudic dictum: It is beneficial to study even *shelo lishmah*, for from *shelo lishmah* one can come to *lishmah* (*Pesachim* 50b; see n.64 below). It is to this last category and the danger of studying *shelo lishmah* that the Rebbe next turns.

24. **to be called rabbi.** Rebbe Nachman has taught that studying Oral Law at night (both of which correspond to *Malkhut*) rectifies speech and, consequently, the voice. This enables a person to rectify song. Now, when a person studies Torah *lishmah*, he strengthens *Malkhut* of

By studying the six orders‿ < of the Mishnah > [19] a person rectifies the six rings of the windpipe, via which the voice emerges.[20] This is (Lamentations 2:19), "Rise, sing out in the night."[21] Song is raised up by means of "the night"—i.e., the six orders of the Talmud.[22]

However, when a person studies not for learning's own sake[23] [but] in order to be called rabbi,[24] < such > study is not all that

---

19. **six orders of the Mishnah.** The six Mishnaic orders are: *Zera'im* (laws of prayer, blessings and agriculture); *Moed* (laws of Shabbat and the festivals); *Nashim* (laws of marriage, divorce, etc.); *Nezikin* (civil and criminal law); *Kodshim* (laws of the Holy Temple and the sacrifices); and *Taharot* (laws of purity and impurity). In total, the Mishnah contains sixty tractates. (There are actually 63, but the 3 tractates of *Bava Kama, Bava Metzia* and *Bava Batra* are counted as 1, and *Avot,* because it does not contain any laws, is not included in the tally of the Sixty Tractates of Law.)

Rebbe Nachman here speaks of the six orders of the Mishnah. Below (§3), he mentions the sixty tractates—i.e., Talmud. The fact that we do not have Talmudic text for every tractate suggests that rectification begins with the study of Mishnah, which is the essence of the Oral Law. Afterwards, one should add Talmud to one's studies—i.e., study Mishnah and Talmud together (*Parparaot LeChokhmah*). The reason for this is that while the Mishnah states the law, it does not analyze or explore its many details. This is the function of the Talmud: to examine the source of the Mishnah, while analyzing and clarifying the law. Therefore, the *Biur Halikutim* adds, the main areas of study nowadays are *Shulchan Arukh* (clarification of *halakhah*) and the hidden teachings of Torah, Kabbalah. The connection between them is indicated by the *Shulchan Arukh* itself, which states: Mishnah should be the primary area of study, and if one has merited insight into the Kabbalah, then a most propitious time for this study is after midnight (*Mishnah Berurah* 1:9).

20. **rings of the windpipe...voice emerges.** This statement is a combination of two separate teachings. The Talmud (*Berakhot* 61a) states that the windpipe (trachea) emits the voice. The *Zohar* (III, 235a) states that the windpipe has six rings (three pairs of cartilage in the larynx), which correspond to the six *sefirot* found in *Z'er Anpin.* Thus, it is from the windpipe's six rings that the voice emerges. Studying the six orders of the Talmud, Rebbe Nachman explains, rectifies these six rings. This is because reciting the Talmud while studying is in essence engaging in holy speech. His speech/*Malkhut* is thus purified, and the *source* of his speech, his voice, is rectified. He can then make use of his voice to arouse his *daat* and enflame his heart, by means of which he comes closer to God (as above, n.2).

Reb Noson explains that the Written Law corresponds to the voice, whereas the Oral Law corresponds to speech. Although the sound that the voice produces is the root of all speech, it is lacking in definition. The same can be said of the Written Law; the laws it prescribes lack clarification and specificity. This clarification of the Written Law only comes with the study of Talmud, the Oral Law. As such, *Oral* Law resembles speech, which gives definition—i.e., rectification—to the voice (*Torat Natan* #1).

21. **Rise, sing out in the night.** Scripture speaks of rising at night to study Torah, as a result of which the *Shekhinah* (Divine Presence) resides with that person (*Tamid* 32b). The Kabbalists teach that this refers specifically to rising for *chatzot* (midnight).

The *Mai HaNachal* adds that these words from Lamentations were spoken by Yirmiyahu

בַּחֲשִׁיבוּת כָּל כָּךְ. וּכְשֶׁלּוֹמֵד בַּלַּיְלָה, חוּט שֶׁל חֶסֶד נִמְשָׁךְ עָלָיו
וּמֵגֵן עָלָיו שֶׁלֹּא יַזִּיק לוֹ הַמַּחֲשָׁבָה הַנַּ"ל:

וְאִיתָא בְּכִתְבֵי הָאֲרִ"י זַ"ל, כִּי צִפֳּרִים שֶׁבְּקְלִפָּה הֵם מֹחִין
שֶׁבְּמַלְכוּת דִּקְלִפָּה, וְהַשְׁתֵּי צִפֳּרִים חַיּוֹת טְהוֹרוֹת, הֵם בְּנְיַן
הַמַּלְכוּת דִּקְדֻשָּׁה.

(though not his motive) is seen and wins him recognition. Studying at night is therefore intrinsically studying *lishmah* (*Chagigah, loc. cit., s.v. hakadosh*).

27. **protects him from . . . this intention.** The lovingkindness that descends upon a person who studies the Oral Torah at night corresponds to the lovingkindness revealed at midnight, which repels and subdues the two birds of the *kelipah*/arrogance. He is therefore protected from the negative affects of studying Torah for *his* sake, his own aggrandizement and personal control over *Malkhut*. Instead, he is able to study *lishmah* (each person on his own level), rectifying *Malkhut* and the six rings of the windpipe—i.e., the voice. This is how the Talmud deduces the thread of lovingkindness from "by *night* His song is with me" (above, n.26), because the concept of night rectifies song (*Mai HaNachal*). The *Parparaot LeChokhmah* adds that this thread of lovingkindness is so beneficial that even while a person studies, he is protected from thoughts that would bring him to *shelo lishmah*.

The *Be'Ibey HaNachal* writes: It often happens that a person wants to study *lishmah* but is diverted by his evil inclination, which awakens in him a desire for personal gain: to be called rabbi, for wealth, and the like. As explained, the means for overcoming these diversions is studying Oral Torah at night. That is, if a person *wants* to study *lishmah*, then studying at night will draw the thread of lovingkindness upon him and protect him from *shelo lishmah*. In contrast to this, study during the day requires actual study *lishmah* and isn't capable of protecting against ulterior motives. Even a person's study at night, if it contains a major element of *shelo lishmah*, draws no lovingkindness upon him. Furthermore, the person who studies *shelo lishmah* can only be protected *before* his song/voice is blemished; the thread of lovingkindness enables him to turn *shelo lishmah* into *lishmah*. But once he has listened to the singing of a wicked person, his voice is blemished and he is exposed to the adverse side of *shelo lishmah*. Then, he must do all he can, look for any way possible, to study *lishmah*.

In review: Listening to the singing of a virtuous person is beneficial to serving God; listening to the singing of a wicked person is detrimental. The reason is that song, which corresponds to prophecy, stems from *Netzach* and *Hod*, the two *sefirot* that nurse *Malkhut*. A person is sustained by the vitality he receives from one of the two manifestations of *Malkhut*. Commensurate with his deeds, he draws either from *Malkhut* of Holiness or *Malkhut* of the Other Side. To protect oneself from harmful singers and song, one should study the Oral Law, Talmud, at night. This will rectify song and protect him from blemishing *Malkhut*.

28. **in the writings of the Ari. . . .** *Etz Chaim, Shaar HaKelipot*, 48:2. The excerpts applicable to our lesson have already been explained above in notes 3 and 10-14.

meritorious.[25] Yet if he studies at night, a thread of lovingkindness is drawn over him < during the day > *(Chagigah* 12b),[26] and it protects him from being adversely affected by this intention.[27]

2. Now, it is brought in the writings of the Ari, of blessed memory, that the birds of the *kelipah* are the intellect of *Malkhut d'Kelipah* (Kingdom of the Other Side), whereas these two live pure birds are the concept of building up *Malkhut d'Kedushah* (Kingdom of Holiness).[28]

Holiness, for his entire being is devoted to serving God. In other words, studying Oral Law *lishmah* returns *Malkhut* to God. But if a person studies to acquire fame, wealth, etc., he forces *Malkhut* to submit to *his* authority and thereby strengthens *Malkhut* of the Other Side. Studying the Oral Law with such intentions cannot possibly rectify *Malkhut* (*Parparaot LeChokhmah; Mai HaNachal*).

25. **not all that meritorious.** A person whose Torah study is truly *lishmah* is a rarity. It is perhaps equally rare that someone studies Torah solely for contentious purposes. In contrast, there are many who would like to study *lishmah*, free of ulterior motives, but have yet to achieve their goal. So they fulfill God's commandment to study Torah, all the while anticipating some personal gain—this being *shelo lishmah*. The Talmud recommends that these people study anyway, for ultimately they will attain the level of *lishmah* they strive for. There is therefore merit to such study, although, as explained, it also carries an inherent danger. For even though their *ultimate* goal is a worthy one, the *Malkhut* they empower through seeking personal gain (see previous note) can cause them to give in completely to the second side of this *shelo lishmah*, studying solely for fame, wealth, etc. And, while even this is not totally devoid of value, for it is still possible to redirect their intentions to attaining the level of *lishmah*, nevertheless, the risk exists that by studying *shelo lishmah*, for gain, they will succumb to the truly reprehensible study whose motive is one-upmanship and argumentation. This is because the *mochin* (mentalities) with which one studies when one's desire is to gain fame, contain the seeds of the *mochin* with which one studies to harass and harangue other scholars. These latter mentalities are the *mochin* of the two birds of the Other Side, *mochin* with a proclivity for arrogance and haughtiness. Whetting one's appetite for fame thus makes one susceptible to becoming arrogant and haughty—the trap of the two birds of the Other Side. Rebbe Nachman therefore concludes that studying Torah in order to be called rabbi cannot be considered all that meritorious.

26. **Yet if he studies at night....** The Talmud (*loc. cit.*) deduces this from the words of King David (Psalms 42:9): "In the day God commands His lovingkindness." What prompts Him to do this? The answer, the Sages say, comes from the conclusion of the verse: "by night His song is with me." Maharsha explains that one who is awake well into the night will generally have a sullen face from lack of sleep. However, when a person studies Torah at night, God draws upon him a thread of lovingkindness and grace (*Maharsha, Avodah Zarah* 3b, *s.v. kol*). The *Iyun Yaakov* adds that Torah study at night is called true Torah, because his meritorious deed is hidden from others. This contrasts with Torah study during the day, when his deed

לְפִיכָךְ נִשְׁתַּבַּח דָּוִד לִפְנֵי שָׁאוּל: "וְיוֹדֵעַ נַגֵּן", כִּי הַנְּגִינָה הִיא בִּנְיַן
הַמַּלְכוּת, לְכָךְ רָאוּי הוּא לְמַלְכוּת. וְזֶה שֶׁכָּתוּב אֶצְלוֹ: "מֵאַחַר
עָלוֹת הֱבִיאוֹ", הַיְנוּ מֵאַחַר הַמֵּינִיקוֹת, הַיְנוּ נֶצַח וָהוֹד. כִּי הֵם
מְנִיקִין לַנְּבִיאִים, וְהֵם בִּנְיַן הַמַּלְכוּת.

וְזֶה שֶׁאָמַר רַבָּה בַּר בַּר חָנָה:
לְדִידִי חָזִי לִי הַהִיא אַקְרוּקְתָּא – וּפֵרֵשׁ רַשְׁבַּ"ם: צְפַרְדֵּעַ, הַיְנוּ

slandered him. In his apparent praise, Doeg, our Sages say, extolled David's Torah knowledge and ability to clarify the law. In fact, he intentionally spoke in a manner that caused Shaul to become jealous of David and desire to kill him. The reason God's spirit left Shaul was because he blemished prophecy. At God's command, Shmuel instructed Shaul to wipe out Amalek. This nation is the personification of *Malkhut* of the Other Side, whose entire aim is to draw nourishment from, and subsequently overwhelm, *Malkhut* of Holiness. Shaul, however, failed in his mission and as a result lost his *malkhut* (kingship), the holy spirit. He was therefore open to receiving Doeg's slander, which, when he did, caused a further blemish in *Malkhut*. David, meanwhile, arose every night at midnight (see n.14), at which time he studied the Oral Law. His Torah was the Torah of lovingkindness (see *Likutey Moharan* I, 283). David also sung many songs in praise of God. He consequently merited rectifying both voice and speech, and was duly deserving of kingship.

In review: Listening to the singing of a virtuous person is beneficial to serving God; listening to the singing of a wicked person is detrimental. The reason is that song, which corresponds to prophecy, stems from *Netzach* and *Hod*, the two *sefirot* that nurse *Malkhut*. A person is sustained by the vitality he receives from one of the two manifestations of *Malkhut*. Commensurate with his deeds, he draws either from *Malkhut* of Holiness or *Malkhut* of the Other Side. To protect one's self from harmful singers and song, one should study the Oral Law, Talmud, at night. This will rectify song and protect him from blemishing *Malkhut* (§1). King David attained kingship because he rectified the voice/song and knew how to draw song—i.e., nurse *Malkhut*—from holiness (§2).

33. **This is the meaning....** Rebbe Nachman now shows how the concepts of this lesson are alluded to within the framework of Rabbah bar bar Chanah's story.

34. **Rashbam.** RaShBaM is an acrostic for Rabbeinu Shmuel ben Meir, Rashi's grandson. It is known that Rashi passed away shortly after he began revising his commentary to the Talmudic tractate *Bava Batra* (29a). Rashbam, his eldest grandchild and a close disciple, completed his grandfather's work. In this lesson, Rebbe Nachman includes Rashbam's commentary together with Rabbah bar bar Chanah's story, relating to it as if it were part of the Talmudic text (cf. Lesson #2, §9). This occurs not infrequently in *Likutey Moharan*, as the Rebbe quotes the basic Talmudic passage, including commentary, within the fabric of his own commentary.

David was therefore lauded before Shaul as one "who is skilled at playing music" (1 Samuel 16:18).[29] This is because song is the concept of building up *Malkhut,* which is why [David] was deserving of *malkhut* (kingship).[30] Thus, of [David] it is written, "From behind the nursing ewes He brought him < to tend His people Yaakov > " (Psalms 78:71). < "From behind the nursing ewes" > — that is, from behind those that suckle.[31] This refers to *Netzach* and *Hod,* for they nourish the prophets and are the concept of building up *Malkhut.*[32]

3. This is the meaning of what Rabbah bar bar Chanah said[33]:
I myself saw this akrukta — Rashbam[34] comments [that this is a]

---

29. **David...skilled at playing music.** After Shmuel anointed David in place of King Shaul, God's spirit left the king. Shaul's counselors advised him to call for someone who would comfort him and calm his spirit with music and song (1 Samuel 16:14-17). David was selected because he was "skilled at playing music, valiant, a warrior, understanding, handsome, and God is with him."

   As is common in Rebbe Nachman's lessons, the Rebbe here shows how a number of elements from a particular episode—in this case the story of King David's appointment as Israel's king—allude to concepts within of our lesson.

30. **deserving of malkhut, kingship.** As we have seen, the voice/song is the source of *Malkhut/ speech.* Because David was "skilled at playing music," he was eminently qualified to rule the *malkhut* of holiness, the kingdom of Israel, for *Malkhut* is built up through song.

31. **the nursing ewes...suckle.** When tending his father's flock, David took special care to ensure that each one received the precise nourishment it needed. First, he took out the young sheep to pasture, so that they might eat the soft upper part of the grass. Next, he took out the elderly sheep to pasture, so that they might eat the middle part of the grass. Finally, David took out the hardy sheep to pasture, so that they might eat the tough bottom part of the grass. God said: "This one is certainly fitting to be the shepherd (king) of My people" (*Shemot Rabbah* 2:2). Thus David, skilled in song, was taken by God from tending the flock to be ruler of the kingdom. See next note.

32. **Netzach and Hod...building up Malkhut.** As mentioned, *Malkhut* has nothing of its own (n.11). It is comprised solely of that which *Netzach* and *Hod* give it: namely, *mochin* (mentalities) and the vessels with which to receive them. In providing these, *Netzach* and *Hod* construct *Malkhut.* This is the meaning of *Netzach* and *Hod* "are the concept of building up *Malkhut*" (*Rabbi Yaakov Meir Shechter;* see above, n.11; see also *Mai HaNachal*). Thus, King David deserved kingship because he was skilled in song—which stems from *Netzach* and *Hod* (see §8)—and because he "nursed" the sheep—i.e., he knew from where to draw the proper nourishment.

   The story of David's being chosen to play music before King Shaul has a further connection with our lesson. At the outset, Rebbe Nachman explained that the two live pure birds, the source of song, are brought as a sacrifice by the leper, who spoke slander. The Talmud (*Sanhedrin* 93b) teaches that Doeg, the one who lauded David (see n.29), actually

צִפּוֹר דֵּעָה. כִּי אַקְרָא דְּהַגְרוֹנְיָא – מִלְּשׁוֹן "קָרָא בְגָרוֹן" הַיְנוּ שֶׁהַנְּגִינָה נִמְשֶׁכֶת מִמֶּנּוּ.

וְאַקְרָא דְּהַגְרוֹנְיָא כַּמָּה הֲוֵי שִׁתִּין בָּתֵּי – הַיְנוּ עַל־יְדֵי מָה תְּתַקֵּן בְּחִינַת קָרָא בְגָרוֹן? עַל־יְדֵי שִׁתִּין בָּתֵּי, הַיְנוּ עַל־יְדֵי שִׁתִּין מַסְכְתּוֹת, וּפֵרֵשׁ רַשְׁבַּ"ם: תַּלְמוּדָא קָאָמַר לָהּ, הַיְנוּ שֶׁיִּלְמַד תַּלְמוּד.

אָתָא תַּנִּינָא בַּלְעָהּ – וּפֵרֵשׁ רַ"שׁ: רַבָּה קָאָמַר לָהּ, הַיְנוּ עַל־יְדֵי שֶׁיִּלְמַד שֶׁלֹּא לִשְׁמָהּ יִבְלַע אוֹתָהּ הַנָּחָשׁ. וְזֶה שֶׁפֵּרֵשׁ רַשְׁבַּ"ם, רַבָּה קָאָמַר לָהּ, הַיְנוּ עַל־יְדֵי שֶׁיִּלְמוֹד בִּשְׁבִיל שֶׁיִּתְקְרָא רַבִּי.

אָתָא פּוּשְׁקַנְצָא – וּפֵרֵשׁ רַשְׁבַּ"ם: עוֹרֵב, הַיְנוּ עַל־יְדֵי שֶׁיִּלְמַד בַּלַּיְלָה, מִלְּשׁוֹן עַרְבִית,

וּבַלְעָהּ – הַיְנוּ וּמֵגֵן עָלָיו מִן הַנָּחָשׁ הַנִּזְכָּר לְעֵיל.

---

39. **RaBbah...RaBbi.** The term *gavra rabba* (literally, "a great man") is used in the Talmud to refer to a rabbinical scholar of repute. Rebbe Nachman explains Rashbam's comment— that it was *RaBbah* (רבה) who said this—as alluding to a person who studies to become a *RaBba* (רבא, great one) for an ulterior motive. He studies not for the sake of study alone, but in order to be called rabbi—not all that meritorious a motive. In the context of Rabbah bar bar Chanah's story, therefore, the *akrukta,* which is his study of the Oral Law, is in danger of being swallowed by a serpent. This swallowing symbolizes turning his *shelo lishmah* study for personal gain (fame, wealth, etc.) into the truly reprehensible study whose motive is one-upmanship and argumentation (see n. 24; *Parparaot LeChokhmah*). How can a person protect himself from this serpent?

40. **OReV...ARVit...night.** The root letters of *orev* (עורב, female raven) and *arvit* (ערבית, night) are the same.

This comparison between *orev* and *arvit* also appears in Rashi's commentary to the Talmudic teaching: "His curly locks are black as a raven" (Song of Songs 5:11). Torah resides with someone who rises early to study and studies late into the night. He shows himself no mercy, "blackening" himself like the raven through self-abnegation (*Eruvin* 22a; cf. *Likutey Moharan* I, 15:5 and n.43).

41. **above mentioned serpent.** It keeps him from the serpent-like behavior of studying so as to harass and harangue other scholars.

tzephardeah—i.e., *tzipor deah.*[35] < As explained, the birds of the *kelipah* are the intellect of *Malkhut* of the Other Side. This is the *tzipor deah.*[36] >

That was as aKRA dehaGRuNia, the city of Hagrunia — This is phonetically similar to *"KRA beGaRoN* (cry out from the throat)" (Isaiah 58:1)—i.e., the song is drawn < from the *tzipor deah* mentioned above > .[37]

And how large was akra dehagrunia? Sixty houses — That is, by what means is the concept of "cry out from the throat" rectified? By means of the "sixty houses," the sixty tractates [of the Talmud]. Thus, Rashbam comments: "the Talmud says this." One should study Talmud.[38]

A serpent came by and swallowed it — Rashbam comments: "Rabbah says this." That is, < his study was > not for its own sake, and so the serpent < swallowed > it. This is why Rashbam comments: "RaBbah says this"—i.e., < he studied > in order to be called RaBbi.[39]

A pushkantza came by — Rashbam explains [that this is an] *OReV*, < which is similar to *ARVit* > —i.e., < at night > . One should study at night.[40]

and swallowed the serpent — [The study of Torah at night] protected him from the above mentioned serpent.[41]

---

35. **tzephardeah...tzipor deah.** The Ari teaches (*Shaar HaPesukim, VaEyrah* p.137) that the term *tzephardeah* is a composite of the Hebrew word for "bird," *tzipor,* and the word *deah,* which means "awareness" or "knowledge." The *tzipor* is *Malkhut,* which is built up with *deah;* the builders of *Malkhut* being *Netzach* and *Hod* (see above, n.32; cf. *Tana deBei Eliyahu* I, 7).

36. **As explained....** See above, the beginning of section 2 and note 28. As mentioned in note 10, *daat,* or *deah,* is the faculty by which man collates and filters the awareness provided by the *mochin.* This can be done in a pure manner—the *deah* of the two live pure *tziporim.* Or, it can be done in a profane manner—the *deah* of the *tziporim* of the *kelipah.*

37. **aKRA dehaGRuNia...KRA beGaRoN....** God instructed Isaiah (a prophet, the voice, the source of *Malkhut*) to cry out in a loud voice, for which one must contract the vocal chords. *Mai HaNachal* explains that *aKRuktA/Malkhut* is rectified through *aKRA dehagrunia,* the voice/song from the birds of *deah,* which draws from the same place as the prophets.

38. **study Talmud.** Quoting Proverbs (24:27), our Sages said: "then you shall build your houses"—this is the study of Talmud (*Sotah* 44a). The "sixty houses" thus alludes to the Talmud. The study of the sixty "houses" (tractates) of Talmud, itself a rectification of *Malkhut,* rectifies the voice.

וְסָלִיק יָתִיב בְּאִילָנָא – פֵּרֵשׁ הַמַּהֲרַשָׁ"א, שֶׁהוּא בְּחִינַת אַבְרָהָם,
שֶׁכָּתוּב אֶצְלוֹ: "וַיִּטַּע אֶשֶׁל" שֶׁהוּא בְּחִינַת חֶסֶד, הַיְנוּ שֶׁהַחוּט שֶׁל
חֶסֶד שֶׁנִּמְשָׁךְ עָלָיו מֵגֵן עָלָיו מִן הַנָּחָשׁ הַנַּ"ל.

תָּא חֲזִי כַּמָּה נָפִישׁ חֵילֵיהּ דְּאִילָנָא – הַיְנוּ שֶׁרַבָּה מַתְמִיהַּ אֶת
עַצְמוֹ, שֶׁכָּל כָּךְ גָּבַר עָלֵינוּ חַסְדּוֹ, שֶׁאֲפִלּוּ עַל זֶה יָכוֹל לְהָגֵן.

וּבָזֶה יִתְיַשֵּׁב הַסְּמִיכוּת שֶׁל הַמִּשְׁנָה: 'עֲשֵׂה לְךָ רַב, וּקְנֵה לְךָ חָבֵר,
וֶהֱוֵי דָן אֶת כָּל הָאָדָם לְכַף זְכוּת'.
כִּי עַל-יְדֵי שֶׁשּׁוֹמֵעַ הַנְּגִינָה כַּנַּ"ל, הוּא מְתַקֵּן בִּנְיַן הַמַּלְכוּת שֶׁלּוֹ,

וְזֶה 'עֲשֵׂה לְךָ רַב', הַיְנוּ שֶׁיְּתַקֵּן בְּחִינַת מַלְכוּת, וְזֶה עַל-יְדֵי 'קְנֵה
לְךָ חָבֵר', הַיְנוּ עַל-יְדֵי קָנֶה, שֶׁהַקּוֹל יוֹצֵא מִמֶּנּוּ,

A pushkantza came by and swallowed the serpent — The way to safeguard against such reprehensible study is by studying the Oral Torah at night (the *pushkantza*/raven).

It ascended and perched on a tree — This is because nighttime study equips a person with the element of lovingkindness (tree/Avraham), which protects him from thoughts that would bring him to studying for the wrong reasons.

Come, see how great the strength of that tree is! — Even Rabbah, a great and learned tzaddik, marveled at the power of the lovingkindness drawn upon the person who studies Oral Torah at night.

46. **in the manner explained above.** In other words, after studying at night.

47. **rectifies the concept of building up Malkhut.** For his speech then reflects the two birds of holiness—i.e., *Malkhut* rectified.

Here, Rebbe Nachman begins to relate to *Malkhut* as it pertains to each person individually. That is, each person, commensurate with his spiritual level, has the ability to rectify *Malkhut*—his aspect of *Malkhut* (*Torat Natan #2*). The *Biur HaLikutim* adds: Rebbe Nachman next comments on the Mishnaic teaching "Get *yourself* a rabbi...." From his words we learn that for a person to rectify his personal aspect of *Malkhut*, he must be very careful not to be misled by his own knowledge of Torah. He must not allow study *shelo lishmah* to have a detrimental affect on him. Much worse, however, is when a person thinks he is worthy of being a rabbi when he is not. Assuming authority not rightfully his can be likened to usurping a *malkhut* (kingdom) from its rightful ruler. He then blemishes *Malkhut* even more. In that case, he benefits from studying at night because of the modesty that it instills (cf. n.26).

48. **as mentioned.** See end of section 2 and note 32.

49. **aspect of Malkhut.** The Talmud (*Gittin* 62a) teaches: How do you know that the rabbis are called *melakhim* (kings)? From the verse in Proverbs (8:15), "With me, kings rule." "Me,"

It ascended and perched on a tree — Maharsha[42] comments that this is the aspect of Avraham, of whom it is written (Genesis 21:33), "He planted a tree." This corresponds to lovingkindness.[43] The thread of lovingkindness that is drawn over him protects him from the serpent.[44]

Come, see how great the strength of that tree is! — Rabbah expressed his amazement that God's lovingkindness on our behalf is so overpowering, that it can even protect us from this.[45]

4. With this, it is possible to reconcile the juxtaposition in the Mishnah: **Get yourself a rabbi, acquire for yourself a companion, and judge everyone favorably** (*Avot* 1:6).

By listening to song in the manner explained above[46] < and becoming absorbed in it—so that when another sings joyously, he, too, rejoices in God; and when another sings with spiritual inspiration, he, too, is inspired and contemplates repentance—he then > rectifies the concept of building up *Malkhut*,[47] < namely, *Netzach* and *Hod,* as mentioned[48] >.

This is, "Get yourself a rabbi"—i.e., < rectify > the aspect of *Malkhut*.[49] It is accomplished by *"K'NeH* (acquire) for yourself a companion." That is, by means of the *KaNeH* (windpipe), via which the voice emerges.[50]

42. **Maharsha.** See *Bava Batra* 73b, *s.v. d'salik.*

43. **He planted a tree...lovingkindness.** Avraham planted a tree so that he could serve his guests fruit with their meals (*Rashi, loc. cit.*). By virtue of his exceptional hospitality Avraham came to personify the quality of lovingkindness, as Scripture itself indicates in: "Give truth to Yaakov, lovingkindness to Avraham" (Micah 7:20).

44. **The thread of lovingkindness....** As explained, by studying the Oral Torah at night a person draws lovingkindness upon himself. This lovingkindness safeguards him from the serpent (see above, nn.26,27). Not only is he protected against having his study descend into contentiousness and one-upmanship, but the thread of lovingkindness even has the power to transform his studying for personal gain into studying *lishmah* (*Parparaot LeChokhmah*). Such is the value of nighttime study of Mishnah, Talmud, the Codes, or Kabbalah!

45. **even protect us from this.** The story thus translates in our text as follows:
Rabbah bar bar Chanah recounted: I myself saw this akrukta that was as akra deHagrunia — Only by rectifying *Malkhut*/speech (*akrukta*) is it possible to rectify the *garon*/voice.
And how large was the city of Hagrunia? Sixty houses — How does one rectify the voice through speech? By studying the Talmud, the sixty tractates.
A serpent came by and swallowed it — But what of the person who studies for personal gain? Can his study still rectify the voice and speech, or will his motive for studying deteriorate still further, to contentiousness and one-upmanship (the serpent)?

שֶׁמְּחַבֵּר הַשְׁנֵי כְּרוּבִים כְּרוּבִים לִהְיוֹת פָּנִים בְּפָנִים "כְּמַעַר אִישׁ וְלֹיוֹת",
'בִּזְמַן שֶׁיִשְׂרָאֵל עוֹשִׂין רְצוֹנוֹ שֶׁל מָקוֹם'.

וַאֲזֵי כְּשֶׁיְתַקֵּן בְּחִינַת מַלְכוּת שֶׁלּוֹ, וְיוּכַל לִמְשֹׁל בְּכָל מַה שֶּׁיִּרְצֶה
וְיוּכַל לְהָמִית לָזֶה וּלְהַחֲיוֹת לָזֶה, וְנִמְצָא עוֹלָם חָרֵב. לָזֶה אָמַר:
'וֶהֱוֵי דָן אֶת כָּל־הָאָדָם לְכַף זְכוּת'. שֶׁצָּרִיךְ לָדוּן אֶת כָּל אָדָם לְכַף
זְכוּת, כִּי אֵין הַקָּדוֹשׁ־בָּרוּךְ־הוּא חָפֵץ בְּחֻרְבַּן־הָעוֹלָם, "כִּי לֹא
לְתֹהוּ בְרָאָהּ, לָשֶׁבֶת יְצָרָהּ".

two of them spent their entire time studying Torah (rectifying *Malkhut*). After twelve years, Eliyahu the prophet appeared at the entrance of the cave to inform Rabbi Shimon that the decree against his life had been rescinded. Leaving the cave, Rabbi Shimon saw people working the fields. This angered him. "How dare they occupy themselves with worldly matters instead of Torah?!" he declared. Fires then erupted wherever Rabbi Shimon and Rabbi Elazar looked, until a Voice rang out from heaven: "You've come out to destroy My world? Return to your cave!" Rabbi Shimon and his son returned to their isolation for another year, after which they were given Heaven's permission to leave. Rabbi Elazar could still not contain his anger. However, as the Talmud relates, Rabbi Shimon rebuilt whatever Rabbi Elazar devastated, for he had begun to judge everyone favorably (see *Shabbat* 33b). There is much in this incident that relates to our lesson. Rabbi Shimon spent his long "night" in exile studying Torah. He rectified his aspect of *Malkhut* and attained such an exalted level that he was granted permission to reveal the esoteric teachings of the Kabbalah (studied during the night, as in n.19). Yet, even someone as great as Rabbi Shimon turned critical and had to be shown the value of judging everyone favorably.

56. to be inhabited. Scripture's words are directed at the belligerent nations who in waging war, plunder and destroy whatever stands in their way: "He did not create [the world] to be a wasteland . . . ."

The Mishnah thus translates in our text as follows: **Get yourself a rabbi** — in order to rectify your aspect of *Malkhut*, **k'neh a companion** — bind your voice to holy speech. But once you've rectified your aspect of *Malkhut*, take care not to become so zealous that you destroy the world in your burning desire to see it rectified as well. Therefore, **judge everyone favorably**.

In the course of a discussion about the mitzvah of bringing children into the world, the Talmud (*Yevamot* 62a) quotes this verse from Isaiah: "He did not create it a wasteland, but formed it to be inhabited." Reb Noson writes: The main reason each person is sent into the world is to rectify his personal aspect of *Malkhut*. To the degree that a person succeeds in his mission, he reveals God's *Malkhut*. Thus, a person should use everything he has at his disposal, all that God has given him, to reveal *Malkhut* of Holiness in the world (*Torat Natan* #2).

In review: Listening to the singing of a virtuous person is beneficial to serving God; listening to the singing of a wicked person is detrimental. The reason is that song, which corresponds to prophecy, stems from *Netzach* and *Hod*, the two *sefirot* that nurse *Malkhut*. A person is sustained by the vitality he receives from one of the two manifestations of *Malkhut*. Commensurate with his deeds, he draws either from *Malkhut* of Holiness or *Malkhut* of the

This joins the two cherubs so that they are face to face, "as the embrace of a man and his consort" (1 Kings 7:36)[51] when the Jewish people perform the will of the Holy One (*Bava Batra* 99a).[52]

But, then, when a person rectifies his aspect of *Malkhut*,[53] he is able to rule over whatever he chooses. He can bring death to one person, or give life to another. The world would then be ravaged. To this [the Mishnah] says, "and judge everyone favorably."[54] It is necessary to judge each person favorably, for the Holy One has no desire in the world's destruction[55]: "He did not create it a wasteland, but formed it to be inhabited" (Isaiah 45:18).[56]

---

our Sages say, refers to the Torah. Likening rabbis and Torah scholars to *melakhim* indicates they are an aspect of *Malkhut*. As Rebbe Nachman explains elsewhere: The Torah scholars are the ones who elevate *Malkhut* (*Likutey Moharan* I, 135:4).

50. **K'NeH...KaNeH....** How does obtaining a rabbi/*Malkhut* rectify the voice? Through "*k'neh* (קנה) for yourself a companion"—i.e., the study of Talmud at night. The holy speech of nighttime Talmud study rectifies the six orders of Mishnah, the six rings of the *kaneh* (windpipe, קנה), the voice. This is the rectification of *Z'er Anpin* (voice) and *Malkhut* (speech).

51. **as the embrace....** When King Solomon built the Holy Temple, he had basins designed to hold water for the Temple's needs. Engraved onto the stands constructed to house these basins were lions, palms and embracing cherubs (see *Rashi, loc. cit.*).

52. **cherubs...face to face...will of the Holy One.** On the cover of the Holy Ark, which held the Tablets of Law, stood two golden cherubs. Similar to the embracing cherubs engraved on the water basins (see previous note), when the Jews performed God's will, the cherubs turned to face each other with the fond look of a man and a woman in love. This was a symbol of God's love for Israel (*Rashbam, loc. cit.*). In our context, the two cherubs symbolize voice and speech. When a person studies Torah (the Ark), voice and speech are united in holiness. Then, *Netzach* and *Hod* (the cherubs) interact, providing prophecy and song in holiness (see nn.3,5-6). Thus Torah study, especially Talmud at night, rectifies song. This enables the one who studies to listen to anyone who sings, and through that song come to serve God.

53. **rectifies his aspect of Malkhut.** He has corrected *his* personal aspect of *Malkhut* and is now a ruler (see n.49). As Rebbe Nachman goes on to explain, "he is able to rule over whatever he chooses...."

54. **would then be ravaged....** For not everyone has the ability to exercise judgment properly. Having acquired the power to rule, an error in judgment can cause untold damage and devastation. The Mishnah therefore concludes: Judge everyone favorably.

55. **world's destruction.** By rectifying the voice of song, a person gains a certain degree of rule and mastery, including the ability to issue decrees for life or death which heaven carries out. It is therefore of the utmost importance that he always look for the good in others. He must not destroy God's creation, because the Creator Himself values lovingkindness and desires the world's continued existence.

The Talmud relates how Rabbi Shimon bar Yochai was forced to flee from the Romans who were occupying the Land of Israel. He hid in a cave with his son Rabbi Elazar, and the

וּבִשְׁבִיל זֶה מַרְגְּלָא בְּפוּמָא דְּאִינְשֵׁי עַכְשָׁו לוֹמַר, שֶׁהַחַזָּנִים הֵם שׁוֹטִים, וְאֵינָם בְּנֵי דֵעָה. כִּי עַכְשָׁו מַלְכוּת דִּקְדֻשָּׁה בַּגָּלוּת. וְעַל כֵּן הַנְּגִינָה שֶׁהִיא נִמְשֶׁכֶת מֵאֲתַר דִּנְבִיאִים מִבְּחִינַת מֹחִין וְדַעַת דְּמַלְכוּת דִּקְדֻשָּׁה, וְעַכְשָׁו שֶׁהַמַּלְכוּת בְּגָלוּת, וְעַל כֵּן הַנְּגִינָה נִפְגֶּמֶת, וְעַל כֵּן הַחַזָּנִים הֵם בְּלֹא דַעַת, כִּי אֵין לָהֶם כֹּחַ עַכְשָׁו לְהַמְשִׁיךְ הַנְּגִינָה מִשָּׁרְשָׁהּ שֶׁבִּקְדֻשָּׁה, שֶׁהוּא בְּחִינַת מֹחִין וְדַעַת שֶׁל מַלְכוּת דִּקְדֻשָּׁה, כַּנַּ"ל.

אֲבָל לֶעָתִיד שֶׁיִּתְעַלֶּה מַלְכוּת דִּקְדֻשָּׁה, וְיִהְיֶה "ה' לְמֶלֶךְ עַל כָּל הָאָרֶץ", אֲזַי תִּתְעַלֶּה וְתֻשְׁלַם הַנְּגִינָה בִּבְחִינַת דַּעַת דְּמַלְכוּת דִּקְדֻשָּׁה, שֶׁמִּשָּׁם נִמְשֶׁכֶת הַנְּגִינָה כַּנַּ"ל.

וְזֶהוּ: "כִּי מֶלֶךְ כָּל הָאָרֶץ אֱלֹהִים, זַמְּרוּ מַשְׂכִּיל". כִּי אֲזַי כְּשֶׁיִּהְיֶה ה' לְמֶלֶךְ עַל כָּל הָאָרֶץ וְיִתְעַלֶּה מַלְכוּת דִּקְדֻשָּׁה, אֲזַי: "זַמְּרוּ מַשְׂכִּיל", הַיְנוּ שֶׁהַחַזָּנִים הַמְזַמְּרִים יִהְיוּ בְּדַעַת וּבְשֵׂכֶל. עַל-יְדֵי שֶׁיִּתְעַלֶּה מַלְכוּת דִּקְדֻשָּׁה, וִיקַבְּלוּ הַנְּגִינָה מִשָּׁרְשָׁהּ שֶׁבִּקְדֻשָּׁה, שֶׁהוּא בְּחִינַת דַּעַת וּמֹחִין שֶׁל מַלְכוּת דִּקְדֻשָּׁה כַּנַּ"ל:

שַׁיָּךְ לְעֵיל.

וְזֶהוּ: "כִּי גָדֹל מֵעַל שָׁמַיִם חַסְדֶּךָ". 'שָׁמַיִם' הוּא בְּחִינַת קוֹל, כְּמוֹ

---

61. **O intelligent one.** Psalm 47 speaks about the future, when God's Kingdom will be revealed to the nations and everyone will accept Him as their King.

62. **ZaMRu maSKiL...m'ZaMRim will have...SeKheL.** This, as opposed to the present, when song is impaired. As explained, when a cantor nowadays sings—although the songs he sings are prayers and praise of God—it cannot generally be considered *zamru maskil* (זמרו משכיל). This is because when today's *chazanim* sing (מזמרים), they do not draw *sekhel* (שכל), the *mochin* of holiness.

63. **by virtue of Malkhut of Holiness having ascended....** This will occur after the coming of Mashiach, a scion from the House of David. King David, the personification of *Malkhut* of Holiness, rectified song and was lauded as one "skilled at playing music"—the level of *zamru maskil*. For with the revelation of *Malkhut* of Holiness, song is also elevated (*Mai HaNachal*).

64. **higher than the heavens.** The Talmud teaches: Rava pointed out an apparent contradiction. One verse states: "For Your lovingkindness is higher than the heavens" (Psalms 108:5). Another states: "For Your lovingkindness is as high as the heavens" (Psalms

5. This is also the reason people are now fond of saying that *chazanim* (cantors) are fools, lacking in *deah* (knowledge).[57] For *Malkhut* of Holiness is presently in exile. Song is [generally] drawn from the place of the prophets, from the mentalities and *daat* of *Malkhut* of Holiness. But now that *Malkhut* is in exile and song is consequently impaired, the *chazanim* lack *daat*.[58] For, at present, they do not have the power to draw song from its source in holiness, which is the mentalities and intellect of *Malkhut* of Holiness.[59]

But in the Future, when *Malkhut* of Holiness ascends and "God will be King over the entire earth" (Zechariah 14:9), then song will be uplifted and perfected in the aspect of the intellect of *Malkhut* of Holiness, from which song is drawn.[60]

This is the meaning of "For the Lord is King of all the earth, *zamru maskil* (sing, O intelligent one)" (Psalms 47:8).[61] For when God will be King over all the earth and *Malkhut* of Holiness ascends, then, "*ZaMRu maSKiL*"—i.e., the *chazanim* who *m'ZaMRim* (sing) will have *daat* and *SeKheL* (intelligence)[62] by virtue of *Malkhut* of Holiness having ascended. They will receive song from its source in holiness, which is the intellect and mentalities of *Malkhut* of Holiness, as explained.[63]

Addendum relating to the lesson:

6. This is the meaning of, "For Your lovingkindness is higher than the heavens" (Psalms 108:5).[64] "Heavens" corresponds to the voice, as is

---

Other Side. To protect one's self from harmful singers and song, one should study the Oral Law, Talmud, at night. This will rectify song and protect him from blemishing *Malkhut* (§1). King David attained kingship because he rectified the voice/song and knew how to draw song—i.e., nurse *Malkhut*—from holiness (§2). And each person must rectify his unique aspect of *Malkhut*. At the same time, he must take care that the power this affords him does not cause him to harm someone else (§4).

57. **lacking in deah.** See above, the beginning of section 3 and note 37, for the connection between the cantors (song) and the birds of *deah*.

58. **Song is generally drawn...But now....** As above, section 1, notes 7-10.

59. **do not have the power to draw....** So that the voice is unable to arouse the mentalities (n.2). Rather, song is presently drawn from the *kelipot,* which are without holy *daat* (see also *Etz Chaim* 48:2).

60. **But in the Future....** As in (Isaiah 11:9), "for the world will be filled with *deah* of God...." This awareness will build *Malkhut* of Holiness, and the song of holiness will be uplifted.

שֶׁכָּתוּב: "מִשָּׁמַיִם הִשְׁמַעְתָּ קוֹלֶךְ", כִּי עַל־יְדֵי הַחֶסֶד, הַיְנוּ בְּחִינַת
חוּט שֶׁל חֶסֶד, הַנִּמְשָׁךְ עַל־יְדֵי שֶׁלּוֹמֵד תּוֹרָה בַּלַּיְלָה עַל־יְדֵי־זֶה
נִתְתַּקֵּן הַקּוֹל כַּנַּ"ל. וְזֶהוּ: "כִּי גָדוֹל מֵעַל שָׁמַיִם חַסְדֶּךְ" כַּנַּ"ל:

הַשְׁתֵּי צִפְּרִים דִּקְדֻשָּׁה, שֶׁמֵּשָׁם הַנְּבוּאָה נִמְשֶׁכֶת, הֵם בִּנְיַן מַלְכוּת
דִּקְדֻשָּׁה, וְעַל כֵּן הַעֲמָדַת מֶלֶךְ הָיָה עַל־פִּי נְבוּאָה, כָּל מַלְכוּת
בֵּית דָּוִד שֶׁהָיָה עַל־פִּי נְבוּאָה. וְהַנְּבוּאָה נִמְשֶׁכֶת מִן הַכְּרוּבִים
שֶׁהֵם בְּחִינַת שְׁתֵּי צִפְּרִים הַנַּ"ל, שֶׁהֵם בִּנְיַן מַלְכוּת דִּקְדֻשָּׁה כַּנַּ"ל:

מֵאַחַר עָלוֹת הֱבִיאוֹ, הַיְנוּ מֵאַחַר הַמֵּינִיקוֹת, כִּי הֵם יַנְקִין לַנְּבִיאִים
וְכוּ' כַּנַּ"ל. וְזֶהוּ "מֵאַחַר עָלוֹת", הַיְנוּ שֶׁדָּוִד הַמֶּלֶךְ, עָלָיו הַשָּׁלוֹם,
הָיָה יָכוֹל לְתַקֵּן וּלְהַעֲלוֹת גַּם הַנְּגִינָה שֶׁאֵינוֹ מֵאָדָם כָּשֵׁר,
לְהַעֲלוֹתָהּ אֶל הַקְּדֻשָּׁה.

69. **appointment of a king...prophecy.** In the manner that Moshe prophetically appointed Joshua, and Shmuel received prophecy to appoint Shaul and, later, David as Israel's king. See Rambam, *Yad HaChazakah, Hilkhot Melakhim* 1:3.

70. **Davidic dynasty....** As regards King David, see 1 Samuel 16:13; as regards King David's descendants, see 2 Samuel 7:14.

71. **prophecy...cherubs...birds...Malkhut of Holiness.** Prophecy, rooted in *Netzach* and *Hod,* builds *Malkhut* (see above, §2).

The *Biur HaLikutim* asks: The two birds that build *Malkhut* are certainly pure and rooted in holiness; *Malkhut* itself is certainly without impurity. How, then, can the evil forces draw nourishment from these birds and from *Malkhut*? Why is there a need for *Malkhut* to be built up? However, this has to do with the way God structured His creation: *Malkhut* of Holiness itself complies with *laylah* (night) and darkness. This is to enable the spark of holiness to descend to the lowest realms and precisely from there bring about rectification. In the process, *Malkhut* must inevitably become a source of sustenance for impurity and the forces of evil; profane song, *YeLaLaH* (wailing), is drawn in the *LaYLaH* from the birds of the *kelipah* that metamorphose from the two birds of holiness. This is how it must be until the voice/song is rectified completely, which will be when Mashiach comes. See also *Rabbi Nachman's Stories,* "The Seven Beggars" ("Fourth Day," pp.390-398).

72. **From behind the nursing ewes....** This excerpt is from section 2. See also notes 31 and 32. The Rebbe now explains the connection between "From behind the nursing ewes" and "behind" holiness or the "back" of holiness.

73. **not virtuous...to holiness.** King David rectified *Malkhut* by rising and studying Torah at night. He thereby merited the qualities of *lishmah* and holy song, and through this was able to rectify the song of even unworthy singers.

written, "You caused Your voice to be heard from heaven."[65] For by means of lovingkindness—i.e., the thread of lovingkindness drawn over one who studies Torah at night—the voice is rectified.[66] This is, "For Your lovingkindness is higher than the heavens."[67]

7. The two birds of holiness, from which prophecy is drawn, are an aspect of building up *Malkhut* of Holiness.[68] This is why the appointment of a king was based on prophecy[69]; as was the case for the entire Davidic dynasty, which was prophetically determined.[70] And prophecy is drawn from the cherubs, which correspond to the two birds, the concept of building up *Malkhut* of Holiness.[71]

8. "From behind the nursing ewes He brought him"—that is, from behind those that suckle. [This refers to *Netzach* and *Hod,*] for they nourish the prophets and are the concept of building up *Malkhut*.[72]

This is the meaning of, "From behind the nursing ewes." King David had the ability to rectify and uplift even the song of someone who was not virtuous, to elevate it to holiness.[73] This is: "From

57:11). How can both statements be true? However, the former applies to those who perform [their religious devotion] for its own sake—*lishmah*. Then, His lovingkindness is *higher than* the heavens. The latter applies to those whose [devotion] is not for its own sake—*shelo lishmah*. Then, His lovingkindness is only *as high as* the heavens. Rabbi Yehudah said in the name of Rav: A person should always engage in Torah study and [perform] mitzvot even if not for their own sake; for even one whose deeds are *shelo lishmah* can eventually come to [study and perform mitzvot] for their own sake (*Pesachim* 50b). Rebbe Nachman here refers solely to the first verse, corresponding to *lishmah,* and he explains "higher than the heavens" within the context of this lesson.

65. **voice...from heaven.** These words appear in the Rosh HaShanah Mussaf prayer and are a paraphrase of Deuteronomy 4:36. Throughout the Kabbalah, heaven and earth conceptually parallel *Z'er Anpin* and *Malkhut.* Thus, "heavens" corresponds to the voice/*Z'er Anpin.*

66. **voice is rectified.** As above, section 1. Previously, Rebbe Nachman indirectly connected lovingkindness to rectifying the voice. By studying at night, a person draws lovingkindness and so merits *lishmah.* His holy speech rectifies his voice. Here, the Rebbe directly ties lovingkindness to the voice: "Higher than the heavens" suggests that lovingkindness is drawn over the voice, rectifying it.

67. **Your lovingkindness is higher than the heavens.** The *Parparaot LeChokhmah* explains: From the verse that teaches that God's lovingkindness is "as high as the heavens" (Psalms 57:11), we learn that *shelo lishmah*—say, to be called rabbi—is also somewhat meritorious. Yet, when that study takes place at night, it is even of greater value. The lovingkindness he engenders then will eventually turn his study *shelo lishmah* into study *lishmah.* This is because study of Torah for its own sake and nighttime study share the more exalted spiritual quality of "*higher* than the heavens."

68. **The two birds...Malkhut of Holiness.** As explained above, sections 1 and 2 (see also nn.32,47).

וְזֶהוּ: "מֵאַחַר עָלוֹת הֱבִיאוּ", הַיְנוּ גַּם הַנְּגִינָה, שֶׁהִיא מֵאֲחוֹרֵי
הַקְּדֻשָּׁה בִּבְחִינַת "מֵאַחַר עָלוֹת", מֵאַחַר הַמֵּינִיקוֹת, כִּי הַנְּגִינָה
דִּקְדֻשָּׁה הוּא מֵאֲתַר דִּנְבִיאִים יַנְקִין, וְהַנְּגִינָה שֶׁאֵינוֹ בִּקְדֻשָּׁה הִיא
בְּחִינַת מֵאַחַר עָלוֹת מֵאֲחוֹרֵי הַקְּדֻשָּׁה. וְדָוִד הַמֶּלֶךְ, עָלָיו הַשָּׁלוֹם,
הָיָה יָכוֹל לְתַקֵּן נְגִינָה זוֹ גַּם כֵּן, וְעַל־יְדֵי־זֶה נִתְעַלָּה מַלְכוּת
דִּקְדֻשָּׁה כַּנַּ"ל. וְזֶהוּ: "מֵאַחַר עָלוֹת הֱבִיאוּ לִרְעוֹת בְּיַעֲקֹב" וְכוּ', כִּי
עַל־יְדֵי־זֶה זָכָה לְמַלְכוּת כַּנַּ"ל.

Although, directly, this lesson was taught regarding the cantor of Ladizin, whose sinful behavior Rebbe Nachman revealed (see n.1), indirectly, it also relates to other *chazanim* with whom the Rebbe had previous dealings. Rebbe Nachman gave this lesson just before he took up residence in the city of Breslov (n.1). Prior to that he had spent two strife-ridden years in Zlatipolia, at the end of which virtually the entire town had turned against him. This discord was sown by two of Zlatipolia's *chazanim*. When Rebbe Nachman first arrived in Zlatipolia just before Rosh HaShanah 5561 (1801), he was received very warmly. The townsfolk spared no effort in welcoming the Rebbe and invited him and his followers to pray in the central synagogue. This they did, although, as it happened, Rebbe Nachman disapproved of the *chazan* and his son-in-law who between them led the Yom Kippur services. When he later criticized them, saying that they were praying just to impress their wives, these cantors became incensed and slandered Rebbe Nachman before the Shpola Zeida. This initiated years of relentless persecution against the Breslover Chassidim (*Tzaddik* #11).

As we've seen over the course of the lesson, the two birds of impurity have the power to lead people astray. However, unlike outright sin, which is obvious, the song of the wicked influences in a far more subtle manner: drawing a person away from God, cooling his heart to holiness, until he eventually succumbs to sin (cf. *Chagigah* 15b, concerning Acher and Greek songs). Also through the power of voice and speech, and frequently in a discreet manner as well, is the undermining of holiness caused by the very severe sin of slander (see above, nn.4,32). Many times slander begins as an apparently benign remark—a defense of one's honor, a righting of a wrong, and the like. As Rebbe Nachman teaches in Lesson #1, the evil inclination will often come to a person in the guise of a mitzvah: the mitzvah of opposing those whose opinions or ways are different than our own. Reb Noson writes that these so-called mitzvot—namely, contentiousness and strife—are decidedly not part of the Torah's 613 mitzvot. As the Rebbe teaches in this lesson, there is a need to judge everyone favorably. Each person hears the Voice differently. And, every person has his own unique aspect of *Malkhut*, which he must strive to better by studying Torah. Using these tools of Torah study and judging others favorably, we can merit the two birds of holiness, the return of prophecy, and the building of the Temple, speedily in our days. Amen.

behind the nursing ewes He brought him..."—referring even to the song that is from the *AChoRey* (back) of holiness; corresponding to "From *AChaR* (behind) the nursing ewes," from *achar* those that suckle.[74] For song that is holy is from the place that the prophets nurse. But song that is not holy corresponds to "From *achar* the nursing ewes..."—from the *achorey* of holiness. King David was able to correct this song as well. And as a result, *Malkhut* of Holiness ascended. This is: "From behind the nursing ewes He brought him to tend [His people] Yaakov...." For it was through this that [David] merited *malkhut* (kingship).[75]

---

74. **AChoRey...AChaR...those that suckle.** Every concept of holiness has an opposite and a reverse. The opposite of holiness, for example, is unholiness or godlessness—there is nothing holy about them. The reverse of a concept, however, does contain a modicum of that concept. Thus, the reverse side or back (אחור) of holiness, though for the most part lacking holiness, does possess a modicum of that quality. It is to the back of holiness that the polar opposite of holiness connects and draws sustenance. In our context, it is "from behind (אחר) the nursing ewes," from the back of *Netzach* and *Hod,* that the wicked draw song.

75. **David merited malkhut.** For he rectified *Malkhut* completely.

Reb Noson writes: Concerning the Revelation at Sinai it is written, "Then God spoke to you out of the fire. You heard the sounds of words, but saw no image—nothing but a voice" (Deuteronomy 4:12). It is the same today for whoever attempts to come close to God and the Torah. In His kindness, God fills each person with ideas on how to come closer to Him. The channel through which these thoughts (*mochin*, intellect) descend to a person is the voice. It calls out to him, often disguised as conscience, reminding him to steer clear of folly and encouraging him to return to God. The choice is the person's. If he wishes, he can hear that voice of holiness calling to him. Alternatively, he can listen for the voice of impurity, which, if he follows it, will lead him astray.

This was the story of the Jewish people's bondage in Egypt. PhaRaOH is *HaORePh* (the nape of the neck), *behind* the throat. His desire was to trap speech, *Malkhut* of Holiness. He enslaved the Jews and constantly burdened them with labor so as to prevent them from praying to God. When the time for the Exodus drew near, as Scripture states (Exodus 2:23-24), "The Jewish people sighed...screamed out...groaned...." God saw that the Jews were beginning to rouse from their slumber and were beginning to hear His Voice calling out to them. In contrast, Pharaoh said, "Who is God that I should listen to His Voice?" Therefore, God redeemed the Jews. And, because they were worthy, they merited hearing His Voice at Sinai, where they received the Torah and became God's Chosen People (*Torat Natan #1*).

* * *

ליקוטי מוהר"ן סימן ד'

לְשׁוֹן רַבֵּנוּ, זִכְרוֹנוֹ לִבְרָכָה

אָנֹכִי ה' אֱלֹהֶיךָ אֲשֶׁר הוֹצֵאתִיךָ מֵאֶרֶץ מִצְרַיִם מִבֵּית עֲבָדִים.

א כְּשֶׁאָדָם יוֹדֵעַ שֶׁכָּל מְאֹרְעוֹתָיו הֵם לְטוֹבָתוֹ, זֹאת הַבְּחִינָה הִיא מֵעֵין עוֹלָם הַבָּא, כְּמוֹ שֶׁכָּתוּב: "בַּה' אֲהַלֵּל דָּבָר בֵּאלֹהִים אֲהַלֵּל

to the two chassidim about confession, they wondered if this practice shouldn't apply to them as well. Yet, since the three of them had been close followers of Rebbe Nachman for a while and he had never mentioned it, they assumed that it did not. That, however, was before the Rebbe gave this teaching. In the lesson (§9), the Rebbe speaks about how *every time* a person comes to the tzaddik he should confess. He also specifies how the tzaddik must attain humility in three major attributes: wisdom, strength, and wealth (§10). It was clear that the Rebbe intended this as an allusion to the three of them (Reb Aharon was wealthy; Reb Shmuel Isaac was extremely strong; Reb Yudel was especially smart). Therefore, immediately after Shavuot they each came before Rebbe Nachman and confessed. They also understood that the Rebbe's reference in the lesson to "the one eye of compassion" had to do with his own concern and "looking out" for their benefit. And, if they needed any further proof that all this applied to them, it came when (as indicated in the lesson, §10) the three of them proved influential in bringing back to God a number of Jews who had gone away from their heritage (*Tovot Zikhronot* #4, p.106).

The Magid of Terhovitza, another of Rebbe Nachman's more prominent chassidim, had a son-in-law by the name of Reb Yitzchak Segal. This Reb Yitzchak had been a follower of Rebbe Zusia of Anipoli. Before Rebbe Zusia passed away, Reb Yitzchak asked him to which tzaddik he should now attach himself. "To the one that tells you to confess," Rebbe Zusia answered. Reb Yitzchak then heard that Rebbe Nachman had his followers confess in his presence and he became a Breslover Chassid (*Oral Tradition*). Rebbe Nachman apparently continued the practice of confession until a short while before his passing (probably after his return from Lemberg in the summer of 1808; cf. *Tzaddik* #491). Reb Yehudah Eliezer, a young man who joined the Rebbe's following at that time, began confessing in his presence. The Rebbe stopped him. Instead, he instructed him to speak to Reb Noson, though not to confess in front of him (*Sichot V'Sipurim* #56, p.143).

2. **Anokhi....** At creation's beginning, God said (Genesis 1:1): בראשית ברא אלהים את ("In the beginning the Lord created the..."). Each of these four words contains the letter *aleph* (א). The Kabbalah speaks of them as "the four *alphin*" (see *Zohar* I, 5a; anglicized as "*alephs*"). Building on this, Rebbe Nachman teaches elsewhere that there are four *alephs* from which Torah is drawn. Those who are virtuous, the tzaddikim, receive their Torah teachings from the *alephs* of holiness, thus increasing the holiness of those who come to hear their lessons. Those who are unworthy receive their Torah teachings from the "fallen *alephs*," which distance people from God (see *Likutey Moharan* I, 28:1 and n.5). Now, it is no coincidence

LIKUTEY MOHARAN #4[1]

"Anokhi YHVH Elohekha (I am God your Lord) Who brought you out
of the land of *Mitzrayim* (Egypt), from the house of slavery."[2]

(Exodus 20:2)

When a person knows that everything that happens to him is for
his benefit, this perception is a foretaste of the World to Come.
As < King David > said, "When He is *YHVH*, I will praise His word;

---

1. **Likutey Moharan #4.** This lesson was given on Shavuot 5561 (May 17, 1801), in Zlatipolia
(*Until The Mashiach*, p.65). The text is *leshon Rabbeinu z'l* (see end of first note to Lesson #2
where this terminology has been explained). The main themes of the lesson are: recognizing
God in all circumstances; confession in the presence of the tzaddik; humility, especially that
of the tzaddik; and the three steps in attachment to tzaddikim.

Prior to giving the lesson, Rebbe Nachman told a story about the Baal Shem Tov. One of
the Baal Shem Tov's followers, a truly pious Jew, had fallen gravely ill. Suffering terrible
pains in his bones, he sent a message to the Baal Shem Tov: "I heard from my master that
anyone who repents fully will certainly not pass away before his time. I've repented fully and
am not that old. Yet my situation is very grave." The Baal Shem Tov realized the chassid was
right, his life was in danger, and so he immediately set off to see him. "It's true," the Baal
Shem Tov explained to the messenger while on the way, "he has repented fully. But if he
wants to save his life, he must confess his iniquities before a true tzaddik." In the Heavenly
Court there were no judgments against the chassid. Yet because of the sins he had committed,
the forces of evil still had the power to harm him in this world. But if he confessed, he would
free himself from the last vestiges of his iniquities, the spiritual markings of which were still
etched upon his bones. Only then could the chassid recover completely.

When the Baal Shem Tov came to the chassid, he said, "Confess what you know, what
God knows, and what I also know. Then you'll be healed." But the chassid was unwilling to
confess in front of the Baal Shem Tov. Again and again the Baal Shem Tov tried, but it was
of no use. Not long after, his condition took a turn for the worse. His bones became so brittle
they began to break. The pain was excruciating, yet the chassid did not confess in the Baal
Shem Tov's presence. A short while later he passed away (*Tzaddik* #184).

That Shavuot, among Rebbe Nachman's chassidim were two men who, like the Baal Shem
Tov's follower, suffered from severe pain in their bones. In his lesson Rebbe Nachman spoke
about confession and how it helps to remove the effects of a person's sins, which are etched upon
the bones (§5). The Rebbe said to these two men: "On Shavuot night we recite the six-hundred
thirteen mitzvot—bundles and bundles of mitzvot. Like the word *tZaVat* (צות), mitZVah (מצוה)
suggests joining the bones together so that 'not one of them is broken' " (Psalms 34:21; see text,
§6). This proved to be a cure for the two followers (*Tovot Zikhronot* #4, p.106).

Also that Shavuot, three of Rebbe Nachman's most prominent followers were with him,
Reb Yudel, Reb Shmuel Isaac and Reb Aharon the Rav (see *Until The Mashiach*, pp.299-
307). Hearing the story about the Baal Shem Tov and the chassid, and how the Rebbe spoke

דָּבָר". וְזֹאת הַבְּחִינָה הִיא מֵעֵין עוֹלָם הַבָּא, כְּמוֹ שֶׁאָמְרוּ חֲכָמֵינוּ,
זִכְרוֹנָם לִבְרָכָה: "בַּיּוֹם הַהוּא יִהְיֶה ה' אֶחָד". וְהִקְשׁוּ: וְכִי הָאִידָנָא
לָאו הוּא אֶחָד? וְתֵרְצוּ חֲכָמֵינוּ, זִכְרוֹנָם לִבְרָכָה: הָאִידָנָא מְבָרְכִין
עַל הַטּוֹבָה הַטּוֹב וְהַמֵּטִיב, וְעַל הָרָעָה דַּיָּן אֱמֶת. וּלְעָתִיד כֻּלּוֹ
הַטּוֹב וְהַמֵּטִיב, שֶׁיִּהְיֶה שֵׁם ה' וְשֵׁם אֱלֹקִים אַחֲדוּת אֶחָד:

which is singular. This, he explains, is because only good comes forth from God. He is one, and a unified good emanates from Him. Changes only appear where there is a negation or absence of good. Rather than coming from God, the evils are determined by those that receive them, namely mankind. Thus, in this world man does not recognize God's oneness (*Pesachim* 50a, *s.v. l'olam haba*). For there are times when punishment, in the form of severe judgments, obscures God's good. However, instead of recognizing the punishment for what it is—a call to repent and a means for effecting forgiveness for our sins—we tend to view these judgments as bad. It is therefore the way we receive whatever comes from God that determines whether it is called good or bad. It is our perception that determines whether we recite "Blessed are You... Who is good and beneficent," or "Blessed are You... the truthful Judge."

The *Be'Ibey HaNachal* adds: Presently, even a person who accepts that everything is for the best also blesses "the truthful Judge" over bad tidings, albeit joyously. This is because his acceptance is based on faith, not knowledge and conscious awareness. He has faith that the punishment is for his benefit, but does not yet *know* this with complete awareness. Were he to reach a level where he truly comprehended this with every fiber of his being, then even in this world he would recite "Who is good and beneficent" in every situation.

7. **entirely Who is good....** Rashi (*loc. cit., s.v. kulo*) explains that in the World to Come there will only be good tidings. That is, whatever happens will be recognized as being beneficial. Only the blessing "Who is good and beneficent" will be said.

8. **totally one.** Since *YHVH* and *Elohim* will be shown to be one, everyone will recognize that God (*YHVH*, compassion) and His Name (*Elohim*, judgment) are actually one.

In review: When a person perceives that whatever happens to him is for his benefit, he has a foretaste of the World to Come.

The *Biur HaLikutim* asks: Why did God create the world in such a way that man knows Him only through duality: either by the attribute associated with *YHVH* or that associated with *Elohim*? What's more, how is it that the forces of evil are allowed to sustain themselves through the holy name *Elohim*? His answer, in brief, is that God's motivation in creating the world was to bestow His creation with everlasting good. This is the Creator manifesting through the holy name that most closely relates to His Essence, *YHVH*. But in order for there to be someone or something to benefit from His lovingkindness, there had to be a separation from God, as it were, so that physical matter might come into existence. It was to this end that the Holy One considered creating the world through the manifestation of *Elohim*, the attribute of judgment that is, as it were, a concealment of His Essence and compassion. However, judgment of this order would have been too severe for the overwhelming majority of His creations to endure. He accordingly created the world with a balance of attributes:

when He is *Elohim,* I will praise His word" (Psalms 56:11).[3]

And this perception is a foretaste of the World to Come, as our Sages taught: "On that day God shall be one and His Name one" (Zechariah 14:9).[4] They asked: Is He now not one?[5] And our Sages answered: At present, the blessing "Who is good and beneficent" is recited over good, whereas "the truthful Judge" is recited over bad.[6] But in the Future, it will be entirely "Who is good and beneficent" (*Pesachim* 50a).[7] The holy name *YHVH* and the holy name *Elohim* will be totally one.[8]

that the titles of the first four lessons of *Likutey Moharan* each begin with the letter *aleph*: *AshreY* (אשרי); *ÆmoR* (אמור); *AkruktA* (אקרוקתא); and *AnokhI* (אנכי). This indicates that all the teachings found in *Likutey Moharan* are rooted in the *four alephs* of holiness (*Rabbi Shmuel Shapiro*). The acrostic formed by the final letters of these four words is YA'IR (יאיר), corresponding to (Psalms 119:130), "The opening of Your words *ya'ir* (illuminates), making simpletons understand." This is *Likutey Moharan*—it brings light to the world and illuminates all those who study it (*Rabbi Zvi Cheshin*).

3. **is YHVH...is Elohim....** *YHVH* is the Tetragrammaton, the holy name that connotes divine compassion. Conversely, the holy name *Elohim* connotes divine justice and judgment. The Talmud teaches that whether good or otherwise befalls a person, he should accept everything joyously—because all that happens is God's will. Nevertheless, in this world a distinction does exist: Over good tidings one blesses "Who is good and beneficent," whereas over bad one blesses "the truthful Judge" (*Berakhot* 60b). Rebbe Nachman takes this a step further. When a person knows that the bad that befalls him is in fact for his good and that its source is ultimately the name *YHVH*, the divine attribute of compassion, then for him there is no difference between compassion and justice, between the names *YHVH* and *Elohim*. This is the meaning of the verse, "When he is *YHVH*, I will praise...when He is *Elohim*, I will praise...." The person who is capable of perceiving all of life this way essentially has a taste of what it will be like in the World to Come, when everything will be absolutely good and beneficial (*Mai HaNachal*).

The verse in Psalms (56:11) in fact reads: "When He is *Elohim*, I will praise His word; when He is *YHVH*, I will praise His word." However, it appears here as brought in the Talmud (*Berakhot* 60b) and the *Eyn Yaakov* (*ibid.*, #131).

4. **On that day....** On the day that Mashiach comes and reveals God to the entire world, then "God shall be one...." This is because all the nations will discard their idolatries and serve only God (*Rashi*, Zechariah *loc. cit.*).

5. **Is He now not one?** Is it not the case that God is always one, and that it is only our perception of Him that undergoes change? And since God is even now one, why only "On *that* day"?

6. **At present...good...bad.** As mentioned (n.3), one must praise God for everything that happens, good and bad. Maharsha relates this to the verse in Lamentations (3:38), "It is not from the mouth of the Most High that evils (רעות) and good (טוב) emanate." He points to the obvious difference between "evils," which Scripture refers to in the plural form, and "good,"

ב וְזֹאת הַבְּחִינָה אִי אֶפְשָׁר לְהַשִּׂיג, אֶלָּא כְּשֶׁמַּעֲלֶה בְּחִינַת מַלְכוּת
דִּקְדֻשָּׁה מֵהַגָּלוּת מִבֵּין הָעַכּוּ"ם. כִּי עַכְשָׁו הַמַּלְכוּת וְהַמֶּמְשָׁלָה
לְהָעַכּוּ"ם, וּבִשְׁבִיל זֶה נִקְרָאִים עֲבוֹדַת אֱלִילִים שֶׁלָּהֶם בְּשֵׁם
אֱלֹהִים, כִּי יוֹנְקִים מִבְּחִינַת מַלְכוּת הַנִּקְרָא אֱלֹהִים, כְּמוֹ שֶׁכָּתוּב:
"אֱלֹהִים מַלְכִּי מִקֶּדֶם". וּכְשֶׁמַּעֲלִין בְּחִינַת מַלְכוּת מִבֵּין הָעַכּוּ"ם,
אֲזַי נִתְקַיֵּם: "כִּי מֶלֶךְ כָּל הָאָרֶץ אֱלֹהִים":

ג וְאִי אֶפְשָׁר לְהָשִׁיב הַמְּלוּכָה לְהַקָּדוֹשׁ־בָּרוּךְ־הוּא אֶלָּא עַל יְדֵי

should either say or write anything disrespectful about them." It was the censor's responsibility to ensure that this or something similar appeared in the book, as otherwise it was forbidden to be printed. See *Through Fire and Water*, Chapter 32.

10. **This is the reason. . . .** The printed edition of *Likutey Moharan* reads: This is the reason their idols are referred to by the name *elohim*. An example of this appears in the verse (Exodus 20:3), "You shall have no other *elohim* (gods) besides Me."

11. **Elohim. . . King from long ago.** Primarily, Rebbe Nachman brings this verse, "*Elohim* is *MaLKi* from long ago," to show the connection between the holy name *Elohim* and *MaLKhut* (Kingship). It is also possible to apply it to the version of the text mentioned in the previous note: Human authority (kingship) stems from God's *Malkhut*/*Elohim*, and so the idols that men worship, by which they seek to undermine God's authority, are known as *elohim*.

On a more subtle level, the Rebbe chose this verse because it specifically refers to *Malkhut* in exile. The words "King from long ago" implies the King Who was once accepted as King of the Universe, but Who now, because of idolatry, has been relegated to being the "King of long ago," barely remembered and recognized. *Malkhut* of Holiness, God's Kingdom, is thus in exile.

12. **Elohim is King. . . .** With *Malkhut*/*Elohim* returned to God/*YHVH*, and all of the world's inhabitants accepting His Kingship, *Elohim* and *YHVH* are then one. People see and understand how everything that happens is for the best (*Mai HaNachal*).

The Talmud teaches: "On that day God shall be one and His Name one." At present, the holy Tetragrammaton is pronounced *Adonai* although it is written *YHVH*. But in the Future, it will be one—written and pronounced *YHVH* (*Pesachim* 50a). The *Parparaot LeChokhmah* asks: How does this align with our lesson, which teaches that *Elohim* is "His Name," *Malkhut*, and that in the Future *YHVH* and *Elohim* will be one? He explains, with the descent of *Malkhut* into exile man lost the right to call God by the name *YHVH* because doing so would enable the Other Side to draw an excess of nourishment from *Malkhut* (see Lesson #3, §1, n.11). To protect the spiritual energy that stems from *YHVH*, we can only refer to God indirectly, by a secondary name. But when *Malkhut* is elevated from the exile and rectified, then, "*Elohim* is King of all the earth." The names *YHVH* and *Elohim* are then unified, with the Tetragrammaton being the revealed—written and spoken—name of God.

In review: When a person perceives that whatever happens to him is for his benefit, he has a

2. Now, it is impossible for a person to grasp this perception except when he uplifts *Malkhut d'Kedushah* (Kingdom of Holiness) from its exile among the nations.[9] For presently, *malkhut* and rule < are in the hands of > the nations. This is the reason < they rule over us with the power of *malkhut* they possess >.[10] They nurse from the aspect of *Malkhut,* which is called *Elohim,* as is written (Psalms 74:12), *"Elohim* is my King from long ago."[11] But when a person raises *Malkhut* from among the nations, it is the fulfillment of the verse (Psalms 47:8), "For *Elohim* is King of all the earth."[12]

3. Yet it is impossible to return the kingdom to the Holy One, except by means of spoken confession in the presence of a *Talmid Chakham*

YHVH and *Elohim* (see *Bereishit Rabbah* 12:15; *Rashi,* Genesis 1:1). And, God manifests either as *YHVH,* for those who recognize Him, or *Elohim,* for those distant from Him. The holy name *Elohim,* as we presently understand it, is therefore the means for sustaining creation when, because of mankind's transgressions, the world is not deserving of His compassion and beneficence. Thus, even the forces of evil are sustained by the name *Elohim.*

9. **nations.** Wherever "nations" appears in the lesson it is a translation of the word *umot,* which the manuscript version of *Likutey Moharan* has in place of *akum,* the word that appears in the printed version. The term *akum* is an acronym for *Aovdey Kokhavim U'Mazalot,* worshippers of stars and planets. Specifically, this term refers to nations or individuals who engage in outright worship of idolatry. More generally, though, it refers to any nation that does not accept God or whose religion misrepresents God's intention for humanity. Thus, any gentile who does not fulfill the seven Noahide Commandments falls into the category of *akum.* When the *akum* have taken control of the *malkhut* (government) and instituted their own religions, cults and statutes, they have subverted *Malkhut* of Holiness and driven it into exile. However, the nations' taking control of *Malkhut* can only happen when *Malkhut* is undermined by sin. When a Jew transgresses God's will, intentionally or unintentionally, he is to some extent denying God's rule, *Malkhut* of Holiness, and *Malkhut* then comes under the control of the *akum.* Rectification will only come about when people return rulership to God and serve Him exclusively (cf. *Be'Ibey HaNachal; Mai HaNachal).* The elevation of *Malkhut* of Holiness from its exile and the accompanying realization that all is good and beneficial will only reach completion in the time of Mashiach. Yet, even now, to the extent that a person elevates *Malkhut* from its exile, he concomitantly attains the awareness that everything is for the best—i.e., a foretaste of the World to Come.

Under the censorship of the Czars, all Jewish books printed in Russia were required to use the term *akum,* rather than *umot,* and carry an explanation that only idol worshippers were being referred to. The wording of this explanatory note essentially read: "But the gentiles in whose lands we currently reside are not like those from the time of the Talmudic Sages. The latter were idolaters who worshipped the stars and the constellations, and were attached to all forms of abomination. They knew not God nor recognized His holy words. But the nations of our day fear God and honor His Torah; doing kindness and justice in their lands, and charity with the Jews who take refuge under their wings. Heaven forbid that we

וִדּוּי דְּבָרִים לִפְנֵי תַּלְמִיד חָכָם. עַל יְדֵי זֶה מְתַקֵּן וּמַעֲלֶה בְּחִינַת
מַלְכוּת לְשָׁרְשָׁהּ.

וְזֶהוּ פֵּרוּשׁ: "קְחוּ עִמָּכֶם דְּבָרִים" – זֶהוּ וִדּוּי דְּבָרִים, זֶה בְּחִינַת
מַלְכוּת, כְּמוֹ דַּבָּר אֶחָד לְדוֹר (סנהדרין ח.). דַּבָּר, לְשׁוֹן מַנְהִיג
וּמוֹשֵׁל. וְשׁוּבוּ אֶל ה' – שֶׁיְּתַקְּנוּ וְיַעֲלוּ אֶת הַדְּבָרִים, אֶת בְּחִינַת
מַלְכוּת, בְּחִינַת אֱלֹהִים אֶל ה'. הַיְנוּ כַּנַּ"ל: "בַּה' אֲהַלֵּל דָּבָר,
בֵּאלֹהִים אֲהַלֵּל דָּבָר", הַיְנוּ שֶׁיֵּדַע, שֶׁכָּל מְאֹרְעוֹתָיו, כֻּלָּם לְטוֹבָתוֹ,

unquestionably Jewish practices and concepts as their own. Nor is confession unique in this regard. Several Jewish practices and concepts have been "forgotten" down through the ages, in part precisely because of their association with other religious doctrines. This includes a number of Kabbalistic teachings, e.g., reincarnation, belief in the existence of demonic forces, and the like. Dismissed by many modern thinkers, these concepts and practices are actually inherent to Torah and Judaism. Thus, from the various branches of Torah we also learn the great significance of a Jew confessing in front of a tzaddik (as will be shown below, in section 8).

14. **Take D'VaRim with you....** This verse is connected to the lesson in three ways, as will be explained (below, n.17). Here, it is that *D'VaRim* ("words," דברים) connotes spoken confession.

15. **DaBoR...generation.** Before Moshe passed away he advised the leader who was to replace him, Yehoshua, to consult with the elders of Israel and not act on his own. But God disagreed. "Take a stick and hit them on the head with it," He told Yehoshua. "There can be only one *DaBoR* (spokesman or leader, דבר) to a generation."

16. **malkhut and ruler.** A ruler's spoken word details what he wants done in his domain, his *malkhut*. For this reason, Rebbe Nachman relates *d'var* and *dabor* to each other and to the concept of *Malkhut*. God, Who is infinite, rules the world by means of divine emanations known as *sefirot*, with each *sefirah* having finite powers. The function of each *sefirah* differs from that of the others and is in accordance with its distinctive characteristics. Thus, in particular, the power of speech stems from *Malkhut*, the last of the *sefirot* (*Tikkuney Zohar, Introduction*) and the one that exemplifies kingship. Here, the Rebbe shows that leadership (kingship and spokesmanship) and speech are synonymous.

17. **elevate the aspect of d'varim...YHVH.** The three connections that "Take *d'varim* with you and return to *YHVH*" has with our text are as follows:

> 1) "Take *d'varim*..." refers to spoken confession, an essential element of *teshuvah* (repentance). This raises *Malkhut* from the control of the nations, for the person who repents recognizes the Kingdom of God.
> 2) "Take *d'varim*..." hints to *Malkhut*, as in, "one *dabor* to a generation." Thus, "Take *d'varim/dabor*" — *Malkhut* itself — "and return *it* to God."
> 3) When the unity between *YHVH* and *Elohim* is achieved and the person is aware that even bad occurrences are really for his good, he has taken *d'varim* — which is *Malkhut/Elohim* — and returned it to *YHVH* (*Mai HaNachal*).

(Torah scholar). Through this, one rectifies the aspect of *Malkhut* and raises it to its source.[13]

{**"Take *d'varim* (words) with you and return to *YHVH* (God)"** (Hosea 14:3).}

This is the meaning of, "Take *D'VaRim* with you..."—i.e., spoken confession.[14] This is the aspect of *Malkhut*, as in, "one *DaBoR* (spokesman) to a generation" (*Sanhedrin* 8a)[15]; *dabor* connotes <*malkhut*> and ruler.[16] "...and return to *YHVH*"—so that they rectify and elevate the aspect of *d'varim/Malkhut/Elohim* to [the level of] *YHVH*.[17] As mentioned above, "When He is *YHVH*, I will praise His word; when He is *Elohim*, I will praise His word." This is, to

foretaste of the World to Come (§1). Attaining this perception is only possible when he frees *Malkhut* of Holiness from the control of the nations and returns it to God (§2).

13. **confession...Torah scholar...source.** In this and the next section Rebbe Nachman explains what one must do to recognize that all that comes from God is good and for one's benefit. To attain this, a person must first elevate *Malkhut* from its exile. This, the Rebbe explains, can be done through spoken confession, through which one attains complete awareness. This perfected awareness is the recognition that both *YHVH* and *Elohim*, namely compassion and judgment, are one. After explaining this, Rebbe Nachman returns to the concept of confession mentioned here (see §§5,6), and explains the vital role it plays in rectifying both *Malkhut* and the person himself.

Over the years many have questioned the importance Rebbe Nachman gives to *viduy d'varim* (confession), primarily because this practice is more commonly associated with other religions. Yet this cannot change the fact that confession is one of the 248 positive commandments (*Rambam, Sefer HaMitzvot, Mitzvot Aseh* #73). The Talmud (*Yoma* 35b-37a) teaches that confession is obligatory for anyone wishing to repent, akin to bringing a sin-offering or Yom Kippur atonement. Without confession, the Temple sacrifices and repentance on Yom Kippur are incomplete (see *Yad HaChazakah, Hilkhot Teshuvah* 1:1-2). In addition, our Sages taught: "They shall confess their iniquities..." (Leviticus 26:40)—as soon as they confess, I will forgive them (*Sifra, Bechukotai* 8:3). One of the reasons why confession is such an essential element of repentance is its special capacity for humbling a person. The humility that comes with admission is a first and crucial step in rectifying one's wrongs (*Mishnah Berurah* 607:8; see §7, n.68). At the same time, confessing a sin without regretting it or without intending to cease repeating it, is worthless (*Yad HaChazakah, Hilkhot Teshuvah* 2:3). As for confessing in front of another human being, which is what the Rebbe suggests in the lesson, the authorities permit this and many even recommend it (*Yad HaChazakah, ibid.* 2:5; *Mishnah Berurah* 607:6; see also *Shaar Tzion* 607:3). Precedents for confession in the presence of a tzaddik are found in the Talmud: the cases of Yehudah and Reuven (*Sotah* 7b) and Akhan (*Sanhedrin* 43b) are discussed below (§§5,7-8). Additional examples include the Jewish people confessing before Moshe (Numbers 21:7); King David before the prophet Natan (2 Samuel 12:13); the nazirite before Shimon HaTzaddik (*Nazir* 4b).

It is important to note that these confessions took place long before the other religions that practice confession were even founded. Moreover, it is common knowledge that these other religions have based their theology on Judaism and the teachings of the Torah, taking

וִיבָרֵךְ עַל כָּל הַדְּבָרִים הַטּוֹב וְהַמֵּטִיב:

ד וּכְשֶׁיֵּדַע כָּל זֹאת נִקְרָא יְדִיעָה שְׁלֵמָה, כִּי עִקַּר הַדַּעַת הוּא
אַחְדוּת שֶׁל חֶסֶד וּגְבוּרָה. זֶה נִקְרָא דַּעַת, הַיְנוּ שֶׁלֹּא יַחֲלֹק בֵּין חֶסֶד
לְדִין, וִיבָרֵךְ עַל כֻּלָּם "הַטּוֹב וְהַמֵּטִיב". וְזֶה נִקְרָא: "ה' אֶחָד וּשְׁמוֹ
אֶחָד" כְּמַאֲמַר חֲכָמֵינוּ, זִכְרוֹנָם לִבְרָכָה, שֶׁלֶּעָתִיד יִהְיֶה אַחְדוּת
גָּמוּר, שֶׁיִּהְיֶה כֻּלּוֹ הַטּוֹב וְהַמֵּטִיב.

וְזֶה ה' אֶחָד, וּשְׁמוֹ – זֶה בְּחִינַת אֱלֹהִים מַלְכוּת, כְּמוֹ שֶׁכָּתוּב:
"וַיַּעַשׂ דָּוִד שֵׁם" אֶחָד גִּימַטְרִיָּא אַהֲבָה,

הַיְנוּ הֵן ה' שֶׁהוּא רַחֲמִים, הֵן שְׁמוֹ שֶׁהוּא בְּחִינַת אֱלֹהִים, בְּחִינַת
דִּין – כֻּלָּם לְטוֹבָתְךָ מֵחֲמַת אַהֲבָה שֶׁהַקָּדוֹשׁ־בָּרוּךְ־הוּא אוֹהֵב

understanding—the proper unification and application of which is *daat*.

20. **lovingkindness and judgment.** The person who sees good/*chasadim* and bad/*gevurot* as separate entities is lacking complete *daat*, whereas the person who has perfected his awareness sees how the *chasadim*/lovingkindness and *gevurot*/judgment are one.

21. **but blesses...over everything.** He knows that the *chasadim*/*YHVH* and the *gevurot*/*Elohim* are in reality one. No matter what happens, he sees how it is actually an expression of God's kindness and love for him. Therefore, he recites "Blessed are You...Who is good and beneficent" over every situation and occurrence.

22. **good and beneficent.** As explained above, in section 1. Rebbe Nachman will next explain why *YHVH* and *Elohim* are referred to as "*YHVH* and His Name."

23. **made a name...malkhut.** Rebbe Nachman brings this proof-text from Scripture to show that "name" corresponds to *Malkhut*. From the verses that follow (2 Samuel 8:14-15), it becomes clear that "made a name for himself" refers to David's consolidation of his rule, his *malkhut*. Scripture states: "He stationed garrisons throughout all of Edom, and all Edom became David's servants. The Lord gave David victory wherever he went. And David reigned over all Israel." King David is thus the personification of *Malkhut* of Holiness; he dedicated his entire life to revealing God's *Malkhut* to the world. In addition, Rashi explains that "David made a name..." means that he buried his enemies after defeating them in battle. This kindness brought Israel a good name among the nations. In our context, this refers to removing and elevating *Malkhut* of Holiness (David) from among the nations (Edom). His burying them alludes to his divesting them of all holiness.

24. **Echod...ahavah.** The numerical value of both *EChaD* (אחד) and *AHaVaH* (אהבה) is 13 (see Appendix: Gematria Chart).

know that everything that happens to him is all for his good, and to recite the blessing "Who is good and beneficent" over everything.[18]

4. Knowing all this is called complete awareness. For the essence of awareness is the union of < *chasadim* (benevolences) and *gevurot* (severities) >. This is called *daat*.[19] In other words, he does not differentiate between lovingkindness and judgment,[20] but blesses "Who is good and beneficent" over everything.[21] This is called "*YHVH* is one and His Name is one." As our Sages taught: In the Future, there will be total oneness and it will be entirely "Who is good and beneficent."[22]

This is: "*YHVH* is *echod* (one) [and His Name is *echod*]." "His Name" corresponds to *Elohim/Malkhut,* as is written (2 Samuel 8:13), "David made a name for himself"— < he being *malkhut* >.[23] *Echod* has the same numerical value as *ahavah* (love).[24]

Therefore, whether it be *YHVH*—which is compassion—or whether it be "His Name"—which corresponds to *Elohim/*

---

18. **over everything.** When a person sins, he causes *Malkhut* of Holiness to be subjugated under the nations (n.9). His punishment then stems from the attribute of judgment associated with the name *Elohim,* and is exacted by means of the nations or the forces of evil, the *kelipot.* There is no way for such a person to attain a clear perception that whatever happens, including his punishment, is for the best, because his relationship to *Malkhut* is blemished. He can, however, still believe that everything is for the best. If he then confesses in a Torah scholar's presence, his sins are totally forgiven, because by confessing he raises *Malkhut* of Holiness from its exile and elevates it to the level of *YHVH.* Then, even if he suffers punishment, the source of his affliction is God's compassion, the attribute associated with the name *YHVH* (see §4). From this suffering it is possible to come to a clear perception that whatever happens is for the best—i.e., that *YHVH* and *Elohim* are one (*Be'Ibey HaNachal*).

In review: When a person perceives that whatever happens to him is for his benefit, he has a foretaste of the World to Come (§1). Attaining this perception is only possible when he frees *Malkhut* of Holiness from the control of the nations and returns it to God (§2). This is accomplished by confession of one's sins in the presence of a Torah scholar, which unites the holy names *YHVH* and *Elohim* (§3).

19. **daat.** This is awareness, also translated as knowledge. *Daat* is indicative of a joining and unification, as in (Genesis 4:1), "Adam *knew* his wife Eve." In the terminology of the Kabbalah, the essence of *daat* is the unity of *chasadim* and *gevurot.* The source of these benevolences is the *sefirah* of *Chokhmah* (Wisdom), whereas the severities are from the *sefirah* of *Binah* (Understanding; see Appendix: Structure of the Sefirot). These two spiritual forces are united in the *sefirah* of *Daat* (see *Etz Chaim* 21:2, p.306; *ibid.* 34:3). Man's objective in this world should be to construct his *daat* with these *chasadim* and *gevurot* so that he comes to complete awareness (see *Likutey Moharan* I, 25:1). In the context of Torah study, for example, he has to combine the wisdom he acquires from his studies with insight and inner

אוֹתְךָ, כְּמוֹ שֶׁכָּתוּב (משלי ג): "אֶת אֲשֶׁר יֶאֱהַב ה' יוֹכִיחַ" וּכְתִיב
(עמוס ג): "רַק אֶתְכֶם יָדַעְתִּי מִכֹּל מִשְׁפְּחוֹת הָאֲדָמָה, עַל כֵּן אֶפְקֹד
עֲלֵיכֶם עֲווֹנוֹתֵיכֶם":

ה. וַעֲווֹנוֹתָיו שֶׁל אָדָם הֵם עַל עַצְמוֹתָיו, כְּמוֹ שֶׁכָּתוּב: "וַתְּהִי

the Other Side rules. But in the Future, when YHVH and Elohim will be united, all judgment
will be mitigated. Evil and suffering will have no place and there will be no bad tidings.
Everything will be good and beneficial. Nevertheless, as Rebbe Nachman teaches here, it is
possible for a person, even in the here and now, to perceive a certain measure of this unity.
Even with Malkhut in exile—the reason mankind suffers, including the righteous tzaddikim
and the penitents—confession in a Torah scholar's presence leads to a degree of rectification
for Malkhut and a measure of complete awareness. Truly knowing that everything is for the
best enables the knower to transcend his suffering to a large extent, for he is aware that even
the hardships and affliction stem from God's love for him.

We can understand from this why our Sages did not institute the blessing "Who is good
and beneficent" over bad tidings as well, even though they knew that all that God does is
good. For it is only from Heaven's perspective that everything is lovingkindness. Humans, on
the other hand, make distinctions. We see some things as beneficial and other things as
harmful (see above, n.6). And, indeed, in our reality, there are times when judgment does
become detrimental—when man's iniquities are themselves the evil forces that punish him
cruelly. Yet, what inevitably happens is that most people interpret their suffering as divine
wrath, punishment inflicted to break us or to exact revenge. However, by taking "words" of
confession and returning to God (unifying YHVH and Elohim; §3), a person comes to know
that his suffering is *not* divine revenge. He comes to an awareness that his suffering is
motivated by God's love for him. This is because he has rectified his aspect of Malkhut/
Elohim, uniting it with YHVH. He still recites the blessing "the truthful Judge," because the
physical suffering he experiences is a reality. But he recites the blessing with joy, because he
has begun to *know* that all his suffering is ultimately for his benefit, for God truly is "good
and beneficent."

In review: When a person perceives that whatever happens to him is for his benefit, he has a
foretaste of the World to Come (§1). Attaining this perception is only possible when he frees
Malkhut of Holiness from the control of the nations and returns it to God (§2). This is
accomplished by confession of one's sins in the presence of a Torah scholar, which unites the
holy names YHVH and Elohim (§3). Knowing that all is for the best, the awareness that one's
suffering also stems from God's love, is considered complete daat (§4).

28. **iniquities...bones.** Rebbe Nachman now returns to explain why confession, especially in
front of a Torah scholar, is such an important element of repentance and so vital to the
process of rectifying Malkhut (Mai HaNachal).

29. **upon their bones.** The commentaries explain that this refers to the negative affect of one's
sins remaining and not being purged (*Rashi, Metzudat David*; see also above, n.1). Although
the verse in Ezekiel does not contain the word etched, in *Kallah Rabbati* (3:1) and the
Tikkuney Zohar (Addendum #3, p.139b) we find: "All man's iniquities are etched upon his

judgment—all is for your benefit and a result of the love which the Holy One has for you.[25] As it is written, "For those whom God loves, He rebukes" (Proverbs 3:12)[26]; and, "Of all the families of the earth, I knew only you [Israel]. That is why I will punish you for all your iniquities" (Amos 3:2).[27]

5. And, a person's iniquities are on his bones,[28] as is written (Ezekiel 32:27), "and their iniquities will be etched upon their bones."[29] Each

---

25. **love...the Holy One has for you.** The verse thus translates in our text as follows: **YHVH is one and His Name** — *YHVH*/kindness and *Elohim*/judgment are one. They are a result of **echod** — the love God has for you.

The Rebbe next explains how suffering can be a result of God's love.

26. **He rebukes.** God rebukes those whom He loves so that they remain on the proper path.

27. **punish you for all your iniquities.** Targum Yonatan, Rashi and Metzudoth all translate "I *knew* only you," as "I *loved* only you."

The verse (*loc. cit.*) refers to God punishing the Jewish people for their sins because He loves them more than all the other nations. This is why He causes them to suffer. The Talmud asks: This is love?! However, the answer is that because God loves the Jews, He punishes them in small measures, as one who is owed a large debt but only asks small sums for each repayment. In contrast, from those whom God despises, He demands repayment in one large sum (*Avodah Zarah* 4a).

The *Biur HaLikutim* points out that these two proof-texts highlight different aspects of God's bringing suffering to those He loves. The first verse teaches that there are times when God afflicts those He loves with *yisurin shel ahavah* (visitations of divine love), knowing that they will accept their suffering willingly and so benefit from it spiritually. The second verse teaches that God punishes those He loves so as to get them to repent for their sins. He does this in order to purify them, so that they might attain the spiritual gifts that are their birthright. Both forms of affliction are thus the result of God's love (*ahavah/echad*)—emanating from "God and His Name," which are in essence one.

In reviewing these concepts, the *Parparaot LeChokhmah* adds the following insight into our lesson: Our Sages taught: A person should always say, "Whatever the Merciful One does is for the best" (*Berakhot* 60b). At one time or another, all people suffer pain or anguish. Those who believe that God sends them this suffering are better able to endure it. This has to do with the connection that human suffering has with *Malkhut*, the medium through which this world is afflicted by judgment (see below, §7 and n.76). The suffering a person experiences is a result of the blemish he's wrought in *Malkhut* by lowering it into the domain of the nations (see n.18). When he realizes that his suffering is God's will—a means of rectifying his sins and thereby restoring *Malkhut*—he can accept his suffering with joy. Logically, he should even recite the blessing "Who is good and beneficent" over that suffering; for if he experienced no pain or anguish, how would he secure atonement for his sins? How would the slate ever be wiped clean? Nevertheless, because there *is* pain and suffering, he recites the blessing "the truthful Judge"—albeit with joy, because it is God's will and therefore for his benefit.

Now, all this applies in the present, because *Malkhut* is in a state of exile and *Malkhut* of

עֲוֹנוֹתָם חֲקוּקָה עַל עַצְמוֹתָם". וְכָל עֲבֵרָה יֵשׁ לָהּ צֵרוּף אוֹתִיּוֹת, וּכְשֶׁעָבַר אֵיזֶה עֲבֵרָה, אֲזַי נֶחְקָק צֵרוּף רַע עַל עַצְמוֹתָיו וְעַל־יְדֵי־ זֶה מַכְנִיס בְּחִינַת הַדִּבּוּר שֶׁל הַלָּאו הַזֶּה שֶׁעָבַר בְּתוֹךְ הַטֻּמְאָה. הַיְנוּ שֶׁמַּכְנִיס בְּחִינַת מַלְכוּת, שֶׁהוּא בְּחִינַת דַּבָּר אֶחָד לַדּוֹר, הוּא מַכְנִיס אוֹתָהּ בְּתוֹךְ הָעַכּוּ"ם, וְנוֹתֵן לָהֶם מֶמְשָׁלָה.

לְמָשָׁל, אִם עָבַר עַל דִּבּוּר שֶׁל הַלָּאו לֹא יִהְיֶה לְךָ. אֲזַי מַחֲרִיב הַצֵּרוּף הַטּוֹב שֶׁל הַדִּבּוּר, וּבוֹנֶה צֵרוּף רַע, וְנֶחְקַק הַצֵּרוּף הַזֶּה עַל עַצְמוֹתָיו, וְנוֹקָם בּוֹ. כְּמוֹ שֶׁכָּתוּב: "עֲוֹנוֹתֵיכֶם הִטּוּ אֵלֶּה", וּכְתִיב: "תְּמוֹתֵת רָשָׁע רָעָה".

35. **etched upon his bones.** See above, note 1, concerning the Baal Shem Tov's follower.

36. **iniquities that have turned away....** Yirmiyahu chastises the Jewish people, attributing their suffering and famine to their own iniquities: "It is your iniquities that have turned away these things, your sins that have withheld the bounty from you." The *Metzudat David* (*loc. cit.*) explains that the Jewish people's sins prevented them from understanding that their suffering was due to their own deeds. In our context, this ties in with the Rebbe's teaching that both suffering and benevolence are from Heaven. If one *understands* this, he has come to a level of awareness that will only be fully revealed in the World to Come. See above, note 27.

The *Mai HaNachal* illustrates this with two examples. The first is what happened to King Shaul, who put to death the priests of the city of Nob (נב) and was also guilty of seeking guidance through the medium AoV (אוב; 1 Samuel 22:19, 28:7). For these transgressions, Shaul and Yonatan—*av* and *BNo* (אב and בנו, a father and his son)—died in battle (*Amud HaAvodah*). The second example involved a student of the Ari who suffered terribly from a pain in his shoulder. "It is because you didn't recite *Birkat HaMazon* right after washing your hands with *mayim acharonim*," the Ari told him. "Our Sages teach (*Berakhot* 42a): 'Teikef (immediately) after washing, one should recite the Grace after Meals.' Now, *TeiKeF* (תכף) has the same letters as the word for shoulder, *KaTeF* (כתף)" (see *Shaar HaMitzvot, Ekev* p.106). Thus, even tzaddikim are punished commensurate with the sin they committed. How much more so the wicked?! May God save us.

37. **deathblow of the wicked.** That is, the evil the wicked person has perpetrated is what slays him (*Rashi, loc. cit.*).

Rebbe Nachman brings these two proof-texts to show that the sins a person commits have negative repercussions. The first verse speaks of a general suffering, which may or may not affect him directly. The second refers to the suffering that affects the sinner personally. The concluding paragraphs of this section deal with how to undo the suffering caused by iniquities.

sin has its own combination of letters.[30] When a person commits a particular sin, a negative letter-combination is etched upon his bones. This brings the spoken aspect of the prohibition which he has transgressed into the realm of impurity. In other words, he brings the aspect of *Malkhut/ < dabor >*[31] among the nations, giving them the power to rule.[32]

For example: If he transgressed the utterance of the prohibition "You shall have no [other gods besides Me]" (Exodus 20:3),[33] then he destroys the utterance's positive letter-combination and forms a negative letter-combination.[34] This letter-combination is etched upon his bones,[35] < in fulfillment of: > "It is your iniquities that have turned away these things" (Jeremiah 5:25).[36] And it is written, "Evil is the deathblow of the wicked" (Psalms 34:22).[37]

bones." The bones are the essential structure of the body (see *Chullin* 58a); they represent wisdom, which is prone to being corrupted by sin (cf. *Likutey Moharan* I, 50).

The *Parparaot LeChokhmah* adds: The bones represent holiness, which is why they remain after a person's passing. Not so the flesh, which begins to rot and decay immediately, for it is representative of the Other Side (*Zohar* III, 170a). But when a person sins, he lowers his holiness/bones into the realm of the Other Side. This is the meaning of the sins being etched upon the bones.

30. **own combination of letters.** Each according to the letters that make up that commandment, as Rebbe Nachman explains in the next paragraph.

31. **dabor.** *Dabor* is *Malkhut*; see above, note 16.

32. **power to rule.** See above, note 9.

33. **no other gods besides Me.** This prohibition from the Ten Commandments bans idol worship. It ties in with our text in that idolatry empowers *Malkhut* of the Other Side and thereby negates *Malkhut* of Holiness (see *Bamidbar Rabbah* 9:45; *Parparaot LeChokhmah*). The subject of idolatry is relevant to section 7, where Rebbe Nachman discusses humility. For as our Sages teach: Haughtiness is akin to idolatry (*Sotah* 4b). The *Biur HaLikutim* takes this further. It is known that the first two of the Ten Commandments, *Anokhi* and *Lo yihiyeh*, are inclusive of all the commandments. *Anokhi* ("I am your God") encompasses all the positive commandments, and *Lo yihiyeh* ("You shall have no other gods") encompasses all the prohibitive commandments (*Tikkuney Zohar* #22, pp.63b,64a). Because a deed that violates God's will lowers *Malkhut/Elohim* into the realm of evil, any commandment transgressed is indirectly also a transgression of *Lo yihiyeh*. Conversely, every mitzvah performed, elevates God's *Malkhut/Anokhi*.

34. **negative letter-combination.** He has vanquished *Malkhut* to the realm of evil. See previous note.

וְעַל יְדֵי וִדּוּי דְּבָרִים יוֹצֵא מֵעַצְמוֹתָיו הָאוֹתִיּוֹת הַחֲקוּקִים עֲלֵיהֶם,
וְנַעֲשֶׂה מֵהֶם הַדִּבּוּר שֶׁל הַוִּדּוּי. כִּי הַדִּבּוּר יוֹצֵא מֵעַצְמוֹתָיו, כְּמוֹ
שֶׁכָּתוּב: "כָּל עַצְמֹתַי תֹּאמַרְנָה". וּמַחֲרִיב הַבִּנְיָן וְהַצֵּרוּף הָרָע,
וּבוֹנֶה מֵהֶם מַלְכוּת דִּקְדֻשָּׁה.

וְזֶה שֶׁאָמְרוּ חֲכָמֵינוּ, זִכְרוֹנָם לִבְרָכָה: בְּשָׁעָה שֶׁהָלְכוּ יִשְׂרָאֵל
בַּמִּדְבָּר, הָיוּ עַצְמוֹתָיו שֶׁל יְהוּדָה מְגֻלְגָּלִין. עַד שֶׁאָמַר מֹשֶׁה:
"שְׁמַע ה' קוֹל יְהוּדָה". שֶׁבִּקֵּשׁ מֹשֶׁה מֵהַקָּדוֹשׁ-בָּרוּךְ-הוּא, שֶׁיִּזְכֹּר
לִיהוּדָה הַוִּדּוּי שֶׁהִתְוַדָּה, וְכֵן הֲוֵי לֵיהּ. וְזֶה דַּוְקָא עַצְמוֹתָיו הָיוּ
מְגֻלְגָּלִין, עַל שֵׁם: "וַתְּהִי עֲוֹנוֹתָם חֲקוּקָה עַל עַצְמוֹתָם", וְעַל-יְדֵי
הַוִּדּוּי נִתְתַּקְּנוּ, וְעָלוּ כָּל חַד לְדוּכְתֵּיהּ.

וִיהוּדָה זֶה בְּחִינַת מַלְכוּת, רֶמֶז, שֶׁבְּחִינַת מַלְכוּת נִתְתַּקֵּן עַל-יְדֵי

relationship between *echad* and *ahavah*—i.e., that unity is love. Therefore, when a person repents out of love for God, his repentance is induced by a complete awareness. He has accordingly rectified *Malkhut,* and so his sins are turned into merits.

40. **Yehudah's bones rolled....** When the Jews left Egypt, they took the bones of Yaakov's twelve sons with them. Yosef had told his brothers, "You shall carry up my bones away from here with you." "With you" implies along with your bones (Exodus 13:19, *Rashi*). Whereas the limbs of the other brothers remained intact, Yehudah's skeleton became disjointed, rolling about in his coffin. This was because Yehudah had agreed to accept excommunication in the event that he failed to return his brother Binyamin safely to their father (Genesis 43:9). The awesome nature of an excommunication dictates that even when made conditionally, it is not without side effects (see *Rashi, Sotah, loc. cit.*). In addition, the word *cherem* (excommunication) has a numerical value of 248, corresponding to the 248 limbs of the human body. This parallel indicates why it was Yehudah's bones that were affected.

41. **just what happened.** Moshe prayed that God remember the confession Yehudah had made in front of Shem (the generation's tzaddik; see Genesis 38:26), and as a result Yehudah's skeleton was rebuilt. Rebbe Nachman now explains this passage within the context of our lesson.

42. **his bones...confession...rectified....** Yehudah's bones were afflicted because, as the Rebbe explained earlier, one's iniquities are etched upon one's bones, turning them into a source of suffering. By the same token, when one confesses, one rectifies the bones and undoes their negative configurations, thereby rebuilding them in holiness. Thus, Yehudah's confession caused his bones to reunite.

43. **Yehudah corresponds to Malkhut.** The royal House of David descended from Yehudah. This was the fulfillment of the blessing Yehudah received from his father Yaakov: "The scepter [of rulership] will not depart from Yehudah...nations will submit to him" (Genesis 49:10). Yehudah thus corresponds to *Malkhut.*

By means of spoken confession, however, the letters disappear from the bones into which they have been etched and are transformed into the words of confession. For speech emanates from one's bones, as is written (Psalms 35:10), "All my bones will say."[38] He tears down the negative structure and combination, and from [the letters] builds *Malkhut d'Kedushah.*[39]

This is what the Sages said: During the time the Israelites traveled in the desert, Yehudah's bones rolled about [in his coffin] until Moshe said (Deuteronomy 33:7), "Hear, O God, the voice of Yehudah" (*Sotah* 7b).[40] Moshe requested that the Holy One remember for Yehudah's sake the confession he had made. And this is just what happened.[41] Thus it was specifically "his bones rolled about," as is written, "and their iniquities will be etched upon their bones." But by means of the confession, they were rectified and each one went into its place.[42]

And Yehudah corresponds to *Malkhut*[43] — an allusion that the

---

38. **All my bones will say.** That is: When my bones say their confession...then *Malkhut* is rectified. The commentaries point out that *atzmotay* ("my bones") can also be understood as "my self," referring to one's *ætzem* (essence). "All my bones" thus implies all of a person's inner thoughts and deeds (*Radak, loc. cit.*).

39. **tears down...builds....** As explained, *Malkhut* is speech (see above, n.16). By using speech constructively — confessing one's sins and orally acknowledging the Kingdom of Heaven — one dismantles *Malkhut* of the Other Side, which was built and empowered through his sins, and rebuilds *Malkhut* of Holiness. Reb Noson adds: *Malkhut,* and in particular God's spoken word, is the manifestation of His will (see §9). When a person sins, he transgresses and sometimes even denies that will. Thus, the blemish sin causes in *Malkhut* is mainly in the letters of speech that give form to His will. Conversely, the essential rectification is through *Malkhut*: taking the blemished configuration of sin and rebuilding it in holiness (*Torat Natan* #3).

This gives us an inkling into just how far-reaching repentance is. A person who sins actually constructs a negative letter-combination, a configuration capable of causing him and the world at large to suffer. However, not only does repentance totally dismantle the negative letter-combination, it actually transforms it by reconfiguring it into holiness. With this, we can better understand our Sages' teaching: Great is repentance for it turns deliberate sin into unintended sin (lessening its liability). Great is repentance for it turns deliberate sin into merit. What is the difference? However, the first case refers to the person whose repentance is motivated by his fear of God, whereas the latter refers to one whose repentance is out of love for Him (*Yoma* 86b). On the face of it, this seems impossible: How can an act that transgressed God's will, a sin, turn into merit? Yet based on Rebbe Nachman's teaching, the process is quite straightforward. By repenting, the person who sinned has totally dismantled the negative configuration he created and has rebuilt it within the realm of holiness. This also ties in with what the Rebbe taught earlier, that when a person attains the awareness that good and bad are actually one, he has attained complete awareness (§4). This is alluded to in the

וִדּוּי דְּבָרִים,

וְזֶה נַעֲשָׂה עַל-יְדֵי מֹשֶׁה, שֶׁזָּכַר מֹשֶׁה הַוִּדּוּי, כִּי כֵן צָרִיךָ, שֶׁיִּהְיֶה הַוִּדּוּי לִפְנֵי תַּלְמִיד חָכָם. וְכָל תַּלְמִיד חָכָם הוּא בְּחִינַת מֹשֶׁה, כְּמוֹ שֶׁאָמְרוּ 'מֹשֶׁה שַׁפִּיר קָאֲמַרְתְּ'. וּבָזֶה שֶׁזָּכַר מֹשֶׁה הַוִּדּוּי, נַעֲשָׂה כְּאִלּוּ הִתְוַדָּה עַכְשָׁו לִפְנֵי מֹשֶׁה, וְעַל-יְדֵי זֶה נִתְתַּקֵּן בְּחִינַת מַלְכוּת, וְנֶחֱרַב הַצֵּרוּף הָרָע שֶׁנֶּחְקַק עַל עַצְמוֹתָיו.

ו. וְזֶה בְּחִינַת הַחֲזָרַת הַמַּלְכוּת לְשָׁרְשָׁהּ, כִּי שֹׁרֶשׁ הַמַּלְכוּת הוּא אֵשׁ, כְּמוֹ שֶׁאָמְרוּ חֲכָמֵינוּ, זִכְרוֹנָם לִבְרָכָה: 'לָמָּה טָעָה נְבָט? שֶׁרָאָה שֶׁיָּצָא אֵשׁ מֵאֲמָתוֹ'; וְהַתּוֹרָה נִקְרֵאת אֵשׁ, שֶׁמִּשָּׁם הַמַּלְכוּת, כְּמוֹ שֶׁכָּתוּב: "הֲלוֹא כֹה דְבָרִי כָּאֵשׁ", וּכְתִיב: "בִּי מְלָכִים

must have attained an excellence akin to Moshe's (n.45). For only then is it possible to attain Nothingness (*Ayin*), the level of total humility (cf. *Chullin* 89a; see below, §9 and n.125).

In review: When a person perceives that whatever happens to him is for his benefit, he has a foretaste of the World to Come (§1). Attaining this perception is only possible when he frees *Malkhut* of Holiness from the control of the nations and returns it to God (§2). This is accomplished by confession of one's sins in the presence of a Torah scholar, which unites the holy names *YHVH* and *Elohim* (§3). Knowing that all is for the best, the awareness that one's suffering also stems from God's love, is considered complete *daat* (§4). A person's sins blemish *Malkhut* and become etched upon his bones. The way to rectify *Malkhut* and remove the blemish is by confessing one's sins in front of a tzaddik/Torah scholar. The bones are thus healed (§5).

47. **This is....** Spoken confession in the presence of a Torah scholar is the same concept as returning and reconnecting *Malkhut* to its source. As Rebbe Nachman will now show, the source of *Malkhut* is fire and the Torah scholar is likened to fire (*Mai HaNachal*).

48. **fire escape from his member.** The Talmud teaches (*loc. cit.*) that Nevat's name was actually Sheva ben Bikhri, whom Scripture describes as "a worthless fellow" who led a rebellion against King David (2 Samuel 20). What possessed him to do this? The Talmud answers that he saw fire (an allusion to kingship; see n.50) emanate from his member and took it as a sign of his future ascent to the throne of Israel. However, Nevat erred tragically. It was his son, Yarovam, who was to reign as king of the Ten Tribes (1 Kings 11:26; *Maharsha, s.v. sheraah; Iyun Yaakov, loc. cit.*).

49. **Torah is called fire....** Rashi (*loc. cit.*) explains: God's word to a prophet is not some dream or a hazy vision. Rather, it is like fire: a mighty emissary that consumes whatever stands in its way. From this we learn that Torah, God's word, is likened to fire.

aspect of *Malkhut* is rectified through spoken confession.

This was accomplished with the aid of Moshe, who recalled the confession. For it is necessary that the confession take place in the presence of a *Talmid Chakham*.[44] And every Torah scholar is an aspect of Moshe, < as the Talmud states: > "Moshe, you said it well" (*Shabbat* 101b).[45] By Moshe's mentioning the confession, it was considered as if [Yehudah] had now confessed < literally in his presence >. This caused the aspect of *Malkhut* to be rectified and the negative letter-combination, which had been etched upon [Yehudah's] bones, to be torn down.[46]

6. This is the aspect of returning *Malkhut* to its source.[47] For the source of *Malkhut* is fire, as our Sages taught: Why did Nevat err? because he saw fire escape from his member (*Sanhedrin* 101b).[48] And the Torah is called fire, because it is from there that *Malkhut* originates. As it is written (Jeremiah 23:29), "Behold, My Word is like fire,"[49] and

---

44. **Talmid Chakham.** In this lesson, Rebbe Nachman uses the terms tzaddik and *Talmid Chakham* (Torah scholar) interchangeably. The term *Talmid Chakham* generally denotes a person who has achieved an exceptional level of Torah knowledge, whereas tzaddik generally refers to a person who has reached very high levels of piety and devotional practice. The spiritual guide who can perform the *tikkunim* (rectifications) delineated in this lesson must possess the qualities of both a *Talmid Chakham* and a tzaddik. (Note that only in the next section does Rebbe Nachman explain why the confession must be made in front of a Torah scholar.)

45. **Moshe...well.** This is how the leading Sages of the Talmud would compliment one another. They would refer to each other as Moshe, the implication being: "You are to your generation what Moshe was to his" (*Rashi, loc. cit.*). We learn from this that every leading tzaddik is in a position to secure rectification for those who need to confess. (See below, section 7, especially note 67, and section 9; cf. *Likutey Moharan* I, 2:6, 9:4, 118).

46. **...in his presence...to be torn down.** Thus, confession in the tzaddik's presence removes the negative letter-combinations and rectifies *Malkhut*. The *Biur HaLikutim* adds that the name YeHuDaH (יהודה) connotes both *HoDaaH* (הודאה, confession) and *HoDaYaH* (הודיה, praise and thanksgiving). In our context, this relates to confession in front of the tzaddik, which rectifies *Malkhut* and enables one to attain the complete awareness that everything is for the best. Such a person—"Yehudah," who confesses—merits to praise God with the blessing "Who is good and beneficent."

The *Parparaot LeChokhmah* asks: From tradition we know that Yehudah's confession took place in front of Shem, who was the tzaddik of that generation. Scripture even reports that Yaakov recalled this confession (*Onkelos,* Genesis 49:8). In that case, why was it necessary for Moshe to once again recall Yehudah's confession in order to restore his skeleton? The answer is that the tzaddik in whose presence one confesses must have attained a deep level of humility if he is to elevate *Malkhut* to the highest spiritual level. That tzaddik

יִמְלֹכוּ". וְעִקַּר הַתּוֹרָה הֵם הַתַּלְמִידֵי חֲכָמִים, כְּמוֹ שֶׁאָמְרוּ חֲכָמֵינוּ,
זִכְרוֹנָם לִבְרָכָה: 'כַּמָּה טִפְּשָׁאֵי דְּקַיְמָא מְקַמֵּי סֵפֶר-תּוֹרָה, וְלָא
קַיְמָא מְקַמֵּי צוּרְבָא מִדְּרַבָּנָן'.

וְזֶהוּ : "כָּל דָּבָר אֲשֶׁר יָבֹא בָאֵשׁ – תַּעֲבִירוּ בָאֵשׁ". 'דָּבָר' זֶה
בְּחִינַת מַלְכוּת, שֶׁנִּמְשָׁךְ בְּתוֹךְ הַטֻּמְאָה בְּתוֹךְ חֲמִימוּת הַיֵּצֶר, כְּמוֹ:
'נוּרָא בֵּי עַמְרָם'. 'תַּעֲבִירוּ בָאֵשׁ' – תִּקּוּנוֹ עַל-יְדֵי אֵשׁ, הַיְנוּ וִדּוּי
דְבָרִים לִפְנֵי תַּלְמִיד חָכָם כַּנַּ"ל.

וְזֶה לְשׁוֹן עֲבֵרָה, שֶׁהַצֵּרוּף שֶׁל עֲבֵרָה עוֹבֵר בְּתוֹךְ עַצְמוֹתָיו, מֵעֵבֶר
אֶל עֵבֶר. וּמִצְוָה – לְשׁוֹן הִתְחַבְּרוּת, כְּשֶׁעוֹשֶׂה חֲבִילוֹת חֲבִילוֹת
שֶׁל מִצְוֹת, אֲזַי נִתְחַבְּרוּ שִׁבְרֵי עַצְמוֹתָיו, כְּמוֹ שֶׁכָּתוּב: "שׁוֹמֵר כָּל

in preparing non-kosher food. Before a Jew may use such utensils, he must heat them until whatever food particles they have absorbed are purged. In this way they "go through fire."

53. **Davar...Malkhut.** As in, "Take *d'varim* with you..." (above, §3 and n.16).

54. **heat of the evil inclination.** For when a person sins, he lowers *Malkhut* into the realm of *Malkhut* of the Other Side (as above, §5).

55. **the fire of Amram.** The Talmud (*loc. cit.*) relates how Rabbi Amram, after withstanding a moral test, called his *yetzer hara* (evil inclination) "the fire of Amram." Thus, just as the fire of Torah is the source of *Malkhut* of Holiness, the fire of the evil inclination is the source of *Malkhut* of the Other Side—with the evil inclination forever seeking ways to draw *Malkhut* of Holiness into the realm of evil.

56. **spoken confession....** As Rebbe Nachman has explained, both *Malkhut* and a *Talmid Chakham* correspond to fire. Thus, because the *d'varim* of confession corresponds to *Malkhut/davar/dabor*, confession in a *Talmid Chakham's* presence is returning *Malkhut* to its source. The verse thus translates as follows: **Every davar that was used in fire —** whenever *Malkhut* is lowered into the realm of *Malkhut* of the Other Side; **must go through fire —** it is rectified by confession in front of a Torah scholar. This is returning *Malkhut* to its source.

57. **AVeyRah...OVeR...from AyVeR to AyVeR.** Rebbe Nachman shows how the word for transgression, *aveyrah* (עברה), is itself indicative of this process whereby the sins are etched upon the bones. They are *over* (עובר) from the bones on one *ayver* (עבר) to those on the other, until the bones become so fragile that they begin to separate and come apart.

58. **bundles of commandments.** The Midrash teaches: If a person has performed bundles upon bundles of transgressions, let him counter them by performing bundles upon bundles of mitzvot (*Vayikra Rabbah* 21:5). The word mitzvah itself connotes "binding together," indicating that a Jew is bound to the commandments of the Torah (*Parparaot LeChokhmah*).

(Proverbs 8:15), "Through me kings rule."[50] And the essence of Torah is the Torah scholar, as our Sages taught (Makkot 22b): How foolish are those who stand up before a Torah scroll and yet do not stand before a rabbinical scholar![51]

This is: "Every *davar* (thing) that was used in fire, must go through fire < to be purged >" (Numbers 31:23).[52] "*Davar*" corresponds to *Malkhut,*[53] which has been < sunk > into the realm of impurity < due to > the heat of the evil inclination,[54] as in, "the fire of Amram" (Kiddushin 81a).[55] "...must go through the fire"—its rectification is by means of fire, i.e., spoken confession before a *Talmid Chakham.*[56]

And this is the connotation of *aveyrah* (transgression): the *AVeyRah* letter-combination *OVeR* (crosses) within his bones, from *AyVeR* to *AyVeR* (side to side).[57] The word mitzvah, however, connotes joining together. When a person performs bundles of commandments,[58] he binds together the shattered fragments of his

---

50. **Through me kings rule.** The "me" to which the verse refers is the Torah. Scripture asserts that the rule of Jewish kings stands on Torah law (see *Rashi, loc. cit.*). These proof-texts therefore show that Torah is fire, and with Torah one can rule. In other words, Rebbe Nachman says, the source of *Malkhut* is fire/Torah. The *Parparaot LeChokhmah* adds: From the Kabbalah we know that the *gevurot,* of which *Malkhut* is comprised, correspond to fire. Therefore, the source of *Malkhut* is fire.

If we apply this to the story of Nevat, we can understand that although he saw the fire of *Malkhut* and correctly took it as a sign of kingship, he misunderstood its application. Although the fire did come from him, he did not consider that the male organ, from which the fire emanated, suggests progeny. In other words, not he but his descendants were destined to rule. Nevat's error led him to rebel against King David, the personification of *Malkhut.* And it was this blemish of *Malkhut*—separating it from the holy *malkhut* of King David and so empowering *Malkhut* of the Other Side—that caused Nevat to be sentenced to death (see above, §5 and nn.36,37).

51. **Torah scroll...rabbinical scholar.** Reb Noson explains this Talmudic teaching (*loc. cit.*) as follows: When a person sanctifies himself through endless Torah study and prayer, his body, or form, becomes totally subservient to spirit, the Torah. His body is thus likened to the parchment of the Torah scroll, while the letters of that scroll are the Torah he has studied and the prayers he has prayed. In this sense, the true Torah scholar *is* a Torah scroll, even holier, and is certainly deserving of the same respect and reverence (*Torat Natan* #4).

And so, from this Talmudic teaching we learn that the true Torah scholar is as exalted as the Torah itself. Therefore, when we say that confession, which is the process of rectifying *Malkhut,* must be performed in such a way that it elevates *Malkhut* back to its source— namely, fire/Torah—we are referring to confession in front of a Torah scholar. Rebbe Nachman clarifies this connection between confession in front of a *Talmid Chakham* and elevating *Malkhut* to fire through the proof-text he brings next.

52. **Every davar...through fire....** On the literal level this verse refers to utensils once used

עַצְמוֹתָיו".

ז. וְזֶה פֵּרוּשׁ: "חֲמַת מֶלֶךְ מַלְאֲכֵי מָוֶת", כִּי חֲמָתוֹ שֶׁל הַקָּדוֹשׁ־
בָּרוּךְ־הוּא בִּשְׁבִיל הַמַּלְכוּת שֶׁהֻשְׁפַּל עַל־יְדֵי עֲווֹנוֹתָיו, "וְאִישׁ
חָכָם יְכַפְּרֶנָּה", הַיְנוּ בְּחִינַת תַּלְמִיד חָכָם, בְּחִינַת מֹשֶׁה, הוּא יְכַפֵּר
לוֹ. כְּמוֹ שֶׁכָּתוּב: "וְעֹבֵר עַל פֶּשַׁע לִשְׁאֵרִית", 'לְמִי שֶׁמֵּשִׂים עַצְמוֹ
כִּשְׁיָרַיִם'.

נִמְצָא, כְּשֶׁבָּא לִפְנֵי תַּלְמִיד חָכָם וּמוֹצִיא כָּל צֵרוּפָיו לִפְנֵי הַתַּלְמִיד
חָכָם, וְהַתַּלְמִיד חָכָם הוּא בְּחִינַת מֹשֶׁה, שֶׁמֵּשִׂים עַצְמוֹ כִּשְׁיָרַיִם,
כְּמוֹ שֶׁכָּתוּב: "וְהָאִישׁ מֹשֶׁה עָנָו מְאֹד", וְעַל־יְדֵי־זֶה נִקְרָא אִישׁ

64. **considers himself as remnants.** "Remnants" alludes to a person who has divested himself of all arrogance and haughtiness (*Maharsha, loc. cit., s.v. shemeitim*). This is why he is called "a wise man," because, as Rebbe Nachman will explain shortly, the source of Wisdom and *Malkhut* is *Ayin* (Nothingness), the Source of all sources. Therefore, a Torah scholar/tzaddik who possesses true and deep humility, as Moshe did, has the power—by virtue of his quality of nothingness—to undo the damage done to *Malkhut* and atone for sins. Thus, when a person confesses in his presence, *Malkhut* returns to its source (*Parparaot LeChokhmah*). The Rebbe next elaborates on the reason why the humility of the tzaddik can atone for sin.

65. **expresses all his letter-combinations....** As above, section 5, note 39.

66. **aspect of Moshe.** As above, note 45. The *Mai HaNachal* adds: The final letters of *v'iSh chakhaM yichaprenaH* ("a wise man can pacify it," ואיש חכם יכפרנה) form the name MoSheH (משה), the tzaddik who has the power to secure God's forgiveness.

67. **Mashiach.** Although the concept of Mashiach is mentioned nowhere else in this teaching, and is included here only in the manuscript version, the connection that Moshe/tzaddik as Mashiach has with the lesson becomes clear in notes 73 and 168 below (see also *Likutey Moharan* I, 9:4, 13:2 and n.27, 20:1 and n.5, where Rebbe Nachman also refers to this concept of Moshe-Mashiach).

Moreover, as Rebbe Nachman quoted earlier from the Talmud (see §5 and n.45), every Torah scholar/tzaddik is an aspect of Moshe Rabbeinu. Indeed, an aspect of Moshe is found in the leaders of every generation (*Zohar* III, 273a). Thus, concerning the verse (Ecclesiastes 1:9), "*Mah Shehayah, Hu sheyihiyeh* (What was, will be)," the *Tikkuney Zohar* (#69, p.111b) points out that the first letters spell MoSheH (משה). Moshe, who was the first redeemer, will also be the final redeemer—namely Mashiach. For only someone of Moshe's caliber can redeem the Jews from exile. At the same time, as the above mentioned *Zohar* indicates, the awesome level of Moshe-Mashiach is found to an extent in the tzaddikim of each era, in those very great teachers who reveal perceptions of Godliness to the people.

68. **Moshe, however, was very humble.** Rashi (*loc. cit.*) explains this as modest and tolerant. The *Biur HaLikutim* sees in Rebbe Nachman's words an allusion to another reason why

bones,[59] as is written (Psalms 34:21), "[God] safeguards all his bones, [not one of them is broken]."[60]

7. {"The King's wrath is a messenger of death, but a wise man can pacify it" (Proverbs 16:14).}

And this is[61] the explanation of the verse: "The King's wrath is a messenger of death." For the wrath of the Holy One is on account of *Malkhut* < that has been demeaned among the nations > .[62] "...but a wise man can pacify it"—i.e., the aspect of *Talmid Chakham*/Moshe, who will atone for [the sinner].[63] As it is written (Micah 7:18), "[The Lord] forgives the transgression for the remnant < of His inheritance > "—for the sake of the one who considers himself as remnants (*Rosh HaShanah* 17a).[64]

We find, then, that when he comes before a Torah scholar and expresses all his letter-combinations in a *Talmid Chakham's* presence....[65] The Torah scholar is an aspect of Moshe[66]- < Mashiach, >[67] who considered himself as "remnants," as is written (Numbers 12:3), "The man Moshe, however, was very humble."[68] This is

---

59. **fragments of his bones.** Either his body remains stable and strong because the mitzvot bind his bones together, or, if he has already sinned and caused his bones to become "shattered," his mitzvot counter this fragmentation by re-binding the bones and restoring them to their former unity (*Mai HaNachal*).

60. **God safeguards all his bones....** In review: When a person perceives that whatever happens to him is for his benefit, he has a foretaste of the World to Come (§1). Attaining this perception is only possible when he frees *Malkhut* of Holiness from the control of the nations and returns it to God (§2). This is accomplished by confession of one's sins in the presence of a Torah scholar, which unites the holy names *YHVH* and *Elohim* (§3). Knowing that all is for the best, the awareness that one's suffering also stems from God's love, is considered complete *daat* (§4). A person's sins blemish *Malkhut* and become etched upon his bones. The way to rectify *Malkhut* is by confessing one's sins in front of the tzaddik/Torah scholar. The bones are thus healed (§5). Confession in front of a Torah scholar corresponds to returning *Malkhut* to its source. This is because fire/Torah is the source of *Malkhut,* and Torah scholars are the essence of the Torah itself. The tzaddik's presence is therefore vital (§6).

61. **And this is.** Until now Rebbe Nachman has focused on the necessity for confessing in front of a Torah scholar. In this section, the Rebbe explains what enables the Torah scholar to rectify *Malkhut* when it is brought before him through confession.

62. **King's wrath...on account of Malkhut....** The Holy One is called "King" to hint that His anger is on account of the debasement of *Malkhut* (Kingship) due to sin. The negative letter-combinations that sin produces are the "messengers of death"—the destroying angels, which attack the sinner (*Parparaot LeChokhmah; Mai HaNachal*).

63. **but a wise man can pacify it....** This is the *Talmid Chakham*/tzaddik, such as Moshe. He can pacify and appease the Divine anger brought about by sin.

חָכָם, כְּמוֹ שֶׁכָּתוּב: "וְהַחָכְמָה מֵאַיִן תִּמָּצֵא". וּבָזֶה יֵשׁ כֹּחַ
לַתַּלְמִיד חָכָם לְכַפֵּר, כְּמוֹ שֶׁנֶּאֱמַר: וְאִישׁ חָכָם יְכַפְּרֶנָּה.

וּבִשְׁבִיל זֶה, כְּשֶׁהִתְפַּלֵּל מֹשֶׁה עַל חֵטְא הָעֵגֶל אָמַר: "אִם תִּשָּׂא
חַטָּאתָם, וְאִם אַיִן מְחֵנִי נָא". כִּי זֶה מִן הַנִּמְנָע שֶׁלֹּא יָבוֹא לְאָדָם
אֵיזֶה גַּדְלוּת, כְּשֶׁשּׁוֹמֵעַ שֶׁמְּסַפְּרִין שִׁבְחוֹ, כָּל שֶׁכֵּן כְּשֶׁמֶּלֶךְ גָּדוֹל
מְשַׁבֵּחַ וּמְפָאֵר אֶת הָאָדָם, אֲזַי בְּוַדַּאי מִן הַנִּמְנָע, שֶׁלֹּא יָבוֹא לוֹ
אֵיזֶה גַּדְלוּת, אֲבָל צָרִיךְ לָזֶה בִּטּוּל כָּל הַרְגָּשׁוֹתָיו וְחָמְרִיּוֹתָיו, אֲזַי
יָכוֹל הָאָדָם, לִשְׁמֹעַ שִׁבְחוֹ, וְלֹא יָבוֹא לוֹ שׁוּם גַּדְלוּת, כְּמוֹ מֹשֶׁה
רַבֵּנוּ, שֶׁרָאָה כָּתוּב בַּתּוֹרָה: "וַיְדַבֵּר ה' אֶל מֹשֶׁה", "וַיֹּאמֶר ה' אֶל
מֹשֶׁה", וְיִשְׂרָאֵל קוֹרִאין בְּכָל יוֹם בַּתּוֹרָה שִׁבְחוֹ שֶׁל מֹשֶׁה, וְהוּא
בְּעַצְמוֹ מְסַפֵּר לָהֶם שְׁבָחָיו, וְלֹא הָיָה לְמֹשֶׁה שׁוּם הִתְפָּאֲרוּת
וְגַדְלוּת מִזֶּה, כְּמוֹ שֶׁכָּתוּב: "וְהָאִישׁ מֹשֶׁה עָנָו מְאֹד", וּבְוַדַּאי עַל־
יְדֵי עַנְוְתָנוּתוֹ, הָיָה כֹּחַ בְּיַד מֹשֶׁה לְכַפֵּר עֲווֹן־הָעֵגֶל. כְּמוֹ שֶׁכָּתוּב:
"וְאִישׁ חָכָם יְכַפְּרֶנָּה".

וְזֶה שֶׁטָּעַן מֹשֶׁה: "וְאִם אַיִן", הַיְנוּ "אִם לֹא תִשָּׂא חַטָּאתָם", בָּזֶה
אַתָּה מַרְאֶה, שֶׁאֵין לִי כָּל כָּךְ עֲנִיווּת, שֶׁאוּכַל לְכַפֵּר לָהֶם עֲווֹן

---

that Torah scholar. By confessing, he elevates *Malkhut*, which he blemished by his sins, to a state of restoration. This rebuilding of *Malkhut* is in essence his renewed acceptance of God's Kingship and Authority. His repentance is thus complete. Therefore, the Torah scholar/tzaddik can elevate *him* to *Ayin*, to the level where there is no difference between good and bad. This is the aspect of the World to Come, attained through confession in front of a Torah scholar (*Mai HaNachal*). The connection that attaining this awareness has with the main corpus of our lesson will be explained below, in section 9.

72. **please blot me out....** When the Jewish people made the Golden Calf, they were guilty of idolatry and deserving of the death penalty. Moshe prayed, "If You would, forgive them...or blot me out," and they were spared. However, the sin was not entirely erased. A certain amount of every generation's suffering is punishment for the sin of the Golden Calf (*Rashi*, Exodus 32:34). In our context, Moshe was able to secure God's forgiveness for the Jews because he was totally humble and negated to God. However, nowhere do we find that the Jews confessed for this in his presence. Therefore, the effects of the sin remain, and the world continues to suffer because of the idolatry of the Golden Calf—i.e., *Malkhut* drawn into the realm of evil. The Rebbe will now explain Moshe's request in greater detail.

the reason he is called a wise man, as is written (Job 28:12), "Wisdom comes from *Ayin* (Nothingness)."[69] Through this the wise man has the power to appease,[70] as is written, "but a wise man can pacify it."[71]

This is why when Moshe prayed that the sin of the Golden Calf [be pardoned], he said (Exodus 32:32), "If You would, forgive their sin. But if not, please blot me out [from the book that You have written]!"[72] It is impossible for a person not to feel some pride when he hears himself being praised. All the more so, when a great king praises and lauds the person; then, it is certainly impossible that he would not be moved to some feelings of self-importance. However, this necessitates the negation of all one's emotions and corporeality. Then, a person can hear himself being praised and not come to any pride. This was the case with Moshe Rabbeinu, who saw it written in the Torah: "God spoke to Moshe," [and] "God said to Moshe." Each day, the Jewish people read in the Torah [God's] praise of Moshe. What's more, he himself related his praise to them. Yet Moshe had no feelings of haughtiness or pride from this, as is written, "The man Moshe, however, was very humble." And, certainly, by means of his humility Moshe had the power to atone for the sin of the Golden Calf, as is written, "...but a wise man can pacify it."

This was Moshe's argument: "But if not"—i.e., if You do not forgive their sin, You are demonstrating that I do not possess the humility needed to atone for the sin of the Golden Calf. This is why I

---

one must specifically confess in the presence of a Torah scholar. In the Torah the words for sin, *AVoN* (עון), and humble, *ANaV* (ענו), share the same letters. A person who has sinned must humiliate himself by confessing that sin in front of the humble tzaddik.

69. **Ayin, Nothingness.** Our Sages said: The words of the Torah remain only with those who make themselves as naught (*Sotah* 21b). The more humble a person is—i.e., the closer he is to *Ayin*—the greater his attachment to Wisdom, God's Torah. From this we see how *Malkhut*, whose source is fire/Torah (see nn.50,51), is connected to Wisdom and *Ayin*. Thus, Moshe, who was extremely humble, epitomized the *wise* man.

70. **the power to appease.** *Ayin* is the ultimate state of humility and self-negation. The power to appease God and secure His absolute forgiveness is granted only to those who possess this quality of nothingness.

71. **a wise man can pacify it.** Having seen how it is that the humble Torah scholar can secure God's forgiveness, we can now apply this to our lesson. When the Torah scholar who has negated himself in *Ayin* returns to a normal state of consciousness, he carries with him an advanced awareness of Godliness. The person who accepts the humiliation that comes with confession in a Torah scholar's presence displays his sincere willingness to negate himself to

הָעֵגֶל. בְּכֵן בַּקָּשָׁתִי – "מְחֵנִי נָא", כְּדֵי שֶׁלֹּא אֶכָּשֵׁל בִּגְדֻלּוֹת, שֶׁאֲנִי
רוֹאֶה וְשׁוֹמֵעַ בְּכָל עֵת סִפּוּר שִׁמִי וְשִׁבְחִי בַּתּוֹרָה, כִּי מִי יוּכַל
לַעֲמֹד בָּזֶה, שֶׁיִּשְׁמַע סִפּוּר שִׁבְחוֹ וְלֹא יִתְגָּאֶה, אִם לֹא עָנָו גָּדוֹל,
וְאִם אֲנִי עָנָו, צָרִיךְ לְךָ שֶׁתִּשָּׂא חַטָּאתָם, כְּמוֹ שֶׁכָּתוּב: "וְעוֹבֵר עַל
פֶּשַׁע לִשְׁאֵרִית" וְכוּ'.

וְזֶה : "וַיְהִי בִישֻׁרוּן מֶלֶךְ" (עייין מ"ר בהעלותך פ' ט"ו א"ל
הקב"ה למשה מלך עשיתיך וכן תרגום יונתן). הַיְנוּ שֶׁמַּלְכוּת
עָלָה לְשָׁרְשָׁהּ, כְּמוֹ שֶׁכָּתוּב: "וַעֲנָוִים יִרְשׁוּ אָרֶץ", וְ'אֶרֶץ' הִיא
דִּינָא דְּמַלְכוּתָא, כְּמוֹ שֶׁכָּתוּב: "וְאֶרֶץ מִתְקוֹמְמָה לוֹ":

number of times in the Talmud (e.g., *Gittin* 10b, *Bava Kama* 113a, *Bava Batra* 54b). It is Aramaic for "the law of the government is the law." A Jew living under the *malkhut* (government) of the non-Jews is obliged to obey their civil laws (see *Rashi, Gittin* 10b).

In our context, Rebbe Nachman reads *dina d'malkhuta* as "the *dinim* (judgments) of *Malkhut*," and he connects this with the concept of earth. Throughout the holy writings, earth is symbolic of *Malkhut*, while *Malkhut* connotes *din* (judgment). Thus, the earth, as an aspect of *Malkhut*, effects judgment against those who have abused it by lowering it into the realm of evil. This is the meaning of (*loc. cit.*), "Earth rises up against him." As the Rebbe explained above (§5), the sins themselves take revenge against those who commit them. In contrast, for the person who has attained deep humility, the earth is a symbol of modesty and humbleness. He will "inherit the earth," namely *Malkhut*, and elevate it to *Ayin*, its source (*Parparaot LeChokhmah*). The *Mai HaNachal* adds: From what the Rebbe has taught, it emerges that the source of *Malkhut* is in essence humility. A person who attains deep humility can attain all the positive attributes of *Malkhut*.

In review: When a person perceives that whatever happens to him is for his benefit, he has a foretaste of the World to Come (§1). Attaining this perception is only possible when he frees *Malkhut* of Holiness from the control of the nations and returns it to God (§2). This is accomplished by confession of one's sins in the presence of a Torah scholar, which unites the holy names *YHVH* and *Elohim* (§3). Knowing that all is for the best, the awareness that one's suffering also stems from God's love, is considered complete *daat* (§4). A person's sins blemish *Malkhut* and become etched upon his bones. The way to rectify *Malkhut* is by confessing one's sins in front of a tzaddik/Torah scholar. The bones are thus healed (§5). Confession in front of a Torah scholar corresponds to returning *Malkhut* to its source. This is because the source of *Malkhut* is fire/Torah, and Torah scholars embody the essence of the Torah itself. The tzaddik's presence is therefore vital (§6). And the tzaddik can effect forgiveness after hearing the confession because, by virtue of his deep humility, the tzaddik can elevate the rectified *Malkhut* to its ultimate source, *Ayin* (§7).

requested, "please blot me out," so as not to be tripped up by pride. For I constantly see and hear the recounting of my name and praise in the Torah. Who can stand up to this—hearing his praise recounted and not become haughty—if not a very humble person? And, if I am humble, You must pardon their sin, as is written, "[The Lord] forgives the transgression for the remnant...."[73]

This is (Deuteronomy 33:5): "There was a *MeLeKh* (king) in Yeshurun"[74]—indicating that *MaLKhut* had risen to its source, as it is written (Psalms 37:11), "But the humble will inherit the earth."[75] "Earth" is *dina d'malkhuta* (the law of the government), as is written (Job 20:27), "Earth rises up against him."[76]

---

73. **You must pardon their sin....** Moshe was so totally humble that he was able to hear his praise and still negate himself completely in *Ayin,* with no feelings of haughtiness whatsoever. He was therefore able to elevate the fallen *Malkhut* back to God, effecting forgiveness for the Jews.

The *Biur HaLikutim* asks: If Moshe had reached such exalted levels, why is the residual punishment for the sin of the Golden Calf spread throughout the ages? His answer is that despite Moshe's incredible self-negation in *Ayin,* as long as he still had a physical form even Moshe was unable to attain the ultimate degree of humility. The *Baal HaTurim* notes that in describing Moshe as an *anav,* Scripture employs the *chaser* (lacking) form, spelling it without the *yod*—ענו. This is because Moshe, recognizing his lack, did not want to overly praise himself. Had he in fact reached the ultimate level of humility, he would not have seen any reason not to praise himself. Thus, lacking the final degree of humility, even Moshe was unable to totally expiate the sin and gain full forgiveness. This level will only be attained by Mashiach, who will erase sin and its effects completely.

74. **There was a MeLeKh in Yeshurun.** *Targum Yonatan* explains that this verse refers to Moshe, who became king over Israel. The Midrash teaches this as well: The Holy One said to Moshe, "I have made you a king," as is written, "There was a king in Yeshurun"—Moshe's kingdom was a reflection of the Kingdom of God (*Bamidbar Rabbah* 15:13, see *MaHarzav*). In our context, the verse alludes to *MaLKhut* residing with Moshe, the Torah scholar/tzaddik (*Parparaot LeChokhmah*).

As he does often throughout *Likutey Moharan,* Rebbe Nachman shows the connection between one concept and another, and then ties that first concept with yet another and another concept. (Later on he returns to show how that second one connects directly to the third and fourth concepts, and so on.) So far, the Rebbe has shown how *Malkhut* must return to its source, tying that source, which is fire, to Torah. Here, he will show how Moshe, the Torah scholar, and *Ayin* (the Source of all sources) are conceptually connected with *Malkhut.*

75. **But the humble...earth.** Once *Malkhut* resided with Moshe, it was considered to have returned to its highest source, which is *Ayin*/total humility, as in, "But the humble will inherit the earth" (*Parparaot LeChokhmah*). See next note.

76. **Earth...dina d'Malkhuta...against him.** The concept of *dina d'malkhuta dina* appears a

ח. וְזֶהוּ שֶׁאָמְרוּ חֲכָמֵינוּ, זִכְרוֹנָם לִבְרָכָה:

מָשָׁל לְאֶחָד, שֶׁהָיָה מְהַלֵּךְ בַּדֶּרֶךְ בְּאִישׁוֹן לַיְלָה וַאֲפֵלָה, וּמִתְיָרֵא
מִן הַקּוֹצִים וּמִן הַפְּחָתִים וּמֵחַיָּה רָעָה וּמִלִּסְטִים, וְאֵינוֹ יוֹדֵעַ
בְּאֵיזֶה דֶּרֶךְ מְהַלֵּךְ וְכוּ':

כִּי זֶה יָדוּעַ, שֶׁכָּל הַמִּדּוֹת רָעוֹת וְתוֹלְדוֹתֵיהֶן נִמְשָׁכִין מֵאַרְבָּעָה
יְסוֹדוֹת, מֵאַרְבַּע מָרוֹת, כַּמּוּבָא בְּמִשְׁנַת חֲסִידִים: 'עַצְבוּת
וְתוֹלְדוֹתֵיהֶן נִמְשָׁכִין מְדּוֹמֵם', 'תַּאֲווֹת רָעוֹת וְתוֹלְדוֹתֵיהֶן
נִמְשָׁכִין מְצוֹמֵחַ', 'דְּבָרִים בְּטֵלִים וְתוֹלְדוֹתֵיהֶן נִמְשָׁכִין מֵחַי'.

Note that in the parable, Torah and mitzvot are spoken of as the power to combat the pitfalls and evil desires of the "night," as well as finding proper direction during the "day." We have previously seen that by elevating *Malkhut* to its source, a person can rectify even those errors and pitfalls to which he has succumbed. As the Rebbe's lesson unfolds, we will see how closely Torah and mitzvot are intertwined with the process of repentance and confession in the presence of a true Torah scholar.

83. **four yesodot...humors.** Rambam explains that below the celestial band within which the moon orbits there are four more bands, each one a source for one of the four fundamental elements: fire, wind, water, earth. These elements are the *yesodot* (literally, foundations) of physical creation in all its forms, mineral, vegetable, animal and human. Of the four *yesodot*, fire is dry and hot, and its corresponding humor (or bile) is red; air is damp and hot, and its corresponding humor is white; water is damp and cold, and its corresponding humor is green; earth is dry and cold, and its corresponding humor is black. All the different forms in creation have their own balance of these *yesodot*, and it is precisely the difference in balance that makes each form unique (*Hilkhot Yesodei HaTorah* 3:10, 4:1,2; *Zohar* III, 227b; cf. *Mishnat Chassidim, Mesikhta HaHarkavah*; cf. *Likutey Moharan* I, 31:2 and n.25 for more on the celestial bands).

84. **Mishnat Chassidim.** An important Kabbalistic work by Rabbi Immanuel Chai Riki (1688-1743) that concisely reviews creation's progression from *ex nihilo* to this physical world and the forces of evil. The passage in our text appears in the chapter *Mesikhta Asiyah Gufanit* 1:1. The *Mishnat Chassidim* explains that the four elements correspond to the four letters of God's holy name *YHVH*, the root of one's good character traits (henceforth, virtues), as well as to the four *kelipot* (see Ezekiel 1:4), the root of one's evil character traits (henceforth, vices). Rebbe Nachman will now explain that the four categories of vice, which correspond to the four elements, also correspond to the four humors and the four classifications of life forms in the universe: mineral, vegetable, animal and human.

85. **Melancholy...mineral life form.** Melancholy stems from earth, the mineral life form, which corresponds to the black humor, and is dry, cold, and inanimate.

86. **evil passions...vegetable life form.** Evil passions stem from water, the vegetable life form, which corresponds to the green humor, and is damp, cold, and animate.

8. This is the meaning of what the Sages said[77]:

It is comparable to someone who was walking along a path in the utter darkness of night.[78] He was afraid of the thorns and the ditches, of wild beasts and bandits; not knowing which path he was on. When he happened upon a lit torch,[79] he was saved from the thorns and the ditches but he was still afraid of wild beasts and bandits[80]; not knowing which path he was on. When dawn broke,[81] he was saved from wild beasts and bandits, yet still did not know which path he was on. When he came to a crossroads, he was saved from all of them.... What is this crossroads? Rabbi Chisda said: It is a *Talmid Chakham* and the day of death (*Sotah* 21a).[82]

It is known that all evil character traits and their derivatives stem from the four *yesodot* (fundamental elements), the four humors.[83] As is brought in *Mishnat Chassidim*[84]: Melancholy and its derivatives stem from the mineral life form[85]; evil passions and their derivatives stem from the vegetable life form[86]; idle chatter and its derivatives

---

77. **the Sages said.** So far, Rebbe Nachman has explained that confession in the tzaddik's presence elevates *Malkhut*—i.e., it is a means for rectifying one's sins. Here, the Rebbe shows that repentance is actually a three step process. Two things must happen prior to confession.

In clarifying these steps, the Rebbe shows how they are alluded to in the Talmudic passage he quotes from *Sotah* (21a). The Talmud states that both the study of Torah and the performance of mitzvot have the power to protect a person. Yet, our Sages differentiate between the two, discussing which is the greater and how far reaching that protective merit is. The notes that explain this passage incorporate the commentaries of Rashi and Maharsha (*loc. cit., s.v. mah*).

78. **utter darkness of night.** "Night" alludes to this world, in which troubles abound. A person must search for his livelihood (thorns/the vegetation) and beware of the pitfalls set by his enemies.

79. **lit torch.** This refers to the mitzvot, which help a person to a certain degree.

80. **wild beasts and bandits.** Alluding to the evil inclination's ability to overwhelm one's power of intellect.

81. **dawn broke.** This refers to the Torah's ability to enlighten a person's way, helping him overcome the obstacles that prevent him from serving God.

82. **crossroads...Talmid Chakham...death.** Even someone who possesses Torah knowledge can err. A person therefore needs a true Torah scholar who will direct him properly. The Talmud offers two other explanations for "crossroads": 1) a Torah scholar and fear of sin; 2) a Torah scholar who reaches the proper conclusions in deciding Torah laws. We will soon see that both these explanations are synonymous with Rabbi Chisda's interpretation: "a Torah scholar and the day of death."

Rebbe Nachman will now review the lesson within the context of our Sages' parable.

גַּאֲוָה וְתוֹלְדוֹתֵיהֶן נִמְשָׁכִין מִמְּדַבֵּר'.

וּמִי שֶׁרוֹצֶה לֵילֵךְ בְּדֶרֶךְ הַקֹּדֶשׁ, צָרִיךְ לְשַׁבֵּר כָּל הַמִּדּוֹת רָעוֹת,
וִיסַפֵּר לִפְנֵי הַתַּלְמִיד חָכָם, הַיְנוּ וִדּוּי דְּבָרִים. וְהַתַּלְמִיד חָכָם יְפָרֵשׁ
וִיבָרֵר לוֹ דֶרֶךְ לְפִי שֹׁרֶשׁ נִשְׁמָתוֹ.

וְיֵשׁ שָׁלֹשׁ בְּחִינוֹת בְּהִתְקָרְבוּת לַצַּדִּיקִים, שֶׁעַל־יְדֵי שָׁלֹשׁ בְּחִינוֹת
אֵלּוּ נִתְתַּקֵּן הַכֹּל, וְאֵלּוּ הֵם הַשְּׁלוֹשָׁה בְּחִינוֹת:

הַבְּחִינָה הָרִאשׁוֹנָה: כְּשֶׁרוֹאֶה אֶת הַצַּדִּיק, כְּמוֹ שֶׁכָּתוּב: "וְהָיוּ
עֵינֶיךָ רוֹאוֹת אֶת מוֹרֶיךָ". וְזֹאת הַבְּחִינָה מְבַטֶּלֶת הַמִּדּוֹת רָעוֹת
הַנִּמְשָׁכִין מִשְּׁנֵי הַיְסוֹדוֹת: 'דוֹמֵם' 'צוֹמֵחַ', הַיְנוּ עַצְבוּת
וְתוֹלְדוֹתֶיהָ, וְתַאֲווֹת רָעוֹת, כִּי צַדִּיק הַדּוֹר נִקְרָא אֵם, עַל שֵׁם
שֶׁהוּא מֵינִיק לְיִשְׂרָאֵל בְּאוֹר תּוֹרָתוֹ, וְהַתּוֹרָה נִקְרָאת חָלָב, כְּמוֹ
שֶׁכָּתוּב: "דְּבַשׁ וְחָלָב תַּחַת לְשׁוֹנֵךְ". וְזֶה אָנוּ רוֹאִים בְּחוּשׁ,
כְּשֶׁהַתִּינוֹק הוּא בְּעַצְבוּת וְעַצְלוּת, כְּשֶׁרוֹאֶה אֶת אִמּוֹ הוּא נִתְעוֹרֵר

direct the person on his proper path. This ties in further with our text in that the lesson revolves around the concept of complete awareness—i.e., an awareness that everything is one. And although this will only be fully revealed in the Future, it is possible to get a glimpse of this even now, through faith (as explained above, n.6). The same is true of the "Teacher." Although God will only fully reveal Himself in the Future, it is possible to get a glimpse of Him even now, through the true tzaddikim.

92. **yesodot, mineral and vegetable.** Although the four elements are fire, air, water and earth (see n.83), here Rebbe Nachman calls the four life forms (mineral, vegetable, animal and human) *yesodot*. However, as has been explained, the four *yesodot,* the four humors, the four classifications of life forms, and the categories of vice are all corresponding concepts.

93. **Mother.** Moshe, the true tzaddik, said to God, "Was I pregnant with all these people? Did I give birth to them?" (Numbers 11:12). We have also seen that the source of *Malkhut* is fire, which corresponds to the *gevurot* (above, n.50). These *gevurot* are rooted in *Binah* (see *Likutey Moharan* I, 15:3), and *Binah* is Mother (see Appendix: The Divine Persona; Proverbs 2:3). This relates to the tzaddik because, as the Rebbe taught earlier, a true Torah scholar is the one who returns *Malkhut* to its highest source (§6, n.51). Thus, our quest to elevate *Malkhut* to its source can be expressed as seeking *Binah,* the true tzaddik, who is the source of Torah.

94. **Honey and milk . . . .** To which the Talmud adds: "Things that are sweeter than honey and milk"—i.e., the Torah—"should be under your tongue" (*Chagigah* 13a).

stem from the animal life form[87]; pride and its derivatives stem from the human life form.[88]

Anyone who would take the path of < God > must break all of the vices < and talk about all his traits > in the presence of a *Talmid Chakham*—i.e., spoken confession. The Torah scholar will then define and clarify a path in line with the root of his soul.

Now, there are three steps in attachment to the tzaddikim. Through these three steps, everything is rectified.[89] The three steps are as follows:

The first step entails seeing the tzaddik,[90] as in (Isaiah 30:20), "your eyes will see your teacher."[91] This step negates the vices that stem from the two *yesodot,* mineral and vegetable[92]—namely, melancholy with its derivatives, and evil passions. For the tzaddik of the generation is called "Mother,"[93] because he nurses the Jewish people with the light of his Torah. And the Torah is called "milk," as is written (Song of Songs 4:11), "Honey and milk under your tongue."[94] We have empirical validation for this: Even when a child is sad and lethargic, if he sees his mother, he very quickly stirs toward her—i.e., toward his source. We also see clearly that when a child is absorbed in his own nonsense, even though he has a great desire for this, if he sees

---

87. **idle chatter...animal life form.** Idle chatter stems from air, the animal life form, which corresponds to the white humor, and is damp and hot. Its derivatives include: flattery, falsehood, slander, and self-praise.

88. **pride...human life form.** Pride stems from fire, the human life form, which corresponds to the red humor, and is dry and hot. Its derivatives include: anger, haughtiness, and hatred.

The Hebrew term for the human life form is *m'daber,* which literally means "speaker." *M'daber* connotes the level of man because the ability to speak is uniquely human.

89. **everything is rectified.** It must be pointed out that this is an ongoing process. One cannot expect to rid oneself of all one's vices in one attempt. It takes much time, patience and effort. Yet when a person is truly devoted to climbing the ladder of holiness, he will certainly attain rectification for everything (*Parparaot LeChokhmah*).

90. **seeing the tzaddik.** The *Parparaot LeChokhmah* explains that this "seeing" of the tzaddik actually refers to attaching oneself to him; more than mere eye contact. That is, a person must come to the tzaddik with the intended goal of seeing him, to learn how to serve God from him. This will be explained in greater detail below, in section 10 (see n.158).

91. **will see your teacher.** This verse refers to the days of Mashiach, when God, "your Teacher," will no longer be hidden. Then, mankind will be able to directly ask Him for all their needs and for proper guidance in their paths (*Metzudat David, loc. cit.*). In our context, this refers to seeing the *Talmid Chakham*/tzaddik, who, after all three steps are fulfilled, will

בִּזְרִיזוּת גָּדוֹל לִקְרַאת אִמּוֹ, הַיְנוּ לְשָׁרְשׁוֹ. גַּם אָנוּ רוֹאִים בְּחוּשׁ, כְּשֶׁהַתִּינוֹק עוֹסֵק בְּדִבְרֵי שְׁטוּת שֶׁלּוֹ, אַף-עַל-פִּי שֶׁיֵּשׁ לוֹ תַּאֲוָה גְּדוֹלָה לָזֶה, אַף-עַל-פִּי כֵן כְּשֶׁרוֹאֶה אֶת אִמּוֹ, הוּא מַשְׁלִיךְ כָּל תַּאֲווֹתָיו אַחַר כְּתֵפָיו, וּמוֹשֵׁךְ אֶת עַצְמוֹ לְאִמּוֹ. נִמְצָא, שֶׁנִּתְבַּטְּלִין הַמִּדּוֹת רָעוֹת שֶׁל שְׁנֵי הַיְסוֹדוֹת: 'דּוֹמֵם' 'צוֹמֵחַ', עַל יְדֵי הִסְתַּכְּלוּת פְּנֵי הַצַּדִּיק.

וְזֶהוּ 'וּמִתְיָרֵא מִן הַקּוֹצִים', שֶׁהוּא בְּחִינַת 'צוֹמֵחַ'. 'וּפְחָתִים' שֶׁהוּא בְּחִינַת 'דּוֹמֵם'. וּכְשֶׁנִּזְדַּמֵּן לוֹ אֲבוּקָה שֶׁל אוֹר, זֶה תַּלְמִיד חָכָם, שֶׁהוּא אָבִיק בְּאוֹר הַתּוֹרָה וְעַל-יָדוֹ נִצּוֹל מִמִּדּוֹת רָעוֹת שֶׁל שְׁנֵי יְסוֹדוֹת: 'דּוֹמֵם' 'צוֹמֵחַ', וְאָז נִצּוֹל מִן הַקּוֹצִים וּמִן הַפְּחָתִים:

הַבְּחִינָה הַשְּׁנִיָּה: הַצְּדָקָה שֶׁנּוֹתֵן לְתַלְמִיד חָכָם, שֶׁעַל-יְדֵי-זֶה נִצּוֹל מִמִּדּוֹת רָעוֹת שֶׁל שְׁנֵי יְסוֹדוֹת: 'חַי' 'מְדַבֵּר', שֶׁהֵן בְּחִינַת 'חַיָּה רָעָה וְלִסְטִים', שֶׁהֵן דְּבָרִים בְּטֵלִים וְגַאֲוָה וְתוֹלְדוֹתֵיהֶן. כִּי עַל-יְדֵי דְּבָרִים בְּטֵלִים וּלְשׁוֹן הָרָע, בָּא עֲנִיּוּת, כְּמוֹ שֶׁכָּתוּב: "כִּי מֵתוּ כָּל הָאֲנָשִׁים", זֶהוּ עֲנִיּוּת. גַּם בְּגַאֲוָה אָמְרוּ: 'סִימָן לְגַסּוּת הָרוּחַ –

---

99. **All the men....** Moshe originally fled Egypt when Datan and Aviram informed Pharaoh that he had killed an Egyptian overseer (Exodus 2:11-15). When Moshe was to return to Egypt, God told him that he need no longer fear these informers, for "All the men have died." The Talmud explains that they had not actually died but had lost their property, and a poor man is as if dead (*Nedarim, loc. cit.*). No one in a position of authority in Egypt would pay attention to these two paupers (see *Rashi, ibid.*). What had caused them to become impoverished? It was the slander they had spoken against Moshe.

100. **poverty...haughty spirit.** Thus, from these Talmudic passages we see that both idle chatter and pride bring poverty. The *Parparaot LeChokhmah* adds that although the context of the Talmud (*Kiddushin, loc. cit.*) is "poverty" in Torah knowledge, not a lack of material wealth, this does not negate the literal meaning. Then again, the Mishnah teaches: If Torah is lacking, so is livelihood (*Avot* 3:17). Thus, haughtiness brings to poverty in Torah, and this in turn leads to material poverty. To clarify this a bit more, it is almost always the case that a wealthy person lacking in the wisdom of Torah is never satisfied with his wealth. Always seeking more, he constantly feels impoverished. This is the significance of poverty's signs and markings—i.e., even the *feelings* of poverty and lack are dispelled from the one who gives charity (cf. *Mai HaNachal*).

his mother, he throws away all of his desires and draws close to her. We find, then, that the vices stemming from the two *yesodot,* mineral and vegetable, are negated by gazing at the countenance of the tzaddik.[95]

This is: **He was afraid of the thorns,** the aspect of the vegetable life form; **and the ditches,** the aspect of the mineral life form. **When he happened upon a lit torch**—this is a *Talmid Chakham,* who < glows > with the light of the Torah.[96] Through him he is saved from the vices that stem from the two *yesodot,* mineral and vegetable; and then he is saved **from the thorns and the ditches.**

The second step is the charity one gives to a *Talmid Chakham*[97] < who embodies a number of souls >.[98] Through this he is saved from the vices that stem from the two *yesodot,* animal and human— the aspects of wild beasts and bandits, which are idle chatter and pride and their derivatives. This is because idle chatter and slanderous gossip engender poverty, as is written (Exodus 4:19), "All the men have died"—this is poverty (Nedarim 64b).[99] Also, concerning pride it is taught: Poverty is a sign of a haughty spirit (Kiddushin 49b).[100] But by

---

95. **...countenance of the tzaddik.** As explained earlier, this refers to actually attaching oneself to the tzaddik. For what the Rebbe says about the child is predicated on the child wanting his mother and wanting to be attached to her. Otherwise, he will not change when he sees her. And it is the same for a person unwilling to overcome his desires will not change just because he looks at the tzaddik (cf. *Likutey Moharan* I, 129).

    The *Parparaot LeChokhmah* adds that hidden in the writings of the tzaddik are his countenance, his intelligence and wisdom. Therefore, true fulfillment of seeing the tzaddik is when one studies and draws from his Torah teachings. This enables people to always "see" and be attached to him, even if they are not physically in the same place. See also, *Likutey Moharan* 192; *Likutey Halakhot, Ketubot* 1.

96. **lit torch...Talmid Chakham....** The lit torch and a Torah scholar are both fire (*Mai HaNachal*).

97. **charity one gives to the Talmid Chakham.** The second step, after seeing the tzaddik, entails giving him charity. Elsewhere (*Likutey Moharan* I, 17:5), Rebbe Nachman teaches that by giving the tzaddik charity, one becomes included in him. Here, the Rebbe will show that being "included" in the tzaddik eliminates the other vices, those that seeing the tzaddik did not eliminate.

98. **embodies a number of souls.** The tzaddik's soul is so great, he can carry any number of additional souls; elevating them together with his own soul to ever greater spiritual levels. This is the concept of being embodied or included in the tzaddik. Similarly, we find in the writings of the Ari that each Torah scholar, each tzaddik, is likened to the trunk of a large tree, with all his followers being the different branches, twigs and leaves that are part of that tree (*Shaar HaGilgulim* #38, pp.144-145).

עֲנִיּוּת'. וְעַל-יְדֵי צְדָקָה נִתְעַשֵּׁר, כְּמוֹ שֶׁאָמְרוּ חֲכָמֵינוּ, זִכְרוֹנָם לִבְרָכָה: 'אִם שְׁלֵמִים וְכֵן רַבִּים וְכֵן נָגוֹזּוּ וְעָבַר וְעִנִּיתִיךְ לֹא אֲעַנֵּךְ, שׁוּב אֵין מַרְאִין לוֹ סִימָנֵי עֲנִיּוּת.

וְזֶהוּ, 'כֵּיוָן שֶׁעָלָה עַמּוּד הַשַּׁחַר נִצּוֹל מֵחַיָּה רָעָה וּמִלְּסְטִים'. 'עַמּוּד הַשַּׁחַר' – רֶמֶז לִצְדָקָה, כְּמוֹ שֶׁכָּתוּב: "כִּי תִרְאֶה עָרֹם וְכִסִּיתוֹ וְכוּ', אָז יִבָּקַע כַּשַּׁחַר אוֹרֶךְ". נִמְצָא, עַל-יְדֵי צְדָקָה נִצּוֹל מִמִּדּוֹת רָעוֹת שֶׁל שְׁנֵי יְסוֹדוֹת: 'חַי' 'מְדַבֵּר' שֶׁהֵם בְּחִינַת חַיָּה רָעָה וְלִסְטִים:

הַבְּחִינָה הַשְּׁלִישִׁית: כְּשֶׁמִּתְוַדֶּה וִדּוּי דְּבָרִים לִפְנֵי תַּלְמִיד חָכָם, שֶׁעַל-יְדֵי-זֶה הַתַּלְמִיד חָכָם מַדְרִיךְ אוֹתוֹ בְּדֶרֶךְ יָשָׁר לְפִי שֹׁרֶשׁ נִשְׁמָתוֹ.

וְזֶה 'הִגִּיעַ לְפָרָשַׁת דְּרָכִים', וְאָמְרוּ חֲכָמֵינוּ, זִכְרוֹנָם לִבְרָכָה: 'זֶה תַּלְמִיד חָכָם וְיוֹם הַמִּיתָה', זֶה בְּחִינַת וִדּוּי דְּבָרִים לִפְנֵי 'תַּלְמִיד חָכָם'. 'יוֹם הַמִּיתָה', רֶמֶז עַל וִדּוּי, כְּמוֹ שֶׁאָמְרוּ רַבּוֹתֵינוּ, זִכְרוֹנָם לִבְרָכָה: 'כָּל הַמּוּמָתִין מִתְוַדִּין'. וְזֶה נִקְרָא פָּרָשַׁת-דְּרָכִים כִּי הַתַּלְמִיד חָכָם מַפְרִישׁ לוֹ דֶרֶךְ לְפִי שֹׁרֶשׁ נִשְׁמָתוֹ,

death will have a portion in the World to Come. This is the reason the Sanhedrin would advise all those sentenced to death to first confess their sins. Even if they had committed terrible crimes, their confession helped to eradicate the negative letter-combinations and rebuild these combinations in holiness. They could therefore merit a taste of the World to Come, where people will attain the awareness that God and His Name are one, and where everything, even one's death, is for the best.

105. **root of his soul.** The *PaRaShat DeRaKhim* (פרשת דרכים, crossroads) alludes to the defining of a path, *maPhRiSh DeReKh* (מפריש דרך), that the Torah scholar does for a person. This is important, because no two people are the same; each of us requires a different balance of devotions. As Reb Noson writes: Even the very great tzaddikim, even those who sat at the feet of the same master, are very different from one another and emphasize very different devotional practices. Consider the disciples of the Magid of Mezritch. One spent much time travelling, another confined himself to his home; one prayed loudly and with great emotion, another prayed silently and with no outward emotion; some engaged in Torah study on the

giving charity, a person becomes wealthy. As the Sages taught: "Though they were united and likewise many, even so they are over and gone; I have afflicted you, but will afflict you no more" (Nahum 1:12)—he is never again made to experience the markings of poverty (*Gittin* 7b).[101]

And this is: **When dawn broke, he was saved from wild beasts and bandits.** The break of dawn is an allusion to charity, as is written (Isaiah 58:7-8), "When you see the naked, and you clothe him.... Then your light shall burst forth like the dawn."[102] We find, then, that through charity one is saved from the vices that stem from the two *yesodot*, animal and human, corresponding to **wild beasts and bandits.**

The third step is when one makes a spoken confession in a Torah scholar's presence. Through this the *Talmid Chakham* guides him on a proper path in line with the root of his soul.[103]

This is: **When he came to a crossroads.** And the Sages comment, **It is a Talmid Chakham and the day of death.** This is the step of spoken confession before a *Talmid Chakham*. **The day of death** is an allusion to confession, as the Sages taught: All those about to be put to death, confess (*Sanhedrin* 43b).[104] This is called *PaRaShat DeRaKhim* (a crossroads), because the Torah scholar *maPhRiSh lo DeReKh* (defines his path) in line with the root of his soul.[105]

---

101. **But by giving charity...afflict you no more....** Because he has given charity, God says, "I will afflict you no more"—i.e., he will be free of poverty and its consequences. As Rashi (*loc. cit.*) comments, the Talmud's exposition of this verse is not based on its plain meaning. Rather, the Talmud reads the verse as if it were saying: If a person's meals are meager, and certainly if they are abundant, then, just as a sheep must be shorn in order for them to ford a river, he must also shear away part of his money for charity so that in reward for his generosity he will prosper. In our context, this teaches that by giving charity a person gains material wealth and thereby negates the causes of poverty—namely, idle chatter and pride.

102. **clothe him...your light shall burst forth....** Charity—"clothing the naked"—is likened to the breaking of dawn.

103. **guides him on a proper path....** This is the most important facet of confession in the presence of the Torah scholar. Prior to this, the negative letter-combinations etched upon his bones prevent a person from finding his proper path. *Malkhut* of the Other Side has been created, which rules and draws that person toward evil even when his desires are good. But, through confession in front of the true tzaddik, he destroys this *Malkhut* of the Other Side and so restores *Malkhut* of Holiness—so that he is then shown his proper path in serving God (see *Parparaot LeChokhmah*).

104. **be put to death, confess.** Our Sages (*loc. cit.*) tell us that whoever confesses before his

אֲזַי נִצוֹל מִכֻּלָם. כִּי קֹדֶם שֶׁהִתְוַדָּה, אַף־עַל־פִּי שֶׁהָיָה אֵצֶל
הַתַּלְמִיד חָכָם, וְנָתַן לוֹ מָמוֹן, עֲדַיִן אֵינוֹ יוֹדֵעַ בְּאֵיזֶהוּ דֶּרֶךְ הוּא
מְהַלֵּךְ, כִּי "יֵשׁ דֶּרֶךְ יָשָׁר לִפְנֵי אִישׁ וְאַחֲרִיתָהּ דַּרְכֵי מָוֶת", אֲבָל
'כְּשֶׁהִגִּיעַ לְפָרָשַׁת דְּרָכִים – זֶה תַּלְמִיד חָכָם וְיוֹם הַמִּיתָה; הַיְנוּ
וִדּוּי דְּבָרִים לִפְנֵי תַּלְמִיד־חָכָם, אֲזַי נִצוֹל מִכֻּלָם:

ט וְזֶה בְּכָל פַּעַם שֶׁבָּא אֵצֶל תַּלְמִיד חָכָם וּמְסַפֵּר לְפָנָיו כָּל לִבּוֹ,
וְהַתַּלְמִיד חָכָם הוּא בְּחִינַת מֹשֶׁה, שֶׁהוּא בְּחִינַת אַיִן, כְּמוֹ שֶׁכָּתוּב:

But he still did not know which path he was on — Although he had rid himself of all the major vices and their derivatives, his previous misdeeds still had the power to mislead him (as above, nn.103,106).

When he came to a crossroads — When he confessed in front of a Torah scholar,

he was saved from all of them — the tzaddik was able to reveal the proper devotional path for him to follow.

In review: When a person perceives that whatever happens to him is for his benefit, he has a foretaste of the World to Come (§1). Attaining this perception is only possible when he frees *Malkhut* of Holiness from the control of the nations and returns it to God (§2). This is accomplished by confession of one's sins in the presence of a Torah scholar, which unites the holy names *YHVH* and *Elohim* (§3). Knowing that all is for the best, the awareness that one's suffering also stems from God's love, is considered complete *daat* (§4). A person's sins blemish *Malkhut* and become etched upon his bones. The way to rectify *Malkhut* is by confessing one's sins in front of the tzaddik/Torah scholar. The bones are thus healed (§5). Confession in front of a Torah scholar corresponds to returning *Malkhut* to its source. This is because the source of *Malkhut* is fire/Torah, and Torah scholars embody the essence of the Torah itself. The tzaddik's presence is therefore vital (§6). And the tzaddik can effect forgiveness after hearing the confession because, by virtue of his deep humility, the tzaddik can elevate the rectified *Malkhut* to its ultimate source, *Ayin* (§7). Confessing in the presence of a tzaddik is actually the third of a three step process for achieving repentance. The first two steps are attaching oneself to the tzaddik and giving charity to the tzaddik. Then the tzaddik can direct him in line with his soul's root, so that he can enter the realm of holiness (§8).

108. **This applies each time....** As explained earlier, the process of eliminating one's vices and thereby attaining higher spiritual levels is ongoing (see n.89). At each stage of a person's ascent on the spiritual ladder he attains a bit more awareness of Godliness. Ultimately, he can come to complete awareness—i.e., recognition that God and His Name are one. In this section, Rebbe Nachman will show how confession in front of the tzaddik leads to this complete awareness, to recognition that everything that happens is for the best.

109. **Talmid Chakham...Moshe...Ayin.** As above, section 7 (n.69).

Then, **he was saved from all of them.** Because, before he confessed, even though he was close to the Torah scholar and had given him money, he still does not know which path he was on. For "A path may seem right to a man, but its end leads to death" (Proverbs 14:12).[106] But when he comes to "a crossroads," which is **a Talmid Chakham and the day of death**—i.e., spoken confession before a *Talmid Chakham*—then, **he was saved from all of them.**[107]

9. This applies each time < you come to > a Torah scholar. < You should tell him all the conundrums in your heart. >[108] The *Talmid Chakham* is an aspect of Moshe, who is an aspect of *Ayin,* as is written, "Wisdom comes from *Ayin.*"[109] And in this way, you become

---

deepest levels, while others focused their major efforts on charity (*Likutey Halakhot, Shomer Sakhar* 2:10). As mentioned above (n.98), some of the tzaddik's followers are like the branches, others like the twigs, and still others like the leaves of a large tree. Therefore, each person requires his own balance of devotional practices in accordance with the root of his soul. Coming to see (being attached to) the tzaddik, giving him charity, and finally confessing in his presence, enable a person to discover his soul's root so that he might be led upon the proper path. Below (n.202), the *Parparaot LeChokhmah* will explain how this is accomplished even today.

106. **A path may seem right....** Rashi (*loc. cit.*) explains that this is a person who, because he thinks he's on the right path, will mislead himself to the bitter end. In our context, this is the person who has eliminated the vices that stem from the four *yesodot,* but who has yet to confess in the presence of a *Talmid Chakham*. The negative structures and letter-combinations formed by the sins he committed before coming to the tzaddik, remain. As a result, he might think he is on the proper path when in fact he is not. Having not yet confessed, he has yet to have the tzaddik direct him on the proper path (*Parparaot LeChokhmah*; see above, n.103).

107. **saved from all of them.** The parable thus translates in our text as follows:
someone who was walking along a path in the utter darkness of night — A person was walking through this world, seeking rectification for his evil deeds.
He was afraid of the thorns and the ditches, of wild beasts and bandits; and he did not know which path he was on — He was subject to the vices that stem from the four elements and the four humors, and did not know how to conduct himself.
When he happened upon a lit torch — When he saw the tzaddik,
he was saved from the thorns and the ditches — he was saved from the vices that stem from the vegetable and mineral life forms, namely melancholy and evil passions.
But he was still afraid of wild beasts and bandits; and did not know which path he was on — Yet there were other vices he hadn't eliminated.
When dawn broke — After seeing the tzaddik he gave him charity.
he was saved from wild beasts and bandits — This eliminated the vices that stem from the animal and human life forms, namely idle chatter and pride.

"וְהַחָכְמָה מֵאַיִן תִּמָּצֵא". וְעַל יְדֵי זֶה אַתָּה נִכְלָל בָּאֵין סוֹף.

וְזֶה בְּחִינַת, 'זַרְקָא דְּאִזְדְּרִיקַת לְאֲתַר דְּאִתְנְטִילַת מִתַּמָּן', שֶׁתַּחֲזִיר אֶת הַמַּלְכוּת לְאֵין סוֹף, שֶׁהוּא רָצוֹן שֶׁבְּכָל הָרְצוֹנוֹת. כִּי הַמַּלְכוּת, שֶׁהוּא בְּחִינַת אוֹתִיּוֹת הַדִּבּוּרִים, כָּל אוֹת וָאוֹת – מְלֻבָּשׁ בָּהּ רָצוֹן הַשֵּׁם יִתְבָּרַךְ. שֶׁרְצוֹן הַשֵּׁם יִתְבָּרַךְ הָיָה, שֶׁזֹּאת הָאוֹת יִהְיֶה לָהּ תְּמוּנָה כָּזוֹ, וְאוֹת אַחֶרֶת יִהְיֶה לָהּ תְּמוּנָה אַחֶרֶת. נִמְצָא, שֶׁרְצוֹנוֹת, הַיְנוּ תְּמוּנוֹת אוֹתִיּוֹת הֵם הִתְגַּלּוּת מַלְכוּתוֹ יִתְבָּרַךְ שְׁמוֹ. וְכָל אֵלּוּ הָרְצוֹנוֹת, הַיְנוּ הַתְּמוּנוֹת נִמְשָׁכִין מֵרָצוֹן אֵין סוֹף, שֶׁאֵין בּוֹ תְּמוּנָה.

וְכָל הַדְּבָרִים וְהַיֵּשׁוּת שֶׁבָּעוֹלָם הֵם מֵהָאוֹתִיּוֹת, הַיְנוּ מִמַּלְכוּת, כִּי יֵשׁוּת הוּא מֵחֲמַת הַמַּלְכוּת, שֶׁרָצָה הַקָּדוֹשׁ־בָּרוּךְ־הוּא שֶׁיִּתְגַּלֶּה מַלְכוּתוֹ בָּעוֹלָם, וְעַל יְדֵי זֶה בָּרָא אֶת הָעוֹלָם מֵאַיִן לְיֵשׁ, וְכָל

known as *Ayin* (Nothingness). At the other end is *Malkhut*, also known as *aniy* (I). Returning *Malkhut* to *Ein Sof* is returning *ANiY* (אני) to *AYiN* (אין)—i.e., returning "I" to "Nothingness."

114. **the will of Ein Sof.** Everything in our world is a garment that clothes some type of will from Above. A bird is an example of one sort of will, a fire is another will, and so on. The source of all these wills is *Ein Sof/Keter*, the Will of Wills. When the tzaddik's soul ascends to the highest heights, he recognizes that *Keter* is the source of everything, and that at this level things no longer exist in the form of myriad separate entities but that all is a unity—i.e., the singular will of the Holy One (*Rabbi Y.M. Shechter*).

However, at the level of *Malkhut*, creation *is* differentiated and appears as myriad separate entities. The singular will of *Ein Sof* manifests as many wills—i.e., many distinct forms. Rebbe Nachman chooses as the paradigm of this change God's one will becoming the shapes of the letters. This ties in with what he taught earlier (see §3 and n.16), that the spoken word corresponds to *Malkhut*. Here we see that the letters of speech are in fact the revelation of His *Malkhut*. This is something that does not happen on the unknowable and ineffable level of *Ein Sof/Keter*. Only in *Malkhut*, where His will is contracted into more finite aspects, does the revelation of His will manifest in all the forms and functions of which creation is comprised.

115. **which has no form at all.** As above, note 110.

116. **originate from the letters....** The letters of speech are the primordial building blocks of creation. God created everything through them, as in (Psalms 33:6), "By the word of God the heavens were made; and by the breath of His mouth all their host" (*Mai HaNachal*).

encompassed in *Ein Sof* (Infinite One).[110]

This is the concept of *zarka*[111]: it is thrown back to the place from which it was taken (*Tikkuney Zohar #21*).[112] This is returning *Malkhut* to *Ein Sof,*[113] which is the will in all the wills. For *Malkhut* corresponds to the letters of speech, with the will of God clothed in each and every letter. It was God's will that one letter have such and such a shape, and another letter have a different shape. We find, then, that [God's] wills—i.e., the forms of the letters—serve to reveal His *Malkhut*. And all these wills, the forms, stem from the will of *Ein Sof*[114]—which has no form <at all>.[115]

And all the objects and material existence in the world originate from the letters, i.e., from *Malkhut*.[116] This is because material existence is a consequence of *Malkhut,* of the Holy One's desire that His *Malkhut* be revealed in the world. Through this He created the

---

110. **Ein Sof, Infinite One.** *Ein Sof* literally means "without end." As explained in Kabbalistic teachings, *Ein Sof* is the ultimate "negative" attribute that can be ascribed to God Himself. It not only implies that God is unlike and incomparable to any "something" that exists, but also that all "somethingness" is nullified in His Presence. God might therefore be described as the Absolute Something. Nevertheless, from our vantage point, the closest we can come to conceiving God is to know that His Essence is not any of the terms we use to describe Him. In this sense, the term *Ein Sof* also carries the connotation of "the Ultimate Nothingness" (*Inner Space,* Rabbi Aryeh Kaplan, p.50). Thus, in the writings of the Ari, God is described as the Infinite Being, Who is ubiquitous, omniscient, omnipotent, and yet also as the Absolute Oneness Who is without any form (*Etz Chaim* 1:2). In terms of the Kabbalistic hierarchy of worlds and *sefirot, Ein Sof* indicates the highest levels, that which is beyond any human comprehension, and aligns with the unknowable *sefirah* of *Keter*.

111. **zarka.** The root letters of ZaRKa (זרק) form the Hebrew word for "throw." *Zarka* is one of the cantillations used when reading the Torah in the synagogue. When singing the *zarka* one raises or "throws" his voice to a higher pitch. The *Zohar* discusses these notes at length and explains their spiritual significance (*Tikkuney Zohar #21,* p.47a*ff*).

112. **thrown back...it was taken.** The *Tikkuney Zohar* (#21, p.60a) explains repentance as throwing something back to its source, from which it had become separated. In our context, this relates to returning *Malkhut* to its source by means of repentance—i.e., confession in front of a Torah scholar. In addition, the *zarka* is symbolic of the tzaddik's ability to free himself from earthly desires and passions. In relation to the root of a person's soul, such desires are extremely vile and despicable. By purifying his body, the tzaddik frees his soul to soar in the realms of holiness. His soul is so to speak thrown—*zarka*—to magnificent heights where it becomes closely attached to its source (*Rabbi Yaakov Meir Shechter*).

113. **Malkhut to Ein Sof.** All the *sefirot* (Divine Emanations) emanated from *Ein Sof,* which corresponds to *Keter,* the highest *sefirah. Ein Sof* is thus the source of all the nine *sefirot* below it, including the final *sefirah, Malkhut*. At one end of the *sefirah* structure is *Keter,* also

הָרְצוֹנוֹת, הַיְנוּ הַתְּמוּנוֹת וְכָל הַיֵּשׁוּת, הַיְנוּ בְּחִינַת מַלְכוּת מְקַבְּלִים
חִיּוּתָם מֵרָצוֹן אֵין סוֹף. כְּמוֹ שֶׁכָּתוּב: 'בְּכָל מָקוֹם שֶׁאַתָּה מוֹצֵא
גְּדֻלָּתוֹ שֶׁל הַקָּדוֹשׁ־בָּרוּךְ־הוּא', הַיְנוּ מַלְכוּתוֹ, הַיְנוּ רְצוֹנוֹת 'שָׁם
אַתָּה מוֹצֵא עַנְוְתָנוּתוֹ', הַיְנוּ רָצוֹן אֵין סוֹף.

וְזֶה בְּחִינַת הִתְפַּשְּׁטוּת הַגַּשְׁמִיּוּת. כִּי כְּשֶׁרוֹצֶה לְהַכְלֵל בְּרָצוֹן אֵין
סוֹף, צָרִיךְ לְבַטֵּל אֶת הַיֵּשׁוּת שֶׁלּוֹ,

וְזֶהוּ שֶׁכָּתוּב בַּזֹּהַר, שֶׁהִסְתַּלְּקוּת מֹשֶׁה בְּשַׁבָּת בְּשַׁעְתָּא דְּמִנְחָה,
שֶׁאָז הִתְגַּלּוּת רַעֲוָא דְּרַעֲוִין, שֶׁהוּא בְּחִינַת רָצוֹן אֵין סוֹף, שֶׁכָּל
הָרְצוֹנוֹת מְקַבְּלִין חִיּוּתָם מִמֶּנּוּ, וְזֶה מֵחֲמַת שֶׁבִּטֵּל מֹשֶׁה כָּל
יֵשׁוּתוֹ, כְּמוֹ שֶׁכָּתוּב: "וְנַחְנוּ מָה".

beneficent. However, he points out, not everybody can attain this level, which requires that a person negate his selfhood entirely—i.e., break all the evil desires that stem from the four elements and confess in front of the tzaddik, as the Rebbe explained above (§8; *Torat Natan* #6-7).

121. **negate his material being.** This is because all material existence is a result of *Malkhut* (as above, nn.117-119). Negating one's material being is returning *Malkhut* to its source.

122. **time of Minchah.** Afternoon, the time for the Minchah Prayer, is a time of judgment. The exception is Shabbat, when the Minchah-time judgments are stayed and kindness alone prevails.

123. **Will of Wills is revealed.** The highest spiritual revelation of the week takes place on Shabbat afternoon, when an influx of spiritual energy from *raava d'raaven* (Will of Wills) is manifest in the world. This spiritual influx emanates from *Keter,* and more specifically from the upper aspect of *Keter,* which is known as *Atika Kadisha* (see Appendix: The Divine Persona). To the degree that this will, the will of *Ein Sof,* is revealed and recognized, *Malkhut* is negated.

124. **receive their vitality.** As above, notes 113-114.

125. **nachnu mah, what are we.** This was the distinct level of humility in which Moshe surpassed all other tzaddikim. Whereas Avraham said (Genesis 18:27), "I am but dust and ashes"; and King David said (Psalms 22:7), "I am a worm, less than human"; Moshe said of himself and Aharon, "After all, what are we?" (*Chullin* 89a)—so total was his negation in the will of *Ein Sof.* And because Moshe negated his material being so completely, he passed away at the time of *Keter's* revelation, when all judgments are mitigated and lovingkindness alone prevails. In our context, this is when *YHVH* and *Elohim* are one, when *Malkhut* is bound with *Keter.*

world *ex nihilo.*[117] All the wills—the forms and all material existence, corresponding to *Malkhut*—receive their vitality from the will of *Ein Sof.*[118] As is taught (*Megillah* 31a): "In every place that you find the greatness of the Holy One"—i.e., His *Malkhut*/wills—"there, you find His humility"—i.e., the will of *Ein Sof.*[119]

And this is an aspect of stripping oneself of corporeality.[120] For when a person wants to be encompassed in the will of *Ein Sof*, he must negate his material being.[121]

This is what is written in the *Zohar* (II, 88b), that Moshe passed away on Shabbat, at the time of Minchah.[122] For that is when *raava d'raaven* (Will of Wills) is revealed.[123] This is the will of *Ein Sof*, from whom all wills < and all material existence > receive their vitality.[124] This was because Moshe had totally negated his material being, as is written, "After all, *nachnu mah* (what are we)?" (Exodus 16:7).[125]

---

117. **ex nihilo.** Fundamental to Jewish belief is that God created the world out of nothingness, *yesh me'ayin* (something from nothing). This is the meaning of *creatio ex nihilo.* In addition, we know that creation was the result of God's will to reveal His *Malkhut* in the world (*Mai HaNachal*).

118. **All the wills...Ein Sof.** Rebbe Nachman makes two points here: The first is that all physical creation stems from *Malkhut*/speech. The second is that *Malkhut* itself is the revelation of God's ultimate will, thus making it an extension of and closely bound with *Ein Sof.* And although our finite conscious minds have difficulty comprehending how this is so, the implication of this connection between *Malkhut* and *Keter/Ein Sof* is that in essence all the different wills are really one will—i.e., the myriad separate forms are in essence part of the unity.

119. **greatness...Malkhut...humility...Ein Sof.** The *Etz Yosef* (*Megillah* 31a, s.v. *kol*) explains this passage in the Talmud as follows: Although people in positions of prestige and authority only cherish the praise of peers and those above them, and put little value in the praise they receive from those beneath them, Scripture points out that, in contrast, wherever God's greatness is mentioned, He is associated with the "lower" echelons of society: the impoverished, widows, orphans, converts, and the like. If anything, His unfathomable greatness manifests in His amazing humility—that despite our unworthiness He values us enough to reveal His greatness and welcome our praise.

In our context, the revelation of God's greatness corresponds to *Malkhut* — the level at which His will becomes manifest. And, as explained, *Malkhut* is actually an extension of *Ayin* (Nothingness), which is His humility (see nn.69,70). Therefore, "In every place that you find greatness/*Malkhut*...there, you find His humility/*Ein Sof.*"

120. **stripping oneself of corporeality.** This concept is mentioned in the *Shulchan Arukh* (*Orach Chaim* 98:1) as the ideal state of mind for prayer. This is because prayer corresponds to *Malkhut*, and ascending to *Ein Sof* during prayer corresponds to elevating *Malkhut* to its source (*Parparaot LeChokhmah*). Reb Noson adds that this is the ultimate goal: stripping oneself of corporeality in order to achieve unity with *Ein Sof*, in Whom all is good and

וְזֶה פֵּרוּשׁ: "וַיִּקְבֹּר אוֹתוֹ בַגַּיְא", זֶה בְּחִינַת אַיִן, כְּמוֹ שֶׁכָּתוּב: "כָּל גֵּיא יִנָּשֵׂא". "בְּאֶרֶץ מוֹאָב", זֶה בְּחִינַת מַלְכוּת, שֶׁדָּוִד בָּא מִמּוֹאָב, שֶׁנִּסְתַּלֵּק מֹשֶׁה בְּתוֹךְ אֵין סוֹף, בְּתוֹךְ רָצוֹן שֶׁבָּרְצוֹנוֹת, בְּתוֹךְ רַעֲוָא דְרַעֲוִין, שֶׁהוּא בְּחִינַת רָצוֹן אֵין סוֹף, הַמְלֻבָּשׁ בִּרְצוֹנוֹת, בִּתְמוּנוֹת אוֹתִיּוֹת, בִּבְחִינַת מַלְכוּת, כְּמוֹ שֶׁכָּתוּב: "בְּכָל מָקוֹם שֶׁאַתָּה מוֹצֵא גְדֻלָּתוֹ", הַיְנוּ מַלְכוּת בְּחִינַת רַעֲוִין, "שָׁם אַתָּה מוֹצֵא" רַעֲוָא, רָצוֹן אֵין סוֹף.

וְזֶה "מוּל בֵּית פְּעוֹר", כִּי אָמְרוּ חֲכָמֵינוּ, זִכְרוֹנָם לִבְרָכָה: 'לָמָּה נִקְרָא שְׁמוֹ פְּעוֹר – עַל שֵׁם שֶׁפּוֹעֵר פִּיו', כִּי כְּשֶׁפּוֹגְמִין בְּמַלְכוּת, אֲזַי יֵשׁ לוֹ כֹּחַ לִפְעוֹר פִּיו בְּצֵרוּפִים רָעִים, אֲבָל מֹשֶׁה שֶׁתִּקֵּן מִדַּת הַמַּלְכוּת, עַל-יְדֵי זֶה לֹא הָיָה בְּיַד פְּעוֹר לִפְעוֹר פִּיו. וְזֶה: "וְלֹא יָדַע אִישׁ", אֲפִלּוּ מֹשֶׁה לֹא יָדַע, כְּמוֹ שֶׁאָמְרוּ רַבּוֹתֵינוּ,

---

significance of Moshe's being buried in Moav as follows: Moshe's rectification of *Malkhut* of Holiness was so complete that even from Moav, a *malkhut* of the *akum* (nations), he was able to bring forth and elevate *Malkhut*—namely, King David.

128. **clothed in the wills....** As explained, the will of *Ein Sof* is the source of *Malkhut*/ creation's letters (see nn.116,118).

129. **Beit Pe'or.** Bilaam counseled the Moabites that if they wanted to conquer the Jews, they would have to first get them to sin. Toward this end, the Moabites sent their daughters to seduce the Jewish men and ultimately induce them to serve Moav's idolatry, Pe'or.

130. **opens its mouth wide.** The name Pe'or suggests an opening. According to tradition, the worship of this idol involved scatological practices, and in particular opening the anus to defecate in its presence (*Sanhedrin* 60b, 64a; *Rashi*, Numbers 25:3).

Elsewhere, the Talmud teaches: Each year, at that time when the Jews sinned with the daughters of Moav, Pe'or rises up to recall their sin and denounce them. But when it sees Moshe's grave opposite it, it sinks back (*Tosafot, Sotah* 14a, *s.v. mipnei*).

131. **negative letter-combinations.** Applying this to our context, Rebbe Nachman explains that Pe'or opens its mouth to blemish *Malkhut* through negative letter-combinations (see above, §5).

132. **Moshe rectified...Malkhut....** Moshe completely rectified *Malkhut*, which corresponds to speech. Thus, Pe'or cannot "say" anything, i.e., cannot open its mouth with negative letter-combinations—it sees Moshe's grave opposite it and sinks back.

The *Be'Ibey HaNachal* expounds on this. Adam's sin and the sins of mankind throughout the generations have caused *Malkhut* of Holiness to descend into the realm of the Other Side.

{**"So Moshe the servant of God died there, in the land of Moav, by the kiss of God. [God] buried him in the valley in the land of Moav, opposite Beit Pe'or. No man knows his burial place to this day"** (Deuteronomy 34:5-7).}

This is the meaning of "[God] buried him in the valley"—it alludes to < *Ein Sof,* > as is written (Isaiah 40:4), "Every valley shall be elevated."[126] "In the land of Moav"—this alludes to *Malkhut,* for King David descended from Moav.[127] Moshe ascended into *Ein Sof,* into Will of Wills, < the aspect of > *raava d'raaven.* This corresponds to the will of *Ein Sof,* which is clothed in the wills/forms of the letters, the aspect of *Malkhut.*[128] As explained, "In every place that you find His greatness"—i.e., *Malkhut,* the aspect of < will > — "there, you find < His humility > "—i.e., the will of *Ein Sof.*

This is: "opposite Beit Pe'or."[129] As the Sages taught: Why was [the idol] called Pe'or? Because it opens its mouth wide.[130] For when one blemishes *Malkhut,* [Pe'or] then has the power to open its mouth wide with negative letter-combinations.[131] But Moshe rectified the aspect of *Malkhut,* and as a result Pe'or could not open its mouth wide (*Sotah* 14a).[132] This is: "No man knows [his burial place]"—even

Rebbe Nachman now connects coming to the tzaddik and confessing in front of him with how the tzaddik, because of his deep humility, secures God's forgiveness for the person and so rectifies everything. This happens because the tzaddik ascends to *Ein Sof,* the highest of levels, Will of Wills. There, he gains the power to vanquish *Malkhut* of the Other Side and elevate a rectified *Malkhut* to *Keter.* This, the Rebbe explains, is the deeper meaning of Moshe's having passed away on Shabbat afternoon: He passed away into Will of Wills and thereby gained forgiveness for the Jewish people's sins, as we shall next see.

Reb Noson adds: The Rebbe's insight into the meaning of Moshe's passing and the site of his burial can be extended to apply even now, to our visiting the gravesites of the tzaddikim— becoming attached to tzaddik by praying there, confessing our sins, and seeking guidance in breaking our evil desires (*Torat Natan* #8; see below, n.202).

126. **elevated.** The *Mai HaNachal* explains: Scripture uses the term "valley" as a metaphor for someone lowly and of minimal status. Thus, the Talmud teaches: If a Torah scholar is haughty, the Holy One will lower him, as in (Numbers 21:20), "From the heights [down] to the valley." But if he then repents, the Holy One raises him up, as in (Isaiah 40:4), "Every valley shall be elevated" (*Nedarim* 55b). The Kabbalah extends this connotation of "valley" to include the quality of nothingness associated with *Ayin.* This is why concerning Moshe's burial place it is written, "Every valley shall be elevated," every humble and unpretentious person will be uplifted in Moshe's merit (*Zohar* III, 280a). In our context, this refers to Moshe being able to effect forgiveness for everybody, even the worst sinner. Thus, Moshe's burial is a metaphor for his negating his selfhood in *Ayin.*

127. **descended from Moav.** King David was the great-grandson of Boaz, who had taken Ruth, a woman from Moav, as his wife (Ruth 4:13). The *Parparaot LeChokhmah* explains the

זִכְרוֹנָם לִבְרָכָה, כִּי נִתְבַּטֵּל לְגַבֵּי אֵין סוֹף.
וְכָל זֶה הָיָה בְּמוֹתוֹ, אֲבָל בְּוַדַּאי גַּם בְּחַיָּיו הָיָה לוֹ הִתְפַּשְּׁטוּת
הַגַּשְׁמִיּוּת, וְהָיָה מְדַבֵּק אֶת עַצְמוֹ בְּאוֹר אֵין סוֹף, אֲבָל
הַהִתְפַּשְּׁטוּת הָיָה בִּבְחִינַת: וְהַחַיּוֹת רָצוֹא וָשׁוֹב. כִּי הַקָּדוֹשׁ־
בָּרוּךְ־הוּא רוֹצֶה בַּעֲבוֹדָתֵנוּ, כְּמוֹ שֶׁכָּתוּב: 'וְאָבִיתָ תְהִלָּה מִגּוּשֵׁי
עָפָר, מִקְּרוּצֵי חֹמֶר', וּבִשְׁבִיל זֶה צָרִיךְ שֶׁלֹּא יִשָּׁאֵר כֵּן, אֶלָּא עַד

These concepts are all found in our lesson as aspects of *Malkhut*. Confession elevates *Malkhut* (§5). The ultimate source of *Malkhut* is humility (§7, see n.76). And, repentance, by which *Malkhut* is elevated to its source, is accomplished through self-sacrifice—i.e., negating one's self entirely in *Ein Sof*. With this, we can better understand the blessing Yaakov gave Yehudah (Genesis 49:8), "Yehudah, your brothers *yodu* (will praise) you. Your hand will be on your enemies' *oreph* (neck); your father's sons will bow to you." The *Targum* renders *yodu* as a variation of *hodaah* (הודאה), referring to Yehudah's confession (see above, n.46), by means of which he rectified *Malkhut*. *Rashbam* (*ad. loc.*) translates *yodu* as a variation of *hod* (הוד, royal splendor), alluding to *Malkhut*. This is the import of the term *yodu*: the brothers recognized him as their leader. And, because Yehudah merited *Malkhut*, he was able to subdue his enemies—"Your hand will be on your enemies' *oreph* (neck)." As the Ari points out, *ORePh* (עורף) corresponds to Pe'OR (פעור). By rectifying *Malkhut*, Yehudah was able to overcome the negative letter-combinations.

134. **during his lifetime....** Scripture relates that Moshe ascended to the heavens three times, each time for forty days and forty nights (see *Rashi*, Deuteronomy 9:18). This shedding of his corporeality for what was essentially 120 consecutive days indicates that self-negation was by no means a rare achievement for Moshe during his lifetime.

135. **the living creatures ran and returned.** This phrase appears in Yechezkel's prophecy of the Divine Chariot. These *chayot* (living creatures) who bore the Chariot were in a constant state of "running and returning." In our context, this parallels the tzaddik/Moshe always seeking to shed his corporeality and becoming absorbed in *Ein Sof,* yet not being able to remain at this level. He is obliged to return to the physical, until God Himself takes his soul.

Reb Noson explains that although "running," becoming nullified in *Ein Sof,* is very precious, and indeed indispensable, the real measure of success is seen in the "returning." He illustrates this with the planting of a kernel of grain. In order for the kernel to produce, it must first be "negated" or totally absorbed in the earth. Then, after it loses its identity as a kernel and its form has all but disappeared, it takes root. Eventually it grows and bears fruit far in excess of its original form. The same is true of man. He must first relinquish his separate identity and negate himself to God. This is "running." Afterwards, when he "returns," it is with a greater level of spirituality (*Likutey Halakhot, Kilaeiy HaKerem* 2:1).

136. **You desire praise from mounds of dust....** This phrase, which is from the Evening Service (Maariv) of Yom Kippur, emphasizes God's preference for the service of flesh-and-blood human beings over the service of beings without corporeality. In a similar vein, Rebbe Nachman once said that he could turn all his followers into complete, awesome tzaddikim—

Moshe did not know (*ibid.*). For he was negated in *Ein Sof.*[133]

All this was at his death. However, also during his lifetime [Moshe] certainly stripped away all corporeality[134] and attached himself to the Light of *Ein Sof.* But then, this stripping was in an aspect of "the living creatures ran and returned" (Ezekiel 1:14).[135] This is because the Holy One desires our service, as is written (Yom Kippur Liturgy), "You desire praise from mounds of dust, from lumps of clay."[136] Therefore, it is imperative not to remain [in this state of

King David's soul, being the personification of *Malkhut* of Holiness, thus became trapped within the nation of Moav. As Rebbe Nachman has explained, *Malkhut* of the Other Side—Moav's idolatry Pe'or—gains control through people's sins and opens its mouth wide with letter-combinations from the realm of the Other Side (§5). This was evident in the nation of Moav from its very inception. When Lot's daughter gave birth to the son she conceived by sleeping with her father, she named him MoAV: this one is *Me'AV*, from her *av* (father; *Rashi*, Genesis 19:37). This negative letter-combination was a sign that King David's soul, *Malkhut* of Holiness, had become trapped in the realm of the Other Side. When, later, the Moabites attempted to overcome the Jews by exposing them to Pe'or, Moshe was able to protect them. His burial in the land of Moav so completely subdued Pe'or that it freed *Malkhut* of Holiness and set the stage for King David's soul to eventually be extricated from there. And King David himself continued to rectify and elevate *Malkhut* of Holiness by composing holy letter-combinations—i.e., the songs and prayers to God that comprise the Book of Psalms.

133. **...negated in Ein Sof.** This is the deeper meaning of even Moshe *not knowing* where he was buried: At his death Moshe became free of the last vestiges of corporeality. He was then so absorbed in *Ein Sof,* had so negated all awareness of self, that he "did not know"—i.e., his *daat* did not differentiate between self and other, because *daat* (awareness) itself was nullified (the Rebbe further clarifies this in the paragraphs that follow). The *Mai HaNachal* explains that this is the concept of confessing in a Torah scholar's presence. When the tzaddik passes away, he becomes included in *Ein Sof.* But even before that, when a person confesses in front of a Torah scholar, that Torah scholar negates himself in *Ein Sof.* At that point, he too is absorbed in the level where there is no differentiation between kindness and judgment. As the Rebbe goes on to explain, when the tzaddik emerges from this level, he too understands that whatever happens is for the best—i.e., that all is one.

The verse thus translates in our text as follows: **God buried him in the valley** — Because Moshe so totally negated himself in *Ein Sof,* **in the land of Moav** — he was able to rectify *Malkhut;* **opposite Beit Pe'or** — and by rectifying *Malkhut,* Moshe dismantled and destroyed the negative letter-combinations. **No man knows...even Moshe did not know** — Moshe was able to do this because he had ascended to the highest of levels, to *Keter,* where there is no form or physical matter, and where all is one and *daat* (awareness) itself is nullified.

The *Parparaot LeChokhmah* shows how this relates to Yehudah, the aspect of *Malkhut* (§5). The Talmud teaches that Yehudah merited *Malkhut* for a number of reasons: because he confessed to his relationship with Tamar; because he humbled himself before Yosef; because of the self-sacrifice the tribe of Yehudah displayed at the Red Sea (*Tosefta, Berakhot* 4:16).

עֵת שֶׁיָּבוֹא הַקָּדוֹשׁ בָּרוּךְ הוּא בְּעַצְמוֹ וְיִטֹּל נִשְׁמָתוֹ.

וְזֶה שֶׁאָנוּ רוֹאִים, שֶׁלְּפְעָמִים נִתְלַהֵב אָדָם בְּתוֹךְ הַתְּפִלָּה וְאוֹמֵר כַּמָּה תֵּבוֹת בְּהִתְלַהֲבוּת גָּדוֹל, זֶה בְּחֶמְלַת ה' עָלָיו, שֶׁנִּפְתַּח לוֹ אוֹר אֵין סוֹף וְהֵאִיר לוֹ. וּכְשֶׁרוֹאֶה אָדָם הַהִתְנוֹצְצוּת הַזֹּאת, אַף־עַל־גַּב דְּאִיהוּ לָא חָזֵי מַזְּלֵיהּ חָזֵי, תֵּכֶף נִתְלַהֵב נִשְׁמָתוֹ לְדַבְקוּת גָּדוֹל, לְדַבֵּק אֶת עַצְמוֹ בְּאוֹר אֵין סוֹף, וּכְשִׁעוּר הִתְגַּלּוּת אֵין סוֹף, לְפִי מִנְיַן הַתֵּבוֹת שֶׁנִּפְתְּחוּ וְהִתְנוֹצְצוּ, כָּל אֵלּוּ הַתֵּבוֹת אוֹמֵר בִּדְבֵקוּת גָּדוֹל וּבִמְסִירַת נַפְשׁוֹ וּבְבִטּוּל כֹּחוֹתָיו. וּבְשָׁעָה שֶׁנִּתְבַּטֵּל לְגַבֵּי אֵין סוֹף, אֲזַי הוּא בִּבְחִינַת: "וְלֹא יָדַע אִישׁ", שֶׁאֲפִלּוּ הוּא בְּעַצְמוֹ אֵינוֹ יוֹדֵעַ מֵעַצְמוֹ. אֲבָל זֹאת הַבְּחִינָה צָרִיךְ לִהְיוֹת רָצוֹא וָשׁוֹב, כְּדֵי שֶׁיִּתְקַיֵּם יְשׁוּתוֹ.

נִמְצָא כְּשֶׁהוּא בִּבְחִינַת וָשׁוֹב, אֲזַי צָרִיךְ לְהַרְאוֹת גַּם לְדַעְתּוֹ. כִּי מִתְּחִלָּה, בִּשְׁעַת דְּבֵקוּת הָיָה נִתְבַּטֵּל הַדַּעַת, כְּמוֹ שֶׁכָּתוּב: "וְלֹא

will next explain). However, if the mind itself has not achieved purity and holiness, it is incapable of properly incorporating these new perceptions. As the Talmud relates (*Chagigah* 14b): Four great Sages ascended to the highest spiritual planes and only Rabbi Akiva returned unscathed (*Torat Natan #7*; see also *Mayim*, Breslov Research Institute).

138. **his mazal sees.** Each person has a guardian angel in heaven, which our Sages called a person's *mazal* (*Rashi, loc. cit., s.v. mazlaihu*). Even though he may not be aware of all the spiritual forces affecting him, nevertheless, "his *mazal* sees" and this inspires his devotion.

139. **devotion...surrender...negation of all his senses.** This is *Malkhut*—the letters revealed to him—seeking its source.

140. **he himself is unaware....** Because he has become absorbed in *Ein Sof,* where all the separate life forms become nullified in God's unity. As a result, he too surrenders his separate identity, relinquishes his selfhood, to the unity of the One.

141. **preserve his soul within him.** For God desires the praise of the "mounds of dust" and the "lumps of clay," as above (n.136). Some explain that this was precisely what two of the four Sages who entered the Orchard (see n.137) were unable to do. They ascended to the highest spiritual planes. But when it came time to descend, BenZoma could not and BenAzai would not (*Mayim* pp.52-55).

142. **state of returning.** After having a taste of the goodness and unity of *Ein Sof.*

negation], until such a time that the Holy One Himself comes and takes one's soul.

This is why we see that now and then a person becomes inspired while praying and he recites several words with tremendous fervor. This is due to God's compassion for him; the Light of *Ein Sof* has been opened to him and shines for him.[137] When a person sees this radiance—and even though he might not see, his *mazal* sees (*Megillah* 3a)[138]—his soul is instantly ignited in great devotion, so that he attaches himself to the Light of *Ein Sof*. And, to the degree that *Ein Sof* is revealed—commensurate with the number of words that have been opened and begun to radiate—he recites all these words with great devotion, with a surrender of self, and with a negation of all his senses.[139] Then, during the time he is negated in *Ein Sof*, he is in a state of "and no man knows," so that he himself is unaware of his own existence.[140] But this must be in the aspect of "running and returning," in order to preserve < his soul within him >.[141]

We find, then, that when he is in a state of "returning,"[142] he must also disclose < this perception > to his *daat*. For at the beginning, at the time of devotion, his *daat* was nullified, as in, "and no man

---

i.e., bring them all to the level of being nullified in *Ein Sof*—but of what value would it be? "It would be like God serving Himself," he explained (*Tzaddik* #330). Therefore, during his lifetime, the tzaddik too must be in a state of "running and returning."

As mentioned, this quote is from the Yom Kippur prayers, which also include confession and are recited at a time when people fast and deny themselves physical pleasure—a shedding of their corporeality.

137. **shines for him.** The Light of *Ein Sof* manifests through the letters, *Malkhut*.

Until now, Rebbe Nachman has spoken about the tzaddik reaching the level of *Keter* and becoming nullified in *Ein Sof*. He has also mentioned that each person can attain a measure of this spiritual nullification by negating himself to the tzaddik who is himself negated in *Ein Sof* (see above, n.133). Here, the Rebbe indicates that the amount of the Light of *Ein Sof* a person perceives is at one and the same time a factor of his own level of achievement and a result of God's compassion. One must work for one's level and at the same time recognize that it is all a gift from God.

Reb Noson adds: A person must also pray to God to save him from out-"running" his capabilities. One whose spiritual ascent is too high or too fast, without the necessary tools for containing the insights he gains, can actually stumble later on as a result of the awareness he's acquired. This happens, Reb Noson explains, when one's *daat* disengages from his conscious mind in order to become absorbed in *Ein Sof*. It has to do this because the conscious mind is finite and so incapable of receiving the Light. Nevertheless, when *daat* returns from its negated state, it carries back to the conscious mind new and awesome insights (as the Rebbe

יָדַע אִישׁ", וּכְשֶׁהוּא בִּבְחִינַת וָשׁוֹב, שֶׁשָּׁב (לְדַעְתּוֹ) לְיֵשׁוּתוֹ, אָז
שָׁב לְדַעְתּוֹ, וּכְשֶׁשָּׁב לְדַעְתּוֹ, אָז הוּא יוֹדֵעַ אַחְדוּת הָאֵין סוֹף
וְטוּבוֹ, וַאֲזַי אֵין חִלּוּק בֵּין ה' לֵאלֹהִים, בֵּין מִדַּת הַדִּין לְמִדַּת
הָרַחֲמִים.

כִּי בְּאֵין סוֹף אֵין שַׁיָּךְ, חַס וְשָׁלוֹם, שִׁנּוּי רָצוֹן, כִּי הַשִּׁנּוּיִים אֵינוֹ
אֶלָּא בְּשִׁנּוּי הַתְּמוּנוֹת, אֲבָל עַל־יְדֵי הַדִּבְקוּת שֶׁל אָדָם בְּאֵין סוֹף,
שֶׁשָּׁם אֵין שִׁנּוּי רָצוֹן, כִּי שָׁם רָצוֹן פָּשׁוּט, וְאַחַר־כָּךְ נִשְׁאָר בּוֹ
רְשִׁימוּ מֵאַחְדוּת הַזֹּאת, וְאַחַר־כָּךְ נַעֲשֶׂה בִּבְחִינַת וָשׁוֹב, אֲזַי
הָרְשִׁימוּ מַרְאֶה לְדַעַת, שֶׁיֵּדַע שֶׁכֻּלּוֹ טוֹב וְכֻלּוֹ אֶחָד:

וְזֶה שֶׁאָמַר מֹשֶׁה לְדוֹרוֹ: "אַתָּה הָרְאֵתָ לָדַעַת כִּי ה' הוּא
הָאֱלֹהִים". כִּי מֹשֶׁה הוּא בְּחִינַת אַיִן, וְדוֹרוֹ הַדְּבוּקִים אֵלָיו רְאוּי
לָהֶם לָדַעַת, הַיְנוּ לְהָאִיר לַדַּעַת, בְּחִינַת אֵין סוֹף, בְּחִינַת רַעֲוָא
דְּרַעֲוִין, בְּחִינַת: ה' הוּא הָאֱלֹהִים:

In our context, the *reshimu* that remains when the *daat* of a person who's been nullified in *Ein Sof* returns to normal consciousness, is a sense of God's unity and the uniformity of His will. The import of this oneness of will is that at their essence, God's judgment and compassion are the same. The Holy One does not start out with a will for judgment and a desire to punish, and—after some new information—change His will to one of compassion and a desire to reward. Rather, from the very beginning all is good and all is one—"entirely Who is good and beneficent" (§1, n.7)—the comprehension of which is called complete awareness, a foretaste of the World to Come. Reb Noson adds that this is because holiness is perpetually in a state of unity, even if to our eyes it appears separated. Not so the forces of the Other Side. Although in their essence they are rooted in holiness and therefore begin in unity, they always conclude in a state of disunity (*Torat Natan* #9).

148. **clearly demonstrated to your daat....** Rashi (*loc. cit.*) explains that when God gave the Torah, He opened the heavens to reveal His oneness. In our context, this alludes to a person whose *daat* has been negated and absorbed in *Ein Sof*. Afterwards, after his *daat* has returned to the conscious mind, he knows clearly—he has a complete awareness—because the oneness of "*YHVH* is the *Elohim*" has been demonstrated to his *daat*.

149. **For Moshe...daat....** See *Etz Chaim* 32:1, and *Likutey Moharan* I, 15:3 and note 16.

150. **his generation...YHVH is the Elohim.** The *Mai HaNachal* explains: At the time of Revelation, the very first of the Ten Commandments was "*Anokhi YHVH Elohekha* (I am God your Lord)." With this, God *demonstrated* to the Jewish people that He/*YHVH* and His

knows." But when he is in a state of "returning," returning to his material being, then he <also> returns to his *daat*.[143] And when he returns to his *daat*, he knows the oneness and beneficence of *Ein Sof*. Then, there is no difference between *YHVH* and *Elohim*, between the divine attribute of judgment and the divine attribute of compassion.[144]

For a change of will is not applicable to *Ein Sof*, Heaven forbid. Changes only occur in the changing of the forms.[145] Nevertheless, by virtue of a person's attachment to *Ein Sof*—where there is no change of will, for there the will is uniform[146]—afterwards, an imprint of this oneness remains within him. Then, later, when he is in a state of "returning," this imprint illuminates <his *daat*>, so that he knows that all is good and all is one.[147]

This is what Moshe said to his generation: "It has been clearly demonstrated to your *daat* that *YHVH* (God) is the *Elohim* (Lord)" (Deuteronomy 4:35).[148] For Moshe corresponds to <*daat*, as is known.>[149] Thus it was fitting for his generation, who were attached to him, to [have] *daat*—i.e., to illuminate the *daat* [with an awareness of] *Ein Sof/raava d'raaven*, the aspect of "*YHVH* is the *Elohim*."[150]

---

143. **returns to his daat.** To his normal state of consciousness. See Reb Noson's explanation in note 137, where he clarifies that his *daat* returns to the conscious mind, which is where it generally resides.

144. **Then, there is no difference....** Because in *Ein Sof* all is one, a unity of all the wills (see above, n.114). And he no longer differentiates between lovingkindness and judgment, but blesses "Who is good and beneficent" over everything (as explained in §4 and notes).

145. **of the forms.** Which are in *Malkhut*, not in *Ein Sof*.

146. **is uniform.** *Ein Sof* is omniscient. With His infinite knowledge and awareness He knows all that ever was, is, and will be. Therefore, a change of will—which happens when something previously unconsidered is now considered, or something considered is now reconsidered—has no place in His oneness and unity. The Holy One's will is thus ultimately simple and uniform (see n.110).

147. **imprint....** The Kabbalistic concept of imprint, *reshimu* in Aramaic, refers to a sensed impression left by any act or attainment, whether in holiness or the opposite. It's what the person carries away with him from his direct experience rather than his intellectual perception. The Kabbalists add that the difference between an imprint of holiness and one left by impurity is that a holy *reshimu* can never be destroyed, whereas an impure *reshimu* can be eradicated. Rebbe Nachman illustrated this above (§5), explaining that sin leaves an imprint upon one's bones and that this imprint, in the form of a negative letter-combination, can be purged through confession.

וְזֶה פֵּרוּשׁ:

רַשְׁבָּ"ם:

אָמַר רַבָּה בַּר בַּר חָנָא: זִימְנָא
חֲדָא הֲוָה קָאזְלִינַן בִּסְפִינְתָּא,
וַחֲזִינַן הַהוּא כַּוְרָא דְּיַתְבָא לֵיהּ
אָכְלָה טִינָא בְּאוּסְיֵהּ, (וּמִית).
וְאִידְּחוּהוּ מַיָּא, וְשַׁדְיוּהוּ לְגוּדָא,
וַחֲרוּב מִינֵּיהּ שִׁיתִין מָחוֹזֵי,
וְאָכְלוּ מִינֵּיהּ שִׁיתִין מָחוֹזֵי,
וּמָלְחוּ מִינֵּיהּ שִׁיתִין מָחוֹזֵי,
וּמָלְאוּ מֵחַד גַּלְגַּלָא דְּעֵינָא תְּלָת
מְאָה גַּרְבֵי מִשְׁחָא. וְכִי הַדְרָן
לְבָתַר תְּרֵיסַר יַרְחֵי שַׁתָּא, חֲזִינַן
דְּהֲוָה קָא מְנַסְרֵי מִגַּרְמֵיהּ
מְטַלְּלְתָּא, וִיהֲבֵי לְמִבְנִינְהוּ הַנֵּךְ
מָחוֹזֵי (בבא בתרא עג:):

כַּוְרָא דָּג: אָכְלָא טִינָא שֶׁרֶץ קָטָן:
בְּאוּסְיֵיהּ בִּנְחִירָיו שֶׁל דָּג נִכְנַס
הַשֶּׁרֶץ: וְאִידְּחוּהוּ מַיָּא הֱדִיחוּהוּ
הַמַּיִם וְהִשְׁלִיכוּהוּ לַיַּבָּשָׁה כְּדֶרֶךְ יָם,
שֶׁאֵינוֹ סוֹבֵל דָּבָר מֵת: חָרְבוּ מִינֵּיהּ
שִׁיתִין מָחוֹזֵי שֶׁהִשְׁלִיכוּהוּ הַמַּיִם עַל
שִׁשִּׁים כְּרַכִּים וּשְׁבָרָן כֻּלָּם, שֶׁהָיָה
גָּדוֹל כָּל כָּךְ: וְאָכְלוּ מִינֵּיהּ שִׁיתִין
מָחוֹזֵי בְּעוֹדֶנּוּ לַח: וּמָלְחוּ מִינֵּיהּ
שִׁיתִין מָחוֹזֵי אֲחֵרִים, שֶׁהָיוּ רְחוֹקִין
מִשָּׁם, מָלְחוּ מִינֵּיהּ וּנְשָׂאוּהוּ
לִמְקוֹמָן: מֵחַד גַּלְגַּלָא דְּעֵינָא
מִגַּלְגַּל עֵינוֹ לָקְחוּ שֶׁמֶן תְּלָת מֵאָה
גַּרְבֵי: הֲוָה מְנַסְרֵי לִבְנוֹת מֵעַצְמוֹת
הַדָּג אוֹתָן מָחוֹזֵי שֶׁהִפִּיל:

פֵּרוּשׁ: סְפִינָה – לְשׁוֹן חֲשִׁיבוּת, בְּחִינַת מַלְכוּת. שֶׁרַבָּה בַּר בַּר
חָנָא חָקַר בְּשִׂכְלוֹ אוֹדוֹת הַמַּלְכוּת, אֵיךְ בְּנֵי-יִשְׂרָאֵל מַעֲלִין אוֹתָהּ.

tzaddik can elevate the rectified *Malkhut* to its ultimate source, *Ayin* (§7). Confessing in the presence of a tzaddik is the third of a three step process for achieving repentance. The first two steps are attaching oneself to the tzaddik and giving charity to the tzaddik. Then the tzaddik can direct him in line with his soul's root, so that he can enter the realm of holiness (§8). And when the tzaddik negates himself in *Ein Sof,* where all is good and beneficent, he also brings the person confessing in his presence to a level of *Ayin* (Nothingness). The repentance thus engendered elevates *Malkhut*/the letters to their ultimate source in *Ein Sof*/Will of Wills, where all is one. And, after the shedding of corporeality and the disengaging of *daat,* which are required in order to be absorbed in *Ein Sof,* that person returns to his conscious mind with complete *daat.* He *knows* that *YHVH* and *Elohim* are one (§9).

151. **This is the explanation.** Rebbe Nachman now shows how the concepts of this lesson are alluded to within the framework of Rabbah bar bar Chanah's story.

152. **importance...Malkhut.** The Hebrew term for ship, *sephina* (ספינה), resembles *sephin* (ספין), which is Aramaic for important. See *Moed Katan* 28a (cf. Lesson #1 and n.65 thereon).

10. This is the explanation[151]:

Rabbah bar bar Chanah recounted: **One time we were traveling on a *sephina* (ship) and we saw this *kavra* in whose nostrils was sitting a mudeater. The *kavra* died and the water tossed it about and cast it ashore. It destroyed sixty cities. Sixty cities then ate from it. Sixty cities salted its flesh. And from one eyeball they filled three *meah* (hundred) kegs with oil. When we returned after twelve months time, we saw them sawing planks from its bones with which to rebuild those cities** (*Bava Batra* 73b).	*Rashbam:* **kavra** - a fish: **mudeater** - a small [parasitic] worm: **in whose nostrils** - the worm entered the nostrils of the fish: **the water tossed it about** - the water tossed it about and threw it on dry land; it being the nature of the sea not to tolerate any dead thing: **It destroyed sixty cities** - the water threw the fish onto sixty cities and it devastated them all; that's how immense it was: **Sixty cities then ate from it** - while it was still fresh: **Sixty cities salted its flesh** - different cities, from afar, salted its meat and carried it back home: **from one eyeball** - from its eyeball they took three hundred kegs of oil: **them sawing** - to rebuild from the bones of the fish those cities which it had leveled:

The explanation is:

SePhiNa — This connotes importance, corresponding to *Malkhut*.[152] Rabbah bar bar Chanah used his intellect to investigate the status of *Malkhut* and the means by which the Jewish people could elevate it.

Name/*Elohim* are one. This followed Moshe's ascent on Mount Sinai, where he shed his corporeality and was absorbed in *Ein Sof*. His generation, those who were attached to Moshe, were therefore also able to *know* (complete awareness) that *YHVH* and *Elohim* are one.

Also, as explained, when the tzaddik is absorbed in *Ein Sof*, his separate identity and selfhood is totally negated (see text above and n.140). Thus, aside from an insight into God's unity, the *reshimu* with which he returns from the state of negation also includes a deeper sense of humility. As has been explained with regard to Moshe (see §7 beginning with n.68), the tzaddik uses this humility as a conduit for bringing an awareness of the unity of *Ein Sof* to others.

In review: When a person perceives that whatever happens to him is for his benefit, he has a foretaste of the World to Come (§1). This perception is only possible when he frees *Malkhut* of Holiness from the control of the nations and returns it to God (§2). This is accomplished by confession of one's sins in the presence of a Torah scholar, which unites the holy names *YHVH* and *Elohim* (§3). Knowing that all is for the best, the awareness that one's suffering also stems from God's love, is considered complete *daat* (§4). A person's sins blemish *Malkhut* and become etched upon his bones. The way to rectify *Malkhut* is by confessing one's sins in front of the tzaddik/Torah scholar. The bones are thus healed (§5). Confession in front of a Torah scholar corresponds to returning *Malkhut* to its source. This is because the source of *Malkhut* is fire/ Torah, and Torah scholars embody the essence of the Torah itself (§6). And the tzaddik can effect forgiveness after hearing the confession because, by virtue of his deep humility, the

וַחֲזִינָן הַאי כַּוְרָא – יִשְׂרָאֵל מְכַנִּין בְּשֵׁם דָּגִים, כְּמוֹ שֶׁכָּתוּב:
"וְיִדְגּוּ לָרֹב בְּקֶרֶב הָאָרֶץ".

דְּיַתְבֵי לֵיהּ אָכְלָא טִינָא בְּנְחִירָיו – זֶה בְּחִינַת תְּפִלָּתָן שֶׁל יִשְׂרָאֵל,
כְּמוֹ שֶׁכָּתוּב: "וּתְהִלָּתִי אֶחֱטָם לָךְ", שֶׁנִּתְעָרֵב שֶׁרֶץ, הַיְנוּ טֻמְאָה
בִּתְפִלָּתוֹ וַעֲבוֹדָתוֹ וּבִלְבֵּל אוֹתוֹ. וְלֹא הָיָה יָכוֹל אִישׁ הַיִּשְׂרְאֵלִי הַזֶּה
לַעֲבֹד עֲבוֹדָתוֹ תַּמָּה. מֶה עָשָׂה הָאִישׁ הַזֶּה? עָשָׂה שָׁלֹשׁ בְּחִינוֹת
הַנַּ"ל. הַיְנוּ הִתְקַשְּׁרוּת לְהַצַּדִּיק וּנְתִינַת הַצְּדָקָה וּוִדּוּי דְּבָרִים.

וְזֶה פֵּרוּשׁ:

וּמֵתָה, וְאִידְחוּהוּ מַיָּא, וְשַׁדְיוּהוּ לְגוּדָא. וְהִזְכִּיר הַשָּׁלֹשׁ בְּחִינוֹת
מֵעֵילָא לְתַתָּא.

וּמֵתָה – זֶה בְּחִינַת וִדּוּי דְּבָרִים, כְּמוֹ שֶׁכָּתוּב: "כָּל הַמּוּמָתִין
מִתְוַדִּין".

וְאִידְחוּהוּ מַיָּא – זֶה בְּחִינַת צְדָקָה, כְּמוֹ שֶׁכָּתוּב: "שַׁלַּח לַחְמְךָ עַל
פְּנֵי הַמָּיִם". וּכְתִיב: "אַשְׁרֵיכֶם זֹרְעֵי עַל כָּל מָיִם".

it is first and foremost the willingness of the Jew—motivated by his attachment to God and a lack in his devotions—that begins the process of repentance. It is the common Jew's desire to change for the better that triggers the rectification of *Malkhut* of Holiness.

157. **three steps mentioned above.** In section 8.

158. **attaching himself to the tzaddik.** Previously, this first step was described as *seeing* the tzaddik. However, as explained there, the purpose of seeing his face is to create a closer bond between the person and the tzaddik. See above, section 8, note 90.

159. **from top to bottom.** For confession and charity must be performed regularly, not only in the presence of the tzaddik. Yet, the intention behind these acts must also be to foster an attachment to the tzaddik (*Parparaot LeChokhmah*).

160. **be put to death, confess.** Thereby causing the tzaddik to lead him on the path most in accord with his soul's root. See above, section 8, note 104.

161. **upon the waters...beside all waters.** Rashi explains that these verses refer to acts of charity and kindness. When a person gives charity, it seems as if he were throwing his food into the water, an act that brings no material benefit. Yet, ultimately, charity always bears

we saw this kavra — The Jewish people are called "fish," as in (Genesis 48:16), "May they increase in the land like fish."[153]

in whose nostrils was sitting a mudeater — This corresponds to the prayers of the Jewish people.[154] As is written (Isaiah 48:9), "For My praise, *echtom* (I will restrain my anger) from you."[155] A worm, an impurity, had become intermingled in his prayer and divine service. It disturbed him and this Jew could not perform his divine service properly.[156] What did this person do? He executed the three steps mentioned above.[157] These are: attaching himself to the tzaddik,[158] donating charity, and spoken confession.

And this is the explanation:
The fish died and the water tossed it about and cast it ashore. The three steps are mentioned from top to bottom.[159]

It died — This is the step of spoken confession, as is said: "All those about to be put to death, confess."[160]

the water tossed it about — This is charity. As is written, "Cast your bread upon the waters" (Ecclesiastes 11:1), and, "Happy are you that sow beside all waters" (Isaiah 32:20).[161]

---

153. **kavra...fish.** This verse is from the blessing Yaakov gave Yosef's sons. Rashi (*loc. cit.*) explains that fish reproduce in great numbers and the evil eye has no mastery over them. The *kavra* or fish of Rabbah bar bar Chanah's story thus alludes to the Jewish people when they guard their covenant with God (see n.172).

154. **prayers of the Jewish people.** Prayer, one of the highest forms of speech, is an aspect of *Malkhut* (both exemplified in the person of King David). The *Shulchan Arukh* explains that the closer a person approaches ultimate perfection in prayer, the more he loses his awareness of self. One who is praying at this level has, at least for the moment, attached himself to *Ein Sof* and thereby causes *Malkhut* to return to its source. Conversely, as long as one has not returned *Malkhut* to its source, he is certainly far from achieving perfection in prayer (*Parparaot LeChokhmah*; see above, n.120).

155. **echtom, I will restrain....** Read literally, *echtom* is "I will plug my nose (*chotem*)," so as to prevent the smoke of anger from escaping (*Rashi, loc. cit.*). Thus, "For My praise, *echtom*" shows the connection between prayer and *chotem* (see also *Likutey Moharan* 2:1). The *kavra's* nostrils therefore allude to a Jew's prayer.

156. **A worm....** This is the mudeater, an allusion to an impurity. The Jew who desired to pray to God found that he could not, as his concentration was being disturbed by an impurity.

    Again it is worth noting that although Rebbe Nachman has spent much time explaining the tzaddik's role in all this (rectifying *Malkhut* and directing the person on the correct path),

וְשַׁדְּיוּהוּ לְגוּדָא – הַצַּדִּיק נִקְרָא גוּדָא, לְשׁוֹן גָּדֵר, שֶׁהוּא גּוֹדֵר
פִּרְצוֹתֵיהֶן שֶׁל יִשְׂרָאֵל. וְזֶה: 'וְשַׁדְּיוּהוּ לְגוּדָא', שֶׁהִקְרִיב אֶת עַצְמוֹ
לַצַּדִּיק.

וְעַל־יְדֵי שָׁלֹשׁ בְּחִינוֹת אֵלּוּ:

וְחָרוּב מִינֵיהּ שִׁיתִּין מְחוֹזָא שֶׁעַל־יְדֵי הַמִּיתָה, הַיְנוּ וִדּוּי דְּבָרִים,
הֶעֱלָה אֶת הַמַּלְכוּת מִבֵּין הַסִּטְרָא אָחֳרָא. וְהַצַּדִּיק הוֹרָה לוֹ אֶת
הַדֶּרֶךְ הַיָּשָׁר,

כְּמוֹ שֶׁכָּתוּב בְּהַפְטָרַת בְּרֵאשִׁית: "אַחֲרִיב הָרִים וּגְבָעוֹת", רֶמֶז עַל
חֻרְבַּן מֶמְשֶׁלֶת הָעַכּוּ"ם. "וְהוֹלַכְתִּי עִוְרִים בְּדֶרֶךְ לֹא יָדָעוּ", זֶה
בְּחִינַת שֶׁהַצַּדִּיק הוֹרָה לוֹ דֶּרֶךְ יָשָׁר. זֶה בְּחִינַת פָּרָשַׁת דְּרָכִים
כַּנַּ"ל. 'וְשִׁיתִּין מְחוֹזָא', רֶמֶז עַל עֲלִיַּת הַמַּלְכוּת, דִּכְתִיב בֵּהּ:
"שִׁשִּׁים הֵמָּה מְלָכוֹת".

166. **haftarah of Bereishit.** The portion of prophets read in the synagogue after the weekly Torah reading (see *Orach Chaim* 284).

167. **mountains and hills...rule of the nations.** *Radak* (Isaiah 42:15) renders this as: "I will destroy the *melakhim* and rulers of the nations."

168. **a crossroads.** By destroying *Malkhut* of the Other Side, the tzaddik can then guide the "blind" person on his proper path of serving God (as above, §8, nn.103-106).

The *Parparaot LeChokhmah* notes that Rebbe Nachman quotes from the "*haftarah* reading of *Bereishit*" instead of directly from Isaiah, and in so doing adds another dimension to his proof. Scripture's account of Creation begins with God creating the world in order to reveal His *Malkhut*. Yet right at the outset Scripture states (Genesis 1:2): "The earth was unformed and void..." which denotes *Malkhut* of the Other Side (of the nations, *Bereishit Rabbah* 2:4) having supplanted *Malkhut* of Holiness. However, Scripture immediately adds: "but the spirit of God hovered"—referring to the spirit of the Mashiach, the tzaddik (*Zohar* I, 192b). He destroys *Malkhut* of the Other Side—as in, "I will destroy mountains and hills"—and elevates *Malkhut* of Holiness to its source. He also guides people on their proper path—as in, "I will lead the blind by a path they did not know"—corresponding to, "Let there be light...." The *Parparaot LeChokhmah* concludes: From this we see that the entire process of Creation, as delineated at the beginning of Genesis, can be understood as God informing all the elements in creation of their proper paths, each in accordance with its root Above.

169. **...sixty M'LaKhoT.** The sixty cities correspond to the "sixty *m'lakhot*," which Rashi explains as "sixty kingdoms," or *Malkhut*.

and cast it ashore — The tzaddik is called a "shore," which has the connotation of fence, because he "fences in the breaches of Israel."[162] This is, **and cast it ashore.** < He gave charity to the tzaddik he had gotten close to >.[163]

And because of these three steps[164]:
It destroyed sixty cities — That is, through death, which is spoken confession,[165] he elevated *Malkhut* from among < the nations >, and the tzaddik taught him the proper path.

{**"I will destroy mountains and hills.... I will lead the blind by a road they did not know"** (Isaiah 42:15-16).}
As is written in the *haftarah* of *Bereishit*,[166] "I will destroy mountains and hills"—this alludes to the destruction of the rule of the nations.[167] < And afterwards, > "I will lead the blind by a path they did not know"—this corresponds to the tzaddik guiding him along the proper path. This is the aspect of "a crossroads."[168] And **sixty cities** alludes to the ascent of *MaLKhuT*, as is written (Song of Songs 6:8), "There are sixty *M'LaKhoT* (queens)."[169]

---

fruit. It is like someone who plants grain on a well-watered field. He can be confident of reaping a fine crop. Likewise, the charitable person is assured that his good deeds will bring him prosperity. Thus, "water tossed it about" in Rabbah bar bar Chanah's story alludes to charity. And, as explained earlier, giving charity to the tzaddik eliminates the vices that stem from the animal and human life forms (above, §8).

162. **fences in the breaches of Israel.** Versions of this phrase appear in Isaiah 58:12 and Ezekiel 22:30. They speak of one, a tzaddik, who can "fence in the breaches" made by the wicked and get them to repent. The Talmud applies this phrase to Moshe, as he was the one who brought the Torah to the Jewish people (*Megillah* 13a, *Maharsha, s.v. kol d'varekha*). Earlier, Rebbe Nachman referred to the tzaddik as "Mother" (§8, n.93), because he nurses the Jews with his Torah. The tzaddik who can nourish the Jewish people with his Torah is the one to draw close to, for with his Torah he can 'fence in all of our breaches.'

163. **tzaddik he had gotten close to.** As explained, closeness to the tzaddik eliminates the vices that stem from the mineral and vegetable life forms (above, §8).
    Thus, by giving charity and getting close to the tzaddik, this Jew of Rabbah bar bar Chanah's story was able to eliminate *all* the vices that stem from the four *yesodot*.

164. **these three steps.** For all three are necessary to rectify *Malkhut*.
    The Rebbe will now show how the three instances of "sixty cities" in the story—"destroyed sixty cities"; "Sixty cities then ate from it"; "Sixty cities salted its flesh"—allude to the three steps of repentance that he discusses in the lesson.

165. **through death...confession....** The destroyed sixty cities allude to the sixty times that Hell is larger than the world. Death, as we have seen, suggests confession: "All those about to be put to death must first confess" (see nn.104 and 160).

וְאָכְלוּ מִינָהּ שִׁיתִין מְחוֹזָא – רֶמֶז עַל שְׁנֵי מִדּוֹת רָעוֹת שֶׁל חַי
מְדַבֵּר, שֶׁעַל־יָדוּ בָּא עֲנִיּוּת כַּנַּ"ל, וְעַל־יְדֵי צְדָקָה מְתַקֵּן אוֹתָם
וְיַמְשִׁיךְ שֶׁפַע. וְזֶה: 'אָכְלוּ מִינֵיהּ'. וְ'שִׁיתִין מְחוֹזָא', רֶמֶז עַל
בְּחִינַת שִׁשִּׁים גִּבּוֹרִים, שֶׁמִּשָּׁם בָּא פַּרְנָסָה, כְּמוֹ שֶׁאָמְרוּ: 'גְּבוּרוֹת
גְּשָׁמִים'.

וּמִלְחוּ מִינָהּ שִׁיתִין מְחוֹזָא – זֶה רֶמֶז עַל תִּקּוּן שְׁתֵּי מִדּוֹת רָעוֹת –
'דּוֹמֵם צוֹמֵחַ', עַל־יְדֵי קָרְבָתוֹ לְהַצַּדִּיק, כִּי הַצַּדִּיק הוּא "בְּרִית
מֶלַח עוֹלָם". גַּם עַצְבוּת וְתַאֲווֹת בָּאִים מִדָּמִים עֲכוּרִים, וְעַל־יְדֵי
מֶלַח פּוֹלֵט הַדָּמִים רָעִים. וְ'שִׁיתִין מְחוֹזָא', זֶה רֶמֶז עַל שִׁשִּׁים
אוֹתִיּוֹת שֶׁבְּבִרְכַּת כֹּהֲנִים, שֶׁהֵם בְּיַד הַצַּדִּיק, כְּמוֹ שֶׁכָּתוּב: "בְּרָכוֹת
לְרֹאשׁ צַדִּיק".

וּמָלְאוּ מְחַד גַּלְגָּלָא דְעֵינָא תְּלָת מֵאָה גַּרְבֵי מִשְׁחָא – גַּרְבֵּי מִשְׁחָא,

bitterness of earning a livelihood by lessening one's desires for material pleasures. Thus, seeing and drawing close to the tzaddik reduces and breaks one's evil desires.

173. **salt expels the bad blood.** This is evident from the process for koshering meat: salt is liberally spread over it in order to remove the blood (*Chullin* 113a). In our context, therefore, salt/the tzaddik removes the bad blood/melancholy.

174. **sixty cities...Birkat Kohanim....** Finally, the sixty cities hint to the sixty letters of *Birkat Kohanim*, the priestly blessing found in Numbers 6:24-26. In the preceding paragraphs it was explained how giving charity to the tzaddik eliminates those vices that lead to poverty. However, the person who escapes poverty is still in danger of falling into the next set of vices, melancholy and evil passions. As the Sages teach: "The more possessions, the more worry" (*Avot* 2:8), and, "When a person has one hundred, he desires two hundred" (*Kohelet Rabbah* 1:34). It is therefore necessary to have the salt/tzaddik that remedies the worry and passionate desire for money that wealth often brings. This, then, is the final "sixty cities": It corresponds to the blessing received through the sixty letters of *Birkat Kohanim*, to "It is God's blessing that enriches; and it contains no sorrow" (Proverbs 10:22). Any trace of melancholy or evil passion that might accompany material abundance is abolished by the *Birkat Kohanim*—i.e., the blessing received from the tzaddik (*Parparaot LeChokhmah*).

So far, Rabbah bar bar Chanah's story translates in our text as follows:
One time we were traveling on a sephina — Rabbah bar bar Chanah went to see how to elevate *Malkhut.*
We saw this kavra in whose nostrils was sitting a mudeater — He saw a Jew whose prayers were

Sixty cities then ate from it — This alludes to the two vices that stem from the animal and human life forms, which, as mentioned, lead to poverty. But by giving charity, they are rectified and abundance is drawn [into the world]. This is: **then ate from it.**[170] And **sixty cities** alludes to the aspect of "sixty men of strength" (Song of Songs 3:7). Livelihood stems from there, as is taught: "strong rains" (*Berakhot* 33a).[171]

Sixty cities salted its flesh — This alludes to the rectification of the two vices [that stem from] the mineral and vegetable life forms. This is accomplished by means of < drawing close to the tzaddikim >, because the tzaddik is "a covenant of salt forever" (Numbers 18:19).[172] Both melancholy and evil passions come from putrid blood, whereas salt expels the bad blood.[173] And **sixty cities** alludes to the sixty letters of the *Birkat Kohanim* (Priestly Blessing), which are in the hands of the tzaddik, as is written (Proverbs 10:6), "Blessings are upon the head of the tzaddik."[174]

And from one eyeball they filled three meah (hundred) kegs with oil —

"Sixty *m'lakhot*" also alludes to the Oral Torah, which is an aspect of speech/*Malkhut*, and is made up of sixty tractates (cf. Lesson #3 and n.24). In our context, when a person confesses in front of the tzaddik (the source of the Torah; above, §6), he elevates *Malkhut* from the realm of evil—a revelation of Torah, particularly Oral Torah.

170. **then ate from it.** They ate from the abundance brought into the world as a result of the charity this Jew gave to the tzaddik (see §8, n.101). Thus, charity counters poverty and eliminates the vices that stem from the animal and human life forms—namely, idle chatter, pride, and their derivatives.

171. **sixty cities...strong rains.** Here Rebbe Nachman connects the sixty cities to "sixty men of strength," and "strength" to strong rains. When the rains are strong and plentiful, crops flourish, and so "strong rains" denotes material abundance. The cold and wind that accompany the rainy season are connected to the *sefirah* of *Gevurah* (Strength). This *sefirah* is thus the source of livelihood and abundance, and its position is on the left of the *sefirah* hierarchy. Hence, Scripture states (Proverbs 3:16): "In its left hand are riches and honor." And to receive a proper and manageable measure of divine abundance, limitations and boundaries must be set. This is the function of *tzimtzum* (constriction), which is an aspect of *Gevurah*. Thus, the "sixty men of strength" alludes to abundance—i.e., the "sixty cities" that "then ate from it" by giving charity.

172. **a covenant of salt forever.** The holiness of the tzaddik is due to his guarding the *brit*, the Covenant (see *Likutey Moharan* I, 2:2,9 and notes, where this is explained in detail). In general, any reference to the Covenant alludes to the tzaddik. See also *Likutey Moharan* 23:2, where Rebbe Nachman explains that the Covenant is an aspect of salt, which sweetens the

זֶה בְּחִינוֹת הַדַּעַת, כִּי "שֶׁמֶן מִשְׁחַת קֹדֶשׁ", זֶה בְּחִינַת שֵׂכֶל. וּתְלָת
מֵאָה, זֶה בְּחִינַת מֹשֶׁה, שֶׁהוּא בְּחִינַת מַה שֶׁהַצַּדִּיק מַקְטִין אֶת
עַצְמוֹ, בִּבְחִינַת מָה. בְּשָׁלֹשׁ בְּחִינוֹת צָרִיךְ לְהַקְטִין אֶת עַצְמוֹ, כְּמוֹ
שֶׁכָּתוּב: "אַל יִתְהַלֵּל חָכָם, גִּבּוֹר וְעָשִׁיר". נִמְצָא שֶׁבְּכָל בְּחִינָה
מֵאֵלּוּ שָׁלֹשׁ בְּחִינוֹת הוּא נַעֲשֶׂה מָה.

וְעַל-יְדֵי זֶה זֶה יֵשׁ לוֹ הִתְפַּשְׁטוּת הַגַּשְׁמִיּוּת, וּמִדַּבֵּק בְּאוֹר אֵין סוֹף,
שֶׁאֵין שָׁם שׁוּם שִׁנּוּי רָצוֹן, אֶלָּא: ה' הוּא הָאֱלֹקִים, כַּנַּ"ל, הַיְנוּ כֻּלּוֹ
הַטּוֹב וְהַמֵּטִיב. וְזֶה בְּחִינַת 'חַד גַּלְגַּלָא דְּעֵינָא', כַּמּוּבָא בְּאִידְרָא:
'וּלְזִימְנָא דְּאָתֵי יִשְׁתַּכַּח בָּהּ עֵינָא חַד דְּרַחֲמֵי', זֶה בְּחִינַת כֻּלּוֹ
הַטּוֹב וְהַמֵּטִיב.

נִמְצָא כְּשֶׁהַצַּדִּיק עוֹשֶׂה עַצְמוֹ מָה, מִדַּבֵּק אֶת עַצְמוֹ לְעֵינָא חַד

MeaH. Rebbe Nachman will now explain why "three *meah*" also relates to Moshe's essence.

177. **wise...strong...rich...he becomes mah.** Wisdom, strength and wealth are the three attributes in which men pride themselves most. At the same time, having these attributes is necessary if one is to be worthy of a revelation from God. As Rabbi Yochanan said, "The Holy One only rests his *Shekhinah* on a person who is strong, rich, and wise. And he must also be humble. We learn all these from Moshe" (*Nedarim* 38a). Moshe had the three attributes; he was wise, strong and wealthy. Yet Moshe was able to negate himself entirely in *Ein Sof.* He had attained a unique level of humility, as evidenced in his words (Exodus 16:7), "*nachnu MaH?*" (see n.125). It was as though *MoSheH* (משה) had removed the *shin* (ש)—i.e., the three attributes that make a man proud—and attained complete humility, *MaH* (מה). This is what Rebbe Nachman referred to above, that by virtue of his deep humility the tzaddik becomes absorbed in Nothingness/*Ein Sof* (see nn.64 and 125).

178. **no change of will...good and beneficent.** As explained above, section 9 and note 147 (see also §4, n.21).

179. **one eye of compassion.** The one eye of compassion is symbolic of God's unceasing compassionate providence, of His guiding all He created with open and infinite lovingkindness. As the *Zohar* (*loc. cit.*) indicates, it will be manifest "in the time to come." This corresponds to the perception of the World to Come, which, as Rebbe Nachman has explained, is a revelation of the unity between God and His Name. Thus, in our context, "from one eyeball" alludes to the oneness of *YHVH* and *Elohim*—i.e., to *Ein Sof,* in which all is one, and entirely good and beneficent.

180. **tzaddik...mah...Ein Sof.** As explained (§9), the tzaddik ascends to *Ein Sof* by negating himself totally to God. There, he experiences *Ein Sof's* oneness and beneficence: there is no difference between *YHVH* and *Elohim,* between the divine attribute of judgment and the divine attribute of compassion (n.144). This corresponds to providence emanating from "the one eye of compassion."

The **kegs with oil** correspond to *daat,* because "holy anointing oil" (Exodus 30:31) is the aspect of intellect.[175]

Now, **three MeaH** alludes to Moshe.[176] This is the concept of the tzaddik contracting himself in the aspect of *MaH.* He must make himself insignificant in three attributes: < wisdom, strength and wealth >. As is written (Jeremiah 9:22), "Let not the wise man...the strong man...the rich man exult." We find, then, that in each of these three steps he becomes *mah.*[177]

In this way he is able to strip himself of corporeality and adhere to the Light of *Ein Sof,* where there is no change of will whatsoever. Rather, "*YHVH* is the *Elohim*"—i.e., "entirely 'Who is good and beneficent.' "[178] This is the aspect of **one eyeball**. As is brought in the *Idra* (Zohar III, 137b): In the time to come, there will be the one eye of compassion.[179] This corresponds to "entirely 'Who is good and beneficent.' "

We find, then, that when the tzaddik makes himself *mah,* he attaches himself to "the one eye of compassion," to *Ein Sof.*[180] And

---

disrupted by an impurity. What did the Jew do to rectify this? He went to see the tzaddik and performed the three steps to repentance.

The kavra died — he confessed;

and the water tossed it about — and he gave charity;

and cast it ashore — and he saw and got close to the tzaddik.

It destroyed sixty cities — His confession rectified *Malkhut* and the tzaddik guided him to his proper path.

Sixty cities then ate from it — As a result of his giving charity he was blessed with abundance. This rid him of the vices of idle chatter and pride, which engender poverty.

Sixty cities salted its flesh — And through seeing the tzaddik and receiving the tzaddik's blessing, he was rid of the vices of melancholy and evil passions.

175. **holy anointing oil...intellect.** Rebbe Nachman continues with his reading of Rabbah bar bar Chanah's story.

The Kabbalah teaches that the term *kodesh* (holy) refers to wisdom (see *Likutey Moharan* I, 21:3, n.22), and it likens the intellect to an oil lamp (*Zohar* III, 39a; see *Likutey Moharan* I, 21:11, n.112). This is because the intellect is a great light that illuminates a person's path in life (Lesson #1, §2). In addition, just as oil is drawn up to the flame, the fatty fluids of the body are drawn up to fuel the mind (*Likutey Moharan* II, 8:12). Thus, *daat*/intellect is the "holy anointing oil." In our context, oil corresponds to Moshe. As mentioned, throughout Torah lore Moshe is synonymous with *daat* (see n.149).

The *Mai HaNachal* adds: The kegs containing the oil allude to the vessel, the conscious mind, that retains the *reshimu* that remains when the person who's been nullified in *Ein Sof* returns to normal consciousness (see above, n.147).

176. **three MeaH alludes to Moshe.** The Hebrew letter *shin* (ש) has a numerical value of 300, three *meah*. The name MoSheH (משה) is comprised of this *Shin* and the primary letters of

דְּרַחֲמֵי, הַיְנוּ לְאֵין סוֹף, וְאַחַר כָּךְ כְּשֶׁחוֹזֵר בִּבְחִינַת רָצוֹא וָשׁוֹב,
אָז מַמְשִׁיךְ מֵאוֹר אֵין סוֹף הָאַחְדוּת הָרָצוֹן הַפָּשׁוּט שָׁם דֶּרֶךְ הַמָּה
שֶׁלּוֹ, וְנַעֲשֶׂה מִמָּה מֵאָה, כְּמוֹ שֶׁנֶּאֱמַר: 'אַל תִּקְרֵי מָה אֶלָּא מֵאָה'.
וְנַעֲשֶׂה תְּלָת מֵאָה מִתְלָת מָה, וּמַמְשִׁיךְ אוֹר הַזֶּה לְדַעְתּוֹ וּלְשִׂכְלוֹ,
הַיְנוּ גַּרְבֵי דְּמִשְׁחָא, שֶׁהוּא בְּחִינַת שֵׂכֶל, כַּנַּ"ל.

אַתָּה הָרְאֵיתָ לָדַעַת, שֶׁמַּמְשִׁיךְ אוֹר אֵין סוֹף לְדַעְתּוֹ, שֶׁיֵּדַע
הָאַחְדוּת, שֶׁה' הוּא הָאֱלֹקִים, וִיבָרֵךְ הַטּוֹב וְהַמֵּטִיב עַל הַכֹּל כְּמוֹ
לֶעָתִיד לָבוֹא:

כִּי הַדְרָן וְאָתְאָן לְבָתַר תְּרֵיסַר יַרְחֵי שַׁתָּא וְקָחֲזֵינָן דַּהֲוֵי מְנַסְרָא
מְגֵרְמַיְהוּ לִכְנִנְאָ הַנָּךְ מָחוֹזָא – כִּי מֵאֲחוֹרֵי הַקְּדֻשָּׁה, שֶׁהֵם שְׁנֵים־
עֶשָׂר שְׁבָטִים, שֶׁעַל־יָדָם נִתְתַּקַּן מַלְכוּת הַנַּ"ל, וְאַחֲרֵיהֶם הוּא
הַטֻּמְאָה.
וְיֵשׁ בְּנֵי־אָדָם שֶׁיּוֹצְאִין מֵהַקְּדֻשָּׁה, וְזֶה שֶׁסִּפֵּר הַתַּנָּא, שֶׁהִדֵּר וְחָזַר

186. **in the Future.** Drawing from the Light of *Ein Sof* leaves his *daat* with an imprint of the good and beneficence that is found there. This enables his mind's eye to see the goodness of God everywhere and in everything; he understands that whatever happens to him is good and beneficial. This, as Rebbe Nachman explained at the outset of the lesson, is a perception that creation in its entirety will only appreciate in the Future, in the World to Come.

187. **twelve tribes...Malkhut is rectified.** Here, Rebbe Nachman begins his explanation of the final part of Rabbah bar bar Chanah's story.

The *Zohar* (I, 240b, 241a) teaches: *Malkhut* is restored by means of twelve rectifications (12 different formations of the *sefirot* from *Chesed* through *Yesod*). These twelve rectifications are personified by the twelve sons of the patriarch Yaakov, the twelve tribes. Each one was a great tzaddik and a paragon of purity and holiness.

188. **Behind holiness...is impurity.** Whoever is within the realm of holiness is said to be included in the twelve tribes. Whoever leaves this realm is "behind holiness," outside of it, and within the realm of impurity.

189. **Tanna.** This refers to Rabbah bar bar Chanah. Actually, Rabbah bar bar Chanah was an *Amora* (from the Talmudic era), not a *Tanna* (from the Mishnaic era). However, this usage is common in Rebbe Nachman's teachings when he wants to refer to one of the early great sages.

afterwards, when he returns in an aspect of "running and returning,"[181] he draws from the Light of *Ein Sof*—the oneness <and> the uniform will—by way of his *mah*.[182] *MaH* is thus transformed into *MeAH*. As is taught: Do not read *mah*, but rather *meah* (*Menachot* 43b).[183] **Three hundred** is made from the three *mah*,[184] and he draws this light to his *daat* and intellect. This is **kegs with oil**, which is intellect, as explained.[185]

[This is the meaning of] "It has been clearly demonstrated to your *daat*" (Deuteronomy 4:35). He draws the Light of *Ein Sof* to his *daat*, so that he might know the oneness: "*YHVH* is the *Elohim*." He then makes the blessing "Who is good and beneficent" over everything, as it will be in the Future.[186]

When we returned after twelve months time, we saw them sawing planks from its bones with which to rebuild those cities — Behind holiness— [holiness being] the twelve tribes, through whom *Malkhut* is rectified[187]—is impurity.[188]

Now, there are people who move outside the realm of holiness. This is what the *Tanna*[189] recounted: He returned to inquire about

---

181. **running and returning.** See above, section 9, note 135.

182. **his mah.** His ascent to *Ein Sof* was by virtue of his *mah*, his complete humility, and it is this deep humility that then serves as his conduit for drawing from the Light of *Ein Sof*.

183. **MaH...transformed into MeaH....** The Talmud (*loc. cit.*) teaches: A person is required to recite one hundred blessings each day, as is written (Deuteronomy 10:12), "So now, Israel, *mah* (what) does God your Lord ask of you?"—do not read *mah* but *meah*. *Tosafot* points out that when *meah* is read in place of *mah* there are one hundred Hebrew letters in the verse, corresponding to the required one hundred blessings.

The *Mai HaNachal* adds: The letter *aleph* (א), which is added to the word *MaH* (מה) to make it *MeAH* (מאה), is the first letter of the Hebrew alphabet and has a numerical value of one. It symbolizes the oneness and unity found in *Ein Sof*, as well as the *reshimu* (imprint) that remains with the tzaddik (or person) when he returns to normal consciousness after being nullified in *Ein Sof*. In other words, the person who makes himself *mah*, humble in the three attributes, becomes absorbed in *Ein Sof* where he gains the awareness that all is good and all is one. He brings *Aleph*, the awareness of oneness, into *mah*, thus making it *meAh*.

184. **Three hundred...from the three mah.** By making himself *mah* in the three attributes of wisdom, strength and wealth, he draws upon himself the awareness of God's oneness, the *Aleph*, in three aspects—thereby making three *meah*. That is, now, the tzaddik himself is able to draw beneficence and good into all areas of material life.

185. **as explained.** See above, note 175, that this is the *daat*/intellect housed within the conscious mind.

לְעֵין בְּאֵלּוּ שֶׁהֵם בָּתַר תְּרֵיסַר יַרְחֵי שַׁתָּא, שֶׁהֵם אֲחוֹרֵי שְׁנֵים־עָשָׂר שְׁבָטִים דִּקְדֻשָׁה, שֶׁיּוֹצְאִין מִכְּלַל יִשְׂרָאֵל עַל־יְדֵי מַעֲשֵׂיהֶם הָרָעִים. וַחֲזִינָן דְּהָווּ מְנַסְרֵי מִגַּרְמַיְהוּ – הַיְנוּ שֶׁעַל־יְדֵי מַעֲשֵׂיהֶם הָרָעִים הַחֲקוּקִים עַל עַצְמוֹתָם, וְהַחֲקִיקָה עוֹבֵר מֵעֵבֶר לָעֵבֶר כִּנְסִירָה מַמָּשׁ.

אֲבָל עַל־יְדֵי שֶׁאִישׁ הַיִּשְׂרְאֵלִי הַנַּ"ל נִתְעוֹרֵר בִּתְשׁוּבָה עַל־יְדֵי שֶׁרֶץ קָטָן שֶׁבְּנְחִירָיו, עַל־יְדֵי שֶׁהִרְגִּישׁ טֻמְאָה קְטַנָּה שֶׁמְּבַלְבֶּלֶת אוֹתוֹ, עַל־יְדֵי תְּשׁוּבָתוֹ גּוֹרֵם, שֶׁגַּם אֵלּוּ הָרְשָׁעִים נַעֲשׂוּ כִּסֵּא לַקְּדֻשָׁה. וִיהַבֵי לִבְנְיָנָא הַנָּךְ מְחוֹזָא – שֶׁעוֹזְרִים גַּם הֵם לְעוֹבְדֵי הַשֵׁם, שֶׁיִּבְנוּ הַנָּךְ מְחוֹזָא הַנַּ"ל:

וְזֶה פֵּרוּשׁ:

אָנֹכִי ה' אֱלֹהֶיךָ – פֵּרוּשׁ הֵן ה' הֵן אֱלֹהֶיךָ תָּבִין, שֶׁכָּל זֹאת אָנֹכִי,

These wicked people disempower *Malkhut*, and they empower the nations and enable them to rule. (Here, the published version was given preference over the manuscript as it was the version the commentaries to *Likutey Moharan* addressed.)

193. **repentance...evildoers to be transformed....** The deeds of every individual have an effect on the entire world. Thus, the person who works to rectify himself brings similar rectification to the world at large. We see this from the Jew who wanted to pray but could not. An impurity, either of his own making or brought about by others, was interfering with his concentration. But by going to the tzaddik, giving charity and confessing, he included himself in the tzaddik and was thereby brought to a perception of the Light of *Ein Sof*. This Jew, although previously trapped in his vices, had reached a most lofty spiritual level—an awareness of God's unity and beneficence. Moreover, when the tzaddik returns from being negated in *Ein Sof*, he brings a *reshimu* into the world. This imprint on the tzaddik's *daat* brings greater recognition of God to others, even those who are distant from Him. Thus, even those Jews who were far from holiness are saved from evil. Because of the process begun by a simple Jew looking to repent, they too ultimately contribute to *Malkhut's* rectification (*Parparaot LeChokhmah*). Reb Noson adds that the more one strives to accomplish these rectifications, the more people are able to perceive the great Light of *Ein Sof* and return to God (*Torat Natan #11*). As mentioned (above, n.1), after hearing these points, three of Rebbe Nachman's followers (Reb Aharon, Reb Yudel and Reb Shmuel Isaac) were influential in bringing back to God a number of Jews who had distanced themselves from their heritage.

194. **rebuilding the above mentioned cities.** Namely, rectifying *Malkhut*. See note 169.

Thus, Rabbah bar bar Chanah's story reads as follows:

Rabbah bar bar Chanah recounted: One time we were traveling on a sephina — Rabbah bar bar

those who are **after twelve months time**—those who are behind the twelve tribes of holiness.[190] They move outside the Jewish community as a result of their evil deeds.[191]

we saw them sawing from its bones — That is, in consequence of their evil deeds, which were etched upon their bones; with the etching crossing over from side to side,[192] exactly like a saw mark.

But because of the Jew mentioned above, who was moved to repentance by the small worm in his nostrils—because [his prayer] had been disturbed by a small impurity—[they can be saved]. By means of his repentance, he causes also these evildoers to be transformed into an abode for holiness.[193]

with which to rebuild those cities — These [evildoers] also help those serving God in rebuilding the above mentioned cities.[194]

11. This is the explanation [of the opening verse]:
{**"*Anokhi YHVH Elohekha* (I am God your Lord) Who brought you out of the land of *Mitzrayim* (Egypt), from the house of slavery."**}

190. **after twelve months time....** Each month of the Jewish calendar corresponds to one of the twelve tribes. Thus, the rectification of *Malkhut* of Holiness takes place, so to speak, within twelve months time. "After twelve months" therefore alludes to behind holiness—i.e., impurity.

191. **He returned to inquire...their evil deeds.** Rabbah bar bar Chanah's returning and inquiring about those behind the twelve tribes alludes to the way the true tzaddikim are always looking for ways to help all Jews, even those outside the fold of holiness.

The *Mai HaNachal* adds: This further explains the verse Rebbe Nachman quoted earlier (end of §7): "There was a king in Yeshurun when...the tribes of Israel were together." When was there a *MeLeKh* in Yeshurun—i.e., when is *Malkhut* rectified within its source? When the tribes of Israel were together—i.e., when the twelve tribes that complete *Malkhut* are united and all together. Knowing this, the tzaddikim seek to elevate *Malkhut* by bringing those behind holiness back within its realm.

192. **evil deeds...crossing over....** As explained above, section 5 (n.57). In investigating how *Malkhut* could be elevated, Rabbah bar bar Chanah took note of a Jew who was having difficulty praying and turned to the tzaddik to help him repent. Rabbah understood that this Jew, by repenting, would bring rectification for himself and his aspect of *Malkhut*. What bothered him, though, was the fate of those outside the realm of holiness, whose bones have etched upon them their sins. Not only would they have no rectification, but they would also continue to blemish *Malkhut* of Holiness and prevent its ascent into *Ein Sof*.

Neither this paragraph nor the explanation that closes this section of the lesson appear in the manuscript version of *Likutey Moharan*. Rather, we find: With this we can understand how it is that the nations are able to rule. It is because of the small impurity mentioned above. For the Jew had performed the three steps, and it was to be expected that *Malkhut* would ascend from among the nations. The answer is that there are people who are behind holiness.

הַיְנוּ שֶׁתְּקַיֵּם: "בַּה' אֲהַלֵל דָּבָר, בֵּאלֹהִים אֲהַלֵל דָּבָר", הַיְנוּ כֻּלּוֹ
הַטּוֹב וְהַמֵּטִיב, כַּנַּ"ל.
אֲשֶׁר הוֹצֵאתִיךָ מֵאֶרֶץ מִצְרַיִם – דְּאִיתָא בַּמִּדְרָשׁ, כִּי כָּל הַגָּלֻיּוֹת
נִקְרָאִים עַל שֵׁם גָּלוּת מִצְרַיִם, מִפְּנֵי שֶׁהֵם מְצֵרִים לְיִשְׂרָאֵל. הַיְנוּ
שֶׁעַל יְדֵי הַצַּדִּיק נִתְבַּטֵּל מַלְכוּתָם וּמֶמְשַׁלְתָּם שֶׁל הָעַכּוּ"ם, כִּי עַל-
יְדֵי זֶה עוֹלָה מִתּוֹכָם מַלְכוּת דִּקְדֻשָּׁה כַּנַּ"ל.

מִבֵּית עֲבָדִים – זֶה רֶמֶז עַל בִּטוּל הַמִּדּוֹת רָעוֹת שֶׁל אַרְבַּע יְסוֹדוֹת,
הַמְכֻנִּים בְּשֵׁם עֲבָדִים, כִּי כָּל הָאַרְבָּעָה יְסוֹדוֹת הֵם מִתַּחַת גַּלְגַּל

of the oneness he had experienced, he returned with the perception that whatever God does, it is always only good and beneficial.

When we returned after twelve months time — Rabbah bar bar Chanah also noticed that even those Jews who are outside the realm of holiness had benefited from this Jew's repentance and spiritual attainments.

we saw them sawing planks from its bones with which to rebuild those cities — He saw how these evildoers were also brought to rebuilding and rectifying *Malkhut*. This is because when even a simple Jew repents and in the process causes *Malkhut* to become bound with *Ein Sof*, it prompts those presently in the realm of impurity to also want to repent and return to God.

195. **Anokhi.** This alludes to God's oneness and unity: "*YHVH* is the *Elohim*." There is only the One.

196. **as above.** See sections 1 and 4. This is the recognition that what is painful and seems bad is really good; praising God for both.

197. **MitZRayIM...MetZeiRIM...to the Jewish people.** Thus, in our context, *Mitzrayim* corresponds to the suffering of *Malkhut* in exile among the nations (as above, §2).

Reb Noson adds: On the personal level, "exile in Mitzrayim" represents a person's enslavement to his own material and evil desires. The suffering of *this* exile is solely because he has yet to shed his attachments, his corporeality. Were he to do so, he would know that God is always good. This awareness is itself freedom, a foretaste of the World to Come (*Torat Natan* #12).

198. **ascends from among them....** See above, sections 3, 4 and 6, that confession in the tzaddik's presence restores the fallen *Malkhut* from its exile. As explained, the confession must be in front of the tzaddik because he is the source of *Malkhut*, and *Malkhut* always seeks to ascend to its source.

199. **beneath the celestial band of the moon.** As explained earlier (n.83), the celestial bands of the four *yesodot* are all below the celestial band within which the moon orbits. The evil in the four *yesodot* is caused by the waning of the moon. This is because the moon corresponds to *Malkhut* (see Appendix: The Divine Persona, alternate names of *Malkhut*). Its waning signifies a disempowering of *Malkhut* of Holiness and an empowering of *Malkhut* of the

Anokhi YHVH Elohekha — Whether it be *YHVH* or *Elohekha,* understand that all this is *Anokhi* ("I").[195] That is, one should fulfill: "When He is *YHVH,* I will praise His word; when He is *Elohim,* I will praise His word"—i.e., "entirely 'Who is good and beneficent,' " as above.[196]

Who brought you out of the land of Mitzrayim, Egypt — The Midrash (*Bereishit Rabbah* 16:4) states: All exiles are known as *MitZRayIM,* because they *MetZeiRIM* (cause anguish and suffering) to the Jewish people.[197] < But when *Malkhut* of Holiness ascends from among them, there is no exile. >[198]

from the house of slavery — This alludes to the nullification of the vices that stem from the four *yesodot,* which are called "slaves." For all four *yesodot* are beneath the celestial band of the moon.[199] And the

Chanah went to discover how to rectify *Malkhut.*

We saw this kavra — He saw this Jew.

in whose nostrils was sitting a mudeater — who wanted to pray but was disturbed by an impurity. He went to the tzaddik and carried out the three steps of repentance, steps by which *Malkhut,* too, is rectified.

The kavra died — He confessed,

and the water tossed it about — and he gave charity,

and cast it ashore — and he saw the tzaddik and attached himself to him.

It destroyed sixty cities — He confessed in order to repent, which destroyed the negative letter-combinations caused by his sins and in so doing reconstructed the positive letter-combinations of *Malkhut* of Holiness.

Sixty cities then ate from it — He gave charity to repent, which brought abundance, and this rid him of the vices that poverty engenders: namely idle chatter, pride, and their derivatives.

Sixty cities salted its flesh — He saw and attached himself to the tzaddik for repentance, and so the tzaddik, who is likened to salt, brought him blessing and helped him expel the vices associated with the blood: namely melancholy, evil passions, and their derivatives.

And from one eyeball — In order for this Jew to complete the third step of repentance, confession in the tzaddik's presence (the order here is reversed), the tzaddik negated his own corporeality and by virtue of his deep humility became absorbed in *Ein Sof.* This achieved a number of things: *Malkhut,* which had been blemished by the Jew's sins, was now rectified and returned to its source, *Ein Sof.* In addition, the tzaddik atoned for the sins of the Jew who had become attached to him, and also brought *him* to a perception of *Ein Sof,* in which God's one eye of compassion alone is manifest.

they filled three hundred kegs with oil — As explained, in order to become nullified in *Ein Sof,* the tzaddik minimized himself with regard to the three attributes in which men pride themselves most: wisdom, strength, and wealth. This brought him to the state of total humility known as *mah*—a total negation of selfhood. When, however, he returned from this absorption in Nothingness to normal consciousness and corporeality, he discovered his conscious mind/keg filled with intellect/oil from the Light of *Ein Sof.* Specifically, as a result

הַיָּרֵחַ. וְהַיָּרֵחַ מְכֻנֶּה בְּשֵׁם עֶבֶד, כַּמּוּבָא בַּזֹּהַר: "הִנֵּה יַשְׂכִּיל עַבְדִּי"
– דָּא סִיהֲרָא.

פֵּרוּשׁ: עַל־יְדֵי הַצַּדִּיק עוֹלָה הַמַּלְכוּת מִן הַסִּטְרָא אַחֲרָא,
וְנִתְבַּטְּלִים הַמִּדּוֹת רָעוֹת, וְעַל־יְדֵי זֶה הָאָדָם בָּא לִבְחִינַת עוֹלָם
הַבָּא, לִבְחִינַת: "בַּה' אֲהַלֵּל דָּבָר, בֵּאלֹהִים אֲהַלֵּל דָּבָר":

who brought you out of the land of Mitzrayim — To make this part of one's awareness, a person must first elevate *Malkhut* out of its exile amongst the nations. How?

from the house of slavery — By seeing the tzaddik and giving charity, which vanquishes the vices/slaves. Then, by confessing in the tzaddik's presence, *Malkhut* is brought out of slavery—i.e., elevated to its source, to *Ein Sof*. As a result, both he and others see that all is good and beneficial—i.e., that *YHVH* and *Elohim* are one.

202. **praise His word.** Having reached the lesson's conclusion, there is one question that still needs to be answered: Where is the tzaddik today who can negate himself in *Ayin* so totally that he can return *Malkhut* to *Ein Sof,* and in the process atone for our sins? When Rebbe Nachman was alive, he spoke of these rectifications and implemented them. But now, with the Rebbe with us only in spirit and not in the flesh, what of the *tikkunim* (rectifications) effected by the three steps of repentance? Is there any way that seeing the tzaddik, giving him charity, and confessing in his presence can presently apply? The *Parparaot LeChokhmah* explains how they do, how the specific *tikkunim* mentioned in the lesson can be fulfilled even today (a comprehensive explanation of the concept of tzaddik appears in *Crossing the Narrow Bridge*, Chapter 17).

The *Parparaot LeChokhmah* writes:

With regard to the rectification achieved by gazing upon the face of the tzaddik, see *Likutey Moharan* #192. There it is explained that the likeness and countenance of the tzaddik can be found in the tzaddik's teachings (see above, n.95).

Joining the tzaddik's followers at the Rosh HaShanah *kibutz* (gathering) is also an aspect of this rectification. At the *kibutz* one realizes that the intense desire of those present to follow the tzaddik's path springs only from the light of the tzaddik's soul and from his Torah lessons. This "light" is his shining countenance, so that being at the Rosh HaShanah *kibutz* is itself an aspect of gazing upon the face of the tzaddik. In this way we can rectify the vices that stem from the mineral and vegetable life forms even today. (The concept of traveling to the tzaddik for Rosh HaShanah, especially to Rebbe Nachman's gravesite in Uman, is explained in two works available from the Breslov Research Institute, *Crossing the Narrow Bridge*, Chapter 18; and *Uman, Uman, Rosh HaShanah*.)

Concerning the rectification achieved by giving charity to the tzaddik, it is clear that this can be accomplished by giving charity to the tzaddik's descendants and his disciples. This also applies to supporting activities that perpetuate the tzaddik's work, including projects dedicated in the tzaddik's name (such as a synagogue) as well as publishing his teachings. In this way we can rectify the vices that stem from the animal and human life forms even today.

Finally, the rectification achieved by confession in the tzaddik's presence can today be performed by traveling to his *tzion* (gravesite), and there engaging in prayer and confession. This may actually be inferred from the lesson itself. Discussing the tzaddik's state of total negation of self, at which time he is absorbed in *Ein Sof*, Rebbe Nachman states: "All this

moon is called "slave," as is brought in the *Zohar* (I 181a): "Behold, My slave will become wise" (Isaiah 52:13)—this refers to the moon.[200]

This means that with the help of the tzaddik, *Malkhut* ascends from the nations and the vices are nullified. Through this, a person achieves [an awareness that is] an aspect of the World to Come[201]—corresponding to, "When He is *YHVH*, I will praise His word; when He is *Elohim*, I will praise His word."[202]

Other Side. This, together with man's sins, subjugates the four *yesodot* to the rule of *Malkhut* of the Other Side. And, conversely, rectifying the four *yesodot*, by seeing the tzaddik and giving charity (§8), strengthens *Malkhut* of Holiness. Then, *Malkhut* seeks to ascend to its source, as in (Isaiah 30:26), "The light of the moon will be as intense as the light of the sun" (*Parparaot LeChokhmah*). Reb Noson adds that the measure of a person's freedom "from the house of slavery" is always commensurate with the degree to which he subjugates his evil desires (as above, n.197; *Torat Natan* #13).

200. My slave...the moon. The *Zohar* (*loc. cit.*) teaches: God created the moon with the intention that it would always shine, with its own light, as brightly as the sun. The moon's role, similar to *Malkhut's,* was to be the conduit for bringing prosperity and good into this world. However, because of the moon's arrogance, God decreed that it be diminished (see *Chullin* 60b). In our context, the moon's waning is symbolic of *Malkhut* being separated from its source. In the words of the *Zohar*: Ever since the moon stopped shining, there's not a day that is not cursed, in which there is no pain or suffering in the world. However, as Isaiah prophesied, in the Future "My slave will become wise"—in the World to Come, the moon will again shine as at Creation. In our context, *Malkhut* will unite with *Ein Sof* and so be filled with complete *daat*, so that all will bless "Who is good and beneficent" over everything.

Reb Noson explains that the moon/*Malkhut* is called a "slave" because, although it seeks to ascend to its source, it is restrained from doing so by its waning/blemish. As explained (§9), the devotion that God desires most from man is when man masters his *yeshut* (physical matter) and negates his material being in His service. But if instead man subjugates his material being to his vices and allows his wills to succumb to evil desires, then *Malkhut* (the wills) is blemished, prevented from ascending to its source. This is slavery. It is unable to ascend to *Ein Sof*, from where it would return with good and beneficence for all the life forms in God's creation (*Torat Natan* #14).

201. This means that with the help of the tzaddik.... By vanquishing the "slaves" and rectifying *Malkhut* it is possible to merit an awareness of the unity of *YHVH* and *Elohim*. Yet, actually achieving this is very difficult. It is not something that the average person manages to accomplish by himself. However, with the help of the tzaddik—by seeing him, giving him charity, and confessing in front of him—a person nullifies his vices and *Malkhut* is freed from the realm of impurity. And, by virtue of the tzaddik's deep humility, the tzaddik elevates *Malkhut* to its source, the Light of *Ein Sof*, and also brings the person who has repented to an awareness that *YHVH*/lovingkindness and *Elohim*/judgment are one—a foretaste of the World to Come (see *Mai HaNachal*).

The verse thus translates in our text as follows:
Anokhi YHVH Elohekha — *YHVH* and *Elohim* are one.

Other Side (the realm of evil) will be destroyed. The letter-combinations in its grasp will be extricated and rebuilt as *Malkhut* of Holiness.

Once this happens, each of us will automatically recognize the path that is right for him. And certainly, when the tzaddik is alive, it is he who informs us of the proper path. But now, with the tzaddik no longer physically present, we must believe that when we perform all these *tikkunim* in their entirety, God sends us the right thoughts concerning the course of action we should pursue. And we must believe that, presently, *this* itself is our proper path.

It is also evident that to find the proper path, we must engage in the study of the tzaddik's works. If we can discuss these ideas with others who are also interested in rectifying themselves, the benefit is even greater. There are times when what someone else has to add makes it that much easier for us to gain insight and awareness into our own quest. Also beneficial is the devotional practice known as *hitbodedut*. This is the secluded personal prayer that Rebbe Nachman always exhorted his followers to practice. We must pour out our hearts in prayer, asking God to guide us on the right path. (*Hitbodedut* is explained in greater detail in: *Outpouring of the Soul; Under the Table,* Chapter 6; and *Crossing the Narrow Bridge,* Chapter 9.)

In conclusion, we must understand that everything happens in accordance with our efforts and yearning. If we are sincere, we believe that these *tikkunim* are actually taking place even if we don't readily see much personal progress in our quest for repentance. We believe that whatever steps we take in the right direction go a very long way in elevating us closer to God. For God is always directing each and every individual in ways that will bring those who want to return, closer to Him. And, even if we see that others find success, whereas we seem to be lagging behind, we should not despair. As indicated at the end of Rebbe Nachman's lesson, one Jew's repentance has the power to benefit many others, even those for whom the holy service of God is presently the furthest thing from their minds. How much more so, then, will another Jew's success help those of us who *are* seeking to repent and return to Him. Unquestionably, if we remain steadfast in our efforts and yearning, we will merit total repentance and rectification of all our sins. We will also attain the awareness of God's oneness we so very much desire.

was at his death. However, also during his lifetime [Moshe] certainly stripped away all corporeality and attached himself to the Light of *Ein Sof*. But then, this stripping was in an aspect of 'the living creatures ran and returned' " (§9). From here we understand that the tzaddik who is the aspect of Moshe/*Ayin* would always be absorbed in the Light of *Ein Sof* were it not that corporeality necessitates his attachment be one of "running and returning." Therefore, when this tzaddik passes away and sheds his material being, his power is that much greater. He can then be totally and perpetually absorbed in *Ein Sof*. The souls of departed tzaddikim also return to visit their graves and we may assume this is especially true of that tzaddik who made a point of promising to intercede on the behalf of whoever prays at his *tzion*, namely Rebbe Nachman himself.

We can learn this from Yehudah's confession (§5). It was only recalled by Moshe several generations after it took place. This shows that the tzaddik's power to rectify blemished *Malkhut* is not governed by time (see above, n.46). Certainly, therefore, once a tzaddik has already been in the world, he has the power to elevate *Malkhut* even after his passing. For, then, he is perpetually ascending ever higher in *Ein Sof*. However, because the rectifications the tzaddik accomplishes are on a greater spiritual plane—further removed from human comprehension—than when he was physically alive, we have to be steadfast in our faith that these rectifications continue to take effect.

We see, then, that all the *tikkunim* can be achieved even today, but in a more refined, spiritual way. Therefore, we must be determined and dedicate ourselves to performing them. We should go to the tzaddik's gravesite and pour out our hearts before God, asking to be shown the straight and proper path that is in harmony with the roots of our souls. We should petition for the opportunity to serve God and to be forgiven for all our transgressions. Then, we will be able to confess from the inner depths of our hearts until the words emerge from our very bones. This is the meaning of "All my bones say"—i.e., the words come from the inner being and essence of the confessor, and the force of all his limbs and bones is actually thrown into the words. After this, we can be confident that the entire structure of *Malkhut* of the

ליקוטי מוהר״ן סימן ה׳

בַּחֲצוֹצְרוֹת וְקוֹל שׁוֹפָר הָרִיעוּ לִפְנֵי וְכוּ׳ (תהלים צ״ח)

א כִּי צָרִיךְ כָּל אָדָם לוֹמַר: כָּל הָעוֹלָם לֹא נִבְרָא אֶלָּא בִּשְׁבִילִי.
נִמְצָא כְּשֶׁהָעוֹלָם נִבְרָא בִּשְׁבִילִי, צָרִיךְ אֲנִי לִרְאוֹת וּלְעַיֵּן בְּכָל עֵת

series of social and educational reforms. The Cantonists kidnapped twelve-year-old (and even younger) Jewish boys, forced them to eat unkosher and baptized them, and then, at age eighteen, conscripted them into the Czar's army for a period of twenty-five years! In addition, conniving with the *Haskalah's* proponents, the Russian government succeeded in foisting secular education upon the Jewish youth and thus uprooting whole segments of Jewish society from their heritage (see *Through Fire and Water*, Chapter 32). It was to mitigate these decrees that Rebbe Nachman taught this Torah lesson, "*B'chatzotzrot* (With Trumpets)," which alludes to these reforms (*Tzaddik* #127; *Parparaot LeChokhmah*; *Siach Sarfei Kodesh* 508, 1-31).

Typical of well nigh all of Rebbe Nachman's teachings, this lesson relates to the general as well as the particular, the communal as well as the personal. Thus, aside from decrees, the topic with which the lesson opens, Rebbe Nachman also discusses the need for being free of undesirable thoughts that sour the mind like *chametz* (§4). While this is a clear reference to the *Haskalah's* efforts to instill alien philosophies and ideologies into Jewish minds and hearts, on the more individual level, it also pertains to being free to concentrate one's thoughts and feelings when praying. At the time, this was of particular importance to the Rebbe's newest follower, Reb Noson. He had long found it difficult to stay focused while praying and was looking to Rebbe Nachman for guidance on this matter.

Nor was focusing in prayer the only matter troubling Reb Noson that Rebbe Nachman addressed in his lesson. Reb Noson hailed from a family of *mitnagdim* (opponents to Chassidism). His father-in-law, Rabbi Dovid Zvi Orbach, though renowned for his piety and a well respected halakhic authority in the Podolia region, was a staunch *mitnaged*. It was therefore with no small degree of personal disquiet that Reb Noson decided to take up the chassidic way, which he did sometime in 1796, at the age of sixteen. Now, some six years later, he was still sensitive to the criticism raised against the path established by the Baal Shem Tov. Not only had the opposition to Chassidism from without not abated, but even worse, for Reb Noson, was what seemed to be the constant in-fighting among the various tzaddikim themselves. At that very time, Rebbe Nachman's move to Breslov had further fueled what proved to be a relentless and vicious campaign by the Shpola Zeida to discredit the Rebbe. Reb Noson was having trouble comprehending how such righteous individuals, whose entire lives were dedicated to serving God, could be involved in such contentiousness and conflict. Rebbe Nachman also addresses this in his lesson (§4), advising Reb Noson not to pay attention to the disputes between tzaddikim because they involved matters more lofty than most people are able to perceive.

2. **only for my sake.** The Talmud teaches that at Creation, everything—all the fish, birds, animals, etc.—was created male and female. The one exception to this was man, Adam. He

LIKUTEY MOHARAN #5[1]

"B'chatzotzrot (With trumpets) and the sound of the shofar shout out before God, the King."

(Psalms 98:6)

Now, each person must say: "The entire world was created only for my sake" (*Sanhedrin* 37a).[2] Consequently, because the world was created for my sake, I must constantly look into and consider

---

1. **Likutey Moharan #5.** Rebbe Nachman taught this lesson on Monday, Rosh HaShanah 5563 (September 27, 1802), shortly after he had taken up residence in the city of Breslov. On Sunday of the previous week (September 19), the man who was to become Rebbe Nachman's closest follower and scribe, Reb Noson, met the Rebbe for the very first time. The text of the lesson is *leshon Rabbeinu z'l* (see end of first note to Lesson #2 where this terminology has been explained). From the Rebbe's own testimony we know that within its sections are concealed the mystical intentions relating to tefillin (see *Likutey Moharan* I, 38:end, in note). Indeed, Reb Noson later composed his own discourse explaining the concepts of tefillin based on this lesson (see *Likutey Halakhot, Orach Chaim, Tefillin* 4). The main themes of the lesson are: mitigating decrees; performing the mitzvot with joy and the reward for the mitzvot; intense prayer; cleansing one's mind of undersirable thoughts; and strife between tzaddikim. Reb Noson once said that the inspiration and guidance he drew from this lesson, the first full discourse he heard from Rebbe Nachman, served him throughout his life.

At the time Rebbe Nachman gave the lesson, decrees were very much an issue in the Jewish communities under Czarist rule. Being considered were several new enactments by the Czar's "Committee for the Amelioration of the Jews." In time, these decrees would lead to enforced secular education, the Cantonist Edicts and ultimately to the establishment of the Pale of Jewish Settlement. In 1802, the Jewish leadership convened to seek ways to avert these disastrous decrees. Their efforts, however, met with much resistance, in particular because of the support the Russian government received from the burgeoning Jewish enlightenment movement known as the *Haskalah.*

Reb Nachman of Tcherin writes: I heard from my father (Reb Zvi Arych, son of Reb Aharon of Breslov) that Rebbe Nachman hinted at the time that the verdict had already been issued in Heaven. Even so, the Rebbe worked the entire year to somehow mitigate these decrees. (Several other of the Rebbe's lessons given in the year 5563 (1802-1803) also relate to the concept of mitigating decrees, e.g., *Likutey Moharan* I, #10, #49.) Some of the other chassidim remember the Rebbe commenting, "If all the tzaddikim joined me in this, I could overturn these decrees completely. As it is, I've pushed them off for some twenty-odd years." This turned out to be precisely what happened.

Through Rebbe Nachman's prayers these decrees were deferred. It was not until 1827, twenty-five years after the Rebbe had taught this lesson, that the Czarist government, under Czar Nikolai I (the "Iron Czar"), revived the matter and the authorities decided to enforce a

בְּתִקּוּן הָעוֹלָם. וּלְמַלְּאוֹת חֶסְרוֹן הָעוֹלָם, וּלְהִתְפַּלֵּל בַּעֲבוּרָם.

וְעִנְיַן הַתְּפִלָּה הֵן בִּשְׁנֵי פָנִים. הַיְנוּ קֹדֶם גְּזַר דִּין מִתְפַּלְלִין כְּסֵדֶר הַתְּפִלָּה, וְאֵין צָרִיךְ לְהַלְבִּישׁ הַתְּפִלָּה, אֲבָל לְאַחַר גְּזַר דִּין צָרִיךְ לְהַלְבִּישׁ הַתְּפִלָּה, כְּדֵי שֶׁלֹּא יָבִינוּ הַמַּלְאָכִים הָעוֹמְדִים לִשְׂמֹאל, וְלֹא יְקַטְרְגוּ. כְּמוֹ שֶׁכָּתוּב: "בִּגְזֵרַת עִירִין פִּתְגָמִין", הַיְנוּ לְאַחַר גְּזַר דִּין, אֲזַי "בְּמֵאמַר קַדִּישִׁין שְׁאֵלְתִּין", אֲזַי הַצַּדִּיקִים מַלְבִּישִׁים שְׁאֵלָתָם בְּמַאֲמָר:

to His left." Rashi asks: Is there [a right or] a left above? No, but there are those [angels] who incline to the right and those who incline to the left. Those to the right speak favorably, whereas those to the left find fault (loc. cit.). The angels on the left, the prosecuting angels, are created by man's sins. They criticize and fault a person's prayers, saying: "This person has sinned. He does not deserve to have his prayers answered!" When this happens, a person must camouflage and disguise his prayers in order to hide them from the prosecuting angels.

7. **decreed by the destroying angels.** That is to say, the verdict has been issued due to the prosecuting angels (*Metzudat David*). It is then made known to the destroying angels, the messengers who are appointed to mete out the punishment decreed by the Holy One (*Parparaot LeChokhmah*).

8. **maamar.** The word *maamar* has several usages. Literally, it connotes any sort of utterance. Thus, in the verse quoted from Daniel, it indicates a decree that is by the word of God. It can also refer to a spoken phrase, an oral discourse on a Torah subject, plain conversation, or even the telling of a story. These are all the different forms the tzaddikim use to disguise their prayers (see n.177).

In general, Rebbe Nachman's intention is for every person to exercise his power of prayer for the benefit of the world. Yet, when the Rebbe speaks about disguising the prayers, he is referring to the tzaddikim, those who know that they must camouflage their prayers in order for them to be effective. In the course of the lesson, once the Rebbe explains how one knows whether it is before or after the decree has been issued, it will become clear that only the very great tzaddikim can attain this knowledge in full. Still, there are many aspects of this teaching that apply to everyone, each in accordance with the spiritual level he has attained. And these aspects make it imperative that each person engage in praying for the world as best he can, and in every manner available. This is especially possible through the practice of *hitbodedut*, the personal, secluded prayer that Rebbe Nachman so strongly advocated (see *Outpouring of the Soul, passim; Crossing the Narrow Bridge*, Chapter 9; *Under the Table*, Chapter 6). Formulating one's *hitbodedut* prayers in one's native tongue, in accordance with the dictates of each new day, allows a person the freedom to pray in either a straightforward manner or in a veiled manner, depending upon what the particular situation calls for. In this way, the Rebbe's teaching applies to all people, and not just to the tzaddikim.

9. **in a maamar.** In review: Every person is responsible to make the world a better place. He can do this by praying for the world's benefit, as prayer has the power to mitigate decrees.

ways of making the world better; to provide what is missing in the world and pray on its behalf.[3]

{"The verdict is decreed by the destroying angels, and the request is through the *maamar* of the holy ones" (Daniel 4:14).}

And in the matter of prayer,[4] there are two approaches. Before the decree has been issued we follow the regular order of prayer and there is no need to veil the prayers.[5] But after the decree has been issued our prayers have to be disguised < within stories >, so that the < accusing angels > standing to the left do not understand and protest.[6] As is written, "The verdict is decreed by the destroying angels"[7] — i.e., when it is after the decree has been issued — then, "the request is through the *maamar*[8] of the holy ones" — then the tzaddikim disguise their requests in a *maamar*.[9]

was created alone, and from him God formed woman, Chavah. Why? Our Sages explain that this was to teach that each individual is considered an entire world in his/her own right. Each person can therefore say that the world was created only for him. In addition, this is to show that each person is born with the innate ability to choose between right and wrong; the extent to which we are influenced by inherited, predetermined qualities in no way denies us our free will (*Maharsha, loc. cit. s.v. l'phikhakh*). See next note.

3. **I must constantly look...on its behalf.** Rebbe Nachman adds a deeper dimension to "The entire world was created only for my sake." He says: If it is for *my* sake, then it is my *responsibility*. It is specifically up to me to see that the world becomes a better place. And, conversely, because the world is *my* responsibility, I must see to flee from all evil — whether in thought, word or deed. This is because all wrongdoing brings harm in its wake, harm that is up to me to prevent (*Mai HaNachal*; see also *Rashi, loc. cit., s.v. bishvili*).

4. **matter of prayer.** Rebbe Nachman will show that the main means by which a person can improve the world is prayer, when coupled with fear of God. Reb Noson writes that without the fear of God the world is incomplete, as we can understand from the converse (Psalms 34:10), "Those who fear Him lack nothing." This indicates that it is the fear of God that makes the world a better place to live (*Likutey Halakhot, Harshaah* 3:20).

5. **no need to veil the prayers.** God created the world with the intention that mankind would serve Him. Towards this end, God prepared man's needs and then gave him the channel of prayer by which man could ask for whatever he might need and thereby directly communicate with Him (see *Rashi,* Genesis 2:5). This was how it was meant to be as long as the channel stayed open. However, as mankind has discovered, sin and iniquity cause the prayer-channel to become clogged and obscured; such as occurred at the decree of the Flood (see below, §2), and again when the decree to destroy the Holy Temple was implemented. Concerning the latter Scripture states (Lamentations 3:8), "Though I would cry out and plead, He shut out my prayer." From this we learn that there is a difference between before and after the decree has been issued. Prior to the decree, the channels are open and one can pray in the usual manner.

6. **angels standing to the left...protest.** The prophet Mikhayhu said (I Kings 22:19), "I saw God seated on His throne, with all the host of heaven standing in attendance to His right and

ב. אֲבָל אֵיךְ יַדְעִינָן בֵּין קֹדֶם גְּזַר דִּין בֵּין לְאַחַר גְּזַר דִּין – עַל־יְדֵי הַמִּצְוֹת שֶׁאָנוּ עוֹשִׂים, יְכוֹלִין אֲנַחְנוּ לֵידַע בֵּין קֹדֶם גְּזַר דִּין לְאַחַר גְּזַר דִּין.

וְדַיְקָא כְּשֶׁעוֹשִׂין הַמִּצְוֹת בְּשִׂמְחָה גְּדוֹלָה כָּל כָּךְ, עַד שֶׁאֵין רוֹצֶה בְּשׁוּם שְׂכַר עוֹלָם הַבָּא, אֶלָּא הוּא רוֹצֶה שֶׁיַּזְמִין לוֹ הַקָּדוֹשׁ־בָּרוּךְ־ הוּא מִצְוָה אַחֶרֶת בִּשְׂכַר מִצְוָה זֹאת, כְּמַאֲמַר חֲכָמֵינוּ, זִכְרוֹנָם לִבְרָכָה: 'שְׂכַר מִצְוָה־מִצְוָה', כִּי הוּא נֶהֱנֶה מֵהַמִּצְוָה בְּעַצְמָהּ.

וְזֶהוּ הַחִלּוּק שֶׁבֵּין נְבוּאַת מֹשֶׁה רַבֵּנוּ לְבֵין נְבוּאַת שְׁאָר נְבִיאִים, כְּפֵרוּשׁ רַשִׁ"י: "וַיְדַבֵּר מֹשֶׁה אֶל רָאשֵׁי הַמַּטּוֹת וְכוּ' זֶה הַדָּבָר אֲשֶׁר צִוָּה ה'". פֵּרֵשׁ רַשִׁ"י: כָּל הַנְּבִיאִים נִתְנַבְּאוּ בְּ"כֹה אָמַר ה'", נוֹסַף עֲלֵיהֶם מֹשֶׁה, שֶׁהִתְנַבֵּא: בְּ"זֶה הַדָּבָר". כִּי בְּחִינַת "כֹּה" הוּא אַסְפַּקְלַרְיָא שֶׁאֵינָהּ מְאִירָה, וְ"זֶה הַדָּבָר" הוּא בְּחִינַת אַסְפַּקְלַרְיָא הַמְּאִירָה.

---

13. **Moshe...other prophets.** Rebbe Nachman gives Moshe as an example of someone who performed the mitzvot without seeking reward. In this he surpassed all the other prophets, just as he surpassed all the other prophets in prophetic ability. As we will see, the Sages associate prophecy with reward. In our context, this implies that just as prophecy enables one to foresee the future and discern impending decrees, so, too, the reward for performing mitzvot for their own sake is the ability to know whether it is before or after the decree has been issued. The Rebbe elaborates:

14. **Zeh hadavar....** This was said to the heads of the tribes regarding the laws of vows. See below, note 21.

15. **Koh...zeh...looking-glass.** Moshe was the greatest of all prophets, and the clarity of his revelations has never been equalled (*Yevamot* 49b). God Himself attests to this: "If someone among you experiences divine prophecy, then when I make Myself known to him in a vision, I will speak to him in a dream. This is not true of My servant Moshe...With him I speak face to face, in a vision not containing allegory, so that he sees a true picture of God" (Numbers 12:6-8). Rabbi Moshe Chaim Luzzatto writes: Yet even in Moshe's case, the Glory could only be revealed to the extent that he was able to accept it. Even he could not see the Glory directly, but only as an image formed in a mirror, since without this, no human being can have a perception of the Creator. The image that Moshe saw, however, was one that was complete and clear, just like an image seen through a highly polished and clear looking-glass, without a trace of dullness.... This was not true of any other prophet, since none could

2. But how do we know whether it is before the decree has been issued or after the decree has been issued? We can determine whether it is before the decree or after the decree by means of the mitzvot we perform.[10]

And this is specifically when a person performs the mitzvot with such great joy, that he has no desire for any reward in the World to Come.[11] Instead, his only desire is that the Holy One provide him with the opportunity to do another mitzvah as a reward for the first mitzvah. As in the saying of the Sages: The reward for a mitzvah is a mitzvah (*Avot* 4:2)—for he derives pleasure from the mitzvah itself.[12]

This is the difference between the prophecy of Moshe Rabbeinu and the prophecy of the other prophets.[13] It is similar to Rashi's commentary to, "Moshe spoke to the tribal heads of the Children of Israel, saying, '*Zeh hadavar* (This is the word) God has commanded'" (Numbers 30:2).[14] Rashi explains: All the prophets prophesied with "*Koh* (Thus) says God." Moshe achieved even more than they in that he prophesied with "*Zeh hadavar*." For *koh* corresponds to a dull looking-glass, whereas *zeh hadavar* corresponds to a clear looking-glass.[15]

However, when decrees are extant and man's prayers are obscured by his sins, he has to disguise his prayers in a *maamar*.

10. **But how...mitzvot we perform.** Having taught that prayer has the power to mitigate decrees but that it must take on a different form once the decree has been issued, Rebbe Nachman now shows how one can tell whether it is before or after the decree has been issued. This entails performing the mitzvot with joy, as the Rebbe next explains, and being sensitive to the constructs of World-Year-Soul, as he explains below.

11. **with such great joy....** The first element in discerning the state of the decree is performing the mitzvot with pure joy, solely for the sake of performing the mitzvot.

12. **The reward for a mitzvah....** The simple explanation of the Mishnah is that God rewards the performance of a mitzvah by providing the person with the means for performing yet another mitzvah and thereby merit even greater reward for his efforts (*Rabbeinu Yonah, loc. cit.*). Rebbe Nachman's interpretation is that the person doing the mitzvah has no desire for reward other than another mitzvah to do. For such a person, the reward is felt in the performance of the mitzvah itself. This is certainly a most exalted spiritual level; a state of awareness that is by no means common in the world. Reb Noson describes it as having reached the ultimate level of perfection (*Torat Natan* #2). Therefore, with this as a prerequisite for determining whether it is before or after the decree has been issued, it is understandable why most people are never capable of such discernment. Nevertheless, this is not to say that the common man has no role to play in mitigating heaven's decrees. On the contrary, the greater the level of joy a person reaches in performing the mitzvot, the greater the level of his prayers and their effectiveness, albeit indirectly, in mitigating a decree.

וְאֵלּוּ הַשְׁתֵּי בְּחִינוֹת נְבִיאוֹת יֵשׁ בַּעֲבוֹדַת הַבּוֹרֵא. יֵשׁ אָדָם הָעוֹשֶׂה
הַמִּצְוָה בִּשְׂכַר עוֹלָם הַבָּא, שֶׁאֵינוּ נֶהֱנֶה מֵהַמִּצְוָה בְּעַצְמָהּ, אֵלּוּ לֹא
הָיוּ נוֹתְנִין לוֹ עוֹלָם הַבָּא בִּשְׂכָרָהּ, לֹא הָיָה עוֹשֶׂה אוֹתָהּ, וְזֶה
בְּחִינַת "כֹּה", אַסְפַּקְלַרְיָא שֶׁאֵינָהּ מְאִירָה. כְּמוֹ אָדָם שֶׁרוֹאֶה אֵיזֶה
דָבָר מֵרָחוֹק, כֵּן הוּא עוֹשֶׂה הַמִּצְוָה בִּשְׁבִיל שָׂכָר הַבָּא לְעֵת
רָחוֹק, הַיְנוּ אַחַר עוֹלָם הַזֶּה.

וְשָׁלוֹם שָׂכָר נִקְרָא בְּשֵׁם נָבִיא, כִּי רָאשֵׁי תֵּבוֹת שֶׁל: יָבֹא בְרִנָּה
נֹשֵׂא אֲלֻמֹּתָיו, [ר"ת נביא],

וְשָׁם בַּפָּסוּק הַזֶּה נִרְמַז עַל שְׁלוֹם שָׂכָר: "הָלוֹךְ יֵלֵךְ וּבָכֹה נֹשֵׂא
מֶשֶׁךְ הַזָּרַע", שֶׁמִּצְטַעֵר בַּעֲשִׂיָּתָהּ, "בֹּא יָבֹא בְרִנָּה נֹשֵׂא אֲלֻמֹּתָיו",

mitzvah, especially when we do it with great joy, we draw from the clarity of vision that
Moshe had. Each of us, commensurate with the spiritual level we've achieved, is then
included in Moshe's *zeh*.

17. **no enjoyment...would not do it.** It is not the most virtuous of intentions to serve God only
for the ultimate reward. Still, the person who does so *is* considered one who serves God. It is
also a fact that the mitzvot provide tremendous reward for those who fulfill them. Then
again, the mitzvot are Divine proclamations, and in recognition of this the Jews have
historically fulfilled His Will even in the most trying times. That being so, why does Rebbe
Nachman say, "If he were not given the World to Come as a reward, he would *not* do it?" It
must therefore be that the Rebbe is in fact referring to someone whose primary enjoyment
when performing the mitzvot stems from the ultimate reward that he knows awaits him. In
his case, "If he were not given the World to Come...he would not do it" means that he
would not do it with any joy and satisfaction in his heart but solely out of obligation
(*Parparaot LeChokhmah*).

   The *Parparaot LeChokhmah* also offers another explanation for "If he were not given the
World to Come as a reward...." He writes: Certain mitzvot are conditional. For example,
tzitzit are required only on one's four-cornered garments. A person who has no four-cornered
garment is exempt from the mitzvah. If, despite this, he acquires a four-cornered garment so
that he might don tzitzit—i.e., for the sake of the mitzvah itself—his act is indeed a most
worthy one. But if his motivation in acquiring the four-cornered garment and affixing the
tzitzit is so that he will be rewarded in the World to Come, then it as though he were looking
through a dull looking-glass: he looks into the distance, lacking clarity of vision.

18. **Yavo Verina Nosay Alumotav...NAVY.** Aside from the direct connection that the verse
has with reward (see next note), in the context of the lesson the letters also hint to reward, or
more specifically to prophecy, which Rebbe Nachman has just connected to reward. As the
Rebbe points out, the Hebrew term for prophet *navy* (נביא) forms an acrostic for the phrase
yavo verina nosay alumotav (יבא ברנה נשא אלמותיו).

These two aspects of prophecy are also found in our service of the Creator.[16] There is the person who does the mitzvah for the reward of the World to Come—he has no enjoyment from the mitzvah itself. If he were not given the World to Come as a reward, he would not do it.[17] This corresponds to *koh,* a dull looking-glass. Just like the person who sees something from a distance, so, too, he performs the mitzvah for the reward it will bring at a distant time, after this world.

{**"He who goes weeping on his way carrying a seed-bag,** *yavo verina nosay alumotav* (**will come back with songs of joy, carrying his sheaves)"** (Psalms 126:6).}

And the payment of reward is called *navy* (prophet). This is because the first letters of "*Yavo Verina Nosay Alumotav*" < spell *NAVY* >.[18]

The payment of reward is also alluded to in the verse itself. < As Rashi explains: > "He who goes weeping on his way carrying a seed-bag"—he is pained by the [mitzvah's] performance. "He will come

attain even such a vision adequately (*The Way of God* 3:5:5, translated by Aryeh Kaplan, Feldheim Publishers).

Rashi points out that the difference in the quality of prophecy between Moshe and the other prophets is indicated by their choice of words. Moshe introduces his vision by using the word *zeh,* which indicates precision: "precisely *this.*" The clarity of his vision can be likened to looking into a highly polished and clear looking-glass. Other prophets introduce their visions by using the word *koh,* which indicates impreciseness: "approximately *thus.*" The lack of clarity of their visions can be likened to looking into a dull and blurred looking-glass. The other prophets all prophesied with *koh* because their visions lacked Moshe's clarity (see *Rashi* on Numbers 30:2, and *Siftei Chakhamin, ad.loc.*)

The *Parparaot LeChokhmah* adds: We can now better appreciate Moshe's desire enter the Holy Land. Not only did he want to enter the Land, a mitzvah unto itself, but he also very much wanted to be able to perform those mitzvot that are only applicable in the Land of Israel. Thus, the reward for the mitzvah of entering the Land would have been the ability to perform more mitzvot.

16. **service of the Creator.** Reb Noson explains that ideally each person must strive to unite the two aspects of *koh* and *zeh.* He should attach himself, his *koh,* to the true tzaddikim, who have attained the level of *zeh.* This is what the prophets themselves did. It was forbidden for them to derive new laws based on their prophetic visions (*Shabbat* 104a). Rather, they all sought to strengthen the observance of the Torah as Moshe taught it, as in (Malachi 3:22), "Remember the Torah of Moshe." This united the prophets/*koh* with Moshe/*zeh,* the two aspects becoming one. Now, in every generation there are great tzaddikim whose perception of Godliness is on the level of *zeh* (see *Sukkah* 45b). Everyone else must attach themselves to these tzaddikim. By doing so, evil is subdued, decrees are mitigated, and whatever was lacking is lacking no more. Everyone then serves God with true joy (*Torat Natan #3*). The *Parparaot LeChokhmah* adds: Moshe has a portion in every mitzvah that a Jew performs (because through him the Jews received the commandments). Inversely, when doing a

שֶׁיִּשְׂמַח לֶעָתִיד, כְּשֶׁיְקַבֵּל שְׂכַר הַמִּצְוֹת. רָאשֵׁי תֵבוֹת שֶׁל יָבֹא
בְּרִנָּה נֹשֵׂא אֲלֻמּוֹתָיו, רָאשֵׁי־תֵבוֹת נָבִיא.

אֲבָל נָבִיא שֶׁמִּתְנַבֵּא בְּ"זֶה הַדָּבָר", שֶׁאֵינוֹ רוֹצֶה בִּשְׂכַר הַמִּצְוֹת,
אֶלָּא רוֹצֶה בַּמִּצְוָה בְּעַצְמָהּ, שֶׁהוּא מְשַׂמֵּחַ כָּל כָּךְ בַּעֲשִׂיָּתָהּ, עַד
שֶׁמְּמָאֵס בְּכָל מִין שָׂכָר, נִמְצָא שֶׁעוֹלָם הַבָּא שֶׁלּוֹ בְּהַמִּצְוָה
בְּעַצְמָהּ.

וְזֶה בְּחִינַת נָבִיא, הַיְנוּ שְׁלוֹם שָׂכָר, בִּבְחִינַת: "זֶה הַדָּבָר", בִּבְחִינַת
אַסְפַּקְלַרְיָא הַמְּאִירָה, כְּמוֹ אָדָם הָרוֹאֶה דָבָר מִקָּרוֹב בִּרְאִיָּה יָפָה
וּבָרָה, כְּמוֹ כֵן הוּא נֶהֱנֶה מֵהַמִּצְוָה בְּעַצְמָהּ, וּשְׂכָרוֹ נֶגֶד עֵינָיו.

וּמִי שֶׁהוּא בַּמַּדְרֵגָה הַזֹּאת, שֶׁעוֹשֶׂה הַמִּצְוָה בְּשִׂמְחָה גְדוֹלָה כָּל
כָּךְ, עַד שֶׁאֵין רוֹצֶה בְּשׁוּם שְׂכַר עוֹלָם הַבָּא בִּשְׁבִילָהּ, הוּא יָכוֹל
לֵידַע בֵּין קֹדֶם גְּזַר דִּין לְאַחַר גְּזַר דִּין.
כִּי הַמִּצְוֹת הֵם קוֹמָה שְׁלֵמָה, וְהֵם מְחַיִּין אֶת כָּל הַקּוֹמוֹת, הֵן

20. **But the prophet.** Based on what he has said, Rebbe Nachman here uses the term "prophet" to refer to anyone who performs mitzvot. There are those who prophesy with the indeterminate and anticipatory *koh*—i.e., they perform mitzvot for future reward in the World to Come. And, there are those who prophesy with the precise and immediate *zeh*—i.e., they perform mitzvot without any thought of future reward. This, as mentioned, was the level of Moshe's service of God.

21. **reward is right before his eyes.** We can now appreciate why Rashi's explanation of *zeh* and *koh* appears specifically in connection with the verses in Numbers that deal with vows (see nn.14-15). When a person takes a vow, he, for reasons of his own, voluntarily obligates himself to do something that he is not required to do. Nonetheless, the Torah stipulates reward for the person who fulfills his self-imposed obligation. Based on Rebbe Nachman's insights, we can say that even in the case of vows Moshe advises the Jewish tribal leaders to volunteer only for the aspect of *zeh*, without any interest in future reward (*Parparaot LeChokhmah*).

22. **And it is the person who is on this level. . . .** This is the second element in knowing whether it is before or after the decree has been issued (see n. 10).

23. **mitzvot form a complete construct.** There are 248 positive commandments, corresponding to the 248 limbs of the human body. And there are 365 prohibitive commandments, corresponding to the 365 veins and sinews of the body (*Mai HaNachal*). It is therefore said of the mitzvot that they form a complete body, or construct.

back with songs of joy, carrying his sheaves"—he will rejoice in the Future, when he will receive reward for the mitzvot.[19]

But the prophet[20] who prophesies with *zeh hadavar* does not desire the reward of the mitzvot. Rather, he desires the mitzvah itself. He rejoices so much in its performance that he rejects any kind of reward. We see, then, that his World to Come is in the mitzvah itself.

This is therefore the concept of *NAVY*—i.e., the payment of reward—corresponding to *zeh hadavar,* a clear looking-glass. Just like the person who sees something from up close, with a splendidly clear view, so, too, he enjoys the mitzvah itself and his reward is right before his eyes.[21]

And it is the person who is on this level—who performs the mitzvah with such great joy that he has no desire for any reward of the World to Come in return—who is able to differentiate between before the decree has been issued and after the decree has been issued.[22]

This is because the mitzvot form a complete construct.[23] And they

---

19. **The payment... for the mitzvot.** Often time the opportunity to do a mitzvah comes with some difficulty or hardship. This is the implied meaning of "He who goes weeping...." But Scripture assures that this person "will come back with songs of joy, carrying his sheaves." Moreover, his reward will be in proportion to the effort expended and the suffering endured, so that his joy will be that much greater (cf. *Metzudat David*).

The question is, how is it that people are able to rejoice in the moment, in this world, when at the very same time they are suffering from the difficulties (physical, psychological and/or monetary) they encounter in the performance of the mitzvot? For we see that Jews are indeed happy to merit performing God's commandments even when they see no tangible reward for their efforts. Where does this joy come from? However, to quote the Talmud, if the Jews are not prophets, they are certainly the descendants of prophets (*Pesachim* 66a). As the Sages taught: Even though a person might not see, his guardian angel sees (*Megillah* 3a). The soul of each Jew is acutely aware of the wonderfully sweet portion reserved for the person who succeeds in doing a mitzvah. This is, "*Yavo Verina Nosay Alumotav*"—*NAVY*. In the sense that he is a "prophet," each Jew is able to perceive the spark and illumination of the future reward for the mitzvot.

Today, this type of perception is the one aspect of prophecy we have left. But even in this respect there are two levels. Some people's joy is only that their soul senses the great reward it will receive in the World to Come. This corresponds to the dull looking-glass. Others, however, succeed in rejoicing in the mitzvah itself. This corresponds to the clear looking-glass, a prophetic vision in the aspect of *zeh*. And although in its fullest such awareness is certainly beyond human comprehension in this world, it does presently exist in the form of a holy spark; a spark incomprehensibly derived from genuine prophecy (*Parparaot LeChokhmah*).

קוֹמַת אָדָם, הֵן קוֹמַת עוֹלָם, הֵן קוֹמַת שָׁנָה, כִּי עוֹלָם שָׁנָה נֶפֶשׁ,
הֵן מְקַבְּלִין הַחִיּוּת מֵהַמִּצְוֹת, כְּמוֹ שֶׁכָּתוּב: "וְכָל מַעֲשֵׂהוּ
בֶּאֱמוּנָה", וּכְתִיב: "כָּל מִצְוֹתֶיךָ אֱמוּנָה". וְהַקָּדוֹשׁ־בָּרוּךְ־הוּא הוּא
אַחְדוּת פָּשׁוּט עִם הַמִּצְוֹת.

וּכְשֶׁמְּעַשֶּׂה הַקָּדוֹשׁ־בָּרוּךְ־הוּא כְּתִקּוּנָן וּכְסִדְרָן, אֲזַי הַקָּדוֹשׁ־בָּרוּךְ־
הוּא מְשַׂמֵּחַ בָּהֶם וּמִתְעַנֵּג בָּהֶם, כְּמוֹ שֶׁכָּתוּב: "יִשְׂמַח ה'
בְּמַעֲשָׂיו". כְּמוֹ בַּעַל־מְלָאכָה, שֶׁעוֹשֶׂה אֵיזֶה כְּלִי, וְהַכְּלִי הוּא יָפֶה,
אֲזַי הוּא מִתְעַנֵּג בָּה, וְהַשִּׂמְחָה שֶׁל הַקָּדוֹשׁ־בָּרוּךְ־הוּא הִיא
מְלֻבֶּשֶׁת בְּהַמִּצְוֹת, כִּי הֵם אַחְדוּתוֹ.

וּמִי שֶׁעוֹשֶׂה הַמִּצְוָה בְּשִׂמְחָה מֵהַמִּצְוָה בְּעַצְמָהּ, נִמְצָא כְּשֶׁנִּכְנָס

same applies to the commandments of the Torah, the mitzvot, which are the spiritual expressions of God's will. This is the reason the Holy One is said to be in simple unity with the mitzvot (*Rabbi Yaakov Meir Shechter*).

The *Mai HaNachal* adds: The Talmud mentions several different methods by which the letters of the Hebrew alphabet can be interchanged. One such method calls for exchanging the first letter, *aleph*, with the last letter, *tav*, and the second letter, *bet*, with the penultimate letter, *shin*, and so on (see *Shabbat* 104a). Using this alphabet, the first two letters of the word *mitzvah* (מצוה), the *mem* and the *tzadi*, become a *yod* and a *heh*, respectively. These are the first two letters of God's holy name, *YHVH* (יהוה). And, since the last two letters of *MitZVaH* and *YHVH* are the same, we can say that they are one.

The *Biur HaLikutim* provides a deeper insight into what it means to experience one's World to Come in the mitzvah itself. The ultimate reward, the reward of the World to Come, is man being given a greater awareness of God so that he might draw closer to Him (see *Likutey Moharan* I, 21). Now, because God and His mitzvot are one, when a person performs the mitzvot with complete joy, he can, even in this world, get a glimpse of this awareness. He is therefore able to enjoy a taste of the joy and reward of the World to Come. As will be explained, in the terminology of the Kabbalah this is known as ascending to the *sefirah* of *Binah*, which corresponds to the World to Come (*Etz Chaim* 15:5, see *Likutey Moharan* 15:5, n.46). When a person performs the mitzvot with great joy, he ascends spiritually to the level of *Binah* (see below, n.167).

28. **proper order.** That is, when people perform mitzvot and keep from committing sins.

29. **God rejoices in His works.** The verse begins, "Let the honor of God be forever." When man performs the mitzvot and keeps away from sin, he honors God. Then, "God rejoices in His works."

30. **...mitzvot...are His unity.** That is, God's joy is felt through the mitzvot, which bring vitality to all parts of the creation.

give life to all other constructs; whether it be the construct of Man, or the construct of World, or the construct of Year.[24] For World-Year-Soul[25] receive vitality from the mitzvot, as in (Psalms 33:4), "All His work is done with faith," and also (*ibid.* 119:86), "All Your mitzvot are faith."[26] Thus, the Holy One is in simple unity with the mitzvot.[27]

Therefore, when the Holy One's works are as they should be and in proper order,[28] the Holy One is happy with them and delights in them, as is written (Psalms 104:31), "God rejoices in His works."[29] Like a craftsman who makes some vessel. If the vessel is beautiful, then he delights in it. And the joy of the Holy One is clothed in the mitzvot, because they are His unity.[30]

Now, when the person who performs the mitzvah with a joy derived from the mitzvah itself enters into the joy of the mitzvah, he

---

24. **give life to all other constructs....** Through the mitzvot spiritual vitality is drawn into all the 248 limbs and 365 sinews and veins that make up the construct of the human body. From the teachings of the Kabbalah we know that the World too is a construct, made up of a head, a heart, and all the other limbs (cf. *Kohelet Rabbah* 1:9; *Sefer Yetzirah* 3:4, 4:5-11, 5:2). Similarly, the Year is a construct, with a head, a heart, etc. (e.g., Rosh HaShanah is the "head" of the year, and the Three Festivals are its "heart"; *Likutey Moharan* I, 30:5). All three of these constructs receive their vitality from the joyous performance of the mitzvot (*Mai HaNachal*). See following two notes.

The *Parparaot LeChokhmah* points out that the letters of the name *Moshe Rabbeinu* (משה רבינו, Moshe our teacher) have a numerical value of 613, equivalent to the total number of mitzvot in the Torah (*Megaleh Amukot*, Section 113). This alludes to the fact that Moshe himself corresponds to the entire construct of the mitzvot. His prophetic level was therefore *zeh*—clarity, and joy in the mitzvot. Reb Noson adds that this is why the tzaddik who performs the mitzvot with great joy—thus becoming an aspect of Moshe—has the ability to bring the entire world to serve God. Through him all the constructs are rectified and all that is lacking in the world is made whole (*Torat Natan* #1).

25. **World-Year-Soul.** In Hebrew, *Olam-Shanah-Nefesh*. Every being—*nefesh*—exists at a particular time—*shanah*—in a particular place—*olam*. In this way the concept of World-Year-Soul encompasses all of creation.

26. **work...mitzvot...faith.** God's creation, which is "all His work," is established with faith, which is synonymous with the mitzvot, as in, "All Your mitzvot are faith." The mitzvot, as a complete construct, correspond to all the different constructs—i.e., they are the vehicle through which God provides spiritual vitality to all His creations.

27. **in simple unity with the mitzvot.** All the many elements and objects that make up the creation can be broken into smaller components. This, however, cannot be said of the Creator, Whose unity is absolute. One ramification of this is that, unlike man, God and His will are one: neither duality nor change are features of His will (cf. Lesson #4, n.146). It is therefore impossible to separate the will of God or His thoughts from God Himself. The

בְּהַשִּׂמְחָה שֶׁבַּמִּצְוָה, הוּא נִכְנָס בְּשִׂמְחַת הַקָּדוֹשׁ־בָּרוּךְ־הוּא, שֶׁמְּשַׂמֵּחַ בְּמַעֲשָׂיו, וְזֶה בְּחִינַת: "יִשְׂמַח יִשְׂרָאֵל בְּעוֹשָׂיו".

נִמְצָא כְּשֶׁיֵּשׁ אֵיזֶה צַעַר וְדִין בְּעוֹלָם שָׁנָה נֶפֶשׁ, אֲזַי בְּוַדַּאי נִגְרַע מִשִּׂמְחַת הַקָּדוֹשׁ־בָּרוּךְ־הוּא, כְּמוֹ שֶׁכָּתוּב: "וַיִּתְעַצֵּב אֶל לִבּוֹ", וּכְמוֹ שֶׁכָּתוּב: 'שְׁכִינָה מָה אוֹמֶרֶת – קַלַּנִי מֵרֹאשִׁי' וְכוּ'. וְזֶה שֶׁנִּכְנָס בְּתוֹךְ הַשִּׂמְחָה. יָכוֹל בְּוַדַּאי לֵידַע לְפִי עִנְיַן הַשִּׂמְחָה אִם הוּא קֹדֶם גְּזַר דִּין, אִם הוּא לְאַחַר גְּזַר דִּין. גַּם יָכוֹל לֵידַע עַל אֵיזֶהוּ חֵלֶק מֵהַקּוֹמָה נִגְזַר הַדִּין, כִּי יוֹדֵעַ לְפִי קוֹמַת הַמִּצְוֹת. אִם אֵין יָכוֹל לַעֲשׂוֹת בְּשִׂמְחָה רָאשֵׁי הַמִּצְוֹת, הַיְנוּ מִצְוֹת הַתְּלוּיִים בָּרֹאשׁ, יֵדַע שֶׁהַדִּין נִגְזַר עַל רָאשֵׁי עוֹלָם שָׁנָה נֶפֶשׁ, וְכֵן בִּשְׁאָר קוֹמַת הַמִּצְוֹת.

connected to God and to His joy clothed in the mitzvot. Therefore, if he is able to perform the mitzvah with joy, he knows that the decree has not been issued. But once the decree has been issued, the joy of the Holy One, which is clothed in the mitzvot, is lessened, and so it will be impossible for him to perform the mitzvah with complete joy. This is how it is possible for a person to know for certain whether it is already after the decree has been issued (*Mai HaNachal*).

The *Mai HaNachal* adds: By including the phrase "the state of the joy," Rebbe Nachman seems to be implying that it is also possible to determine the severity of the judgment once it has been decreed. Thus, if a person sees that he can perform a certain mitzvah joyously, but his joy is incomplete, he can conclude that although the decree has been issued, it is not a particularly harsh one. If, on the other hand, he encounters tremendous difficulty in performing the mitzvah joyously, to the extent that he feels little or no joy at all, he can safely assume the decree is a harsh one. In this way, the performance of each mitzvah serves as a barometer for measuring the extent to which the world has been beset by decrees.

35. **World-Year-Soul...mitzvot.** It is also possible to determine the specific part of the construct against which the decree has been pronounced. In general, World-Year-Soul receive their spiritual energy from the mitzvot. Specifically, the heads of the different constructs receive vitality from those mitzvot that relate to the head, the arms from those mitzvot that relate to the arm, and so on. So, for example, putting tefillin on the arm and head provide spiritual vitality not only for the corresponding parts of that person's Soul construct, but also for the corresponding parts in the constructs of World and Year. And this is equally true for all the other limbs, because the construct of mitzvot and the constructs of World-Year-Soul are aligned and spiritually connected (see *Tikkuney Zohar* #70, p.131a; *Sefer Charedim,* by Rabbi Elazar Azikri, explains how all the mitzvot are applicable today and how they correspond to the various parts of the body: e.g., listening to the blowing of the

enters into the joy of the Holy One, who rejoices in His works. This corresponds to "Israel rejoices in its Maker" (Psalms 149:2).[31]

We find, therefore, that if there is any misfortune or harsh decree affecting World-Year-Soul, then certainly the joy of the Holy One is lessened, as in (Genesis 6:6), "He grieved in His heart."[32] As < the Sages taught: When a person sins, > what does the *Shekhinah* say? "My head is heavy! My arms are heavy!" (*Sanhedrin* 46a).[33]

Thus, this person who has entered into the joy [of the mitzvah] will certainly know, by the state of the joy, whether it is before the decree has been issued or after the decree has been issued.[34] He can also discern the part of the structure against which the judgment has been decreed. He knows this based on the structure of the mitzvot. If he cannot joyfully perform the "head" of the mitzvot—i.e., those mitzvot that relate to the head—he will know that a judgment has been decreed against the "heads" of World-Year-Soul. And it is likewise for the rest of the structure of the mitzvot.[35]

---

31. **enters into the joy of the mitzvah....** His joy is found in that mitzvah itself. In this sense, he becomes united with the mitzvah—i.e., with God Himself. Reb Noson adds that the tzaddikim, by performing the mitzvot with great joy, elevate the entire structure of the world so that it becomes united with God (*Torat Natan #5*). This is how God, the mitzvot, and the entire world become a single unity.

32. **He grieved in His heart.** This verse refers to God's decision to destroy the world by flood in the time of Noach. In contrast to the joy of the mitzvot, which sustains the constructs, the sadness brought about by mankind's sins led to the near total destruction of all the world's constructs.

33. **My head...arms are heavy.** The Talmud teaches that when a death sentence is carried out against an evildoer, God's Divine Presence suffers along with the sinner, even though he brought the suffering upon himself. This shows that when suffering and misfortune—i.e., decrees—beset the world, God's joy is incomplete. And this lack of joy is felt in all His works, the constructs of World-Year-Soul.

Rebbe Nachman has brought two proof-texts, one indicating that God's anguish is in His heart, the other that it is in His head and arms. This adds support for the Rebbe's next statement, that from the different parts of the mitzvah construct which are lacking joy—be it head, heart, arm, etc.—one can tell which parts of the World-Year-Soul constructs have been affected by a decree.

The *Biur HaLikutim* adds: As mentioned, Rebbe Nachman included this lesson among those in which he alluded to the mystical intentions of tefillin (see n.1). An obvious example is this proof-text the Rebbe brings concerning the head and the arm, which clearly connects to the head tefillin and the arm tefillin. Then, too, the arm tefillin are placed next to the heart, which is the subject of his earlier proof. See *Likutey Halakhot, Tefillin*, 4, on how this lesson contains the intentions of tefillin.

34. **certainly know by the state of the joy....** The person who performs a mitzvah is

וְזֶהוּ שֶׁאָמְרוּ רַבּוֹתֵינוּ, זִכְרוֹנָם לִבְרָכָה: 'בְּשַׁבָּת – זָכְרֵהוּ מֵאֶחָד בְּשַׁבָּת', הַיְנוּ שִׂמְחַת וְתַעֲנוּג עוֹלָם הַבָּא, שֶׁהוּא בְּחִינַת שַׁבָּת, יַרְגִּישׁ בְּשֵׁשֶׁת יְמֵי הַמַּעֲשֶׂה, שֶׁהֵן בְּחִינַת מַעֲשֵׂה הַמִּצְוֹות, שֶׁבָּהֶם נִבְרְאוּ עוֹלָם שָׁנָה נֶפֶשׁ.

[וְזֶהוּ]: "בְּיוֹמוֹ תִתֵּן שְׂכָרוֹ", שֶׁיְּהֵא שְׂכָרוֹ מֵהַמִּצְוֹות בְּעַצְמָן, "וְלֹא תָבוֹא עָלָיו הַשֶּׁמֶשׁ", שֶׁלֹּא יַעֲשֶׂה הַמִּצְוֹות בִּשְׂכַר עוֹלָם הַבָּא, שֶׁהִיא אַחַר בִּיאַת שִׁמְשׁוֹ אַחַר מוֹתוֹ:

ג. וְעִקַּר הַשִּׂמְחָה הוּא בַּלֵּב, כְּמוֹ שֶׁכָּתוּב: "נָתַתָּה שִׂמְחָה בְלִבִּי". וְאִי אֶפְשָׁר לַלֵּב לִשְׂמֹחַ, אֶלָּא עַד שֶׁיָּסִיר עַקְמוּמִיּוֹת שֶׁבְּלִבּוֹ, שֶׁיְּהֵא לוֹ יַשְׁרוּת לֵב, וְאָז יִזְכֶּה לְשִׂמְחָה, כְּמוֹ שֶׁכָּתוּב: "וּלְיִשְׁרֵי לֵב שִׂמְחָה".

Rashi, loc. cit.). From the Ari we learn that the first letters of *B'yomo Titain Secharo* ("You must pay him his wages on the same day," ביומו תתן שכרו) spell *ShaBbaT* (שבת) (*Shaar HaPesukim*, p.198). See next note.

40. **sun sets...death.** Rebbe Nachman explains the connection between Shabbat and paying wages in the context of our lesson: A person should seek his wages/reward/Shabbat for performing the mitzvot "on the same day"—i.e., from the mitzvot themselves—rather than waiting until after "the sun sets," after his passing—i.e., in the World to Come.

In review: Every person is responsible to make the world a better place. He can do this by praying for the world's benefit, as prayer has the power to mitigate decrees. However, when decrees are extant and man's prayers are obscured by his sins, he has to disguise his prayers in a *maamar* (§1). To know whether it is before or after the decree one must perform the mitzvot with joy—with no expectation of future reward, but feeling reward in the performance itself. Then, the degree to which he succeeds in feeling joy is indicative of whether God, Whose own joy is clothed in the mitzvot, is joyous or the decree has already been issued (§2).

41. **joy in my heart.** Having taught that joy is the key for discerning the state of the decree, Rebbe Nachman now teaches how to attain it.

42. **crookedness in his heart.** Crookedness of the heart refers to the perversity and bad character traits that possess a person's heart. As in King David's prayer (Psalms 101:4), "A perverse heart will depart from me; I will know no evil" (*Mai HaNachal*). The Rebbe will shortly explain how one can make straight the heart's crookedness.

43. **straight of heart.** Because of his heart's uprightness, he will be able to perform the mitzvot with a joy derived from the mitzvah itself. This is the level of the clear looking-glass, mentioned above (*Mai HaNachal*). Reb Noson adds that this is the main vitality and joy of the heart: its uprightness (*Torat Natan #6*).

This is the meaning of what the Sages said concerning Shabbat: Remember it from the first day of the week *(Mekhilta, Yitro 7; Beitza 16a)*.[36] The joy and pleasure of the World to Come, which is an aspect of Shabbat,[37] should be experienced during the six days of work. [These six weekdays] correspond to the performance of the mitzvot, because World-Year-Soul were created on them.[38]

{**"You must pay him his wages on the same day, before the sun sets"** (Deuteronomy 24:15).}

This is, "You must pay him his wages on the same day"[39] — the person's reward will come from the mitzvot themselves. "Before the sun sets" — because he does not perform the mitzvot for the reward of the World to Come, which is after his "sun sets," after his death.[40]

3. Now, the essence of joy is found in the heart, as is written *(Psalms 4:8)*, "You have put joy in my heart."[41] But it is impossible for the heart to rejoice unless a person removes the crookedness in his heart,[42] so that he might have a straight heart. Then he will merit < true > joy, as is written *(ibid. 97:11)*, "and joy for the straight of heart."[43]

shofar, to the ear; walking to synagogue, to the feet; giving charity, to the hands; praying and studying Torah, to the mouth; etc.; see *Anatomy of the Soul*). Therefore, when one cannot joyously perform the mitzvot that relate to the head, he knows a decree has been issued against the heads of World-Year-Soul, and likewise for the remaining parts of each of the different constructs (*Mai HaNachal*).

36. **Remember it....** Our Sages teach that as soon as one Shabbat ends, we are to start thinking about the next one and begin preparing for it. Though we have the whole week ahead of us, our longing for Shabbat should be such that we are always mindful of Shabbat, even during the weekdays. The Rebbe now shows how this ties in with our lesson.

37. **an aspect of Shabbat.** The Talmud states: Shabbat is one-sixtieth of the World to Come (*Berakhot* 57b). The joy of Shabbat is a taste, an experience in this world, of the joy and reward of the World to Come.

38. **were created on them.** World-Year-Soul, that is, everything, was created during the Six Days of Creation. As explained earlier (nn.24-26), these constructs correspond to the construct of the mitzvot. By performing the mitzvot with joy—joy in the mitzvot themselves—a person draws his ultimate reward/Shabbat into the Six Days of Creation— i.e., into all the aspects of this world. Through this he can know whether it is before or after the decree (*Mai HaNachal*).

39. **his wages on the same day.** In its plain meaning, this verse prohibits employers from delaying payment to their workers. If the arrangement between them calls for the employee to be paid for each day's labor by the end of that day, the employer may not put it off (see

וְעַקְמוּמִיּוּת שֶׁבַּלֵּב מַפְשִׁיטִין עַל־יְדֵי רְעָמִים, כְּמוֹ שֶׁאָמְרוּ חֲכָמֵינוּ,
זִכְרוֹנָם לִבְרָכָה: 'לֹא נִבְרְאוּ רְעָמִים אֶלָּא לְפַשֵּׁט עַקְמִימִיּוּת
שֶׁבַּלֵּב', וּרְעָמִים הוּא בְּחִינַת קוֹל שֶׁאָדָם מוֹצִיא בְּכֹחַ בִּתְפִלָּתוֹ,
וּמִזֶּה נַעֲשֶׂה רְעָמִים.

כִּי אִיתָא בַּזֹּהַר, 'כַּד קָלָא נָפִיק וְאַעֲרַא בְּעָבֵי מַטְרָא אִשְׁתַּמַּע קָלָא
לִבְרִיָּתָא וְדָא אִינּוּן רְעָמִים', וְעִקַּר הָרְעָמִים הֵם מִגְּבוּרוֹת, כְּמוֹ
שֶׁכָּתוּב: "וְרַעַם גְּבוּרוֹתָיו מִי יִתְבּוֹנָן".

וּבִשְׁבִיל זֶה אָנוּ מְבָרְכִין: שֶׁכֹּחוֹ וּגְבוּרָתוֹ וְכוּ'. וְהַגְּבוּרוֹת הֵם

like sound they emit resembles the shofar blast of the *AyIL* (איל, ram) of Yitzchak (see n.69)—corresponding to the *bnei AyLIm* (אלים). This powerful sound that the *bnei aylim*-angels emit encounters the rain clouds and is transmitted to the creation. Concerning this it is written, "Who can understand the thunder of His strength?" (explained in next note). For they certainly are from the side of *Gevurah*. This is (Psalms 29:3), "The voice of God is upon the waters, the God of Glory thunders...." No one understands the source of this shofar for it stems from *Binah* (Understanding), and "who can understand the thunder of His strength?"

Now, the windpipe encompasses three elements: the first is the flaming of the heart (the hot air expelled by the windpipe, corresponding to the *gevurot*, severities), the second is the cool air drawn in by the windpipe (which corresponds to the *sefirah* of *Tiferet*), and the third is the moisture drawn into the lungs that are attached to the windpipe (water corresponding to the *chasadim*, benevolences). The combination of these forces—water, wind and fire—produces the *kol* (voice).... When the flames of the heart encounter the moisture of the lungs, this is, "Who can understand the thunder of His *gevurot*?" This [thunder] brings understanding to the heart, which is in *Binah*. For the [flames of the] heart are the *gevurot* to the left; whereas the moisture of the lungs is the *chasadim* to the right (see nn.48 and 114). The source of these *chasadim* is *Chokhmah* (Wisdom), the intellect, from which flows "A garden spring, a well of fresh water, and drops from Lebanon" (Song of Songs 4:15)—this being the *libuna* (whiteness) of the mind dripping on the windpipe of the lungs (see n.53).... *ChoKhMaH* (חכמה) is *KoaCh MaH* (כח מה): *koach* in the heart, *mah* in the mind. And *kaneh* (windpipe) is *Tiferet*, corresponding to the six *sefirot* of *Z'er Anpin* (see Appendix: The Divine Persona)...and so, "*K'neh* wisdom, *k'neh* understanding" (see n.94).

The Rebbe shows how these concepts apply within the context of our lesson.

48. ...**the thunder of His gevurot.** All natural phenomena evolve from corresponding spiritual elements. Thunder derives from the spiritual forces known as *gevurot* (severities). The source of these *gevurot* is the *sefirah* of *Binah*, although they permeate the entire left side of the *sefirah* structure (see Appendix: The Structure of the Sefirot), which in general the *Zohar* refers to as the side of *Gevurah* (as in previous note).

49. **gevurah fill the universe.** See *Berakhot* 54a, 59a; *Orach Chaim* 227:1. Aside from the obvious connection to *gevurot*, Rebbe Nachman implies that the very act of reciting a blessing over thunder, or even any blessing, is to be equated with prayer.

And the heart's crookedness is made straight by means of thunder. As our Sages taught: Thunder was only created to straighten the crookedness of the heart (*Berakhot* 59a).[44] Thunder corresponds to the voice[45] a person releases < with great force > while praying. From this [voice], thunder is generated.[46]

As stated in the *Zohar* (III, 235b)[47]: When the voice is released and encounters the rain clouds, the voice is transmitted to the creation — and this is thunder. For thunder is essentially from *gevurot* (severities), as is written (Job 26:14), "Who can understand the thunder of His *gevurot* (strength)?"[48]

This is the why [when hearing thunder] we recite the blessing "...for His might and *gevurah* fill the universe."[49] These *gevurot* are

---

44. **Thunder...of the heart.** After stating which blessing to recite when hearing thunder, the Talmud (*loc. cit.*) provides a short discussion on the nature of thunder and the purpose it serves. Our Sages say that thunder was created in order to bring fear into people's hearts, as in (Ecclesiastes 3:14), "The *Elohim* (Lord) made [everything] in order that mankind fear Him." Maharsha explains that on the face of it, the world has no real benefit from thunder. Why, then, did God include it in His creation. The conclusion is that it was created to shake up and "straighten out" those hearts that have no fear of God (*s.v. lifshote*). This is indicated by Scripture's choice of God's holy name *Elohim*, which itself alludes to judgment — the severities from the *sefirah* of *Binah* soon to be discussed in our text.

45. **voice.** The Hebrew term *kol* has alternatively been translated in our text as "sound" and "voice." There are a number of instances where another term — such as "blast" for the *kol* of a shofar, or "rumble" for the *kol* of thunder — might have been a more appropriate choice. However, in order to highlight the connections that Rebbe Nachman makes between all these various "voices" the translation of *kol* has been limited to the former two.

46. **great force while praying...thunder....** Literally, *b'koach* means "with strength" or "forcefully," and can be understood as praying with such intense fervor and enthusiasm that the sound of his voice rumbles and roars like thunder. For there is another kind of thunder, akin to the natural phenomenon we call thunder, through which it is possible to come to true joy. Rebbe Nachman explains that commensurate with the energy a person puts into reciting the words of prayer, the resultant "thunder" has the power to straighten the crookedness of his heart and so cause him to merit joy. The Rebbe now explains how this works.

47. **stated in the Zohar.** Rebbe Nachman refers to this passage from the *Zohar* (*loc. cit.* and *Raaya Mehemenah, ibid.*) in both this section of the lesson and the next. Although the following translation includes all the pertinent concepts he will mention (based on the commentary of *Matok Midvash*), individual explanatory notes are provided only at the point each concept appears in the text. The *Zohar* states:

The six rings of the larynx (henceforth, windpipe) correspond to six levels of angels that join together and are called "*bnei aylim* (powerful ones)" (Psalms 29:1; see *Metzudat David*). These angels, which come from the side of *Gevurah* (Strength; see next note), give forth the wind that blows in the world. (A relaxed windpipe emits a quiet sound, whereas a "joined" or contracted windpipe emits a loud sound.) When the angels/six rings unite, the loud shofar-

בְּחִינַת כֹּחַ וּגְבוּרָה, שֶׁאָדָם מוֹצִיא אֶת הַקּוֹל בְּכֹחַ גָּדוֹל, וְהַקּוֹל
הַזֶּה פּוֹגֵעַ בְּעָבֵי מִטְרָא, הַיְנוּ בְּחִינַת מֹחִין, שֶׁמִּשָּׁם יוֹרְדִין טִפִּין
טִפִּין, כְּמוֹ שֶׁכָּתוּב בַּזֹּהַר: "בְּאֵר מַיִם חַיִּים וְנוֹזְלִים מִן לְבָנוֹן" –
'מִן לְבוּנָא דְמֹחָא'.

וּכְשֶׁפּוֹגֵעַ בְּעָבֵי מִטְרָא, אֲזַי אִשְׁתְּמַּע קָלָא לִבְרִיָּתָא, הַיְנוּ בְּחִינַת
רְעָמִים, וְזֶהוּ: "קוֹל רַעַמְךָ בַּגַּלְגַּל", הַיְנוּ בְּגַלְגַּלְתָּא דְמֹחָא, כַּד
אֲעַרָא בְּגַלְגַּלְתָּא דְמֹחָא, נַעֲשֶׂה מֵהַקּוֹל רְעָמִים, וְנִשְׁמָע לִבְרִיָּתָא.

וְזֶה: "פִּי יְדַבֵּר חָכְמוֹת", הַיְנוּ הַדִּבּוּר הַיּוֹצֵא מִפִּי פּוֹגֵעַ בַּחָכְמָה,
הַיְנוּ בְּגַלְגַּלְתָּא דְמֹחָא, וְעַל־יְדֵי־זֶה: "וְהָגוּת לִבִּי" וְכוּ', הַיְנוּ
שֶׁנִּתְעוֹרֵר עַל־יְדֵי־זֶה הָרַעַם, נִתְעוֹרֵר הַלֵּב, כְּמוֹ שֶׁאָמְרוּ: 'קוֹל
מְעוֹרֵר הַכַּוָּנָה'.

---

55. **sphere of the mind.** In our context, the sphere refers to that place where a person's voice, his heart's enthusiasm, encounters his intellect. In the physical, this is the skull, which houses the mind. The thunder is generated there.

56. **transmitted to the creation.** People hear that person praying earnestly, and his voice of thunder arouses them to fear of Heaven (see n.44). This brings all of creation closer to God (*Mai HaNachal*).

On a deeper level, one sees that Rebbe Nachman has introduced two phases of thunder: potential and actual. The thunder of one's voice as he recites the prayers is potential thunder; the thunder generated when his voice strikes the mind, the thunder transmitted to the creation, is actual thunder. The difference is that the voice only turns to thunder after it reaches the mind. Yet, even beforehand, by safeguarding his mind a person rectifies the *gevurot* (as will be explained in §4) and so his voice already has the element of thunder in potential (*Biur HaLikutim*).

57. **the voice stimulates kavanah.** The Hebrew term *kavanah* is generally translated "concentration" or "directed consciousness" both of which are associated with the mind. However, the term often appears in the writings of the Sages (e.g., *Berakhot* 13a,b; *Zohar* I, 72a) and afterwards as "*kavanah* of the heart." In that case *kavanah* might likewise be translated as "fervor" or "inspiration." The fact is that when a person prays with fervor, his mind *is* concentrated. As Rebbe Nachman teaches here, lifting one's voice in prayer, by being an aspect of thunder, stirs the heart so that a person can truly focus on what he himself is saying. The inner depths of the words straighten the inner crookedness of his heart and he merits joy (*Mai HaNachal*). See also *Likutey Moharan* I, 20:10, and note 81. Elsewhere, Rebbe Nachman teaches that just as the voice awakens *kavanah*, *kavanah* awakens the voice (*Rabbi Nachman's Wisdom* #293).

Thus, thunder in the sphere of the mind is not only transmitted outward to the creation, but also inward—to enhance one's own *kavanah* and purify one's own heart. Elsewhere

an aspect of might and strength. A person releases the voice with great force,[50] and this voice strikes the rain clouds—i.e., the aspect of < upper > mentalities[51] from where drop after drop descends.[52] As is brought in the *Zohar* (III, 235b): "a well of fresh water, and drops from LeBaNon" (Song of Songs 4:15)—from the *LiBuNa* (whiteness) of the mind.[53]

And when [this voice] strikes the rain clouds, then "the voice is transmitted to the creation"—i.e., the aspect of thunder.[54] This is the meaning of "The sound of Your thunder was in the sphere" (Psalms 77:19)—i.e., in the sphere of the mind.[55] For when it encounters the skull, the voice is converted into thunder and is transmitted to the creation.[56]

{"My mouth will speak wisdom and the meditation of my heart will be understanding" (Psalms 49:4).}

This < corresponds to > "My mouth will speak wisdom...." The speech that leaves my mouth strikes wisdom—i.e., the sphere of the mind. As a result, "the meditation of my heart will be understanding"—i.e., < the heart > will be stirred by the thunder. < This is because > the voice stimulates *kavanah* (Berakhot 24b).[57]

50. **great force.** As mentioned, this refers to praying with intense fervor and enthusiasm—*koach* (see n.46; see also n.67 that the *geborei koach* are those God-fearing people who voice their prayers with great strength).

51. **rain clouds...upper mentalities.** The Kabbalah refers to the upper *sefirot* of *Chokhmah* and *Binah* as mentalities—*mochin* in Hebrew. More generally, *mochin* indicates a person's intellect and mental capacity. Water, as rain or in any of its other forms, often symbolizes *mochin* and intellect, as in the verse (Isaiah 11:9), "As the water covers the sea, so will the earth be filled with the knowledge of God." The symbol of water appears throughout this lesson, with the Rebbe referring to the sea of wisdom; "the sea returned to its might"; the Waters of Conflict; and "let the sea roar."

52. **drop after drop descends.** As indicated in note 47, these raindrops are the *chasadim* that stem from *Chokhmah*/mentalities. They are the moisture that tempers the flames of the *gevurot*. (See below, note 99, where the nature of these drops is further explained.)

53. **whiteness of the mind.** Brain matter is basically white. In nature, when vapors from the earth rise and encounter rain clouds, thunder is generated and people become frightened. Likewise, when a man prays loudly, with power and strength (the flames of his heart), his voice strikes his mind (the moisture) and thunder is generated (in the windpipe, from which the voice emanates). See also *Likutey Moharan* I, 29 and notes 56 and 57, that the "whiteness of the mind" connotes a pure mind and so is likened to the clean waters of Lebanon.

54. **the voice is...thunder.** That is, when one's burning desire to serve God is channeled into awareness while praying—so that his prayers are a combination of intense concentration upon the words he recites and the intense fervor with which he recites them—then thunder is produced.

וְזֶה שֶׁאָמְרוּ חֲכָמֵינוּ, זִכְרוֹנָם לִבְרָכָה, 'מִי שֶׁיֵּשׁ בּוֹ יִרְאַת שָׁמַיִם,
דְּבָרָיו נִשְׁמָעִין', כִּי מִי שֶׁיֵּשׁ בּוֹ יִרְאָה, קוֹלוֹ נַעֲשָׂה רְעָמִים, כִּי רַעַם
מִסִּטְרָא דִּיצְחָק, כְּמוֹ שֶׁכָּתוּב: "וְרַעַם גְּבוּרוֹתָיו", וְעַל־יְדֵי־זֶה
דְּבָרָיו נִשְׁמָעִין, הַיְנוּ מִשְׁתַּמַּע קָלָא לִבְרִיָּתָא, כִּי תַּמָּן תַּלְיָא
שְׁמִיעָה, כְּמוֹ שֶׁנֶּאֱמַר: "ה', שָׁמַעְתִּי שִׁמְעֲךָ יָרֵאתִי".

וְזֶה פֵּרוּשׁ: "גִּבּוֹרֵי כֹחַ עוֹשֵׂי דְבָרוֹ לִשְׁמֹעַ בְּקוֹל דְּבָרוֹ". אִיתָא
בַּזֹּהַר, 'זַכְיָן לְמִשְׁמַע קָלִין מִלְעֵילָא', הַיְנוּ עַל יְדֵי הַגְּבוּרוֹת נַעֲשָׂה
רְעָמִים, וְעַל־יְדֵי־זֶה הַלֵּב שׁוֹמֵעַ, וְהַיְנוּ: "וְהָגוּת לִבִּי תְבוּנוֹת",
וּכְמוֹ שֶׁכָּתוּב: "וְנָתַתָּ לְעַבְדְּךָ לֵב שׁוֹמֵעַ", וְגַם דְּבָרָיו נִשְׁמָעִין

properly and intensely one's voice is transformed into thunder, so that those who hear him are naturally aroused to return to God and serve Him.

62. geborei...sound of His word. The "mighty ones" to whom the verse refers are the angels. They do God's bidding not for reward, but solely to hearken to the word of God (*Metzudat David*). In our context, this refers to the person who performs mitzvot without seeking reward. The term *GeBoRei koach* (גבורי כח) connotes *GeVuRot* (גבורות), which the Rebbe earlier called "an aspect of *koach* and strength." Rebbe Nachman explains this further and shows how it is in line with our lesson.

63. hearing voices from Above. The *Zohar* (*loc. cit.*) teaches that the "mighty ones" of whom the Psalmist speaks are actually the tzaddikim who use their inner strength to totally subdue their evil inclination. In our context, "Above" can be understood as alluding to the upper *mochin*, the intellect (see n.51). These mighty ones/tzaddikim, who use the flaming of their heart for serving God (while subduing their burning desire for the mundane), merit to hear the voice as it strikes the sphere of the mind. See also next note.

64. gevurot, thunder is generated. Subduing the evil inclination requires strength. The tzaddikim, who with their fear of Heaven/*gevurot*/strength subdue their evil inclination, are thus able to generate thunder.

65. heart will be understanding. For when the voice is transmitted and strikes the mind (see n.57), it brings fear into the heart.

66. a hearing heart.... This was King Solomon's prayer: he wanted a heart that would both hear and understand. On the simple level, Rebbe Nachman brings this proof-text to show that the heart hears. Yet, it also teaches that just as King Solomon *prayed* for a "hearing heart," a person must pray if he wants to attain fear of Heaven. That is, though it takes fear of Heaven to pray with fervor, true fear of Heaven only comes when a person prays for it. This is a classic example of *hitbodedut*, the special type of prayer the Rebbe so strongly promoted (see n.8).

This is what our Sages taught: When a person has fear of Heaven, his words are heard (*Berakhot* 6b).[58] For when someone possesses fear of Heaven, his voice is converted into thunder. This is because thunder is from the side of Yitzchak, as in, "the thunder of His *gevurot*."[59] This causes his words to be heard—i.e., "the voice is transmitted to the creation."[60] For hearing is linked to [the fear of Heaven], as is written (Habakkuk 3:2), "O God, I heard of Your message; I feared" (*Zohar* III, 230a).[61]

And this is the explanation of "*geborei kouch* (mighty ones) who do His bidding, hearkening to the sound of His word" (Psalms 103:20).[62] [As] the *Zohar* (I, 90a) states: "They merit hearing voices from Above."[63] In other words, by means of the *gevurot,* thunder is generated.[64] This causes the heart to hear—i.e., "the meditation of my heart will be understanding"[65]—as is written (1 Kings 3:9), "Give Your servant a hearing heart [to judge Your people]."[66] And then his words

---

(*Likutey Moharan* I, 270), Rebbe Nachman teaches that sometimes a person prays with inspiration as a result of seeing someone else praying with *kavanah* (i.e., hearing his voice of thunder). Other times, he draws inspiration from his own prayers; he begins praying with a bit of enthusiasm and, stimulated by his initial modest success, puts even greater effort into his devotions.

58. **fear of Heaven...words are heard.** A person who rebukes others when he himself is not free of sin has little chance of being listened to. But when a person fears Heaven, he is free of sin, and so his words are heard (*Iyun Yaakov, loc. cit.*). Rebbe Nachman adds another dimension to this Talmudic assertion.

59. **Yitzchak...of His gevurot.** The *Mai HaNachal* explains: It is a person's fear of Heaven that enables him to pray with a powerful voice—i.e., thunder. This is because the voice of *koach* and the fear of Heaven are both from the *gevurot*, the side of *Gevurah* (see nn.48-50). And the paragon of the God-fearing tzaddik, Yitzchak, also corresponds to the side of *Gevurah*. Hence, Scripture refers to the fear of Heaven as "Yitzchak's fear" (Genesis 31:42).

60. **causes his words to be heard....** As explained above, notes 54-56.

61. **hearing...I feared.** The *Zohar* (*loc. cit.*) links Yitzchak/fear with hearing, and teaches that hearing (i.e., accepting) another's words or rebuke only comes when there is fear. In our context, a person's intense and fervent prayer corresponds to the flames of the *gevurot*. His voice is thus the thunder that can be heard by others and instill in them fear of Heaven (see *Biur HaLikutim*). Hence, that which our Sages said, "When a person has fear of Heaven, his words are heard," can be understood as: When a person has fear of Heaven, when he has aroused the *gevurot*, he can pray intensely and his voice is heard by the creation. As explained, this instills in them fear of Heaven, making straight the heart's crookedness.

Incidentally, we learn from this that outright rebuke is not always necessary. By praying

לִבְרִיָּתָא, וְזֶהוּ: "לִשְׁמֹעַ בְּקוֹל דְּבָרוֹ".

וְזֶה בְּחִינַת קוֹל הַשּׁוֹפָר, דָּא שׁוֹפָר שֶׁל אַיִל, אֵילוֹ שֶׁל יִצְחָק (עי"ז
שֶׁנִּתְעוֹרֵר הָרַעַם - כצ"ל). בְּחִינַת: "וְרַעַם גְּבוּרוֹתָיו".

וְזֶהוּ: "אַשְׁרֵי הָעָם יוֹדְעֵי תְרוּעָה", 'יוֹדְעֵי' דַּיְקָא, שֶׁיִּפָּגַע הַקּוֹל
בַּמֹּחַ, בְּחִינוֹת עָבֵי מִטְרָא, וְיִהְיֶה בִּבְחִינַת רְעָמִים, וּמִי שֶׁשּׁוֹמֵעַ
תְּקִיעַת שׁוֹפָר מֵאִישׁ יָרֵא וְחָרֵד, בְּוַדַּאי לֹא יִדְאַג כָּל הַשָּׁנָה
מֵרְעָמִים, כְּמוֹ שֶׁכָּתוּב: "בְּקוֹלוֹת וּבְרָקִים עֲלֵיהֶם נִגְלֵיתָ, וּבְקוֹל
שׁוֹפָר עֲלֵיהֶם הוֹפַעְתָּ", שֶׁבְּקוֹל הַשּׁוֹפָר הוֹפִיעַ עֲלֵיהֶם מְקוֹלוֹת
וּבְרָקִים:

they know how to arouse God's compassion on Rosh HaShanah and mitigate the decrees (*Rashi, loc. cit.*). The Midrash also speaks of the shofar's ability to abolish harsh decrees, as we find, "God said, 'When you stand before Me on Rosh HaShanah, take shofars and blow them. And even if there are many adversaries speaking against you, they will all be destroyed' " (*Pesikta d'Rav Kahane*). Rebbe Nachman will now connect the shofar to intense prayer, as both have the ability to mitigate decrees.

The *Biur HaLikutim* points out that the very next verse in Psalms (89:17) states: "They rejoice in Your name all day long...." That is, when a Jew arouses the voice of thunder, he merits rejoicing in God—i.e., feeling the joy of the mitzvot.

71. **Specifically knows...thunder.** That is, the shofar's sound/intense prayer strikes the mind and awakens the intellect, which then arouses fear in the heart. This makes straight the heart's crookedness, enabling it to feel joy. And through the joy of his "straightened heart," a person knows the nature and state of the decree and can effectively pray to mitigate it.

72. **And whoever hears the shofar...no fear of thunder....** Both the voice of the God-fearing person and the sound of the shofar possess the potential aspect of thunder. In reward for listening to them and being moved to divine service, God protects a person from being harmed by any external manifestation of thunder (*Mai HaNachal*).

73. **As it is written....** This stanza, which is part of the Rosh HaShanah Mussaf liturgy, does not appear in the manuscript version of *Likutey Moharan*.

In review: Every person is responsible to make the world a better place. He can do this by praying for the world's benefit, as prayer has the power to mitigate decrees. However, when decrees are extant and man's prayers are obscured by his sins, he has to disguise his prayers in a *maamar* (§1). To know whether it is before or after the decree one must perform the mitzvot with joy—with no expectation of future reward, but feeling reward in the performance itself. Then, the degree to which he succeeds in feeling joy is indicative of whether God, Whose own joy is clothed in the mitzvot, is joyous or the decree has already been issued (§2). To feel this joy, one must have a straight heart, a heart whose crookedness has been eliminated by thunder—i.e., a revelation of intellect. This thunder is generated by arousing the fear of Heaven through intense prayer (§3).

are "transmitted to the creation"; this being "hearkening to the sound of His word."[67]

This also corresponds to the sound of the shofar[68]—i.e., the shofar-horn of the ram, the ram of Yitzchak (*Zohar* III, 235b)—which is an aspect of "the thunder of His *gevurot*."[69]

This, then, is the meaning of (Psalms 89:16), "Happy is the nation who knows the shofar's blast."[70] Specifically "knows," because the voice hits the mind—corresponding to rain clouds—and is converted into the aspect of thunder.[71] And whoever hears the shofar blown by a man who is God-fearing and pious, will certainly have no fear of thunder the entire year.[72] As it is written: "With sounds [of thunder] and lightning You revealed Yourself to them, and with the shofar-sound You appeared to them." You appeared to them through the sound of the shofar, [protecting them] from thunder and lightning.[73]

67. **hearkening to the sound of His word.** Thus, Rebbe Nachman interprets this verse in two different ways. First, the *geborei koach* are those God-fearing people who voice their prayers with great strength. They are said to be "hearkening to the voice of His word" because their hearts are attentive to the meaning of the words of prayer. The other interpretation of "hearkening to the voice of His word" is that other people also hear and are affected by the sound of his prayer, because his voice generates thunder that is "transmitted to the creation" (*Mai HaNachal*).

68. **the sound of the shofar.** Here, Rebbe Nachman shows that the thunder generated by a God-fearing person corresponds to the blast of the shofar.

This lesson was given on Rosh HaShanah (see n.2). As is evident from the collected teachings of many a chassidic leader, it was customary for the rebbes to discourse on the "subject of the day." It seems surprising, therefore, that our lesson makes no mention of the holy day. However, as was often the case in his lessons, Rebbe Nachman here alludes to "subject of the day" without mentioning it specifically. Thus, he makes a number of connections to Rosh HaShanah, starting with this reference to the shofar.

69. **ram of Yitzchak...thunder....** This refers to the ram sacrificed by Avraham after he was commanded not to harm Yitzchak (Genesis 22:13). Our Sages teach (*Rosh HaShanah* 16a): Why do we blow a ram's horn? It is because God said, "Blow a ram's horn before Me so that I will recall the *akedah* of Yitzchak, when he was bound to the altar."

As quoted earlier from the *Zohar* (n.47), this ram's horn corresponds to the thunder of the *gevurot*: "...the loud shofar-like sound they emit resembles the shofar blast of the ram of Yitzchak.... This mighty sound that the *bnei aylim* emit encounters the rain clouds and is transmitted to the creation. Concerning this it is written, 'Who can understand the thunder of His *gevurot?*'"

Thus, the thunder generated by the voice of a person who fears God parallels the shofar/ the ram of Yitzchak—Yitzchak personifying the fear of Heaven (see n.59; *Mai HaNachal*). Yitzchak, the voice of thunder, is thus symbolic of the fear that is aroused by intense prayer.

70. **knows the shofar's blast.** Scripture is referring to the Jewish people. By blowing the shofar,

ד אֲבָל צָרִיךְ לְפַנּוֹת אֶת הַמֹּחִין מֵחָכְמוֹת חִיצוֹנִיּוֹת וּמִמַּחֲשָׁבוֹת
זָרוֹת. מֵחֲמַת שֶׁלֹּא יַחֲמִיץ אֶת חָכְמָתוֹ בְּחָכְמוֹת חִיצוֹנִיּוֹת
וּבְתַאֲווֹת, כְּדֵי כְּשֶׁיּוֹצִיא אֶת הַקּוֹל וְיִפְגַּע בְּמֹחוֹ, יִתְעַבֵּד מִמֶּנּוּ
רַעַם, אֲבָל כְּשֶׁגַּלְגַּלְתָּא דְמֹחָא אָטוּם בְּטֻמְאָה, כְּמוֹ שֶׁכָּתוּב:
"וְנִטְמֵתֶם בָּם", אֲזַי אֵין קוֹלוֹ נִשְׁמָע.

גַּם יִשְׁמֹר יִרְאָתוֹ, שֶׁמִּמֶּנּוּ תּוֹצָאוֹת הַקּוֹל, כְּמוֹ שֶׁכָּתוּב: "וְרַעַם
גְּבוּרוֹתָיו", שֶׁלֹּא יִהְיֶה לוֹ יִרְאָה חִיצוֹנִית, וְזֶה: 'אִם אֵין חָכְמָה אֵין
יִרְאָה'; אִם אֵין יִרְאָה אֵין חָכְמָה.

וְזֶהוּ : 'יָרַד גַּבְרִיאֵל וְנָעַץ קָנֶה בַּיָּם'. פֵּרוּשׁ: מֵהִשְׁתַּלְשְׁלוּת
הַגְּבוּרוֹת, הַיְנוּ יִרְאָה חִיצוֹנִית, נָעַץ קָנֶה בְּיָם הַחָכְמָה. קָנֶה דָא

insensitive (see *Living Torah*, on Leviticus 11:43). If either of the two channels—the mind or the heart—is clogged by impurities, the voice cannot penetrate the sphere of the mind and so thunder cannot be generated.

78. **his voice is not heard.** This indirectly explains why so many of those who presume to have influence over others are not really very effective: They lack true fear of Heaven. Because they have yet to subdue their own evil inclination, and because their secular wisdom and passions distance them from God, their words are not heard or hearkened to.

The *Biur HaLikutim* explains that defiling the mind with impurity leads to its becoming clogged and insensitive. In response, God, as it were, clogs His ear and makes Himself insensitive to that person's prayers. And this leads to decrees, God forbid.

79. **no extrinsic fears....** A person should never fear anything except God (*Advice*, p. 119). If all he ever fears is the Holy One, then even when something peripheral causes him to be afraid, he is fully aware that these fears are actually a reminder for him to fear only God (*Likutey Halakhot, Pesach* 9:15-17). Fearing extrinsic fears, on the other hand, automatically undermines one's fear of Heaven.

80. **no wisdom...no fear...no wisdom.** Man must always safeguard both his heart (fear) and his intellect (wisdom). Each complements and depends upon the other. Thus: when his mind is exposed to secular wisdom, the fear in his heart becomes tainted; and when the fear in his heart is caused by extrinsic fears, the intellect turns to secular wisdom and the mind becomes clogged (*Parparaot LeChokhmah; Mai HaNachal*). This explains why later on in the lesson both Rebbe Nachman and the commentaries quoted in the notes include evil passions as one of the mind's enemies, even though, like fear, these passions are actually rooted in the heart.

Rebbe Nachman now brings a proof-text showing the connection between the heart/fear and the mind/wisdom.

81. **Gavriel...reed into the sea.** When King Solomon married Pharaoh's daughter, Gavriel descended and plunged a reed into the sea. Around this reed a swamp gathered and upon this

4. But it is [first] necessary[74] to clear the mentalities of secular wisdom and undesirable thoughts—of *chametz*.[75] A person must not sour his wisdom with secular wisdom or < evil > passions,[76] so that the voice emerges < pure and clean. > It will then strike the < upper mentalities > and be converted into thunder. But when the sphere of the mind is clogged with impurity—as in (Leviticus 11:43), "... because *nitmeitem* (you will be made unclean) by them"[77]—then his voice is not heard.[78]

He must also safeguard his fear of Heaven—from which the voice emerges, as in, "the thunder of His *gevurot*"—so that he has no extrinsic fears < but only a fear of the Holy One >.[79] This is: Where there is no wisdom, there is no fear of Heaven; where there is no fear of Heaven, there is no wisdom (*Avot* 3:21).[80]

And < this corresponds to that which our Sages taught: When King Shelomoh married Pharaoh's daughter, > the angel GaVRiel descended and plunged a reed into the sea (*Shabbat* 56b; *Sanhedrin* 21b).[81]

---

74. **But it is first necessary.** Having established that a person must awaken a burning desire in his heart to serve God, so that it will in turn arouse his intellect and generate thunder, Rebbe Nachman now advises against those elements that interfere with the *mochin* (mentalities) and even harm a person's chances of attaining intellect.

75. **chametz.** *Chametz* (leaven) is symbolic of man's inner inclination towards evil. As taught in the Talmud (*Berakhot* 17a): When Rabbi Alexandri finished praying, he would say: "Master of all the worlds, it is revealed and known to You that our desire is to do Your will. What prevents us? Only the leaven in the dough (the evil inclination)."

   The *Biur HaLikutim* adds: Although Rebbe Nachman has just taught that the heart's crookedness needs to be made straight, he will next explain that what is most essential is the guarding of the mind. This shows that everything actually stems from the mind (*Chokhmah*) and then descends to the heart (*Binah*). The initial step must therefore be to eliminate anything that might sour the mind.

76. **secular wisdom or evil passions.** These are actually two separate concepts, corresponding respectively to the mind and the heart. Over-indulging one's natural desire for food, sex, etc. turns these needs into what in our lesson the Rebbe calls evil passions. Controlling them is therefore known as subduing the evil inclination; rather than accommodating his burning desire for the mundane, he employs the flaming of his heart to serve God (see n.63). Conversely, the secular wisdom that distances people from God relates to the intellect, from which wisdom is drawn. Thus, in order for a person's voice to generate thunder, he must purify both his mind and his heart, as the Rebbe now explains.

77. **made unclean by them.** Rebbe Nachman alludes here to the Talmudic teaching that points to the similarity between the words *NiTMeiTeM* and *NeTaMTeM* (literally, "you will be clogged up"). Our Sages teach (*Yoma* 39a): Sins clog a person's heart. We learn this from the verse, "Do not defile yourselves with [non-kosher foods], because *nitmeitem* by them." Do not read *NiTMeiTeM* (נטמאתם) but *NeTaMTeM* (נטמתם)—they will make you spiritually

בְּחִינַת קוֹל הַיּוֹצֵא מֵהַקָּנֶה. הַיְנוּ עַל־יְדֵי הִשְׁתַּלְשְׁלוּת הַגְּבוּרוֹת,
שֶׁהִיא בְּחִינַת סוֹסְפִּיתָא דְּדַהֲבָא, יְרָאָה חִיצוֹנִית, נִשְׁאָר הַקּוֹל נָעוּץ
בַּאֲטִימַת הַשֵּׂכֶל, וְלֹא יִשְׁתַּמַּע לִבְרִיָּתָא.

וְעִקָּר לִשְׁמֹר מֹחוֹ שֶׁלֹּא יַחְמִיץ, וְזֶהוּ: "גְּעַר חַיַּת קָנֶה", כִּדְאִיתָא
בַּזֹּהַר: קָנֶה חֵי"ת תְּשַׁבֵּר וְתַעֲשֶׂה מִמֶּנָּה הֵ"א, וְתַעֲשֶׂה מֵאוֹתִיּוֹת
חָמֵץ – מַצָּה, הַיְנוּ שֶׁלֹּא תַּחְמִיץ חָכְמָתְךָ.
וְזֶהוּ לְשׁוֹן גְּעַר – לְשׁוֹן מְרִיבָה, כִּי מַצָּה – לְשׁוֹן מְרִיבָה.

not excise it immediately, that thought becomes a post to which the "gold dross" of secular wisdom and extrinsic fears are attracted. Eventually, this causes him to fall into the spiritual exile that is Rome.

86. **safeguard his mind from becoming chametz.** Understandably, never succumbing to an evil trait or never allowing a undesirable thought to enter one's mind is an ideal. This is the ultimate level of safeguarding the mind from souring like *chametz*. Most of us, however, find ourselves easily drawn in and even overwhelmed by our traits and thoughts. What then?

87. **Rebuke the beast of the reed.** This was King David's prayer for God to destroy the kingdom of evil. Rashi explains that the "beast" is Amalek, whom Rebbe Nachman equates with secular wisdom (see *Likutey Moharan* II, 19).

88. **As the Zohar states....** The passage in the *Zohar* reads as follows: When King Shelomoh married Pharaoh's daughter, Gavriel descended and plunged a reed into the sea...rose the city of Rome. This gave life to the Other Side. The *kaneh* (reed) refers to the life-force of the evil beast. (The Hebrew term *chayah* means both beast and life.) This is the reed that gave the forces of evil dominion over the world. Why a reed? Because a reed is easily snapped and broken. This is Egypt. The Egyptians ruled the entire world. Yet when the time came, the Egyptians, who are like *chametz*, were broken; the Jews, who are like *matzah*, were redeemed. How are the Egyptians broken? By breaking the leg of the *chet*, thereby turning it into a *heh* (*Zohar* III, 251b, 252a and *Matok Midvash* thereon). Phonetically, the Hebrew letter *CheT* (spelled חית) is similar to the word *ChayaT* (חית, the beast of). When the left leg of the letter *Chet* (ח) is separated from its roof, the letter *Heh* (ה) is formed. Thus, when the *chet* in the word *ChaMetZ* (חמץ) is broken, the word *MatZaH* (מצה) is formed. And the *chet* is likened to a *kaneh*, because like the reed it is easy to break. See next note.

89. **wisdom will then not turn sour.** In our context, the verse and commentary can be understood as follows: The "beast" (*chayah*) alludes to evil and specifically the evil thoughts that enter a person's mind. The "rebuke" is a person's cry or shout of protest against these undesirable thoughts. This breaks the beast. Thus: **Rebuke** — crying out in prayer, **the beast of the reed** — breaks and chases away evil thoughts.

90. **rebuke...conflict.** For safeguarding the mind is a constant battle. Rebbe Nachman now explains an additional significance of this battle.

The explanation is: From the devolution of the *GeVuRot*[82]— < which correspond to gold dross, > extrinsic fears[83]—he "plunged a reed into the sea" of wisdom. A *kaneh* (reed) is the aspect of the voice released from the *kaneh* (windpipe).[84] Thus, < because of the secular wisdom and > extrinsic fears, the voice remains plunged in the mire of the intellect and will not be transmitted to the creation.[85]

But the most important thing is that a person safeguard his mind from becoming *chametz*.[86] This is (Psalms 68:31), "Rebuke *ChayaT* (the beast of) the reed."[87] As the *Zohar* (III, 252a) states: Break the reed of the *CheT* and make it a *heh,* thus transforming the letters *ChaMetZ* into *MatZaH*.[88] Your wisdom will then not turn sour.[89]

This is the connotation of "rebuke," which conveys conflict.[90] For the word *MatZah* also implies conflict: the tzaddikim engage in

swamp rose the city of Rome (*Shabbat, loc. cit.,* and *Rashi*; Rome is representative of the fourth and final exile of the Jewish people.)

82. **devolution of the gevurot.** The angel GaVRiEL (גבריאל)—*GeVuRah EL* (אל גבורה, the Might of the Almighty)—corresponds to the *GeVuRot* (גבורות). His having descended is thus depicted as the devolution of the *gevurot*, indicating that there has been a decline in spirituality. These corrupted *gevurot* become enclothed in extrinsic fears rather than a direct fear of God.

83. **gold dross, extrinsic fears.** From the Kabbalah we learn that gold corresponds to the aspect of fear and the *gevurot* (cf. *Zohar* II, 90b; *Tikkuney Zohar* #24, p.69b). The impurities that form on the surface of gold—gold dross—is thus an aspect of extrinsic fears (*Mai HaNachal*).

84. **kaneh, reed...kaneh, windpipe.** Rebbe Nachman connects the *kaneh* of Gavriel with one's personal *kaneh*, the windpipe. In the Talmud we find: The voice is released through the *kaneh* (*Berakhot* 61a); the windpipe being a sort of reed or shaft through which the air in the lungs is passed on to the larynx, where it is transformed into the sounds of the voice.

85. **voice remains plunged....** At their source, the *gevurot* emanate from an extremely lofty level: the *sefirah* of *Binah* (Understanding; *Zohar* III, 10b; see also *Likutey Moharan* I, 41). However, as the *gevurot* descend into this material world, they assume the form of "gold dross"—i.e., secular wisdom and extrinsic fears. Either of these two evils can become the first step in a person's falling from his devotion to God, hence, "Where there is no wisdom, there is no fear of Heaven...," as above (see n.80; *Parparaot LeChokhmah*; *Mai HaNachal*).

The passage from *Shabbat* and *Sanhedrin* (n.81) thus reads: **When King Shelomoh** — **When wisdom married Pharaoh's daughter** — became secular wisdom, **Gavriel descended** — this caused the *gevurot* to descend into extrinsic fears, etc. **and plunged a kaneh into the sea** — and the voice that emerged from the *kaneh* became mired in the sea of wisdom, the intellect. As a result, the voice was unable to resound like thunder in order to arouse the creation to serve God.

Then, **Around this reed a swamp gathered and upon this swamp rose the city of Rome.** The reed became a post around which debris in the sea began to collect, until a swamp formed... (*Rashi, s.v. naatz*). That is, if a person succumbs to even one undesirable thought and does

דְּצַדִּיקַיָּא עָבְדִין מַצּוּתָא בְּסִטְרִין אָחֳרָנִין, דְּלָא יִתְקְרִיבוּ לְמִשְׁכְּנָא דִּקְדֻשָּׁה.

הַיְנוּ כְּשֶׁתִּשְׁמֹר אֶת חָכְמָתְךָ שֶׁלֹּא יִכָּנֵס בּוֹ חָכְמוֹת חִיצוֹנִיּוֹת, שֶׁלֹּא תְּהַרְהֵר בְּהִרְהוּרִים רָעִים, שֶׁהֵם בְּחִינַת קָנֶה דְּסִטְרָא אָחֳרָא, כְּנֶגֶד 'קָנֶה חָכְמָה קָנֶה בִּינָה' דִּקְדֻשָּׁה, עַל־יְדֵי־זֶה תְּנַצֵּל מִבְּחִינַת חָמֵץ, שֶׁהִיא סִטְרָא דְּמוֹתָא, כִּדְאִיתָא מַחְמֶצֶת, תַּמָּן סִטְרָא דְּמוֹתָא. וְתָאֲמִין, כִּי כָּל מַצּוּתָא וּמְרִיבָה שֶׁיֵּשׁ בֵּין הַצַּדִּיקִים הַשְּׁלֵמִים, אֵין זֶה אֶלָּא כְּדֵי שֶׁיְּגָרְשׁוּ סִטְרִין אָחֳרָנִין.

וְזֶה פֵּרוּשׁ: "אֹזֶן שֹׁמַעַת תּוֹכַחַת חַיִּים בְּקֶרֶב חֲכָמִים תָּלִין" –

95. **MaChMetZeT...ChaMetZ...MeT.** The letters of the word *machmetzet* (מחמצת, sours or leavens) can be arranged to form the words *chametz* (חמץ, leaven) and *met* (מת, death). Thus, the letters themselves hint to the connection between leavened dough and the Other Side, the side of death (cf. *Zohar* III, 251b, "One who eats *chametz* on Pesach"). And since the Other Side is considered *chametz*, death, a person who safeguards his mind against evil thoughts has banished the Other Side and spared himself a spiritual death.

96. **to dispel the Other Side.** As mentioned at the end of note 92, it is a mistake to take the strife between true tzaddikim at face value. Rather, the battle one tzaddik wages against another is in actuality a battle, in disguised form, against the *Sitra Achra*. Then again, this is only one explanation. Further on in the lesson Rebbe Nachman will give another reason for the strife between tzaddikim (see text and nn.99,100; see also *The Aleph-Bet Book*, Strife). It is clear, therefore, that understanding the true intentions of the tzaddikim is no simple matter. Their disputes should thus not become the concern or talk of the common folk, as is unfortunately all too common today. See also *Likutey Halakhot, Ribit* 5.

The *Parparaot LeChokhmah* explains this form of strife in a manner that ties together the different points of the lesson. He writes: The mind of a Jew is likened to a holy encampment. The secular wisdom that seeks to infiltrate this encampment stems from the corrupted *gevurot*, the gold dross, which are elements of the Other Side (see nn.82,83). Their attempt at infiltration in itself denotes strife, because the intention of the Other Side is to pursue the person and oppose his striving for holiness. He, in turn, must mitigate this decree (the pursuit of the Other Side) and thereby reconnect the fallen *gevurot* to their source in holiness. This requires his using precisely the same means, namely conflict. However, in his case it is "holy conflict." He battles against his evil inclination—against his interest in secular wisdom and his desire for evil passions—thereby transforming the forces of evil into holiness, the *chet* into a *heh*, and *chametz* (impurity) into *matzah* (holy conflict).

Unfortunately, not everyone is capable of waging this battle. It is therefore incumbent upon the tzaddikim, who can do battle, to engage in conflict against the Other Side and so prevent it from infiltrating the encampment of holiness. They battle to keep secular wisdom and heresy away from the Jews. And so people must have faith in the tzaddikim and

MatZuta (battle)[91] with the Other Side in order to keep it from approaching the dwelling place of holiness *(Zohar III, 251b).*[92]

That is, when you protect your wisdom so that secular wisdom does not penetrate it, <and> you do not entertain evil thoughts—which is the *KaNeH* (reed) of the Other Side,[93] in contrast to <the *KaNeH* (windpipe) of holiness, i.e.,> "*K'NeH* wisdom, *K'NeH* understanding"[94] of holiness—you will be saved from the aspect of *chametz,* which is the side of death. As is stated *(Zohar, ibid.)*: *MaChMetZeT*—it contains <*ChaMetZ* and *MeT*>.[95] And believe that all strife and conflict between those tzaddikim who have reached perfection is only to dispel the Other Side.[96]

This is the meaning of (Proverbs 15:31), "He whose ear hears the

---

91. **MatZah...conflict...MatZuta.** As in (Isaiah 41:12), "You may seek, but will not find *MatZutekha* (those who contend with you)." Thus *matzah* (מצה), which shares the same root letters as *matzuta* (מצותא), suggests conflict and rebuke.

92. **...keep it from...holiness.** As explained above (n.8), Rebbe Nachman's lessons are simultaneously relevant to the very greatest tzaddikim and the simplest people alike. After teaching the need for battling against undesirable thoughts, he now shows that each person's efforts in this is a microcosm of the larger battle that the tzaddikim constantly wage against the *Sitra Achra* (Other Side). The tzaddikim pray and engage in daily struggle against the forces of evil, to keep them from gaining a foothold in holiness. The person who struggles against his evil thoughts is waging the same battle, albeit on a smaller scale. And, just as it can be said that in the overall scheme of things the tzaddikim have succeeded in protecting holiness—keeping the Jewish people alive and flourishing despite a national history replete with devastating decrees—so, too, each individual, commensurate with the effort he has put into the battle, has succeeded in building and safeguarding his own "holy encampment" (see n.96)—i.e., his mind.

The *Biur HaLikutim* adds that there are times when the struggle and strife the tzaddikim engage in seems not to be with the Other Side but with each other. In truth, their intent is to banish the forces of evil—the decrees. However, because they know the decree has already been issued, they disguise their prayers and struggle in a *maamar,* giving the impression that they are at odds with each other. See text and note 96, below.

93. **KaNeH of the Other Side.** For from the *kaneh* the Other Side draws its sustenance and life-force, as in note 88 above.

94. **K'NeH wisdom...understanding.** In Proverbs (4:5), King Solomon says: "Acquire wisdom, acquire understanding." Rebbe Nachman plays on the phonetic similarity between the words *KaNeH* and *K'NeH* (acquire). That is, by using his *kaneh* (windpipe) to cry out in prayer against the evil thoughts, a person can overcome the *kaneh* (reed) of the Other Side and *k'neh* (acquire) true wisdom and understanding. In addition, "wisdom" and "understanding" correspond to *Chokhmah* and *Binah,* the mind and the heart—i.e., the two organs which when united form the voice of holiness that arouses fear of Heaven (as above, §3 and nn.47-58).

לְשׁוֹן תְּלוּנָה וּמְרִיבָה. כְּשֶׁאַתָּה שׁוֹמֵעַ מְרִיבוֹת שֶׁבֵּין הַצַּדִּיקִים
תֵּדַע, שֶׁזֶּה מַשְׁמִיעִין אוֹתְךָ תּוֹכָחָה, עַל שֶׁפָּגַמְתָּ בְּטִפֵּי מֹחֲךָ, שֶׁעַל
זֶה נֶאֱמַר: "כָּל בָּאֶיהָ לֹא יְשׁוּבוּן, וְלֹא יַשִּׂיגוּ אָרְחוֹת חַיִּים",
שֶׁאַתָּה דָּבוּק בְּסִטְרָא דְּמוֹתָא, בְּחִינַת חָמֵץ, בְּחִינַת יָרַד גַּבְרִיאֵל

because this person has blemished the drops of his mind and become attached to the aspect of *chametz*, he hears of the conflict and interprets it superficially—considering it no different than the rivalry and bickering of ordinary people. However, it is precisely this interpretation that indicates that his mind is blemished. If only he would realize that he is being shown this for his own benefit, as a test. He is being given an opportunity to catch himself from falling further; a chance to turn *chametz*-thoughts into *matzah*, so that with the aspect of *matzah*— i.e., holy conflict—he himself can battle the Other Side. And, even if this proves too much for him, so that the tzaddikim are obliged to wage the battle for him, his belief in the holy intention behind their conflict is itself enough to mitigate the decrees against him. Conversely, if he chooses to not recognize his blemish and deny responsibility for the conflict between tzaddikim, then this conflict will only cause him to be even further distanced from God (see also *Torat Natan* #7).

100. **None that go...return...regain....** In its simple meaning the verse relates to immorality, yet it also refers to undesirable thoughts and heresies (*Rashi*, Proverbs 2:16). Rebbe Nachman shows that the two are actually connected. Not safeguarding the mind from secular wisdom (heresies) blemishes the mind. Sexual sin blemishes one's fear of Heaven, which in turn blemishes the mind. The Talmud teaches that it is very difficult to repent for either of these sins (*Avodah Zarah* 17a), which is why Scripture states: "None that go...return, nor do they regain the paths of life."

On the surface, this seems to indicate that repentance for sins associated with blemishing the Covenant (sexual purity) is well nigh impossible. Yet, from the teachings of Rebbe Nachman we know that this is certainly not so. Reb Noson explains: As mentioned, conflict between tzaddikim has the power to distance a person from God. In one sense, this is precisely the purpose of the conflict! Certain sins engender such devastating spiritual harm that, as the *Zohar* states, repentance is impossible for these iniquities (see *Zohar* I, 188a; see *Rabbi Nachman's Wisdom* #71). Even so, God's capacity for compassion is unlimited and He wants everyone to repent. Repentance is therefore always possible. Why then does the *Zohar* state that one cannot repent? However, this is the same as the strife between tzaddikim. That is, by rights, when a person has sinned so terribly, he deserves to be distanced from holiness. He is therefore put to a test. It is only natural that if shown the conflict between tzaddikim, or told by the holy writings that he can never repent, he will turn even further away from holiness. This is his trial. If he refuses to be fooled and pushed away, if he stands at the gates of holiness and refuses to depart, if he cries out to God to help him regardless of his murky past and the crookedness in his heart—then even he will merit repentance. There can be no better proof of this than those very terrible sinners who have successfully repented. From their example we learn that being driven away from holiness is actually the initial stage toward repentance (*Torat Natan* #7).

reproof of life *talin* (lodges) among the wise."[97] < *TaLiN* > is similar to *TeLuNah* (complaint) and conflict.[98] When you hear the tzaddikim arguing, know that this is to let you hear reproof for having blemished the drops of your mind.[99] Concerning this it is said (Proverbs 2:19), "None that go to her return, nor do they regain the paths of life."[100] You have become attached to the side of death, the aspect of

understand that their conflicts and disagreements are only for the benefit of the Jewish people. Indeed, any suggestion that these disputes are indicative of actual enmity between the tzaddikim is in itself a foreign thought, one that only adds more strength to the Other Side (by clogging one's mind).

97. **hears the reproof of life....** The simple meaning is that the person who is willing to listen to rebuke will be counted among the wise (*Metzudat David*).

98. **TaLiN...TeLuNah...conflict.** The *Zohar Chadash* teaches: When Yaakov lodged in Bethel on his way to Lavan's house (Genesis 28:11), he took issue with God that Esav was being granted control over this world. We learn this from the word *LaN* (lodged), which resembles *vayaLoNu* (they argued) (*Zohar Chadash, Vayetze* p.27; marginal note from the Tcheriner Rav). Similarly, in our text, the Rebbe makes the connection between *talin* (חלין) and *telunah* (חלונה).

99. **drops of your mind.** Earlier in this section Rebbe Nachman spoke of safeguarding the mind from becoming *chametz*. Here, he adds another dimension: keeping the drops of the mind from becoming blemished. Essentially, this entails guarding the Covenant, i.e., refraining from sexual sin (e.g., having relations with a *niddah*, non-Jewess, or any woman one is proscribed from marrying, as well as not engaging in homosexuality or masturbation). As is taught, the origin of semen or seed is in the mind (cf. *Yevamot* 53b; *Zohar Chadash, Bereishit* 15a; see *Likutey Moharan* I, 7:3, n.39; *ibid.* 11:4, n.42; see also *Rabbi Nachman's Tikkun*, Breslov Research Institute, 1984, especially pp.74-76). Seed is therefore known as the "drops of the mind." As mentioned above (nn.47,53), these drops, which descend from the whiteness of the mind, are the *chasadim* that descend from *Chokhmah* and temper the *gevurot*. A blemish of the Covenant is therefore considered a blemish of one's intellect and an inflaming of the *gevurot*.

Now, as explained, conflict between the true tzaddikim is actually spiritual conflict, a battle against the Other Side. Therefore, when a person hears this conflict, he should realize that the strife and blemish is actually in his own mind—a dispute between the sacred and the secular, between holiness and impurity. He is being rebuked for having soured his mind with undesirable thoughts.

The *Parparaot LeChokhmah* explains this in greater depth: Had this person been worthy of defeating his evil inclination and expelling all evil thoughts—engaging the Other Side on his own—the tzaddikim would not have had to engage in conflict for his benefit. Their battles would then not pertain to him, and certainly he would not have been made to hear about them. On the contrary, he would have understood that this was not conflict and contention, but a way of mitigating decrees and overcoming the forces of evil for everyone's benefit. But,

וְכוּ', וְתֵדַע שֶׁנַּעַץ קָנֶה, הַיְנוּ חָכְמוֹת חִיצוֹנִיּוֹת נְעוּצִים בְּיָם חָכְמָתֶךָ,

וּבְוַדַּאי אִם לֹא הָיָה נִפְגָּם מֹחַךְ, לֹא הָיָה נִשְׁמָע לְךָ מְרִיבוֹת שֶׁבֵּין הַצַּדִּיקִים, וְאֵין הַמְּרִיבָה אֶלָּא בִּשְׁבִילְךָ, כְּדֵי שֶׁתָּשׁוּב מִמָּוֶת לְחַיִּים, מֵחָמֵץ לְמַצָּה, מֵחָי"ת לְהֵ"א, וְתָשׁוּב מִיִּרְאָה רָעָה, מִקּוֹל פָּגוּם, מֵחָכְמָה פְּגוּמָה לְיִרְאָה טוֹבָה, לְקוֹל טוֹב, לְחָכְמָה טוֹבָה.

וּכְשֶׁתִּשְׁמֹר אֶת מֹחַךְ מִבְּחִינַת חָמֵץ, שֶׁלֹּא יִהְיֶה אָטוּם, אֲזַי יִפָּגַע קוֹלְךָ בְּגֻלְגָּלְתְּךָ, וְיִתְעַבֵּד רַעַם, וְיִתְפַּשֵׁט עַקְמִימִיּוּת שֶׁבְּלִבְּךָ, וְאָז תִּזְכֶּה לְשִׂמְחָה, כְּמוֹ שֶׁכָּתוּב: "וּלְיִשְׁרֵי לֵב שִׂמְחָה", וְזֶה פֵּרוּשׁ: "אֶעֶנְךָ בְּסֵתֶר רַעַם, אֶבְחָנְךָ עַל מֵי מְרִיבָה סֶלָה", 'מֵי מְרִיבָה' זֶה

105. **from death to life....** See above, notes 88 and 95.

106. **This conflict is only for your sake...true wisdom.** As explained above (see n.100), a person has to understand and believe that the real reason for the tzaddikim arguing is only so as to put *him* to the test. The very fact that he hears of this discord should serve as a warning that according to the dictates of strict justice he deserves to be pushed away from holiness for having abused the drops of his intellect. If he stands up to this test by ignoring the disputes and acknowledging the gravity of his previous wrongdoing, he will be able to come closer to God rather than be rejected. For the truth is that God loves mercy and desires that those distant from Him be drawn closer, despite their being unworthy. But the only way this can happen is by their being subjected to this test. If instead of turning away from the tzaddikim because of their arguing a person draws closer to them out of a desire to repent, they will teach him how to "return...and regain the paths of life" (*Advice*, p. 203f; *Parparaot LeChokhmah*).

107. **guard your mind...chametz.** By fighting the evil thoughts and rejecting secular wisdom. As we have seen (nn.46,89), this is best accomplished through prayer.

108. **strike your skull.** The flames of the heart strike the moisture of the mind (see n.55).

109. **converted into thunder.** As above, note 47.

110. **heart's crookedness...straight...joy....** As in section 3, and notes 42-44.

111. **When you called...I tested you....** This verse from Psalms (*loc. cit.*) refers to the Jewish people's bondage in Egypt. In our context, their enslavement corresponds to the implementation of severe decrees. The Psalmist says that when they prayed to God, He answered them. Rebbe Nachman, who has discussed the importance of prayer in overturning decrees, next explains how the rest of the verse corresponds to our lesson.

Interestingly, Rashi explains "I answered you thunderously" as: I openly displayed My *gevurot* and awesomeness. This supports Rebbe Nachman's earlier statement: For thunder is

chametz,[101] of "Gavriel descended."[102] Know also that "a reed has been plunged"—extrinsic wisdom has been plunged—into your sea of wisdom.[103]

And, certainly, if your mind had not been blemished, you would not have been given to hear the conflicts among the tzaddikim.[104] This conflict is only for your sake, in order that you return from death to life, from *chametz* to *matzah,* from *chet* to *heh*[105]; and so that you repent from unwholesome fear < to fear of His exaltedness >, from a marred voice < to a flawless voice >, from blemished wisdom < to complete and true wisdom >.[106]

But when you guard your mind from the aspect of *chametz,*[107] so that it does not become clogged, then your voice will strike your skull[108] and be converted into thunder,[109] and the heart's crookedness will be made straight. Then, you will merit joy, as in, "and joy for the straight of heart."[110] This is the meaning of (Psalms 81:8), "When you called in secret, I answered you thunderously; I tested you at the Waters of Conflict, Selah."[111] The Waters of Conflict are an aspect of

---

101. **death...chametz.** As above, note 95.

102. **...Gavriel descended.** See above, notes 82 and 88. As has been explained in earlier lessons, what appears to be a restatement of associations already established is actually Rebbe Nachman's way of directly connecting yet another concept to the equation. Rebbe Nachman has already connected a blemished mind to *chametz*/death. Here, he adds the above mentioned concept of corrupted *gevurot* (Gavriel) to this equation.

The *Parparaot LeChokhmah* adds: Rebbe Nachman mentions three aspects: death, *chametz,* and the letters *chet* and *heh.* They can be understood as symbolizing three levels of spiritual decline. On one level are those whose descent is so total that they are considered spiritually dead. On a second level are those whose minds have leavened spiritually. They are linked to death, or as the Rebbe said, "have become attached to the side of death," though not to the same degree as those on the former level. Finally, there are those who are only slightly separated from holiness, just as there is only a slight difference between the *chet* and the *heh.* What the people on these different levels have in common is the responsibility to make the world a better place (see §1). To do this, they must do their best to repent—no matter what level they are on. And by doing so, they can then merit the three positive levels (which Rebbe Nachman discusses next): fear of God's exaltedness, a flawless voice, and complete and true wisdom.

103. **extrinsic wisdom....** As above, notes 82, 83 and 85.

104. **not have been given to hear the conflict....** The verse thus translates in our text as follows: **The ear that hears the reproof of life** — There is a personal lesson to be learned when a person hears **lodges among the wise** — the tzaddikim arguing.

בְּחִינַת מַצָּה, בְּחִינַת מֹחִין. עַל־יְדֵי־זֶה נַעֲשֶׂה רְעָמִים:

ה וְתֵדַע, שֶׁצָּרִיךְ לְשַׁתֵּף הַגְּבוּרוֹת בַּחֲסָדִים, שְׂמֹאלָא בִּימִינָא, כְּמוֹ

eliminated by thunder—i.e., a revelation of intellect. This thunder is generated by arousing the fear of Heaven through intense prayer (§3). But for thunder to be generated when his voice strikes his mind, a person must safeguard his fear of Heaven, and more importantly keep his mind free of secular wisdom and evil passions, especially blemishes of the Covenant. This battle waged by the intellect against evil thoughts parallels the one waged by the tzaddikim against the Other Side. Thus, when this latter battle manifests as conflict between tzaddikim, the person who hears it should understand that he is being advised to repent and rectify his own blemished intellect. Only then can he come to the voice of thunder that straightens the heart's crookedness, and so perform the mitzvot with proper joy. (With this joy he can discern whether it is before or after the decree and pray properly for the world) (§4).

114. ...chasadim...right. Previously, Rebbe Nachman taught that a person must awaken his fear of Heaven. Here he emphasizes the importance of also serving God out of love—for Him and His commandments. In the Kabbalah, the *sefirah* of Chesed (Lovingkindness), the *chasadim* (benevolences), and the qualities of love, hospitality and unconditional giving are associated with the right side (see also nn.47,48); whereas the *sefirah* of Gevurah (Strength), the *gevurot* (severities), judgments and decrees, and the qualities of fear and restriction are all associated with the left (see Appendix: Structure of the Sefirot).

As desirable as it initially seems, a world influenced exclusively by Chesed and the *chasadim* would not work all that well. Unconditional giving and unbounded love would be just too overwhelming. It would also result in no boundaries, and therefore no restraint, discipline or accountability. On the other hand, a world governed solely by Gevurah and the *gevurot* would certainly not be desirable. The constriction and judgment would be impossible to bear. Only a combination of Chesed and Gevurah, a balance of *chasadim* and *gevurot*, in which the extreme qualities of each is tempered by the other, produces a workable solution for living in this world. This is the main concept of this section, a concept alluded to earlier (§3, n.47) when Rebbe Nachman spoke of the tempering of the heart's flaming (*gevurot*) with the mind's moisture (*chasadim*) to produce the voice (*Tiferet*). Rather than remaining separate influences, one to the right and the other to the left, the *chasadim* and the *gevurot* must be joined together to provide the world with a balance of tempered benevolences and tempered severities.

The *Mai HaNachal* adds that tempering the *gevurot*/fear with *chasadim*/joy mitigates the decrees, so that a person's prayers—whether recognizable or disguised—can nullify them entirely.

115. saving strength...right arm. That is, God's "saving," or salvation, comes about when His acts of strength (*Gevurah*/left) emanate from His right arm (*Chesed*). The *Mai HaNachal* explains that although the angels on the left stand ready to accuse, by coupling the left/ *gevurot* with the right/*chasadim*, the "right" becomes a salvation in that it prevents the angels on the left from protesting against the prayer that is veiled in a *maamar* (cf. n.6 above).

matzah, of mentalities,[112] through which thunder is generated.[113]

5. Know as well that a person must couple the *gevurot* (severities) with *chasadim* (benevolences), left with right,[114] as is written (Psalms 20:7), "with the saving *gevurot* (strength) of His right arm."[115] For the main

essentially from *gevurot*, as is written, "...the thunder of His *gevurot* (strength)" (see §3 and n.48).

The *Biur HaLikutim* points out that Psalm 81 has a further link to Rebbe Nachman's lesson in that it also speaks of Rosh HaShanah and the shofar.

112. **Waters of Conflict...matzah...mentalities.** When Miriam passed away, the well Israel was given in her merit to provide them with water in the wilderness, departed. The people began demanding water from Moshe and Aharon and demonstrating against them. The place where Israel disputed with God, where Moshe failed to sanctify God's name by hitting the rock instead of talking to it, was called Waters of Conflict, *Mey Merivah* (Numbers 20:13). In our context, "Waters" connotes the moisture of the mind, the intellect/*mochin*, and "Conflict" corresponds to *matzah* (as above, nn.91,96). Thus, "Waters of Conflict" alludes to the conflict between tzaddikim that rectifies the intellect.

113. **...thunder is generated.** By bringing this verse from Psalms, Rebbe Nachman ties together a number of the lesson's points: "In your distress you called out and I strengthened you. When you called in secret, I answered you thunderously...Selah." That is, what was it that made you worthy of My answering and strengthening you when you called out to Me in distress? It was that your voice was an aspect of thunder. "I tested you at the Waters of Conflict"—i.e., I tested you with the conflict between tzaddikim and saw that your intellect was pure, an aspect of *matzah*. You were not put off or confused by their arguments. And so your voice was like thunder, straightening your heart's crookedness. As a result, you merited joy and knew to differentiate between before and after the decree. This enabled you to pray even after the decree had been issued, by disguising your prayer in a *maamar*. This is, "you called in secret," for the prayer is veiled and concealed in the *maamar*, and because of this "I answered you" (*Mai HaNachal*).

In particular, these last two sections of the lesson were intended by Rebbe Nachman as a guide for Reb Noson on how to remain focused while praying (see n.1). This was a major concern for Reb Noson, who had already sought help from a number of that era's great chassidic masters (see *Through Fire and Water*, Chapters 3-6). In addition, Rebbe Nachman addressed Reb Noson's personal dilemma regarding the ongoing conflict and strife between the leading tzaddikim of the day. We can also assume that the Rebbe's references to secular wisdom were meant as criticism of the *Haskalah* movement, and his mention of "battles" as a possible veiled reference to the forthcoming decrees of forced conscription (see n.1).

In review: Every person is responsible to make the world a better place. He can do this by praying for the world's benefit, as prayer has the power to mitigate decrees. However, when decrees are extant and man's prayers are obscured by his sins, he has to disguise his prayers in a *maamar* (§1). To know whether it is before or after the decree one must perform the mitzvot with joy—feeling reward in the performance itself. Then, the degree to which he succeeds in feeling joy is indicative of whether God is joyous or the decree has already been issued (§2). To feel this joy, one must have a straight heart, a heart whose crookedness has been

שֶׁכָּתוּב: "בִּגְבוּרוֹת יֵשַׁע יְמִינוֹ", כִּי עִקַּר הַהִתְגַּלּוּת עַל יְדֵי הַחֲסָדִים,
כְּמוֹ שֶׁכָּתוּב: "שֵׁב לִימִינִי"...

וְכֵן צָרִיךְ לְשַׁתֵּף הָאַהֲבָה עִם הַיִּרְאָה, כְּדֵי שֶׁיִּתְעַבֵּד רְעָמִים, וְזֶה
מִסִּטְרָא דִּימִינָא, מֹחָא חִוָּרָא כְּכַסְפָּא.
וְזֶה "וַיָּשָׁב הַיָּם", הַיְנוּ יָם הַחָכְמָה, "לִפְנוֹת בֹּקֶר" – דָּא בֹּקֶר

tie together the different proof-texts and supports found throughout a lesson. Thus, the *gevurot* and *chasadim* of the previous paragraph are referred to here as fear and love, though the order is reversed (see next note).

119. **to generate thunder.** The previous "joining" taught that revelation of God's salvation/ *gevurot* comes through the *chasadim*. This "coupling" teaches that combining love with fear generates thunder (see n.47).

120. **a mind as white as silver.** The *Tikkuney Zohar* (*loc. cit.*) applies this to Avraham, who personified *Chesed* (the *sefirah* and the attribute), love of God, and the right side generally. All the qualities associated with the right side emanate from the first right-sided *sefirah*, *Chokhmah* (Wisdom)—from the mind as white as silver, the "whiteness" of the mind (see n.53)—but are only perfected once the mind has been purged of secular wisdom, foreign thoughts and evil passions. These come from the dark side of love and are the "enemies" bent on preventing a person from developing his potential in holiness. It is necessary to rebuke and expel them, as in, "Rebuke the beast of the reed," thereby transforming the *chametz* of the mind into *matzah* (see §4 and nn.87,88). The strength for this stems from the love for God, holy love. This is the meaning of the verse, "Sit at my right hand while I make your enemies your footstool." And when his love of God saves him from these enemies so that his mind is cleared of secular wisdom and evil passions, then his voice will strike the sphere of the mind and generate the thunder that will bring him to joy (*Mai HaNachal*).

121. **When it turned morning. . . .** Earlier (see n.88), Rebbe Nachman quoted from a passage in the *Zohar* that includes the following reference to Egypt: "Why a reed? Because a reed is easily snapped and broken. This is Egypt. The Egyptians ruled the entire world. Yet when the time came, the Egyptians, who are like *chametz*, were broken; the Jews, who are like *matzah*, were redeemed." The Rebbe also quoted Psalm 81, which refers to the Jewish people's bondage in Egypt (see n.111), though not directly. Here, by quoting this verse from Exodus that relates to the splitting of the Red Sea, the Rebbe directly connects the Egyptians— subdued enemies of the Jewish people—to the lesson.

122. **sea of wisdom.** The Midrash teaches that the splitting of the Red Sea was a time of great judgment (*Shemot Rabbah* 21:7). In our context, it was a time of a clogging of the intellect, the sea of wisdom.

123. **morning of Avraham.** In the terminology of the Kabbalah, the attribute of *chesed* corresponds to the day, whereas the attribute of *gevurah* corresponds to the night. Thus, each morning, when night turns to day, the *sefirah* of Chesed (Lovingkindness) is in ascendance. This corresponds to Avraham, who exemplified the attribute of lovingkindness. More specifically, the *Zohar* here adds: Avraham is symbolic of the morning, as Scripture points

revelation comes about <through the right,> by means of *chasadim,*[116] as is written (*ibid.* 110:1), "Sit at My right hand [while I make your enemies your footstool]."[117]

It is likewise necessary to couple love with fear of Heaven,[118] in order to generate thunder.[119] This [love] is from the right side, from "a mind as white as silver" (*Tikkuney Zohar* #70).[120]

This is <the meaning of "When it turned morning, the sea returned to its might"> (Exodus 14:27).[121] "The sea" alludes to the sea of wisdom[122]; "when it turned morning"—this is the morning of Avraham (*Zohar* II, 170b),[123] corresponding to "Avraham My beloved"

---

116. **For the main revelation....** In general, *Keter, Chokhmah* and *Binah,* the upper three *sefirot,* are said to be concealed. The attributes of God that these three *sefirot* represent, *mochin* (see n.51), are for the most part not manifest. In contrast, the seven lower *sefirot,* from *Chesed* to *Malkhut,* are said to be revealed. The attributes of God that these seven *sefirot* represent are manifest. Thus, the main revelation of God begins with *Chesed,* the first of the lower *sefirot* and one situated on the right side of the *sefirah* structure (see Appendix: Structure of the Sefirot). Also in terms of the *gevurot* and *chasadim,* revelation—or in this case tempering—comes from the right. For whereas the *gevurot* descend from *Binah* to *Gevurah* along the left side, they are tempered by the *chasadim* descending from *Chokhmah* on the right. See next note.

117. **Sit at My right hand....** Rashi (*loc. cit.*) explains that here "sit" means "wait." That is, "Wait at My right hand while I...." In our context, this refers to the *gevurot*/decrees "waiting" to become joined with *chasadim* before descending to *Gevurah.* This, so that they can be tempered and not develop into harsh decrees. The end of the verse, "while I make your enemies your footstool," indicates this as well: "your enemies," the decrees, will be "your footstool," subdued and vanquished. The *Mai HaNachal* adds that "enemies" alludes to secular wisdom and one's evil thoughts and passions, all of which sour the mind (see n.80). The Talmud teaches (*Bava Batra* 16a): "Satan is the seducer, the accuser, and the Angel of Death." That is, the angels on the left side entice a person with physical desires and secular wisdom. Then, having seduced him into sinning, they become his accusers, calling for decrees to be issued against him for these sins. And, like the Angel of Death, they are only too willing to be the ones sent to carry out the decrees issued. The only way to counter this seduction and mitigate the decrees is through one's love for God—an aspect of the right side—which makes it possible to pray and disguise the prayers from the angels on the left.

The *Biur HaLikutim* concurs that these "enemies" are of a spiritual nature. Specifically, they are the elements of the Other Side mentioned previously, the forces that sour and clog the mind and block its proper functioning. And although the voice of thunder and the attribute of fear do subdue these forces and open the mind, the essential means for overcoming them and achieving total purity is only the qualities that stem from the right side—i.e., love and *chesed.*

118. **love with fear of Heaven.** This is combining *Chesed* with *Gevurah,* the right with the left (*Mai HaNachal*). It is common for Rebbe Nachman to interchange the various corresponding names and attributes of a particular concept. This is an additional way to

דְּאַבְרָהָם. בְּחִינַת: "אַבְרָהָם אוֹהֲבִי". "לְאֵיתָנוּ" – דָּא גְּבוּרוֹת. הַיְנוּ בְּחִינַת: "קוֹל רַעַמְךָ בַּגַּלְגַּל".

וְזֶהוּ : "מַיִם רַבִּים לֹא יוּכְלוּ לְכַבּוֹת אֶת הָאַהֲבָה", כִּי עִקָּר הַתְגַּבְּרוּת עַל יְדֵי הָאַהֲבָה, כְּמוֹ שֶׁכָּתוּב: "שֵׁב לִימִינִי" וְכוּ'. וְזֶהוּ פֵּרוּשׁ: "אֵל הַכָּבוֹד". 'אֵל' – דָּא חֶסֶד. 'כָּבוֹד' – דָּא חָכְמָה, כְּמוֹ שֶׁכָּתוּב: "כָּבוֹד חֲכָמִים יִנְחָלוּ". 'הִרְעִים' – דָּא בְּחִינַת רְעָמִים, הַיְנוּ הַגְּבוּרוֹת בְּחִינַת רְעָמִים, צָרִיךְ לְשַׁתֵּף עִמָּהֶם אַהֲבָה, כְּדֵי שֶׁיִּפָּגְעוּ בַּכָּבוֹד, בִּבְחִינַת חָכְמָה, שֶׁיִּתְעַבֵּד מֵהֶם רְעָמִים,

126. **Many waters....** The "many waters" are the many nations who attempt to overwhelm and crush the Jewish people (*Shir HaShirim Rabbah* 8:7). In our context, this refers to the secular wisdom and many vices that seek to drown the intellect, the holy encampment of the Jew. How can a person counter these "many waters"?

127. **conquer...by means of love.** That is, through acts of lovingkindness, the attribute of *chesed.* Performing the mitzvot with love and joy helps a person wage the battle against his enemies—i.e., secular wisdom and evil passions—who are constantly attempting to overwhelm him and undermine his fear of Heaven. Thus, after first developing fear of Heaven (which brings one to perform the mitzvot), a person must perform the mitzvot with joy (out of love for God). This alone will give him the ability to conquer and vanquish all the elements opposed to his spiritual development.

Rebbe Nachman's advice applies to our daily lives as well. The key to overcoming any opposition, the source of which is the *gevurot,* is through love, the *chasadim.* This, as opposed to fighting the *gevurot* with *gevurot,* as we so often seem to do.

128. **Sit at My right.** For the "enemy," the fallen *gevurot*/Other Side, must be tempered and conquered by love (as above, n.117).

129. **El is chesed.** God's holy name *El* indicates kindness, as in (Psalms 52:3), "The *chesed* (lovingkindness) of *El* lasts throughout the day" (see Appendix: Sefirot and Associated Names of God).

130. **wise...inherit glory.** Both *Chokhmah* (Wisdom) and *Chesed* (Lovingkindness) are on the right side of the *sefirah* structure. From this verse in Proverbs we see that wisdom and glory are synonymous. Thus, when a person performs the mitzvot with joy—i.e., love/*chesed*—he merits glory—i.e., wisdom/a pure intellect.

131. **thunders...thunder.** He then merits thunder—i.e., to arouse fear of Heaven in others as well as in himself, for his intellect and fear are pure and tempered with love.

The verse thus translates in our text as follows: **El** — When *chesed* is performed, **of glory** — one merits intellect, and so he **thunders** — his voice arouses fear of Heaven.

(Isaiah 41:8)[124]; "to its might"—this is *gevurot,* corresponding to "The sound of Your thunder was in the sphere."[125] And this is (Song of Songs 8:7), "Many waters cannot extinguish the love."[126] For the ability to conquer is mainly by means of love,[127] as in, "Sit at My right...."[128]

And this is the explanation of (Psalms 29:3), "the *El* (God) of Glory thunders." "*El*" is *chesed* (lovingkindness)[129]; "glory" is wisdom, as is written (Proverbs 3:35), "The wise will inherit glory"[130]; "thunders" alludes to the thunder.[131] In other words, the *gevurot,* an aspect of thunder, must be coupled with love, so that they will strike the glory, the aspect of wisdom, and be converted into thunder. Then, you will

---

out (Genesis 22:3), "Avraham got up early in the morning" to do the will of the Holy One. Hence the phrase "the morning of Avraham." The *Zohar* therefore understands "when it turned morning..." as alluding to Avraham, and says: The judgments against the Israelites at that time were so great that had God not recalled the merit of Avraham, all of Israel would have drowned in the Red Sea. It split for the Jews only in his merit, for his having gotten up early in the morning to do the will of God, and they passed through (*Zohar* II, 170b). In our context, with "the sea" connoting the sea of wisdom, God's splitting the sea for the Israelites alludes to His opening their clogged minds and giving them minds "as white as silver" in Avraham's merit (see n.120). See note 125 for the completion of Rebbe Nachman's explanation of this verse.

Rebbe Nachman's references here to Avraham, the personification of *Chesed,* is also intended to highlight the contrast between him and Yitzchak, the personification of *Gevurah.* Yitzchak's *gevurot* are tempered by Avraham's *chasadim.* This is especially necessary on Rosh HaShanah, when fear is the dominant attribute, for Rosh HaShanah is the Day of Judgment. The sounding of the shofar (thunder) is thus a means for arousing fear of Heaven but also love for God (cf. nn.68 and 69).

124. **Avraham my beloved.** Avraham—who is love—is God's *beloved.*

125. **might...gevurot...sphere.** As Rebbe Nachman explained earlier: Thunder is an aspect of *gevurot...* These *gevurot* correspond to might and strength. A person releases the voice with great force and...when it encounters the skull (sphere of the mind), the voice is converted into thunder and is transmitted to the creation (see §3 and nn.48-50,55).

Thus, although when the Jews came to the Red Sea it was a time of judgment, of fallen *gevurot,* by tempering these *gevurot* with *chasadim* the decree against the Jewish people was mitigated and all of Israel passed through the sea—the sea of wisdom, the intellect. This was because at the Red Sea the Jewish people had attained the devotions mentioned in our lesson. They separated from *chametz*/death/secular wisdom and ate *matzah,* representative of a pure intellect. Their fear of Heaven/*gevurot*/"might" was also complete, as in (Exodus 14:31), "the people feared God." With purified intellect and fear, their prayers were like thunder and so were hearkened to by God (Exodus 14:10). This also gives us a deeper understanding of Rashi's explanation of the verse in Song of Songs (1:11), "We will make for you necklaces of gold studded with silver." Rashi says it refers to the gold and silver booty the Jews acquired at the splitting of the Red Sea. In our context, this refers to the gold *gevurot* and silver *chasadim,* fear and love, that the Jewish people then attained (*Mai HaNachal*).

וְתִתְגַּבֵּר עַל אוֹיְבֶיךָ, כְּמוֹ שֶׁכָּתוּב: "שֵׁב לִימִינִי" וְכוּ':

וְזֶה פֵּירוּשׁ:

אָמַר רַבָּה בַּר בַּר חָנָא: זִימְנָא
חֲדָא הֲוָה אַזְלִינַן בִּסְפִינְתָּא,
וְסַגָּאי סְפִינְתָּא בֵּין שִׁיצָא
לְשִׁיצָא דְּכַוְרָא תְּלָתָא יוֹמָא
וּתְלָתָא לֵילוֹתָא, אִיהוּ בִּזְקִיפוּ
וַאֲנָן בִּשְׁפּוּלֵי. וְכִי תֵּימָא, לָא
מַסְגֵּי סְפִינְתָּא טוּבָא? כִּי אָתָא
רַב דִּימִי אָמַר כְּמֵיחַם קַמְקוּמָא
דְּמַיָּא מַסְגֵּי שִׁתִּין פַּרְסֵי, וְשָׁדֵי
פָּרָשָׁא גִּירָא וְקַדְמָה לֵיהּ אִיהִי.
וְאָמַר רַב אַשִׁי הַהוּא גִּילְדָּנָא
דְּיַמָּא הֲוַאי, דְּאִית לֵיהּ תְּרֵי
שִׁיצָא (בבא בתרא עג:).

רַשְׁבָּ"ם:

שִׁיצָא סְנַפִּיר: בֵּין שִׁיצָא לְשִׁיצָא
סְנַפִּירִין בְּגַב הַדָּג, אֶחָד לְצַד הָרֹאשׁ
וְאֶחָד לְצַד הַזָּנָב: אִיהוּ בִּזְקִיפוּ
שֶׁהָיָה הוֹלֵךְ כְּנֶגֶד הָרוּחַ: וַאֲנָן
אַזְלִינַן בִּשְׁפּוּלֵי כְּמוֹ שֶׁהָרוּחַ הוֹלֵךְ,
דְּמַיִם שֶׁל יָם אֵינָם נוֹבְעִין, אֶלָּא עַל-
יְדֵי רוּחַ הוֹלְכִין בָּהֶן: כְּמֵיחַם
קַמְקוּמָא דְּמַיָא כְּשִׁיעוּר שֶׁמְּחַמְּמִים
קַמְקוּמָא שֶׁל מַיִם חַמִּין: וְשָׁדֵי
פָּרָשָׁא גִּירָא כְּשֶׁהָיָה שׁוּם אָדָם יוֹרֶה
בְּחֵץ וּבְקֶשֶׁת עַל שְׂפַת הַיָּם לָאָרֶץ,
הֲרֵי חֲזִינַן דְּקַדְמָה לָהּ סְפִינְתָּא לַחֵץ:

סְפִינְתָּא – לְשׁוֹן חֲשִׁיבוּת, דָּא בְּחִינַת גְּבוּרָה יִרְאָה, כְּמוֹ שֶׁכָּתוּב:
יִרְאַת ה' הִיא אוֹצָרוֹ", שֶׁהִיא עִקַּר הַחֲשִׁיבוּת.

between love and fear enables a person to battle his evil thoughts and desires, and even overcome them (§5).

133. **This is the explanation.** Rebbe Nachman now shows how the concepts of this lesson are alluded to within the framework of Rabbah bar bar Chanah's story.

134. **sephinta...importance.** The Aramaic term for ship, *sephinta* (ספינתא), resembles *sephin* (ספין), which is Aramaic for important. See *Moed Katan* 28a (cf. Lesson #1 and n.65).

135. **fear...His treasure.** Rashi explains that a person who fears God merits God's treasure, and the Talmud associates God's treasure with *gevurot geshamim* (mighty rains; *Taanit* 2a). This shows the connection between fear and *gevurot,* as above (§3).

136. **fear...is most important.** Expounding on this verse from Isaiah, "The fear of God...," the Talmud states that God's greatest treasure is the Torah. Yet when a person has Torah knowledge but lacks fear of God, he is like one who has the keys to the inner doors but has no key to open the outer gates. How can he enter? (*Shabbat* 31a). And although in our lesson

conquer your enemies, as in, "Sit at My right hand while I make your enemies your footstool."[132]

6. This is the explanation[133]:

Rabbah bar bar Chanah recounted: One time we were traveling on a *sephinta* **(ship). To sail between a fish's two** *shitza* **(fins) took the ship three days and three nights, [even though] it was swimming upwind and we were sailing downwind. And lest you think the ship was not sailing quickly, when Rav Dimi came, he said, "In the time it takes to heat a kettle of water, it went sixty** *parsay* **(parasangs). And a** *parsha* **(rider) shot an arrow, yet [the ship] preceded it." Rav Ashi said, "This [fish] was a sea** *gyldena,* **which has two fins"** *(Bava Batra* 73b).

Rashbam:

shitza - a fin: **between two shitza -** these are the fins on the back of the fish, one to the side of the head and one to the side of the tail: **it was swimming upwind** - it was going against the wind: **and we were sailing downwind** - in the same direction as the wind; for the waters of the sea do not flow and one sails using the wind: **In the time it takes to heat a kettle of water** - in the amount of time it would take to boil a kettle of water: **And a rider shot an arrow** - if anyone on the seashore would shoot an arrow from his bow, we would see the ship outrace the arrow:

sephinta — This connotes importance.[134] It corresponds to *gevurah/* fear, as is written (Isaiah 33:6), "The fear of God is His treasure."[135] For [the fear of Heaven] is what is most important.[136]

---

132. ...**footstool.** As explained, when a person's love and fear of God are properly balanced, he has the weapons to battle and overcome his enemies.

In review: Every person is responsible to make the world a better place by praying to mitigate decrees. However, when decrees are extant and man's prayers are obscured by his sins, he has to disguise his prayers in a *maamar* (§1). To know whether it is before or after the decree one must perform the mitzvot with joy—feeling reward in the performance itself. Then, the degree to which he succeeds in feeling joy is indicative of whether God is joyous or the decree has already been issued (§2). To feel this joy, one must have a heart whose crookedness has been eliminated by thunder—i.e., a revelation of intellect. This thunder is generated by arousing the fear of Heaven through intense prayer (§3). But for thunder to be generated when his voice strikes his mind, a person must safeguard his fear of Heaven, and more importantly keep his mind free of secular wisdom and evil passions, especially blemishes of the Covenant. This battle waged by the intellect against evil thoughts parallels the one waged by the tzaddikim against the Other Side. Thus, when this latter battle manifests as conflict between tzaddikim, the person who hears it should understand that he is being advised to repent and rectify his own blemished intellect. Only then can he come to the voice of thunder that straightens the heart's crookedness, and so perform the mitzvot with proper joy (§4). He must also have love for God and perform the mitzvot with joy. For the proper balance

שִׁיצָא – לְשׁוֹן צָרָה, כְּמוֹ שֶׁכָּתוּב: "וַאֲכַלֶּה אֹתָם כְּרָגַע", וְתַרְגּוּמוֹ: 'וַאֲשֵׁיצֵי יַתְהוֹן'.

תְּלָתָא יוֹמָא וְלֵילוּתָא – דָּא בְּחִינַת מִצְווֹת, שֶׁיֵּשׁ בָּהֶם מְשְׁכָּלוֹת וּמְקַבָּלוֹת וְחֻקּוֹת, וּכְתִיב בָּהֶם: "וְהָגִיתָ בּוֹ יוֹמָם וָלָיְלָה". אִיהוּ בְּזָקִיפוּ וְאָנַן בִּשְׁפּוּלֵי – זֶה בְּחִינַת: "יִשְׂמַח ה' בְּמַעֲשָׂיו, יִשְׂמַח יִשְׂרָאֵל בְּעוֹשָׂיו". כְּמֵיחַם קֵמְקוּמָא דְמַיָא – דָּא מֹחָא, כְּמוֹ שֶׁכָּתוּב: "וְנוֹזְלִים מִן לְבָנוֹן". מַסְגָּא שָׁתִין פַּרְסֵי – דָּא בְּחִינַת גְּבוּרוֹת, שָׁשִׁים גִּבּוֹרִים, וְרַעַם גְּבוּרוֹתָיו.

וְכִי שָׁדֵי פַּרְשָׁא גִּירָא – 'פַּרְשָׁא' : דָּא בְּחִינַת חֶסֶד, שֶׁהוּא מוֹצִיא

---

eternally unfathomable—e.g., the Red Heifer (cf. *Yad HaChazakah, Hilkhot Me'ilah* 8:8; *Or HaChaim*, Numbers 19:2).

139. **day and night.** Thus, "three days and three nights" also alludes to performing the mitzvot.

140. **God rejoices...Israel rejoices....** This corresponds to performing the mitzvot with joy, as a result of which a person can enter into and feel the joy of God (as above, §2, nn.29-31).

141. **heat...water...mind....** As explained, the mind corresponds to moisture, the rain clouds (nn.47,51-53). "To heat a kettle of water" thus corresponds to combining the heart's burning desire to serve God (fear, *gevurot*) with a pure mind (intellect, *chasadim*) in order to produce thunder. See also *Rabbi Nachman's Wisdom* #79.

142. **sixty parsay...gevurot.** The term *parsay* is the plural of *parsa* (parasang, a Persian measure of distance) and resembles the Hebrew term for one of Persian descent, *Parsi*. The Talmud indicates that as a people, the Persians were particularly strong and mighty (cf. *Kiddushin* 72a), which in our context corresponds to the *gevurot*.

143. **sixty mighty men...thunder....** "Sixty *parsay*" thus alludes to the "sixty mighty men" from the verse (*loc. cit.*), "Here is Shelomoh's bed, encircled by sixty mighty men...." God had given King Solomon the ability to rule over all of creation, including the demons. But after he married Pharaoh's daughter, King Solomon was beset by extrinsic fears and so had sixty warriors stand guard around his bed (*Shir HaShirim Rabbah* 3:7). In our context, King Solomon's error caused the *gevurot* to descend and assume the form of extrinsic fears. To rectify this he needed "sixty mighty men"—i.e., "the thunder of His *gevurot*."

From the teachings of the Kabbalah we learn that each one of the *Ten Sefirot* contains a

ShitZa — This connotes misfortune, as is written (Numbers 16:21), "[Separate yourselves from this congregation,] and I will destroy them in an instant." The Aramaic translation [of "and I will destroy them"] is *v'aShaytZay yas'hone*.[137]

three days and three nights — This corresponds to the mitzvot, which are [divided into three categories]: the rational, the tradition-based, and the statutes.[138] Concerning them it is written (Joshua 1:8), "You shall study [Torah] day and night."[139]

it was swimming upwind and we were sailing downwind — This corresponds to "God rejoices in His works; Israel rejoices in its Maker."[140]

In the time it takes to heat a kettle of water — This is the mind, as in, "and drops from Lebanon."[141]

it went sixty parsay — This corresponds to *gevurot*[142]: "sixty *geborim* (mighty men)" (Song of Songs 3:7), and "the thunder of His strength."[143]

And a parsha shot an arrow — *PaRSha* is the aspect of *chesed* (lovingkindness). It refers to someone who brings to light that which

Rebbe Nachman has not explicitly mentioned the concept of Torah, it is implied in what he says concerning the intellect, for Torah wisdom is the very opposite of secular wisdom. Thus, just as it is impossible to have a pure intellect without fear of Heaven (see n.80), it is impossible to attain the inner depths and truth of Torah without fear of Heaven. Even if he studies Torah, his Torah is likened to secular wisdom, the side of death, *chametz*. Therefore, the Rebbe says: The fear of Heaven is what is most important. The *Mai HaNachal* adds that interpreting *sephinta* (ship) as a metaphor for fear of Heaven is most appropriate. For it is through the *sephinta*/fear that a person traverses the sea of wisdom/intellect, as in, "where there is no fear of Heaven, there is no wisdom" (as above, §4, n.80).

137. **ShitZa... v'aShaytZay yas'hone.** God said this to Moshe and Aharon when Korach led a band of his supporters to rebel against them. On the surface, their disagreement seems to be what in our lesson Rebbe Nachman calls a conflict between tzaddikim. However, in rebelling against Moshe, Korach blemished his mind, causing it to sour like *chametz*, and so was punished with death (cf. n.95). This is *shitza*, indicative of misfortune and decrees.

138. **the rational, the tradition-based, and the statutes.** Rational mitzvot are those commandments that are self-evident and can be arrived at intellectually, without any prophetic inspiration—e.g., honoring one's parents and the prohibitions against murder and theft. Tradition-based mitzvot are those that are handed down, originally through prophetic inspiration, and once given are understood to be in the individual's or nation's best interest—e.g., celebrating Shabbat and the Festivals. Statutes are the commandments that remain

לְאוֹר תַּעֲלוּמוֹת, דְּבָרִים הַמִּצְמְצָמִין הוּא מְפָרֵשׁ אוֹתָם.

גִּירָא – דָּא: "שְׁלַח חִצֶּיךָ וּתְהֻמֵּם", דָּא בְּחִינַת: "שֵׁב לִימִינִי" וְכוּ'.

קַדְמָה לֵיהּ אִיהִי – דָּא בְּחִינַת יִרְאָה שֶׁהִיא קֹדֶם, שֶׁהַיִּרְאָה הִיא
קוֹדֶמֶת, כְּמוֹ שֶׁכָּתוּב: "רֵאשִׁית חָכְמָה" וְכוּ'.

שֶׁרַבָּה בַּר בַּר חָנָא סְפֵר, שֶׁהָלַךְ כָּל כָּךְ בְּמִדַּת הַיִּרְאָה, וְרָאָה גֹּדֶל
כֹּחַ הַיִּרְאָה, עַד שֶׁיָּכוֹל לְהָבִין עַל יָדָהּ בֵּין קֹדֶם גְּזַר דִּין לְאַחַר גְּזַר
דִּין, וְזֶהוּ בֵּין שִׁיצָא וְכוּ'.

וְהָדָר מְפָרֵשׁ אֵיךְ יָכוֹל לְהָבִין, הַיְנוּ עַל־יְדֵי הַמִּצְווֹת, שֶׁהֵם בְּחִינַת
תְּלָתָא יוֹמָא וְכוּ', יָכוֹל לְהָבִין. וְדַוְקָא כְּשֶׁעוֹשִׂין אוֹתָן בְּשִׂמְחָה,
וְעַל־יְדֵי שִׂמְחַת הַמִּצְווֹת יָכוֹל לְהָבִין. כִּי הַקָּדוֹשׁ־בָּרוּךְ־הוּא מְשַׂמֵּחַ
בְּמַעֲשָׂיו, וְהַשִּׂמְחָה הִיא מְלֻבֶּשֶׁת בְּמִצְווֹת, כַּנַּ"ל, וַאֲנַחְנוּ מְשַׂמְּחִין
לְמַטָּה גַּם כֵּן בְּהַקָּדוֹשׁ־בָּרוּךְ־הוּא, כְּמוֹ שֶׁכָּתוּב: "יִשְׂמַח יִשְׂרָאֵל
בְּעוֹשָׂיו", וְאֵין רְצוֹנֵנוּ בְּשׁוּם שָׂכָר, אֲפִלּוּ שְׂכַר עוֹלָם הַבָּא, כַּנַּ"ל.

n.117). King David spent his life fighting Israel's enemies. On a deeper level, his battles signified the battles tzaddikim wage against the Other Side in order to keep it from entering the holy encampment (§4). Thus, those of King David's prayers and psalms that he composed to invoke God's assistance in battle are also heartfelt requests for assistance in countering all spiritual opposition. This is the deeper intent behind "Shoot Your arrows..." and "Sit at My right hand...," as well as the many other similar verses Rebbe Nachman quotes in his lessons from the Book of Psalms.

147. **preceded it... is the fear of God.** The Psalmist says that preceding wisdom—i.e., before a person can attain wisdom—he must first have the fear of God. In our context, the *chasadim*/ love of God must be preceded by the *gevurot*/fear of God.

Having shown how the different elements in Rabbah bar bar Chanah's story allude to concepts discussed in the lesson, Rebbe Nachman pauses here to tie them together by means of a review.

148. **delved so deeply into... fear of Heaven.** "One time we were traveling on a ship (fear)..." (n.134-136).

149. **discern between....** Discern between the different misfortunes, which correspond to decrees. See above, note 137.

150. **mitzvot...three days....** As above, and note 139.

151. **as explained.** See section 2 and notes 29,30.

is hidden, someone who *mePhaReSh* (explains) those matters which are obscure.[144]

an arrow — As in, "Shoot Your arrows and panic them" (Psalms 144:6).[145] This corresponds to "Sit at My right hand while I make your enemies your footstool."[146]

the ship preceded it — This is the aspect of fear, which "precedes." For fear of Heaven precedes all else, as is written (Psalms 111:10), "The beginning of wisdom is the fear of God."[147]

Rabbah bar bar Chanah recounted that he had delved so deeply into the attribute of the fear of Heaven,[148] and had seen the great power of this fear, that he was now able to use it to discern between before the decree has been issued and after the decree has been issued—i.e., **between two shitza**.[149]

He then explains how he could discern: by means of the mitzvot, which are the aspect of **three days...**,[150] it is possible to discern. And this is only when one performs [the mitzvot] with joy; for through the joy of the mitzvot it is possible to discern. This is because the Holy One rejoices in His works and this joy is clothed in the mitzvot, as explained.[151] And we below also rejoice in the Holy One, as in, "Israel rejoices in its Maker." We desire no reward, even the reward of the World to Come. This is, **It was swimming upwind and we were sailing**

---

measure of all the other *sefirot* (e.g., *Malkhut* consists of *Keter* of *Malkhut*, *Chokhmah* of *Malkhut*, *Binah* of *Malkhut*, and so on to *Malkhut* of *Malkhut*). In this way, the six rings of the windpipe that emit the shofar blast/thunder (see n.47), which correspond to the six *sefirot* from *Chesed* through *Yesod*, are actually sixty—i.e., the sixty strong men that rectify the corrupted *gevurot*/extrinsic fears and thereby generate a voice of thunder.

144. **PaRSha...mePhaReSh...obscure.** The *Zohar* explains: The difference between *tov* (good) and *chesed* (lovingkindness) is that the nature of *tov* is constricted, such that the good is contained within itself. *Chesed,* on the other hand, expands outward, extending beneficence to both the righteous and the wicked (*Zohar* II, 168b; see *Likutey Moharan* I, 283). This connects to what Rebbe Nachman explained earlier, that the main revelation begins with the *sefirah* of *Chesed* (§5 and n.116). Thus, *parsha* (פרשא, rider) alludes to revealing the hidden, as in one who is *mepharesh* (מפרש, explains) and reveals the meaning of that which is difficult and obscure.

145. **Your arrows...panic them.** The *Metzudat David* renders "Your arrows" as "Your thunder." Thus, King David asks God to assist him in battle: "Shoot Your thunder and panic them."

146. **Sit...right hand....** As explained, this is the coupling of *gevurot* with *chasadim* (see §5,

וְזֶה, 'אִיהוּ בִּזְקִיפוּ וְאָנָן בִּשְׁפּוֹלֵי', לְפִי שִׂמְחָתוֹ כֵּן שִׂמְחָתֵנוּ, וְעַל־
יְדֵי־זֶה אֲנַחְנוּ יְכוֹלִין לְהָבִין.

וְהָדָר מְפָרֵשׁ אֵיךְ לְהַשִּׂיג בְּחִינַת שִׂמְחָה, עַל־יְדֵי בְּחִינַת רַעַם.
וְזֶהוּ: כִּי אָתָא רַב דִּימִי אָמַר: כְּמֵיחַם קַמְקוּמָא דְּמַיָּא וְכוּ', הַיְנוּ
בְּחִינַת: קוֹל רַעַמְךָ בַּגַּלְגַּל. שִׁיתִּין זֶה בְּחִינַת גְּבוּרוֹת, הַפּוֹגְעִין
בְּגַלְגַּלְתָּא, וְנַעֲשֶׂה מִמֶּנּוּ רְעָמִים. וְאִשְׁתַּמַּע קָלָא: זֶה בְּחִינַת הַקּוֹל
מְעוֹרֵר הַכַּוָּנָה, בְּחִינַת: לֹא נִבְרְאוּ רְעָמִים וְכוּ'.

וְהָדָר אָמַר, שֶׁעִקַּר הִתְגַּבְּרוּת הַגְּבוּרוֹת אֵינוֹ אֶלָּא עַל־יְדֵי חֲסָדִים.
וְצָרִיךְ לְאַכְלְלָא שְׂמָאלָא בִּימִינָא, כַּנַּ"ל, וְאַף־עַל־פִּי־כֵן צָרִיךְ
לְאַקְדָּמָא אֶת הַיִּרְאָה. כִּי בַּעַל אֲבֵדָה מַחֲזִיר עַל אֲבֵדָתוֹ (כְּמוֹ
שֶׁאָמְרוּ רַבּוֹתֵינוּ, זִכְרוֹנָם לִבְרָכָה [קִדּוּשִׁין ב:]: 'דַּרְכּוֹ שֶׁל אִישׁ לְחַזֵּר
אַחַר אִשָּׁה. מָשָׁל לְאָדָם, שֶׁאָבְדָה לוֹ אֲבֵדָה' וְכוּ'.

פֵּרוּשׁ: כִּי אַהֲבָה הוּא בְּחִינַת אִישׁ וְיִרְאָה הִיא בְּחִינַת אִשָּׁה,
כַּיָּדוּעַ. וְעַל כֵּן צָרִיךְ לְהַקְדִּים אֶת הַיִּרְאָה, כִּי אָז תָּבוֹא אֵלָיו
הָאַהֲבָה מִמֵּילָא, כִּי הָאַהֲבָה הוֹלֶכֶת וּמְחַזֶּרֶת אַחַר הַיִּרְאָה תָּמִיד,
כִּי בַּעַל אֲבֵדָה מַחֲזִיר אַחַר אֲבֵדָתוֹ, כַּנַּ"ל; כָּךְ שָׁמַעְתִּי מִפִּיו

157. **necessary to encompass the left....** Above, section 5.

158. **fear...first.** As in note 147 above (see also n.129).

159. **As the Sages taught.** This did not appear in Rebbe Nachman's original manuscript. Reb Noson, who added it, writes: "I heard this example explicitly from Rebbe Nachman's holy lips."

160. **It is the way of man to search after....** The Talmud asks why it is that the man is the one who takes the initiative in searching for a mate. The answer, the Sages say, is that this search is like searching for a lost object. Who searches for whom? Obviously the person who lost an object does the searching and not the other way around. Well, Chavah, the first woman, was created from Adam's rib. It was taken from him and so he must go searching for what he has lost (*Kiddushin, loc cit., Rashi, s.v. aveidah*).

161. **as is known.** Male and female correspond to the *sefirot* of *Chesed* and *Gevurah*, love and fear, right and left, respectively (see *Zohar* I, 70a).

Earlier, Rebbe Nachman taught that the main revelation begins in *Chesed* (§5). Thus, at Creation, Adam/man/*chesed* was created first. But as Scripture states (Genesis 2:18): "It is not

downwind—our joy < below > is in accordance with His joy < Above >. In this way we can discern [whether it is before or after the decree has been issued].[152]

[Rabbah bar bar Chanah] then explains how to achieve this joy: by means of the aspect of thunder.[153] This is, **when Rav Dimi came, he said: In the time it takes to heat a kettle of water it went sixty parsay**— i.e., corresponding to "The sound of Your thunder was in the sphere," < and to "The voice stimulates *kavanah*" > .[154] **Sixty** is an allusion to *gevurot,* which strike the skull and are converted into thunder.[155] And then "the voice is transmitted"—this corresponds to "The voice stimulates *kavanah*," and to "Thunder was only created [to straighten the crookedness of the heart]."[156]

He then said that, in essence, the conquering-ability of the *gevurot* is only due to *chasadim*. Thus, it is necessary to encompass the left within the right, as explained.[157] But even so, a person must put the fear of Heaven first,[158] because "the owner of a lost object searches after what he has lost." {As the Sages taught[159]: It is the way of the man to search after the woman. This is analogous to a person who has lost something. Who searches after whom? Certainly, the owner of the object searches after what he has lost (*Kiddushin* 2b).[160] The explanation of this is: Man is the aspect of love, whereas woman is the aspect of fear, as is known.[161] It is therefore necessary to put the fear of Heaven first, as, then, love will automatically follow. For the love [of God] constantly goes out and searches after the fear of Heaven,

152. **we can discern. . . .** As above, section 2.

153. **how to achieve this joy. . . thunder.** Having just explained that performing the mitzvot with joy is the key for discerning whether it is before or after the decree, Rabbah bar bar Chanah's words raise the question, Of what value is fear? He therefore makes the point that to attain joy one must have the aspect of thunder. Rebbe Nachman has explained that true joy is only possible once the heart's crookedness has been made straight by the thunder that comes from the *gevurot*. These *gevurot,* as we have seen, are an aspect of fear. Thus fear, too, is a fundamental component in the process. And, because it is not possible to generate this thunder unless the mind has been made pure, Rabbah bar bar Chanah goes on the quote the words of Rav Dimi (*Parparaot LeChokhmah*).

154. **water. . . sphere. . . kavanah.** Rebbe Nachman has already shown that "kettle of water" alludes to a mind pure enough to generate thunder (see n.141), and so here he links it to two previously quoted verses that speak of the heart and its relationship to the thunder/voice.

155. **Sixty. . . gevurot. . . thunder.** As above, notes 142-143.

156. **voice is transmitted. . . .** This relates back to section 3 and note 57.

הַקָּדוֹשׁ בְּפֵרוּשׁ). וְזֶהוּ בְּחִינַת: וְכִי שָׁדָא פָּרְשָׁא גִּירָא וְכוּ',

וְאָמַר רַב אַשִׁי: הַאי גִּלְדָּנָא דְיָמָא וְכוּ': גִּי'יל'דָּנָ'א – הוּא בְּחִינַת

שֵׁם אג"לא, שֶׁהוּא בְּחִינַת גְּבוּרוֹת, כִּי הוּא רָאשֵׁי תֵּבוֹת: אַ'תָּה

גִּ'בּוֹר לְ'עוֹלָם אֲ'דֹנָי, כַּמּוּבָא, כִּי גִּלְדָּנָא הוּא אוֹתִיּוֹת אג"ל, וְשֵׁם

אֲדֹנָ"י בִּשְׁלֵמוּת הַיְנוּ שֵׁם אגל"א, כַּנַּ"ל.

then receives the blessings associated with *Atah Gebor:* sustenance, vitality, and even resurrection of the dead—i.e., restoring his intellect to holiness and breaking free of secular wisdom/*chametz*/death.

165. **AGL...ADoNoY.** The holy name *Adonoy* (Master) is associated with *Malkhut*, which in itself indicates judgments. *AGL* (אגל) has a numerical value of thirty-four, the number of letters in the holy name *ADoNoY* (אדני) when it is expanded to the third power, or *milui-d'milui* (this is done as follows: דלת ואו יוד = יוד ; נון ואו נון = נון ; דלת למד תיו = דלת ; אלף למד פא = אלף). The holy name *AGLA* (= 35) is thus the *milui-d'milui* expansion of *Adonoy* with one more added for the word itself, and therefore indicative of several judgments (see *Pri Etz Chaim, Shaar HaAmidah* #18, p.241; *Shaar HaKavanot, Inyan Kavanat HaAmidah, Drush* #5, p.225). The *Parparaot LeChokhmah* explains that these judgments are the decrees which emanate from *Binah*. In our context, the *several* judgments corresponds to the different decrees: those that have yet to be issued and those that have already been issued.

166. **GYLDeNA...AGLA.** The *GYLDeNA* (גילדנא) of Rabbah bar bar Chanah's story thus alludes to the two holy names of the *gevurot* just mentioned: *ADoNoY* (אדני) and *AGLA* (אגלא; using the א in both).

167. **two fins.** The Kabbalah teaches that the *gevurot* from *Binah* descend as judgments all the way to *Malkhut*/*Adonoy*. It also teaches that where *milui-d'milui* expansion is used—as in turning *Adonoy* into *AGLA* (see n.165)—the degree of *gevurot* is all the more magnified and severe. In our context, we might therefore align the holy name *Adonoy* with the holy *gevurot* before they are revealed (issued), and *AGLA* with the *gevurot* after the decree has been issued. These are the two *shitza* (fins)—misfortunes/decrees—of the sea *gyldena*.

The *Parparaot LeChokhmah* reviews all this in the context of our lesson. He writes: Rabbah bar bar Chanah's entire story revolves around rectifying the *gevurot* by tempering them at their source, the source of all judgments, *Binah* (see §1 and also n.85). These *gevurot* produce fear in people (§3). And if they are extrinsic fears, corrupted *gevurot,* they cause a "souring" of the mind (gold dross), making it impossible for that person to rectify his intellect (§4). Conversely, when the *gevurot* are attached to holiness, when the fear a person feels is the fear of Heaven, then he automatically merits love of God. Such love/*chesed* is indicative of a pure mind (as white as silver) (§5). This is the ultimate rectification, for then the *gevurot* are tempered with *chasadim* and so do not turn into severe judgment/decrees. Tempering these *gevurot*/decrees at their source enables a person to discern through the joy of the mitzvot he performs whether it is before or after the decree. And the way to come to this joy is by generating thunder, which is itself an aspect of *gevurot* (§3). Thunder makes straight the heart's crookedness (§2). Specifically the heart, because the heart is the seat of joy and also corresponds to the source of the *gevurot, Binah* (see Appendix: The Sefirot and Man). By performing the mitzvot with great joy a person ascends to the level of *Binah*, and from the

just as the owner of the object searches after what he has lost.}[162] This is, **And a rider shot an arrow....**[163]

Rav Ashi said, This [fish] was a sea gyldena. *Gyldena* alludes to the holy name *AGLA,* which is an aspect of *gevurot* in that it is an acronym for *"Atah Gebor L'olam Adonoy* (You are mighty forever, O Lord!)" (*Amidah* Prayer),[164] as is brought (*Zohar Chadash, Terumah*). *GYLDeNA* is made up entirely of the letters *AGL* and the holy name *ADoNoY*[165] — i.e., the holy name *AGLA*.[166] < And this is what is alluded to by **two fins.**[167] >

good for man to be alone"—it is not good for love to be without fear. God therefore followed His creation (revelation) of Adam with the creation (revelation) of Chavah/woman/*gevurah*.

162. **put the fear of Heaven first....** Similarly, the *Zohar* teaches: Fear of Heaven must precede love (*Zohar* II, 216a). Thus, although the main revelation begins in *Chesed,* and from there rectification extends to all the *sefirot* below it, love of God cannot be properly attained unless one has first achieved fear of Heaven. It is this fear, the thunder, that rouses the intellect so that thunder can be generated and heard (*Torat Natan #9*). All service of God must therefore begin with the search for fear of Heaven: man searching for woman.

163. **And a rider shot an arrow....** This is the coupling of *chasadim* (rider) and *gevurot* (arrow), man and woman...as in note 146.

The *Parparaot LeChokhmah* adds: If the *chasadim* are what give power to the *gevurot,* then we are back to our previous question (see n.153), Of what value is fear? In other words, if the primary means for overcoming evil thoughts and passions is through one's love of God—if the left has to be encompassed in the right—then why does Rabbah bar bar Chanah emphasize the importance (*sephinta*) of fear, as if it were the key attribute for bringing a person closer to God? Rebbe Nachman's answer is that even though the *"parsha* (rider) shot an arrow..."—i.e., love was combined with fear—"the ship preceded it." That is, fear of Heaven must precede all else. Fear must always be the initial, primary motivating attribute if a person is to then achieve a true level of love and the subsequent rectification of his mind and intellect. As in the verse the Rebbe quoted earlier, "The beginning of wisdom is the fear of God."

164. **AGLA...Atah Gebor....** *Atah gebor l'olam,* the opening words of the second blessing of the *Amidah* prayer, recalls God's might (*gevurot*). The blessing also recalls God's power to provide the world with rain (sustenance) and His power to resurrect the dead. The *Zohar* teaches that the blessing *Atah Gebor* has forty-nine words (including *morid haTal,* "Who sends down the dew"). This corresponds to *Binah* (*Zohar Chadash, Terumah* p.42a), which is the source of all judgments and decrees (see n.85). A person must seek to mitigate the decrees that emanate from *Binah* with *chasadim* from *Chokhmah* (which corresponds to the first blessing of the *Amidah*). And, since this blessing corresponds to the *gevurot,* the holy names associated with it—*AGLA* in particular—are holy names of *gevurot*. The *Parparaot LeChokhmah* brings additional support to show that the holy name *AGLA* relates to fear/ judgment. In our text, we have seen that the *gevurot* correspond to rain/sustenance (see n.135), whereas the fallen *gevurot* correspond to *chametz*/death (§4). Thus, when the *gevurot* are in a rectified state, connected to holiness, they lead a person to the fear of Heaven. He

וְזֶה פֵּרוּשׁ:

בַּחֲצֹצְרוֹת וְקוֹל שׁוֹפָר – וְכוּ', הַיְנוּ עַל־יְדֵי בְּחִינַת קוֹל דְּנָפִיק,
כַּנַּ"ל,

עַל־יְדֵי־זֶה יִרְעַם הַיָּם וְכוּ', נַעֲשָׂה בְּחִינַת רְעָמִים, בְּחִינַת: "קוֹל
רַעַמְךָ בַּגַּלְגַּל".

תֵּבֵל וְיֹשְׁבֵי בָהּ – דָּא בְּחִינַת לִבָּא וְעָרְקִין דִּילֵהּ, כְּמוֹ שֶׁאָמְרוּ: לֹא
נִבְרְאוּ רְעָמִים וְכוּ',

כִּי תֵּבֵל – אוֹתִיּוֹת תָּיו לֵב. תָּיו – לְשׁוֹן רְשִׁימָה, כְּמוֹ שֶׁכָּתוּב:
"וְהִתְוִיתָ תָּו", שֶׁנִּרְשָׁם הַקּוֹל בַּלֵּב, כְּמוֹ שֶׁנֶּאֱמַר: לֹא נִבְרְאוּ
רְעָמִים וְכוּ'. וְעַל־יְדֵי־זֶה:

thunder generated when the voice strikes a mind cleansed of secular wisdom and evil passions (§§3-4). This straightens the heart by elevating the fallen *gevurot* and arousing fear of Heaven.

And a parsha shot an arrow — And to generate thunder it is also necessary for the *chasadim*/ love to temper the *gevurot*/fear. This gives the thunder of the *gevurot* the power it needs to overcome the mind's enemies: secular wisdom, evil passions, and the like (§5).

the ship preceded it — Even so, the love of God must be preceded by fear of Heaven, which Scripture states is "the beginning of wisdom."

Rav Ashi said: This fish was a sea gyldena, which has two fins — Thus, when a person tempers the *gevurot*/fear with love, he generates the thunder that produces a straightened heart so that he can then feel the joy in the mitzvot. This joy enables him to discern whether a decree has yet to be issued, in which case it can be mitigated through regular prayer, or if it has already been issued, in which case it can only be mitigated or nullified through prayer disguised in a *maamar*.

168. **This is the explanation. . . .** Rebbe Nachman now shows how the concepts of this lesson are alluded to in the opening verse.

169. **sound of the shofar. . . released during prayer.** When a person who has attained fear of Heaven prays loudly and with fervor, his voice is like a shofar, thunder (§3; *Mai HaNachal*).

170. **Let the sea thunder . . . in the sphere.** His voice thunders in the sphere of the mind, a pure intellect—i.e., the sea of wisdom (§3; *Mai HaNachal*).

171. **TeVeL. . . Tav LeV. . . imprinted on the heart.** The letters of the word *TeVeL* (תבל) can be understood as a compound for *Tav* (ת) *LeV* (לב). When spelled out, the letter *TaV* (תו) means a sign or mark; and *lev* is the Hebrew term for heart. *Tevel* thus alludes to an imprint on the heart—i.e., thunder.

172. **crookedness of the LeV.** As explained, when a person's voice strikes his purified mind, thunder is generated. This voice of thunder purges the crookedness of his *lev* (§3).

7. This is the explanation [of the opening verse][168]:
{**"With trumpets and the sound of the shofar shout out before God, the King. Let the sea thunder and all within it, the** *tevel* **(world) and all its inhabitants. Let the rivers clap their hands, the mountains** *y'ranainu* **(sing joyously) together. At the presence of God, for He is coming to judge the earth"** (Psalms 98:6-9).}

With trumpets and the sound of the shofar — That is, by means of the voice that is released [during prayer][169]

Let the sea thunder — thunder is generated. This corresponds to "The sound of Your thunder was in the sphere."[170]

the tevel and all its inhabitants — This alludes to the heart and its arteries.

TeVeL is made up of the letters *Tav LeV*. *TaV* connotes a mark, as is written (Ezekiel 9:4), "and *hitvita TaV* (inscribe a mark)." The voice is imprinted on the heart,[171] as in, "Thunder was only created to straighten the crookedness of the *LeV*."[172] And because of this:

---

extent of his joy—which mirrors the degree of joy Above—he can discern whether the decree (*gevurot*) has already been issued from *Binah*/heart or not. If the decree has yet to be issued, he can pray a regular prayer to have it overturned. Otherwise, the only way to have the decree postponed or even nullified is by disguising his prayer in a *maamar* (§1; see nn.7-8). The reason is that until the decree is issued, a person can pray openly, giving voice to the words of his prayer without concern for the accusing angels. But after the decree has been issued— corresponding to "He grieved in His *heart*" (see §2 and n.32)—one must bear the decree in thought alone. He dare not articulate it lest these messengers of the Other Side arouse further accusations. However, keeping the decree in thought is precisely what is needed to rectify the fallen *gevurot* because this returns them to their source, *Binah*—the World of Thought—and so undoes the grief of "His heart" that led to the decree in the first place. Thus, by praying in thought to nullify the decree, and in the meantime disguising his prayer in a *maamar,* a person can effect mitigation even after the decree has been issued.

Rabbah bar bar Chanah's story thus reads as follows:
One time we were traveling on a sephinta — Rabbah bar bar Chanah delved into the nature of fear of Heaven and came to recognize its great importance.
between a fish's two shitza — He learned that the attribute of fear is the initial step for distinguishing between the two states of a misfortune/decree—i.e., before or after it has been issued.
To sail...took the ship three days and three nights, even though it was swimming upwind and we were sailing downwind — The way to know whether it is before or after the decree has been issued is by performing the mitzvot joyously. The joy of the mitzvot operates in two directions, up and down: our rejoicing in God and God's rejoicing in us. Through this joy it is possible to feel whether God's joy is complete and, if not, to gauge the severity of the decree (§2).
And lest you think the ship was not sailing quickly, when Rav Dimi came, he said: In the time it takes to heat a kettle of water it went sixty parsay — But to arouse joy, a person must first free his heart of crookedness. This is accomplished through an element of fear, namely the

נְהָרוֹת יִמְחֲאוּ כָף – בְּחִינַת שִׂמְחָה, כַּנַּ"ל, "וּלְיִשְׁרֵי לֵב שִׂמְחָה".
וְעַל יְדֵי הַשִּׂמְחָה

יַחַד הָרִים יְרַנֵּנוּ – רִנָּה: לְשׁוֹן תְּפִלָּה, כְּמוֹ שֶׁכָּתוּב: "לִשְׁמֹעַ אֶל
הָרִנָּה" וְכוּ'.

הָרִים בְּחִינַת צַדִּיקִים. הַיְנוּ עַל יְדֵי שִׂמְחַת הַלֵּב יְכוֹלִין לְהִתְפַּלֵּל
וּלְהַלְבִּישׁ אֶת תְּפִלָּתָן בְּמַאֲמָר, כְּשֶׁיָּבִינוּ כִּי נִגְזַר הַדִּין, וְזֶה פֵּרוּשׁ
יַחַד, שֶׁמַּלְבִּישִׁים תְּפִלָּתָם בְּסִפּוּרִים יַחַד.

through love of God he can disguise his prayer in a *maamar* and nullify the decree even after it has been issued. This is also the meaning of the words from the Tachanun Prayer: "Hearken to our cry"—i.e., the regular prayer—"and give heed to our *maamar*"—i.e., the disguised prayer.

Reb Noson explains that Rebbe Nachman's use of the word "together" teaches that when a person performs the mitzvot with such great joy that he becomes one with Holy One (§2), he joins "his world" together with God. Then, he will certainly be able to disguise his prayers in whatever he talks about, and it can be said of him, "The entire world has been created only for *his* sake!" (see §1; *Torat Natan* #10).

The verse thus translates in our text as follows:

With trumpets and the sound of the shofar — When a person prays loudly and with fervor, his voice is akin to the blast of the shofar and the rumble of thunder.

Let the sea thunder and all within it — To generate this thunder his voice must issue from the flaming (fear) of his heart and resound in the sphere of his purified mind (love).

the tevel and all its inhabitants — And this thunder is the *tav* that makes straight his *lev*.

Let the rivers clap their hands — And once the crookedness of the heart has been removed, he merits to feel joy in his heart.

the mountains y'ranainu — Having achieved this level of righteousness, his personal aspect of tzaddik, he can discern through this joy if a decree is pending or if it has already been issued. He can mitigate a pending decree with regular prayer. And if it has already been issued, he can mitigate or even nullify the decree by disguising the prayer,

together — by putting it together with a *maamar*.

At the presence of God, for He is coming to judge the earth — When God comes to judge the earth—i.e., issue decrees against it—then through the concepts mentioned in this lesson the tzaddikim know how to compose their prayers for the benefit of the world (*Mai HaNachal*).

Let the rivers clap their hands — This alludes to joy, as mentioned above: "and joy for the straight of heart."[173] And by means of this joy...

the mountains y'RaNainu together — *RiNah* connotes prayer, as is written (1 Kings 8:28), "Hearken to the *rinah* and to the prayer."[174]

mountains — This alludes to tzaddikim.[175] By means of the heart's joy they are able to pray, and once they realize that the judgment has already been decreed, they disguise their prayer in a *maamar*.[176] This is the explanation of < **mountains** > **together**—[the tzaddikim] disguise their prayers together with stories.[177]

---

173. **joy for the straight of heart.** And with a straight heart, a person can feel joy in his heart from the mitzvot he performs (§2).

174. **y'RaNainu...RiNah....** When a person has joy in his heart, he knows in which manner to pray.

175. **mountains...tzaddikim.** Scripture often calls the patriarchs (and other tzaddikim) "mountains," as in, "jumping over the mountains" (Song of Songs 2:8), and "Listen you mountains" (Micah 6:2; *Zimrat HaAretz*). Though Rebbe Nachman specifies tzaddikim, as mentioned earlier, every person, in accordance with the spiritual level he's achieved, is capable of praying for the benefit of the world (as above, nn.8,92).

176. **By means of the heart's joy they are able to pray....** As explained above, in sections 1 and 2. Through the true joy in their hearts they are able to discern whether it will suffice to articulate a regular prayer, or only by disguising their prayers in a *maamar*—restricting the direct prayer for nullifying the decree to thought alone—will it be possible to overturn it (*Parparaot LeChokhmah*; see n.167).

177. **together with stories.** A *maamar*. They tell stories and engage in everyday conversations, yet hidden in what they say is their praise of God and their pleading for His salvation (see §1 and n.8). As our Sages taught: The ordinary conversation of the tzaddik requires study (*Sukkah* 21b).

The *Mai HaNachal* adds: Regular prayer corresponds to fear, as in (Proverbs 31:30), "The woman who fears God, she will be praised" (see note 161, that man corresponds to love and woman to fear). Prayer disguised in a *maamar*, an aspect of "together," corresponds to love, as in (Psalms 133:1), "How good and how pleasant it is when brothers dwell together." Thus, through fear of Heaven a person can pray a regular prayer and nullify a decree, and

לִיקוּטֵי מוֹהֲרַ"ן סִימָן ו

וַיֹּאמֶר ה' אֶל מֹשֶׁה, קְרָא אֶת יְהוֹשֻׁעַ וְכוּ'

א כִּי צָרִיךְ כָּל אָדָם לְמַעֵט עַצְמוֹ בִּכְבוֹד עַצְמוֹ וּלְהַרְבּוֹת בִּכְבוֹד הַמָּקוֹם.
כִּי מִי שֶׁרוֹדֵף אַחַר הַכָּבוֹד, אֵינוֹ זוֹכֶה לִכְבוֹד אֱלֹקִים, אֶלָּא לִכְבוֹד

After Shabbat, the Rebbe again spoke about this lesson. In particular he mentioned the section which discusses Moshe, Yehoshua and the Tent of Meeting, and how they parallel the upper point, lower point and *vav* of the *aleph*. Then he said to me, "Whenever teacher and disciple come together, the aspect of Moshe, Yehoshua and the Tent of Meeting exists."

Reb Noson continues: All this took place at the very beginning of my relationship with Rebbe Nachman. At that time I had not yet begun to record and present for his approval the larger lessons. I wrote down only the smaller discourses and kept them for myself. For a long time, I was hoping to get a copy of this lesson as written by the Rebbe personally, but was only able to do so after Purim (more than five months after the lesson was given), when I was with him in Medvedevka. Then I sat with him and transcribed this lesson as he dictated it to me from his own manuscript. It was nearly nighttime when I finished. The Rebbe was already sitting on his bed, preparing to retire. Yet, before I left, we talked for a while longer and he revealed to me how the three mitzvot the Jews were commanded to fulfill upon entering the Land of Israel are related to this lesson. This also appears as part of the published lesson. And the Rebbe concluded our conversation by saying that each of these three mitzvot—i.e., to appoint a king; to kill off the seed of Amalek; to build the Holy Temple—is an aspect of repentance (*Tzaddik* #128; *Until the Mashiach* pp.86, 94-95; *Parparaot LeChokhmah*).

[Translator's note: Aside from offering valuable background information for Lesson #6, the above also explains why the printed lesson is somewhat repetitive. As mentioned, a fair amount of the text serves to expand and elaborate on topics mentioned only in passing when it was given orally. These additions were recorded at different times, and therefore necessitated review of the subject matter to which they applied. This is why the printed version appears sometimes redundant.]

2. **minimize his own...maximize...the Omnipresent.** This is based on the teaching in Midrash (*Bamidbar Rabbah* 4:20 and *Tana debei Eliyahu* 13) that everyone should seek to honor God and do everything possible to increase His glory. Consider the example of King David. Once crowned sovereign ruler over all the people, King David established Jerusalem as the capital of Israel and immediately arranged for God's Holy Ark to be brought up to its rightful place there. During the festive ceremonies held in honor of the Ark's return, as King David joyfully danced with all his might, his arms and legs became inadvertently uncovered. His wife Mikhal, daughter of his predecessor, King Shaul, chastised her husband for what she considered his undignified behavior—in her eyes behavior more befitting a lowlife than a king. But King David saw the matter differently. "It was before God...," he responded. "I frolicked before God. And I will dishonor myself even more, be lowly in my own esteem...."

LIKUTEY MOHARAN #6[1]

"Then God said to Moshe, 'The time is coming for you to die. *Kra et Yehoshua* (summon Yehoshua) and present yourselves in the Tent of Meeting, where I will appoint him.' "

(Deuteronomy 31:14)

E ach person is required to minimize his own *kavod* (honor) and maximize the honor of the Omnipresent One.[2] For anyone who pursues honor does not attain *kavod Elohim* (God's glory), but *kavod*

---

1. **Likutey Moharan #6.** Rebbe Nachman taught this lesson on Shabbat Shuvah, 6 Tishrei 5563 (October 2, 1802). It was shortly after Reb Noson had joined the Rebbe's following and, in a sense, the lesson can be seen as Rebbe Nachman personally initiating him into the role Reb Noson would one day fill as the Rebbe's leading disciple (cf. Lesson #5, n.1). Indeed, Reb Noson himself testifies that he drew a lifetime of encouragement from this teaching (see *Through Fire and Water*, Chapter 8). Through section 7 (see n.156) of the lesson's text is *leshon Rabbeinu* (this terminology has been explained at the end of the first note to Lesson #2). Its main themes are: humility; remaining quiet and silent in the face of embarrassment; repentance; and strengthening oneself spiritually—accomplishing more when things are good, and holding on when things are difficult. The lesson also explains the Ari's *kavanot* (Rabbi Yitzchak Luria's mystical meditations) for Elul, the month of repentance, and shows how they are applicable to learned and simple Jew alike.

Reb Noson writes: At the time Rebbe Nachman gave the lesson, he quoted the verse, "...and above it, upon the form of the throne, there was a form resembling an *adam* (man)." As he said this, the Rebbe grabbed hold of the chair he was sitting on and began to rock it. Gripped with intense fear and awe, he declared, "When one sits on the chair, one is an *adam!*" (In Yiddish: *Az min zitst ohf der shteel, demult iz min a mensch!*). The meaning of his statement remains a mystery.

Afterwards, Rebbe Nachman completed the teaching, as printed in *Likutey Moharan*. At the time he gave the lesson, however, he made no mention of the mystical meditations of Elul. Only later, after praying Maariv and reciting *Havdalah,* did the issue of the *kavanot* come up. As he would often do, the Rebbe reviewed the lesson he had just given. Then, turning to the respected elders in his following, those who were accustomed to praying from the *Siddur* of the Ari, he said, "Tell me, how are all the *kavanot* of Elul hinted at in this lesson?" Silence. Not one of those present was able to give the Rebbe an answer. For in truth, it was impossible to discern on our own how the meditations of Elul were alluded to within his teaching. The Rebbe then asked for a copy of the *Siddur Ari*, which he opened to the *kavanot* of Elul. A moment later he was revealing truly incredible wonders, showing how he had alluded to all these *kavanot* in what was a most fantastically remarkable way. This too has been published as part of the lesson, although it was impossible to put into writing the sweetness and sensation of perfect knowledge which I then felt in my heart.

שֶׁל מְלָכִים, שֶׁנֶּאֱמַר בּוֹ: "כְּבֹד מְלָכִים חֲקֹר דָּבָר", וְהַכֹּל חוֹקְרִים אַחֲרָיו וְשׁוֹאֲלִים: מִי הוּא זֶה וְאֵיזֶהוּ, שֶׁחוֹלְקִים לוֹ כָּבוֹד הַזֶּה, וְחוֹלְקִים עָלָיו, שֶׁאוֹמְרִים שֶׁאֵינוֹ רָאוּי לַכָּבוֹד הַזֶּה.

אֲבָל מִי שֶׁבּוֹרֵחַ מִן הַכָּבוֹד, שֶׁמְּמַעֵט בִּכְבוֹד עַצְמוֹ וּמַרְבֶּה בִּכְבוֹד הַמָּקוֹם, אֲזַי הוּא זוֹכֶה לִכְבוֹד אֱלֹהִים, וְאָז אֵין בְּנֵי־אָדָם חוֹקְרִים עַל כְּבוֹדוֹ אִם הוּא רָאוּי אִם לָאו, וְעָלָיו נֶאֱמַר: "כְּבֹד אֱלֹהִים הַסְתֵּר דָּבָר", כִּי אָסוּר לַחֲקֹר עַל הַכָּבוֹד הַזֶּה.

person who does this is "minimizing his own glory" and transforming everything into honor for God. In this way he repents and through repentance attains *kavod Elohim*. As explained later, this is the aspect of slaughtering the evil inclination, of which it is said, "Whoever brings a sacrifice of thanksgiving honors Me." And when he honors God in this way, God honors him in return, as is written, "For I honor those who honor Me"—this honor corresponding to "The glory of the Lord is a concealed matter" (*Parparaot LeChokhmah*).

7. **deserving...or not.** Because this Godly honor is a byproduct of one's being embarrassed and shamed—a minimizing of one's personal honor. See previous note.

8. **a concealed matter.** In contrast to *kavod melakhim* (n.4), God's greatness is unlimited and impossible to delineate. Any attempt to describe it will, by definition, fall short of the truth. It is therefore best to say nothing—keeping *kavod Elohim* as hidden as possible. "A concealed matter" thus becomes the greatest honor, because such concealment attests to God's infiniteness (see *Metzudat David, ad. loc.*).

9. **forbidden to inquire into this type of glory.** For this honor is conferred upon a person by God, in reward for his humility. It is therefore forbidden to question or investigate it. Reb Noson explains that all the honor a person receives in this world is concrete and corporeal. As long as one does not strive to direct this honor to God, he is open to being scrutinized and challenged: Does he deserve such honor or not? But, by elevating whatever honor he receives to God, even when he has not yet attained true humility, he is at least binding the *kavod melakhim* to the *kavod Elohim* (*Torat Natan* #1).

Based on the above, an obvious question comes to mind. It is well known that Moshe exemplified, better than anyone else in Scripture, the person who most attained *kavod Elohim*. Yet, time and again Scripture itself informs us that Moshe's authority and honor were challenged. If he had attained *kavod Elohim*, why was he so often opposed? However, as we will see, *kavod Elohim* corresponds to the highest levels of repentance, which only the greatest tzaddikim truly attain. The embarrassment and harassment that Moshe had to endure was necessary so that he could attain *kavod Elohim* on his level—the highest of all levels.

In review: Every person must minimize his own honor and maximize God's honor.

melakhim (glory of kings),[3] of which it is said (Proverbs 25:2), "but the glory of kings is an investigated matter."[4] Everyone inquires about him < to see if he is deserving of such honor, asking, > "Who is he and what is he?" (Esther 7:5) that he is afforded such honor. And they oppose him, saying that he is not deserving of such *kavod*.[5]

However, the person who flees from glory—minimizing his own glory while maximizing the glory of God—attains *kavod Elohim*.[6] Then, < they > do not investigate whether he is deserving of his glory or not.[7] Of him it is said (Proverbs, *ibid*.), "The glory of the Lord is a concealed matter."[8] For it is forbidden to inquire into < this type of > glory.[9]

David's only concern was honoring God as best he could. It mattered not what anyone thought of him, even though he was king of Israel (2 Samuel 6:12-22; see *Rashi*, and *Radak*). With this proof-text Rebbe Nachman has introduced the topic of humility. A person should always seek to do whatever possible in order to enhance and increase God's glory. Conversely, he should show no concern for his own personal honor, even to the point where its being diminished does not bother him at all. This is because diminishing one's own prestige in order to honor God is in fact the greatest honor one could ever hope for, as we shall now see.

3. **kavod Elohim...kavod melakhim.** The term *kavod Elohim*, here translated as "God's glory," is whatever prestige and honor that comes to a person which he accepts, not for himself, but for the Holy One's sake. That is, he in no way looks to personally benefit from the honor, but rather, because he has attained true humility and considers himself as nothing, passes all the honor on to God. Conversely, *kavod melakhim*, here translated as "glory of kings," is that prestige and honor shown a person which he basks and revels in. Thinking himself to be worthy of this honor, such a person lacks humility and therefore has no share in *kavod Elohim* (*Be'Ibey HaNachal*).

4. **glory of kings is an investigated matter.** The greatness of a flesh and blood king is finite. While one king may be deserving of greater glory than another, all *kavod melakhim* is limited. Moreover, it can be investigated and scrutinized. Thus, when a king demands tributes and glory in excess of the honor he truly deserves, he encounters opposition (see *Metzudat David, ad. loc.*).

5. **not deserving....** The arrogance of the person seeking *kavod melakhim* causes not just other people but also the quality of honor itself to demand an accounting: Is this person really worthy of the glory bestowed upon him?

6. **flees from glory...attains kavod Elohim.** Similar to King David (above, n.2), who disregarded his own prestige and honor in order to honor God. It will be explained in the next section that this entails maintaining one's silence even when insulted and disgraced. The

ב. וְאִי אֶפְשָׁר לִזְכּוֹת לַכָּבוֹד הַזֶּה, אֶלָּא עַל־יְדֵי תְּשׁוּבָה. וְעִקַּר הַתְּשׁוּבָה – כְּשֶׁיִּשְׁמַע בְּזִיּוֹנוֹ, יִדֹּם וְיִשְׁתֹּק.

כִּי לֵית כָּבוֹד בְּלֹא כָּ"ף. וְהַכָּ"ף הוּא כֶּתֶר, בְּחִינַת, בְּחִינַת אֶהְיֶה, בְּחִינַת

From this we see that the way to "become embarrassed" is to fully acknowledge one's shortcomings and sins. This is the meaning of "the essence of repentance is hearing one's embarrassment...." That is, a person who has committed a sin will generally rationalize: "My sin wasn't all that serious," "It wasn't so terrible...," "That should only be my worst...," and so on. This leads to a denial of the sin, or at least to the denial of the severity of the sin. Such a person never properly repents, for he has rationalized the sin away. Only his feelings of embarrassment and shame will bring about full acknowledgment of his sin (see below, n.43).

As we will see below in our text, remaining quiet and silent in the face of embarrassment elevates a person to the highest of levels. Reb Avraham Chazan once said, "Considering the great value of embarrassment, as demonstrated by the Rebbe in this lesson, a person ought to immerse in a *mikvah* and perform other devotions so as to be in as pure a state as possible before being embarrassed! However, the nature of embarrassment is not that way. Rather, it is sprung upon a person suddenly and one never has time to prepare for it" (*Rabbi Eliyahu Chaim Rosen*).

Both the *Parparaot LeChokhmah* and the *Mai HaNachal* point out that the advice to keep silent in the face of embarrassment is not meant for all situations. A person should remain silent only when his own honor is diminished by not replying. If, however, someone reviles God or in other ways profanes Him or His Torah, then a person must certainly stand up to the blasphemer and in no uncertain terms take issue with him. Yet, even this is only where the blasphemer might take heed or be silenced in some manner. Where those who profane God and seek to diminish His glory are very powerful, so that action is not possible (e.g., Nazi Germany), then one has no choice but to remain silent. (Taking a counter-stand is also necessary when one's family has been unjustly shamed. One is then obliged to actively speak out in order to protect their good name.) Thus, the *Parparaot LeChokhmah* concludes: A person should pray that when he suffers abuse, only his own honor is diminished and not, God forbid, the honor of God Himself.

12. **no Kavod without a Kaf....** As a rule, the first letter of any word in the Holy Tongue is the most dominant in determining the properties of that word. The Hebrew word for honor, *kavod* (כבוד), shares the same first letter with *Keter* (כתר)—the *Kaf* (כ). This common first letter indicates that when *kavod* lacks the aspect of *Keter* it is devoid of the essence of spiritual glory and can only be the glory given to kings. Only that *kavod* which contains the light of *Keter* is truly *kavod* (*Rabbi Y.M. Shechter*).

13. **Kaf is...Keter.** The *kavod* to which the *Zohar* refers is *kavod Elohim*. Moshe beseeched God to reveal this exalted *kavod* to him, but the Holy One informed him that no man could have a vision of His glory and live (Exodus 33:18-20). This is because *kavod Elohim* corresponds to *Keter*, which is above human comprehension (*Zohar, loc. cit.*). The light of *Keter*, the highest of the *sefirot*, permeates each of the other nine *sefirot* as it descends to

2. Now, it is impossible to attain this *kavod* [*Elohim*] except by means of *teshuvah* (repentance).[10] And the essence of repentance is that when a person hears himself being insulted, he remains quiet and silent.[11]

For there can be no *Kavod* without a *Kaf,* and the *Kaf* < is an aspect of > *Keter* (Crown)[12] (*Zohar* III, 255b).[13] This corresponds to

---

10. **teshuvah, repentance.** Having stated that one must minimize one's own honor and maximize the honor of God, Rebbe Nachman now explains how one can go about doing this. The key, he says, is repentance. As will be explained below (§3), the motivation to repent stems from a recognition of God and His awesomeness. A person experiences a sense of God's greatness and so regrets his blemishes against God. He feels remorse and looks to rectify his wrongs. Thus, the way of repentance is that of recognizing God. The greater a person's recognition, the more he will attempt to maximize God's honor, even as he reduces and negates his own.

11. **quiet and silent.** "Silent" refers to one's speech, when one simply does not retort. "Quiet" refers to the stillness in one's heart, when he realizes that he deserves the insult, that it is coming from God, and that this is part of his repentance. Obviously, the latter is the more complete level. For there are times when a person feels the insults very deeply but does not retort because the insult has left him at a loss for words, or because he feels that responding will only open him to further embarrassment, or because, at that moment, silence is the best retort (see *Likutey Moharan* I, 82:2). Thus, Rebbe Nachman teaches that in the face of insult one must be "quiet and silent"—in one's heart as well as with one's mouth (*Rabbi Eliyahu Chaim Rosen*). Rebbe Nachman taught above that one must minimize his own honor for the Holy One's sake, by means of which he then merits *kavod Elohim* (§1). Here, the Rebbe teaches that one who truly seeks *kavod Elohim* will willingly overlook his embarrassment for the Holy One's sake (*Mai HaNachal; Biur HaLikutim*). The *Be'Ibey HaNachal* adds that by reflecting upon one's own insignificance vis-a-vis God, a person comes to see himself as "vile and despised in his own eyes" (cf. Psalms 15:4) and so can receive any honor without seeking personal benefit from it. Such a person will make certain that all honor is passed on to God. Not so one who harbors ill feelings when insulted. He has not yet attained true humility, and so his pride prevents him from meriting *kavod Elohim*.

The *Biur HaLikutim* asks: If the essence of repentance is hearing oneself embarrassed and remaining silent, how is it that the Torah does not include this in the laws of repentance? Furthermore, is it possible that the essence of repentance—embarrassment—is dependent upon the actions of someone else? (And a wicked person who embarrasses others, at that!) The *Biur HaLikutim* answers: The main expression of repentance is confession (*Yad HaChazakah, Hilkhot Teshuvah* 1:1). Confessing one's sin is a major source of embarrassment. Therefore, although it does not say so outright, the Torah clearly alludes to this embarrassment as the essence of repentance. Moreover, the person who truly feels ashamed of his sin as he confesses before God *knows* that his embarrassment is not really dependent upon others. One can achieve this embarrassment by oneself. In fact, after giving this lesson, Rebbe Nachman remarked to Reb Noson, "Do you ever feel yourself getting red in the face before God?" (*Siach Sarfei Kodesh* 730). The *Biur HaLikutim* thus adds that an important measure of a person's desire to repent is his willingness to admit fault and openly confess.

תְּשׁוּבָה,

כִּי אֶהְיֶה דָּא אָנָא זָמִין לְמֶהֱוֵי. הַיְנוּ קֹדֶם הַתְּשׁוּבָה, עֲדַיִן אֵין לוֹ
הֲוָיָה, כְּאִילוּ עֲדַיִין לֹא נִתְהַוָּה בָּעוֹלָם, כִּי טוֹב לוֹ שֶׁלֹּא נִבְרָא
מִשֶּׁנִּבְרָא, וּכְשֶׁבָּא לְטַהֵר אֶת עַצְמוֹ וְלַעֲשׂוֹת תְּשׁוּבָה, אָז הוּא
בִּבְחִינַת אֶהְיֶה, הַיְנוּ שֶׁיִּהְיֶה לוֹ הֲוָיָה בָּעוֹלָם, הַיְנוּ אָנָא זָמִין
לְמֶהֱוֵי.

וְזֶה בְּחִינַת כֶּתֶר, כִּי כֶּתֶר לְשׁוֹן הַמְתָּנָה, בְּחִינַת תְּשׁוּבָה, כְּמוֹ
שֶׁאָמְרוּ חֲכָמֵינוּ, זִכְרוֹנָם לִבְרָכָה: 'הַבָּא לְטַהֵר מְסַיְּעִין לוֹ מָשָׁל

produces unification in *YHVH*. This is because all physical creation—not only the tangible but the intangible as well—has existence, *HaVaYaH* (*YHVH*). And so, the way to come closer to God is by having everything acquire being—the revelation of *YHVH*. However, a person cannot come to this revelation except by first establishing his *preparedness* to acquire being—i.e., through the holy name *Ehyeh* (*Torat Natan* #5; *Likutey Halakhot, Onaah* 3:1). Reb Noson's further commentary on these holy names and their application within our lesson appears below, in section 3, where Rebbe Nachman himself discusses the concept of *ehyeh* in greater depth.

18. **had he not been created.** Our Sages taught: For two and a half years the school of Shamai debated with the school of Hillel: Is there a real advantage to man's existence or would it have been better had he never been created? At the end of that period, with each side still convinced of its position, a tally was taken. The majority were of the opinion that because of man's many sins, it would have been better had he not been created. But, having already been created, it behooves man to examine his deeds (*loc. cit.*). *Tosafot* explains that this refers to most people, for it is human nature to be susceptible to sin. As for a tzaddik, however, happy is he and happy is his generation (*s.v. noach*). Concerning the Talmud's remark about examining one's deeds, see below (§3) that the tzaddik is constantly engaged in repentance, which also includes his teaching the pathways of *teshuvah* to his generation.

19. **then exist...to be.** A person whose life is full of sin is likened to an animal in human form. He is not a human being. Thus, his decision to repent is the first step in preparing himself to become truly human, with being. Therefore, *ehyeh* indicates "I am prepared to be"—I am prepared to shed my animalistic passions and way of life and am prepared to become a human being. *Ehyeh* is thus an aspect of repentance.

Reb Noson adds: In truth, mankind has no being in this world. This is because man has no real future—his death is inevitable and he takes nothing with him. His only being is that which he prepares for the future, the eternal world. In other words, his repenting in this world is his preparation for having being once he merits his portion of the eternal world. *Ehyeh* is thus true preparation for the future. Yet, even in the present, it is of great value. For *ehyeh* is the joy in one's heart: "I am prepared to be"—for, through repentance, there will certainly be some being and benefit to my having been created (*Torat Natan* #2).

20. **Keter.** Rebbe Nachman now explains how *Keter* (Crown) corresponds to repentance.

Ehyeh, <as is known, >[14] which corresponds to repentance.[15]

For <the meaning of> *ehyeh* is "I am prepared to be."[16] That is, before repenting a person does not yet have being.[17] It is as if he does not yet exist in the world. Indeed, he would be better off had he not been created *(Eruvin* 13b).[18] But when he prepares to purify himself and repent, he is then in the aspect of *ehyeh.* In other words, he will then exist in the world—i.e., "I am prepared to be."[19]

This is an aspect of *Keter,*[20] because the word *keter* suggests waiting, <which is> an aspect of repentance. As our Sages taught: Anyone who undertakes to purify himself is assisted [from Above]. It

Malkhut. From *Malkhut* the light returns by way of the *sefirot* to *Keter.* In total, twenty *sefirot* are traversed, twenty being the numerical value of the letter *kaf.*

14. **Keter...Ehyeh.** *Ehyeh* is one of God's holy names. On the *sefirah* hierarchy it parallels *Keter* (see Appendix: Sefirot and Associated Names of God).

15. **...corresponds to repentance.** Rebbe Nachman will next explain how the term *ehyeh,* from which the holy name *Ehyeh* derives, is conceptually an aspect of repentance.

Thus far, Rebbe Nachman has introduced four interrelated concepts: *kavod, Keter, Ehyeh* (*ehyeh*) and repentance. They will appear again and again throughout the lesson. In the remainder of this section the Rebbe shows the correlation between *Ehyeh,* repentance and *Keter,* and also how they are related to embarrassment (which is the essence of repentance) and *kavod.*

16. **ehyeh...I am prepared to be.** See *Zohar* III, 65b. In Scripture, the term *ehyeh* appears in God's response to Moshe, who had asked what name he was to use when informing Israel that God was about to redeem them from Egypt: "*Ehyeh asher ehyeh* (I will be Who I will be)...This is what you must say to the Israelites: *Ehyeh* sent me to you" (Exodus 3:14). The Rebbe now explains why *ehyeh* corresponds to repentance.

17. **being.** This connotes true existence, *havayah* in Hebrew. Rebbe Nachman explains that in the preparatory stage, prior to repentance, a person is said to be in a state of *ehyeh.* He is prepared to be, but has not yet attained the state of being, *havayah.* Below, Rebbe Nachman will explain how these terms relate to God's holy names *Ehyeh* and *YHVH* (*HaVaYaH,* הויה, has the same letters as *YHVH,* יהוה).

Reb Noson explains: When God sent His message of redemption to the Jews and said, "*Ehyeh asher ehyeh...Ehyeh* sent me to you," He added, "Tell the Israelites, '*YHVH,* the God of your fathers...has sent me to you' " (Exodus 3:14-15). Under Egyptian bondage the Jews were not a nation. To acquire being, they first had to experience the embarrassment of the bondage and bear it in silence—the stage of *ehyeh.* Only then could they acquire *havayah* as a nation unto *YHVH* (cf. *Likutey Tefilot*). The Tetragrammaton, *YHVH* (יהוה), is the name of God which denotes the level where past (*HaYaH,* היה), present (*HoVeH,* הוה), and future (*YiHiYeH,* יהיה) are one (*Tur, Orach Chaim* 5). This name also denotes the creative power that constantly sustains the universe (*The Living Torah* on Exodus 3:15). Thus, Reb Noson adds, with the holy name *YHVH* being the Source of everything in creation, any sin a person commits causes blemish, as it were, in *YHVH,* and, conversely, rectification for evil deeds

לְאֶחָד, שֶׁבָּא לִקְנוֹת אֲפַרְסְמוֹן. אוֹמְרִים לוֹ: הַמְתֵּן' וְכוּ', וְזֶה בְּחִינַת כֶּתֶר, כְּמוֹ שֶׁכָּתוּב: "כַּתַּר לִי זְעֵיר וַאֲחַוֶּךָ".

אֲבָל קֹדֶם הַתְּשׁוּבָה אֲזַי בְּחִינַת אֶהְיֶה בְּהַסְתָּרַת פָּנִים מִמֶּנּוּ, כִּי עֲדַיִן לֹא הֵכִין אֶת עַצְמוֹ לִמְהֱוִי בָּעוֹלָם, וְהַסְתָּרַת פְּנֵי אֶהְיֶה גִּימַטְרִיָּא דָם*, הַיְנוּ שְׁפִיכוּת דָּמִים וּבִזְיוֹנוֹת, עַל שֵׁם: "וּבֹזַי יֵקָלּוּ", כִּי עֲדַיִן הַדָּם

*פֵּרוּשׁ: כִּי אֲחוֹרֵי שֵׁם אֶהְיֶה הוּא בְּגִימַטְרִיָּא דָּם, כַּמּוּבָא. הַיְנוּ כְּשֶׁכּוֹתְבִין הַשֵּׁם בַּאֲחוֹרַיִם, דְּהַיְנוּ א, אה, אהי,

---

25. **achoraim of . . . Ehyeh.** The Ari teaches that the method of numerical calculation known as *achoraim* infers a concealment of holiness. This method calls for adding the sum of the numerical value of all a word's previous letters to the value of its next letter, until all the letters are used. In our case, the *achoraim* of the holy name *Ehyeh* (אהיה) is as follows: *aleph* (א = 1); *aleph heh* (אה = 6); *aleph heh yud* (אהי = 16); *aleph heh yud heh* (אהיה = 21).

26. **same numerical value as dam.** The numerical value of the *achoraim* of *Ehyeh* adds up to 44 (see previous note), the same value as *dam* (דם = 44).

27. **spilt blood and scorn.** As explained, as long as a person has yet to repent, the holy name *Ehyeh* is hidden from him. Yet it is never very far away, because it is hidden within—in his very blood. As a result of which, he is subject to spilt *dam* and embarrassment from without.

The *Be'Ibey HaNachal* teaches that, conceptually, this is what took place in Egypt. God wanted to reveal Himself and told Moshe that the way the people could know Him was through His name *Ehyeh*. God was, as it were, preparing Himself to be known. Moshe informed the Israelites of this and also that *YHVH*, the God of their fathers, had sent him to them as their redemption was at hand (see n.17). The Israelites believed that God would indeed fulfill His promise of redemption. Not so Pharaoh, who upon hearing God's name said, "Who is *YHVH* that I should listen to Him?" (Exodus 5:2). In return, most of the plagues with which God then punished Pharaoh and the Egyptians were accompanied with a warning to acknowledge God's mastery over the world. But Pharaoh remained obstinate and was not willing to recognize his wickedness. The name PhaRaOH (פרעה) has the same letters as the word HaORePh (הערף), the nape or back of the neck. That is, Pharaoh remained in the backpart of *Ehyeh*, which is *dam* (blood), refusing to repent and acknowledge God. Therefore, the first plague visited upon him and the Egyptians was the Plague of Blood.

28. **dishonored.** The sons of Eli the High Priest were lax in their priestly duties, behavior which indicated a laxness in their honor of God as well. God therefore told Eli, "I intended for you and your father's house to have the honor of serving Me forever. But now, far be it from Me! For I honor those who honor Me, but those who scorn Me will be dishonored" (*loc. cit.*). We see then that those who honor God, God rewards with honor—*kavod Elohim*. Conversely, those who scorn God and fail to repent and honor Him, are embarrassed and shamed.

is like the allegory of the person who comes to buy sweet smelling oil. They tell him, "Wait..." (*Yoma* 38b).[21] This corresponds to *KeTeR,* as is written (Job 36:2), "*KaTaR* (wait) for me awhile and I will tell you."[22]

Before repentance, however, the aspect of *ehyeh* is hidden from him.[23] For he has not yet prepared himself to exist in the world. And the hidden face of *Ehyeh*[24]— < i.e., the *achoraim* of the holy name *Ehyeh*[25] > —has the same numerical value as *dam* (blood)[26]—i.e., spilt blood and scorn,[27] as is written (1 Samuel 2:30), "[For I honor those who honor Me,] but those who scorn Me will be dishonored."[28] The blood

---

21. **Wait....** The Talmud teaches that if a person seeks to defile himself by sinning, the way is opened for him; similarly, if a person seeks to purify himself, he is assisted. Liken this to a merchant who sells both kerosene and perfume. When someone comes to buy kerosene, the merchant says to him, "Measure the quantity you need by yourself." But if someone comes to buy perfume, the merchant says, "Wait, we will both measure it, so that I may also inhale its fragrance" (*Yoma, loc. cit.*). Reb Noson adds that even though a person must save himself by hurriedly escaping the darkness of sin, he should not be disturbed if he finds himself still far from prayer and holiness. It is necessary to be patient, to wait until he achieves a complete *tikkun* (rectification). For it is not possible to draw close to the Holy One until one has been purified and has guarded himself from sin for an extended period of time. In this way the forces of evil and impurity, which had a hold on him, are dispelled and he is able to receive a complete rectification (*Torat Natan* #4; *Mai HaNachal*).

22. **KeTeR...KaTaR....** Iyov maintained that he had been wrongly made to suffer by God. His friend Elihu challenged him, saying, "*Katar* (wait) for me...." He wanted a moment to prove to Iyov that God was righteous and that, in fact, Iyov's suffering was the result of his sins. Elihu was thus defending God's honor. In our context, Elihu was telling Iyov that in order for him to attain *kavod Elohim,* Iyov would have to repent—i.e., wait. This is the only way to merit spiritual glory.

Reb Noson explains that waiting is necessary because a person who sins does not wait. He does not restrain himself, but instead proceeds to commit the sin posthaste (cf. *Bereishit Rabbah* 18:6). Therefore, part of his rectification when entering holiness entails his waiting patiently for salvation and rectification; he becomes purified slowly and in stages (*Torat Natan* #3).

23. **ehyeh is hidden from him.** Rebbe Nachman now explains why embarrassment is the essence of repentance and where it stems from. Essential to understanding his explanation is the recognition that, as mentioned above (n.19), before a person repents his sin he is likened to an animal. He has no being (*havayah*), nor does he even think of being. Therefore, even the indispensable preparatory stage of *ehyeh* is hidden from him.

24. **hidden face of Ehyeh.** When in the Kabbalah the term "face" (*panim*) is used in conjunction with some concept, it indicates that concept's essence and, more specifically, that it is in a rectified state, a state of holiness. Conversely, when the term "backpart" (*achoraim*) is used, it indicates that concept's secondary features, that which is as yet unrectified and unsanctified. The "face" of that concept is thus hidden. In our context, the person has not yet begun to repent—i.e., the holy name *Ehyeh* is hidden from him.

שֶׁבֶּחָלָל הַשְּׂמָאלִי שֶׁבַּלֵּב, שֶׁשָּׁם   אֶהְיֶה, שֶׁחוֹזְרִין בְּכָל פַּעַם לְאָחוֹר, הוּא
מְדוֹר הַיֵּצֶר הָרָע, כְּמוֹ שֶׁכָּתוּב: בְּגִימַטְרִיָּא דָּם, וְזֶהוּ בְּחִינַת הַחֲזָרַת
"וְלֵב כְּסִיל לִשְׂמֹאלוֹ", עֲדַיִן   וְהַסְתָּרַת פְּנֵי אֶהְיֶה, שֶׁעוֹלֶה דָּם:

הוּא בְּתֹקֶף וָעֹז. וּבִשְׁבִיל זֶה בָּאִין עָלָיו בִּזְיוֹנוֹת וּשְׁפִיכוּת דָּמִים, כִּי

זֶה בְּחִינַת הַסְתָּרַת וְהַחְזָרַת פְּנֵי אהי"ה, גִּימַטְרִיָּא – דָּם.

וְתִקּוּן לָזֶה, שֶׁיַּהֲפֹךְ דָּם לְדָם, שֶׁיִּהְיֶה מִן הַשּׁוֹמְעִים חֶרְפָּתָם וְאֵינָם
מְשִׁיבִים, וְלֹא יְדַקְדֵּק עַל בִּזְיוֹן כְּבוֹדוֹ. וּכְשֶׁמְּקַיֵּם דֹּם לַה', אָז
הַקָּדוֹשׁ-בָּרוּךְ-הוּא מַפִּיל לוֹ חֲלָלִים חֲלָלִים, כְּמוֹ שֶׁכָּתוּב: "דֹּם
לַה' וְהִתְחוֹלֵל לוֹ – וְהוּא יַפִּיל לְךָ חֲלָלִים", (כְּמוֹ שֶׁדָּרְשׁוּ רַבּוֹתֵינוּ,
זִכְרוֹנָם לִבְרָכָה), הַיְנוּ: "וְלִבִּי חָלַל בְּקִרְבִּי", הַיְנוּ עַל-יְדֵי-זֶה נִתְמַעֵט
הַדָּם שֶׁבֶּחָלָל הַשְּׂמָאלִי,

וְזֶה בְּחִינַת זְבִיחַת הַיֵּצֶר הָרָע, וְעַל-יְדֵי-זֶה זוֹכֶה לְכָבוֹד אֱלֹקִי, כְּמוֹ
שֶׁכָּתוּב: "זֹבֵחַ תּוֹדָה יְכַבְּדָנְנִי", וְדָרְשׁוּ חֲכָמֵינוּ, זִכְרוֹנָם לִבְרָכָה עַל

(be quiet): waiting patiently for God's salvation, and being quiet while awaiting that salvation. In our context, the two translations are synonymous. A person must be quiet and silent, enduring embarrassment in order to repent. And he must also be patient, the aspect of *Keter*, while "waiting" to fully repent. This is the implied meaning of the word *hitcholel* in the verse; "hope longingly" suggests entreaty and prayer to God, an aspect of repentance.

35. **ChaLoLim, dead.** The Talmud teaches that when a person is beset by enemies and finds it impossible to withstand them, the best thing he can do is "be quiet before God...." That is, by praying to God and patiently waiting for His salvation (both implying repentance), he will eventually prevail over his enemies. See next note.

36. **my heart...hollowed....** The verse in Psalms begins, "I am impoverished and poor...." King David said this, declaring that he had successfully defeated his evil inclination. In our context, this means that King David had minimized his own honor, hence was "impoverished," and was therefore able to master his evil inclination.

37. **bad blood...is lessened.** The defeated enemy is the blood in the left hollow of the heart, the sins accumulated due to the hidden face of *Ehyeh*. When a person endures silence in the face of embarrassment, when he patiently awaits salvation despite his torment, this suffering reduces and weakens the potency and strength of the blood in the left hollow of the heart. He is then on the proper path to repentance.

38. **sacrifice of thanksgiving....** The thanksgiving sacrifice is called a *korban todah*, from the

which is in the left hollow of the heart—the abode of the evil inclination, as is written (Ecclesiastes 10:2), "but a fool's heart inclines to his left"—still retains its strength and power.[29] This is the reason he is subjected to ridicule and spilt blood. They are the aspect of a hidden and turned face of *Ehyeh,* which has the same numerical value as *dam.*[30]

Now, the rectification for this[31] is to turn <from> *DaM* to *DoMe* (quiet).[32] He should be among those who hear themselves ridiculed and yet do not retort. Nor should he be vexed by affronts to his honor.[33] For when he fulfills "be quiet before God," then the Holy One strikes [his enemies] dead. As it is written (Psalms 37:7), "Be *dome* before God and *hitChoLeL* (hope longingly) for Him"[34]—God will strike them *ChaLoLim* (dead) (*Gittin* 7a).[35] This is (Psalms 109:22), "and my heart is *ChoLoL* (hollowed) within me"[36]—i.e., through [his quiet and silence] the <bad> blood in the left hollow is lessened.[37]

This is an aspect of slaughtering the evil inclination, through which he merits *kavod Elohim.* As is written (Psalms 50:23), "Whoever brings a sacrifice of thanksgiving honors Me,"[38] and the Sages

---

29. **fool's heart...left....** Kohelet states: "A wise man's heart inclines to his right, but a fool's heart inclines to his left" (*loc. cit.*). Rashi indicates that the right side denotes the good and proper path, whereas the left side denotes the reverse. In our context, the fool, one who fails to repent and prepare himself for the state of being, is one whose blood is overpowering and at full strength. *Ehyeh* is thus hidden from him. Where is this blood? In the left side of his heart, the seat of the evil inclination. The spilling of this blood through embarrassment therefore weakens the evil inclination.

30. **hidden...as dam.** One must therefore endure embarrassment in order to repent. A person who refuses to repent endures embarrassment anyway, because his blood, which is at full strength, must be suppressed. But, because he never "prepares" himself—the aspect of *ehyeh*—he suffers embarrassment and still does not repent. It never occurs to him to look into why he is being made to suffer. As a result, his blood eventually returns to its previous strength and the cycle begins again: he is made to suffer further embarrassment and torment in the hope that he might eventually ask himself, "Why?"

31. **rectification for this.** For the blood is at full strength and bringing him embarrassment.

32. **DaM to DoMe.** The Hebrew letters of *dam* and *dome* are identical, דם. They differ only in their *nikud* (Hebrew vowel signs). Whereas *dam* is punctuated with a *patach,* a straight line under the letter *dalet* (דַם), *dome* is punctuated with a *cholem,* a point on the upper left side of the *dalet* (דֹם).

33. **affronts to his honor.** For he realizes that his true honor—his *kavod Elohim*—is not at stake, but only his corporeal honor—*kavod melakhim.* He therefore remains silent, minimizing and reducing his own self-importance in repentance before God.

34. **Be dome before God and hitChoLeL....** Rashi brings two explanations for the word *dome*

זְבִיחַת הַיֵּצֶר הָרָע:

ג וְצָרִיךְ לֶאֱחֹז תָּמִיד בְּמִדַּת הַתְּשׁוּבָה, כִּי מִי יֹאמַר: "זִכִּיתִי לִבִּי,
טָהַרְתִּי מֵחַטָּאתִי", כִּי בְּשָׁעָה שֶׁאָדָם אוֹמֵר: חָטָאתִי, עָוִיתִי,
פָּשַׁעְתִּי, אֲפִלּוּ זֶה אִי אֶפְשָׁר לוֹמַר בְּבַר לְבָב בְּלִי פְּנִיָּה.
(וְזֶהוּ: מִי יֹאמַר: "זִכִּיתִי לִבִּי, טָהַרְתִּי מֵחַטָּאתִי", הַיְנוּ מִי יוּכַל
לוֹמַר, שֶׁלְּבּוֹ זַךְ וְטָהוֹר מִפְּנִיּוֹת, אֲפִלּוּ בְּשָׁעָה שֶׁאוֹמֵר: חָטָאתִי
וְכוּ'. וְזֶהוּ: "מִי יֹאמַר וְכוּ': טָהַרְתִּי מֵחַטָּאתִי", הַיְנוּ שֶׁיִּהְיֶה טָהוֹר
מִן הֶחָטָאתִי, עָוִיתִי, פָּשַׁעְתִּי שֶׁאָמַר, כִּי גַם אָז אֵינוֹ זַךְ וְטָהוֹר בְּלִי
פְּנִיּוֹת, כַּנַּ"ל).

נִמְצָא, שֶׁצָּרִיךְ לַעֲשׂוֹת תְּשׁוּבָה עַל הַתְּשׁוּבָה הָרִאשׁוֹנָה, הַיְנוּ עַל
חָטָאתִי, עָוִיתִי, פָּשַׁעְתִּי שֶׁאָמַר, כִּי עָלָיו נֶאֱמַר: "בִּשְׂפָתָיו

41. **I have cleansed my heart...ulterior motive.** The simple meaning of this verse from Proverbs is that a person must recognize the all-encompassing nature of God's awareness. That being the case, no one can deny his sins before God, no one can claim to have totally cleansed himself and fully repented for his sin (*Metzudat David*). Here, Rebbe Nachman adds a new dimension to this, showing how even the very confession "I have cleansed my heart, I am purged..." is not uttered with complete honesty and sincerity.

42. **This is the meaning of....** This paragraph was added by Reb Noson as an explanation of the Rebbe's statement concerning ulterior motives.

43. **without ulterior motives....** Simply, this refers to making a sincere attempt at truly repenting for one's misdeeds. For even though everyone might know his shortcomings and transgressions, a person still finds it hard to fully acknowledge his wrongdoing and feel true remorse. Therefore, it is necessary for him to repent over and over again, until he finally cleanses his heart and, with absolute sincerity, says "I have sinned..."—doing so without any ulterior motive and rationalization for why he sinned. Elsewhere, Rebbe Nachman speaks about ulterior motives and insincerity when repenting and explains that people often repent because of physical suffering, or financial or emotional needs (see *Likutey Moharan* I, 22:7, n.71). All these and similar concepts are ulterior motives and so result in incomplete repentance, which is nevertheless of some value.

   The Be'Ibey HaNachal explains that constant repentance and accepting embarrassment go hand in hand. The more an individual is concerned with his own prestige and honor, the more ulterior motives he will harbor when repenting. Therefore, one must be willing to endure embarrassment for the Holy One's sake alone. Only in this way will he slaughter the evil inclination and merit *kavod Elohim*.

44. **must repent for his first act....** This, so as to purify his previously impure confession. Reb Noson writes that this is why God's answer to Moshe was not just "*Ehyeh*," but "*Ehyeh asher*

explain that this refers to slaughtering the evil inclination (*Sanhedrin* 43b).[39]

3. Thus, a person should perpetually embrace the attribute of repentance.[40] For "Who can say, 'I have cleansed my heart, I am purged of my sin?' " (Proverbs 20:9). Even at the moment a person says, "I have sinned, I have transgressed, I have acted wantonly," it is impossible for him to say this with a pure heart and without an ulterior motive.[41]

{This is the meaning of[42] "Who can say I have cleansed my heart, I am purged of my sin." In other words, who can say that his heart is sincere and pure of ulterior motives even at the time he is saying "I have sinned...." This is the meaning of "Who can say...I am purged of my sin"—i.e., that he is purged of the "I have sinned, I have transgressed, I have acted wantonly," which he utters. For even then, his confession is not completely sincere and pure, without ulterior motives.[43]}

We find, therefore, that he must repent for his first act of repentance, for the "I have sinned, I have transgressed, I have acted wantonly" that he uttered.[44] Of such a person it is said (Isaiah 29:13),

word *HoDayaH*, which is similar to *HoDaaH* (confession, admission). As Rashi explains, a person who confesses and repents honors God.

39. **slaughtering the evil inclination.** That is, when a person remains quiet though insulted and maligned, his silence for the Holy One's sake reduces the power of the blood in the left hollow of his heart—i.e., a weakening and slaughtering of the evil inclination. This is considered true glorification and honor of God. Below, in section 3, Rebbe Nachman returns to this Talmudic statement and provides deeper insight into its meaning (see there and n.52).

With this, Rebbe Nachman has shown the connection between silence, which is repentance—i.e., an admission of guilt and the confession of sin—and *kavod Elohim*. Thus, remaining quiet and silent when embarrassed, *Ehyeh*, and *Keter* are all one concept: the essence of repentance. The person who has these can achieve being.

In review: Every person must minimize his own honor and maximize God's honor (§1). This requires repentance, returning to God and recognizing His greatness, which is best accomplished by enduring insult in silence—doing so for the Holy One's sake. A person thereby increases God's honor and himself merits *kavod Elohim* (§2).

40. **perpetually embrace...repentance.** Recognizing the great value of repentance and its power to slaughter the evil inclination, a person might make the effort to remain quiet and silent in the face of embarrassment and then assume that he has already attained true repentance. Therefore, Rebbe Nachman teaches: "A person should *perpetually* embrace the attribute of repentance." Reb Noson explains that the concept of *teshuvah* exists at every level. A person must therefore always begin his devotions with a fresh attitude—i.e., start each day's devotions anew with the preparatory stage, *ehyeh*. Even someone who has already merited a lofty level in serving God must see himself in a state of *ehyeh* with regard to the higher levels, where he does not yet have *havayah* (*Torat Natan* #7).

כְּבֵדוּנִי", כִּי עַל־יְדֵי תְּשׁוּבָה זוֹכֶה לִכְבוֹד ה', "וְלִבּוֹ רָחַק מִמֶּנִּי".

וַאֲפִלּוּ אִם יוֹדֵעַ אָדָם בְּעַצְמוֹ, שֶׁעָשָׂה תְּשׁוּבָה שְׁלֵמָה, אַף עַל־פִּי־
כֵן צָרִיךְ לַעֲשׂוֹת תְּשׁוּבָה עַל תְּשׁוּבָה הָרִאשׁוֹנָה. כִּי מִתְּחִלָּה
כְּשֶׁעָשָׂה תְּשׁוּבָה עָשָׂה לְפִי הַשָּׂגָתוֹ, וְאַחַר־כָּךְ בְּוַדַּאי כְּשֶׁעוֹשֶׂה
תְּשׁוּבָה, בְּוַדַּאי הוּא מַכִּיר וּמַשִּׂיג יוֹתֵר אֶת הַשֵּׁם יִתְבָּרַךְ. נִמְצָא
לְפִי הַשָּׂגָתוֹ שֶׁמַּשִּׂיג עַכְשָׁו, בְּוַדַּאי הַשָּׂגָתוֹ הָרִאשׁוֹנָה הוּא בְּחִינַת
גַּשְׁמִיּוּת. נִמְצָא, שֶׁצָּרִיךְ לַעֲשׂוֹת תְּשׁוּבָה עַל הַשָּׂגָתוֹ הָרִאשׁוֹנָה, עַל
שֶׁהִתְגַּשֵּׁם אֶת רוֹמְמוּת אֱלֹקוּתוֹ.

וְזֶה בְּחִינַת עוֹלָם הַבָּא, שֶׁיִּהְיֶה כֻּלּוֹ שַׁבָּת, הַיְנוּ כֻּלּוֹ תְּשׁוּבָה, כְּמוֹ

person knows inside himself that he has been totally sincere in his *teshuvah....*" This refers to someone who has attained complete repentance for his sins; his confession "I have sinned" is pure. This person then recognizes that his original perception of Godliness was mundane. He therefore repents on an even higher level, for he has now attained greater spiritual heights and a much greater perception of Godliness. He has attained complete, pure *teshuvah,* and so recognizes that God is far greater than any previous conception he may have had — this being the third level of *teshuvah.*

Reb Noson associates the three levels of repentance with the three times *ehyeh* is mentioned in Exodus 3:14 (see n.17). That is, at their inception as a nation, the Israelites were told to enter the state of *ehyeh,* preparing themselves to have being. Having achieved that first level of repentance, they would then have to repent again in order to acquire a sincere and purified motive, free of external considerations. And once that second level of repentance was accomplished, they would then have to repent for their earlier, more mundane perception of Godliness. Only then would they be able to ascend to ever greater perceptions of Godliness — the reward for true repentance. Thus, no matter how many obstacles stood in their way, as long as they were prepared to constantly go through the stages of *ehyeh,* the Israelites would eventually be able to eliminate their impurities, conquer their material desires, and achieve their objective: the Exodus. Hence, *ehyeh* appears in the verse three times (*Torat Natan #5*).

47. This...World to Come. "This" is *teshuvah al teshuvah,* perpetual repentance.

The Ari explains that the name *Olam HaBa* (World to Come) literally means "the world that is coming." That is, it is in a constant state of coming, always bringing with it new *mochin* (mentalities) and revelations of Godliness (*Etz Chaim,* 15:5, p.231; see also *Likutey Moharan* I, 15:5, n.46). In our context, this refers to the newer and greater perceptions of Godliness attained after each repentance.

48. World to Come...Shabbat. The Talmud teaches that this world was created to last for six thousand years (corresponding to the Six Days of Creation, the six days of the week). The seventh millennia, the World to Come, is likened to the seventh day, Shabbat (*Sanhedrin* 97a).

"and he honors Me with his lips"—because through repentance he attains *kavod Elohim*—"but his heart is far from Me."[45]

And even if a person knows inside himself that he has been totally sincere in his repentance, he must still repent for his first act of repentance. This is because when he first repented, he did so according to his level of perception [then]. But afterwards, when he [again] repents, he certainly recognizes and perceives even more about God. So that relative to his present perception, his first perception was certainly < crude in comparison >. We find, therefore, that he must repent for his original < repentance >, for having made crass the exalted nature of His Godliness.[46]

This is an aspect of the World to Come,[47] which will be completely *ShaBbaT*[48]—i.e., completely *TeShuVah,* as is written (Deuteronomy 30:2),

---

ehyeh" (see above, n.17). God was alluding to the fact that to repent, a person must always begin anew, over and over again, by repenting for his earlier act of repentance—*teshuvah al teshuvah.* For this is the only way to truly repent (*Torat Natan #5*).

45. **draws near...his lips...heart is far from Me.** God laments that the Jews would honor Him with their lips, as if drawing near to Him, yet their hearts were very distant from truly serving Him (*Rashi, loc. cit.*). Even though the people's *teshuvah* referred to in this verse was superficial, Rebbe Nachman indicates that it might still have resulted in *kavod Elohim.* For while this original expression of *kavod* was not particularly lofty, based as it was on ulterior motives, it nevertheless could have prepared the way for subsequent acts of *teshuvah,* which continuously increase a person's awareness and sincerity. As we have seen, through perpetual repentance one attains *kavod Elohim.* And so, had the Jews truly repented, they would have attained *kavod Elohim,* as their service with their lips (their prayers and words) indicated. Yet, because they only achieved the first level of repentance, their hearts were not purified from their "I have sinned...." As a result, their hearts remained distant from God. They never attained *kavod Elohim.*

Deeper study of this verse from Isaiah (*loc. cit.*) suggests that the Jews saw themselves as having already succeeded in drawing nearer to God (see *Rashi, ibid.*). This was haughtiness on their part, the very reverse of humility. Thus, their "lip service" was not an indication of true humility but of true arrogance. They assumed they were drawing closer to God and giving Him honor, yet they never advanced to the stage of purifying their hearts. Therefore, God said of the people, "its heart is far from Me."

46. **totally sincere...was certainly crude....** Reb Noson explains that Rebbe Nachman has actually specified three levels of *teshuvah.* The very first time a person repents he slaughters the evil inclination on that level. Yet, as we have seen, he has still to repent purely and without ulterior motives. He must therefore repent for that first repentance, *teshuvah al teshuvah,* always starting anew until he can repent with absolute sincerity. By doing this, he goes from one cycle of *ehyeh* to *havayah* to another on a higher level, and so on. There are many, many such levels through which a person must ascend until he can repent completely, until he totally purifies his heart and confession. Therefore, the Rebbe states: "And even if a

שֶׁכָּתוּב: "וְשַׁבְתָּ עַד ה' אֱלֹקֶיךָ", כִּי עִקַּר עוֹלָם הַבָּא הוּא הַשָּׂגַת אֱלֹקוּתוֹ, כְּמוֹ שֶׁכָּתוּב: "וְיָדְעוּ אוֹתִי לְמִקְּטַנָּם וְעַד גְּדוֹלָם". נִמְצָא בְּכָל עֵת שֶׁיַּשִּׂיגוּ הַשָּׂגָה יְתֵרָה, אֲזַי יַעֲשׂוּ תְּשׁוּבָה עַל הַהַשָּׂגָה הָרִאשׁוֹנָה.

aimed at producing an ascent. The reason a person is tested is to see whether he is capable and willing to strengthen himself against the onslaught of his evil inclination. If he is, and does, then every step he takes towards further spirituality, especially those that require great effort, is an aspect of *teshuvah al teshuvah*. He thereby comes closer to God; he achieves the level he had previously tasted but had not earned. For these tests that a person must pass on each new level of spiritual advancement is what Rebbe Nachman earlier called *Keter*/waiting. Before accomplishing true *teshuvah al teshuvah* a person must wait and be tested. This is where his desire and resolve to repent show themselves. If he remains determined, his determination will lead him to constant repentance, *teshuvah al teshuvah* (*Torat Natan* #8-9, #11).

Reb Noson then adds that in reality, only the very great tzaddikim actually merit complete repentance. As we have seen, *teshuvah al teshuvah* is accomplished when one has achieved a pure heart and so is free of any ulterior motive whatsoever. And, while it is true that every person, commensurate with his level of spiritual development, merits some degree of *teshuvah al teshuvah*—which for his level is indeed an accomplishment—absolute purity is attained only by the very great tzaddikim. These tzaddikim are constantly engaged in *teshuvah al teshuvah*. They forever strive to reveal ever greater levels and perceptions of Godliness—disclosing His kindness and goodness, which is never-ending and all-encompassing—so that everyone will repent and seek God. This is seen in their *teshuvah al teshuvah*. Initially, the tzaddikim assume the aspect of *ehyeh*, corresponding to the holy name *Ehyeh*. This paves the way for their acquiring an aspect of *havayah*, YHVH. But they do not stop there. Rather, they immediately repent again, *teshuvah al teshuvah*, again yearning for God and assuming an aspect of *ehyeh*. Twice *EHYeH* (אהיה = 21) and *YHVH* (יהוה = 26) add up to 68, the same numerical value as *ChaYIM* (חיים), life. True life is the revelation of *mochin*, man's knowledge of God (cf. Deuteronomy 30:20) as it will be revealed in the World to Come (see also n.47). Thus, the tzaddikim constantly begin over again; seeking new revelations, new life. The average person, however, lacks the ability to always be engaged in *teshuvah al teshuvah*. Instead, his spiritual accomplishments correspond to *Ehyeh*, YHVH, and *ADoNoY*—the holy name that denotes *Malkhut*, faith, a limited revelation of Godliness (אדני = 65). Faith/*Malkhut* is thus compared to a *reshimu* (imprint or impression) of the *mochin*, as opposed to full and complete mentalities or intellect. The point is, that a person must strive for ever-greater intellect by engaging in *teshuvah al teshuvah*. This is the level of tzaddikim. If, however, he finds himself incapable of maintaining a prolonged attempt at repentance, he can, and should, draw encouragement from the perceptions he has already attained, and use them as stepping stones to future perceptions of Godliness (*Torat Natan* #6, #8, #10).

Rebbe Nachman once said that several of his lessons, from among those given in 1802-1803, reflect the *kavanot* (Kabbalistic intentions) of tefillin (*Likutey Moharan* I, 38:end). The earlier point, about the holy names of God being reflected in one's repentance, and its connection to the mitzvah of tefillin are discussed by Reb Noson in *Likutey Halakhot, Tefillin* 5, sections 25-26. His discourse has been translated into English and appears in *Tefillin: A Chassidic Discourse* (see Chapter 4, pp.61-69), published by Breslov Research Institute, 1989.

"Then, *ShaVTa* (you will return) to God your Lord."[49] For the essence of the World to Come will be the ability to have a perception of His Godliness, as is written (Jeremiah 31:33), "they will know Me, from the least of them to the greatest."[50] Therefore, each time < he comes to > a deeper perception, < it will be necessary > to repent for the preceding perception.[51]

49. **Shabbat...TeShuVah...Then ShaVTa....** The word *ShaVTa* (שבת), in this case returning to God, contains the same letters as ShaBbaT (שבת; the letters *b* and *v* are interchangeable as both correspond to the Hebrew letter ב). This indicates that Shabbat and *TeShuVah* (תשבה, repentance) are one concept. This can be understood in light of Shabbat being the aspect of the World to Come, which is the ultimate good—the place where all separation and limitation disappear and creation coalesces into a single unity. Then, everything will be one and totally good. Sin and harsh judgment will have absolutely no place; on the contrary, the World to Come is the essence of forgiveness of sin. Thus, Shabbat/ the World to Come *is* repentance. As our Sages taught: Whoever delights in the Shabbat will be granted boundless prosperity...and have his sins forgiven (*Shabbat* 118a,b). This is because keeping Shabbat brings one to the ultimate truth, which is also one, without separation and limitation, and in which total forgiveness is supreme.

Reb Noson adds that this is the explanation of the Talmudic teaching: Were the Jews to twice keep all the laws of Shabbat, they would be redeemed immediately (*Shabbat* 118b). These two Shabbatot correspond to *teshuvah al teshuvah* (*Torat Natan* #9).

50. **they will know Me...least...greatest.** The verse from Jeremiah concludes, "for I will forgive their iniquities and disregard their sins." In our context, Rebbe Nachman quotes this verse as a proof-text that because the Jews will merit *teshuvah al teshuvah* in the World to Come (i.e., G-d will "forgive their iniquities..."), they will then come to *know* God through their greater perceptions. Thus, the World to Come suggests attaining ever greater perceptions of Godliness. As the Rebbe teaches in our lesson, this can be accomplished even in the present, in this world, through repentance. In fact, the verse itself alludes to this when it says, "from the least...to the greatest." In our context, this translates as ascending in one's recognition of God from the lower perceptions ("the least") to recognizing Him through the loftier perceptions ("the greatest").

Similarly, Rebbe Nachman will show below (§4) that to walk the pathways of repentance, a person must know how to ascend to the highest levels while at the same time not fall from the lower ones. Actually, the Rebbe has already alluded to this with this verse, "from the least...to the greatest." That is, one must know how to serve God in all situations and from all the different levels of spiritual achievement or lack thereof (*Mai HaNachal*).

51. **repent for the preceding perception.** For in order to merit the new and ever greater revelations of Godliness in the World to Come, a person has to repent for his earlier, more mundane perceptions of Godliness.

Reb Noson explains this concept of *teshuvah al teshuvah:* It is impossible to attain true repentance without first being tested. As the Baal Shem Tov taught: A person's first motivation towards repentance is sent to him by God. This is an ascent for him. He is given a taste of a level he personally has not yet achieved. But then he is tested. And more often than not, he finds himself backsliding, perhaps even committing a sin. Actually, this is a descent

וְזֶה שֶׁאָמְרוּ חֲכָמֵינוּ, זִכְרוֹנָם לִבְרָכָה: 'כָּל הַזּוֹבֵחַ אֶת יִצְרוֹ', הַיְנוּ
בְּחִינַת תְּשׁוּבָה, בְּחִינַת: "וְלִבִּי חָלָל בְּקִרְבִּי", בְּחִינַת דֹם לַה',
בְּחִינַת אהיה, בְּחִינַת כֶּתֶר, בְּחִינַת כָּבוֹד, כַּנַּ"ל, 'וּמִתְוַדֶּה עָלָיו',
הַיְנוּ שֶׁמִּתְוַדֶּה עַל זְבִיחַת יִצְרוֹ, הַיְנוּ שֶׁעוֹשֶׂה תְּשׁוּבָה עַל תְּשׁוּבָתוֹ
וְהַשָּׂגָתוֹ הָרִאשׁוֹנָה, 'כְּאִלּוּ כִּבְּדוֹ לְהַקָּדוֹשׁ בָּרוּךְ הוּא בִּשְׁנֵי
עוֹלָמוֹת'. כִּי תְּשׁוּבָה הָרִאשׁוֹנָה, בְּחִינַת כְּבוֹד עוֹלָם הַזֶּה. וְאַחַר
הַתְּשׁוּבָה שֶׁזּוֹכֶה לְהַשָּׂגָה יְתֵרָה, וּמַכִּיר בְּיוֹתֵר אֶת רוֹמְמוּת
אֱלֹקוּתוֹ, וְעוֹשֶׂה תְּשׁוּבָה עַל תְּשׁוּבָתוֹ, זֹאת הַתְּשׁוּבָה הוּא בְּחִינַת
כְּבוֹד עוֹלָם הַבָּא.

וְזֶה שֶׁאָמְרוּ חֲכָמֵינוּ, זִכְרוֹנָם לִבְרָכָה: "אוֹר יְקָרוֹת וְקִפָּאוֹן", 'אוֹר
שֶׁהוּא יָקָר בָּעוֹלָם הַזֶּה, יִהְיֶה קָפוּי וְקַל לָעוֹלָם הַבָּא'. נִמְצָא

55. **in two worlds.** By repenting, he minimizes his own honor and thereby adds to God's honor in this world. By repenting for the way he originally repented, he maximizes God's honor even further. His *teshuvah al teshuvah* corresponds to the World to Come. Thus, "it is as if he honored the Holy One in two worlds" (*Be'Ibey HaNachal*).

56. **kavod of the World to Come.** The *Be'Ibey HaNachal* writes: The two worlds are this world and the World to Come, yet they actually comprise three levels. The first level applies to someone who desires honor and glory. This person attains the "honor of kings," so that everyone questions his right to glory. He stands on the level of the backpart of *Ehyeh* receiving embarrassment instead of the honor he believes he deserves. (Examples of this type of glory seeker are politicians and self-appointed leaders of communities). The second level is one who does not seek glory, but gets irritated when embarrassed. This person wants to minimize his own honor and glorify God and therefore does not respond to his embarrassment. But, this level of honor is only that of this world. He has not yet attained full repentance, a pure heart. The minimizing of his own honor and the increase in God's honor go together, for his silence when enduring embarrassment slaughters his evil inclination and is thus turned into honor for God. But, were this person to be given honor, he would most likely receive it for his own sake and would not increase God's honor. The third level, on the other hand, is that of the person who has attained true humility. No matter what is given to him, glory or embarrassment, he always manages to honor God. This is someone who has achieved a pure heart and the honor of the World to Come. Thus, the first repentance is the *teshuvah* of this world. The second repentance, the *teshuvah al teshuvah*, is that of the World to Come.

57. **neither...light nor thick darkness.** Scripture refers to the days just prior to the coming of the Mashiach. At that time, there will be a day with no "natural" light, just a vague light

And this is the meaning of what the Sages taught: Whoever slaughters his evil inclination <and then confesses, it is as if he honored the Holy One in two worlds> *(Sanhedrin 43b).*[52] This <slaughtering of the evil inclination> is an aspect of repentance—corresponding to "My heart is hollowed within me," and "Be quiet before God"—an aspect of the holy name *Ehyeh/Keter/kavod.*[53] "...and then confesses"—i.e., he confesses for slaughtering his evil inclination, repenting for his first repentance and for his original level of perception[54]—[so that] "it is as if he honored the Holy One in two worlds."[55] This is because the first repentance corresponds to the *kavod* of this world. After he has repented and attained a greater perception and a greater recognition of the exalted nature of His Godliness, he then repents for his [earlier] repentance. This [second] repentance is the *kavod* of the World to Come.[56]

This is the meaning of *(Zechariah 14:6):* "[On that day,] there will be neither bright light nor thick darkness"[57]—concerning which the Sages said: The light which is substantial in this world will be

---

52. **the Sages taught....** Rabbi Yehoshua ben Levi taught: Whoever slaughters his evil inclination and then confesses, it is as if he honored the Holy One in two worlds, in this world and the World to Come, as is written (Psalms 50:23), "Whoever brings a sacrifice of thanksgiving, *y'khabdan'ni* (honors Me)" *(loc. cit.).* Rashi explains that after the evil inclination provokes someone to sin, if that person then overcomes his desires, repents and confesses his sins, he slaughters his evil inclination. This gives honor to God. Scripture, Rashi adds, uses the word *y'khabdan'ni* (from *kavod*), in which the letter *nun* appears twice, when it could just as well have used *y'khabdaini,* which has only one *nun.* However, the double *nun* indicates a double honor—in this world and the World to Come *(Rashi, loc. cit., s.v. zovei'ach).* Although Rashi doesn't say why the letter *nun* implies glory and honor, from our lesson it is possible to conclude the following: The *nun* (= 50) is generally associated with the highest of the Fifty Gates of Wisdom, which corresponds to *Binah. Binah* is also known as the World to Come. In our context, this refers to the *mochin* (mentalities), greater revelations and perceptions of Godliness. Thus, by repenting and confessing (bearing embarrassment to honor God), one achieves the first level of repentance, *kavod Elohim* of this world. This is his initial perception of Godliness—i.e., one *nun.* If he then purifies his confession and repents for his earlier insincerity, his *teshuvah al teshuvah* brings him to repentance of the World to Come—i.e., a second *nun.* Thus, two *nuns* suggest honoring God twice—perceiving two separate levels of Godliness.

53. **repentance...heart...quiet...Ehyeh/Keter/kavod.** The connection between all these concepts is explained above in section 2 and the accompanying notes.

54. **confesses...original level....** He does this because he recognizes that his first repentance was impure. He must therefore strive for *teshuvah al teshuvah.*

בָּעוֹלָם הַבָּא, כְּשֶׁיִּזְכּוּ לְהַשָּׂגָה יְתֵרָה בֶּאֱלֹקוּתוֹ, בְּוַדַּאי יִתְחָרְטוּ
וְיַעֲשׂוּ תְּשׁוּבָה עַל הַשָּׂגַת עוֹלָם הַזֶּה, כִּי הַשָּׂגַת עוֹלָם הַזֶּה בִּבְחִינַת
גֶּשֶׁם נֶגֶד הַשָּׂגַת עוֹלָם הַבָּא.

וְזֶה כְּאִלּוּ כִּבְּדוּ לְהַקָּדוֹשׁ-בָּרוּךְ-הוּא בִּשְׁנֵי עוֹלָמוֹת, כִּי זְבִיחַת
הַיֵּצֶר הִיא הַתְּשׁוּבָה הָרִאשׁוֹנָה, הוּא בְּחִינַת כְּבוֹד עוֹלָם הַזֶּה,
וְהַוִּדּוּי עַל זְבִיחַת הַיֵּצֶר, הַיְנוּ תְּשׁוּבָה שְׁנִיָּה, הִיא בְּחִינַת כְּבוֹד
עוֹלָם הַבָּא, שֶׁהַכָּבוֹד הָרִאשׁוֹן נַעֲשָׂה קָפוּי וְקַל, נֶגֶד הַכָּבוֹד הַשֵּׁנִי.

וְזֶה שֶׁאוֹמֵר הַקָּדוֹשׁ-בָּרוּךְ-הוּא: "אֵלֶּה עָשִׂיתָ וְהֶחֱרַשְׁתִּי, דִּמִּיתָ
הֱיוֹת אֶהְיֶה כָמוֹךָ", כִּי הָאָדָם עַל-יְדֵי שֶׁמַּחֲרִישׁ, נַעֲשֶׂה בְּחִינַת

---

60. **original glory...second glory.** The *Mai HaNachal* explains: When in the process of repenting a person minimizes his own honor, he slaughters the evil inclination by remaining quiet and silent when embarrassed, and therefore merits *kavod Elohim*. God Himself bestows this honor upon him. However, this *kavod Elohim* is minimal, as it reflects only the honor of this world. But, by then engaging in *teshuvah al teshuvah,* that person has honored God even more, thereby meriting a greater level of *kavod Elohim*—a level of *kavod Elohim* that will only be universally revealed in the World to Come!

Rebbe Nachman has already mentioned *kavod Elohim* several times and in different aspects. Below, in section 4, the Rebbe will add yet another aspect to the two levels of *kavod Elohim* (this worldly and next worldly) and explain how one attains them.

61. **I kept silent when....** In this next paragraph, Rebbe Nachman relates to what is an obvious question: How can *Ehyeh,* "I am prepared to be," or "I will be," be one of God's names when God never undergoes change? He has no need to prepare to be. He already *is!* This is why God's essential name is *YHVH.* To better understand this, consider the preceding and subsequent verses to the one the Rebbe quotes in the lesson: "When you see a thief, you join him; you throw in your lot with adulterers. Your mouth speaks evil...You sit around speaking against your brother...I kept silent when you did these things, [and so] you imagined that I am *ehyeh* (prepared to be) like you. I will rebuke you and lay it right before your eyes. Ponder this now, you who have forgotten God...Whoever offers a thanksgiving offering honors Me..." (Psalms 50:18-23).

62. **...by keeping silent.** A key to serving God is emulating His ways. Just as God is forgiving, generous, kind, etc., so must the person who strives to be His servant act with forgiveness, generosity, kindness, etc. Yet, whereas a human being's nature is affected by his actions and his character is improved by good deeds, it would be wrong, as Rebbe Nachman next explains, to assume that this process has a parallel in God. Take, for example, the act of remaining silent mentioned earlier in the lesson. Although a person who keeps silent in the

insignificant and slight in the World to Come (*Pesachim* 50a).[58] We see, therefore, that in the World to Come, when people will merit a greater perception of His Godliness, they will surely be contrite and repent for their perception in this world. For perception in this world is <materialistic> in comparison with perception in the World to Come.[59]

Thus, "it is as if he honored the Holy One in two worlds." The slaughter of the evil inclination is the first repentance <and> corresponds to the glory of this world. And the confession for having slaughtered the evil inclination is the second repentance, corresponding to <*kavod Elohi*>. This is because the original glory <is> thick and negligible in comparison with the second glory.[60]

{"I kept silent when you did these things, [and so] you imagined that I *ehyeh* like you. I will rebuke you and lay it right before your eyes" (Psalms 50:21).}[61]

This is what the Holy One says, "I kept silent when you did these things, [and so] you imagined that I *ehyeh* (will be) like you" — because, as explained, man becomes an aspect of *ehyeh* by keeping silent.[62] But when the Holy One keeps silent for a person it is not

which will be neither brightness nor darkness—i.e., no one will know whether salvation or annihilation is near. Nevertheless, this dawning of the new era will be the proof that the light heralds salvation, the revelation of God (*Rashi, Metzudat David, loc. cit.*, v.6-7).

58. **light...this world...World to Come.** Our Sages commented (*loc. cit.*) that the verse from Zechariah seems contradictory, as it states that there was neither light nor darkness. However, they explained, Scripture is in fact referring to a single light. It is a light that seems very bright in this world, but will be considered dull and negligible in the World to Come. For what seems precious now will be commonplace and mundane in the World to Come.

The *Mai HaNachal* points out that "light" corresponds to glory, as in (Ezekiel 43:2), "The earth was illuminated with His glory" (see *Likutey Moharan* I, 14:2). Furthermore, Rebbe Nachman's text reads: "*Or shehu yakar*..." (light that is substantial). The Hebrew *yakar* is the Aramaic term for honor. Thus, "Light (that) is glory." In our context, this indicates that the honor/repentance of this world will be negligible when compared to the honor/repentance of the World to Come, as the Rebbe next explains.

59. **World to Come.** In our context, the verse from Zechariah and our Sages' explanation refer to a person who has sinned and feels remorse. That person is now standing at the threshold of being, but must first prepare himself. By doing so—the aspect of *ehyeh*—he attains honor/ repentance, the light of this world. Yet, his work is not done. He must repent further. He must realize that his present perception of Godliness is only a very limited one, materialistic relative to the reality of God's spirituality. Realizing this, he recognizes the need to repent for his earlier repentance, *teshuvah al teshuvah*. For in the World to Come, he will certainly have greater awareness of God's exaltedness and repent for his earlier limited perceptions, which are the lowly perceptions of this world.

אהיה, כַּנַ"ל. אֲבָל הַקָּדוֹשׁ־בָּרוּךְ־הוּא, מַה שֶּׁמַּחֲרִישׁ לָאָדָם, אֵין זֶה
בִּשְׁבִיל אהיה, חַס וְשָׁלוֹם, כִּי זֶה אֵין שַׁיָּךְ אֵצֶל הַקָּדוֹשׁ בָּרוּךְ הוּא.
אֵין זֶה אֶלָּא כְּדֵי שֶׁיְּקַבְּלוּ עָנְשָׁם בָּעוֹלָם הַבָּא, שֶׁאָז מְסַדְּרִין לְעֵינָיו
עֲווֹנוֹתָיו, וְיוֹכִיחַ אוֹתוֹ עַל פָּנָיו, וְזֶה: אוֹכִיחֲךָ וְאֶעֶרְכָה לְעֵינֶיךָ:

ד וּכְשֶׁרוֹצֶה אָדָם לֵילֵךְ בְּדַרְכֵי הַתְּשׁוּבָה, צָרִיךְ לִהְיוֹת בָּקִי בַּהֲלָכָה,
וְצָרִיךְ לִהְיוֹת לוֹ שְׁנֵי בְּקִיאוּת, הַיְנוּ בָּקִי בְּרָצוֹא, בָּקִי בְּשׁוֹב, כְּמוֹ

ability to turn to God, and never with an assurance. But in the World to Come, all free choice will be negated. Then, God will turn to a sinner and 'lay his sins right before his eyes,' so that he knows exactly the reason for his punishment. Thus, God's keeping silent for a person is not at all intended as an act of vengeance. Rather, His desire is to maintain that person's free choice, which he then applies for better or otherwise.

65. **before your eyes.** Elsewhere (*Likutey Moharan* I, 98), Rebbe Nachman teaches that the worst possible punishment a person can suffer is to be shown outright the severity of the blemish he has caused by sinning (*Parparaot LeChokhmah*). Therefore, God will "lay it right before your eyes."

In review: Every person must minimize his own honor and maximize God's honor (§1). This requires *teshuvah*, returning to God and recognizing His greatness, which is best accomplished by enduring insult in silence—doing so for the Holy One's sake. A person thereby increases God's honor and himself merits *kavod Elohim* (§2). Even so, he must never cease repenting. He must engage in *teshuvah al teshuvah*, always seeking greater revelations of God. In this way, he will merit the repentance of the World to Come (§3).

66. **wants to walk....** Initially, Rebbe Nachman taught that a person merits repenting by bearing embarrassment in silence. However, to merit *teshuvah al teshuvah*, to constantly walk the pathways of *teshuvah*, to be able to repent at all times—a person needs a certain type of expertise.

67. **expert in Halakhah.** Most simply, *Halakhah* refers to the body of Jewish Law or to any specific law contained therein. It is comprised of that specific set of laws and rules originally derived from the Five Books of Moshe and presently concisely set forth in the *Shulchan Arukh* (Code of Jewish Law). The word *halakhah* (a single law) is similar to *halikhah*, which means "walking." Thus, in order for someone to "*walk* the pathways of repentance," he must know how and by what means to walk—i.e., *Halakhah*.

Expertise in *Halakhah*, at its most fundamental level, requires knowledge of the Torah's laws and their fine points as they relate to each and every one of the mitzvot. For all the various elements of Torah are needed when reviving those weak souls who have descended from high levels of holiness. Each person strays in his own way and then needs *his* specific mitzvah to help him find his way back. This is because each mitzvah, with its laws, rules and fine points, has a unique life-sustaining power, as is written (Deuteronomy 30:20), "For it is your life"—"it" being the Torah.

because of < the aspect of > *ehyeh,* God forbid. Such a concept is in no way applicable to the Holy One. It is only so that < this person might receive his punishment > in the World to Come.[63] For, then, his transgressions are set before his eyes and he is rebuked to his face.[64] And this is, "I will rebuke you and lay it right before your eyes."[65]

4. Now, when a person wants to walk the pathways of repentance,[66] he must be *baky* (expert) in *Halakhah.*[67] This demands that he have two types of expertise: *baky b'ratzo* (expert at "running") and *baky*

---

face of embarrassment thereby repents and increases his awareness, these changes are inapplicable to God; God's intention in remaining silent is certainly *not* so that He might repent or increase awareness.

63. **punishment in the World to Come.** When God causes a person to suffer, He takes on the aspect of the holy name *Ehyeh.* This is because God's intention in sending this person suffering is to arouse him to repent. For at that time, his sins have brought him to the backpart of *Ehyeh* so that he does not yet recognize God. But if he then suffers the ignominy of embarrassment or some other form of anguish and as a result turns to God—whom he now recognizes as the initiator of his suffering—*he* takes on the aspect of *ehyeh* and God in turn advances, as it were, to the aspect of *havayah,* as in (Exodus 16:12), "And you shall know that I am *YHVH.*" However, when a person persists in the path of wrongdoing, God will often cease manifesting to him as *Ehyeh.* This is, "You sit around speaking against your brother . . ." (Psalms, *ibid.*). Not only does he not remain silent and repent, but he persists in slandering others. The embarrassment he deserves, he transfers to others—especially those who embarrass him! And so God makes no further attempt to awaken him to repentance through suffering. Thus, there are two possibilities. If a person arouses himself to the need for repentance, if he ponders the meaning of his suffering—as in (*ibid.*), "Ponder this now, you who have forgotten God"—and repents, thereby slaughtering his evil inclination, he merits *kavod Elohim.* But, if he does not, if he refuses to awaken, then God says: "I kept silent when you did these things," because I no longer wished to arouse you to repentance. This, in fact, is a very severe punishment. For, then, this person remains oblivious to his sins and so fails to repent. His punishment is thus stored away for the Future, in the World to Come, where God will lay the matter of his sins right before his eyes and punish him for every single thing he did wrong (*Be'Ibey HaNachal; Mai HaNachal*).

64. **rebuked to his face.** The *Parparaot LeChokhmah* offers another explanation for why God will not always reprove a person in this world. He writes: There are times when God refrains from exacting punishment from someone because He knows that this person will not ponder his situation and come to realize the reason for his suffering. In all likelihood, quite the reverse will happen. The sinner will feel he is being punished for no reason at all and as a result rebel even further against God. At the same time, in this world people are not meant to always understand the meaning of their suffering, for then they would be denied the power of free choice—knowing with certainty the relationship between cause and effect obviates choosing. Therefore, a person is only made to suffer for his sins commensurate with his

שֶׁכָּתוּב: 'זַכָּאָה מָאן דְּעָיֵל וְנָפִיק'. וְזֶה בְּחִינַת: "אִם אֶסַּק שָׁמַיִם –
שָׁם אָתָּה", בְּחִינַת עָיֵל, בְּחִינַת בָּקִי בְּרָצוֹא. "וְאַצִּיעָה שְּׁאוֹל –
הִנֶּךָּ", בְּחִינַת וְנָפִיק, בְּחִינַת בָּקִי בְּשׁוֹב.

(*Torat Natan* #14, #16).

Reb Noson explains further that each person has his own level to which he ascends. He can run up the spiritual ladder to a position that is uniquely his. Likewise, others have their unique levels (with one person's running being another person's returning). Expertise is therefore necessary. How else can a person know his unique capabilities and find his level? For it would be wrong to mimic another's devotions and achievements, as this invariably leads to seeking honor rather than the right pathways to repentance (*Torat Natan* #15, #20).

69. **enters and exits.** This passage from the *Zohar* (*loc. cit.*) is referring to someone who enters the upper realms of knowledge of God. This is a very lofty level, and no one can remain there forever. Just as a person must know how to "enter in peace" into these higher realms, he must know how to "exit in peace" (*Chagigah* 15b). Therefore, an expertise in running and returning is also necessary if one is to descend from the lofty heights and be stronger for having ascended. Indeed, it is this security that enables him to ascend to ever greater heights in the first place. As the *Zohar* concludes: Someone who cannot descend properly might be better off never ascending, for the greater his exposure to the loftier levels, the greater the possibility of error in his descent (as happened to Acher, see *Chagigah* 14b *ff*; see also n.76).

Reb Noson provides a further understanding of "ascending and descending." He explains that a person who wants to repent must inevitably be tested in circumstances similar to those in which he succumbed. By "entering" those realms and remaining steadfast in his devotion to God, he has ascended and descended—i.e., "entered in peace" and "exited in peace"—and merited rectifying his transgressions (*Torat Natan* #18, #19).

70. **You are there...ascending...running.** Specifically "*there*"—indicating that God is to be found at an even greater level than the one he has already attained. He is therefore obliged to seek further.

71. **here You are...descending...returning.** Specifically "*here*"—indicating that God is extremely close to him even, or especially, in these lowest of levels to which he has fallen. He need only open his eyes to see this.

The *Mai HaNachal* adds that these two levels, *baky b'ratzo* and *baky b'shov* correspond to the two levels of *kavod Elohim* discussed earlier. *Baky b'shov* corresponds to the first level of repentance, the *kavod Elohim* of this world, where people's perception of Godliness is limited. *Baky b'ratzo* refers to ascending to the higher level, to *teshuvah al teshuvah*, the *kavod Elohim* of the World to Come, where people's awareness of God will be increased. As we've seen (§1, nn.2-6), this second level of *kavod Elohim* is one in which the honor belongs entirely to God. The person has attained such a great degree of humility that he no longer feels himself a separate entity. Rather, he negates himself totally to God, and in so doing attains a deeper perception of Godliness.

The *Biur HaLikutim* points out that God's greatest honor is when someone who is distant from Him, someone on a low spiritual level, recognizes Him. This is seen in the verse, "You are *there*"—distant...."*here* You are"—revealed and right next to me.

b'shov (expert at "returning").[68] As stated < in the *Zohar* (III, 292a) > : "Deserving is he who enters and exits."[69] This corresponds to (Psalms 139:8), "If I ascend to heaven, You are there"—an aspect of ascending, of being expert at running[70]; "and if I make my bed in Hell, here You are"—an aspect of descending, of being expert at returning.[71]

This is (Song of Songs 6:3), "I am my beloved's, and my beloved is

And this is why it is necessary to be very diligent in Torah study, which literally revives a person from the spiritlessness which sin engenders. This is especially true of the study of *Shulchan Arukh,* in which clarifying the laws differentiates good from bad and the permissible from the forbidden—as a result of which, evil loses its power to drag a person down from his spiritual level. This is the inner meaning of being expert in *Halakhah* (*Likutey Halakhot, Birkhot HaPeirot* 5:19; *Torat Natan* #12).

Rebbe Nachman once said, "Everyone must study the *Shulchan Arukh* each day without fail" (*Rabbi Nachman's Wisdom* #29; see also *Likutey Moharan* I, 8:6; *ibid.* 62:2). On the same topic, Reb Noson writes: Our Sages taught that a time will come when people will not be able to clarify *Halakhah* (see *Shabbat* 138b *ff*)—a situation that will only be rectified when Mashiach comes. This is why it is necessary to acquire as much expertise as one can: to do one's best to ascertain the law, in order to serve God properly and come as close as possible to Him (*Torat Natan* #27). Conversely, Reb Noson says elsewhere that the reason our exile has lasted as long as it has, can be traced to the fact that people are not well versed in *Halakhah.* More specifically, they fail to draw closer to the true tzaddikim who can teach them how to achieve the necessary expertise in *Halakhah/halikhah* (*Torat Natan* #34).

68. **running...returning.** These terms, *ratzo* and *shov,* come from Yechezkel's vision of the Divine Chariot: "The living creatures ran and returned, in appearance like a flash of lightning" (Ezekiel 1:14). This Vision of the Chariot, another part of which is discussed below in greater detail (§5), depicts some of the most sublime spiritual levels and states a person can experience (see *Innerspace,* by R. Aryeh Kaplan, Moznaim Pub., Part Two: Meditation and Prophecy).

This running and returning, Rebbe Nachman says, implies ascent and descent. A person who is expert in *Halakhah* knows how to ascend to higher spiritual levels when things are going well, as well as how to not fall even further when they are not. For when a person uses his knowledge of Torah/*Halakhah* in order to ascend to the highest levels he can attain, he must keep in mind that there are greater levels still. This will spur him to carry on striving and searching for God in ever higher realms—beginning anew again and again and again. Conversely, when he begins to feel low and powerless to continue on in his devotions, he must use his knowledge of Torah/*Halakhah* to strengthen himself so as not to succumb to sin. This will save him from despair. For the fact is that God is everywhere. "His glory fills the whole world" (Isaiah 6:3). Thus, even if someone falls to the lowest depths, he must not lose sight of the *takhlit* (ultimate goal), so as not to backslide even more. Rather, he must maintain his present level. This requires realizing that God is everywhere, even in the lowest of places— even in *his* lowest places. He can reach out to Him even there (*Torat Natan* #13). The key for maintaining one's achievements, regardless of what one has to endure, is faith. Believing that "God is first and God is last" (cf. Isaiah 44:6), instills in a person the awareness that God can be found on every single level, from the highest to the lowest, and thus is always available

וְזֶה: "אֲנִי לְדוֹדִי וְדוֹדִי לִי". 'אֲנִי לְדוֹדִי', – זֶה בְּחִינַת עַיל. 'וְדוֹדִי
לִי' – זֶה בְּחִינַת וְנָפִיק. [וְזֶה סוֹד כַּוָּנַת אֱלוּל], וְזֶה עִקַּר כְּבוֹדוֹ.

וְזֶה: "וְכִבַּדְתּוֹ מֵעֲשׂוֹת דְּרָכֶיךָ". 'דְּרָכֶיךָ' – לְשׁוֹן רַבִּים. הַיְנוּ עַיל
וְנָפִיק, וּכְשֶׁיֵּשׁ לוֹ אֵלוּ הַשְּׁנֵי בְּקִיאוּת הַנַּ"ל, אֲזַי הוּא הוֹלֵךְ בְּדַרְכֵי
הַתְּשׁוּבָה וְזוֹכֶה לִכְבוֹד ה', כְּמוֹ שֶׁכָּתוּב: "וְכִבַּדְתּוֹ מֵעֲשׂוֹת
דְּרָכֶיךָ", הַיְנוּ שֶׁזּוֹכֶה לְכֶתֶר, כִּי לֵית כָּבוֹד בְּלָא כָּף, וְאָז יְמִין ה'
פְּשׁוּטָה לְקַבֵּל תְּשׁוּבָתוֹ.

something from a public to a private domain, which is prohibited on Shabbat. Yet, it is also a readily recognizable aspect of our daily lives as the *going out* to *bring home* one's livelihood.

This applies to the spiritual as well. Through a person's involvement in the external, the physical activities necessitated by the body, he filters out and extracts that which is holy within the physical and brings it into the realm of *kedushah* (holiness). On Shabbat, however, there is no process of sifting and filtering. Quite the opposite. On Shabbat all that was extracted during the week ascends to a place of peace, tranquility and rest. Then, the pathways of *teshuvah*—aspects of going and coming, running and returning—are perfected. All work is therefore unnecessary, indeed forbidden. Shabbat is thus the time when we are occupied with the ways of God, not our own ways. This is the honor of Shabbat.

The verse Rebbe Nachman quotes here from Isaiah begins: "If you restrain your foot on Shabbat [from walking beyond the permissible limit], from pursuing your business on My holy day...and you honor the Shabbat...." As the Rebbe has just taught, to repent one must be an expert in *Halakhah*/walking. He must know how to walk forward (running) and back (returning). This is repentance. And, as we have seen earlier (§3), Shabbat is also the concept of repentance. Thus, when a person knows how to properly "walk" on the Shabbat (he knows how to run and return), he has merited repentance. And because of this, he merits "you honor"—i.e., *kavod Elohim* (see *Parparaot LeChokhmah*; *Biur HaLikutim*).

78. **Ways is plural....** The Rebbe explains why the verse uses the plural, "ways." This is to show that the expertise must be both in running and returning to attain repentance. Then, and only then, is he "walking the pathways of *teshuvah*."

79. **merits...Godly kavod....** As above, section 2. Through repentance one merits *kavod Elohim* (see n.77).

80. **Keter...kaf.** See above, section 2, note 13.

81. **right hand...repentance.** When a person repents, God stretches out His hand to receive his repentance. See also Rashi and *Siftei Chakhamim* on Deuteronomy 3:24, *Tanchuma*, *BeShalach* 15, and *Or HaChaim*, Deuteronomy 32:11. Below, Rebbe Nachman will show how the concept of *yemin* (the right hand) ties in with other aspects of the lesson (§§10,12).

mine."[72] "I am my beloved's" is the aspect of ascending[73]; "and my beloved is mine" is the aspect of descending.[74] [This is the hidden meaning of the meditations of Elul,[75]] and this is the essence of His glory.[76]

And this is (Isaiah 58:13), "and you honor [the Shabbat] by refraining from your routine ways."[77] "Ways" is plural, indicating ascending and descending.[78] When a person possesses these two types of expertise, then he is walking the < true > pathways of repentance, and merits the above mentioned < Godly > *kavod*. As it is written, "and you honor it by refraining from your routine ways"[79] — i.e., he attains *Keter,* for there can be no *kavod* without a *kaf*.[80] Then, the right hand of God is outstretched to accept his repentance (cf. *Sifri,* Deuteronomy 3:29; *Tachanun* Prayer).[81]

72. **I am...is mine.** In Hebrew, אני לדודי ודודי לי — "*Ani L'dodi V'dodi Li.*" The first letters of these words spell ELUL (אלול). The Jewish month of Elul is reserved for repentance, as the Jewish people prepare for Rosh HaShanah and Yom Kippur. With repentance being the main theme of our lesson, the Rebbe now connects Elul to the lesson and will show how all the concepts discussed so far are related to the month of Elul.

73. **I am...ascending.** In other words, "I am endeavoring to ascend to my Beloved" — i.e., to higher spiritual levels.

74. **and my beloved is...descending.** For God sustains even those on the lowest of levels, especially if they truly seek Him from there.

75. **hidden meaning of the meditations of Elul.** Here, Rebbe Nachman specifically refers to the name Elul, whereas below (see end of this section and n.82) he refers to the hidden meaning of the month's *kavanot* (meditations).

76. **the essence of His glory.** God's glory is perfected by man's deeds here on earth. Thus, when we serve God from this lowly world, which is so very distant from Him, His glory increases and reaches completion, as it were. This is because the glory revealed by God's own mighty and awesome deeds is, so to speak, lacking — in a sense, it is as if the Holy One were serving Himself. The completion of glory, therefore, can only be achieved by Divine service performed in this physical world, especially by those who are on low spiritual levels. Thus, the meaning of "Deserving is he who enters and exits" is: Deserving is he who is an expert at ascending to God and yet has the expertise to remain strong even in the difficult times and to hold on even when falling to lower rungs of the spiritual ladder. Such a person has truly merited and revealed the glory of God. We see, then, that the element of ascending and descending produce a true revelation of God's glory.

77. **honor the Shabbat...from your routine ways.** The work of the six days of the week can, in a general sense, be viewed as the process of separating that which is holy from the externalities, and bringing that holiness into the inner realm. This is the concept of carrying

[וְזֶה סוֹד כַּוָּנַת אֱלוּל:]

ה וְעַל-יְדֵי הַדְּמִימָה וְהַשְׁתִיקָה נַעֲשֶׂה בְּחִינַת חִירִיק, כַּמּוּבָא
בְּתִקּוּנִים: "וְתַחַת רַגְלָיו כְּמַעֲשֵׂה לִבְנַת הַסַּפִּיר" – דָּא חִירִיק, וְזֶה
בְּחִינַת: "וְהָאָרֶץ הֲדֹם רַגְלָי". 'הֲדֹם' – זֶה בְּחִינַת דְּמִימָה, וְזֶה

forming the letter *aleph*. This was the *aleph* that Yechezkel saw. The *Zohar* next describes what these parts of the *aleph* allude to.

The upper point alludes to *Keter*, which hovers up above *Chokhmah* and *Binah*. The lower point is likened to the *chirik* (a single vowel sign; see next note), which is a single dot (*yod*), corresponding to the earth/*Malkhut*, as in (Isaiah 66:1), "the earth is My footstool." The line between the two, the *vav*, is the firmament between the two levels, corresponding to *Z'er Anpin* (the Divine persona comprised of six *sefirot*). Thus, the letter *aleph*—its two dots/*yods* (=20) and its line/*vav* (=6)—has a numerical value of twenty-six, the same as God's holy name *YHVH*. The *aleph* also encompasses all of the Ten *Sefirot*: from *Keter* (*Chokhmah* and *Binah*), through the six central *sefirot*, to *Malkhut*.

The *Zohar* then says: "and above it, upon the semblance of the throne, there was a *mareh* (form) resembling an *adam* (man)." Everything is found in the *aleph*, for there can be no *ADaM* without the *Aleph*. That is, this *mareh* (form) denotes the holy name of *YHVH* in its expansion *MaH* (=45, the same numerical value as *ADaM*; see Appendix: Expansions of the Holy Names). Thus, the *adam* on the throne is *Z'er Anpin*. This holy name *YHVH* was lacking an *aleph*—it comprised only *dam*, the backpart of *Ehyeh*. But, when the *aleph* of *Ehyeh* was formed and placed within the holy name *YHVH*, then *ADaM* (*MaH*) was made—"a form resembling a man." Therefore: If you think you can enter the upper chambers and determine anything about God's holy name, return! For His name is totally hidden (*Tikkuney Zohar*, Introduction, p.6b,7a; *Matok Midvash, loc. cit.*).

The different parts of this passage will be explained in greater detail as they appear in the lesson. Rebbe Nachman now shows how the mysteries of Yechezkel's vision are applicable to each and every person on his particular level and how it is possible for even mortal beings to achieve them.

85. **the chirik.** The *chirik* is the name of one of the vowel signs in the Hebrew *nikud* system. Pronounced as the *ea* in the word "easy," the *chirik* (.) is a single dot placed below the feet or base of a letter (a stone, the lower point, as in n.84). The verse Rebbe Nachman quotes from Exodus refers to the revelation Israel's sages attained at Mount Sinai. In our context, this can be understood as the Jews at Sinai having repented for their sins and being ready for *teshuvah*—i.e., to serve God anew. They thereby merited the first level of repentance: the *chirik*, the lower point, the *teshuvah* of this world.

86. **earth is hadome ragli . . . .** The earth is likened to a *foot*stool, and both allude to the lower point of the *aleph*/the *chirik*.

The *Mai HaNachal* adds that if we examine the entire verse, we find within it all three elements of the *aleph*. Isaiah (*loc. cit.*) said, "The heavens are My *kisay*, and the earth is *haDoMe ragli*." That is, "the heavens"—the *vav*—"are My *kisay*"—the upper point; "and the earth is *haDoMe ragli*"—the lower point. This will become clearer further on in the lesson.

{This is the hidden meaning of the *kavanot* (meditations) of Elul}.[82]

5. Now, by means[83] of quiet and silence the aspect of the *chirik* is formed.[84] As is brought in the *Tikkunim* < on the verse > , "and under His feet was something like a sapphire brick" (Exodus 24:10) — this is the *chirik* (*Tikkuney Zohar* 7a).[85] And this corresponds to "the earth is *hadome ragli* (My footstool)" (Isaiah 66:1)[86] — "*haDoMe*" corresponds to

---

82. **kavanot of Elul.** *Kavanot* are Kabbalistic meditations based on the various permutations of God's holy names. These *kavanot* apply not only to prayer, but to all aspects of life. The meditations that relate to the month of Elul are elaborated upon below (§§10-13).

In review: Every person must minimize his own honor and maximize God's honor (§1). This requires *teshuvah*, returning to God and recognizing His greatness, which is best accomplished by enduring insult in silence — doing so for the Holy One's sake. A person thereby increases God's honor and himself merits *kavod Elohim* (§2). Even so, he must never cease repenting. He must engage in *teshuvah al teshuvah*, always seeking greater revelations of God. In this way, he will merit the repentance of the World to Come (§3). And in order to walk the pathways of repentance, a person must be expert at running and returning — i.e., at knowing how to both ascend and descend the spiritual ladder in accordance with his unique capabilities (§4).

83. **Now, by means.** In this section, Rebbe Nachman introduces two new concepts: the letter *aleph*, and the rabbi/disciple relationship. In addition, the Rebbe returns to the statement he made prior to giving the lesson, "When one sits on the chair, one is an *adam!*" (see above, n.1). The Rebbe now ties all these concepts together within the context of our lesson. He also offers a commentary to Ezekiel's vision, connecting the concept of creatures running and returning to the appearance of a man sitting on the throne (see n.68).

84. **the chirik is formed.** The following passage from the *Tikkuney Zohar* with the commentary of the *Matok Midvash* is vital for understanding this section of the lesson. In this part of Yechezkel's vision (verses 26-28), he mentions the Hebrew term *mareh*, "form" or "appearance" (lit. "vision"), nine times. The first two are found in verse 26: "Above the firmament that was over their heads was the semblance of a throne, in appearance (*mareh*) like sapphire stone; and above it, upon the semblance of the throne, there was a form (*mareh*) resembling an *adam* (man)."

The *Zohar*, in discussing these *marot* (plural of *mareh*) states: "Above the firmament that was over their heads" there was the letter *aleph*, "in appearance like sapphire stone." A stone resembles a round dot, the letter *yod*, similar to the upper and lower points of the letter *aleph*. This was the "sapphire stone" that was *d'mut kisay* ("the semblance of a throne"). The word *kisay* is akin to *d'mitkasya*, which means "covers over" or "hides." The upper point of the *aleph* is hidden above the line of the *aleph*. The line resembles the letter *vav*, similar to the firmament that divides upper from lower. Thus, "the semblance of a *kisay* (throne)" corresponds to the upper *yod* being hidden from sight above the *vav*.

The *Zohar* then quotes another verse which refers to sapphire (Exodus 24:10): "and under His feet was something like a sapphire brick." This refers to the lower point of the *aleph*. Thus, the "stone" and "brick" of sapphire refer to the upper and lower points of the letter *aleph*, respectively. They are positioned above and below, and united by the slanted *vav*, thus

בְּחִינַת הַנְּקֻדָּה הַתַּחְתּוֹנָה שֶׁל תְּמוּנַת א.

וּנְקֻדָּה הָעֶלְיוֹנָה שֶׁעַל הָאָלֶף זֶה בְּחִינַת כֶּתֶר, בְּחִינַת: "וּמִמַּעַל לָרָקִיעַ אֲשֶׁר עַל רֹאשָׁם אֶבֶן סַפִּיר דְּמוּת כִּסֵּא", 'דְּמִתְכַּסְיָא לְעֵילָא מִנָּא"ו שֶׁבְּאָלֶ"ף, דְּמִתְקַרְיָא רָקִיעַ', וְהַנְּקֻדָּה הִיא כִּסֵּא דְּמִתְכַּסְיָא, כְּמוֹ שֶׁכָּתוּב: "בַּמֻּפְלָא מִמְּךָ אַל תִּדְרֹשׁ, וּבַמְכֻסֶּה מִמְּךָ אַל תַּחְקֹר", וְזֶה בְּחִינַת: "כְּבוֹד אֱלֹקִים הַסְתֵּר דָּבָר", בְּחִינַת כֶּתֶר.

וְהַוָא"ו שֶׁבְּתוֹךְ הָאָלֶף, הוּא רָקִיעַ, שָׁמַיִם, אֵשׁ וּמַיִם, בְּחִינַת הַבּוּשָׁה שֶׁנִּשְׁתַּנָּה פָּנָיו לְכַמָּה גְוָנִין. וְזֶה בְּחִינַת רָקִיעַ כְּלָלִיּוּת הַגְּוָנִין.

וְנַעֲשֶׂה עַל־יְדֵי־זֶה אָדָם לָשֶׁבֶת עַל הַכִּסֵּא, כְּמוֹ שֶׁכָּתוּב: "וּדְמוּת

95. **ShaMaYiM.** The Hebrew term for the heavens, the firmament.

96. **...aiSh and MaYiM.** The Talmud (*Chagigah* 12a) teaches: The word *shamayim* (שמים) is a compound of *aiSh* (אש, fire) and *MaYiM* (מים, water). The Maharsha explains that these two elements, fire and water, represent the attributes of judgment and kindness, respectively. These are the attributes used to create the heavens (*Maharsha, loc. cit., s.v. tana aish umayim*). They are also the attributes found in *Z'er Anpin*, which is said to contain many colors (see *Zohar* I, 71b). See next note.

97. **face changes colors.** The Talmud (*Berakhot* 6b) likens suffering embarrassment to being judged in fire and water. This is because a person who is shamed undergoes changes of facial color, from red to white, until his blood finally simmers down (*Maharsha, loc. cit., s.v. mai krum*). Thus, embarrassment parallels the heavens, the firmament, for they both contain the elements of fire and water.

98. **firmament...all the colors.** In our context, this teaches that the *vav* of the *aleph* corresponds to embarrassment—i.e., one's face changing color when suffering embarrassment. Thus, a person who wants to repent must learn to remain silent (the lower point) and endure the embarrassment (the *vav*). Only by doing so will he slaughter his evil inclination and thereby attain *Keter, kavod Elohim* (the upper point). He has thus completed the letter *aleph*. And, by completing the *aleph*...

99. **adam...on the throne is made.** The *Zohar* (*loc. cit.*) teaches: Scripture refers to man by several names: *adam, gever, enosh, ish.* Each is indicative of a different spiritual level, the greatest of all being *adam.* And when is there perfection Above? When the Holy One, *YHVH*—specifically the aspect of the holy name *MaH* (*ADaM*)—sits on His Throne. For until the Holy One sits on His Throne, there can be no more than a semblance of perfection, as in, "upon the semblance of the throne, there was a form resembling an *adam.*" The *Zohar* adds: Adam was created on the sixth day of Creation, at the same moment the Throne was

< *haDeMimah* (the quiet) and silence >,[87] an aspect of the ⊠ lower point of the shape of the *aleph*.[88]

And the upper point of the *aleph* is the aspect of *Keter*,[89] ⊠ corresponding to "Above the firmament that was over their heads was the semblance of a *kisay* (throne), in appearance like sapphire stone" (Ezekiel 1:26). [This is the point] that covers from above the *vav* of the *aleph*, which is called "firmament" (see *Tikkuney Zohar, ibid.*).[90] This point is *kisay d'mitKaSya* (a throne that is covered).[91] As is taught: Do not inquire about that which is hidden from you, and into what is *miKhuSeh* (covered) from you do not investigate (Chagigah 13a).[92] This corresponds to "The *kavod* of the Lord is a concealed matter," the aspect of *Keter*.[93]

And the *vav* in the middle of the *aleph* is the firmament,[94] ⊠ *ShaMaYiM*[95] — *aiSh* and *MaYiM* (fire and water),[96] which corresponds to embarrassment, when one's face changes colors.[97] This is the aspect of the firmament, which encompasses all the colors.[98]

In this way, "an *adam* to sit on the throne" is made (Zohar III, 48a).[99] As it is written (Ezekiel 1:26), "and above it, [upon the semblance of the

---

87. **HaDoMe...HaDeMimah....** The term *haDoMe* (הדם) is similar to *DeMimah* (דמימה, quiet). Thus, in our context the verse reads: "The earth/*chirik* is made by being *DoMe* (quiet)."

88. **lower point...of the aleph.** When, out of his desire to repent, a person remains quiet and silent in the face of embarrassment, he forms the *chirik*, the lower point of the *aleph*.

89. **upper point...Keter.** As above, note 84.

90. **vav...firmament.** See below, note 94.

91. **...kisay d'mitKaSya.** That is, the upper point corresponds to *Keter*, which is concealed above the firmament (as above, n.84). It is called *kisay* (כסא) because it is *mitkasya* (מתכסיא) above the firmament, beyond the reach of the mind, as the Rebbe next explains.

92. **hidden from you...miKhuSeh....** That which is considered *kisay*, hidden from a person, cannot be questioned or scrutinized.

93. **a concealed matter...Keter.** That is, the upper point is considered something hidden, similar to *kavod Elohim*. It is forbidden to question this *kavod*—the aspect of *Keter*. Thus, someone who wants to repent must remain quiet and silent when embarrassed. He thereby attains the lower point of the *aleph*. If he then merits *teshuvah*, he attains *kavod Elohim/Keter* (as in §2), which is the upper point of the *aleph*.

94. **vav...is the firmament.** Throughout the Kabbalah, *Z'er Anpin* is associated with the heavens, whereas *Malkhut* is associated with the earth. *Z'er Anpin* is also aligned with the letter *vav*, by virtue of its six *sefirot* (see n.84). Thus, in our context, the *vav* corresponds to the firmament.

כְּמַרְאֵה אָדָם עָלָיו מִלְמָעְלָה", 'כִּי לֵית אָדָם בְּלָא אֶלֶ"ף'. וְזֶה
אוֹתִיוֹת אָדָם, אֶלֶף דָּם. הַיְנוּ עַל־יְדֵי דֹם לַה', נַעֲשֶׂה אֶלֶ"ף, וְנַעֲשֶׂה
אָדָם לָשֶׁבֶת עַל הַכִּסֵּא.

כִּי הַנָּא"ו שֶׁבְּתוֹךְ הָאֶלֶף הוּא רָקִיעַ כְּלָלִיוּת הַגְּוָנִין, הַיְנוּ הַבּוּשָׁה,
כַּנַּ"ל. וְהַנְּקֻדָּה הַתַּחְתּוֹנָה הִיא הַשְּׁתִיקָה וְהַדְמִימָה, כְּמוֹ שֶׁכָּתוּב:
"וְהָאָרֶץ הֲדֹם רַגְלָי", וְזֶה בְּחִינַת חִירִיק, בְּחִינַת: "וְתַחַת רַגְלָיו",
וְהַנְּקֻדָּה הָעֶלְיוֹנָה הוּא כִּסֵּא דְּמִתְכַּסְיָא, בְּחִינַת תְּשׁוּבָה, בְּחִינַת:
"כְּבוֹד אֱלֹקִים הַסְתֵּר דָּבָר", בְּחִינַת: "בַּמְכֻסֶּה מִמְּךָ אַל תַּחְקֹר",
בְּחִינַת: "וּמִמַּעַל לָרָקִיעַ דְּמוּת כִּסֵּא וְכוּ', וְנַעֲשֶׂה אָדָם לָשֶׁבֶת עַל
הַכִּסֵּא", בְּחִינַת: "כְּמַרְאֵה אָדָם עָלָיו מִלְמָעְלָה".

repentance. This is the level of *Keter*, which denotes a level of silence that is even higher than speech, for it corresponds to the hidden levels. And there, in *Keter*, a person must wait. It would be wrong for him delve into something above his level. Rather, he must wait patiently, until he can ascend to the next level (*Torat Natan* #22).

The *Mai HaNachal* adds: We can now better understand why a person must endure embarrassment in silence. The firmament, the *vav*, corresponds to the Hebrew vowel *patach* (*Tikkuney Zohar*, Introduction, p.7b). Pronounced as the *a* in "Shabbat," the *patach* (-) is shaped like a *vav*, a straight line. When a person seeks honor, he finds only the honor given to kings, the type of honor everyone questions and scrutinizes. People therefore have what can be called a *peh patuach* (an open mouth) to speak against him. Now, the source of this questioning and open criticism (*PaTuaCh*) to which he is subjected is the *vav* (*PaTaCh*). His embarrassment, caused by his "bad" blood (*dam*), can only be undone by his keeping quiet and silent—turning from *DaM*, with a *patach*, to *DoMe*, with a *cholem* (see n.33). Then, in place of *kavod melakhim* he finds *kavod Elohim*, true honor. The *ChoLeM* of *dome*—which denotes *haChLaMah*, healing and sealing a wound—closes the mouths that were open.

The *Mai HaNachal* adds that both *kavoD melakhiM* and *kavoD ElohiM* end with the letters *DM*. However, whereas *kavod melakhim* is *dAm*, with a *pAtach*, *kavod Elohim* is *dOme* with a *chOlem*.

105. **an adam to sit...resembling a man.** The passage quoted earlier from the *Tikkuney Zohar* (n.84) explains that the *adam* sitting on the throne is actually God (in His manifestation as *Z'er Anpin*). Rebbe Nachman, on the other hand, sees this as referring to man himself. The explanation, the *Parparaot LeChokhmah* says, comes from the teaching that "the Holy One and the Jewish people are one" (*Zohar* III, 93b; see §6:end). Thus, when the Jews perfect themselves and their devotions, they bring rectification to the Supernal Worlds as well. So that when any Jew repents and achieves the level of *adam*, God's rulership becomes even more complete, as it were, and He sits on His Throne. As we will see below (§§7,9), this is connected to the Final Redemption, when the Jewish people's archenemy, Amalek, will be obliterated—"for God took an oath that His Name and Throne will not be complete until Amalek is destroyed" (*Rashi*, Exodus 17:16).

throne,] there was a form resembling an *adam* (man)."[100] For there can be no *Adam* without an *Aleph* (Tikkuney Zohar, ibid.).[101] Hence, the letters of *ADaM* are *Aleph-DaM*.[102] That is, his being *dome* (quiet) before God forms the *aleph*,[103] and also "an *adam* to sit on the throne."

For the *vav* in the middle of the *aleph* is the firmament, the encompassing of all the colors—i.e., the above mentioned embarrassment. The lower point is the *DeMimah* and silence, as in, "the earth is *haDoMe ragli* (My footstool)."[104] This is also the aspect of *chirik*, corresponding to "and under His feet...." And the upper point is the "*kisay d'mitkasyah* <Above>," the aspect of repentance, corresponding to "The glory of the Lord is a concealed matter," and to "Do not inquire about that which is hidden from you," and to "Above the firmament that was over their heads was the semblance of a *kisay*." Then, "an *adam* to sit on the throne" is made, corresponding to "above it...a form [resembling] a man."[105]

completed.... Therefore, man, who was created on the sixth day, is fit to sit on the throne (*Zohar* III, 48a; *Matok Midvash, loc. cit.; Parparaot LeChokhmah*).

100. **resembling an adam.** *Z'er Anpin*, the holy name *MaH*, as above (nn.84,99).

101. **no Adam without...Aleph.** The *aleph* in the word *adam* is its most important letter (see above, n.13). Without it, *adam* (man) would only be *dam* (blood). The root letters of *ALePh* also connote "to learn." This refers to the higher awareness a person achieves by remaining silent when his blood is spilt by insult.

102. **ADaM...Aleph-DaM.** The *aleph* (= 1) is joined with *dam* (= 44), the backpart of *Ehyeh*. Together they equal 45, *ADaM* (as above, n.84).

The *Mai HaNachal* explains that this is alluded to in the beginning of the lesson, where Rebbe Nachman mentions humility. The Hebrew term *mah* ("what") implies nothingness and complete humbleness. As our Sages (*cf. Chulin* 89a) taught: When Moshe and Aharon said (Exodus 16:7), "We are *mah*," they meant "We are considered as nothing." Thus, when a person attains true humility, he attains *kavod Elohim, teshuvah al teshuvah*, the level of *adam/mah* (both equal 45). He is therefore worthy of sitting on the throne.

103. **dome...forms the aleph.** As explained above, remaining quiet and silent correspond to the lower point of the *aleph*, and the embarrassment corresponds to the *vav* above it. When a person endures the embarrassment by remaining quiet, he attains the *Keter/kavod Elohim*, the upper point. Rebbe Nachman now reviews the lesson, showing how the *aleph* is formed.

104. **DeMimah and silence....** Reb Noson adds another dimension to the concept of remaining quiet and silent. He writes: There are two types of silence. The first is the silence demanded of a person due to his many sins; he ought to recognize his faults and be too embarrassed to speak out before God. Yet, as appropriate as this level of devotion is, it is incomplete. A person must strive for the level where he can speak words of Torah and prayer before God. His speech—not his silence—is thus indicative of his having ascended the spiritual ladder. If he then keeps quiet and silent when embarrassed, he achieves full

וְאָז נַעֲשֶׂה יְחוּד בֵּין חַמָּה לִלְבָנָה, שֶׁהַשֶּׁמֶשׁ מֵאִיר לַלְבָנָה, וְנַעֲשֶׂה
יְחוּד בֵּין מֹשֶׁה וִיהוֹשֻׁעַ, כִּי 'פְּנֵי מֹשֶׁה כִּפְנֵי חַמָּה', וְדָא נְקֻדָּה
הָעֶלְיוֹנָה, בְּחִינַת כִּסֵּא, בְּחִינַת מֹשֶׁה, כְּמוֹ שֶׁכָּתוּב: "וְכִסְאוֹ כַשֶּׁמֶשׁ
נֶגְדִּי", בְּחִינַת: "וּמִמַּעַל לָרָקִיעַ דְּמוּת כִּסֵּא".

(§3). As mentioned earlier, he must attach himself to the truly great tzaddikim, those who have already attained the *aleph's* upper point (*Torat Natan* #26).

106. sun and the moon. Rebbe Nachman now introduces the concept of teacher and disciple. Reb Noson was then in the early stages of becoming one of the Rebbe's followers. This section of the lesson was Rebbe Nachman's way of alluding to Reb Noson's future role as his leading disciple (see above, n.1).

Reb Noson explains that all sin stems from the diminishing of the moon. At Creation, the sun and the moon were the same size. However, the moon was jealous and complained to God. This caused the moon to be diminished (see *Chulin* 60b). But when Mashiach comes and the entire world is rectified, then "the light of the moon will be like the light of the sun" (Isaiah 30:26). Thus, rectification of all sin is the unification of the moon with the sun, the lower point with the upper point (*Torat Natan* #24). The *Mai HaNachal* adds that were the Jewish people to follow the teachings in this lesson, the moon's blemish would be eradicated. In our context, this refers to everyone perceiving the "light of God," *kavod Elohim*—the repentance of the World to Come (see above, n.58).

107. sun illuminates the moon. That is, the upper point illumines the lower point. *Keter* shines into *Malkhut*, bringing vitality even to the lowest of spiritual levels (see nn.68,69,76).

108. Moshe and Yehoshua. Moshe is the prototypical teacher and Yehoshua the prototypical disciple. As we will see, nowhere do we find a disciple so devoted to his teacher as Yehoshua was to Moshe. Rebbe Nachman therefore uses their example as his proof. Still, as the author of the *Biur HaLikutim,* Reb Avraham Chazan, once said: Rebbe Nachman's mention of Moshe and Yehoshua was intended as more than just a hint to Reb Noson's future role as the Rebbe's main follower. When one examines Reb Noson's lifetime, one finds more than just a few similarities between Reb Noson's devotion to the Rebbe and Yehoshua's devotion to Moshe Rabbeinu (see *Through Fire and Water: The Life of Reb Noson of Breslov, passim*).

109. Moshe's...face of the sun. The Talmud (*loc. cit.*) likens the shine on Moshe's face to the brightness of the sun, and the shine on Yehoshua's face to the light of the moon. Obviously, Moshe's glow was far greater than Yehoshua's. The elders of the generation, who had earlier seen Moshe and could now observe Yehoshua, said, "Woe, what an embarrassment!" That is, in such a short period, the level of their leader's prestige had descended so greatly (see *Rashbam, s.v. oy lo*). In our context, as the Rebbe will soon point out, the moon reflects the sun's light, but only when there is a unity between them. Thus, every Jew must strive to promote unity between Moshe and Yehoshua, between the upper point and the lower point, so that *Keter* can illumine *Malkhut* with vitality (as above, n.107).

110. throne...like the sun...kisay. From these proof-texts we learn that the throne is like the sun. And, we have already seen that the *kisay* (throne) corresponds to the *kisay d'mitkasya,* the point that is hidden—i.e., the upper point. Thus, the sun/Moshe corresponds to the upper point.

As a result, there is a union between the sun and the moon,[106] so that the sun illuminates the moon.[107] This also creates a oneness between Moshe and Yehoshua[108] — for Moshe's face was like the face of the sun *(Bava Batra* 75a).[109] This is the upper point, which is the aspect of the *kisay,* of Moshe. As it is written (Psalms 89:37), "and his throne will be like the sun before Me"; corresponding to "Above the firmament...was the semblance of a *kisay.*"[110]

Reb Noson shows how, in light of Rebbe Nachman's lesson, we can get an inkling of what transpired in Yechezkel's Vision of the Chariot (Ezekiel 1). Rashi comments that the righteous are known as "God's Chariot" (see Genesis 17:22). Indeed, each person, commensurate with his level of repentance, ascends to become a part of the Chariot. But, as the prophet describes, before the chariot he saw a "storm wind...a great cloud, and flashing fire...and the likes of the *chashmal* (Speaking Silence) emanating from the midst of the fire." The wind, cloud and fire correspond to the *kelipot*—the obstacles and the burning lusts that rage within that person who yearns to serve God. A person cannot perceive the Chariot unless he first overcomes the obstacles and triumphs over his lusts. In addition, he must endure embarrassment from those who oppose his devotions. How does he do this? Through the *chashmal: chash* (silence) and *mal* (speech) (*Chagigah* 13a). That is, before he can achieve the level of speech, he must endure all his embarrassment in silence (see above, n.104). Inside the fire, Yechezkel also saw four four-faced creatures; the faces were those of a lion, an ox, an eagle, and a man. These "living creatures ran and returned, like a vision of lightning," carrying the throne. He also mentions seeing an even higher level—"and above it, upon the form of the throne, there was a form resembling an *adam.*" This is the man, "an *adam* to sit on the throne," who has completed all the aspects of the letter *aleph,* as has been explained in our text. And although only the very great tzaddikim can attain this level in full, still, by engaging in *teshuvah al teshuvah* countless times over, each person, commensurate with the level of his spiritual development, can become a part of that tzaddik who does sit on the throne (*Torat Natan* #25).

In addition, the three animal creatures correspond to the mind, the heart and the lungs. The mind is the upper point of the *aleph,* the heart where the blood flows is the lower point, and the lungs through which wind (air) passes is the *vav.* When a person completes his *aleph,* his organs are complete and he merits being called *adam*—one worthy of sitting on the throne (*Torat Natan* #25).

Reb Noson then adds: The main thrust of Rebbe Nachman's lesson is to show how every Jew can succeed in attaining the highest levels and perceptions of Godliness, until he himself becomes an aspect of "an *adam* to sit on the throne." For this world corresponds to the lower point of the *aleph.* Knowledge of God is the upper point, *Keter,* which is presently hidden from man. A person's main objective in life should be to draw these perceptions of Godliness into this world by means of the *vav*—the aspect of the six days of the week, the workdays, the mundane. The Midrash teaches that everything was created for man (*Pesikta Rabbati* 46:3). That is, everything was created for man to use in his striving to attain Godly perceptions, so that he too could become "an *adam* to sit on the throne." The way to achieve this is by suffering embarrassment in silence. He thereby subdues the blood in the left ventricle of his heart—the simmering blood of the liver, gall and spleen, which oppose the heart, lungs and mind. And by refining these aspects of the mundane world, he elevates himself to the upper point, but only when his silence brings to *teshuvah al teshuvah,* the aspect of Shabbat/tzaddik

וְהַנְּקֻדָּה הַתַּחְתּוֹנָה הִיא יְהוֹשֻׁעַ, בְּחִינַת לְבָנָה, בְּחִינַת: "וְתַחַת רַגְלָיו כְּמַעֲשֵׂה לִבְנַת", דָּא לְבָנָה.

וְהַוָּא"ו שֶׁבְּתוֹךְ הָאָלֶף הוּא הָרָקִיעַ, הוּא בְּחִינַת הָאֹהֶל, כְּמוֹ שֶׁכָּתוּב: "וִיהוֹשֻׁעַ בִּן נוּן לֹא יָמִישׁ מִתּוֹךְ הָאֹהֶל". וְ'אֹהֶל' הוּא רָקִיעַ, כְּמוֹ שֶׁכָּתוּב: "וַיִּמְתָּחֵם כָּאֹהֶל לָשָׁבֶת", וּכְתִיב: "נוֹטֶה שָׁמַיִם כַּיְרִיעָה", וְזֶה: "יְרִיעוֹת הָאֹהֶל".

וְכִסֵּא הָעֶלְיוֹן, הַיְנוּ נְקֻדָּה הָעֶלְיוֹנָה נֶחְלֶקֶת לְשָׁלֹשׁ טִפִּין. כִּי תְּשׁוּבָה צָרִיךְ לִהְיוֹת בִּשְׁלֹשׁ תְּנָאִים, כְּמוֹ שֶׁכָּתוּב: "פֶּן יִרְאֶה בְעֵינָיו, וּבְאָזְנָיו יִשְׁמָע, וּלְבָבוֹ יָבִין וְשָׁב".

light brings darkness in its wake, causing many "souls to go lost." This is why repentance is imperative, so that its revelation of the upper point will illumine the lower point with undiminished light. Then, the person who returns to God is able to retrieve all the holiness he lost in the darkness because of his misdeeds (*Torat Natan* #31).

115. **Tent...firmament....** Rebbe Nachman now shows why the tent, which unites the concepts of Moshe and Yehoshua, is compared to the heavens. For God "spread the heavens like a thin covering, and He stretched them out like a tent to dwell in." The *Metzudat David* explains that God Who resides on High spread out the heavens like a "tent" for His Divine Presence to dwell in. Thus, this verse alludes to the *vav*, a firmament/line attached to the upper point.

116. **heavens like an overhanging sheet.** The *Metzudat David* explains that God spread out the heavens as if to enclose the earth within them. Thus, this verse alludes to the *vav* being attached to the lower point, earth. This proof-text together with the next (Exodus, *loc. cit.*) shows the connection between *shamayim* and tent; here heaven is likened to a sheet, and in the next verse sheet is connected to tent.

The *Mai HaNachal* adds that the reason Rebbe Nachman brings this extra verse as a proof-text is that it refers to the same firmament that Yechezkel saw in his vision (see *Tikkuney Zohar*, p.7a).

117. **sheets of the tent.** That is, the upper point and the lower point must unite in order to bring *Keter's* illumination into *Malkhut*. This is the meaning of the Tent of Meeting—it is the "meeting place" (*vav*) of the upper and lower points.

118. **kisay on High.** Rebbe Nachman now adds another dimension to the hidden upper point.

119. **repentance must meet three conditions....** These conditions correspond to the three divisions of the intellect, *Chokhmah, Binah* and *Daat.* In order for a person to gain the new awareness that comes with *teshuvah*, he must first remove the obstructing layers of "fat" from his eyes, ears and heart. He must 'see with his eyes, hear with his ears, and understand with his heart.' This requires his focusing his eyes on the path he chooses to follow; his listening well to the words of the holy tzaddikim; and his concentrating his heart on the ultimate goal.

And the lower point is Yehoshua, the aspect of the moon,[111] corresponding to "and under His feet was something like a < sapphire > LiVNat (brick)"—i.e., LeVaNah (moon).[112]

And the vav in the middle of the aleph is the firmament, the aspect of the tent,[113] as is written (Exodus 33:11), "Yehoshua the son of Nun did not depart from the tent."[114] "Tent" alludes to the firmament, as is written (Isaiah 40:22), "and He stretched them out like a tent to dwell in."[115] And as is written (Psalms 104:2), "Who spreads the heavens like an overhanging sheet"[116]—this is "...the sheets of the tent" (Exodus 26:12).[117]

{"Make the heart of this people fat, stop up its ears, and seal its eyes: lest it see with its eyes, hear with its ears, understand with its heart—and so repent and be healed" (Isaiah 6:10).}

And the kisay on High,[118] the upper point, is divided into three dots, < as is known >. This is because repentance must meet three conditions, as is written, "...lest it see with its eyes, hear with its ears, understand with its heart—and so repent < and be healed >."[119]

---

111. **lower point...Yehoshua...moon.** "...and Yehoshua's face was like the face of the moon" (Bava Batra 75a; see n.109).

112. **LiVNat...LeVaNah.** "Under His feet" corresponds to the lower point, as explained (nn.84,85). Scripture states that there was a livnat (brick) under his feet. LiVNat (לבנת) resembles LeVaNah (לבנה), the moon. Thus, the lower point is the moon, Yehoshua.

113. **vav...firmament...tent.** As above, note 94. Rebbe Nachman now mentions the element that joins Moshe to Yehoshua: the tent. This is explained below (§7), where the Rebbe says that the tent is the light the teacher shines into his disciple. This light is daat (knowledge), perceptions of Godliness.

114. **depart from the tent.** When the teacher meets with his disciple they create the aspect of the aleph. Moshe/teacher symbolizes the sun, wisdom (the upper point). He shines to Yehoshua/disciple, the moon (the lower point), who receives the illumination by way of the Tent of Meeting, the Heavens (the vav). In our context, the verse teaches that in order for Yehoshua to receive from Moshe, he must always be attached to the upper point. Hence, "Yehoshua...did not depart from the tent."

Reb Noson explains that Moshe, the tzaddik, the upper point, is so lofty and hidden— "The glory of the Lord is a concealed matter"—that not everyone is able to receive directly from his light. Hence the need for Yehoshua, the disciple, the lower point— "Yehoshua...did not depart from the tent"—whose dissemination of the tzaddik's teachings is of paramount importance. And their union, a union between the sun and the moon, leads to the ultimate rectification. For the disciple knows how to reveal the tzaddik's light indirectly, in a reflected manner, so that everyone can look at it and benefit (Torat Natan #28). And, Reb Noson adds: When a person sins, he causes a concealment of the upper point. The spiritual light that then reaches the lower point is very limited and incapable of preventing forces of the Other Side from taking charge. Therefore, this diminished spiritual

וְאֵלּוּ הַשָּׁלֹשׁ בְּחִינוֹת הֵם נְקֻדַּת סְגוֹ"ל, 'וְסָגוֹל דָּא חַמָּה', הַיְנוּ פְּנֵי
מֹשֶׁה כִּפְנֵי חַמָּה.

Noson explains this as follows. As mentioned, *teshuvah* is best accomplished by remaining quiet and silent when embarrassed. Through this, a person merits becoming "an *adam* to sit on the throne." But, to achieve this level, he must be willing to endure *repeated* suffering, hardship and embarrassment that is often associated with drawing closer to the true tzaddikim. This perseverance is vital, because only the very great tzaddikim actually attain *teshuvah al teshuvah*, rising up to the level of *Keter*, the throne. Moreover, such tzaddikim never rest. They constantly strive for even greater revelations of God, and always engage in *teshuvah al teshuvah*. They are also always working from their exalted level to draw down God's awesome *chesed* (lovingkindness) and reveal it to the world. This *chesed* translates as a message of eternal hope: The opportunity is always there for each and every person to partake of God's goodness—to taste, savor, and benefit from it.

Yet, as mentioned, in order to receive this *chesed* through the tzaddikim, it is necessary to endure the accompanying hardship. A person has to be willing to bend his shoulder to the yoke. This is actually a test of how determined and willing he is to sacrifice in order to acquire Godliness. For the more a person is willing to struggle for his attainments, the greater his gain. He learns how to be *baky b'ratzo*—to strive for the greatest heights, where God is waiting for him. And, even when he finds himself feeling low, backsliding from his devotions, he learns how to find God. He becomes *baky b'shov*—knowing that God is always with him and He will not let him down. Thus, the struggle itself is his primary repentance. Moreover, the closer he comes to the tzaddik, the more likely he is to experience these stumbling blocks and hardships, which hinder his drawing near and so distance him from *teshuvah*. The increased effort and longing which these difficulties produce in him are thus only for his benefit.

Therefore, the ideal way to repent is by drawing closer to the true tzaddikim. They reveal God's *chesed* through the upper point of the *aleph* and shine it into the lower point, so that all those less exalted than they can draw from the light and be filled with the hope that they can always find God. Thus, despite all the stumbling blocks and hardships that have the power to distance a person from God, by enduring suffering and embarrassment one realizes that there certainly is hope, for he has now formed the channel, the *vav*, by which to draw the light from the tzaddik, from the upper point. He has successfully subdued his evil inclination, the blood in the left hollow of his heart, and can now merit true repentance (*Torat Natan* #21).

The *Parparaot LeChokhmah* explains that this is why we find such fierce opposition to the tzaddikim. The controversy surrounding the tzaddik is a test, to see if the disciple will remain steadfast in his faith in the tzaddikim and continue trying to draw closer to them. This is also why we find that the tzaddikim will occasionally treat their disciples with indifference, and even rejection. The disciple is being tested. If he remains steadfast in his faith in the tzaddik and in the devotions the tzaddik prescribes, the embarrassment he endures at the hands of the tzaddik will be transformed into an illuminating light from the *aleph's* upper point.

Elsewhere, Reb Noson says that due to the many blemishes caused by our sins, it sometimes becomes necessary for the tzaddik, who is the upper point, to pass away. That is, the blemishes block the light of the upper point and prevent it from shining into this world to motivate people to repent. Then, with the tzaddik no longer in the world physically, it becomes necessary to seek the tzaddik's legacy—i.e., his disciples. To the extent a person does this, to the extent he seeks the truth, he is likewise able to attain true repentance (*Torat Natan* #27).

These three aspects [of repentance] are the vowel sign *segol*.[120] And "the *segol* is the sun" (*Tikkuney Zohar* 7b) — i.e., "Moshe's face was like the face of the sun."[121]

Then he is able to absorb new insights and achieve true repentance (*Torat Natan* #30; see *Likutey Moharan* 7:8). These, then, are the three dots of the *aleph's* upper point. And, as we have seen, the motivation for *teshuvah* stems from the upper point/Moshe/the tzaddik.

120. **vowel sign segol.** *Segol* is the name of one of the vowel signs in the Hebrew *nikud* system. Pronounced as the *ai* in the word "said," the *segol* (ֶ) is comprised of three dots placed below the feet or base of a letter. See next note.

121. **segol . . . Moshe's face . . . face of the sun.** Earlier, Rebbe Nachman showed the connection between Moshe and the sun (see n.109); like the sun, Moshe/teacher shines his light from above. The Rebbe has also shown how Moshe represents the *kisay*, the hidden upper point of the *aleph*. This upper point, like *teshuvah*, is divided into three, *Chokhmah, Binah* and *Daat* (as in n.119), and in this way resembles the three dots of the *segol*. Hence the *Zohar's* likening the *segol* to the sun.

This passage from the introduction to the *Tikkuney Zohar* (*loc. cit.*) also explains the Kabbalistic intentions of all the vowels signs, together with their *gematria*, or numerical value, and what their names imply. The *segol*, which corresponds to the *sefirah* of *Chesed*, consists of three dots (a dot = 10), for a value of thirty (3x10 = 30). Each dot is drawn from the letter *vav* (a *vav* = 6), and this adds to *segol's* value another eighteen (3x6 = 18). This totals 48 (*ChaM*, חם). The word *segol* (סגול) itself has four (ד) letters, which brings the value to 52 (*CheMeD*, חמד). One of the translations of *chemed* is "special," which is akin to the word *segulah*, a virtuous attribute or quality. Adding 1 more to the total, for the word *chemed* itself, changes the value to 53, the same as *ChaMaH* (חמה), the sun. Thus, "Moshe's face was like . . . the sun," for Moshe illuminates *Chesed*, to which the *segol* corresponds (*Matok Midvash, loc. cit.*). With this proof, Rebbe Nachman has connected the *segol*, which is the three points of *teshuvah*, with the upper point of the *aleph*, which is Moshe and the sun.

In review: Every person must minimize his own honor and maximize God's honor (§1). This requires *teshuvah*, which is best accomplished by enduring insult in silence for the Holy One's sake. A person thereby increases God's honor and himself merits *kavod Elohim* (§2). Even so, he must never cease repenting. He must engage in *teshuvah al teshuvah*, always seeking greater revelations of God. In this way, he will merit the repentance of the World to Come (§3). And in order to walk the pathways of repentance, a person must be expert at running and returning — i.e., at knowing how to both ascend and descend the spiritual ladder in accordance with his unique capabilities (§4). Walking the pathways of repentance enables a person to complete and perfect the letter *aleph* — i.e., "an *adam* to sit on the throne." He unites sun and moon, teacher and disciple, bringing rectification from the upper point to the lower point. But only when his repentance is complete, when he meets the three conditions for *teshuvah* (§5).

*

Reb Noson writes: After giving this lesson Rebbe Nachman said, "Whenever a teacher and a disciple come together, the aspect of Moshe, Yehoshua and the Tent of Meeting exists." Reb

ו וְזֶה פֵּרוּשׁ:

רַשְׁבַּ"ם:

דְּשָׁמְיטִין גַּדְפַיְהוּ נָפְלוּ נוֹצָה שֶׁלָּהֶם מֵרֹב שׁוּמָן: דְּלָיָא לִי גַּדְפָא הִגְבִּיהַּ לִי הַכָּנָף, רָמַז – זֶהוּ חֶלְקְךָ לֶעָתִיד לָבוֹא: לָתֵן עֲלֵיהֶם אֶת הַדִּין שֶׁבַּחֲטָאתָם מִתְעַכֵּב מָשִׁיחַ, וְיֵשׁ לָהֶם צַעַר בַּעֲלֵי-חַיִּים, לְאוֹתָן אַוָּזִין, מֵחֲמַת שׁוּמָנָן:

אָמַר רַבָּה בַּר בַּר חָנָה: זִימְנָא חֲדָא הֲוָה אָזְלִינָן בְּמִדְבָּרָא, וַחֲזִינָן הָנֵי אַוָּזֵי דְּשָׁמְיטִין גַּדְפַיְהוּ מְשַׁמְנַיְהוּ, וְקָא נַגְדֵי נַחֲלֵי דְּמַשְׁחָא מִתּוּתַיְהוּ. וְאָמִינָא לְהוּ: אִית לִי מִנַּיְכוּ חוּלְקָא לְעָלְמָא דְּאָתֵי? חֲדָא דַּלְיָא לִי אַטְמָא, וְחֲדָא דַּלְיָא לִי גַּדְפָא. כִּי אֲתַאי לְקַמֵּיהּ דְּרַבִּי אֶלְעָזָר, אָמַר לִי: עֲתִידִין יִשְׂרָאֵל לָתֵן עֲלֵיהֶם אֶת הַדִּין: (כבא בתרא עג:)

שֶׁהָלַךְ – לַחֲקֹר בַּמִּדָּה הַטּוֹבָה שֶׁל עֲנָוָה, שֶׁאָדָם מֵשִׂים עַצְמוֹ כַּמִּדְבָּר לָדוּשׁ. שֶׁהַכֹּל דָּשִׁין עָלָיו.

וְרָאָה חֲכָמִים, וְזֶה בְּחִינַת אַוָּזֵי, כְּמוֹ שֶׁאָמְרוּ חֲכָמֵינוּ, זִכְרוֹנָם לִבְרָכָה: 'הָרוֹאֶה אַוָּז בַּחֲלוֹם יְצַפֶּה לְחָכְמָה'.

דְּשָׁמְיטִין גַּדְפַיְהוּ – פֵּרֵשׁ רַשִׁ"י: נוֹצוֹת, זֶה בְּחִינַת מַחֲלֹקֶת וּבִזְיוֹנוֹת, כְּמוֹ שֶׁכָּתוּב: "כִּי יִנָּצוּ אֲנָשִׁים", הַיְנוּ שֶׁאֵין מַשְׁגִּיחִין עַל מַחֲלֹקֶת וּבִזְיוֹנוֹת שֶׁמְּבַזִּין אוֹתָן, וְשׁוֹמְעִים חֶרְפָּתָן וְאֵינָם מְשִׁיבִים. וְעַל שֵׁם הַשְּׁתִיקָה נִקְרָאִים חֲכָמִים, כִּי: 'סְיָג לַחָכְמָה – שְׁתִיקָה':

---

126. **goose…anticipate wisdom.** The Talmud (*loc. cit.*), in discussing the meanings of different dream symbols, offers proof-texts in support its interpretations. The verse for geese and wisdom is (Proverbs 1:20), "[Torah] wisdom will be declared openly in the streets." The Sages are drawing an analogy between geese, whose nature it is to squawk loudly, and the Torah's wisdom being energetically proclaimed in public. Thus, geese correspond to *chokhmah* (wisdom).

127. **silence is a fence for wisdom.** Rabbeinu Yonah opines (*loc. cit.*) that when a person is wise, he listens attentively to someone else's view or opinion and is open to learning something from that person. Silence is thus a means of achieving wisdom.

128. **Silence is also…Keter.** By means of silence one achieves repentance, which is the aspect of *Keter*, as explained above (§2). This is alluded to in, "Silence is a fence for *chokhmah*." This

6. This is the explanation[122]:

Rabbah bar bar Chanah recounted: One time we were traveling in the desert and we saw these geese who were so fat that their plumes *shamitan* (fell off). Rivers of oil were flowing from beneath them. So I asked them, "Will I have a piece of you in the World to Come?" One lifted a foot towards me and one lifted a wing towards me. When I came before Rabbi Elazar, he said to me, "In the Future, the Jewish people's judgment will be on their account" (*Bava Batra* 73b).

Rashbam:

their plumes shamitan - their feathers fell off because of their abundant fat: **lifted a wing towards me** - it lifted a wing in my direction, hinting, "This is your portion in the World to Come": **judgement will be on their account** - the sins [of the Jewish people] delay the arrival of the Mashiach, causing pain to living creatures—to those geese, [who suffer] due to their fatness:

[traveling in the desert] — [Rabbah bar bar Chanah] set out to investigate the fine trait of humility,[123] when a person considers himself as a desert to be tread upon (*Eruvin* 54a)[124]—everyone steps on him.[125]

He saw *ChaKhaMim* (Torah sages). This is an allusion to **geese**, as the Sages taught (*Berakhot* 57a): Anyone who sees a goose in his dream can anticipate *ChoKhMah* (wisdom).[126]

their plumes shamitan, fell off — Rashbam translates [*gadfayhu* (plumes) as] *NotZot* (feathers). This alludes to controversy and insult, as is written (Deuteronomy 25:11), "If two men *yeNatZu* (get into a fight)...." The [*chakhamim*] do not pay attention to the controversy or insults directed at them. They hear themselves ridiculed and yet do not retort. As a result of this silence they are called sages, because silence is a fence for wisdom (*Avot* 3:13).[127] {Silence is also the aspect of *Keter*.[128]}

122. **This is the explanation.** Rebbe Nachman now shows how the concepts of this lesson are alluded to within the framework of Rabbah bar bar Chanah's story.

123. **trait of humility.** A major theme of this lesson, as above, section 1 and note 2.

124. **desert to be tread upon.** The Talmud asks: What is the meaning of (Numbers 21:18), "and from the desert to Matanah"? If a person humbles himself, making himself like a desert for all to tread upon, Torah knowledge will be given to him as a present, *matanah* (*Eruvin* 54a). That is, the revelation of Godliness sought by a person who studies Torah, i.e., *kavod Elohim,* can only occur when one has humility. This person seeks to reveal God and honor Him, willingly doing so at the expense of his own honor—i.e., he allows himself to become a "desert."

125. **everyone steps on him.** His humbleness is such that he allows all sorts of embarrassment and humiliation to pass over him.

כִּי הַשְּׁתִיקָה הִיא בְּחִינַת כֶּתֶר.

(כִּי עַל־יְדֵי הַשְּׁתִיקָה זוֹכִין לִתְשׁוּבָה, שֶׁהִיא בְּחִינַת כֶּתֶר, כַּנַּ"ל. וְזֶה בְּחִינַת: 'סְיָג לַחָכְמָה שְׁתִיקָה'. 'סְיָג' דַּיְקָא, זֶה בְּחִינַת כֶּתֶר, שֶׁהוּא בְּחִינַת סְיָג וְגֶדֶר סָבִיב סָבִיב, שֶׁמְּסַבֵּב וּמַכְתִּיר וּמַעֲטִיר אֶת הַחָכְמָה, וְזֶה הַכֶּתֶר, שֶׁהוּא בְּחִינַת סְיָג, נַעֲשֶׂה מֵהַשְּׁתִיקָה, כַּנַּ"ל. וְזֶהוּ: 'סְיָג לַחָכְמָה שְׁתִיקָה', כַּנַּ"ל).

וְזֶה לְשׁוֹן דִּשְׁמְטִין, כְּמוֹ שֶׁכָּתוּב: "שָׁמוֹט כָּל בַּעַל מַשֵּׁה יָדוֹ", הַיְנוּ שֶׁלֹּא יִתְבַּע עֶלְבּוֹנוֹ.

וְזֶה פֵּרוּשׁ מִשַּׁמְנַיְהוּ – מִלְּשׁוֹן: "שָׁמַנְתָּ עָבִיתָ", (כְּלוֹמַר: מֵחֲמַת שֶׁאוֹחֲזִין עַצְמָן בִּבְחִינַת: "שָׁמַנְתָּ עָבִיתָ"), הַיְנוּ בִּשְׁבִיל זֶה שׁוֹמְעִין חֶרְפָּתָן וְאֵינָם מְשִׁיבִים, כִּי זֶה עוֹשִׂין בִּשְׁבִיל תְּשׁוּבָה עַל עֲווֹנוֹתָם, כְּמוֹ שֶׁכָּתוּב: "וַיִּשְׁמַן יְשֻׁרוּן". (בִּבְחִינַת הַשֶּׁמֶן לֵב כוּ', וְאָזְנָיו כוּ', פֶּן יִרְאֶה כוּ', שֶׁהַתְּשׁוּבָה צָרִיךְ לִהְיוֹת בִּשְׁלֹשָׁה תְּנָאִים אֵלּוּ).

וְנִגְדֵּי נַחֲלֵי דְמַשְׁחָא מִתְּחוֹתַיְהוּ – הַיְנוּ עַל־יְדֵי הַשְּׁתִיקָה זוֹכִין לִכְבוֹד אֱלֹקַי, שֶׁהוּא בְּחִינַת שֶׁמֶן, כְּמוֹ שֶׁכָּתוּב: "אָהַבְתָּ צֶּדֶק

shine into him. Worse yet, the fact is that many of those who fail to shed their evil desires are the very same people who seek honor! Not only do they not maximize God's honor by trying to repent, but they labor to maximize their own standing and position—mostly at the expense of those who are endeavoring to honor God. This is why repentance always seems such a distant thing for them. They fail to perceive the great light which the tzaddikim shine upon them.

Reb Noson explains this as the meaning of the Mishnah: Jealousy, lust and honor remove *adam* (a man) from the world (*Avot* 4:21). "Jealousy" refers to those who are resentful of truly God-fearing people. Rather than honoring those whose devotion to God they fail to match, they oppose and ridicule them. This is the polar opposite of the lower point; instead of maintaining silence, these jealous people abuse others. "Lust" refers to the blood in the left hollow of the heart which a person has failed to subdue or slaughter by remaining silent. As a result, there is no *vav*. Finally, "honor" refers to those who seek to increase their own glory, thereby negating the aspect of *Keter/kavod Elohim/*the upper point. Thus, these three evil characteristics—which blemish the heart, ears and eyes—"remove *adam* from the world." That is, the blemish they cause assures that the level of *adam*, a man who has truly repented, cannot be achieved (*Torat Natan* #30).

133. **from beneath them...silence.** "Beneath" alludes to the lower point, remaining silent in the face of insult and humiliation (*Mai HaNachal*).

134. **anointed you with oil.** Rashi explains that moving up to a higher, more prestigious position is comparable to being "anointed with oil." At his coronation, a king of Israel was

This is the term *ShaMiTan,* as is written (Deuteronomy 15:2), "Every creditor will *ShaMoTe* (remit) any debt owed him"—i.e., a person should not demand satisfaction for his humiliation.[129]

. And < this is > **who were so fat,** similar to (Deuteronomy 32:15), "...you grew fat and gross."[130] {In other words, [because of their humility the *chakhamim*] consider themselves to be in a state of "grew fat and gross."} That is, as a result, they hear themselves ridiculed and yet do not retort. This, in order to repent for their transgressions, < corresponding to > (*ibid.*), "But Yeshurun grew fat."[131] {This corresponds to (Isaiah 6:10), "Make the heart of this people fat, stops up its ears, and seal its eyes: lest it see...," because repentance must meet these three conditions.[132]}

Rivers of oil were flowing from beneath them — That is, by means of silence[133] a person achieves *kavod Elohim,* which is the aspect of oil, as is written (Psalms 45:8), "You love righteousness and hate wickedness, therefore [the Lord, your Lord,] has anointed you...."[134] And this

"fence" is the aspect of *Keter,* which is a boundary that goes all around—encircling and crowning the *sefirah* of *Chokhmah.* And this *Keter*/fence is made by remaining silent. This is, "Silence is a fence for *Chokhmah*" (*marginal note*). Thus, when people remain quiet and silent when insulted, they are wise.

129. **ShaMiTan...ShaMoTe....** One of the laws of *Shemitah,* the sabbatical year, is that every creditor must remit all debts owed him. (There are several exceptions; see *Yad HaChazakah, Hilkhot Shemitah v'Yovel,* Chapter 9). Thus, in one sense, *shamitan* alludes to overlooking the past and letting bygones be bygones. In our context, this refers to a person who wants to repent and have his past wrongdoing "remitted" and overlooked by God. He must then repent by remaining quiet and silent in the face of embarrassment.

130. **...who were so fat...and gross.** That is, the "feathers" (insults) were "*shamitan*" (not returned in kind) because they "were so fat" (wanted to repent). Rebbe Nachman now shows how "so fat" refers to repentance.

131. **grew fat.** The verse reads, "But Yeshurun (the Jewish people) grew fat and rebelled [against God]; you grew fat and gross...[the nation] abandoned its Maker." Thus, "growing fat" refers to veering off the path to God. A person who wants to repent views himself as one who has "grown fat" and strayed from the path. He therefore remains quiet and silent. See next note.

132. **heart...ears...eyes...repentance....** See above, note 119, where this is explained. Rebbe Nachman has shown how "fat" refers to a person's sins and that anyone who wants to rectify these three major parts of the human form must meet the conditions for repentance. Reb Noson notes that these three conditions relate to a person's lusts and evil traits. His evil desires have travelled throughout his blood system, infiltrated it, so that now he no longer even attempts to subdue his evil inclination. However, as long as a person refuses to shed these desires, he will be unable to receive the light that the tzaddik (upper point) attempts to

וַתִּשְׂנָא רֶשַׁע, עַל־כֵּן מְשָׁחֲךָ", וְזֶה בְּחִינַת: "מֶלֶךְ הַכָּבוֹד".

וְאָמִינָא לְהוּ: אִית לִי מִינַּיְכוּ חוּלְקָא לְעָלְמָא דְּאָתֵי? חֲדָא דַּלְיָא לִי אַטְמָא – זֶה בְּחִינַת: "וְהָאָרֶץ הֲדֹם רַגְלָי", בְּחִינַת נְקֻדָּה הַתַּחְתּוֹנָה, כַּנַּ"ל.

וְחַדָא דַּלְיָא לִי כָּנָף – זֶה בְּחִינַת כְּסֵא, כְּמוֹ שֶׁכָּתוּב: "וְלֹא יִכָּנֵף עוֹד מוֹרֶיךָ", זֶה בְּחִינַת הַנְּקֻדָּה הָעֶלְיוֹנָה. הַיְינוּ שֶׁהֶרְאוּ לְרַבָּה בַּר בַּר חָנָה, שֶׁגַּם הוּא זָכָה לְאֵלּוּ הַבְּחִינוֹת.

'אָמַר רַבִּי אֶלְעָזָר: עֲתִידִין יִשְׂרָאֵל לִתֵּן עֲלֵיהֶם אֶת הַדִּין' – כִּי יִשְׂרָאֵל נִקְרָאִים אָדָם, וְקוּדְשָׁא בְּרִיךְ הוּא וְיִשְׂרָאֵל – כֻּלָּא חַד. וְיִשְׂרָאֵל, שֶׁהֵם בְּחִינַת אָדָם, יֵשְׁבוּ עַל הַכִּסֵּא. כְּמוֹ שֶׁכָּתוּב: "וְעַל הַכִּסֵּא דְּמוּת כְּמַרְאֵה אָדָם", וְיִשְׂרָאֵל יִתְּנוּ דִין לְכָל בָּאֵי עוֹלָם,

of the *aleph*.

139. **he too had attained...levels.** Like them, Rabbah was also considered a wise man. He too had merited *teshuvah al teshuvah*, the *teshuvah* of the World to Come.

140. **Jews are called adam....** Aside from applying certain laws exclusively to the Jewish people, this passage from the Talmud (*Yevamot* 61a) also confers upon them a distinctive status. In general, Jews are considered to be *adam* vis-a-vis non-Jews (see also *Zohar* II, 86a).

141. **the Holy One and the Jewish people are one.** See above, note 105.

142. **Jews, who are called adam.** A marginal note in the text of *Likutey Moharan* refers the reader to a passage in the *Zohar* which explains the concept of *adam*. The Serpent seduced Chavah, forever polluting all her descendants (see also *Shabbat* 146a). However, when the Jews received the Torah at Sinai, they were purified of this pollution (*Zohar* I, 126b). This is *adam*, the man who is free of the Serpent's pollution—i.e., he has attained *teshuvah al teshuvah*, and risen above the lusts and desires of the mundane world. In our context, Rebbe Nachman is referring to the exalted status the Jews will achieve in the Future. By repenting, they will ascend to the level of *adam*, and thereby merit sitting on the throne.

143. **aleph dome, as above.** See section 5 and notes 83 and 99.

144. **a form resembling an adam.** When the Jewish people are perfect in their devotions, they bring perfection to all the worlds (cf. n.105). In this sense, they achieved the level of "an *adam* to sit on the throne." And, since the Jews are then one with God, they merit to actually sit on the throne.

corresponds to (*ibid.* 24:8,10), "The King of glory."[135]

**So I asked them, "Will I have a piece of you in the World to Come?"[136]
One lifted a foot towards me** — This corresponds to "the earth is My footstool," alluding to the lower point.[137]

and one lifted a KaNaF, wing, towards me — This is the aspect of the *kisay*, as is written (Isaiah 30:20), "Your Teacher will not *KaNeF* (cover) Himself anymore." This alludes to the upper point.[138]

In other words, [the geese] showed Rabbah bar bar Chanah that he too had attained these spiritual levels.[139]

Rabbi Elazar said: In the Future, the Jewish people's judgment will be on their account — For the Jews are called *adam,* < as is written, "For you My flock...are *adam*" (Ezekiel 34:31) >.[140] And, the Holy One and the Jewish people are one (*Zohar* III, 93b).[141] The Jews, who are called *adam*[142] — < *aleph-dome,* as above[143] > — will sit on the throne, as in, "upon [the semblance of] the throne, there was a form resembling an *adam*"[144] Then, the Jews will provide judgement for all the world's

anointed with oil (*Horayot* 11b), a sign of his having attained *kavod Elohim.* Thus, in our context the verse reads: "You love righteousness and hate wickedness"—you regret your evil past and have repented, therefore—"your Lord has anointed you with oil"—you have merited *kavod Elohim.* The *Mai HaNachal* adds: Earlier (§2, n.21), Rebbe Nachman quoted the Talmud that a person who wants to repent and purify himself is analogous to someone who wants to enjoy the fragrance of pure spices and oils: he is told to wait. As is evident from here, this is because oil corresponds to *kavod Elohim,* which is attained only by "waiting" and repenting.

135. **The King of glory.** In its simple meaning, this verse is a reference to God. In our context, however, this alludes to spiritual glory, *kavod Elohim,* given to those who reach the higher rungs on the spiritual ladder.

136. **in the World to Come.** The World to Come corresponds to repentance, as explained in section 3. Rabbah asked the geese/Torah sages whether he had reached a true level of humility and so attained repentance.

137. **foot...footstool...lower point.** The first step is silence, the footstool, as explained in section 5. One of the geese—a wise man, one who had already attained the level of *Keter,* true repentance—answered that Rabbah had indeed attained the lower point of the *aleph.*

138. **Your Teacher will not....** The prophet Isaiah prophesies that although God is presently hidden from us, in the Future He will reveal Himself: "Your Teacher will not *KaNeF* (cover) Himself anymore." In this sense, the *KaNaF* (wing) alludes to that which is hidden, the upper point. In our context, this also refers to Moshe/the teacher, who taught Torah to all of Israel. He represents the aspect of running to higher spiritual levels—i.e., "a wing"—the upper point

הַיְנוּ הֵם יִשְׁפְּטוּ בְּעַצְמָן כָּל הַדִּינִין:

ז. וְזֶה פֵּרוּשׁ: "יַדְבֵּר עַמִּים תַּחְתֵּינוּ וּלְאָמִּים תַּחַת רַגְלֵינוּ", זֶה בְּחִינַת חִירִיק נְקֻדָּה הַתַּחְתּוֹנָה שֶׁל אָלֶף, שֶׁהוּא בְּחִינַת: "וְתַחַת רַגְלָיו", בְּחִינַת: "וְהָאָרֶץ הֲדֹם רַגְלָי".

"יִבְחַר לָנוּ אֶת נַחֲלָתֵנוּ", זֶה בְּחִינַת מֹשֶׁה, בְּחִינַת נְקֻדָּה הָעֶלְיוֹנָה שֶׁל הָאָלֶף, בְּחִינַת: "וּמִמַּעַל לָרָקִיעַ דְּמוּת כִּסֵּא", וְכִסְאוֹ כַשֶּׁמֶשׁ. פְּנֵי מֹשֶׁה כִּפְנֵי חַמָּה, כְּמַאֲמַר חֲכָמֵינוּ, זִכְרוֹנָם לִבְרָכָה: 'ר' שִׁמְעוֹן

So I asked them, "Will I have a piece of you in the World to Come?" — Rabbah asked if he, too, had attained true repentance.

One lifted a foot towards me — Indicating that Rabbah had already attained the lower point.

and one lifted a wing towards me — Indicating that Rabbah had also attained the upper point. He had thus completed the *aleph*, and attained the level of *adam*.

When I came before Rabbi Elazar, he said to me, "In the Future, the Jewish people's judgment will be on their account" — That is, just as Rabbah bar bar Chanah attained the level of repentance, of "an *adam* to sit upon the throne," so, too, in the Future all the other Jews will merit repenting and ascending to the level of *adam*, where they will provide judgement and justice for the world.

In review: Every person must minimize his own honor and maximize God's honor (§1). This requires *teshuvah,* which is best accomplished by enduring insult in silence for the Holy One's sake. A person thereby increases God's honor and himself merits *kavod Elohim* (§2). Even so, he must never cease repenting, engaging in *teshuvah al teshuvah* until he merits the repentance of the World to Come (§3). And in order to walk the pathways of repentance, a person must be expert at running and returning—i.e., at knowing how to both ascend and descend the spiritual ladder in accordance with his unique capabilities (§4). Walking the pathways of repentance enables a person to complete and perfect the letter *aleph*—i.e., "an *adam* to sit on the throne." He unites sun and moon, teacher and disciple, bringing rectification from the upper point to the lower point. But only when his repentance is complete, when he meets the three conditions for *teshuvah* (§5). And though the highest levels are presently attainable only by the very great tzaddikim, in the Future all Jews will be able to attain the level of *adam* (§6). Provided, that is, that each person strengthens himself in his *baky b'ratzo* and *baky b'shov,* as will be discussed below.

147. **He subdues...footstool.** "Beneath our feet" alludes to the lower point, the footstool, as explained in section 5. To the same degree that a person achieves the lower point, he subdues the nations—symbolically, the evil traits—beneath his feet. This is comparable to the slaughtering of the evil inclination, and is connected to the time of the Final Redemption, when Amalek will be totally destroyed. As Rashi explains the verse in Exodus (17:16): "God took an oath that His Name and Throne will not be complete until Amalek is destroyed" (*Parparaot LeChokhmah; Mai HaNachal*). In other words, when the lower point is rectified,

inhabitants[145]—i.e., they alone will judge all judgments.[146]

7. {**"He subdues peoples under us, and nations beneath our feet. He chooses our heritage for us, the pride of Yaakov whom He loves"** (Psalms 47:4-5).}

"He subdues peoples under us, and nations beneath our feet" refers to the aspect of *chirik*. This is the lower point of the *aleph*, corresponding to "and under His feet...," and to "the earth is My footstool."[147]

"He chooses our heritage for us" is the aspect of Moshe, the upper point of the *aleph*. It corresponds to "Above the firmament...was the semblance of a throne"/"and his throne will be like the sun"/ "Moshe's face was like the face of the sun." As the Sages taught:

---

145. **the Jews will provide judgment....** All that happens Above is dependent upon *adam* below. All the *tikkunim* (rectifications) of the Supernal Worlds are in accordance with the actions of a Jewish person in this world. Therefore, when Israel perfects itself in the service of God, the holy name of God is, as it were, also made whole and perfected (cf. *Zohar* III, 4b). And by performing the rectifications outlined here, forming the *aleph*, they achieve the level of *adam*. Then, too, all these aspects are correspondingly perfected in the upper worlds, to the point where these *tikkunim* ascend unto the throne. Thus, any Jew who remains quiet and silent in the face of humiliation—thereby reducing the blood in the left hollow of his heart and slaughtering his evil inclination—attains, commensurate with his personal level, true spiritual glory/*Keter*. And, finally, once Israel receives from the upper point of the *aleph*/ Moshe/the teacher, they will become "an *adam* to sit on the throne" and provide judgment for all living creatures (*Parparaot LeChokhmah; Mai HaNachal*; see also n.105).

146. **judge all judgments.** For the throne that the Jewish people sit on indicates the throne of judgment. That is, the Jews will have the power to rule over the world and subjugate the nations to God's will. This becomes evident later on in the lesson (see §§7-9), which speaks of the Jews being required to destroy Amalek—i.e., the personification of evil—and build the Holy Temple—i.e., the revelation of Godliness in the world. This is also confirmed in Rashbam's commentary: "The sins [of the Jewish people] delay the arrival of the Mashiach, causing pain to living creatures." That is, because the Jews have yet to attain the level of *adam*, they cannot reveal Godliness in the world. This causes pain and suffering to all the living creatures, who are not called *adam*.

The story thus translates in our text as:
Rabbah bar bar Chanah recounted having traveled in the desert — He set out to investigate the great value of humility.
and he saw these geese — he met some wise men
who were so fat — who after sinning, repented.
that their plumes fell off — They were wise (had attained *Chokhmah*) because they remained quiet and silent in the face of insult and humiliation.
Rivers of oil were flowing from beneath them — As a result of their silence (repentance), they merited *kavod Elohim*.

אוֹמֵר: נַחֲלָה זוֹ שִׁילָה', 'שִׁילָה דָּא מֹשֶׁה'.

"אֶת גְּאוֹן יַעֲקֹב", זֶה בְּחִינַת וָא"ו שֶׁבְּתוֹךְ אָלֶף, בְּחִינַת אֹהֶל,

בְּחִינַת אוֹר, שֶׁמֹּשֶׁה מֵאִיר לִיהוֹשֻׁעַ, כְּמוֹ שֶׁכָּתוּב: "וְיַעֲקֹב אִישׁ תָּם

יֹשֵׁב אֹהָלִים".

וְזֶה בְּחִינַת: 'שְׁלֹשָׁה דְּבָרִים שֶׁנִּצְטַוּוּ יִשְׂרָאֵל, שֶׁיְּכַלּוּ זַרְעוֹ שֶׁל

עֲמָלֵק', זֶה בְּחִינַת: "יְדַבֵּר עַמִּים תַּחְתֵּינוּ", 'וּלְמַנּוֹת לָהֶם מֶלֶךְ',

זֶה בְּחִינַת "גְּאוֹן יַעֲקֹב", בְּחִינַת: "דָּרַךְ כּוֹכָב מִיַּעֲקֹב", בְּחִינַת

מֶלֶךְ, 'וְלִבְנוֹת לָהֶם בֵּית הַבְּחִירָה', זֶה בְּחִינַת מֹשֶׁה, בְּחִינַת דַּעַת,

(Genesis 6:5), "raK rA koL hayoM (nothing but evil all day long)," the last letters of which spell AMaLeK (Biur HaLikutim). In our context, this refers to slaughtering the evil inclination, and to the mitzvah of wiping out all that Amalek is and represents—thereby attaining the lower point of the aleph.

Although Rebbe Nachman's order of the three mitzvot differs from Rabbi Yehudah's—beginning with killing off Amalek rather than first appointing a king—Rabbi Yehudah himself admitted that he did not know which came first.

152. star...from Yaakov...king. "A star will go forth from Yaakov, and a scepter will arise from Israel..." destroying all of Israel's enemies.

"A star...a scepter..." refers to a king arising from the Jewish people (Rashi, loc. cit.). More specifically, it refers to the Mashiach. Below (§9), Reb Noson explains that just as the stars reside in the heavens, "star" itself refers to the heavens. Yaakov thus corresponds to the vav/tent/firmament, and to the mitzvah of appointing a king. The Be'Ibey HaNachal asks: How can Yaakov/king be compared to the vav, which also alludes to embarrassment and the changes in one's facial coloring (as above, §5)? The answer is that the letter vav corresponds to the sefirah of Tiferet (Beauty, the central sefirah of Z'er Anpin), which comprises all the Supernal Colors. In holiness, the blend of these colors is truly majestic. But if a person sins, he must later endure a blending of colors in his face. If he remains quiet and silent when shamed, he merits rectifying these colors. In this way, Yaakov/king corresponds to the letter vav.

The Parparaot LeChokhmah takes this a step further. If a person remains quiet and silent when humiliated, he rectifies the lower point. He is then worthy of the vav, opening a channel through which he receives the light from the upper point. He thus attains kavod Elohim. But if a person is insulted and responds in kind, he cannot merit the lower point. Then, the embarrassment he endures (the vav) is likened to the "honor of kings"—the honor that everyone scrutinizes. The mitzvah of appointing a king thus corresponds to the vav. The Parparaot LeChokhmah adds: This is the meaning of "the Jewish people's judgment..." (above, §6). They have suffered terribly during their long exile. However, by accepting the suffering for the Holy One's sake—i.e., in order to adhere to Torah and mitzvot—the Jews merit the level of adam. They can then sit on the throne. Of course, complete rectification will only take place when Mashiach comes, when "a star will go forth from Yaakov"—the king. Then, the suffering the Jews endured will transform them into the aspect of the lower point,

Rabbi Shimon said, " 'Heritage' refers to Shiloh" *(Zevachim* 119a).[148] [And] " 'Shiloh' is Moshe" *(Zohar* I, 25b).[149]

"...the pride of Yaakov" is the *vav* in the middle of the *aleph,* the tent. It is the light that Moshe shone into Yehoshua, as is written (Genesis 25:27), "but Yaakov was a man of perfection who remained in the tents."[150]

{Rabbi Yehudah taught: Upon entering the Holy Land, the Jewish people were charged with three mitzvot—to appoint a king; to kill off the seed of Amalek; and to build a Holy Temple for themselves—though I don't know which comes first *(Sanhedrin* 20b).}

This corresponds to the three things that Israel was commanded: To kill off the seed of Amalek corresponds to "He subdues peoples under us."[151] To appoint a king corresponds to "the pride of Yaakov"; to "A star will go forth from Yaakov, [and a scepter will arise from Israel]..." (Numbers 24:17), which alludes to a king.[152] To build a Holy Temple for themselves is the aspect of Moshe, of *daat*

Amalek is destroyed. Then, the rectification of the upper point, the *kisay,* is set in motion. And when the *kisay* is completed, *adam*—the Jewish people—can sit on the throne.

148. **Heritage refers to Shiloh.** Shiloh was the site of the Tent of Meeting for the vast majority of years from the time the Jewish people entered the land until they built the Holy Temple in Jerusalem. Shiloh is called "heritage" because the portions allocated to the twelve tribes, their heritage in the Land, were apportioned there *(Maharsha, loc. cit., s.v. v'Rabbi Shimon).* Though Moshe corresponds to the upper point/Shiloh, it was Yehoshua who divided the Land. In our context, this is because the light of Moshe/the teacher is too great, and only the true disciple, Yehoshua, can properly receive and apportion it to the rest of Israel.

     In the following sections, Shiloh and the Holy Temple are used interchangeably, and so each one's corresponding aspects are also linked and considered the same.

149. **Heritage...Shiloh...Moshe.** Rebbe Nachman first reminded the reader that Moshe is the upper point. Then, to show that Moshe is "heritage," he brought a proof-text that "heritage" corresponds to Shiloh. Here, he shows that Shiloh is in fact Moshe—as the *Zohar (loc. cit.)* teaches, both Shiloh (שילה) and Moshe (משה) have a numerical value of 345 (see Lesson #2 and n.58). (In addition, the roots of Shiloh and Moshe—שלה and משה—both mean "to draw.")

150. **pride of Yaakov...in the tents.** The Hebrew term for tent is *oHeL* (אהל). This is similar to (Job 29:3), "When *HiLo* (His light, הלו) shone over my head." Tent is therefore associated with light. Thus, the "pride of Yaakov"—i.e., the light of the teacher that filters down to the disciple—corresponds to the tent—i.e., the *vav*-channel through which that light is filtered.

     Thus, in our context the verse reads: "He subdues...beneath our feet"—by maintaining silence when embarrassed a person slaughters his evil inclination and attains the lower point. "He chooses our heritage for us"—having attained the lower point, a person is able to receive the light of the upper point; channeled to him through "the pride of Yaakov"—the *vav.*

151. **Amalek...peoples under us.** As mentioned, the nation Amalek is the personification of all that is evil, the embodiment of all evil traits. This is alluded to in Scripture's words

כְּמוֹ שֶׁאָמְרוּ חֲכָמֵינוּ, זִכְרוֹנָם לִבְרָכָה: 'מִי שֶׁיֵּשׁ בּוֹ דֵּעָה, כְּאִלּוּ
נִבְנָה בֵּית הַמִּקְדָּשׁ בְּיָמָיו', וְזֶה בְּחִינַת: "יִבְחַר לָנוּ אֶת נַחֲלָתֵנוּ":

(מְסִימָן ד' עַד כָּאן לְשׁוֹן רַבֵּנוּ, זִכְרוֹנוֹ לִבְרָכָה)

by Rabbi Yehudah in the Talmud is to appoint a king; only afterwards does he mention
wiping out Amalek. This seems at odds with our lesson, in which Rebbe Nachman states that
first a person must endure humiliation in silence, the lower point, before he can attain the
rectification of the *vav,* appointing a king. However, because his intention in suffering in
silence is to minimize his own honor and thereby subdue Amalek and all those who seek to
minimize God's honor, the first act must be to appoint a king. A person must realize that the
objective in minimizing his own honor is not so that he is left without any self-esteem; for
Jewish honor is intimately bound up with God's honor. Rather, the main reason for the
suffering is so that the rectification of the lower point comes from the Jews themselves. Thus,
when God bestows kingship upon a person, He does so with the intention of revealing His
honor, *kavod Elohim,* which is the revelation of the upper point. Then, with this initial
revelation illuminating the lower point, the Jews have the power to subdue the evil of
Amalek. This is also the reason that the Talmud states (*Kiddushin* 32b): Although a king
might want to set aside his honor, his honor is not waived.

The *Parparaot LeChokhmah* sums up the lesson to this point. He writes: Before a person
repents, he is an aspect of pre-*ehyeh,* with the blood in the left hollow of his heart (his evil
inclination) in full force. Now, it is known that for any object or concept to be balanced, it
must include aspects from both its extremes. The same is true of embarrassment, which is a
balance between the upper and lower points. Thus, a person who accepts humiliation
properly, with silence (the lower point), has the channel through which to draw the light from
the upper point. If, on the other hand, he does not deal properly with the humiliation, that
embarrassment becomes merely a precursor of the far greater shame and humiliation he will
have to suffer. Therefore, when a person remains quiet and silent for the Holy One's sake, he
subdues his enemies (Amalek) who cause him this embarrassment, and he slaughters his main
enemy, the evil inclination. This embarrassment, the changes of his facial coloring (the king),
becomes the radiance of the upper point's light, *kavod Elohim* (the Temple). Furthermore, the
embarrassments represent the Tent of Meeting, where Moshe and Yehoshua come together.
Thus, each person, to the degree that he remains quiet before God, merits effecting this
union, which is epitomized by the building of the Holy Temple—i.e., the drawing of *daat,* the
revelation of God, into the mundaneity that is this world.

156. **leshon Rabbeinu.** See end of first note to Lesson #2 where this terminology has been
explained. The text from the beginning of Lesson #4 to here comes from Rebbe Nachman's
own manuscript. The last portion, regarding the three mitzvot which the Jews were
commanded upon entering the Land of Israel, the Rebbe told to Reb Noson after Purim. He
concluded by saying that each of these three mitzvot are the aspect of *teshuvah.* When Reb
Noson asked for an explanation of this, the Rebbe responded, "You tell me." On his way
back to his lodgings, Reb Noson thought of the possible connections and indeed came up
with some beautiful new insights. He recorded his ideas and showed them to Rebbe Nachman
on the following day. The Rebbe was pleased with Reb Noson's explanation and told him so.
Indeed, it was this episode which began Rebbe Nachman's training Reb Noson in composing

(holy knowledge),[153] as our Sages taught: When someone has *daat*, it is as if the Holy Temple was built in his lifetime (*Berakhot* 33a).[154] And this corresponds to "He chooses our heritage for us."[155]

{From Lesson #4 until here is *leshon Rabbeinu*.[156]}

which will in turn bring the King Mashiach, the *vav*. He will totally destroy the forces of evil, Amalek, and when this rectification is also complete, he will focus on the third rectification, building the eternal Holy Temple (see also n.155).

153. **Moshe...daat.** Moshe is the personification of *daat* (knowledge, awareness). In the profound teachings of the holy Ari, Moshe is equated with *Daat* of the Divine persona *Z'er Anpin* (*Etz Chaim*, 32:1; see also *Likutey Moharan* I, 15:3, n.16).

154. **daat...Holy Temple was built....** In the verse "...Your dwelling place is Your accomplishment, God; the Temple, Lord, Your hands have established" (Exodus 15:17), the word Temple appears between the two holy names *YHVH* and *Adonoy*. Maharsha (*loc. cit., s.v. kol*) explains that the *sefirah* of *Daat* is a combination of *Chokhmah* and *Binah*, the fountainheads of compassion and justice, respectively. The person who knows how to unite the two holy names associated with these *sefirot*, knows how to unite the letters with which heaven (compassion) and earth (judgment) were created (built). Thus, through a combination of these attributes, the attributes of *Chokhmah* and *Binah*, the Temple, too, is built. The same is presently true when a person attains *daat*. As the Sages taught: It is as if he built the Holy Temple. Reb Noson points out that the Temple served as a means for the revelation of Godliness. In our context, he says, this indicates that the hidden upper point is revealed for all to see, even, or especially, for those who correspond to the lower point (*Torat Natan #33*).

155. **Moshe...Temple...heritage for us.** Rebbe Nachman has just shown how the mitzvah of building the Holy Temple corresponds to Moshe: the Temple/"our heritage" corresponds to knowledge and Moshe is *daat*. The mitzvah of building the Temple thus corresponds to the upper point. Therefore, the three mitzvot the Jewish people were charged with correspond to the three parts of the *aleph*: the lower point corresponds to destroying Amalek; the *vav* corresponds to appointing a king; and the upper point corresponds to building the Holy Temple. These three mitzvot were given to the Jews specifically when they entered the Holy Land. In our context, this relates to a person's wanting to enter holiness. He must first accomplish the devotions mentioned in this lesson.

Reb Noson adds: In fact, all Torah law emanated from the Holy Land, from the Holy Temple. True expertise in *Halakhah* came from there. This was similarly true of Moshe, who gave the Jews the Torah. Had Moshe entered the Holy Land and performed the three mitzvot, this would have insured a permanent shining of the upper point's light. Then, the expertise in *Halakhah—baky b'ratzo* and *baky b'shov—*would have remained revealed for all to know and practice. But, because of their sins, the Jews lost this expertise. Instead, Moshe had to plead for forgiveness on their behalf. In the forty days he spent in heaven, from the beginning of Elul until after Yom Kippur, he was able to invoke Elul's special capacity for repentance—i.e., the expertise of *baky b'ratzo* and *baky b'shov*, as explained in our lesson. We, however, must now work very hard to attain this necessary expertise in *Halakhah* (*Torat Natan #32*).

The *Parparaot LeChokhmah* says: Interestingly, the first of the three mitzvot mentioned

וְזֶה פֵּרוּשׁ:

"וַיֹּאמֶר ה' אֶל מֹשֶׁה: קְרָא אֶת יְהוֹשֻׁעַ" – מֹשֶׁה הוּא נְקֻדָּה הָעֶלְיוֹנָה וִיהוֹשֻׁעַ הוּא נְקֻדָּה הַתַּחְתּוֹנָה.

"וְהִתְיַצְּבוּ בָאֹהֶל" – זֶה בְּחִינַת הָרָקִיעַ, בְּחִינַת הַוָּא"ו שֶׁבְּתוֹךְ הָאָלֶף.

"וַאֲצַוֶּנּוּ" – כִּי מֹשֶׁה הָיָה צָרִיךְ אָז לִמְסֹר הַכֹּל לִיהוֹשֻׁעַ, "וְאֵין שִׁלְטוֹן בְּיוֹם הַמָּוֶת", כִּי בִּשְׁעַת הִסְתַּלְּקוּת הַצַּדִּיק אֵין לוֹ שְׁלִיטָה וְכֹחַ לְהָאִיר לִיהוֹשֻׁעַ, עַל כֵּן דַּיֵּק וַאֲצַוֶּנּוּ, אֲנִי בְּעַצְמִי, כִּי חָזְרָה הַמֶּמְשָׁלָה לְהַקָּדוֹשׁ-בָּרוּךְ-הוּא:

וּכְלָל כָּל הָעִנְיָן כָּלוּל בִּתְמוּנַת אָלֶף, שֶׁהוּא נְקֻדָּה הָעֶלְיוֹנָה, וּנְקֻדָּה הַתַּחְתּוֹנָה וּוָא"ו. וְדוֹק מְאֹד.

וְהוּא עִנְיָן שֶׁאָמְרוּ חֲכָמֵינוּ, זִכְרוֹנָם לִבְרָכָה: שֶׁקֹּדֶם כְּנִיסַת יִשְׂרָאֵל לָאָרֶץ הֻזְהֲרוּ לְקַיֵּם שָׁלֹשׁ מִצְווֹת: 'לְהַכְרִית זַרְעוֹ שֶׁל עֲמָלֵק' 'וְלִבְנוֹת לָהֶם בֵּית הַבְּחִירָה' 'וּלְמַנּוֹת מֶלֶךְ'.

mentioned that because of our many sins it is sometimes necessary for the tzaddik/upper point to pass away. The many blemishes caused by sin block the light of the upper point and prevent it from shining into this world so that people might repent. This was certainly so in Moshe's case; because of the behavior of the Jewish people he was denied entry into the Holy Land (see also n.155). But, God's rule always remains. When the time comes for the tzaddik's light to be concealed, God sees to it that there remain followers of the true tzaddik who continue illuminating his true *daat* in this world. Thus, depending upon how seriously a person seeks the truth through the tzaddik's legacy, or heritage, to that same degree he will be able to attain true repentance (see *Likutey Halakhot, Shluchin* 5:12).

Thus, in our context the verse reads: Moshe was about to pass away. The illumination he had brought into the world was in danger of disappearing. Therefore, **God said to Moshe** — the upper point. In order for your illuminating light to continue shining, **summon Yehoshua** — your light must be directed into the lower point. To do this, **present yourselves in the Tent of Meeting** — a channel must be created to filter the light downward. This is accomplished by **I will appoint him** — by returning one's rulership to God. When a person minimizes his honor and maximizes God's (as above, §1), he has attained true humility. He accepts that everything is under God's domain and is willing to suffer embarrassment in silence for the Holy One's sake, to give honor to God. In so doing, he gives over all rulership to God. Then, God will see to it that the light of the *aleph's* upper point is filtered down through the *vav* in the *aleph* until it descends to the *aleph's* lower point. The *aleph* will thus be perfected and *adam* will be made

8. This is the explanation [of the opening verse][157]:

{**"Then God said to Moshe, 'The time is coming for you to die.** *Kra et Yehoshua* **(summon Yehoshua) and present yourselves in the Tent of Meeting, where I will appoint[158] him.' "**}

Then God said to Moshe...summon Yehoshua — Moshe represents the upper point of the *aleph* and Yehoshua the lower point.[159]

and present yourselves in the Tent of Meeting — This alludes to the firmament, to the *vav* in the middle of the *aleph*.[160]

where I will appoint him — It was then necessary for Moshe to hand everything over to Yehoshua, however, "There is no authority on the day of death" (Ecclesiastes 8:8). For at the time of the tzaddik's passing he does not have the authority and strength to shine into < another >.[161] Therefore, < God said, > "where I will appoint him"—*I*, Myself, for rulership returned to the Holy One.[162]

9. In general, this entire matter is encompassed in the shape of the *aleph*, which consists of an upper point, a lower point, and a *vav*. Consider this very carefully.

This is also connected to what the Sages taught: Upon entering the Holy Land, the Jewish people were charged with three mitzvot: to kill off the seed of Amalek; to build a Holy Temple for themselves; and to appoint a king.

---

his own original Torah insights (see end of n.1; *Through Fire and Water*, Chapter 8).

157. **explanation of the opening verse.** Rebbe Nachman shows how the concepts of this lesson are alluded to in the opening verse. The *Biur HaLikutim* points out that this verse appears in the Shabbat Torah reading of *VaYeilekh*, which is known as Shabbat *Shuvah*, the Shabbat of Repentance. This corresponds to our lesson, in that rearranging the letters of *ShUVaH* (שובה) produces the word *BUShaH* (בושה, embarrassment).

158. **appoint.** *Atzavenu* in Hebrew, which is generally translated "I will instruct him," or "I will give him charge." The translation here follows Rav Saadia Gaon, as "I will appoint him" is more in line with our text.

159. **Moshe...Yehoshua...lower point.** As above, section 5.

160. **Tent...firmament...vav....** As above, section 5. See notes 91, and 110-111.

161. **no authority on the day of death....** Rashi explains that although he is mentioned throughout Scripture as King David, on the day of his passing he is referred to merely as "David" (1 Kings, 2:1). This indicates that a king's rule and authority are taken from him on the day he dies.

162. **rulership returned to the Holy One.** Earlier (n.121), in Reb Noson's commentary, it was

'לְהַכְרִית זַרְעוֹ שֶׁל עֲמָלֵק' הִיא בְּחִינַת יְהוֹשֻׁעַ, נְקֻדָּה הַתַּחְתּוֹנָה. כִּי
עִקַּר מְחִיַּת עֲמָלֵק תָּלוּי בִּיהוֹשֻׁעַ, כְּמוֹ שֶׁכָּתוּב: "צֵא הִלָּחֵם
בַּעֲמָלֵק", וְכַמְבֹאָר בַּדֹּהַר הָעִנְיָן.

'וְלִבְנוֹת בֵּית הַבְּחִירָה' הוּא בְּחִינַת מֹשֶׁה, נְקֻדָּה הָעֶלְיוֹנָה, כִּי 'מִי
שֶׁיֵּשׁ בּוֹ דֵעָה, כְּאִלּוּ נִבְנֶה בֵית-הַמִּקְדָּשׁ בְּיָמָיו', וּמֹשֶׁה הוּא בְּחִינַת
הַדַּעַת.

'וּלְמַנּוֹת מֶלֶךְ' הוּא בְּחִינַת רָקִיעַ, הַנָּא"ו שֶׁבְּתוֹךְ הָאָלֶ"ף, כְּמוֹ
שֶׁכָּתוּב: "דָּרַךְ כּוֹכָב מִיַּעֲקֹב", שֶׁקָּאֵי עַל שֶׁיָּקוּם מֶלֶךְ מִיַּעֲקֹב,
"וְדָרַךְ כּוֹכָב" הוּא בְּחִינַת רָקִיעַ, שֶׁיֵּשׁ בּוֹ כּוֹכָבִים וּמַזָּלוֹת. וְהַיְנוּ
"מִיַּעֲקֹב", כִּי "יַעֲקֹב אִישׁ תָּם יֹשֵׁב אֹהָלִים", בְּחִינַת רָקִיעַ, כְּמוֹ
שֶׁכָּתוּב: "וַיִּמְתָּחֵם כָּאֹהֶל", כַּמְבֹאָר בַּדֹּהַר, שֶׁיַּעֲקֹב הוּא בְּחִינַת
וָא"ו.

כִּי שָׁלֹשׁ מִצְווֹת אֵלּוּ הֵן בְּחִינַת תְּשׁוּבָה, וְהָבֵן.
(מִן וּכְלָל עַד כָּאן כָּפוּל לְעֵיל בְּשִׁנּוּי לָשׁוֹן קְצָת):

---

himself epitomized this ability to connect the highest wisdom to the mundaneity of this world (see Lesson #1, §2). As the tzaddik of his generation, he was also able to transmit this wisdom and teaching to his sons, the twelve tribes.

167. **three mitzvot...repentance.** As explained above in section 7. In the manuscript version of *Likutey Moharan* the following appears here: Simply, entering the Holy Land is an aspect of *teshuvah*, a sign that he wants to *shuv* (return) to God. This is because entering the Holy Land indicates entering the boundaries of holiness, which is accomplished by means of the three mitzvot mentioned earlier. Killing off the seed of Amalek is an aspect of slaughtering the evil inclination, for Amalek signifies the impurity which stems from the primordial snake in Gan Eden.

168. **Understand this.** At this point in the printed edition there appears the following: From "In general" until here is a review of what was said earlier, with only slight changes in terminology.

Being that Rebbe Nachman gave over his handwritten manuscript of this teaching a while after he taught it publicly, it is safe to assume that Reb Noson had in the interim recorded the lesson for his own study. Later on, when *Likutey Moharan* was printed, it became clear that Reb Noson had inserted numerous additions to the Rebbe's manuscript, apparently from his own notes. There are times when he restates an entire lesson based on his own recording of the teaching (see *Likutey Moharan* I, 46, 47, 53, etc.). Thus, it is fair to postulate that this section was from Reb Noson's notes, which explains why it seems to be a repetition of section 7.

Killing off the seed of Amalek is the aspect of Yehoshua, the lower point. This is because blotting out Amalek is essentially dependent upon Yehoshua, as is written (Exodus 17:9), "[Moshe said to Yehoshua, 'Pick some men for us, and] go out and battle against Amalek,' " and as < this > is explained in the *Zohar* (II, 65b).[163]

Building themselves a Holy Temple is the aspect of Moshe, the upper point. This is because "When someone has knowledge, it is as if the Holy Temple was built in his lifetime." And Moshe is the aspect of knowledge, < as is known >.[164]

Appointing a king is the aspect of firmament, the *vav* in the middle of the *aleph*. As is written, "A star will go forth from Yaakov," which indicates that a king will arise out of Yaakov.[165] "A star will go forth" alludes to the firmament, which contains stars and constellations. Thus, "from Yaakov," because "Yaakov was a man of perfection who remained in the tents"—an aspect of firmament, as in, "and He stretched them out like a tent." [And] as is explained in the *Zohar* (III, 244b): Yaakov is the aspect of *vav*.[166]

For these three mitzvot are the aspect of repentance.[167] Understand this.[168]

---

to sit on the throne—for God and the Jewish people are one. And, being one with God, the Jews can provide judgment for all living creatures.

163. **blotting out Amalek...dependent upon Yehoshua....** Amalek is the personification of all the evil in Esav and his descendants. Yehoshua, meanwhile, was a descendent of Yosef, who was Esav's prime adversary. The Sages teach: Our forefather Yaakov foresaw that the descendants of Esav would only be vanquished by the descendants of Yosef (*Bava Batra* 123b). The *Zohar* (*loc. cit.*) adds that the reason Yehoshua, more than anyone else, was chosen to blot out Amalek was because he "did not depart from the tent" (see n.114). In our context, this means that he was constantly attached to the upper point of the *aleph*, to Moshe, by means of the *vav*, the tent of the Holy Temple. Through this attachment, he was able to draw the strength to vanquish Amalek.

164. **Moshe is the aspect of knowledge....** As above, section 7, notes 149-150.

165. **star...king...out of Yaakov.** As above, section 7 and note 152.

166. **firmament...Yaakov...aspect of vav.** In the terminology of the Kabbalah, Yaakov corresponds to *Z'er Anpin*, which has six *sefirot* (see Appendix: The Divine Persona). Thus, Yaakov is the *vav*. The *vav* connects the upper and lower points and so represents the ability to draw the knowledge found Above to lower levels. When an individual is quiet and silent in the face of insult, his embarrassment becomes this bridge, the *vav*. Yehoshua placed himself totally at the feet of Moshe and so the place of their meeting also served as a bridge, connecting the master with the disciple. As Rebbe Nachman teaches elsewhere, Yaakov

(שַׁיָּךְ לְעֵיל), וְזֶה סוֹד כַּוָּנוֹת אֱלוּל. שָׁמַעְתִּי קְצָת כְּטִפָּה מִן הַיָּם.
עַיֵּן שָׁם בַּכַּוָּנוֹת שֶׁל אֱלוּל, מְבֹאָר שָׁם, שֶׁכְּלָל כַּוָּנוֹת אֱלוּל הוּא,
"הַנּוֹתֵן בַּיָּם דֶּרֶךְ", שֶׁצְּרִיכִין לְהָאִיר בְּחִינַת דֶּרֶךְ בַּיָּם וְכוּ', וְזֶה
הַדֶּרֶךְ הוּא בְּחִינַת שְׁתֵּי פְּעָמִים הַשֵּׁם יב"ק, כִּי שְׁתֵּי פְּעָמִים יב"ק
עוֹלֶה דֶּרֶךְ, וְזֶה נִמְשָׁךְ מִבְּחִינַת שְׁנֵי שֵׁמוֹת, שֶׁהֵם קס"א ס"ג, כִּי
אֵלּוּ שְׁנֵי שֵׁמוֹת – קס"א ס"ג, הֵם עוֹלִים בְּגִימַטְרִיָּא שְׁתֵּי פְּעָמִים
יב"ק, שֶׁהוּא בְּגִימַטְרִיָּא דֶּרֶךְ, כַּנַּ"ל.

underpinnings, which are explained in the writings of the Ari. Elul, for example, is the month of repentance. To achieve the greatest possible spiritual levels this month has to offer, one must meditate on the holy name *Ehyeh* punctuated with the *segol* vowel sign, and also on the holy name *YHVH* punctuated with the *chirik,* as we will next see. In other months, or for different occasions, one would meditate on other configurations and punctuations. See also note 199. (At this point, it would be most beneficial for the reader to familiarize himself with Appendix: Expansions of the Holy Names, specifically those of *YHVH* and *Ehyeh,* in order to understand the upcoming sections better. See also Appendix: Gematria Chart.)

The following is Reb Noson's introductory comment to these meditations: Everyone should know and firmly believe that each and every Jew, by means of his repentance (even if he has no understanding of the Kabbalistic meditations), effects incredible rectifications in heaven during the month of Elul. This is because every attempt at repentance brings about a "sweetening of decrees"—i.e., a defeat of the forces of evil. The main thing is to walk the pathways of repentance with total simplicity and keep from turning back to sin. By doing so, a person makes awesome *tikkunim* (*Torat Natan* #35).

171. **Who makes a way through the sea....** The Kabbalah teaches that it is possible to associate every Hebrew word to one of God's holy names. "Through the sea," *BaYaM* (בים = 52), is the key word in these meditations, which focus on the holy name *YHVH* in its expansion equivalent to *BaN* (בן = 52). This name is associated with *Malkhut,* in which a person must make a "way" for his rectifications.

172. **twice Yabok...derekh.** The letters of *YaBoK* have a numerical value of 112 (יבק = 10 + 2 + 100). Twice that, 224, is the numerical value of *DeReKh* (דרך = 4 + 200 + 20). See Appendix: Gematria Chart.

173. **KaSA and SaG.** See Appendix: Expansions of the Holy Names. *KaSA* is one of the expansions of the holy name *Ehyeh* (אלף הי יוד הי), while *SaG* is one of the expansions of *YHVH* (יוד הי ואו הי).

174. **KaSA...SaG...derekh.** *KaSA* is equal to 161 (קסא = 100 + 60 + 1). *SaG* is equal to 63 (סג = 60 + 3). Together, they equal the 224 of *DeReKh.* See Appendix: Gematria Chart.

10. This relates to above: **This is the hidden meaning of the *kavanot* (meditations) of Elul.**[169]

I heard a little about this [from Rebbe Nachman], but it was only like a drop in the sea. Study the meditations of Elul,[170] where it is explained that the general *kavanot* of Elul are [based on the verse] (Isaiah 43:16), "...Who makes a way through the sea." For one must take the aspect of "way" and shine it into the "sea."[171] This *derekh* (way) is the aspect of two times the holy name *Yabok,* because twice *Yabok* equals *derekh.*[172] This proceeds from the aspect of two holy names, *KaSA* [and] *SaG.*[173] For these two names, *KaSA* and *SaG,* have a numerical value equal to two times *Yabok,* which is the numerical value of *derekh.*[174]

---

169. **hidden meaning of the kavanot of Elul.** This is mentioned above in section 4, where Rebbe Nachman speaks about being expert in running and returning, *baky b'ratzo* and *baky b'shov.* When a person attains this expertise, he merits *kavod Elohim, Keter.* Then the right hand of God is outstretched to accept his *teshuvah.* Beginning with this section and on through section 13, Reb Noson explains the Rebbe's remark, "This is the hidden meaning of the *kavanot* of Elul." Here, he quotes from the Ari's esoteric teachings and begins to explain them based on Rebbe Nachman's teachings—making the Kabbalistic meditations an open book for all those whose desire is to serve God.

It was a common practice for Rebbe Nachman to encompass whole series of Kabbalistic teachings in lessons of practical advice, explaining how people can aspire to and attain the greatest of levels. After giving one such lesson, the Rebbe would offer a few hints as to where in the Kabbalah one could find these concepts. Prior to Reb Noson's becoming one of the Rebbe's followers, Rebbe Nachman said, "I long for a follower who is both learned and gifted with a power of language. Then, I will be able to explain the teachings of the Ari so clearly that even young people will understand them" (*Tzaddik* #363). Considering that this lesson was given just after Reb Noson became the Rebbe's follower, it does seem that the Rebbe's intention in revealing these *kavanot* was to see if Reb Noson could record them properly.

170. **meditations of Elul.** In Rebbe Nachman's time, this appeared in the *Siddur of the Ari,* which contained the prayers along with their mystical meditations. These meditations are also found in *Shaar Ruach HaKodesh,* 16, pp.121-126. We must emphasize that the purpose of these footnotes is to explain the Rebbe's lessons and not to elucidate the Kabbalah. Thus, the notes adhere to the flow of the text and clarify matters solely as they relate to the lesson itself. Having said this, a short introduction to the meditations found in the Ari's teachings is necessary here:

Kabbalistic meditations are in the main based on the various combinations of God's holy names. Each name, even each letter and part thereof, has its own special intention. This is true of all the twenty-two letters of the Hebrew alphabet, as well as each of the vowel signs. Thus, each month of the Jewish calendar is represented by its own configuration of God's name combined with a particular vowel sign. Each of these representations has its

וְצָרִיךְ לְכַוֵּן שֵׁם קס"א בְּסֶגּוֹל, וְשֵׁם ס"ג בְּחִירִיק.

וְסֶגּוֹל דִקס"א וְחִירִיק דס"ג הֵם עוֹלִים תָּי"ו, כִּי שֵׁם קס"א הוּא שֵׁם אהי"ה בְּמִלּוּאוֹ כָּזֶה: אלף הי יוד הי, שֶׁהֵם יוּד אוֹתִיּוֹת, וְכָל אַחַת נְקֻדָּה בְּסֶגּוֹל, וְסֶגּוֹל הוּא שָׁלֹשׁ נְקֻדּוֹת, וְעַל כֵּן הוּא עוֹלֶה שְׁלֹשִׁים, וְעַל כֵּן יוּד פְּעָמִים סֶגּוֹל עוֹלֶה שי"ן. וס"ג הֵם יוּד אוֹתִיּוֹת שֶׁל מִלּוּי הֲוָי"ה, יוד הי ואו הי, וְכָל אַחַת נְקֻדָּה בְּחִירִיק, עוֹלֶה ק', וּשְׁנֵיהֶם – חִירִיק דס"ג וְסֶגּוֹל דִקס"א עוֹלִים יַחַד תָּיו, בְּגִימַטְרִיָּא פְּשׁוּטָה, וְאָז עַל-יְדֵי כָּל בְּחִינוֹת הַנַּ"ל, הַיָּמִין פְּשׁוּטָה לְקַבֵּל תְּשׁוּבָתוֹ,

כִּי יָמִין בְּמִלּוּאוֹ עוֹלֶה דֶּרֶךְ עִם הַשָּׁלֹשׁ אוֹתִיּוֹת, שֶׁהוּא שְׁתֵּי פְּעָמִים יב"ק וְכוּ', עַיֵּן שָׁם. כָּל זֶה מְבֹאָר מִתּוֹךְ כַּוָּנַת אֱלוּל.

וְעַתָּה בּוֹא וּרְאֵה וְהָבֵן אֵיךְ כָּל הַכַּוָּנוֹת הַנַּ"ל מְרֻמָּזִים וְנֶעֱלָמִים בְּדֶרֶךְ נִפְלָא וְנוֹרָא מְאֹד בְּתוֹךְ הַתּוֹרָה הַנַּ"ל, כִּי מְבֹאָר שָׁם, שְׁמִי שֶׁרוֹצֶה לַעֲשׂוֹת תְּשׁוּבָה, צָרִיךְ שֶׁיִּהְיֶה לּוֹ שְׁנֵי בְּקִיאוּת, הַיְנוּ בָּקִי בְּרָצוֹא בָּקִי בְּשׁוֹב, שֶׁהוּא בְּחִינַת עַיִל וְנָפִיק, בְּחִינַת: "אִם אֶסַּק שָׁמַיִם שָׁם אָתָּה", שֶׁהוּא בְּחִינַת בָּקִי בְּרָצוֹא, "וְאַצִּיעָה שְּׁאוֹל הִנֶּךָ", שֶׁהוּא בְּחִינַת בָּקִי בְּשׁוֹב וְכוּ', כַּמְבֹאָר לְעֵיל, עַיֵּן שָׁם.

---

178. **four hundred... PeShUTaH.** The five letters of *PeShUTaH* (פשוטה, $80 + 300 + 6 + 9 + 5$) equal 400. See Appendix: Gematria Chart.

179. **repentance.** See Lesson #1, note 48, that the letter *Tav*, which has a value of 400, indicates *Teshuvah* (repentance).

180. **yemin...derekh...three letters.** As explained, *DeReKh* (דרך) equals 224. Add 1 for each of its 3 letters and its numerical value is 227. *YeMIN* (ימין), with its letters spelled out (יוד מם יוד נון), equals 226 (see Gematria Chart). Then add 1 for the word itself, as the rules of *gematria* allow, and the word *yemin* also equals 227.

181. **And now! Come see and understand....** Before Reb Noson begins to show how the *kavanot* are alluded to in our lesson, he reviews the concepts of *baky b'ratzo* and *baky b'shov*, which is the theme of the meditations for Elul.

182. **is explained.** A more extensive review appears in section 4 and notes 63-79.

[Here,] it is required to think of the name *KaSA* as being punctuated with a *segol,* and the name *SaG* with a *chirik.*[175]

Now, the *segol* of *KaSA* and the *chirik* of *SaG* together equal four hundred. For the name *KaSA* is actually the name *Ehyeh* with its letters spelled out *ALePh HeY YOD HeY.* Together there are ten letters, each one punctuated with a *segol.* And the *segol* consists of three dots, and is [itself] therefore equal to thirty. Thus, the *segol* times ten [letters] is equal to three hundred.[176] And *SaG* consists of the ten letters of *YHVH* with its letters spelled out *YOD HeY VAV HeY,* each one punctuated with a *chirik.* [The *chirik* consists of one dot, whose value is ten, and so the *chirik* times ten letters] equals one hundred.[177]

Thus, the both of them, the *chirik* of *SaG* and the *segol* of *KaSA,* have a combined value of four hundred. This is the numerical value of *PeShUTaH* (outstreched).[178] And so, by virtue of all the above mentioned concepts, the *yemin* (right hand)...is outstretched to accept his repentance.[179]

For when the letters *yemin* are spelled out, it is equal to *derekh* with its three letters.[180] This is twice *Yabok*...see there. All this is explained in the *kavanot* of Elul.

11. And now! come see and understand how, in a fantastically awesome manner, all the above *kavanot* are hinted at and concealed in the above Torah lesson.[181] For there it is explained that a person who wants to repent must have two types of expertise: at running and at returning. This is the aspect of ascending and descending, corresponding to "If I ascend to heaven, You are there"—the expertise of running; "and if I make my bed in Hell, here You are"—the expertise of returning. See above, where this is explained.[182]

---

175. **punctuated....** It is possible to affix any of the nine basic vowel signs to each of the twenty-two Hebrew letters. In the meditations of Elul, each of the ten letters of *KaSA* are punctuated with a *segol* (.), while each of the ten letters of *SaG* are punctuated with a *chirik* (.) (see nn.85,120).

176. **three dots...equal to three hundred.** The smallest letter in the Hebrew alphabet is the *yod,* which is basically a simple dot. The *yod* has a gematria of 10. Thus, the three dots of the *segol* are actually three *yods,* and are equal to 30. Since there are ten letters in *KaSA,* each with three dots, 30x10 = 300: אֶלֶף הֵי יוֹד הֵי.

177. **chirik...one hundred.** There are ten letters in *SaG,* each with a *chirik,* a single dot. Thus, 10 letters x 10 dots = 100: יוֹד הֵי וָאו הֵי.

וְהַפֵּרוּשׁ הַפָּשׁוּט הוּא, שֶׁמִּי שֶׁרוֹצֶה לֵילֵךְ בְּדַרְכֵי הַתְּשׁוּבָה, צָרִיךְ
לַחְגֹּר מָתְנָיו, שֶׁיִּתְחַזֵּק עַצְמוֹ בְּדַרְכֵי ה' תָּמִיד, בֵּין בַּעֲלִיָּה בֵּין
בִּירִידָה, שֶׁהֵם בְּחִינַת: "אִם אֶסַּק שָׁמַיִם וְאַצִּיעָה שְּׁאוֹל" וְכוּ', הַיְנוּ
בֵּין שֶׁיִּזְכֶּה לְאֵיזוֹ עֲלִיָּה, לְאֵיזוֹ מַדְרֵגָה גְּדוֹלָה, אַף־עַל־פִּי־כֵן אַל
יַעֲמֹד שָׁם, וְלֹא יִסְתַּפֵּק עַצְמוֹ בָּזֶה, רַק צָרִיךְ שֶׁיִּהְיֶה בָּקִי בָּזֶה מְאֹד,
לֵידַע וּלְהַאֲמִין שֶׁהוּא צָרִיךְ לָלֶכֶת יוֹתֵר וְיוֹתֵר וְכוּ', שֶׁזֶּהוּ בְּחִינַת
בָּקִי בְּרָצוֹא, בִּבְחִינַת עַיִל, שֶׁהוּא בְּחִינַת: "אִם אֶסַּק שָׁמַיִם שָׁם
אָתָּה".

וְכֵן לְהֵפֶךְ, שֶׁאֲפִלּוּ אִם יִפֹּל, חַס וְשָׁלוֹם, לְמָקוֹם שֶׁיִּפֹּל אֲפִלּוּ
בִּשְׁאוֹל תַּחְתִּיּוֹת, גַּם כֵּן אַל יִתְיָאֵשׁ עַצְמוֹ לְעוֹלָם, וְתָמִיד יְחַפֵּשׂ
וִיבַקֵּשׁ אֶת הַשֵּׁם יִתְבָּרַךְ, וִיחַזֵּק עַצְמוֹ בְּכָל מָקוֹם שֶׁהוּא, בְּכָל מַה
שֶּׁיּוּכַל, כִּי גַּם בִּשְׁאוֹל תַּחְתִּיּוֹת נִמְצָא הַשֵּׁם יִתְבָּרַךְ, וְגַם שָׁם יְכוֹלִין
לְדַבֵּק אֶת עַצְמוֹ אֵלָיו יִתְבָּרַךְ, וְזֶה בְּחִינַת: "וְאַצִּיעָה שְּׁאוֹל הִנֶּךָ".
וְזֶה בְּחִינַת בָּקִי בְּשׁוֹב, כִּי אִי אֶפְשָׁר לֵילֵךְ בְּדַרְכֵי הַתְּשׁוּבָה, כִּי אִם
כְּשֶׁבָּקִי בִּשְׁנֵי הַבְּקִיאוּת הָאֵלּוּ.

וְדִקְדֵּק רַבֵּנוּ, זִכְרוֹנוֹ לִבְרָכָה, וְקָרָא עִנְיָן זֶה בִּלְשׁוֹן בָּקִי, כִּי הִיא
בְּקִיאוּת גְּדוֹלָה מְאֹד מְאֹד, שֶׁיִּזְכֶּה לֵידַע לְיַגֵּעַ עַצְמוֹ וְלִטְרֹחַ
בַּעֲבוֹדַת ה' תָּמִיד, וּלְצַפּוֹת בְּכָל עֵת לְהַגִּיעַ לְמַדְרֵגָה גְּבוֹהָה יוֹתֵר,
וְאַף־עַל־פִּי־כֵן אַל יִפֹּל מִשּׁוּם דָּבָר, וַאֲפִלּוּ אִם יִהְיֶה אֵיךְ שֶׁיִּהְיֶה,
חַס וְשָׁלוֹם, אַף־עַל־פִּי־כֵן אַל יִפֹּל בְּדַעְתּוֹ כְּלָל, וִיקַיֵּם: "וְאַצִּיעָה
שְּׁאוֹל הִנֶּךָ", כַּנַּ"ל:

וְעַל־פִּי סוֹד נֶעְלָם בָּזֶה סוֹד כַּוָּנוֹת אֵלּוּ הַנַּ"ל, כִּי בָּקִי הוּא בְּחִינַת
שֵׁם יב"ק הַנַּ"ל, שֶׁהוּא אוֹתִיּוֹת בָּקִי. וְזֶה שֶׁזּוֹכֶה לִשְׁנֵי הַבְּקִיאוּת
הַנַּ"ל, שֶׁהֵם שְׁתֵּי פְּעָמִים בָּקִי, דְּהַיְנוּ בָּקִי בְּרָצוֹא בָּקִי בְּשׁוֹב, עַל־
יְדֵי־זֶה זוֹכֶה לְדֶרֶךְ הַתְּשׁוּבָה, כִּי שְׁתֵּי פְּעָמִים בָּקִי, שֶׁהֵם בְּחִינַת

The simple meaning of all this is that the person who wants to walk the pathways of repentance must summon up his fortitude and constantly strengthen himself in the ways of God—whether in a state of spiritual ascent or descent, corresponding to "If I ascend to heaven...and if I make my bed in Hell." In other words, even if he is experiencing an ascent and a high spiritual level, he must not remain there nor be satisfied with this. Rather, he must be extremely expert at this, knowing and believing that he must go further and further. This is the expertise of running, an aspect of ascent, which corresponds to "If I ascend to heaven...."

The opposite is also true. Even if, God forbid, he falls to wherever he falls—even into the deepest Hell—he must still never give himself over to despair, but constantly seek and search for God. No matter where he is, he must strengthen himself with all means available. For God is to be found even in the deepest Hell, and there too it is possible to attach oneself to Him. This corresponds to "and if I make my bed in Hell, here You are," the expertise of returning. For it is impossible to walk the pathways of repentance unless one possesses both these types of expertise.

Rabbeinu, of blessed memory, was very precise in referring to this concept by the term *baky*. For it is indeed a very, very great expertise when a person merits knowing how to exert himself and toil continuously in the service of God, hoping all the while to reach a higher spiritual level, and yet not allowing anything to bring him down. Even if he is as he is, God forbid, he still does not get discouraged at all, as he fulfills, "and if I make my bed in Hell, here You are."

12. Based on Kabbalistic teaching we know that concealed in this is the hidden meaning of the *kavanot* of Elul. For *baky* is the aspect of the above mentioned holy name *YaBoK,* which has the same letters as *BaKY*.[183] When a person attains the two types of expertise mentioned earlier, which is twice *baky*—i.e., *baky b'ratzo* (running) and *baky b'shov* (returning)—he also attains the *derekh* (way) of repentance.

183. **YaBoK...BaKY.** As is taught, the holy name *Yabok* denotes *baky,* a thorough knowledge of Torah law (*Zohar* III, 223a).

Here, the name *YaBoK* (112) is comprised of three holy names *YHVH* (26), *EHYeH* (21) and *ADoNoY* (65) which together also equal 112 (see n.51 above). See below, note 199, for how these holy names are connected to man.

שְׁתֵּי פְּעָמִים יב״ק, הַנַּ״ל, עוֹלֶה בְּגִימַטְרִיָּא דֶּרֶךְ כַּנַּ״ל, כִּי עַל־פִּי הַכַּוָּנוֹת נַעֲשֶׂה זֶה הַדֶּרֶךְ מִבְּחִינַת סֶגּוֹל דְּקס״א וְחִירִיק דְּס״ג, שֶׁהֵם בְּגִימַטְרִיָּא שְׁתֵּי פְּעָמִים יב״ק, כַּנִּזְכָּר לְעֵיל.

וְזֶה בְּעַצְמוֹ סוֹד, בְּחִינַת שְׁנֵי הַבְּקִיאוּת הַנַּ״ל, כִּי בָּקִי בְּרָצוֹא, שֶׁהוּא בְּחִינַת "אֶסַּק שָׁמַיִם", זֶה בְּחִינַת סֶגּוֹל דקס״א, כִּי אֶסַּק אוֹתִיּוֹת קס״א.

וּבָקִי בְּשׁוּב, שֶׁהוּא בְּחִינַת: "וְאַצִּיעָה שְׁאוֹל הִנֶּךָּ", זֶה בְּחִינַת חִירִיק דְּס״ג, מִלְּשׁוֹן: "אַל תַּסֵּ״ג גְּבוּל עוֹלָם", שֶׁהוּא בְּחִינַת שֶׁמַּסִּיג גְּבוּלוֹ וּמַחֲזִירוֹ לַאֲחוֹרָיו, שֶׁזֶּה בְּחִינַת יְרִידָה, שֶׁהָאָדָם נוֹפֵל, חַס וְשָׁלוֹם, מִמַּדְרֵגָתוֹ, וְהוּא נָסוֹג אָחוֹר, חַס וְשָׁלוֹם. אַף־עַל־פִּי־כֵן יְחַזֵּק אֶת עַצְמוֹ, וְאַל יִתְיָאֵשׁ עַצְמוֹ לְעוֹלָם, כִּי גַּם שָׁם נִמְצָא הַשֵּׁם יִתְבָּרַךְ, וְזֶה בְּחִינַת: "וְאַצִּיעָה שְׁאוֹל הִנֶּךָּ", כַּנַּ״ל, וְזֶה בְּחִינַת שֵׁם ס״ג, כַּנַּ״ל.

כִּי סֶגּוֹל דָּא חַמָּה, שֶׁהוּא הַנְּקֻדָּה הָעֶלְיוֹנָה שֶׁעַל הָאָלֶף, הַנֶּחֱלֶקֶת לְשָׁלֹשׁ טִפִּין, שֶׁזֶּהוּ בְּחִינַת "אֶסַּק שָׁמַיִם", בְּחִינַת סֶגּוֹל דְּקס״א,

---

denotes returning—i.e., remaining steadfast with God. That is, a person knows he has fallen but recognizes that God is with him nonetheless. He is then an aspect of *YHVH*. Moreover, that same person who wants to repent might find himself returning not from his evil ways but from his good deeds and thoughts. If he then mistakenly concludes that he is not worthy of *teshuvah*, he might begin to fall even lower than the low level he is presently on. In that case, he must draw spiritual nourishment from the holy name *YHVH*, particularly in its formation as *SaG*, which brings life and support to all those distant from God who have not yet repented. And, the *Mai HaNachal* adds, although we might construe from this that *YHVH* is the holy name most associated with repentance, in essence, *teshuvah* is actually *Ehyeh*. The reason is that a person attempting to get closer to God discovers that his earlier perceptions of Godliness are mundane when compared with his current perceptions (as above, §3). Thus, the moment he realizes the need for *teshuvah*, he takes on the aspect of *ehyeh*. But he requires support. The support that comes from *YHVH/SaG*. This is why Rebbe Nachman calls this having expertise, because a person requires proficiency at both running and returning; to be successful in seeing his repentance through to the end he must always be attached to both *Ehyeh* and *YHVH*.

189. **segol...aleph...three dots.** See above, section 5, notes 116-118.

This is because twice *baky,* which is the aspect of twice the holy name *Yabok,* is equal to the numerical value of *derekh.*[184] For by following the method of the *kavanot,* this *derekh* is made from the *segol* of *KaSA* and the *chirik* of *SaG,* which [also] have the numerical value of twice *Yabok.*[185]

This in itself is the deeper meaning of the two types of expertise. The *baky* of running, which corresponds to "*esak shamayim* (I ascend to heaven)," is related to the *segol* of *KaSA*—because *eSAK* and *KaSA* have the same letters.[186]

The *baky* of returning, which corresponds to "and if I make my bed in Hell," is related to the *chirik* of *SaG,* as in (Proverbs 22:28), "Do not *taSeG* (moves back) the ancient boundary stone." This is when a person retreats from his limit and turns back, < resembling "*naSoGu* backwards" (Isaiah 42:17) > .[187] It is a spiritual fall; a person falls from his original level and turns back, God forbid. Nevertheless, [a person who is *baky*] will strengthen himself and never give himself over to despair. For even in such a place God can be found, corresponding to "and if I make my bed in Hell, here You are." This is an aspect of the name *SaG.*[188]

For "*segol* is the sun," the upper point of the *aleph,* which is divided into three dots.[189] It corresponds to "If I ascend to heaven," an aspect of the *segol* of *KaSA,* which has the same letters as *eSAK*

---

184. **attains the derekh of repentance....** For one must be an expert at both running and returning—the two areas of *bakiut* (expertise). Only a person who has both can go on the *derekh* (way) of *teshuvah.* That is, his twice *baky* (112x2) is what reveals the *derekh* (224).

185. **derekh...twice Yabok.** For the *derekh* (224) is made by a combination of the two holy names *KaSA* (161) and *Sag* (63). But, for them to be revealed to a person, he must first attain twice *baky*—the *baky b'ratzo* and the *baky b'shov.*

186. **eSAK and KaSA....** Thus, the word *esak,* which implies running, is an allusion to *KaSA.*

187. **SaG...taSeG...naSoGu backwards.** Thus, the word *taSeG,* which implies returning, is an allusion to *SaG.*

188. **name SaG.** The *Mai HaNachal* shows how this has a further connection with our lesson. As we have seen, for a person to repent, he must first prepare himself to be. That is, he must take on the quality of "I will be" (*ehyeh*), so that he can then take on being (*havayah,* *YHVH*). It has also been explained that *KaSA* is related to *Ehyeh,* while *SaG* is related to *YHVH.* For these two holy names are the keys to repentance. *Ehyeh/KaSA* denotes running—i.e., preparing oneself to ascend the spiritual ladder. At this moment, however, he has not yet attained the higher level. He is an aspect of *ehyeh.* On the other hand, *YHVH/SaG*

שֶׁהוּא אוֹתִיּוֹת אֶסַּק, כַּנַּ"ל. וְחִירִיק הוּא בְּחִינַת נְקֻדָּה הַתַּחְתּוֹנָה שֶׁל הָאָלֶף, שֶׁהוּא בְּחִינַת: "וְאַצִּיעָה שְׁאוֹל הִנֶּךָּ", שֶׁהוּא בְּחִינַת חִירִיק דְּסַ"ג הַנַּ"ל.

וְזֶה שֶׁכָּתַב שָׁם לְמַעְלָה בְּהַתּוֹרָה הַנַּ"ל: "וּכְשֶׁיֵּשׁ לוֹ אֵלּוּ הַשְּׁנֵי בְקִיאוּת הַנַּ"ל אֲזַי הוּא הוֹלֵךְ בְּדַרְכֵי הַתְּשׁוּבָה", כִּי מִשְּׁנֵי פְּעָמִים בָּקִי, שֶׁהֵם בְּחִינַת קְסָ"א וּסַ"ג, "אֶסַּק שָׁמַיִם וְאַצִּיעָה שְׁאוֹל" וְכוּ', עַל־יְדֵי־זֶה נַעֲשֶׂה בְּחִינַת דֶּרֶךְ, שֶׁהוּא בְּגִימַטְרִיָּא שְׁתֵּי פְּעָמִים בָּקִי, שֶׁהֵם קְסָ"א וְסַ"ג וְכוּ', כַּנַּ"ל.

כִּי עִקַּר דֶּרֶךְ הַתְּשׁוּבָה זוֹכִין עַל־יְדֵי שְׁנֵי הַבְּקִיאוּת הַנַּ"ל, וְאָז יְמִין ה' פְּשׁוּטָה לְקַבֵּל תְּשׁוּבָתוֹ, כִּי יָמִין בְּגִימַטְרִיָּא דֶּרֶךְ, שֶׁהֵם שְׁתֵּי פְּעָמִים בָּקִי, כַּנַּ"ל. וּפְשׁוּטָה בְּגִימַטְרִיָּא סֶגּוֹל דְּקְסָ"א וְחִירִיק דְּסַ"ג,

שֶׁהֵם בְּעַצְמָם בְּחִינַת נְקֻדָּה הָעֶלְיוֹנָה וּנְקֻדָּה הַתַּחְתּוֹנָה, שֶׁהֵם בְּחִינַת מַה שֶּׁצְּרִיכִין לְבַקֵּשׁ הַשֵּׁם יִתְבָּרַךְ תָּמִיד, הֵן לְמַעְלָה הֵן לְמַטָּה, בְּחִינַת: "אִם אֶסַּק שָׁמַיִם שָׁם אָתָּה, וְאַצִּיעָה שְׁאוֹל הִנֶּךָּ", שֶׁהֵם בְּחִינַת שְׁנֵי הַבְּקִיאוּת הַנַּ"ל, וְעַל כֵּן כְּשֶׁיֵּשׁ לוֹ שְׁנֵי הַבְּקִיאוּת הַנַּ"ל, אָז הוּא הוֹלֵךְ בְּדַרְכֵי הַתְּשׁוּבָה, וְאָז יְמִין ה' פְּשׁוּטָה לְקַבֵּל תְּשׁוּבָתוֹ. וְהָבֵן הַדְּבָרִים הֵיטֵב, כִּי הֵם דְּבָרִים עֲמֻקִים מְאֹד.

וְעַל־פִּי־זֶה תָּבִין לְקַשֵּׁר הַתּוֹרָה הֵיטֵב, שֶׁמַּה שֶּׁכָּתַב בַּסּוֹף מֵעִנְיַן נְקֻדָּה הָעֶלְיוֹנָה וּנְקֻדָּה הַתַּחְתּוֹנָה שֶׁל הָאָלֶף, זֶהוּ בְּעַצְמוֹ בְּחִינַת שְׁנֵי הַבְּקִיאוּת הַנַּ"ל, (כִּי זֶה אֵינוֹ מְבֹאָר בְּפֵרוּשׁ בְּהַתּוֹרָה הַנַּ"ל,

outstretched towards him in order to receive his *teshuvah.*

194. **explained above.** See section 10, note 178. *KaSA* with its vowel signs equals 300 and *SaG* with its vowel signs equals 100, thus together they equal 400, the numerical value of *peshutah* (outstretched). That is, they cause God's *yemin* to become outstretched to receive him in repentance.

195. **themselves the aspect of . . . point.** As above, section 5.

(ascend).[190] And *chirik* is the lower point of the *aleph*, corresponding to "and if I make my bed in Hell," which is an aspect of the *chirik* of *SaG*.[191]

This is the meaning of what was said above in the lesson: **When a person possesses these two types of expertise (*baky*), then he is walking the pathways (*derekh*) of repentance.**[192] For from twice *baky*—which are the aspects of *KaSA* and *SaG*, "ascend to heaven" and "make my bed in Hell"—the aspect of *derekh*—which has a numerical value of twice *baky,* corresponding to *KaSA* and *SaG*—is made.

For the essence of the pathways of repentance is reached through these two types of expertise. And then, the *yemin* of God is *peshutah* (outstreched) to accept his repentance. This is because *yemin* has the same numerical value as *derekh,* which is twice *baky*[193]; and *peshutah* has the same numerical value as the *segol* of *KaSA* and the *chirik* of *SaG,* as explained above.[194]

[Furthermore, the *segol* and the *chirik*] are themselves the aspects of the upper point and the lower point.[195] They represent the need to constantly search for God, whether it be above or below. These are the two types of expertise: "If I ascend to heaven, You are there; and if I make my bed in Hell, here You are." Therefore, when a person possesses these two types of expertise, he is walking the pathways of repentance. And then, the right hand of God is outstretched to accept his repentance. Understand this well, for the matters discussed here are very deep.

13. Based on this, it is possible to link together the elements of this Torah lesson. What was written at the end about the upper and lower points of the *aleph* is the very same aspect as the two types of expertise. {This was not actually explained in the body of the lesson.

---

190. **If I ascend....** For the sun is the upper point, the aspect of running, ascending (n.186), which has the three points of *teshuvah*. Therefore, in the *kavanot, KaSA* is punctuated with the *segol,* corresponding to these three points.

191. **chirik of SaG.** The lower point of the *aleph* only has the one point. Therefore, *SaG* is punctuated with the *chirik,* one dot. The three points of *teshuvah* in the upper point must shine into the one point of the lower point. That is, the three points must unite in order for a person to properly repent and attain the pathways of *teshuvah.*

192. **said above in the lesson....** See section 4.

193. **yemin...twice baky.** That is, when a person merits the two *bakiut,* he has made the *derekh* of *teshuvah.* Now that the way is secured, he causes God's right hand, His *yemin,* to be

רַק עַל-פִּי כַוָּנוֹת הַנַּ"ל מוּבָן זֹאת מְמֵילָא לַמַּשְׂכִּיל),

וְזֶהוּ בְּעַצְמוֹ בְּחִינַת תְּשׁוּבָה עַל תְּשׁוּבָה, שֶׁכָּתַב שָׁם, כִּי זְבִיחַת הַיֵּצֶר הָרָע, שֶׁהוּא בְּחִינַת דֹם לַה', שֶׁהוּא בְּחִינַת תְּשׁוּבָה הָרִאשׁוֹנָה, שֶׁהוּא בְּחִינַת כְּבוֹד עוֹלָם הַזֶּה, זֶה בְּחִינַת נְקֻדָּה הַתַּחְתּוֹנָה, שֶׁנַּעֲשֵׂית מִבְּחִינַת הַדְּמִימָה וְהַשְּׁתִיקָה, מִבְּחִינַת דֹם לַה'. וְכָל זֶה הוּא בְּחִינַת חִירִיק דְּס"ג וְכוּ', שֶׁהוּא בְּחִינַת בָּקִי בְּשׁוֹב, כַּנַּ"ל.

וּתְשׁוּבָה הַשְּׁנִיָּה שֶׁעוֹשֶׂה עַל תְּשׁוּבָתוֹ הָרִאשׁוֹנָה, שֶׁהוּא בְּחִינַת כְּבוֹד הָעוֹלָם הַבָּא, בְּחִינַת: "כְּבוֹד אֱלֹקִים הַסְתֵּר דָּבָר", זֶה בְּחִינַת נְקֻדָּה הָעֶלְיוֹנָה, בְּחִינַת כֶּתֶר, שֶׁהוּא בְּחִינַת מֹשֶׁה, בְּחִינַת סֶגּוֹל וְכוּ'. וְהָבֵן הַדְּבָרִים הֵיטֵב, אֵיךְ כָּל הַדְּבָרִים הַנֶּאֱמָרִים שָׁם, בְּהַתּוֹרָה הַנַּ"ל, נִקְשָׁרִים וְנִכְלָלִים אַחַר-כָּךְ בְּיַחַד בְּקֶשֶׁר נִפְלָא וְנוֹרָא, וְהַמַּשְׂכִּילִים יָבִינוּ קְצָת:

וְעִקַּר הַדָּבָר, שֶׁעַל יְדֵי שֶׁהָאָדָם, כְּשֶׁהוּא בַּמַּדְרֵגָה הַתַּחְתּוֹנָה מְאֹד, וְאַף-עַל-פִּי-כֵן הוּא מְחַזֵּק עַצְמוֹ וּמַאֲמִין שֶׁגַּם שָׁם יֵשׁ לוֹ תִּקְוָה עֲדַיִן, כִּי גַם שָׁם נִמְצָא הַשֵּׁם יִתְבָּרַךְ, בִּבְחִינַת: "וְאַצִּיעָה שְּׁאוֹל הִנֶּךָּ", אֲזַי מַמְשִׁיךְ עַל עַצְמוֹ הַקְּדֻשָּׁה מִשֵּׁם הַקָּדוֹשׁ הֲוָיָה בְּמִלּוּי ס"ג, שֶׁהוּא מְחַיֶּה אֶת כָּל הַנְּסוֹגִים אָחוֹר מִקְּדֻשָּׁתוֹ לְהַחֲזִיקָם לְבַל

must be meditated on punctuated with the *segol*.

On the other hand, being *baky* at returning, as in, "and if I make my bed in Hell . . . ," is the aspect of the name *SaG*. This is when the person is in a state of *naSoG* (retreat), God forbid. He is very distant from that which is holy, but despite this does not totally despair. In keeping with the concept "and if I make my bed . . . here You are," he continues to search for the Holy One and struggles to attain *teshuvah*. But then the name *Ehyeh* is hidden from him (see nn.23-27), so that he suffers insult and humiliation.

When this happens, he must strengthen himself to accept his suffering and embarrassment with love, and to be as quiet and silent as the earth—corresponding to "let my soul be like earth to everyone" (*Daily Liturgy, Amidah*), and "the earth is My footstool." His hope is that by ignoring attacks to his prestige, he will merit *teshuvah*. For by being quiet and silent the lower point of the *aleph* is made, this being the aspect of the *chirik*. Therefore, the name *SaG* must be meditated on punctuated with the *chirik*.

The relationship is only made clear by understanding the *kavanot* mentioned above.[196]}

This is also the concept of "repentance upon repentance" mentioned in the lesson. The slaughtering of the evil inclination— corresponding to "Be quiet before God"/the first repentance/the *kavod* of this world—is the lower point. This is accomplished by means of the *DeMimah* and silence, corresponding to "Be *DoMe* before God." And all of these concepts form the aspect of the *chirik* of *SaG,* which is the expertise of returning.

The second repentance, which one does for his first repentance— the aspect of the glory of the World to Come, corresponding to "The glory of the Lord is a concealed matter"—is the upper point. It is *Keter,* which is the aspect of Moshe, and the *segol.*[197]

Understand this well, how all the subjects mentioned in this lesson are later tied together in a wonderfully awesome manner. Those who delve into it will understand a little.[198]

14. The essence of the matter is: When a person is on a very low level and yet still fortifies himself—believing that even there he still has hope and that there too God may be found, corresponding to "and if I make my bed in Hell, here You are"—he then draws holiness upon himself from the sacred name *YHVH* in its permutation of *SaG.* This

---

196. **kavanot mentioned above.** The *aleph* is explained in section 5, whereas the two types of *baky* are explained in section 4. Although, as we have seen above, Rebbe Nachman generally makes a point of tying together the different concepts he introduces, he has not shown a direct connection between the *aleph* and the twice-*baky.* It is apparent only from the *Kavanot* of the Ari, which states that one requires twice-*baky* corresponding to *Ehyeh*/upper point and *YHVH*/lower point, as has just been explained.

197. **Keter...Moshe...segol.** See section 5 and note 110 for the details of these connections.

198. **understand a little.** The *Parparaot LeChokhmah* explains that from this it is possible to see how the different concepts of the lesson tie together. To be *baky* at running means that one is not content with his present spiritual level, but time after time seeks to go higher and higher. This is what is meant in section 3 that one must be constantly involved with the attribute of *teshuvah.*

For it is necessary to attain *teshuvah al teshuvah.* This is the aspect of the name *Ehyeh* in its permutation of *KaSA,* as in, "If I *eSAK* (ascend) to Heaven." For the name *Ehyeh* is the aspect of *teshuvah,* the main perfection and fullness of which is only achieved when one ascends constantly by engaging in *teshuvah al teshuvah*—being *baky* at running. And this *teshuvah* is the aspect of the upper point of the *aleph,* corresponding to "the *segol* (three dots, three conditions for repentance) is the sun." Therefore, each of the letters of the name *KaSA*

יִפְּלוּ לְגַמְרֵי, חַס וְשָׁלוֹם, וְזֶה בְּחִינַת בָּקִי בְּשׁוֹב, שֶׁזֶּה הַבְּקִיאוּת הוּא בְּחִינַת שֵׁם יב"ק הַקָּדוֹשׁ, בְּחִינַת שֵׁם ס"ג.

וְכֵן כְּשֶׁאָדָם זוֹכֶה לָבוֹא לְאֵיזוֹ מַדְרֵגָה בַּקְּדֻשָּׁה הָעֶלְיוֹנָה, וְאַף-עַל-פִּי-כֵן אֵינוּ עוֹמֵד שָׁם, וְהוּא מִתְחַזֵּק וּמִתְגַּבֵּר לַעֲלוֹת יוֹתֵר וְיוֹתֵר, אֲזַי מַמְשִׁיךְ הַקְּדֻשָּׁה עַל עַצְמוֹ מִשֵּׁם הַקָּדוֹשׁ אהי"ה בְּמִלּוּי קס"א, שֶׁהוּא בְּחִינַת בָּקִי בְּרָצוֹא.

כִּי הָאָדָם – כְּפִי תְּנוּעוֹתָיו וּכְפִי הִתְחַזְּקוּתוֹ בַּעֲבוֹדָתוֹ יִתְבָּרַךְ, כֵּן גּוֹרֵם לְיַחֵד הַשֵּׁמוֹת לְמַעְלָה, וּמַמְשִׁיךְ עַל עַצְמוֹ הַקְּדֻשָּׁה מִשָּׁם. וְהָבֵן הֵיטֵב:

וְהִנֵּה מְבֹאָר לְעֵיל, שֶׁעַל-יְדֵי הַדְּמִימָה וְהַשְּׁתִיקָה שֶׁשּׁוֹתְקִין לַחֲבֵרוֹ כְּשֶׁמְּבַזִּין אוֹתוֹ, עַל-יְדֵי-זֶה זוֹכֶה לִתְשׁוּבָה, שֶׁהִיא בְּחִינַת כֶּתֶר כַּנַּ"ל, עַיֵּן שָׁם, כִּי 'סְיָג לַחָכְמָה שְׁתִיקָה' כַּנַּ"ל, כִּי צְרִיכִין לִזָּהֵר מְאֹד לָדוּן אֶת כָּל אָדָם לְכַף זְכוּת, וַאֲפִלּוּ הַחוֹלְקִים עָלָיו וּמְבַזִּין אוֹתוֹ, צָרִיךְ לְדוּנָם לְכַף זְכוּת וְלִשְׁתֹּק לָהֶם, וְעַל-יְדֵי-זֶה נַעֲשֶׂה בְּחִינַת כֶּתֶר.

כַּמּוּבָא בַּמִּדְרָשׁ:

'מָשָׁל לְאֶחָד, שֶׁמָּצָא אֶת חֲבֵרוֹ שֶׁהוּא עוֹשֶׂה כֶּתֶר. אָמַר לוֹ: בִּשְׁבִיל מִי, אָמַר לוֹ: בִּשְׁבִיל הַמֶּלֶךְ. אָמַר לוֹ: כֵּיוָן שֶׁהוּא לְצֹרֶךְ

levels, and occasionally even higher!

200. **silence...repentance...Keter....** See above, section 2.

201. **Silence is a fence for wisdom.** As above, section 6 and note 128.

202. **judge everyone favorably.** This is a very major topic in Rebbe Nachman's teachings: judging others, as well as one's own self, favorably (see Lesson #3 and *Likutey Moharan* I, 282). In our context, this relates to recognizing one's own worth, so that a person will attempt repentance and not think that he is "too far gone" to ever come close to God. The Rebbe now shows how this applies in our lesson.

   The principles involved in judging everyone favorably are fully explained in *Azamra!*, published by the Breslov Research Institute, 1984.

203. **Kaf zekhut.** Literally, this means "the scale of merit," כף זכות in Hebrew. Rebbe Nachman connects this *kaf*, כ, with the *kaf* of *keter*, כתר.

[name] sustains all those who have *naSoG* (retreated) from His holiness. It strengthens them and prevents them from falling away entirely, God forbid. This is the aspect of being expert at returning, which is the expertise that corresponds to the holy names *Yabok* and *SaG*.

Similarly, when a person merits reaching a certain high level of holiness and yet does not stand still—rather, he strengthens himself and strives to ascend higher and higher—he then draws holiness upon himself from the holy name *Ehyeh* in its permutation of *KaSA*. This is the aspect of being expert at running.

For [each] person, in accordance with his actions and the manner in which he strengthens himself in the service of God, causes the holy names above to unite.[199] He, in turn, draws holiness upon himself from there. Understand this well.

15. It has been explained above that by means of the quiet and silence he displays when his friend insults him, a person merits repentance, which is the aspect of *Keter,* as explained.[200] This is because "Silence is a fence for wisdom."[201] For it is necessary to be very careful to judge everyone favorably.[202] Even when others attack and insult him, a person must judge them favorably and maintain his silence. This forms the aspect of *Keter,* < for there is no *Keter* without a *Kaf,* and this is precisely *Kaf zekhut* (favorably).[203] Understand this. >

As is brought in the Midrash:

> **It is like the allegory of someone who saw his friend making a *keter* (crown). "Who is it for?" he asked him. "For the king,"**

---

199. **holy names above to unite.** The Divine names of God represent and are bound up with the forces or energies from Above. Causing these names to unite essentially means bringing them, through one's deeds, to a state of greater perfection or completion. He is activating these spiritual energies. Man has the ability to do this because: "Man embodies the mysteries of all the worlds" (*Zohar Chadash, Shir HaShirim* 4). Thus, every part of the human body has its corresponding feature in creation which exists only for man's benefit and upon which his actions and behavior have a direct affect (cf. *Tzaddik* #504, #505).

This, in effect, is the reason for the various *kavanot* (meditations). When a person reflects and meditates upon a given holy name, he arouses the forces encompassed in that name and draws its energy upon himself. This is why the Ari emphasized the need for purity for one who wants to properly and safely engage in these meditations. For his part, Rebbe Nachman shows here and in many other lessons how we can turn these meditations into action, so that even if we are not capable of engaging in the *kavanot,* our deeds can bring us to the same

הַמֶּלֶךְ, כָּל אֶבֶן טוֹב שֶׁתִּמְצָא, תִּקְבָּעֶנּוּ בּוֹ',

כָּךְ כָּל אֶחָד מִיִּשְׂרָאֵל הוּא בְּחִינַת כֶּתֶר לְהַשֵּׁם יִתְבָּרַךְ, וְצָרִיךְ לְהַכְנִיס בּוֹ כָּל מִין אֲבָנִים טוֹבוֹת שֶׁאֶפְשָׁר לִמְצֹא, דְּהַיְנוּ שֶׁצְּרִיכִין לְהִשְׁתַּדֵּל לְחַפֵּשׂ וּלְבַקֵּשׁ אַחַר כָּל צַד זְכוּת וְדָבָר טוֹב שֶׁאֶפְשָׁר לִמְצֹא בְּיִשְׂרָאֵל, וְלָדוּן אֶת הַכֹּל לְכַף זְכוּת, כִּי הֵם בְּחִינַת כֶּתֶר לְהַשֵּׁם יִתְבָּרַךְ כַּנִּזְכָּר לְעֵיל. וּכְמוֹ שֶׁאָמְרוּ רַבּוֹתֵינוּ, זִכְרוֹנָם לִבְרָכָה: 'הֱוֵי דָן אֶת כָּל אָדָם לְכַף זְכוּת'.

נִמְצָא, שֶׁעַל יְדֵי שֶׁדָּנִים אֶת הַכֹּל לְכַף זְכוּת, שֶׁעַל־יְדֵי־זֶה שׁוֹתְקִין לוֹ כְּשֶׁמְּבַזֶּה אוֹתוֹ, כִּי מוֹצְאִין בּוֹ זְכוּת, שֶׁאֵינוּ חַיָּב כָּל כָּךְ בַּמֶּה שֶׁמְּבַזֶּה אוֹתוֹ, כִּי לְפִי דַּעְתּוֹ וּסְבָרָתוֹ נִדְמֶה לוֹ שֶׁרָאוּי לוֹ לְבַזּוֹת אוֹתוֹ וְכוּ', עַל־יְדֵי זֶה נַעֲשֶׂה בְּחִינַת כֶּתֶר, הַיְנוּ כַּנַּ"ל, שֶׁעַל־יְדֵי

person who honestly sees himself as undeserving of insult could only be one who has sincerely repented, so that his is the exalted repentance of the World to Come (see §3, n.46). This could only be the tzaddik, who always seeks to honor God and has himself attained *kavod Elohim*. But, as we have seen, it is forbidden to remain quiet and silent when God's honor is disparaged (above, n.11 end). And since the tzaddik has attained *kavod Elohim*, how can he remain quiet and silent when insulted? However, the tzaddik remains quiet and silent by judging others favorably: "It seems to them that I deserve to be insulted," he says. On the other hand, were they to know for certain that the tzaddik's honor is *kavod Elohim*, they would surely not insult him. Thus, with his silence the tzaddik attains another aspect of repentance and can ascend to an even greater level of *Ehyeh/Keter*. The tzaddik then reveals a greater level of *Keter*, which is a greater revelation of *kavod Elohim*. Therefore, rather than God's honor being minimized, it is actually made greater by his silence.

With this, the *Parparaot LeChokhmah* explains why it is that the true tzaddikim are inexorably surrounded by great controversy. It is well known that the opposition to the Baal Shem Tov, and indeed all the Chassidic masters, was extremely bitter. Worse yet was the persecution suffered by Rebbe Nachman (and Reb Noson). The reason is that true tzaddikim are only those who have attained *teshuvah al teshuvah* and seek to ascend higher, to an even greater level of *Keter*. Achieving this goal is only possible if they quietly and silently endure the humiliation heaped upon them by their opponents.

On a more profound level, the reason for this opposition is that a person must experience a descent before he can ascend to the next rung on the spiritual ladder (see *Likutey Moharan* I, 22:11). This is *baky b'ratzo* and *baky b'shov*. However, the tzaddik, who yearns to always be *baky b'ratzo*, finds the descent very disturbing. He is embarrassed before God and feels shame and disgrace, as if he has been banished from the Holy One's presence. When this happens, the tzaddik must show his expertise in *baky b'shov*. For this embarrassment before God is precisely what enables him to ascend to the next level. We see, therefore, that the

he replied. "Since it's for the king," he said, "set into it every jewel you find" (*Vayikra Rabbah* 2:5).[204]

So, too, every Jew is an aspect of a crown for God. One must therefore set in him every sort of jewel one can possibly find. That is, it is necessary to make an effort to seek out and search for every merit and positive quality one can possibly find in a fellow Jew. Everyone must be judged favorably, for they are an aspect of a *Keter* for God.[205] This is as the Sages taught: Judge every *adam* favorably (*Avot* 1:6).

We find, then, that by judging everyone favorably he remains silent when others insult him. He finds some merit in the person who insulted him: "He is not all that responsible for shaming me, because to that person's knowledge and way of thinking it seems that I *am* deserving of insult." This creates the aspect of *Keter*—i.e., the quiet and silence form the aspect of *Keter,* as mentioned above.[206]

---

204. **It is like the allegory....** This Midrash expounds on the verse "Speak to the children of Israel" (Leviticus 1:2): God instructed Moshe to command the Jews concerning the sacrifices. Why command the Jews? Because they are precious to Me. The Midrash goes on to say that Moshe found many reasons to praise the Jews, showing God how special they were, particularly when compared to the nations. This is the allegory Rebbe Nachman quotes: Moshe was making a crown (praise). God asked him, "Who is it for?" Moshe answered, "For the King" (to show God how precious every Jew is). "If it is for the King, set into it every jewel you find" (use every reason for praise that you can think of), as is written (Isaiah 49:3), "You are My servant, Israel, through whom I will be glorified" (*Vayikra Rabbah, loc. cit*).

In our context, the Midrash relates to Moshe, who was always striving towards greater spiritual heights. He attained *teshuvah al teshuvah* and therefore merited *Keter* (Crown). In a sense, Moshe was always making "a crown." Furthermore, by always finding merit in the Jews and judging them favorably, Moshe was able to obtain forgiveness for their sins from God. Moshe thus brought the Jews to *teshuvah,* showing them that they too could attain *Keter* (see §2). This is understood by virtue of the Midrash basing itself on the verse that speaks about the sacrifices, which in our context refers to repenting and confessing—i.e., slaughtering the evil inclination (§§2,3). The lesson now points out another dimension of this allegory.

205. **So, too, every Jew....** That is, every Jew is precious to God and God wants him to repent and attain *Keter.*

206. **as mentioned above.** See section 2. As explained there, a person should realize that the insults he suffers are the result of his own sins. Rebbe Nachman adds here that even when he is convinced that these insults are unjustified, he should keep quiet for the Holy One's sake and judge the other person favorably. The *Parparaot LeChokhmah* points out that this is actually referring to the tzaddik. The embarrassment comes from the blood that has yet to be rectified, which is why a person must remain quiet and silent to atone for his sins. But the

הַדְּמִימָה וְהַשְּׁתִיקָה נַעֲשֶׂה בְּחִינַת כֶּתֶר, כַּנַּ"ל. וְהָבֵן:

"Yehoshua," the disciple who "did not depart from the tent." Thus, Rebbe Nachman was "Moshe," *baky b'ratzo*, the upper point of the *aleph*, shining into Reb Noson more than the other disciples; and Reb Noson was "Yehoshua," *baky b'shov*, the lower point of the *aleph*, receiving the illumination directly from the Rebbe. Although during his lifetime Reb Noson was time and again made the target of the slings and arrows of his opposition, he saw the deeper purpose of this humiliation and each time withstood the test. This becomes apparent from Reb Noson's writings. Whereas those familiar with *Likutey Moharan* will readily note Rebbe Nachman's emphasis on constantly striving for and attaining the highest spiritual levels, those familiar with Reb Noson's *magnum opus, Likutey Halakhot*, will readily note that it is filled with words of encouragement and support—exhorting anyone who will listen to never give up, never despair, and to always seek out God no matter how acute his spiritual descent. Worth noting in this connection is the teaching of the Ari: On three separate occasions after Moshe's passing, God told Yehoshua, "*Chazak* (Be strong)!" He did this to illumine Yehoshua with Moshe's light (*Likutey Torah, Yehoshua*, p.288). Now, three times *ChaZaK* (חזק = 115) equals MoSheH (משה = 345). In our context, this corresponds to the *segol*, the three dots of the upper point that illumine the lower point. And though it is known that Rebbe Nachman favored Reb Noson at the helm of the Breslover Chassidim after his passing, nowhere is it recorded that the Rebbe said so specifically. This, too, was no different than the way Moshe's leadership was transferred to Yehoshua. As quoted above in our lesson (§7), God said, "where *I* will appoint him"—i.e, God and not Moshe would do the appointing. Thus, Reb Noson was left to decide for himself how best to hand over the Rebbe's teachings. He had no one to ask for guidance other than God Himself.

For a detailed description of the impact this lesson had upon Reb Noson and the legacy he left through his writings, see *Through Fire and Water: The Life of Reb Noson of Breslov* (Breslov Research Institute, 1992).

Understand this.[207]

tzaddik's expertise is the key to rebound from his descent and ascend to a higher level. But if in the face of opposition he remains quiet and silent, he has suffered the embarrassment on the spiritual level he was on even without descending. The embarrassment itself is considered the descent and so the tzaddik can then ascend without suffering the humiliation of a real descent. Such is the benefit of remaining quiet and silent by judging one's opponents favorably. A classic example of this appears in the Book of Samuel. When King David fled from his son Avshalom, he passed through Bachurim. A Benjaminite by the name of Shim'iy the son of Gerah came out to curse him. When Avishai, the king's nephew and a powerful warrior, asked for permission to kill Shim'iy for his insolence, King David replied (2 Samuel 16:10), "God must have instructed him to curse me." After this episode with Avshalom, King David reascended the throne stronger than before.

With this, the *Parparaot LeChokhmah* explains the Talmudic teaching: In the World to Come, each tzaddik will be singed by the canopy of his neighbor (*Bava Batra* 75a). Could it be that the reward of the righteous in the World to Come is the "pleasure" of being singed and embarrassed by one's neighbor? The answer is that man's true pleasure in the World to Come will be his ever greater perceptions of Godliness. This is something which, in this world, the tzaddik can only attain through a descent or embarrassment. But what about in the future world, where there will be no descent? Then, "each tzaddik will be singed...," so that this humiliation will enable him to ascend to even higher spiritual levels and enjoy even greater pleasure and reward in the World to Come.

207. **Understand this.** The *Parparaot LeChokhmah* concludes his commentary to this lesson with an interesting piece about the relationship between Rebbe Nachman and Reb Noson. As we have seen (nn.1,121) any meeting between a teacher and a disciple corresponds to the meeting between Moshe and Yehoshua. Anyone who studies Reb Noson's life in detail will see that the Rebbe's main legacy was left with him. Indeed, Reb Noson became the Rebbe's

APPENDIX

CHARTS

THE ORDER OF THE TEN SEFIROT

KETER

CHOKHMAH

BINAH

CHESED

GEVURAH

TIFERET

NETZACH

HOD

YESOD

MALKHUT

THE STRUCTURE OF THE SEFIROT

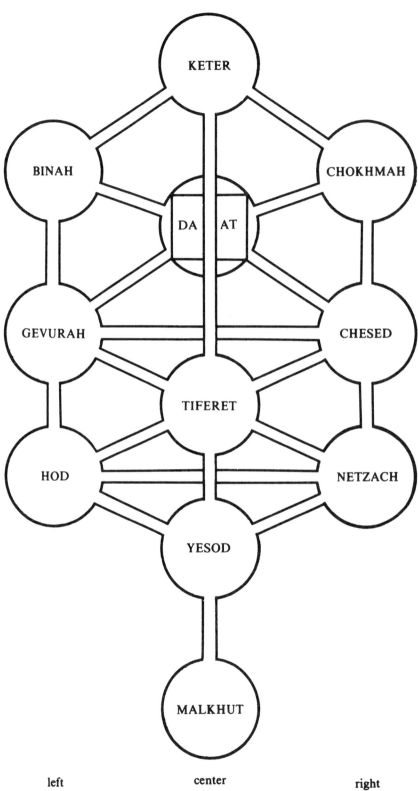

left   center   right

THE PARTZUFIM - THE DIVINE PERSONA

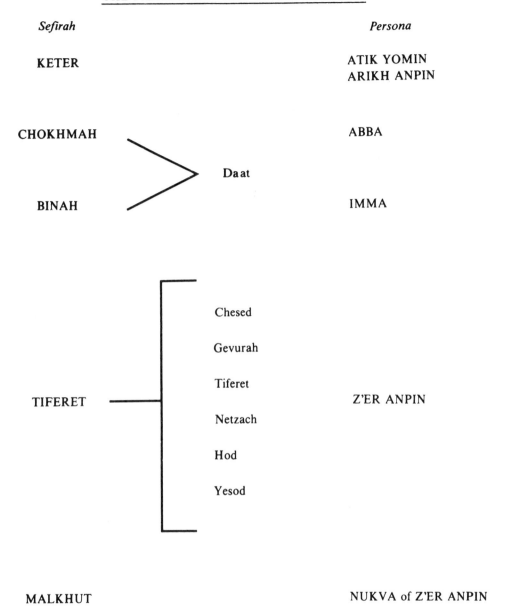

Sefirah   *Persona*

KETER   ATIK YOMIN
                                               ARIKH ANPIN

CHOKHMAH   ABBA

                        Daat

BINAH   IMMA

                    Chesed

                    Gevurah

                    Tiferet
TIFERET   Z'ER ANPIN
                    Netzach

                    Hod

                    Yesod

MALKHUT   NUKVA of Z'ER ANPIN

Alternate names used in the Kabbalah and our text for Z'er Anpin and Malkhut:

Z'er Anpin: Yaakov, Yisrael Sava, Torah, Written Law, Holy King, Sun.

Malkhut: Leah, Rachel, Prayer, Oral Law, Divine Presence/Shekhinah, Moon.

THE SEFIROT AND MAN

Keter-Crown	Skull
Chokhmah-Wisdom	Right brain
Binah-Understanding	Left brain
(Daat-Knowledge)	(Middle brain)
Chesed-Lovingkindness	Right arm
Gevurah-Strength	Left arm
Tiferet-Beauty	Torso
Netzach-Victory	Right leg
Hod-Splendor	Left leg
Yesod-Foundation	Sexual organ (brit)
Malkhut-Kingship	Mate/feet

Alternatively, Chokhmah corresponds to brain/mind; Binah to heart.

LEVELS OF EXISTENCE

World	Manifestation	Sefirah	Soul	Letter
Adam Kadmon		Keter	Yechidah	Apex of Yod
Atzilut	Nothingness	Chokhmah	Chayah	Yod
Beriyah	Thought	Binah	Neshamah	Heh
Yetzirah	Speech	Tiferet [six sefirot]	Ruach	Vav
Asiyah	Action	Malkhut	Nefesh	Heh

World	Inhabitants	T-N-T-A
Adam Kadmon	Tetragrammatons	
Atzilut-Nearness	Sefirot, Partzufim	Taamim-Cantillations
Beriyah-Creation	The Throne, Souls	Nekudot-Vowels
Yetzirah-Formation	Angels	Tagin-Crowns
Asiyah-Action	Forms	Aotiyot-Letters

EXPANSIONS OF THE HOLY NAMES OF GOD

YHVH — Expansions of the Tetragrammaton — יהוה

Expansion		Partzuf	Value		Expansion
YOD HY VYV HY	AB	Chokhmah	72	עב	יוד הי ויו הי
YOD HY VAV HY	SaG	Binah	63	סג	יוד הי ואו הי
YOD HA VAV HY	MaH	Z'er Anpin	45	מה	יוד הא ואו הא
YOD HH VV HH	BaN	Malkhut	52	בן	יוד הה וו הה

EHYH — Expansions of the Holy Name EHYeH — אהיה

ALePH HY YOD HY	KSA	161	קסא	אלף הי יוד הי
ALePH HH YOD HH	KNA	151	קנא	אלף הה יוד הה
ALePH HA YOD HA	KMG	143	קמג	אלף הא יוד הא

THE SEFIROT AND ASSOCIATED NAMES OF GOD

Sefirah	Holy Name
Keter-Crown	*Ehyeh Asher Ehyeh*
Chokhmah-Wisdom	*YaH*
Binah-Understanding	*YHVH* (pronounced *Elohim*)
Chesed-Lovingkindness	*El*
Gevurah-Strength	*Elohim*
Tiferet-Beauty	*YHVH* (pronounced *Adonoy*)
Netzach-Victory	*Adonoy Tzevaot*
Hod-Splendor	*Elohim Tzevaot*
Yesod-Foundation	*Shaddai, El Chai*
Malkhut-Kingship	*Adonoy*

THE SUPERNAL COLORS

Sefirah	Color
Keter-Crown	blinding invisible white
Chokhmah-Wisdom	a color that includes all color
Binah-Understanding	yellow and green
Chesed-Lovingkindness	white and silver
Gevurah-Strength	red and gold
Tiferet-Beauty	yellow and purple
Netzach-Victory	light pink
Hod-Splendor	dark pink
Yesod-Foundation	orange
Malkhut-Kingship	blue

THE SEVEN SUPERNAL SHEPHERDS

Sefirah	Shepherd
Chesed-Lovingkindness	Avraham
Gevurah-Strength	Yitzchak
Tiferet-Beauty	Yaakov
Netzach-Victory	Moshe
Hod-Splendor	Aharon
Yesod-Foundation	Yosef
Malkhut-Kingship	David

HEBREW LETTER NUMEROLOGY — GEMATRIA

ק=100	י=10	א=1
ר=200	כ=20	ב=2
ש=300	ל=30	ג=3
ת=400	מ=40	ד=4
	נ=50	ה=5
	ס=60	ו=6
	ע=70	ז=7
	פ=80	ח=8
	צ=90	ט=9